THE

TWO LITURGIES

WITH OTHER

DOCUMENTS

SET FORTH BY AUTHORITY

IN THE REIGN OF

KING EDWARD THE SIXTH.

THE
TWO LITURGIES,

A.D. 1549, AND A.D. 1552:

WITH OTHER

DOCUMENTS

SET FORTH BY AUTHORITY

IN THE REIGN OF KING EDWARD VI.

VIZ.

THE ORDER OF COMMUNION, 1548.
THE PRIMER, 1553.
THE CATECHISM AND ARTICLES, 1553.
CATECHISMUS BREVIS, 1553.

EDITED FOR

The Parker Society,

BY THE

REV. JOSEPH KETLEY, M.A.
OF QUEENS' COLLEGE, CAMBRIDGE:
CURATE OF ST MARK'S, KENNINGTON.

PUBLISHERS
Eugene, Oregon

Wipf and Stock Publishers
199 W 8th Ave, Suite 3
Eugene, OR 97401

Two Liturgies, A.D. 1549 and A.D. 1552
with other documents set forth by authority in the reign of King Edward VI
By Ketley, Joseph
ISBN 13: 978-1-55635-064-11
ISBN: 1-55635-064-3
Publication date 12/4/2006
Previously published by Cambridge, 1844

TABLE OF CONTENTS.

		PAGE
	Preface	iii
	Various Readings and Title of copy collated.....................	xiv
I.	The Order of Communion	xv
	Facsimile of Title of copy followed, Grafton, March, 1548	xvi
	Facsimile of Colophon of same..	8
II.	The Book of Common Prayer, and Administration of the Sacraments and other Rites and Ceremonies in the Church of England, Whitchurch, 1549	9
	Facsimile of Title of copy followed, Whitchurch, May, 1549	10
	Facsimile of Title and Colophon of copy collated, Whitchurch, June, 1549	11
	Facsimiles of Titles and Colophons of three copies collated, of Grafton, March, 1549	12—14
	Facsimile of Title and Colophon of copy collated, Oswen, July 15, 1549	15
	Contents of the Book of Common Prayer, 1549...............	16
	Facsimile of Colophon, Whitchurch, May, 1549	158
	Prices of the Book of Common Prayer, order concerning...	158
III.	The Form and Manner of Making and Consecrating of Archbishops, Bishops, Priests, and Deacons, Grafton, 1549.	159
	Facsimile of Title of above...	160
	Facsimile of Colophon of the same...................................	186
IV.	The Book of Common Prayer, and Administration of the Sacraments, and other Rites and Ceremonies in the Church of England, Whitchurch, 1552	187
	Facsimile of Title of copy followed, Whitchurch, Second Edition, 1552...	188
	Facsimile of Title and Colophon of copy collated, Whitchurch, First Edition, 1552	189
	Facsimiles of Titles and Colophons of two copies collated, Grafton, August, 1552	190, 191
	Contents of the Book of Common Prayer, 1552...............	192
	Facsimile of Colophon of copy followed, Whitchurch, Second Edition, 1552	354
	Prices of the Book of Common Prayer, order concerning...	355

[DOCUMENTS, EDW. VI.]

CONTENTS.

                                                                                          PAGE

V. THE PRIMER; OR BOOK OF PRIVATE PRAYER, NEEDFUL TO BE USED OF ALL CHRISTIANS. AUTHORISED AND SET FORTH BY ORDER OF KING EDWARD VI. SERES, 1553 357
      Facsimile of Title of the above 358
      Contents of the Primer 483
      Facsimile of Colophon of the same 484

VI. A SHORT CATECHISM; OR PLAIN INSTRUCTION, CONTAINING THE SUM OF CHRISTIAN LEARNING, SET FORTH BY THE KING'S AUTHORITY, FOR ALL SCHOOLMASTERS TO TEACH. DAY, 1553. 485
      Facsimile of Title of copy followed 486
      Contents of Short Catechism 489
      Articles adjoined, agreed upon by the Bishops and other learned men in the last convocation at London, 1552, to root out the discord of opinions and establish the agreement of true religion. Published by the King's Majesty's authority, 1553 526
      Prayers added to the above 538
      Facsimile of Colophon of Catechism, Articles, and Prayers 540

VII. CATECHISMUS BREVIS CHRISTIANÆ DISCIPLINÆ SUMMAM CONTINENS, OMNIBUS LUDIMAGISTRIS AUTHORITATE REGIA COMMENDATUS. HUIC CATECHISMO ADJUNCTI SUNT ARTICULI, DE QUIBUS IN ULTIMA SYNODO LONDINENSI, ANNO DOM. 1552, AD TOLLENDAM OPINIONUM DISSENSIONEM, &c. APUD WOLFIUM, 1553 541
      Facsimile of Title page of copy of Catechismus Brevis followed 542
      Facsimile of Title of copy of Catechismus Brevis collated... 543
      Articuli de quibus, &c.. 571
      Facsimile of Colophon of Catechismus brevis.................. 581

PREFACE.

In conformity with the plan of the Parker Society, as announced to its members, it was deemed highly necessary to reprint the two Liturgies and some important authorised Documents of the reign of King Edward the Sixth. In the present volume seven articles are given: concerning which it may be proper to make a few brief preliminary remarks.

I. THE ORDER OF THE COMMUNION. This has been printed from a copy in the possession of Dr Routh, President of Magdalene College, Oxford. There is another in the Public Library at Cambridge, containing several variations, which will be found stated at the end of this Preface: but this work is not in Sion College, the Archiepiscopal Library at Lambeth, the British Museum, or the Bodleian Library. It is reprinted in Bishop Sparrow's Collection, in L'Estrange's Alliance of Divine Offices, in Wilkins' Concilia, in Cardwell's Two Books of Common Prayer of the reign of Edward the Sixth compared, and in Clay's Book of Common Prayer Illustrated [1].

II. THE BOOK OF COMMON PRAYER, &c. 1549. The copy which has been followed, is Whitchurch, May, in the

---

[1] The Act referred to in the Proclamation, passed at Westminster, was compounded of two, and passed both houses of parliament, Dec. 20th 1547. It is entitled "An Acte against suche as shall unreverentlie speake against the Sacrament of the bodie and bloude of Christe commonlie called the Sacrament of the Altar, and for the receiving thereof in both kyndes." About three weeks previously, the clergy in convocation assembled had agreed, that the Sacrament should be so received. Wake, pp. 592, 593. See note by Rev. W. K. Clay, in the Appendix to the Book of Common Prayer Illustrated. Mr Clay also remarks that "merely such parts of the Communion service, as this short formulary contains, were in English, because they alone related particularly to the general communicant. All the previous portions of the ceremony, and even the consecration of the elements, as well as the receiving of them by the priest himself, continued still in Latin." See his note to the order of Communion.

British Museum. This copy has been compared with other editions, (of which there were several,) namely,

(1) Whitchurch, June; in the British Museum.
(2) Grafton, March; in Brasenose College, Oxford.
(3) Grafton, March; in the possession of the Right Reverend the Lord Bishop of Cashel; and formerly the property of Heber.
(4) Grafton, March; in the British Museum.
(5) Oswen, July; also in the British Museum.

The differences in these copies, noticed at the bottom of the pages in the present volume, may be thus distinguished. Whitchurch, June, refers to (1); Grafton, 1, 2, and C, to (2), (4), and (3), respectively; and Oswen, to (5).

There are some peculiarities in these several impressions of 1549, especially as between the copies of Grafton, March, 1, and C, and the others; and also between the three copies of the Grafton, March, 1, 2, and C, respectively.

And first, of the differences between the March 1, and C, and the other impressions. The Te Deum Laudamus, Benedictus, Magnificat, Nunc Dimittis, and the Litany and Suffrages, are not found in their proper places in the Morning and Evening Services; but are inserted in a separate sheet towards the close of the volume in C, the Bishop of Cashel's copy, and distributed throughout the volume in separate sheets in Grafton 1, the Brasenose copy. The headings to these hymns, as they stand in the Primer of Henry the Eighth, are retained in some of the sheets, which were afterwards inserted, for the purpose, apparently, of remedying the defect.

Secondly, there are differences between the three copies of Grafton, March, marked 1, 2, and C, in the notes of collation. Each of these copies has *Mense Martij* in the title-page. The Bishop of Cashel's copy has the same publisher and date in the colophon as in the title-page, which is given at the end of the Communion, and thus far corresponds with the copy in Brasenose College: but it differs from that in the British Museum, which has *Mense Martij* in the title-page, but *Mense Junij* in the colophon; a circumstance which has given rise to the conjecture that this copy was made up from more than one edition. Again, the Bishop of Cashel's copy has only one colophon, that at the end of the communion; but the Brasenose copy has three:—the first colophon at the end of the communion agrees literally with the Bishop of Cashel's copy, and has also the same folio cxxxiiij: the second colophon is placed after two leaves containing the Te Deum, the Benedictus, the Magnificat, and the Nunc Dimittis, in these words: "Imprinted at London, the .xvi. daye of Marche in the thirde yere of the reigne of our Souereigne Lord Kyng Edvvarde the .vi. by Richard Grafton, printer to his most royall majestie. Cum priuilegio ad imprimendum solum:" and the third colophon, which comes after the occasional offices, with which the remainder of the volume is occupied, is the one given with the facsimile of title-page.

There are also slight variations in the order of prices.

In Whitchurch, June, after the colophon, and on a separate leaf, it is thus: "The Kinges Maiestie, by the aduise of his moste dere uncle the Lorde Protector, and other his highness Counsell, streightly chargeth and commaundeth, that no maner of person doe sell thys presente booke unbounde, aboue the price of .ii. Shyllynges & .ii. pence the piece. And the same bounde in paste or in boordes couered with calues leather, not aboue the price of .iiii. Shillinges the piece. God saue the King."

In the Brasenose copy there is no order of price.

In the Bishop of Cashel's copy, it is thus given at the end of the book; "The Kynges Maiestie, by the aduise of his most dere uncle the lorde Protector, and other his highness Counsail, straightley chargeth and commaundeth, that no maner of persone shall sell this presente Booke unbounde, aboue the price of twoo shillynges and two pence. And the same bound in past or bordes, in Calues Lether, not aboue the price of four shillynges the peice. God saue the King." And immediately after is given, without date,

"Imprinted in the house of Richard Grafton, Printer to the Kynges Maiestie, Cum priuilegio ad imprimendum solum."

In Grafton 2, the copy in the British Museum, and placed just before the colophon, on the same page, the order of price is as follows, "The Kynges Maiestie, by the aduise of his most dere Uncle the Lord Protector, and other his highness counsaill, straightly chargeth and commaundeth, that no maner of persone, shall sell this present Booke unbounde, aboue the price of two shillynges and two pence. And the same bounde in paste or in bordes, in Calues Lether, not aboue the price of foure shillynges the pece. God save the Kyng."

In Oswen, and placed after the colophon, on the back of the leaf, the order of price is thus: "The Kynges Maiestie, by the aduyse of his most deare uncle the Lord Protector, and other his highness Counsell, streightlye chargeth and commaundeth, that no maner of person, do sell this present boke unbound, aboue the price of .ii. Shyllinges, .vi. pence ẙ piece. And the same bound in paste, or in boordes, not aboue the price of foure shyllynges the piece. God Saue the King."

In the border around the title-page of Oswen, there is the following passage in black letter:—

(1) Let euerye soule submyt hymselfe unto the auc-
(2) thoritie of the higher powers. For there is no power but of God.
(3) The powers that be, are ordained of God. Whosoeuer
(4) therefore resisteth power: resisteth the ordinaunce of God. Rom. xiii.

(1) at the top; (2) at the right hand side; (3) at the bottom; and (4) at the left hand side.

Dr. Cardwell has noticed another copy of Oswen, the colophon of which differs from that of the copy collated. In the copy collated the date of the colophon is the 30th of July; in that noticed by Dr Cardwell, it is the 23rd of May. After "At Worcester by Jhon Oswen," is added,

"They be also to sell at Shrewesburye," which is not in the copy in the British Museum[1].

III. THE FORM AND MANNER OF MAKING AND CONSECRATING ARCHBISHOPS, BISHOPS, PRIESTS, AND DEACONS. The copy, from which this has been printed, is in the library of the Archiepiscopal Palace, Lambeth. It is published in a separate form, and not at the end of the form of prayer, as in 1552: and is rarely to be met with. It differs in several places from the copy in 1552, as may be seen by comparing the two together. In the title-page of the copy of 1552, the word "Archbishop" is omitted.

IV. THE BOOK OF COMMON PRAYER, &c. 1552. The edition which has been followed in this reprint is that of Whitchurch, from a copy in the British Museum. This has been collated with three other copies:

(1) Whitchurch, first edition, in the possession of Lea Wilson, Esq. Norwood, Surrey.
(2) Grafton, first edition, in the Archiepiscopal Library, Lambeth.
(3) Grafton, second edition, in the British Museum.

The differences in these copies, as noticed in the present volume, are thus distinguished: Whitchurch, 1, refers to his first edition; and Grafton, 1, and 2, to his first and second editions respectively.

In the first impressions both of Whitchurch and Grafton, there is at the end a leaf, with a correction of faults escaped; following which is the order of prices. The errors, thus noticed, do not appear in the second impressions: and hence they are distinguished here as the first and second editions. Just before the order of prices, this notice is given, which is peculiar to the second editions: "This book is truly and diligently imprinted;" as may be seen in page 355, in the facsimile given at the end of the common prayer for 1552.

"An Act for the Uniformity of Common Prayer" is the

---

[1] Notes to Dr. Cardwell's second edition of the Two Books of Common Prayer compared, p. xliii.

first article in the contents of the copy of Grafton's second edition, while the Act itself is given in the same order as it is in Whitchurch's second edition; but in Grafton's first edition it is given at the end of the volume after the colophon. There is an edition by Whitchurch without the Act.

It is worthy of notice also, that the last rubric at the end of the Communion, page 283, "Although no order can be so perfectly devised, &c." appears fourth in order in Grafton's second edition. This rubric is printed on a separate leaf in other copies; and, as is evident from the signatures, it was added subsequently to the first impression. It was not in the copy used by Dr Cardwell[1]. In Grafton 1, the leaf has been pasted in since the copy was bound. The book as first published did not contain this rubric. See Burnet, History of the Reformation[2].

The order of prices is, with slight variations, the same as page 355; but in the first edition of Whitchurch there is a curious supernumerary leaf, rarely, if ever, found in other copies, containing a second order of prices, as follows: "This boke is to be solde in queres for ii. shillinges .viii. pence, and bounde in forel .iii. shillinges .iiii. pence, and in paste or bordes .iiii. shillinges, *and to be allowed for the carriage of every hundreth myles .ii. pence in a boke.*" The passage in italics is probably peculiar to this copy: it is noticed as such in a manuscript note in one of the fly-leaves at the beginning.

It may here be noticed, that the Books of Common Prayer of 1549 and 1552 are here reprinted with the contents in *regular order,* and not in *comparison,* as in the volumes of Dr Cardwell, the Rev. Wm. Keeling, and the Rev. W. K. Clay; their plan being different from that adopted by the Parker Society. In Dr Cardwell's work the two Liturgies of Edward VI. are presented in comparison with each other, from copies in the Bodleian Library[3]. In the Rev. W. Keeling's volume the books of Common Prayer of the

---

[1] See note B, preface to second edition, p. xliv.

[2] Burnet, Hist. Ref. II. i. p. 351. Oxford, 1829.

[3] See "Two Books of Common Prayer, set forth by Authority of

Church of England, from the first compilation to the last revision, together with the Liturgy of the Church of Scotland, are presented so as to shew the variations; and the copies of the Books of Common Prayer of King Edward's reign used in that work are the one of May, 1549, by Whitchurch, in the Library of St John's College, Cambridge, and the other of 1552, by Whitchurch, in the Library of the University of Cambridge[4]. In the Rev. W. K. Clay's work, "The Book of Common Prayer illustrated," the object is "to shew its various modifications; the date of its several parts, and the authority on which they rest: with an Appendix, containing the Order of the Communion, the four Acts of Uniformity, the Long Parliament Directory, and sundry other documents[5]."

It was not thought necessary in the present volume to reprint the Psalms, Gospels, and Epistles at length, but merely the references to them, in order that the book might not be of inconvenient size, and that space might be reserved for the valuable pieces which follow.

V. THE PRIMER. The copy of this work, which has been followed, now for the first time reprinted correctly, is in the Bodleian Library, Oxford. By comparing it with a copy in the possession of the Rev. Henry Walter[6], of Hasilbury Bryan, but without minute collation, the Editor

Parliament, in the Reign of King Edward the Sixth; compared with each other," and edited by Edward Cardwell, D.D., Principal of St Alban's Hall, Oxford. Second edition, Oxford, 1841, preface, p. xxxviii.

[4] See "Liturgiæ Britannicæ, or the several editions of the Book of Common Prayer of the Church of England, from its compilation to its last revision; together with the Liturgy set forth for the use of the Church of Scotland: arranged to shew their respective variations, by Wm. Keeling, B.D., Fellow of St John's College, Cambridge." Pickering, London, 1842. Preface.

[5] See "The Book of Common Prayer Illustrated; by Wm. Keatinge Clay, B.D., of Jesus College, Cambridge, and Minor Canon of Ely." Parker, London, 1841.

[6] Editor of "The Primer: A Book of Private Prayer, needful to be used of all Christians, which book was authorised and set forth by order of King Edward VI. to be taught, learned, read, and used, of all his subjects: second edition, with an Appendix." London, 1828.

is able to notice the following variations. Mr Walter's copy has no printed date on the title-page, but there is a written one, 1566, through which some one has drawn the pen, and written underneath, 1553. This, judging from internal evidence, has been done without sufficient authority; for at the end of the extract of the King's privilege is, "God save the Queen," and not, as in the Bodleian copy, "God save the King." In this copy the Order of the Calendar, to the extent of five octavo pages, is omitted; and the Calendar itself is quite different. Before the "Summa[1]," instead of "And in thy faithful prayers remember Thomas Cottesford, the preparer of this preparative," as in the Bodleian copy, in the other it is thus: "And in thy faithful prayers remember that thou pray for Mary, our most virtuous and sovereign Queen." Instead of the fourth collect "for the King[2]," it is "for the Queen;" and in the prayer itself, instead of "our most gracious sovereign King Edward the Sixth," it is, "Our gracious sovereign Lady, Queen Mary;" and so in other parts. The utmost that can be supposed is, that the book without a date in the possession of Mr Walter was in the press when King Edward expired: but this cannot be stated as certain.

VI. A SHORT CATECHISM. This is a very rare book: the copy from which it has been reprinted is in the possession of the Right Honourable Thomas Grenville, London.

This Catechism appears to have been first printed *in Latin* in the year 1552: the articles appended to it, though agreed to in 1552, in the synod at London, were published by the King's commandment on the 20th May, 1553. See Herbert's Ames, i. 628, 602, 536; Strype, Mem. ii. 368; Strype, Cranmer, cap. 27; Wake's Catechism, Preface; Foxe's Martyrs, 1340. The same Articles are printed by Grafton, 1553; and by Wolfe, in Latin, 1553.

Of this Short Catechism there are two reprints: the one

---

[1] See page 377 of this volume.
[2] Page 393.

in the Fathers of the English Church, by the Rev. Legh Richmond, A.M.; and the other, in the Enchiridion Theologicum, or Manual for the use of Students in Divinity, by Dr Randolph.

In the former of these reprints there are some omissions; viz. the copy of the King's Majesty's Letters, &c. some short prayers at the end, and the table of contents; and there are several variations, some of them of importance. It is not stated from what copy the reprint in the "Fathers of the English Church" was made. In the second of these reprints, the Articles, and copy of the King's Majesty's Letters, are omitted. The Table of Contents is given at the end, not at the beginning, in which also there is a slight variation; but in the other parts there is no variation of importance, and but few of any kind. Dr Randolph remarks in his preface, that it is "a Catechism published in the time of King Edward VI., and was the last work of the Reformers in that reign; whence it may be fairly understood to contain, as far as it goes, their ultimate decision, and to represent the sense of the Church of England as then established. In this, according to Archbishop Wake[3], the complete model of our church catechism was laid; and it was also in some measure a public work, 'the examination of it having been committed (as the injunction justifies) to certain bishops and other learned men,' after which it was published by the King's authority. It was printed both in English and Latin, in the same year[4]."

The changes made in the articles from their first promulgation by Edward VI. to their final establishment by the Act of Elizabeth, 1571, have been shewn by Dr Lamb[5].

[3] Preface to his "Principles of the Christian Religion explained; in a brief Commentary on the Church Catechism." London, 1708.

[4] Enchiridion Theologicum, Vol. I. p. vi. Oxford, 1812.

[5] "An Historical Account of the Thirty-nine Articles, from the first promulgation of them in M.D.LII. to their final establishment in M.D.LXXI.; with exact copies of the Latin and English MSS.; and facsimiles of the signatures of the Archbishops and Bishops, &c. By

VII. CATECHISMUS BREVIS. The copy of this document which has been followed, is in the possession of G. Stokes, Esq. Cheltenham, and it has been compared with another edition in the British Museum[1]. Of the two, the latter is the more rarely to be met with: there is no colophon, and the articles are unnumbered. There are three copies of the former in the Lambeth Library, and by comparing them it appears that they are exactly alike in every particular: of the latter there is one copy in that Library.

Heylyn, in his Historia Quinquarticularis[2], says, that this Catechism was set forth by Bishop Poinet[3]: this he has repeated in his Certamen Epistolare[4]; and says also, that "it was so hard to come by, that scarce one scholar in 500 hath ever heard of it, and hardly one of a thousand hath ever seen it."

Among the letters obtained by the Parker Society from Zurich is one from Sir John Cheke to Bullinger, dated June 7, 1553, in which, referring to King Edward, he writes as follows: "Nuper etiam J. Wintoniensis Episcopi Catechismum auctoritate sua scholis commendavit, et articulos synodi Londinensis promulgavit; quos tu si cum Tridentina compares, intelliges spiritus spiritui quid præstet."

The Liturgies and other Formularies here presented to the members of the Parker Society have been prepared with considerable labour, pains, and expense. It is hoped that, considering the great difficulty of securing absolute correctness in every minute particular, these reprints will be found as accurate as can reasonably be expected in works of this description; and the Editor ventures to express his belief that they will bear a comparison with other reprints of the same works. The whole are reprinted from the copies

John Lamb, D.D. Master of Corpus Christi College, Cambridge." London, 1829. See also Bennett's Essay on the Articles, 1715.

[1] The former is denoted by G. S. and the latter by B. M.
[2] Part II. chap. xv, sect. 1. London, 1660.
[3] John, Bishop of Winchester, whose name is spelt indifferently Poinet and Poynet, and sometimes Ponet, and Ponnet.
[4] Certamen Epistolare, pp. 160, 161. London, 1659.

with scrupulous accuracy, with the exception of a few slight variations, obviously required by the sense, and which are always explained in the notes. The punctuation of the original editions has not been departed from beyond what was necessary for correctness and perspicuity.

The Editor thankfully acknowledges his obligations to those gentlemen who kindly favoured him with some valuable communications; particularly to the Rev. W. K. Clay, Minor Canon of Ely; the Rev. Thomas Lathbury, of Bath; the Rev. W. Maskell, Broadleage, Devizes; the Rev. W. H. Cox, Vice-Principal of St Mary's Hall, Oxford; the Rev. H. O. Coxe, Sub-Librarian of the Bodleian; and J. B. Collings, Esq. London. He also gratefully acknowledges the kindness of Dr Routh, President of Magdalene College, Oxford; the Rev. the Principal and Fellows of Brasenose College; the Rev. Dr Bandinel, Librarian of the Bodleian; and the Rev. S. R. Maitland, Librarian to his Grace the Archbishop of Canterbury, in granting him access to the copies collated; and to Antonio Panizzi, Esq., in the facilities afforded in collating in the British Museum. His especial thanks are due to the Right Rev. the Lord Bishop of Cashel, the Right Hon. Thos. Grenville, Lea Wilson, Esq., G. Stokes, Esq., and the Rev. H. Walter, for the loan of valuable copies, referred to in the titles and preface of this work.

For the collation of the Brasenose copy, the Society is indebted to the Rev. W. Kay, Fellow of Lincoln College: this is the only part of the work which has not passed under the review of the Editor. Mr Kay also corrected the proofs of the Primer, and the Rev. H. O. Coxe, Sub-Librarian at the Bodleian, the proof of the Order of Communion; but both of these were subsequently revised by the Editor himself; and the copy of the Book of Common Prayer in Brasenose College was carefully examined, though not collated, by him.

In the Cambridge copy of "The Order of the Communion" (see page iii.) are the following variations from the edition reprinted in this volume.

PAGE	LINE	
1.	19.	of *all* our realms.
	25.	lest *that* by . . . . . *they* become.
2.	9, 10.	with *this* our direction.
	21.	*so* to set forth.
3.	8.	where*of.*
	10.	*for* our offences.
4.	38.	shall *yet* continue still.
5.	7.	*and* drink of.
	8.	*truly* penitent.
	19.	desire *to* sin.
	31.	thus *doing.*
6.	3.	advouterer (om. *an.*)
8.	8.	*unto* everlasting.
	16.	*of* his Son.
	ult.	lifting (om. *up.*)

The following is a facsimile of the Title of the Cambridge copy.

¶ The or=
der of the
Com=
munion.

The Colophon agrees with that of the copy followed (see p. 8.) with only the following variations:

eyght daie	*for*	VIII daye.
second	*for*	seconde.
Edvvard the .VI:	*for*	Edward the sixt.
Rychard	*for*	Richard.
moste	*for*	most.

THE ORDER

OF

THE COMMUNION.

¶ THE ORDER OF THE COM- MV- NION.

[The copy of this edition, which has been followed, is in the possession of the Rev. Dr Routh, President of Magdalene College, Oxford.]

¶ THE PROCLAMATION.

EDWARD by the grace of God King of England, France, and Ireland, defender of the faith, and of the church of England and Ireland in earth the supreme head: To all and singular our loving subjects, greeting: for so much as in our high Court of Parliament lately holden at Westminster, it was by us with the consent of the Lords spiritual and temporal, and Commons there assembled, most godly and agreeably to Christ's holy Institution enacted, that the most blessed Sacrament of the body and blood of our Saviour Christ, should from thenceforth be commonly delivered and ministered unto all persons, within our Realm of England and Ireland, and other our dominions under both kinds, that is to say, of bread and wine (except necessity otherwise require) lest every man phantasyng and devising a sundry way by himself, in the use of this most blessed Sacrament of unity, there might thereby arise any unseemly and ungodly diversity: Our pleasure is, by the advice of our most dear Uncle the Duke of Somerset, Governor of our person, and Protector of our Realms, Dominions, and Subjects, and other of our privy Council, that the said blessed Sacrament be ministered unto our people, only after such form and manner as hereafter, by our authority, with the advice before mentioned is set forth and declared. Willing every man with due reverence and Christian behaviour to come to this holy Sacrament and most blessed Communion, lest they by unworthy receiving of so high mysteries become guilty of the Body and Blood of the Lord, and so eat and drink their own damnation: but rather diligently trying themselves, that they may so come to this holy Table of Christ, and so be partakers of this holy communion, that they may dwell in

Christ, and have Christ dwelling in them: And also with such obedience and conformity, to receive this our ordinance, and most Godly direction, that we may be encouraged from time to time, further to travail for the reformation and setting forth of such Godly orders, as may be most to God's glory, the edifying of our subjects, and for the advancement of true religion. Which thing we (by the help of God) most earnestly intend to bring to effect: Willing all our loving subjects in the mean time, to stay and quiet themselves with our direction, as men content to follow authority, (according to the bounden duty of subjects,) and not enterprising to run afore, and so by their rashness, become the greatest hinderers of such things, as they more arrogantly than Godly would seem (by their own private authority) most hotly to set forward. We would not have our subjects, so much to mislike our judgment, so much to mistrust our zeal, as though we either could not discern what were to be done, or would not do all things in due time: God be praised, we know both what by his word is meet to be redressed, and have an earnest mind, by the advice of our most dear Uncle, and other of our privy Council, with all diligence and convenient speed, to set forth the same, as it may most stand with God's glory, and edifying and quietness of our people: which we doubt not but all our obedient and loving subjects will quietly and reverently tarry for.

GOD SAVE THE KING.

THE ORDER OF THE COMMUNION.

First the Parson, Vicar, or Curate, the next Sunday or holy day, or at the least, one day before he shall minister the Communion, shall give warning to his Parishioners, or those which be present, that they prepare themselves thereto, saying to them openly and plainly as hereafter followeth, or such like.

DEAR friends, and you especially, upon whose souls I have cure and charge, upon   day next I do intend by God's grace to offer to all such as shall be thereto Godly disposed, the most comfortable Sacrament of the body and blood of Christ, to be taken of them in the remembrance of his most fruitful and glorious Passion: by the which Passion we have obtained remission of our sins, and be made partakers of the kingdom of heaven, wherefore we be assured and ascertained, if we come to the said Sacrament with hearty repentance of our offences, steadfast faith in God's mercy and earnest mind to obey God's will, and to offend no more: wherefore our duty is, to come to these holy mysteries with most hearty thanks to be given to almighty God for his infinite mercy and benefits, given and bestowed upon us, his unworthy servants, for whom he hath not only given his body to death, and shed his blood, but also doth vouchsafe in a Sacrament and mystery to give us his said body and blood spiritually: to feed and drink upon. The which Sacrament being so divine and holy a thing, and so comfortable to them which receive it worthily, and so dangerous to them that will presume to take the same unworthily, my duty is to exhort you, in the mean season to consider the greatness of the thing, and to search and examine your own consciences, and that not lightly, nor after the manner of dissimulers with God: but as they which should come to a most godly and heavenly banquet, not to come, but in the marriage garment required of God in scripture, that you may, so much as lieth in you, be found worthy to come to such a table: the ways and means thereto is,

First, that you be truly repentant of your former evil life, and that you confess with an unfeigned heart to Almighty

God your sins and unkindness towards his majesty committed either by will, word, or deed, infirmity or ignorance, and that with inward sorrow and tears you bewail your offences, and require of Almighty God, mercy, and pardon, promising to him, from the bottom of your hearts, the amendment of your former life. And amongst all others, I am commanded of God, especially to move and exhort you, to reconcile yourselves to your neighbours whom you have offended, or who hath offended you, putting out of your hearts all hatred and malice against them, and to be in love and charity with all the world, and to forgive other, as you would that God should forgive you. And if there be any of you whose conscience is troubled and grieved in any thing, lacking comfort or counsel, let him come to me, or to some other discreet and learned Priest taught in the law of God, and confess and open his sin and grief secretly, that he may receive such ghostly counsel, advice, and comfort that his conscience may be relieved, and that of us, as a minister of God and of the Church, he may receive comfort and absolution, to the satisfaction of his mind, and avoiding of all scruple and doubtfulness: requiring such as shall be satisfied with a general Confession, not to be offended with them that doth use, to their further satisfying, the auricular and secret Confession to the Priest; nor those also which think needful or convenient for the quietness of their own consciences particularly to open their sins to the Priest, to be offended with them which are satisfied with their humble confession to God, and the general confession to the Church: but in all these things to follow and keep the rule of charity; and every man to be satisfied with his own conscience, not judging other men's minds or acts, where as he hath no warrant of God's word for the same.

> The time of the communion shall be immediately after that the Priest himself hath received the sacrament, without the varying of any other rite or ceremony in the Mass (until other order shall be provided), but as heretofore usually the Priest hath done with the sacrament of the body, to prepare, bless and consecrate so much as will serve the people: so it shall continue still after the same manner and form, save that he shall bless and consecrate the biggest chalice or some fair and convenient cup or cups full of wine with some water put unto it; and that day, not drink it up all himself, but taking one only sup or draught, leave the rest upon

the altar covered, and turn to them that are disposed to be partakers of the Communion, and shall thus exhort them as followeth.

DEARLY beloved in the Lord, ye coming to this holy communion, must consider what S. Paul writeth to the Corinthians, how he exhorteth all persons diligently to try and examine themselves, or ever they presume to eat of this bread or drink of this cup. For as the benefit is great, if with a true penitent heart, and lively faith we receive this holy Sacrament (for then we spiritually eat the flesh of Christ, and drink his blood; then we dwell in Christ and Christ in us, we be made one with Christ and Christ with us) so is the danger great, if we receive the same unworthily: for then we become guilty of the body and blood of Christ our Saviour, we eat and drink our own damnation (because we make no difference of the Lord's body), we kindle God's wrath over us, we provoke him to plague us with divers diseases and sundry kinds of death. Judge therefore yourselves (brethren) that ye be not judged of the Lord: let your mind be without desire of sin: repent you truly for your sins past, have an earnest and lively faith in Christ, our Saviour, be in perfect charity with all men; so shall ye be meet partakers of these holy mysteries: but above all things you must give most humble and hearty thanks to God the Father, the Son and the Holy Ghost, for the redemption of the world by the death and passion of our Saviour Christ, both God and man, who did humble himself even to the death upon the cross for us miserable sinners, lying in darkness and the shadow of death, that he might make us the children of God, and exalt us to everlasting life. And to the end that we should alway remember the exceeding love of our Master and only Saviour Jesus Christ thus doying for us, and the innumerable benefits which by his precious blood shedding he hath obtained to us, he hath left in these holy mysteries, as a pledge of his love, and a continual remembrance of the same, his own blessed body and precious blood, for us spiritually to feed upon, to our endless comfort and consolation. To him therefore, with the Father and the Holy Ghost, let us give as we are most bounden continual thanks, submitting ourselves wholly to his holy will and pleasure, and studying to serve him in true holiness and righteousness all the days of our life. Amen.

Then the Priest shall say to them which be ready to take the Sacrament.

IF any man here be an open blasphemer, an advouterer, in malice, or envy, or any other notable crime, and be not truly sorry therefore, and earnestly minded to leave the same vices, or that doth not trust himself to be reconciled to Almighty God, and in charity with all the world, let him yet a while bewail his sins, and not come to this holy table, lest after the taking of this most blessed bread the Devil enter into him as he did into Judas, to fulfil in him all iniquity, and to bring him to destruction, both of body and soul.

Here the Priest shall pause a while, to see if any man will withdraw himself: and if he perceive any so to do, then let him commune with him privily at convenient leisure, and see whether he can with good exhortation bring him to grace: and after a little pause, the Priest shall say.

YOU that do truly and earnestly repent you of your sins and offences committed to Almighty God, and be in love and charity with your neighbours, and intend to lead a new life, and heartily to follow the commandments of God, and to walk from henceforth in his holy ways, draw near, and take this holy Sacrament to your comfort, make your humble Confession to Almighty God, and to his holy Church, here gathered together, in his name, meekly kneeling upon your knees.

Then shall a general Confession be made in the name of all those that are minded to receive the holy Communion, either by one of them, or else by one of the Ministers, or by the Priest himself, all kneeling humbly upon their knees.

ALMIGHTY God, Father of our Lord Jesus Christ, maker of all things, judge of all men, we knowledge and bewail our manifold sins and wickedness, which we from time to time most grievously have committed by thought, word, and deed, against thy divine majesty, provoking most justly thy wrath and indignation against us: we do earnestly repent, and be heartily sorry, for these our misdoings: the remembrance of them is grievous unto us, the burthen of them is intolerable. Have mercy upon us, have mercy upon us, most merciful Father, for thy Son our Lord Jesus Christ's sake: forgive us all that is past, and grant that we may ever hereafter serve and please thee, in newness of life, to the

THE ORDER OF THE COMMUNION.

honour and glory of thy name, through Jesus Christ our Lord.

Then shall the Priest stand up, and turning him to the people, say thus.

OUR blessed Lord, who hath left power to his church, to absolve penitent sinners from their sins, and to restore to the grace of the heavenly Father such as truly believe in Christ, have mercy upon you, pardon and deliver you from all sins, confirm and strength you in all goodness, and bring you to everlasting life.

Then shall the Priest stand up, and turning him toward the people, say thus.

Hear what comfortable words our Saviour Christ saith to all that truly turn to him.

COME unto me all that travail and be heavy loden, and I shall refresh you. So God loved the world, that he gave his only begotten Son, to the end that all that believe in him should not perish, but have life everlasting.

Hear also what Saint Paul saith.

This is a true saying, and worthy of all men to be embraced and received, that Jesus Christ came into this world to save sinners.

Hear also what Saint John saith.

If any man sin, we have an Advocate with the Father, Jesus Christ the righteous, he it is that obtained grace for our sins.

Then shall the Priest kneel down and say, in the name of all them that shall receive the communion, this prayer following.

WE do not presume to come to this thy table (O merciful Lord) trusting in our own righteousness, but in thy manifold and great mercies: we be not worthy so much as to gather up the crumbs under thy table: but thou art the same Lord, whose property is always, to have mercy: grant us therefore gracious Lord, so to eat the flesh of thy dear Son Jesus Christ, and to drink his blood, in these holy Mysteries, that we may continually dwell in him, and he in us, that our sinful bodies may be made clean by his body, and our souls washed through his most precious blood. Amen.

Then shall the Priest rise, the people still reverently kneeling, and the Priest shall deliver the Communion, first to the Ministers, if any be there present, that they may be ready to help the Priest, and after to the other. And when he doth deliver the sacrament of the body of Christ he shall say to every one these words following.

THE body of our Lord Jesus Christ, which was given for thee, preserve thy body unto everlasting life.

And the Priest delivering the Sacrament of the blood, and giving every one to drink once and no more, shall say.

THE blood of our Lord Jesus Christ, which was shed for thee, preserve thy soul to everlasting life.

If there be a Deacon or other Priest, then shall he follow with the Chalice, and as the Priest ministereth the bread, so shall he for more expedition minister the Wine, in form before written.

Then shall the Priest, turning him to the people, let the people depart with this blessing.

THE peace of God, which passeth all understanding, keep your hearts and minds, in the knowledge and love of God, and in his Son Jesus Christ our Lord.

To the which the people shall answer.

Amen.

Note, that the Bread that shall be consecrated shall be such as heretofore hath been accustomed. And every of the said consecrated Breads shall be broken in two pieces, at the least, or more by the discretion of the Minister, and so distributed. And men must not think less to be received in part, than in the whole, but in each of them the whole body of our Saviour Jesu Christ.

Note, that if it doth so chance, that the wine hallowed and consecrate doth not suffice or be enough for them that do take the Communion, the Priest, after the first Cup or Chalice be emptied, may go again to the altar, and reverently, and devoutly, prepare, and consecrate another, and so the third, or more, likewise beginning at these words, *Simili modo postquam cœnatum est,* and ending at these words, *qui pro vobis et pro multis effundetur in remissionem peccatorum,* and without any levation or lifting up.

¶ Imprinted at London, the viij
daye of Marche, in the seconde
yere of the reigne of our souereigne lorde Kyng Ed-
ward the sixt. By
Richard Graf
ton, prin-
ter to
his most royall
Maiestie.

In the yere of our Lorde
M.D.XLVIII.
Cum priuilegio ad impri-
mendum solum.

THE
BOOK OF COMMON PRAYER

AND

ADMINISTRATION OF THE SACRAMENTS

AND OTHER

RITES AND CEREMONIES

IN THE

CHURCH OF ENGLAND.

1549.

THE

booke of the common
prayer and admi-
nistracion of
the
Sacramentes, and other
rites and ceremonies of
the Churche: after the
use of the Churche
of England.

LONDINI IN OFFICINA
Edouardi Whitchurche.

Cum priuilegio ad imprimendum folum.
ANNO DO. 1549. *Menfe*
Maij.

[The copy of this edition of Whitchurch, which has been followed, is in the British Museum, 468, b. 4.]

THE

booke of the common
prayer and admi=
nistracion of
the
Sacramentes, and other
rites and Ceremonies of
the Churche: after the
use of the Churche
of England.

LONDINI IN OFFICINA
Edouardi Whitchurche.

Cum priuilegio ad imprimendum folum.

ANNO. DO. 1549. *Mense
Junii.*

[*The colophon of this edition is as follows.*]

Imprinted at London in
Fleteftrete, at the figne of the Sunne ouer againft
the conduyte, by EdVVarde VVhitchurche
The .xvi. daye of Iune, the
yeare of our Lorde,
1549.

[The copy of this edition of Whitchurch, which has been collated, is in the British Museum, C. 9, c. 11.]

THE
booke of the common praier
and adminiftracion of the
Sacramentes, and
other rites and
ceremonies
of the
Churche: after the
use of the Churche of
Englande.

LONDINI, *in officina Richardi Graftoni,*
Regij impreſſoris.

Cum priuilegio ad imprimendum ſolum.

Anno Domini. M.D.XLIX.
Menſe Martij.

[*The colophon of the whole book is as follows: besides which there are two other colophons noticed in the Preface.*]

Imprinted at London in
Flete ftrete, at the signe of the Sunne ouer against
the conduyte, by Edvvarde VVhitchurche.
The seuenth daye of Marche, the
yeare of our Lorde
1549.

[*The copy of this edition, which has been collated, is in Brazen Nose College, Oxford.*]

THE

booke of the common praier
and adminiſtracion of the
Sacramentes, and
other rites and
ceremonies
of the
Churche: after the
use of the Churche of
Englande.

LONDINI, *in officina Richardi Graftoni,*
Regij impreſſoris.

Cum priuilegio ad imprimendum ſolum.

Anno Domini. M.D.XLIX.
Menſe Martij.

[*The colophon, at the end of the Communion, of this edition is as follows.*]

Imprinted at London viij daye of Marche, in the third
yere of the reigne of our ſouereigne Lorde Kyng
Edward the vi. by Richard Grafton, prin-
ter to his most royal Maiestie.

Cum priuilegio ad imprimendum ſolum.

[The copy of this edition, which has been collated, is in the possession of the Right Reverend Bishop of Cashel, Palace, Waterford.]

THE

𝔟𝔬𝔬𝔨𝔢 of 𝔱𝔥𝔢 𝔠𝔬𝔪𝔪𝔬𝔫 𝔭𝔯𝔞𝔦𝔢𝔯

𝔞𝔫𝔡 𝔞𝔡𝔪𝔦𝔫𝔦𝔰𝔱𝔯𝔞𝔠𝔦𝔬𝔫 of 𝔱𝔥𝔢

𝔖𝔞𝔠𝔯𝔞𝔪𝔢𝔫𝔱𝔢𝔰, 𝔞𝔫𝔡

𝔬𝔱𝔥𝔢𝔯 𝔯𝔦𝔱𝔢𝔰 𝔞𝔫𝔡

𝔠𝔢𝔯𝔢𝔪𝔬𝔫𝔦𝔢𝔰

of 𝔱𝔥𝔢

𝔎𝔥𝔲𝔯𝔠𝔥𝔢: after 𝔱𝔥𝔢

𝔲𝔰𝔢 of 𝔱𝔥𝔢 𝔎𝔥𝔲𝔯𝔠𝔥𝔢 of

𝔈𝔫𝔤𝔩𝔞𝔫𝔡𝔢.

LONDINI, *in officina Richardi Graftoni,*
Regij impreſſoris.

Cum priuilegio ad imprimendum ſolum.

Anno Domini M.D.XLIX.
Menſe Martij.

[*The colophon of this edition is as follows.*]

Excuſum Londini, in ædibus Richardi Graftoni,
Regij impreſſoris.
Menſe Junij. M.D.xlix.

Cum priuilegio ad imprimendum ſolum.

[The copy of this edition, which has been collated, is in the British Museum, 468, b. 3.]

The Boke

of the common praier and administration of ye Sacramentes & other rites
and ceremonies
of the church:
after the
use
of the Church
of Eng-
land.

Wigorniæ in officina Ioannis Ofwæni.

Cum priuilegio ad imprimendum folum.

ANNO Do. 1549.
Menfe Iulii.

[*The colophon of this edition is as follows.*]

Imprinted the xxx
day of July,
ANNO DO. M.D.XLIX.
At Worcester by Jhon
Olwen.

Cum priuilegio ad imprimendum folum.

[The copy of this edition, which has been collated, is in the British Museum, 468, b. 5.]

THE CONTENTS OF THIS BOOK.

1. A PREFACE.
2. A Table and Kalendar for Psalms and Lessons, with necessary rules pertaining to the same.
3. The Order for Matins and Evensong, throughout the year.
4. The Introits, Collects, Epistles and Gospels, to be used at the celebration of the Lord's Supper and holy Communion through the year, with proper Psalms and Lessons, for divers feasts and days.
5. The Supper of the Lord and holy Communion, commonly called the Mass.
6. [1]The Litany and Suffrages.
7. Of Baptism, both public and private.
8. Of Confirmation, where also is a Catechism for children.
9. Of Matrimony.
10. Of Visitation of the Sick, and Communion of the same.
11. Of Burial.
12. The purification of women.
13. A declaration of Scripture, with certain prayers to be used the first day of Lent, commonly called Ashwednesday.
14. Of Ceremonies omitted or retained.
15. Certain notes for the more plain explication and decent ministration of things contained in this book.

[[1] The Litany and Suffrages omitted in Grafton, 1, but given in a separate sheet at the end.]

THE PREFACE.

There was never any thing by the wit of man so well devised, or so surely established, which (in continuance of time) hath not been corrupted: as (among other things) it may plainly appear by the common prayers in the Church, commonly called divine service: the first original and ground whereof if a man would search out by the ancient fathers, he shall find that the same was not ordained, but of a good purpose, and for a great advancement of godliness: for they so ordered the matter, that all the whole Bible (or the greatest part thereof) should be read over once in the year, intending thereby, that the Clergy, and specially such as were Ministers of the congregation, should (by often reading and meditation of God's word) be stirred up to godliness themselves, and be more able also to exhort other by wholesome doctrine, and to confute them that were adversaries to the truth. And further, that the people (by daily hearing of holy scripture read in the Church) should continually profit more and more in the knowledge of God, and be the more inflamed with the love of his true religion. But these many years passed, this godly and decent order of the ancient fathers hath bee[1] so altered, broken, and neglected, by planting in uncertain stories[2], Legends, Responds, Verses, vain repetitions, Commemorations, and Synodals, that commonly when any book of the Bible was begun, before three or four chapters were read out, all the rest were unread. And in this sort, the book of Esaie was begun in Advent, and the book of Genesis in Septuagesima: but they were only begun, and never read thorow[3]. After a like sort were other books of holy scripture used. And moreover, whereas St Paul would have such language spoken to the people in the church, as they might understand and have profit by hearing the same; the service in this Church of England

[1 *been*, Grafton, 2; *be*, Oswen.]
[2 See an explanation of these and the following terms in Wheatly on the Common Prayer, Chap. III. Sect. 9.]
[3 *through*, Grafton, 2.]

(these many years) hath been read in Latin to the people, which they understood not; so that they have heard with their ears only; and their hearts, spirit, and mind, have not been edified thereby. And furthermore, notwithstanding that the ancient fathers had divided the Psalms into seven portions, whereof every one was called a nocturn; now of late time a few of them have been daily said (and oft repeated) and the rest utterly omitted. Moreover, the number and hardness of the rules called the Pie[1], and the manifold changings of the service, was the cause, that to turn the book only was so hard and intricate a matter, that many times there was more business to find out what should be read, than to read it when it was found out.

These inconveniences therefore considered, here is set forth such an order, whereby the same shall be redressed. And for a readiness in this matter, here is drawn out a Kalendar for that purpose, which is plain and easy to be understood; wherein (so much as may be) the reading of holy scripture is so set forth, that all things shall be done in order, without breaking one piece thereof from another. For this cause be cut off Anthems, Responds, Invitatories[2], and such like things, as did break the continual course of the reading of the scripture. Yet because there is no remedy, but that of necessity there must be some rules: therefore certain rules are here set forth, which as they be few in number, so they be plain and easy to be understood. So that here you have an order for prayer (as touching the reading of holy scripture) much agreeable to the mind and purpose of the old fathers, and a great deal more profitable and commodious, than that which of late was used. It is more profitable, because here are left out many things, whereof some be untrue, some uncertain, some vain and superstitious: and is ordained nothing to be read, but the very[3] pure word of God, the holy scriptures, or that which is evidently grounded upon the same; and that in such a language and order, as is most easy and plain for the under-

[[1] *Pie*, a directory for devotional services, so called because it was pied, or parti-coloured.]

[[2] *Invitatories*. Hymns of invitation to prayer. In the Latin Services the 95th psalm is called the Invitatory.]

[[3] *very*, omitted in Oswen.]

standing, both of the readers and hearers. It is also more commodious, both for the shortness thereof, and for the plainness of the order, and for that the rules be few and easy. Furthermore, by this order, the curates shall need none other books for their public service, but this book and the Bible: by the means whereof, the people shall not be at so great charge for books, as in time past they have been.

And where heretofore there hath been great diversity in saying and singing in churches within this realm: some following Salisbury use, some Hereford use, some the use of Bangor, some of York, and some of Lincoln: Now from henceforth, all the whole realm shall have but one use. And if any would judge this way more painful, because that all things must be read upon the book, whereas before, by the reason of so often repetition, they could say many things by heart: if those men will weigh their labour, with the profit in knowledge, which daily they shall obtain by reading upon the book, they will not refuse the pain, in consideration of the great profit that shall ensue thereof.

And forsomuch as nothing can, almost, be so plainly set forth, but doubts may rise in the use and practising of the same: to appease all such diversity (if any arise), and for the resolution of all doubts, concerning the manner how to understand, do, and execute the things contained in this book, the parties that so doubt, or diversely take any thing, shall always resort to the Bishop of the Diocese, who by his discretion shall take order for the quieting and appeasing of the same: so that the same order be not contrary to anything contained in this book.

¶ Though it be appointed in the afore written preface, that all things shall be read and sung in the church, in the English tongue, to the end that the congregation may be thereby edified: yet it is not meant, but when men say Matins and Evensong privately, they may say the same in any language that they themselves do understand. Neither that any man shall be bound to the saying of them, but such as from time to time, in Cathedral and Collegiate Churches, Parish Curches, and Chapels to the same annexed, shall serve the congregation.

THE
TABLE AND KALENDAR,
EXPRESSING THE
ORDER OF THE PSALMS AND LESSONS,
TO BE SAID AT

MATINS AND EVENSONG, THROUGHOUT THE YEAR,

EXCEPT CERTAIN PROPER FEASTS, AS THE RULES FOLLOWING MORE PLAINLY DECLARE[1].

The order how the Psalter is appointed to be read.

THE Psalter shall be read through once every month: and because that some months be longer than some other be, it is thought good to make them even by this means.

To every month, as concerning this purpose, shall be appointed just 30 days.

And because January and March hath one day above the said number, and February, which is placed between them both, hath only 28 days, February shall borrow of either of the months of January and March one day, and so the Psalter which shall be read in February, must be begun the last day of January, and ended the first day of March.

And whereas May, July, August, October and December have 31 days apiece, it is ordered that the same Psalms shall be read the last day of the said months[2], which were read the day before: so that the Psalter may be begun again the first day of the next months ensuing.

Now to know what Psalms shall be read every day, look in the Kalendar the number that is appointed for the Psalms, and then find the same number in this Table, and upon that number shall you see, what Psalms shall be said at Matins, and Evensong.

And where the 119th Psalm is divided into 22 portions, and is over long to be read at one time: it is so ordered,

[1 "A Table and Kalendar for Psalms and Lessons, with necessary rules pertaining to the same." Grafton, 2.]
[2 month, Grafton, 2.]

that at one time shall not be read above 4 or 5 of the said portions, as you shall perceive to be noted in this Table.

And here is also to be noted, that in this Table, and in all other parts of the service, where any Psalms are appointed, the number is expressed after the great English Bible, which from the 9th Psalm unto the 148th Psalm (following the division of the Ebrues) doth vary in numbers from the common Latin translation.

A Table for the Order of the Psalms, to be said at Matins and Evensong.

	Matins.	Evensong.
i.	1, 2, 3, 4, 5.	6, 7, 8.
ii.	9, 10, 11.	12, 13, 14.
iii.	15, 16, 17.	18.
iv.	19, 20, 21.	22, 23.
v.	24, 25, 26.	27, 28, 29.
vi.	30, 31.	32, 33, 34.
vii.	35, 36.	37.
viii.	38, 39, 40.	41, 42, 43.
ix.	44, 45, 46.	47, 48, 49.
x.	50, 51, 52.	53, 54, 55.
xi.	56, 57, 58.	59, 60, 61.
xii.	62, 63, 64.	65, 66, 67.
xiii.	68.	69, 70.
xiv.	71, 72.	73, 74.
xv.	75, 76, 77.	78.
xvi.	79, 80, 81.	82, 83, 84, 85.
xvii.	86, 87, 88.	89.
xviii.	90, 91, 92.	93, 94.
xix.	95, 96, 97.	98, 99, 100, 101.
xx.	102, 103.	104.
xxi.	105.	106.
xxii.	107.	108, 109.
xxiii.	110, 111, 112, 113.	114, 115.
xxiv.	116, 117, 118.	119 Inde. 4.
xxv.	Inde. 5.	Inde. 4.
xxvi.	Inde. 5.	Inde. 4.
xxvii.	120, 121, 122, 123, 124, 125.	126, 127, 128, 129, 130, 131.
xxviii.	132, 133, 134, 135.	136, 137, 138.
xxix.	139, 140, 141.	142, 143.
xxx.	144, 145, 146.	147, 148, 149, 150.

The Order how the rest of holy Scripture (beside the Psalter) is appointed to be read.

¶ The Old Testament is appointed for the first Lessons, at Matins and Evensong, and shall be read through every year once, except certain books and chapters, which be least edifying, and might best be spared, and therefore are left unread.

¶ The New Testament is appointed for the second Lessons, at Matins and Evensong, and shall be read over orderly every year thrice, beside the Epistles and Gospels; except the Apocalypse, out of the which there be only certain Lessons appointed upon divers proper feasts.

And to know what Lessons shall be read every day: find the day of the month in the Kalendar following: and there ye shall perceive the books and chapters, that shall be read for the Lessons, both at Matins and Evensong.

And here is to be noted, that whensoever there be any proper Psalms or Lessons appointed for any feast, moveable or unmoveable; then the Psalms and Lessons appointed in the Kalendar shall be omitted for that time.

Ye must note also, that the Collect, Epistle, and Gospel, appointed for the Sunday, shall serve all the week after, except there fall some feast that hath his proper.

¶ This is also to be noted, concerning the leap years, that the 25th day of February, which in leap years is counted for two days, shall in those two days alter neither Psalm nor Lesson: but the same Psalms and Lessons, which be said the first day, shall serve also for the second day.

Also, wheresoever the beginning of any Lesson, Epistle, or Gospel is not expressed, there ye must begin at the beginning of the chapter.

JANUARY.

JANUARY.		Psalms.	MATINS.		EVENSONG.	
			1 Less.	2 Less.	1 Less.	2 Less.
A	1	Circumci.	Gen. 17	Roma. 2	Deut. 10	Collos. 2
b	2		Gene. 1	Math. 1	Gene. 2	Roma. 1
c	3		3	2	4	2
d	4 No.		5	3	6	3
e	3 No.		7	4	8	4
f	Prid. No.	Epiphani.	Esai. 60	Luke 3	Esai. 49	John 2
g	Nonas.		Gen. 9	Math. 5	Gen. 11	Roma. 5
A	8 Id.		12	6	13	6
b	7 Id.		14	7	15	7
c	6 Id.		16	8	17	8
d	5 Id.		18	9	19	9
e	4 Id.		20	10	21	10
f	3 Id.		22	11	23	11
g	Prid. Id.		24	12	25	12
A	Idus.		26	13	27	13
b	19 kl.		28	14	29	14
c	18 kl.		30	15	31	15
d	17 kl.		32	16	33	16
e	16 kl.		34	17	35	1 Cor. 1
f	15 kl.		36	18	37	2
g	14 kl.		38	19	39	3
A	13 kl.		40	20	41	4
b	12 kl.		42	21	43	5
c	11 kl.		44	22	45	6
d	10 kl.	Con. Pauli.	46	Act. 22	47	Act. 26
e	9 kl.		48	Mat. 23	49	1 Cor. 7
f	8 kl.		50	24	Exod. 1	8
g	7 kl.		Exod. 2	25	3	9
A	6 kl.		4	26	5	10
b	5 kl.		6	27	7	11
c	4 kl.		8	28	9	12
	Prid. kl.					

FEBRUARY.

FEBRUARY.		Psalms.	MATINS.		EVENSONG.	
			1 Less.	2 Less.	1 Less.	2 Less.
d	1		Exod. 10	Mark 1	Exod. 11	1 Cor. 13
e	2	Puri. Ma.	12	2	13	14
f	3		14	3	15	15
g	4 No.		16	4	17	16
A	Prid. No.		18	5	19	2 Cor. 1
b	Nonas.		20	6	21	2
c	8 Id.		22	7	23	3
d	7 Id.		24	8	32	4
e	6 Id.		33	9	34	5
f	5 Id.		35	10	40	6
g	4 Id.		Leui. 18	11	Leui. 19	7
A	3 Id.		20	12	Nume.10	8
b	Prid. Id.		Num. 11	13	12	9
c	Idus.		13	14	14	10
d	16 kl.		15	15	16	11
e	15 kl.		17	16	18	12
f	14 kl.		19	Luk. di. 1	20	13
g	13 kl.		21	di. 1	22	Galath. 1
A	12 kl.		23	2	24	2
b	11 kl.		25	3	26	3
c	10 kl.		27	4	28	4
d	9 kl.		29	5	30	5
e	8 kl.		31	6	32	6
f	7 kl.		33	7	34	Ephes. 1
g	6 kl.	Mathias.	35	8	36	2
A	5 kl.		Deut. 1	9	Deut. 2	3
b	4 kl.		3	10	4	4
c	3 kl.		5	11	6	5
	Prid. kl.					

σ 1 [dimidium primi, half of ch. i.]

MARCH.

MARCH.		Psalms.	MATINS.		EVENSONG.	
			1 Less.	2 Less.	1 Less.	2 Less.
d	1		Deu. 7	Luk. 12	Deu. 8	Ephe. 6
e	2		9	13	10	Philip. 1
f	3		11	14	12	2
g	4	Kalend.	13	15	14	3
A	5	6 No.	15	16	16	4
b	6	5 No.	17	17	18	Collos. 1
c	7	4 No.	19	18	20	2
d	8	3 No.	21	19	22	3
e	9	Prid. No.	23	20	24	4
f	10	Nonas.	25	21	26	1 Thes. 1
g	11	8 Id.	27	22	28	2
A	12	7 Id.	29	23	30	3
b	13	6 Id.	31	24	32	4
c	14	5 Id.	33	John. 1	34	5
d	15	4 Id.	Josue. 1	2	Josue. 2	2 Thes. 1
e	16	3 Id.	3	3	4	2
f	17	Prid. Id.	5	4	6	3
g	18	Idus.	7	5	8	1 Timo. 1
A	19	17 kl.	9	6	10	2, 3
b	20	16 kl.	11	7	12	4
c	21	15 kl.	13	8	14	5
d	22	14 kl.	15	9	16	6
e	23	13 kl.	17	10	18	2 Tim. 1
f	24	12 kl.	19	11	20	2
g	25	11 kl. Annuncia.	21	12	22	3
A	26	10 kl.	23	13	24	4
b	27	9 kl.	Judic. 1	14	Judic. 2	Titus 1
c	28	8 kl.	3	15	4	2, 3
d	29	7 kl.	5	16	6	Phile. 1
e	30	6 kl.	7	17	8	Hebre. 1
f	31	5 kl.	9	18	10	2

APRIL.

APRIL.		Psalms.	MATINS.		EVENSONG.	
			1 Less.	2 Less.	1 Less.	2 Less.
g	1	Kalend.	Judi. 11	John 19	Judi. 12	Hebre. 3
A	2	4 No.	13	20	14	4
b	3	3 No.	15	21	16	5
c	4	Prid. No.	17	Acts 1	18	6
d	5	Nonas.	19	2	20	7
e	6	8 Id.	21	3	Ruth 1	8
f	7	7 Id.	Ruth 2	4	3	9
g	8	6 Id.	4	5	1 Regum 1	10
A	9	5 Id.	1 Regum 2	6	3	11
b	10	4 Id.	4	7	5	12
c	11	3 Id.	6	8	7	13
d	12	Prid. Id.	8	9	9	Jacob. 1
e	13	Idus.	10	10	11	2
f	14	18 kl.	12	11	13	3
g	15	17 kl.	14	12	15	4
A	16	16 kl.	16	13	17	5
b	17	15 kl.	18	14	19	1 Peter. 1
c	18	14 kl.	20	15	21	2
d	19	13 kl.	22	16	23	3
e	20	12 kl.	24	17	25	4
f	21	11 kl.	26	18	27	5
g	22	10 kl.	28	19	29	2 Peter. 1
A	23	9 kl.	30	20	31	2
b	24	8 kl. Mar. Evan.	2 Reg. 1	21	2 Reg. 2	3
c	25	7 kl.	3	22	4	1 John. 1
d	26	6 kl.	5	23	6	2
e	27	5 kl.	7	24	8	3
f	28	4 kl.	9	25	10	4
g	29	3 kl.	11	26	12	5
A	30	Prid. kl.	13	27	14	2, 3 Joh.

MAY.

MAY.		Psalms.	MATINS.		EVENSONG.	
			1 Less.	2 Less.	1 Less.	2 Less.
b	Kalend.	1 Phil. & Ja.	2 Re. 15	Acts 8	2 Re. 16	Judas. 1
c	6 No.	2	17	28	18	Roma. 1
d	5 No.	3	19	Math. 1	20	2
e	4 No.	4	21	2	22	3
f	3 No.	5	23	3	24	4
g	Prid. No.	6	3 Reg. 1	4	3 Reg. 2	5
A	Nonas.	7	3	5	4	6
b	8 Id.	8	5	6	6	7
c	7 Id.	9	7	7	8	8
d	6 Id.	10	9	8	10	9
e	5 Id.	11	11	9	12	10
f	4 Id.	12	13	10	14	11
g	3 Id.	13	15	11	16	12
A	Prid. Id.	14	17	12	18	13
b	Idus.	15	19	13	20	14
c	17 kl.	16	21	14	22	15
d	16 kl.	17	4 Reg. 1	15	4 Re. 2	16
e	15 kl.	18	3	16	4	1 Cor. 1
f	14 kl.	19	5	17	6	2
g	13 kl.	20	7	18	8	3
A	12 kl.	21	9	19	10	4
b	11 kl.	22	11	20	12	5
c	10 kl.	23	13	21	14	6
d	9 kl.	24	15	22	16	7
e	8 kl.	25	17	23	18	8
f	7 kl.	26	19	24	20	9
g	6 kl.	27	21	25	22	10
A	5 kl.	28	23	26	24	11
b	4 kl.	29	25	27	1 Esd. 1	12
c	3 kl.	30	1 Esd. 2	28	3	13
d	Prid. kl.	30	4	Mark 1	5	14

JUNE.

JUNE.		Psalms.	MATINS.		EVENSONG.	
			1 Less.	2 Less.	1 Less.	2 Less.
e	Kalend.	1	1 Esd. 6	Mark 2	1 Esd. 7	1 Cor. 15
f	4 No.	2	8	3	9	16
g	3 No.	3	10	4	2 Esd. 1	2 Cor. 1
A	Prid. No.	4	2 Esd. 2	5	4	2
b	Nonas.	5	4	6	5	3
c	8 Id.	6	6	7	7	4
d	7 Id.	7	8	8	9	5
e	6 Id.	8	10	9	11	6
f	5 Id.	9	12	10	13	7
g	4 Id.	10	Hester 1	11	Hester 2	8
A	3 Id.	11 Barna. apo.	3	Act. 14	4	Acts 15
b	Prid. Id.	12	5	Mar. 12	6	2 Cor. 9
c	Idus.	13	7	13	8	10
d	18 kl.	14	9	14	Job 1	11
e	17 kl.	15	Job 2	15	3	12
f	16 kl.	16	4	16	5	13
g	15 kl.	17	6	Luke 1	7	Gala. 1
A	14 kl.	18	8	2	9	2
b	13 kl.	19	10	3	11	3
c	12 kl.	20	12	4	13	4
d	11 kl.	21	14	5	15	5
e	10 kl.	22	16	6	17. 18	6
f	9 kl.	23	19	Mat. 3	20	Ephe. 1
g	8 kl.	24 Na. Jo. Ba.	Mala. 3	Lu. 8	Mal. 3[1]	Math. 14
A	7 kl.	25	Job 21	9	Job 22	Ephe. 2
b	6 kl.	26	23	10	24. 25	3
c	5 kl.	27	26. 27	11	28	4
d	4 kl.	28	29	Acts 3	30	5
e	3 kl.	29 S. Peter.	31	Luke 12	32	Acts 4
f	Prid. kl.	30	33		34	Ephe. 6

[1] [Mal. 4. Whitchurch Junii, Grafton, 1 and 2; and Oswen.]

26

AUGUST.

		AUGUST.	Psalms.	MATINS. 1 Less.	MATINS. 2 Less.	EVENSONG. 1 Less.	EVENSONG. 2 Less.
c	1	Kalend.		Jere. 12	John. 20	Jere. 13	Hebr. 4
d	2	4 No.		14	21	15	5
e	3	3 No.		16	Acts 1	17	6
f	4	Prid. No.		18	2	19	7
g	5	Nonas.		20	3	21	8
A	6	8 Id.		22	4	23	9
b	7	7 Id.		24	5	25	10
c	8	6 Id.		26	6	27	11
d	9	5 Id.		28	7	29	12
e	10	4 Id.		30	8	31	13
f	11	3 Id.		32	9	33	Jacob. 1
g	12	Prid. Id.		34	10	35	2
A	13	Idus.		36	11	37	3
b	14	19 kl.		38	12	39	4
c	15	18 kl.		40	13	41	5
d	16	17 kl.		42	14	43	Peter. 1
e	17	16 kl.		44	15	45, 46	2
f	18	15 kl.		47	16	48	3
g	19	14 kl.		49	17	50	4
A	20	13 kl.		51	18	52	5
b	21	12 kl.		Lament. 1	19	Lamen. 2	2 Peter. 1
c	22	11 kl.		3	20	4	2
d	23	10 kl.		5	21	Ezech. 2	3
e	24	9 kl.	Bart. Apost.	Ezech. 3	22	6	1 John 1
f	25	8 kl.		7	23	13	2
g	26	7 kl.		14	24	18	3
A	27	6 kl.		33	25	34	4
b	28	5 kl.		Dani. 1	26	Dani. 2	5
c	29	4 kl.		3	27	4	2.3 John
d	30	3 kl.		5	28	6	Jude 1
e	31	Prid. kl.		7	Math. 1	8	Roma. 1

JULY.

		JULY.	Psalms.	MATINS. 1 Less.	MATINS. 2 Less.	EVENSONG. 1 Less.	EVENSONG. 2 Less.
g	1	Kalend.		Job 35	Luk. 13	Job 36	Philip. 1
A	2	6 No.		37	14	38	2
b	3	5 No.		39	15	40	3
c	4	4 No.		41	16	42	4
d	5	3 No.		Prover. 1	17	Prov. 2	Collos. 1
e	6	Prid. No.		3	18	4	2
f	7	Nonas.		5	19	6	3
g	8	8 Id.		7	20	8	4
A	9	7 Id.		9	21	10	1 Thes. 1
b	10	6 Id.		11	22	12	2
c	11	5 Id.		13	23	14	3
d	12	4 Id.		15	24	16	4
e	13	3 Id.		17	John 1	18	5
f	14	Prid. Id.		19	2	20	2 Thes. 1
g	15	Idus.		21	3	22	2
A	16	17 kl.		23	4	24	3
b	17	16 kl.		25	5	26	1 Timo. 1
c	18	15 kl.		27	6	28	2, 3
d	19	14 kl.		29	7	30	4
e	20	13 kl.		31	8	Eccles. 1	5
f	21	12 kl.		Eccles. 2	9	3	6
g	22	11 kl.	Magdalen.	4	10	5	2 Tim. 1
A	23	10 kl.		6	11	7	2
b	24	9 kl.		8	12	9	3
c	25	8 kl.	James Ap.	10	13	11	4
d	26	7 kl.		12	14	Jere. 1	Titus. 1
e	27	6 kl.		Jere. 2	15	3	2, 3
f	28	5 kl.		4	16	5	Phile. 1
g	29	4 kl.		6	17	7	Hebre. 1
A	30	3 kl.		8	18	9	2
b	31	Prid. kl.		10	19	11	3

SEPTEMBER.

SEPTEMBER.		Psalms.	MATINS.		EVENSONG.	
			1 Less.	2 Less.	1 Less.	2 Less.
f	Kalend.	1	Dani. 9	Math. 2	Dani. 10	Roma. 2
g	4 No.	2	11	3	12	3
A	3 No.	3	13	4	14	4
b	Prid. No.	4	Ose. 1	5	Ose. 2. 3	5
c	Nonas.	5	4	6	5. 6	6
d	8 Id.	6	7	7	8	7
e	7 Id.	7	9	8	10	8
f	6 Id.	8	11	9	12	9
g	5 Id.	9	13	10	14	10
A	4 Id.	10	Joel 1	11	Joel 2	11
b	3 Id.	11	3	12	Amos 1	12
c	Prid. Id.	12	Amos. 2	13	3	13
d	Idus.	13	4	14	5	14
e	18 kl.	14	6	15	7	15
f	17 kl.	15	8	16	9	16
g	16 kl.	16	Abdias. 1	17	Jonas. 1	1 Cor. 1
A	15 kl.	17	Jon. 2. 3	18	4	2
b	14 kl.	18	Miche. 1	19	Miche. 2	3
c	13 kl.	19	3	20	4	4
d	12 kl.	20	5	21	6	5
e	11 kl.	21	7	22	Naum. 1	6
f	10 kl.	22	Naum. 2	23	3	7
g	9 kl.	23	Abacu. 1	24	Abacu. 2	8
A	8 kl.	24	3	25	Sopho. 1	9
b	7 kl.	25	Soph. 1	26	3	10
c	6 kl.	26	Agge. 1	27	Agge. 2	11
d	5 kl.	27	Zech. 1	28	Zech. 2.3	12
e	4 kl.	28	4. 5	Marke 1	6	13
f	3 kl.	29	7	2	8	14
g	Prid. kl.	30	9	3	10	15

Mathewe. (21) Michael. (29)

OCTOBER.

OCTOBER.		Psalms.	MATINS.		EVENSONG.	
			1 Less.	2 Less.	1 Less.	2 Less.
A	Kalend.	1	Zacha.11	Mark 4	Zacha.12	1 Cor. 16
b	6 No.	2	13	5	14	2 Cor. 1
c	5 No.	3	Mala. 1	6	Mala. 2	2
d	4 No.	4	3	7	4	3
e	3 No.	5	Toby. 1	8	Toby. 2	4
f	Prid. No.	6	3	9	4	5
g	Nonas.	7	5	10	6	6
A	8 Id.	8	7	11	8	7
b	7 Id.	9	9	12	10	8
c	6 Id.	10	11	13	12	9
d	5 Id.	11	13	14	14	10
e	4 Id.	12	Judith 1	15	Judit. 2	11
f	3 Id.	13	3	16	4	12
g	Prid. Id.	14	5	Lu. di. 1	6	13
A	Idus.	15	7	di. 1	8	Gala. 1
b	17 kl.	16	9	2	10	2
c	16 kl.	17	11	3	12	3
d	15 kl.	18	13	4	14	4
e	14 kl.	19	15	5	16	5
f	13 kl.	20	Sapi. 1	6	Sapi. 2	6
g	12 kl.	21	3	7	4	Ephe. 1
A	11 kl.	22	5	8	6	2
b	10 kl.	23	7	9	8	3
c	9 kl.	24	9	10	10	4
d	8 kl.	25	11	11	12	5
e	7 kl.	26	13	12	14	6
f	6 kl.	27	15	13	16	Philip. 1
g	5 kl.	28	17	14	18	2
A	4 kl.	29	19	15	Eccls. 1	3
b	3 kl.	30	Eccls. 2	16	3	4
c	Prid. kl.	31	4	17	5	Collos. 1

Luc. Evan. (18) Sy. & Ju. (28)

28

DECEMBER.

DECEMBER.			Psalms.	1 Less.	2 Less.	EVENSONG.	2 Less.
f	1	Kalend.	1	Esai. 7	Actes 2	1 Less. Esai. 8	Hebr. 7
g	2	4 No.	2	9	4	10	8
A	3	3 No.	3	11	5	12	9
b	4	Prid. No.	4	13	6. 7	14	10
c	5	Nonas.	5	15	6. 7	16	11
d	6	8 Id.	6	17	8	18	12
e	7	7 Id.	7	19	9	20. 21	13
f	8	6 Id.	8	22	10	23	Jacob. 1
g	9	5 Id.	9	24	11	25	2
A	10	4 Id.	10	26	12	27	3
b	11	3 Id.	11	28	13	29	4
c	12	Prid. Id.	12	30	14	31	5
d	13	Idus.	13	32	15	33	1 Peter. 1
e	14	19 kl.	14	34	16	35	2
f	15	18 kl.	15	36	17	37	3
g	16	17 kl.	16	38	18	39	4
A	17	16 kl.	17	40	19	41	5
b	18	15 kl.	18	42	20	43	2 Peter. 1
c	19	14 kl.	19	44	21	45	2
d	20	13 kl.	20	46	22	47	3
e	21	12 kl.	Tho. Apost. 21	48	23	49	1 John. 1
f	22	11 kl.	22	50	24	51	2
g	23	10 kl.	23	52	25	53	3
A	24	9 kl.	24	54	Math. 1	55	4
b	25	8 kl.	Nati.Domini. 25	Esay. 9	Act 6. 7	Esay. 7	Tit. 3
c	26	7 kl.	Stephan. 26	56	Apoc. 1	57	Actes 7
d	27	6 kl.	John Evan. 27	58	Acte 25	59	Apo. 22
e	28	5 kl.	Innocen. 28	Jer. 31	26	(¹)Esay.60	1 John 5
f	29	4 kl.	29	Esay. 61	27	62	2 John 1
g	30	3 kl.	30	63	28	64	3 John 1
A	31	Prid. kl.	31	65		66	Jude 1

¹ [Is, not in Grafton, 1 and 2.]

NOVEMBER.

NOVEMBER.			Psalms.	1 Less.	MATINS. 2 Less.	EVENSONG. 1 Less.	2 Less.
d	1	Kalend.	All Saints. 1	Sap. 3	He.11.12	Sap. 5	Apoc. 19
e	2	4 No.	2	Eccle. 6	Lu. 18	Eccle. 7	Collos. 2
f	3	3 No.	3	8	19	9	3
g	4	Prid.	4	10	20	11	4
A	5	Nonas.	5	12	21	13	1 Thes. 1
b	6	8 Id.	6	14	22	15	2
c	7	7 Id.	7	16	23	17	3
d	8	6 Id.	8	18	24	19	4
e	9	5 Id.	9	20	John 1	21	5
f	10	4 Id.	10	22	2	23	2 Thes. 1
g	11	3 Id.	11	24	3	25	2
A	12	Prid. Id.	12	26	4	27	3
b	13	Idus.	13	28	5	29	1 Timo.1
c	14	18 kl.	14	30	6	31	2. 3
d	15	17 kl.	15	32	7	33	4
e	16	16 kl.	16	34	8	35	5
f	17	15 kl.	17	36	9	37	6
g	18	14 kl.	18	38	10	39	2 Tim. 1
A	19	13 kl.	19	40	11	41	2
b	20	12 kl.	20	42	12	43	3
c	21	11 kl.	21	44	13	45	4
d	22	10 kl.	22	46	14	47	Titus 1
e	23	9 kl.	23	48	15	49	2. 3
f	24	8 kl.	24	50	16	51	Phile. 1
g	25	7 kl.	25	Baruc. 1	17	Baruc. 2	Hebre. 1
A	26	6 kl.	26	3	18	4	2
b	27	5 kl.	27	5	19	6	3
c	28	4 kl.	28	Esay. 1	20	Esay. 2	4
d	29	3 kl.	29	3	21	4	5
e	30	Prid. kl.	Andre. Apo. 30	5	Acts 1	6	6

AN

ORDER FOR MATINS,

DAILY THROUGH THE YEAR.

The Priest being in the quire, shall begin with a loud voice the Lord's Prayer, called the Pater noster.

OUR Father, which art in heaven, hallowed be thy name. Thy kingdom come. Thy will be done in earth as it is in heaven. Give us this day our daily bread. And forgive us our trespasses, as we forgive them that trespass against us. And lead us not into temptation. But deliver us from evil. Amen.

Then likewise he shall say,

O Lord, open thou my lips.

Answer. And my mouth shall shew forth thy praise.

Priest. O God, make speed[1] to save me.

Answer. O Lord, make haste to help me.

Priest. Glory be to the Father, and to the Son, and to the Holy Ghost.

As it was in the beginning, is now, and ever shall be world without end. Amen.

Praise ye the Lord.

And from Easter to Trinity Sunday,

Alleluia.

Then shall be said or sung without any Invitatory this Psalm. Venite, exultemus, *&c. in English, as followeth:*

Psalm xcv[2].

Glory be to the Father, and to the Son, and to the Holy Ghost;

As it was in the beginning, is now, and ever shall be: world without end. Amen.

Then shall follow certain Psalms in order as they been[3] appointed in a table made for that[4] purpose, except there be proper Psalms appointed for that day. And at the end of every Psalm throughout

[1 Good speed, Grafton, 2.]

[2 After the Psalms follows the *Gloria Patri;* sometimes abbreviated, and sometimes at length; but variously in the editions collated.]

[3 be, Oswen. In the margin of this and most of the Rubrics, Oswen has "*note.*"]   [4 for the, Oswen.]

the year, and likewise in the end of *Benedictus, Benedicite, Magnificat,* and *Nunc Dimittis,* shall be repeated.

Glory be to the Father, and to the Son, &c.

Then shall be read two lessons distinctly with a loud voice, that the people may hear. The first of the Old Testament, the second of the New; like as they be appointed by the Kalendar, except there be proper lessons assigned for that day: the minister that readeth the lesson, standing and turning him so as he may best be heard of all such as be present. And before every lesson, the minister shall say thus. The first, second, third or fourth chapter of *Genesis* or *Exodus*, Matthew, Mark, or other like as is appointed in the Kalendar. And in the end of every Chapter, he shall say.

¶ Here endeth such a chapter of such a book.

And (to the end the people may the better hear) in such places where they do sing, there shall the lessons be sung in a plain tune after the manner of distinct reading: and likewise the Epistle and Gospel.

¶ After the first lesson shall follow *Te Deum laudamus*, in English, daily throughout the year, except in Lent, all the which time in the place of *Te Deum* shall be used *Benedicite omnia Opera Domini Domino,* in English as followeth:

Te Deum Laudamus[1].

We praise thee, O God, we knowledge thee to be the Lord.

All the earth doth worship thee, the Father everlasting.

To thee all Angels cry aloud, the heavens and all the [2] powers therein.

To thee Cherubim, and Seraphim continually do cry,

Holy, holy, holy, Lord God of Sabaoth.

Heaven and earth are [3]replenished with the majesty of thy glory.

The glorious company of the Apostles, praise thee.

The goodly fellowship of the Prophets, praise thee.

The noble army of Martyrs praise thee.

The holy church throughout all the world doth knowledge thee.

The Father of an infinite majesty.

Thy honourable, true, and only Son.

[1 The praise of "God the Father, the Son, and the Holy Ghost." Grafton, 1. *Laudamus* omitted, Grafton, 2.]

[2 the, omitted by Grafton, 1.]

[3 full of, Grafton, 1 and 2.]

The Holy Ghost[4] also being the Comforter.
Thou art the King of Glory, O Christ.
Thou art the everlasting Son of the Father.
When thou tookest upon thee to deliver man, thou didst not abhor the virgin's womb.
When thou hadst overcomed[5] the sharpness of death, thou didst open the kingdom of heaven to all believers.
Thou sittest on the right hand of God, in the Glory of the Father.
We believe that thou shalt come to be our judge.
We therefore pray thee, help thy servants, whom thou hast redeemed with thy precious blood.
Make them to be numbered with thy saints, in glory everlasting.
O Lord, save thy people : and bless thine heritage.
Govern them and lift them up for ever.
Day by day we magnify thee.
And we worship thy name ever world without end.
Vouchsafe, O Lord, to keep us this day without sin.
O Lord, have mercy upon us : have mercy upon us.
O Lord, let thy mercy lighten upon us : as our trust is in thee.
O Lord, in thee have I trusted : let me never be confounded.

Benedicite, omnia Opera Domini Domino.

O ALL ye works of the Lord, speak good of the Lord : praise him, and set him up for ever.
O ye Angels of the Lord, speak good of the Lord : praise him, and set him up for ever.
O ye heavens, speak good of the Lord : praise him, and set him up for ever.
O ye waters that be above the firmament, speak good of the Lord : praise him, and set him up for ever.
O all ye powers of the Lord, speak good of the Lord : praise him, and set him up for ever.
O ye Sun, and Moon, speak good of the Lord : praise him, and set him up for ever.

[4 Also the Holy Ghost, the Comforter. Grafton, 1 and 2.]
[5 overcome, Grafton, 1.]

O ye stars of heaven, speak good of the Lord : praise him, and set him up for ever.

O ye showers, and dew, speak good of the Lord : praise him, and set him up for ever.

O ye winds of God, speak good of the Lord : praise him, and set him up for ever.

O ye fire and heat, praise ye the Lord : praise him, and set him up for ever.

O ye winter and summer, speak good of the Lord : praise him, and set him up for ever.

O ye dews and frosts, speak good of the Lord : praise him, and set him up for ever.

O ye frost and cold, speak good of the Lord : praise him, and set him up for ever.

O ye ice and snow, speak good of the Lord : praise him, and set him up for ever.

O ye nights and days, speak good of the Lord : praise him, and set him up for ever.

O ye light and darkness, speak good of the Lord : praise him, and set him up for ever.

O ye lightnings and clouds, speak good of the Lord : praise him, and set him up for ever.

O let the earth speak good of the Lord : yea, let it praise him, and set him up for ever.

O ye mountains and hills, speak good of the Lord : praise him, and set him up for ever.

O all ye green things upon the earth, speak good of the Lord : praise him, and set him up for ever.

O ye wells, speak good of the Lord : praise him, and set him up for ever.

O ye seas, and floods, speak good of the Lord : praise him, and set him up for ever.

O ye whales, and all that move in the waters, speak good of the Lord : praise him, and set him up for ever.

O all ye fowls of the air, speak good of the Lord : praise him, and set him up for ever.

O all ye beasts, and cattle, speak ye good of the Lord : praise him, and set him up for ever.

O ye children of men, speak good of the Lord : praise him, and set him up for ever.

O let Israel speak good of the Lord : praise him, and set him up for ever.

MATINS. 33

O ye priests of the Lord, speak good of the Lord : praise him, and set him up for ever.

O ye servants of the Lord, speak good of the Lord : praise him, and set him up for ever.

O ye spirits and souls of the righteous, speak good of the Lord : praise him, and set him up for ever.

O ye holy and humble men of heart, speak ye good of the Lord : praise ye him, and set him up for ever.

O Ananias, Azarias, and Misael, speak ye good of the Lord : praise ye him, and set him up for ever.

Glory be to the Father, and to the Son, &c.

As it was in the beginning, is now, &c.

And after the Second Lesson, throughout the whole year, shall be [1] used *Benedictus Dominus Deus Israel*, &c. in English, as followeth :

[2]*Benedictus.* Luc. i.

BLESSED be the Lord God of Israel : for he hath visited and redeemed his people ;

And hath lifted up an horn of salvation to us : in the house of his servant David ;

As he spake by the mouth of his holy Prophets : which [3]hath been since the world began ;

That we should be saved from our enemies : and from the hands of all that hate us ;

To perform the mercy promised to our fathers : and to remember his holy covenant ;

To perform the oath which he sware to our father Abraham : that he would give us ;

That we being delivered out of the hands of our enemies : might serve him without fear ;

[[1] As followeth, omitted in Grafton, 1, and C : also in C is added here, "Then shall be said daily, &c.," which in the other copies is in the Rubric after the *Benedictus*.]

[[2] The Song of Zachary ; Benedictus : and Thanksgiving for the performance of God's promises. Grafton, 1, and C. The Magnificat, &c. are not found in their proper places in the Morning and Evening Service, but are inserted in a separate sheet towards the close of the volume in C ; and distributed throughout the volume in separate sheets in Grafton, 1. See Preface by the Editor.]

[[3] have, Oswen.]

In holiness and righteousness before him : all the days of our life.

And thou, Child, shalt be called the Prophet of the Highest : for thou shalt go before the face of the Lord, to prepare his ways ;

To give knowledge of salvation unto his people : for the remission of their sins,

Through the tender mercy of our God : whereby the day-spring from [1] an high hath visited us ;

To give light to them that sit in darkness, and in the shadow of death : and to guide our feet into the way of peace.

Glory be to the Father, and to the Son, &c.

As it was in the beginning, is now, and ever, &c.

Then shall be said daily through the year, [2] the prayers following, as well at Evensong as at Matins, all devoutly kneeling.

Lord, have mercy upon us. [3] Christ, have mercy upon us. Lord, have mercy upon us.

Then the Minister shall say the *Creed* and the Lord's Prayer in English, with a loud voice, &c.

Answer. But deliver us from evil. Amen.
Priest. O Lord, shew thy mercy upon us.
Answer. And grant us thy salvation.
Priest. O Lord, save the king.
Answer. And mercifully hear us when we call upon thee.
Priest. Endue thy ministers with righteousness.
Answer. And make thy chosen people joyful.
Priest. O Lord, save thy people.
Answer. And bless thine inheritance.
Priest. Give peace in our time, O Lord.
Answer. Because there is none other that fighteth for us, but only thou, O God.
Priest. O God, make clean our hearts within us.
Answer. And take not thine holy Spirit from us.
Priest. The Lord be with you.
Answer. And with thy spirit.

[1] *an high,* like the *a* in *a*loft.]
[2] these, Grafton, 2.]
[3] These two versicles are not in one line in Grafton, 2.]

¶ Then shall daily follow three Collects. The first of the day, which shall be the same that is appointed at the Communion. The second for peace. The third for grace to live well. And the two last Collects shall never alter, but daily be said at Matins throughout all the year, as followeth: the Priest standing up, and saying,

Let us pray.

¶ Then the Collect of the day.

¶ *The second Collect: for peace.*

O GOD, which art author of peace, and lover of concord, in knowledge of whom standeth our eternal life, whose service is perfect freedom: defend us, thy humble servants, in all assaults of our enemies, that we, surely trusting in thy defence, may not fear the power of any adversaries: through the might of Jesu Christ our Lord. Amen.

¶ *The third Collect: for grace.*

O LORD, our heavenly Father, almighty and everliving God, which hast safely brought us to the beginning of this day: defend us in the same with thy mighty power; and grant that this day we fall into no sin, neither run into any kind of danger, but that all our doings may be ordered by thy governance, to do always that is righteous in thy sight: through Jesus Christ our Lord. Amen.

AN

ORDER FOR EVENSONG

THROUGHOUT THE YEAR.

¶ The Priest shall say.

Our Father, &c.

Then likewise he shall say.

O God, make speed to save me.

Answer. O Lord, make haste to help me.

Priest. Glory ¹be to the Father, and to the Son: and to the Holy Ghost;

As it was in the beginning, is now, and ever shall be: world without end. Amen.

Praise ye the Lord.

And from Easter to Trinity Sunday,

Alleluia.

As before is appointed at Matins.

Then Psalms in order as they be appointed in the Table for Psalms, except there be proper Psalms appointed for that day. Then a Lesson of the Old Testament, as ²it is appointed likewise in the Calendar, except there be proper Lessons appointed for that day. After that, ³(*Magnificat anima mea Dominum*) in English, as followeth.

⁴*Magnificat.* Luc. i.

My soul doth magnify the Lord.

And my spirit ⁵hath rejoiced in God my Saviour.

For he hath regarded the lowliness of his handmaiden.

For behold, from henceforth all generations shall call me blessed.

[¹ *be*, omitted in Grafton, 1.]
[² *it*, omitted by Grafton, 1 and 2, C, and Oswen.]
[³ ¶ The Song of Mary rejoicing and praising God, Grafton, 1, and C.]
[⁴ *Magnificat*, in a separate sheet at the close of the volume, Grafton, 1, and C. (See note, page 33.) Luc. i. omitted by Grafton, 2: but the Magnificat is given at length. Also, "as followeth," just before, omitted Grafton, 1, and C.]
[⁵ hath, omitted by Oswen, and Grafton, 1.]

For he that is mighty hath magnified me : and holy is his name.

And his mercy is on them that fear him : throughout all generations.

He hath shewed strength with his arm : he hath scattered the proud in the imagination of their hearts.

He hath put down the mighty from their seat : and hath exalted the humble and meek.

He hath filled the hungry with good things : and the rich he hath sent empty away.

He remembering his mercy, hath holpen his servant Israel: as he promised to our fathers, Abraham and his seed, for ever.

Glory be to the Father, and to the Son, &c.

As it was in the beginning, &c.

Then a Lesson of the New Testament. And after that (*Nunc dimittis servum tuum*) in English [6]as followeth.

[7]*Nunc Dimittis.* Luc. ii.

LORD, now lettest thou thy servant depart in peace : according to thy word.

For mine eyes have seen : thy salvation,

Which thou hast prepared : before the face of all [8]people;

To be a light [9]to lighten the Gentiles : and to be the glory of thy people Israel.

Glory be to the Father, and to the Son : and to the Holy Ghost.

As it was in the beginning, is now, and ever shall be : world without end. Amen.

Then the suffrages before assigned at Matins, the clerks kneeling likewise, with three Collects. First of the day: Second of peace : Third for aid against all perils, as here followeth. Which two last Collects shall be daily said at Evensong without alteration.

The second Collect at Evensong.

O GOD, from whom all holy desires, all good counsels, and all just works do proceed : Give unto thy servants that

[[6] *as followeth,* omitted in Grafton, 1. Luc. ii. omitted in Grafton, 2, but Nunc Dimittis given at length. Also this and the following Rubric is given with the previous Rubric in Grafton, C.]

[[7] ¶ The Song of Symeon the Just, Grafton, 1, and C.]

[[8] of thy, Grafton, 1. all thy, Oswen.]   [[9] for to, Oswen.]

peace, which the world cannot give; that both our hearts may be set to obey thy commandments, and also that by thee we being defended from the fear of our enemies, may pass our time in rest and quietness: through the merits of Jesu Christ our Saviour. Amen.

The third Collect for aid against all perils.

LIGHTEN our darkness, we beseech thee, O Lord, and by thy great mercy, defend us from all perils and dangers of this night, for the love of thy only Son, our Saviour Jesu Christ. Amen.

¶ In the feasts of *Christmas, the Epiphany, Easter, the Ascension, Pentecost,* and upon *Trinity Sunday,* shall be sung or said immediately after *Benedictus* this Confession of our Christian Faith.

Quicunque vult, &c.

WHOSOEVER will be saved : before all things it is necessary that he hold the Catholic faith.

Which faith except every one do keep holy and undefiled : without doubt he shall perish everlastingly.

And the Catholic faith is this : That we worship one God in Trinity, and Trinity in Unity ;

Neither confounding the persons : nor dividing the substance.

For there is one person of the Father, another of the Son : and another of the Holy Ghost.

But the Godhead of the Father, of the Son, and of the Holy Ghost, is all one : the glory equal, the majesty co-eternal.

Such as the Father is, such is the Son : and such is the Holy Ghost.

The Father uncreate, the Son uncreate : and the Holy Ghost uncreate.

The Father incomprehensible, the Son incomprehensible : and the Holy Ghost incomprehensible.

The Father eternal, the Son eternal : and the Holy Ghost eternal.

And yet they are not three eternals : but one eternal.

As also there be not three incomprehensibles, nor three uncreated : but one uncreated, and one incomprehensible.

So likewise the Father is almighty, the Son almighty : and the Holy Ghost almighty.

And yet are they not three almighties : but one almighty.

So the Father is God, the Son God : and the Holy Ghost God.

And yet are they not three Gods : but one God.

So likewise the Father is Lord, the Son Lord : and the Holy Ghost Lord.

And yet not three Lords : but one Lord.

For like as we be compelled by the Christian verity[1] : to acknowledge every person by himself to be God and Lord ;

So are we forbidden by the Catholic religion : to say there be three Gods, or [2]thee Lords.

The Father is made of none : neither created nor begotten.

The Son is of the Father alone : not made nor created, but begotten.

The Holy Ghost is of the Father and of the Son : neither made nor created, nor begotten, but proceeding.

So there is one Father, not three Fathers ; one Son, not three Sons : one Holy Ghost, not three Holy Ghosts.

And in this Trinity none is afore [3]nor after other : none is greater nor less than other.

But the whole three persons : be co-eternal together and co-equal.

So that in all things, as [4]it is aforesaid : the Unity in Trinity, and the Trinity in Unity is to be worshipped.

He therefore that will be saved : must thus think of the Trinity.

Furthermore, it is necessary to everlasting salvation : that he also believe rightly in the Incarnation of our Lord Jesu Christ.

For the right faith is that we believe and confess : that our Lord Jesus Christ, the Son of God, is God and man ;

God of the Substance of the Father, begotten before the worlds : and man of the substance of his mother, born in the world.

Perfect God, and perfect man : of a reasonable soul, and human flesh subsisting.

[1 unity, Grafton, 2.]
[2 Evidently a misprint for three ; the other copies have "three."]
[3 or, Grafton, 2.]   [4 as is, Grafton, 2.]

Equal to the Father as touching his Godhead : and inferior to the Father ¹touching his manhood.

Who although he be God and man : yet he is not two, but one Christ;

One, not by conversion of the Godhead into flesh : but by taking of the manhood into God;

One altogether, not by confusion of substance : but by unity of person.

For as the reasonable soul and flesh is one man : so God and man is one Christ.

Who suffered for our salvation : descended into hell, rose again the third day from the dead.

He ascended into heaven, he sitteth on the right hand of the Father, God Almighty : from whence he shall come to judge the quick and dead.

At whose coming all men shall rise again with their bodies : and shall give account of their own works.

And they that have done good, shall go into life everlasting : and they that have done evil, into everlasting fire.

This is the Catholic faith : which except a man believe faithfully, he cannot be saved.

Glory be to the Father, and to the Son : and to the Holy Ghost.

As it was in the beginning, is now, and ever shall be : world without end. Amen.

Thus endeth the Order of Matins and Evensong through the whole Year.

[¹ as touching, Oswen.]

[2]THE

INTROITS[3], COLLECTS, EPISTLES, AND GOSPELS,

TO BE USED AT THE CELEBRATION OF THE LORD'S SUPPER AND HOLY COMMUNION, THROUGH THE YEAR: WITH PROPER PSALMS AND LESSONS FOR DIVERS FEASTS AND DAYS.

¶ *The first Sunday in Advent.*

Beatus vir. Psalm i.

Glory be to the Father, and to the Son, and to the Holy Ghost;
As it was in the beginning, is now, and ever shall be: world without end. Amen.

And so must every Introit be ended.

Let us pray.

The Collect.

ALMIGHTY God, give us grace that we may cast away the works of darkness, and put upon us the armour of light, now in the time of this mortal life, (in the which thy Son Jesus Christ came to visit us in great humility:) that in the last day, when he shall come again in his glorious majesty, to judge both the quick and the dead, we may rise to the life immortal, through him, who liveth and reigneth with thee and the Holy Ghost, now and ever. Amen.

The Epistle. Rom. xiii. [v. 8 to end.]
The Gospel. [4]Matt. xxi. [v. 1—13.]

[[2] From this place to the end of the first Sunday in Advent, is in MS. in Oswen.]

[[3] *Introits* were Psalms said or sung, while the Priest was entering within the rails of the Communion Table. See Wheatly, chap. v. sec. 8.]

[[4] Matt. xx. Grafton, 2; but the same Gospel as above.]

The second Sunday.

Ad Dominum cum tribularer[1]. Psalm cxx.

The Collect.

BLESSED Lord, which hast caused all holy scriptures to be written for our learning: grant us that we may in such wise hear them, read, mark, learn, and inwardly digest them, that by patience and comfort of thy holy word, we may embrace and ever hold fast the blessed hope of everlasting life, which thou hast given us in our Saviour Jesus Christ.

The Epistle. Roma. xv[2]. [v. 4—13.]
The Gospel. Luc. xxi. [v. 25—33.]

¶ *The third Sunday.*

Cum invocarem. Psalm iv.

The Collect.

LORD, we beseech thee, give ear to our prayers, and by thy gracious visitation lighten the darkness of our heart, by our Lord Jesus Christ.

The Epistle. 1 Cori. iv. [v. 1—5.]
The Gospel. Math. xi. [v. 2—10.]

¶ *The fourth Sunday.*

Verba mea auribus. Psalm v.

The Collect.

LORD, raise up (we pray thee) thy power, and come among us, and with great might succour us, that whereas through our sins and wickedness we be sore let and hindered, thy bountiful grace and mercy, through the satisfaction of thy Son our Lord, may speedily deliver us; to whom with thee and the Holy Ghost be honour and glory world without end.

The Epistle. Philip. iv. [v. 4—7.]
The Gospel. John i. [v. 19—28.]

[1 cum tribularar, Grafton, 2.]
[2 Roma. xx. Grafton, C; but the same Epistle as above.]

Proper Psalms and Lessons on Christmas day.

¶ *At Matins.* Psalms xix. xlv. lxxxv.
The first lesson, Esai. ix. *unto the end.*
The second lesson, Math. i³. *unto the end.*

¶ *At the first Communion.*
Cantate Domino. Psalm xcviii.

The Collect.

GOD, which makest us glad with the yearly remembrance of the birth of thy only Son Jesus Christ: grant that as we joyfully receive him for our Redeemer, so we may with sure confidence behold him, when he shall come to be our Judge, who liveth and reigneth &c.

The Epistle. Tit. ii⁴. [v. 11—15.]
The Gospel. Luc. ii. [v. 1—14.]

¶ *At the second Communion.*
Domine Dominus noster. Psalm viii.

The Collect.

ALMIGHTY God, which hast given us thy only-begotten Son to take our nature upon him, and this day to be born of a pure virgin; Grant that we being regenerate, and made thy children by adoption and grace, may daily be renewed by thy holy Spirit, through the same our Lord Jesus Christ, who liveth and reigneth &c.

The Epistle. Hebre. i. [v. 1—12.]
The Gospel. John i. [v. 1—14.]

Proper Psalms and lessons at Evensong. Psalms lxxix. cx. cxxxii.
The first lesson, Esai. vii. "God spake once again to Achas," &c. *unto the end.*
The second lesson, Tit. iii. "The kindness and love of our Saviour," &c. *unto* "foolish questions."

¶ St. Stephin's Day.

¶ *At Matins.*
The second lesson, Acts vi. vii. "Stephin full of faith and power," *unto,* "And when forty years."

At the Communion.
Quid gloriaris in malicia? Psalm lii.

[³ i. omitted in Grafton, C.]
[⁴ Luc. ii. and Tit. ii. inverted by mistake in Grafton, C.]

The Collect.

GRANT us, O Lord, to learn to love our enemies by the example of thy martyr Saint Stephin, who prayed to thee for his persecutors: which livest and reignest, &c.

Then shall follow a collect of the Nativity.

The Epistle. Acts vii. [v. 55 to end.]
The Gospel. Math. xxiii. [v. 34 to end.]

The second Lesson at Evensong.

Acts vii. ¶ "And when forty years were expired, there appeared unto Moses," *unto* "Stephin full of the Holy Ghost," &c.

¶ St. John Evangelist's Day.

At Matins.

¶ The second lesson, Apoca. i. *unto the end.*

At the Communion.

In Domino confido. Psalm xi.

The Collect.

MERCIFUL Lord, we beseech thee to cast thy bright beams of light upon thy Church: that it being lightened by the doctrine of thy blessed Apostle and Evangelist John may attain to thy everlasting gifts: through Jesus Christ our Lord.

The Epistle. 1 John i. [v. 1 to end.]
The Gospel. John xxi. [v. 19 to end.]

¶ At Evensong.

¶ The second lesson, Apoca. xxii. *unto the end.*

¶ The Innocents' Day.

¶ At Matins.

¶ The first lesson, Hiere. xxxi. *unto,* "Moreover I heard Ephraim."

Deus, venerunt gentes. Psalm lxxix.

The Collect.

ALMIGHTY God, whose praise this day the young innocents thy witnesses hath confessed, and shewed forth, not in speaking, but in dying: mortify and kill all vices in us, that in our conversation, our life may express thy faith, which with our tongues we do confess: through Jesus Christ our Lord.

The Epistle. Apoca. xiv. [v. 1—5.]
The Gospel. Math. ii. [v. 13—18.]

¶ *The Sunday after Christmas Day.*

Levavi oculos. Psalm cxxi.

The Collect.

ALMIGHTY God, which hast given us, &c. *as upon Christmas Day.*

The Epistle. Gala. iv. [v. 1—7.]
The Gospel. Math. i. [v. 1 to end.]

¶ *The Circumcision of Christ.*

At Matins.

The first lesson, Gene. xvii. *unto the end.*
The second lesson, Rom. ii. *unto the end.*

At the Communion.

Lætatus sum. ¹Psalm cxxii.

The Collect.

ALMIGHTY God, which madest thy blessed Son to be circumcised and obedient to the law for man: grant us the true circumcision of thy Spirit: that our hearts, and all our members, being mortified from all worldly and carnal lusts, may in all things obey thy blessed will, through the same thy Son Jesus Christ our Lord.

The Epistle. Rom. iv. [v. 8—14.]
The Gospel. Luc. ii. [v. 15—21.]

¶ *At Evensong.*

The first lesson, Deute. x. "And now Israel," *unto the end.*
The second lesson, Coloss. ii. *unto the end.*

¶ *The Epiphany.*

At Matins.

The first lesson, Esai. lx. *unto the end.*
The second lesson, Luke iii. "And it fortuned," *unto the end.*

[¹ Psal. cii. Oswen; but Psal. cxxii. given.]

At the Communion[1].

Cantate Domino. Psalm xcvi.

The Collect.

[2] O GOD, which by the leading of a star didst manifest thy only-begotten Son to the Gentiles; Mercifully grant, that we, which know thee now by faith, may after this life have the fruition of thy glorious Godhead; through Christ our Lord.

The Epistle. Ephe. iii. [v. 1—12.]
The Gospel. Mat. iii[3]. [v. 1—12.]

At Evensong.

The first lesson, Esai. xlix. *unto the end.*
The second lesson, John ii. "After this he went down to Capernaum," *unto the end.*

The first Sunday after the Epiphany.

Usquequo Domine? Psalm xiii.

The Collect.

LORD, we beseech thee, mercifully to receive the prayers of thy people which call upon thee: and grant that they may both perceive and know what things they ought to do, and also have grace and power faithfully to fulfil the same.

The Epistle. Roma. xii. [v. 1—5.]
The Gospel. Luc. ii. [v. 41 to end.]

¶ *The second Sunday.*

Dixit insipiens. Psalm xiv.

The Collect.

ALMIGHTY and everlasting God, which dost govern all things in heaven and earth: mercifully hear the supplications of thy people, and grant us thy peace all the days of our life.

The Epistle. Rom. xii. [v. 6—16.]
The Gospel. John ii. [v. 1—11.]

[1 *At the Communion*, omitted by Grafton, 2, and Oswen; *Cantate Domino*, omitted by Grafton, 1 and 2.]
[2 O, omitted by Oswen.]
[3 Misprint for ii, as in the other copies.]

¶ *The third Sunday.*

Domine, quis habitabit? Psalm xv.

The Collect.

ALMIGHTY and everlasting God, mercifully look upon our infirmities, and in all our dangers and necessities, stretch forth thy right hand to help and defend us, through Christ our Lord.

The Epistle. [4]Rom. xii. [v. 16 to end.]
The Gospel. Math. viii. [v. 1—13.]

¶ *The fourth Sunday.*

Quare fremuerunt gentes? Psalm ii.

The Collect.

GOD, which knowest us to be set in the midst of so many and great dangers, that for man's frailness we cannot always stand uprightly: Grant to us the health of body and soul, that all those things which we suffer for sin, by thy help we may well pass and overcome, through Christ our Lord.

The Epistle. Rom. xiii. [v. 1—7.]
The Gospel. Math. viii. [v. 23 to end.]

¶ *The fifth Sunday.*

Exaudiat te Dominus[5]. Psalm xx.

The Collect.

LORD, we beseech thee to keep thy church and household continually in thy true religion: that they which do lean only upon hope of thy heavenly grace, may evermore be defended by thy mighty power; through Christ our Lord.

The Epistle. Colos. iii. [v. 12—17.]
The Gospel. Math. xiii. [v. 24—30.]

The sixth Sunday (if there be so many) shall have the same Psalm, Collect, Epistle, and Gospel, that was upon the fifth.

[4 Rom. xiii. Oswen: but the Epistle given as above.]
[5 *Deus*, Grafton, 2. *Domine ne*, Psalm vi. in Grafton, 1, and C; but the xxth Psalm is given at length.]

¶ *The Sunday called Septuagesima.*

Dominus regit. Psalm xxiii.

The Collect.

O LORD, we beseech thee favourably to hear the prayers of thy people; that we, which are justly punished for our offences, may be mercifully delivered by thy goodness, for the glory of thy name; through Jesu Christ our Saviour, who liveth and reigneth, &c.

The Epistle. 1 Cor. ix. [v. 24 to end.]
The Gospel. Math. xx. [v. 1—16.]

¶ *The Sunday called Sexagesima.*

¶ *At the Communion*[1].

Domini est terra. Psalm xxiv.

The Collect.

LORD GOD, which seest that we put not[2] our trust in any thing that we do: mercifully grant that by thy power we may be defended against all adversity, through Jesus Christ our Lord.

The Epistle. 2 Cor. xi[3]. [v. 19—31.]
The Gospel. Luc. viii. [v. 4—15.]

¶ *The Sunday called Quinquagesima*[4].

Judica me Domine. Psalm xxvi[5].

The Collect.

O LORD, which dost teach us, that all our doings without charity are nothing worth: send thy Holy Ghost, and pour into our hearts that most excellent gift of charity, the very bond of peace and all virtues, without the which, whosoever liveth is counted dead before thee: Grant this, for thy only Son Jesus Christ's sake.

The Epistle. 1 Cor. xiii. [v. 1 to end.]
The Gospel. Luc. xviii. [v. 31 to end.]

[1 At the Communion, omitted by Grafton, 1 and 2, and Oswen: also Ps. xxiii. Oswen; but Ps. xxiv. is given.]

[2 not, omitted by Oswen.]

[3 2 Cor. iii. Oswen. But the same chapter is given at length in all the copies.] [4 Quadragesima, Oswen.]

[5 Ps. cxxvi. Grafton, 2; but Ps. xxvi. is given.]

¶ The first day of Lent, commonly called Ashwednesday.

⁶Domine ne. Psalm vi.

The Collect.

ALMIGHTY and everlasting God, which hatest nothing that thou hast made, and dost forgive the sins of all them that be penitent: Create and make in us new and contrite hearts, that we worthily lamenting our sins, and knowledging our wretchedness, may obtain of thee, the God of all mercy, perfect remission and forgiveness, through Jesus Christ.

The Epistle. Joel ii. [v. 12—17.]
The Gospel. Math. vi. [v. 16—21.]

¶ The first Sunday in Lent.

Beati quorum. Psalm xxxii.

The Collect.

O LORD, which for our sake didst fast forty days and forty nights: Give us grace to use such abstinence, that, our flesh being subdued to the Spirit, we may ever obey thy godly motions[7], in righteousness and true holiness, to thy honour and glory, which livest and reignest, &c.

The Epistle. 2 Cor. vi. [v. 1—10.]
The Gospel. Math. iv. [v. 1—11.]

¶ The second Sunday.

De profundis. Psalm cxxx.

The Collect.

ALMIGHTY God, which dost see that we have no power of ourselves to help ourselves: keep thou us both outwardly in our bodies, and inwardly in our souls, that we may be defended from all adversities which may happen to the body, and from all evil thoughts which may assault and hurt the soul; through Jesus Christ, &c.[8]

The Epistle. 1 Tess.[9] iv. [v. 1—8.]
The Gospel. Math.[10] xv. [v. 21—28.]

[⁶ *Exaudiat te Deus,* Grafton 1; but Ps. vi. given at length. See 5th Sunday after Epiphany.]

[⁷ Monitions, Whitchurch, June.]   [⁸ Amen, Oswen.]

[⁹ 1 Tessa. iii. Whitchurch, June, but same Epistle.]

[¹⁰ Mark xv. Grafton, 2, but Mat. xv. given; also reference omitted, Grafton, 1.]

¶ The third Sunday.

Judica me Deus[1]. Psalm xliii.

The Collect.

WE beseech thee, almighty God, look upon the hearty desires[2] of thy humble servants: and stretch forth the right hand of thy majesty, to be our defence against all our enemies: through Jesus Christ our Lord.

The Epistle. Ephe. v.[3] [v. 1—14.]
The Gospel. Luc. xi. [v. 14—28.]

¶ The fourth Sunday.

Deus noster refugium[4]. Psalm xlvi.

The Collect.

GRANT, we beseech thee, almighty God, that we, which for our evil deeds are worthily punished: by the comfort of thy grace may mercifully be relieved, through our Lord Jesus Christ.

The Epistle. Gala. iv. [v. 21 to end.]
The Gospel. John vi. [v. 1—14.]

¶ The fifth Sunday.

Deus, in nomine tuo[5]. Psalm liv.

The Collect.

WE beseech thee, almighty God, mercifully to look upon thy people: that by thy great goodness, they may be governed and preserved evermore, both in body and soul: through Jesus Christ our Lord.

The Epistle. Hebrues ix.[6] [v. 11—15.]
The Gospel. John viii.[7] [v. 46 to end.]

[1 *Deus*, omitted by Grafton, 2.]   [2 desire, Oswen.]
[3 Ephes. v. omitted by Grafton, 2; but same Epistle given.]
[4 *refugium*, omitted by Grafton, 2.]
[5 *tuo*, omitted by Grafton, 2.]
[6 Heb. xi. Grafton, 2, and C; but the same Epistle.]
[7 John ix. Grafton, 2; but the same Gospel.]

DAYS BEFORE EASTER. 51

¶ *The Sunday next before Easter.*
Exaudi deus deprecationem[8]. Psalm lxi.
The Collect.

ALMIGHTY and everlasting God, which of thy tender love toward man, hast sent our Saviour Jesus Christ to take upon him our flesh, and to suffer death upon the cross, that all mankind should follow the example of his great humility: mercifully grant, that we both follow the example of his patience, and be made partakers of his resurrection: through the same Jesus[9] Christ our Lord.

The Epistle. Philip. ii. [v. 5—11.]
The Gospel. Math. xxvi.[10] [v. 1 to end.] and xxvii. [v. 1—56.]

¶ *Monday before Easter.*
The Epistle. Esai. lxiii.[11]
The Gospel. Mar. xiv.[12] [v. 1 to end.]

¶ *Tuesday before Easter.*
The Epistle. Esai. 1. [v. 5 to end.]
The Gospel. Mar. xv.[13] [v. 1 to end.]

¶ *Wednesday before Easter.*
¶ *At the Communion.*
The Epistle. Hebr. ix. [v. 16 to end.]
The Gospel. Luc. xxii. [v. 1 to end.]
¶ *At Evensong.*
The first lesson, Lamenta. i. *unto the end.*

¶ *Thursday before Easter.*
¶ *At Matins.*
The first lesson, Lamenta. ii. *unto the end.*
The Epistle. 1 Cor. xi. [v. 17 to end.]
The Gospel. [14] Luc. xxiii. [v. 1 to end.]
At Evensong.
The first lesson, Lamenta. iii. *unto the end.*

[8 *Deprecationem*, omitted by Grafton, 2, and C.]   [9 Jesu, Oswen.]
[10 The xxvii. in the margin, at the end of the xxvi. ch.: a part of these chapters is in MS. in Oswen.]   [11 Esai. xliii. Oswen.]
[12 Mark xiii. Grafton, 2; but the same Gospel.]
[13 Math. xxvii. Oswen. Math. xv. Grafton, 2.]
[14 Luc. xxii. Grafton, 2, and Oswen; but the same Gospel.]

On Good Friday.

At Matins.

The first lesson, Gen. xxii. *unto the end.*

The Collect.

ALMIGHTY God, we beseech thee graciously to behold this thy family: for the which our Lord Jesus Christ was contented to be betrayed, and given up into the hands of wicked men, and to suffer death upon the cross: who liveth and reigneth, &c.

At the Communion.

Deus, deus [1]*meus.* Psalm xxii.

¶ After the two Collects at the Communion, shall be said these two Collects following.

The Collect.

ALMIGHTY and everlasting God, by whose Spirit the whole body of the Church is governed and sanctified: receive our supplications and prayers, which we offer before thee for all estates of men in thy holy congregation, that every member of the same, in his vocation and ministry, may truly and godly serve thee: through our Lord Jesus Christ.

MERCIFUL God, who hast made all men, and hatest nothing that thou hast made, nor wouldest the death of a sinner, but rather that he should be converted and live: Have mercy upon all Jews, Turks, Infidels, and Heretics, and take from them all ignorance, hardness of heart, and contempt of thy word: and so fetch them home, blessed Lord, to thy flock, that they may be saved among the remnant of the true Israelites, and be made one fold under one shepherd, Jesus Christ our Lord: who liveth and reigneth, &c.

The Epistle. Heb. x. [v. 1—25.]
The Gospel. John xviii. [v. 1 to end; xix. v. 1 to end.]

At Evensong.

¶ The first lesson, Esai. liii. *unto the end.*

[[1] *meus,* omitted by Grafton, 2.]

Easter Even.

At Matins.

¶ The first lesson, Lamenta. iv. v. *unto the end.*

At the Communion.

Domine deus [2]*salutis,* Psal. lxxxviii.

The Epistle.   1 Pet. iii. [v. 17 to end.]
The Gospel.   Mat. xxvii. [v. 57 to end.]

¶ Easter day.

In the morning[3] afore Matins, the people being assembled in the church: these Anthems shall be first solemnly sung [4]or said.

CHRIST rising again from the dead, now dieth not. Death from henceforth hath no power upon him. For in that he died, he died but once to put away sin: but in that he liveth, he liveth unto God. And so likewise, count yourselves dead unto sin, but living unto God in Christ Jesus our Lord. Alleluia, Alleluia.

CHRIST is risen again, the firstfruits of them that sleep: for seeing that by man came death, by man also cometh the resurrection of the dead. For as by Adam all men do die, so by Christ all men shall be restored to life. Alleluia.

The Priest. ¶ Shew forth to all nations the glory of God.
The Answer. ¶ And among all people his wonderful works.

Let us pray.

O GOD, who for our redemption didst give thine only begotten Son to the death of the cross: and by his glorious resurrection hast delivered us from the power of our enemy: Grant us so to die daily from sin, that we may evermore live with him in the joy of his resurrection: through the same Christ our Lord. Amen.

[2 *salutis,* omitted by Grafton, 2.]
[3 before, Grafton, 2.]
[4 *or said,* omitted by Oswen.]

AT THE COMMUNION.

¶ *Proper Psalms and Lessons.*

At Matins.

Psalms ii. lvii. cxi.

The first lesson, Exo. xii. *unto the end.*
The second lesson, Roma. vi. *unto the end.*

At the first Communion.

Conserva me [1]*domine.* Psalm xvi.

The Collect.

ALMIGHTY God, which through thy only begotten Son Jesus Christ, [2]hast overcome death, and opened unto us the gate of everlasting life: we humbly beseech thee, that as by thy special grace, preventing us, thou dost put in our minds good desires; so by thy continual help, we may bring the same to good effect, through Jesus Christ our Lord: who liveth and reigneth, &c.

The Epistle. Coloss. iii. [v. 1—7.]
The Gospel. John xx. [v. 1—10.]

At the [3]second Communion.

Domine quid [4]*multiplicati?* Psalm iii.

The Collect.

ALMIGHTY Father, which hast given thy only Son to die for our sins, and to rise again for our justification: Grant us so to put away the leaven of malice and wickedness, that we may alway serve thee in pureness of living and truth, through Jesus Christ our Lord.

The Epistle. 1 Cor. v. [v. 6—8.]
The Gospel. Mar. xvi. [v. 1—8.]

At Evensong.

¶ *Proper Psalms and Lessons.*

Psalms cxiii. cxiv. cxviii.

The second lesson, Act. ii. *unto the end.*

[[1] *Domine*, omitted by Grafton, 2.]
[[2] hath. Oswen, and Amen after who liveth and reigneth &c.]
[[3] *second*, omitted by Oswen.]
[[4] *multiplicati*, omitted by Grafton, 2.]

¶ Monday in Easter Week.

At Matins.

The second lesson, [5]Mat. xxviii. *unto the end.*

At the Communion.

Nonne deo [6]*subjecta?* [7]Psalm lxii.

The Collect.

ALMIGHTY God, which through thy only begotten Son Jesus Christ, hast overcome death, and opened unto us the gate of everlasting life: we humbly beseech thee, that as by thy [8]special grace, preventing us, thou dost put in our minds good [9]desires; so by thy continual help, we may bring the same to good effect, through Jesus Christ our Lord: who liveth and reigneth, &c.[10]

The Epistle. Acts x. [v. 34—43.]
The Gospel. Luc. xxiv. [v. 13—35.]

At Evensong.

¶ The second lesson, Acts iii. *unto the end.*

¶ Tuesday in Easter Week.

At Matins.

The second lesson, Luke xxiv. *unto* "And behold [11]two of them."

At the Communion.

Laudate pueri. Psalm cxiii.

The Collect.

ALMIGHTY Father, which hast given thy only Son to die for our sins, and to rise again for our justification: Grant us so to put away the leaven of malice and wickedness, that we may alway serve thee in pureness of living and truth, through Jesus Christ our Lord.

The Epistle. Acts xiii. [v. 26—41.]
The Gospel. Luc. xxiv. [v. 36—48.]

At Evensong.

The second lesson, 1 Cor. xv. *unto the end.*

[[5] Matt. xviii. Grafton, 2.]   [[6] *subjecta*, omitted by Grafton, 2.]
[[7] Psal. lxviii. Grafton, 1 and 2; but Ps. lxii. given.]
[[8] especial, Oswen.]   [[9] desire, Oswen.]
[[10] &c., omitted by Oswen.]   [[11] of them, omitted by Grafton, 2.]

¶ *The first Sunday after Easter.*

Beatus vir. Psalm [1]cxii.

The Collect.

ALMIGHTY Father, &c. As at the second Communion on Easter day.

The Epistle. 1 John v. [v. 4—12.]
The Gospel. John xx. [v. 19—23.]

¶ *The second Sunday after Easter.*

Deus in adjutorium. Psalm lxx.

The Collect.

ALMIGHTY God, which hast given thy holy Son to be unto us, both a sacrifice for sin, and also an example of Godly life: Give us the grace that we may always most thankfully receive that his inestimable benefit, and also daily endeavour ourselves to follow the blessed steps of his most holy life.

The Epistle. 1 Peter ii. [v. 19 to end.]
The Gospel. John x. [v. 11—16.]

¶ *The third Sunday.*

Confitebimur. Psalm lxxv.

The Collect.

ALMIGHTY God, which shewest to all men that be in error the light of thy truth, to the intent that they may return into the way of righteousness: Grant unto all them that be admitted into the fellowship of Christ's religion, that they may eschew those things that be contrary to their profession, and follow all such things as be agreeable to the same: through our Lord Jesus Christ.

The Epistle. 1 Peter ii. [v. 11—17.]
The Gospel. John xvi. [v. 16—22.]

¶ *The fourth Sunday.*

Deus stetit in synagoga. Psalm [2]lxxxiii.

The Collect.

ALMIGHTY God, which dost make the minds of all faithful men to be of one will: grant unto thy people, that they

[[1] Psal. cxxii. Grafton, 2; but Ps. cxii. given.]
[[2] Ps. lxxxii. in Grafton, 1 and 2, and Oswen; but Ps. lxxxiii. is given in all the copies.]

may love the thing, which thou commandest, and desire that which thou dost promise, that among the sundry and manifold changes of the world, our hearts may surely there be fixed, where as true joys are to be found: through Christ our Lord.

The Epistle. James i. [v. 17—21.]
The Gospel. John xvi. [v. 5—14.]

¶ *The fifth Sunday.*

Quam dilecta tabernacula. Psalm ³lxxxiv.

The Collect.

LORD, from whom all good things do come; grant us thy humble servants, that by thy holy inspiration we may think those things that be good, and by thy merciful guiding may perform the same; through our Lord Jesus Christ.

The Epistle. James i. [v. 22 to end.]
The Gospel. John xvi. [v. 23 to end.]

¶ *The Ascension Day.*

¶ *Proper Psalms and Lessons.*

At Matins.

Psalms viii. xv. xxi.

The second lesson, John xiv. *unto the end.*

¶ *At the Communion.*

Omnes gentes plaudite. Psalm xlvii.

The Collect.

GRANT, we beseech thee, almighty God, that like as we do believe thy only begotten Son our Lord to have ascended into the heavens: so we may also in heart and mind thither ascend, and with him continually dwell.

The Epistle. Acts i. [v. 1—11.]
The Gospel. Mar. xvi. [v. 14 to end.]

¶ *Proper Psalms and Lessons at Evensong.*
Psalms xxiv. lxviii. cxlviii.[4]

The second lesson, Ephe. iv. *unto the end.*

[³ Psal. xxxiv. Grafton, 2; but Ps. lxxxiv. given.]
[⁴ Ps. cviii. Whitchurch, June; and clxviii. Grafton, 1.]

¶ *The Sunday after the Ascension.*

Dominus regnavit. Psalm xciii.

The Collect.

O GOD, the King of glory, which hast exalted thine only Son Jesus Christ, with great triumph unto thy kingdom in heaven: we beseech thee leave us not comfortless, but send to us thine Holy Ghost to comfort us, and exalt us unto the same place, whither our Saviour Christ is gone before; who liveth and reigneth, &c.

The Epistle. 1 Peter iv. [v. 7—11.]
The Gospel. John xv. [v. 26 to end.] John xvi. [v. 1—4.]

¶ *Whit-Sunday.*

¶ *Proper Psalms and Lessons at Matins.*

Psalms xlviii. lxvii. cxlv.

The second lesson, Act. x. "Then Peter opened his mouth," *unto the end.*

¶ *At the Communion.*

Exultate justi in Domino. Psalm xxxiii.

The Collect.

GOD, which as upon this day hast taught the hearts of thy faithful people, by the sending to them the light of thy Holy Spirit: Grant us by the same Spirit to have a right judgment in all things, and evermore to rejoice in his holy comfort, through the merits of Christ Jesus our Saviour, who liveth and reigneth with thee in the unity of the same Spirit one God, world without end[1].

The Epistle. Acts ii. [v. 1—11.]
The Gospel. John xiv. [v. 15—21.]

¶ *Proper Psalms and Lessons at Evensong.*

Psalms civ. cxlv.

The second lesson, Acts xix. "It fortuned when Apollo went to Corinthum," *unto* "After these things."

[[1] Amen, Grafton, 2, and Oswen.]

¶ *Monday in Whitsun-week.*

Jubilate Deo. Psalm c.

The Collect.

¶ GOD, which, &c., *as upon Whit-Sunday.*

The Epistle. Act. x. [v. 34 to end.]
The Gospel. John iii. [v. 16—21.]

¶ *Tuesday.*

¶ *At the Communion*[2].

Misericordiam. Psalm[3] ci.

The Collect.

GOD, which, &c., *as upon Whit-Sunday.*

The Epistle. Acts viii. [v. 14—17.]
The Gospel. John x. [v. 1—10.]

¶ *Trinity-Sunday.*

¶ *At Matins.*

The first lesson, Gene. xviii. *unto the end.*
The second lesson, Math. iii. *unto the end.*

¶ *At the Communion.*

Deus misereatur[4]. Psalm lxvii[5].

The Collect.

ALMIGHTY and everlasting God, which hast given unto us thy servants grace by the confession of a[6] true faith to acknowledge the glory of the eternal Trinity, and in the power of the divine majesty to worship[7] the Unity: We beseech thee that through the steadfastness of this faith, we may evermore be defended from all adversity: which livest and reignest, one God, world without end[8].

The Epistle. Apoca. iv. [v. 1 to end.]
The Gospel. John iii. [v. 1—15.]

[2 *At the Communion,* Not in Grafton, 1.]
[3 Ps. cl. Whitchurch, June; but Ps. ci. given.]
[4 *Miseriatur,* Grafton, 2.]
[5 Psal. lxviii. Grafton, 2; but Ps. lxvii. given.]
[6 of true faith, Grafton, 2.]
[7 to worship thee in Unity, Grafton, 2.]   [8 Amen, Grafton, 2.]

AT THE COMMUNION.

¶ *The first Sunday after Trinity Sunday.*

Beati immaculati. Psalm cxix. [v. 1—8.]

The Collect.

GOD, the strength of all them that trust in thee, mercifully accept our prayers; and because the weakness of our mortal nature can do no good thing without thee, grant us the help of thy grace, that in keeping of thy commandments, we may please thee both in will and deed; through Jesus Christ our Lord.

The Epistle. 1 John iv. [v. 7 to end.]
The Gospel. Luc. xvi. [v. 19 to end.]

¶ *The Second*[1] *Sunday.*

In quo corriget[2]? Psalm cxix. [v. 9—16.]

The Collect.

LORD, make us to have a perpetual fear and love of thy holy name: for thou never failest to help and govern them whom thou dost bring up in thy steadfast love. Grant this, &c.

The Epistle. 1 John iii. [v. 13 to end.]
The Gospel. Luke xiv. [v. 16—24.]

¶ *The third Sunday.*

Retribue[3] *servo tuo.* Psalm cxix. [v. 17—24.]

The Collect.

LORD, we beseech thee mercifully to hear us, and unto whom thou hast given an hearty desire to pray, grant that by thy mighty aid we may be defended: through Jesus[4] Christ our Lord.

The Epistle. 1 Peter v. [v. 5—11.]
The Gospel. Luc. xv. [v. 1—10.]

[1 *Seventh*, in Oswen; through which some one has drawn the pen.]
[2 *corrigit*, Grafton, 1.]
[3 *Retribuo*, Grafton, 2.]   [4 Jesu, Oswen.]

¶ The fourth Sunday.

¶ *At the Communion*[5].
Adhæsit pavimento anima[6]. Psalm cxix. [v. 25—32.]

The Collect.

GOD, the Protector of all that trust in thee, without whom nothing is strong, nothing is holy: increase and multiply upon us thy mercy, that thou being our ruler and guide, we may so pass through things temporal, that we finally lose not the things eternal: Grant this, heavenly Father, for Jesu[7] Christ's sake our Lord.

The Epistle. Roma. viii. [v. 18—23.]
The Gospel. Luc. vi. [v. 36—42.]

¶ The fifth Sunday.

Legem pone. Psalm cxix.[8] [v. 33—40.]

The Collect.

GRANT Lord, we beseech thee, that the course of this world may be so peaceably ordered by thy governance: that thy congregation may joyfully serve thee in all godly quietness: through Jesus Christ our Lord.

The Epistle. 1 Peter iii. [v. 8—15.]
The Gospel. Luc. v. [v. 1—11.]

¶ The sixth Sunday.

Et veniat super me[9]. Psalm cxix. [v. 41—48.]

The Collect.

GOD, which hast prepared to them that love thee, such good things as pass all man's understanding: Pour into our hearts such love toward thee, that we loving[10] thee in all things, may obtain thy promises, which exceed all that we can desire; Through Jesus Christ our Lord.

The Epistle. Roma. vi. [v. 3—11.]
The Gospel. Mat. v. [v. 20—26.]

[5 *At the Communion*, omitted by Grafton, 2, and Oswen.]
[6 *anima*, omitted by Whitchurch, June; *anima mea* in Grafton, 1 and 2.]
[7 Jesus, Oswen.]
[8 Psal. cxx. Grafton, 2; but Ps. cxix. is given.]
[9 *me*, omitted by Grafton, 2.]
[10 living in all things, Grafton, 1.]

¶ The seventh Sunday.

Memor esto. Psalm cxix. [v. 49—56.]

The Collect.

LORD of all power and might, which art the author and giver of all good things: graff in our hearts the love of thy name, increase in us true religion, nourish us with all goodness, and of thy great mercy keep us in the same: Through Jesus Christ our Lord.

The Epistle. Roma. vi. [v. 19 to end.]
The Gospel. [1]Mar. viii. [v. 1—9.]

¶ The eighth Sunday.

¶ *At the Communion.*[2]

Portio mea Domine.[3] Psalm cxix. [v. 57—64.]

The Collect.

GOD, whose providence is never deceived, we humbly beseech thee, that thou wilt put away from us all hurtful things, and give those things which be profitable for us: Through Jesus Christ our Lord.

The Epistle. Roma. viii. [v. 12—17.]
The Gospel. Mat. vii. [15—21.]

¶ The ninth Sunday.

Bonitatem. Psalm cxix. [v. 65—72.]

The Collect.

GRANT to us, Lord, we beseech thee, the spirit to think and do always such things as be rightful: that we, which cannot be without thee, may by thee be able to live according to thy will: Through Jesus Christ our Lord.

The Epistle. 1 Cor. x. [v. 1—13.]
The Gospel. Luc. xvi. [v. 1—9.]

[[1] Math. viii., Grafton, 2; but the same Gospel is given.]
[[2] *At the Communion*, omitted by Grafton, 1 and 2.]
[[3] *Domine*, omitted by Grafton, 2.]

SUNDAYS AFTER TRINITY.

The tenth Sunday.

Manus tuæ. Psalm cxix.[4] [v. 73—80.]

The Collect.

LET thy merciful ears, O Lord, be open to the prayers of thy humble servants: and that they may obtain their petitions, make them to ask such things as shall please thee: Through Jesus Christ our Lord.

The Epistle. 1 Cor. xii. [v. 1—11.]
The Gospel. Luc. xix.[5] [v. 41—47.]

The eleventh Sunday.

Defecit. Psalm cxix. [v. 81—88.]

The Collect.

GOD, which declarest thy almighty power, most chiefly in shewing mercy and pity: Give unto us abundantly thy grace, that we running to thy promises, may be made partakers of thy heavenly treasure: through Jesus Christ our Lord.

The Epistle. 1 Cor. xv. [v. 1—11.]
The Gospel. Luc. xviii.[6] [v. 9—14.]

The twelfth Sunday.

In eternum Domine. Psal. cxix. [v. 89—96.]

The Collect.

ALMIGHTY and everlasting God, which art always more ready to hear than we to pray; and art wont to give more than either we desire or deserve: Pour down upon us the abundance of thy mercy, forgiving us those things whereof our conscience is afraid, and giving unto us that that our prayer dare not presume to ask; through Jesus Christ our Lord.

The Epistle. 2 Cor. iii. [v. 4—9.]
The Gospel. Mar. vii.[7] [v. 31 to end.]

[[4] Ps. cix. Grafton, 1; but Ps. cxix. given as above.]
[[5] Luc. xviii. Grafton, 1 and 2; but same Gospel.]
[[6] Luke xvii. Grafton, 1 and 2; but same Gospel.]
[[7] Math. vii. Grafton, 1 and 2; but same Gospel.]

AT THE COMMUNION.

The thirteenth Sunday.

Quomodo dilexi. Psalm cxix. [v. 97—104.]

The Collect.

ALMIGHTY and merciful God, of whose only gift it cometh, that thy faithful people do unto thee true and laudable service: grant, we beseech thee, that we may so run to thy heavenly promises, that we fail not finally to attain the same: through Jesus Christ our Lord.

The Epistle. Gala. iii. [v. 16—22.]
The Gospel. Luc. x. [ver. 23—37.]

The fourteenth Sunday.

Lucerna pedibus meis. Psalm cxix. [v. 105—112.]

The Collect.

ALMIGHTY and everlasting God, give unto us the increase of faith, hope, and charity: and, that we may obtain that which thou dost promise, make us to love that which thou dost command, through Jesus Christ our Lord.

The Epistle. Gala. v. [v. 16—24.]
The Gospel. Luc. xvii. [v. 11—19.]

The fifteenth Sunday.

Iniquos odio habui[1]. Psalm cxix. [v. 113—120.]

The Collect.

KEEP, we beseech thee, O Lord, thy church with thy perpetual mercy, and, because the frailty of man without thee cannot but fall, keep us ever by thy help, and lead us to all things profitable to our salvation: through Jesus Christ our Lord.

The Epistle. Gala. vi. [v. 11 to end.]
The Gospel. Matt. vi. [v. 24 to end.]

[[1] *habui,* omitted by Grafton, 2.]

SUNDAYS AFTER TRINITY.

The sixteenth Sunday.

¶ *At the Communion*[2].
Feci judicium. Psalm cxix. [v. 121—128.]

The Collect.

LORD, we beseech thee, let thy continual pity cleanse and defend thy congregation: and because it cannot continue in safety without thy succour, preserve it evermore by thy help and goodness; through Jesus Christ our Lord.

The Epistle. Ephes. iii. [v. 13 to end.]
The Gospel. Luc. vii. [v. 11—17.]

¶ *The seventeenth Sunday.*

Mirabilia. Psalm cxix. [v. 129—136.]

The Collect.

LORD, we pray thee that thy grace may always prevent and follow us, and make us continually to be given to all good works; through Jesus Christ our Lord.

The Epistle. Ephes. iv. [v. 1—6.]
The Gospel. Luc. xiv. [v. 1—11.]

¶ *The eighteenth Sunday.*

Justus es domine. Psalm cxix. [v. 137—144.]

The Collect.

LORD, we beseech thee, grant thy people grace to avoid the infections of the devil, and with pure heart and mind to follow thee, the only God: Through Jesus Christ our Lord.

The Epistle. 1 Cor. i. [v. 4—8.]
The Gospel. Math. xxii. [v. 34 to end.]

¶ *The nineteenth Sunday.*

Clamavi. Psalm cxix. [v. 145—152.]

The Collect.

O GOD, forasmuch as without thee we are not able to please thee: Grant that the working of thy mercy may in

---

[2 *At the Communion,* omitted by Grafton, 1 and 2.]

all things direct and rule our hearts: Through Jesus Christ[1] our Lord.

The Epistle. Ephe. iv. [v. 17 to end.]
The Gospel. Mat. ix. [v. 1—8.]

The twentieth Sunday.

Vide humilitatem meam. Psalm cxix. [v. 153—160.]

The Collect.

ALMIGHTY and merciful God, of thy bountiful goodness, keep us from all things that may hurt us: that we being ready both in body and soul, may with free hearts accomplish those things, that thou wouldest have done; through Jesus Christ our Lord.

The Epistle. Ephe. v. [v. 15—21.]
The Gospel. Math. xxii. [v. 1—14.]

¶ *The twenty-first Sunday.*

Principes persecuti. Psalm cxix. [v. 161—168.]

The Collect.

GRANT, we beseech thee, merciful Lord, to thy faithful people, pardon and peace; that they may be cleansed from all their sins, and serve thee with a quiet mind: Through Jesus Christ our Lord.

The Epistle. Ephe. vi. [v. 10—20.]
The Gospel. John iv. [v. 46 to end.]

¶ *The twenty-second Sunday.*

Appropinquet deprecatio. Psalm cxix. [v. 169—176.]

The Collect.

LORD, we beseech thee to keep thy household the church in continual godliness: that through thy protection, it may be free from all adversities, and devoutly given to serve thee in good works, to the glory of thy name: Through Jesus Christ our Lord.

The Epistle. Phil. i. [v. 3—11.]
The Gospel. Math. xviii.[2] [v. 21 to end.]

[[1] Jesus Christ, &c. Grafton, 2.]
[[2] Matt. xxviii. Grafton, 2; but the same Gospel.]

¶ The twenty-third Sunday.

Nisi quia dominus. Psalm cxxiv.

The Collect.

GOD our refuge and strength, which art the author of all godliness, be ready to hear the devout prayers of thy church: and grant that those things which we ask faithfully, we may obtain effectually: through Jesu[3] Christ our Lord.

The Epistle. Phil. iii. [v. 17 to end.]
The Gospel. Math. xxii. [v. 15—22.]

¶ The twenty-fourth Sunday.

Qui confidunt. Psalm cxxv[4].

The Collect.

LORD, we beseech thee, assoil[5] thy people from their offences: that through thy bountiful goodness, we may be delivered from the bands of all those sins, which by our frailty we have committed: Grant this, &c.

The Epistle. Coloss. i. [v. 3—12.]
The Gospel. Math. ix. [v. 18—26.]

¶ The twenty-fifth Sunday.

Nisi dominus. Psalm cxxvii.

The Collect.

STIR up, we beseech thee, O Lord, the wills of thy faithful people, that they plenteously bringing forth the fruit of good works, may of thee be plenteously rewarded: through Jesus Christ our Lord.

The Epistle. Jere. xxiii. [v. 5—8.]
The Gospel. John vi. [v. 5—14.]

[3 Jesus, Grafton, 2.]
[4 Psalm xxv. Grafton, 2; but Psalm cxxv. is given.]
[5 to release, to absolve. ED.]

Saint Andrew's Day.

At the Communion.

Sepe expugnaverunt. Psalm cxxix.

The Collect.

ALMIGHTY God, which hast given such grace to thy Apostle saint Andrewe, that he counted the sharp and painful death of the cross to be an high honour, and a great glory: Grant us to take and esteem all troubles and adversities which shall come unto us for thy sake, as things profitable for us toward the obtaining of everlasting life: through Jesus Christ our Lord.

The Epistle. Roma. x. [v. 9 to end.]
The Gospel. Math. iv. [v. 18—22.]

Saint Thomas the Apostle.

At the Communion[1].

Beati omnes. Psalm cxxviii.

The Collect.

ALMIGHTY everliving[2] God, which for the more confirmation of the faith, didst suffer thy holy apostle Thomas to be doubtful in thy Son's resurrection: Grant us so perfectly, and without all doubt, to believe in thy Son Jesus Christ, that our faith in thy sight never be reproved: hear us, O Lord, through the same Jesus Christ; to whom with thee and the Holy Ghost be all honour, &c.

The Epistle. Ephes. ii. [v. 19 to end.]
The Gospel. John xx. [v. 24 to end.]

¶ The Conversion of Saint Paul.

At Matins.

The second lesson, Acts xxii. *unto,* "They heard him."
Confitebor tibi. Psalm cxxxviii.

The Collect.

GOD, which hast taught all the world, through the preaching of thy blessed Apostle Saint Paul: grant we beseech thee,

[[1] *At the Communion,* not in Grafton, C.]
[[2] everlasting, Grafton, 2.]

that we which have his wonderful conversion in remembrance, may follow and fulfil the holy doctrine that he taught: through Jesus Christ our Lord.

The Epistle. Acts ix. [v. 1—22.]
The Gospel. Math. xix. [v. 27 to end.]

¶ At Evensong.
¶ The second lesson, Acts xxvi. unto the end.

¶ The Purification of Saint Mary the virgin.

Ecce nunc benedicite. Psalm cxxxiv.

The Collect.

ALMIGHTY and everlasting God, we humbly beseech thy Majesty, that as thy only begotten Son was this day presented in the Temple, in the substance of our flesh: so grant that we may be presented unto thee with pure and clear minds: By Jesus Christ our Lord.

The Epistle.
The same that is appointed for the Sunday.
The Gospel. Luc. ii. [v. 22—27.]

¶ Saint Mathies day.

Eripe me. Psalm cxl.

The Collect.

ALMIGHTY God, which in the place of the traitor Judas, didst choose thy faithful servant Mathie to be of the number of thy twelve Apostles: Grant that thy church being alway preserved from false Apostles, [3]may be ordered and guided by faithful and true pastors: Through Jesus Christ our Lord.

The Epistle. Acts i. [v. 15 to end.]
The Gospel. Math. xi. [v. 25 to end.]

[3 and may, Oswen.]

The Annunciation of the virgin Mary.

¶ *At the Communion.*[1]
Domine, non est exal. Psalm cxxxi.

The Collect.

WE beseech thee, Lord, pour thy grace into our hearts, that as we have known Christ thy Son's incarnation, by the message of an Angel; so by his cross and passion, we may be brought unto the glory of his resurrection: Through the same Christ our Lord.

The Epistle. Esai. vii. [v. 10—15.]
The Gospel. Luc. i. [v. 26—38.]

¶ Saint Mark's Day.
Domine clamavi. Psalm cxli.[2]

The Collect.

ALMIGHTY God, which hast instructed thy holy Church with the heavenly doctrine of thy Evangelist Saint Mark: give us grace so to be established by thy holy gospel, that we be not, like children, carried away with every blast of vain doctrine: Through Jesus Christ our Lord.

The Epistle. Ephes. iv. [v. 7—16.]
The Gospel. John xv. [v. 1—11.]

¶ Saint Philip and James.

¶ *At Matins.*
The second lesson, Acts viii. *unto,* "When the apostles."

¶ *At the Communion.*
Ecce quam bonum! Psalm cxxxiii.

The Collect.

ALMIGHTY God, whom truly to know is everlasting life: Grant us perfectly to know thy Son Jesus Christ, to be the way, the truth, and the life, as thou hast taught Saint Philip, and other the Apostles: Through Jesus Christ our Lord.

The Epistle. James i. [v. 1—12.]
The Gospel. John xiv. [v. 1—14.]

[[1] *At the Communion,* not in Grafton, 1 and C.]
[[2] Psalm cxl. Grafton, 2.; but Ps. cxli. is given.]

Saint Barnabe Apostle.

At Matins.
¶ The second lesson, Acts xiv. *unto the end.*
¶ *At the Communion.*
Voce mea ad Dominum. Psalm cxlii.

The Collect.
LORD Almighty, which hast endued thy holy Apostle Barnabas with singular gifts of thy Holy Ghost: let us not be destitute of thy manifold gifts, nor yet of grace to use them alway to thy honour and glory: Through Jesus Christ our Lord.

The Epistle. Act. xi. [v. 22 to end.]
The Gospel. John xv. [v. 12—16.]

¶ *At Evensong.*
¶ The second lesson, Act. xv. *unto,* "After certain days."

¶ Saint John Baptist.

¶ *Proper Lessons at Matins.*
The first lesson, Malach. iii. *unto the end.*
The second lesson, Mat. iii. *unto the end.*

At the Communion.
Domine exaudi. Psalm cxliii[3].

The Collect.
ALMIGHTY God, by whose providence thy servant John Baptist was wonderfully born, and sent to prepare the way of thy Son our Saviour by preaching of penance: make us so to follow his doctrine and holy life, that we may truly repent according to his preaching, and after his example constantly speak the truth, boldly rebuke vice, and patiently suffer for the truth's sake: through Jesus Christ our Lord.

The Epistle. Esai. xl. [v. 1—11.]
The Gospel. Luc. i. [v. 57 to end.]

Proper Lessons at Evensong.
The first lesson, Malach. iii. *unto the end*[4].
The second lesson, Mat. xiv. *unto,* "When Jesus heard."

[3 Psalm cxliv. Whitchurch, June: but Ps. cxliii. is given.]
[4 Malach. iv. Whitchurch, June, and Grafton, 2.]

¶ Saint Peter's Day.

At Matins.
The second lesson, Acts iii. *unto the end.*

At The Communion.
Benedictus dominus. Psalm cxliv[1].

The Collect.

ALMIGHTY God, which by thy Son Jesus Christ hast given to thy Apostle Saint Peter many excellent gifts, and commandedst him earnestly to feed thy flock; make, we beseech thee, all bishops and pastors diligently[2] to preach thy holy word, and the people obediently to follow the same, that they may receive the crown of everlasting Glory, through Jesus Christ our Lord.

The Epistle. Acts xii. [v. 1—11.]
The Gospel. Mat. xvi. [v. 13—19.]

At Evensong.
The second lesson, Acts iv. *unto the end*[3].

¶ Saint Mary Magdalene.

Lauda anima mea. Psalm cxlvi.

The Collect.

MERCIFUL Father, give us grace, that we never presume to sin through the example of any creature, but[4] if it shall chance us at any time to offend thy divine majesty, that then we may truly repent, and lament the same, after the example of Mary Magdalene, and by lively faith obtain remission of all our sins: through the only merits of thy Son our Saviour Christ.

The Epistle. Prov. xxxi. [v. 10 to end.]
The Gospel. Luc. vii. [v. 36 to end.]

[1 Ps. cxliii. Grafton, 1 and C, but Ps. cxliv. is given.]
[2 diligently, omitted by Oswen.]   [3 Acts iii. Grafton, C.]
[4 but and if, Oswen.]

¶ Saint James the Apostle.

Laudate Dominum de celis.   Psalm cxlviii.[5]

The Collect.

GRANT, O merciful God, that as thine holy Apostle James leaving his father and all that he had, without delay, was obedient unto the calling of thy Son Jesus Christ, and followed him : So we forsaking all[6] worldly and carnal affections, may be evermore ready to follow thy commandments : through Jesus Christ our Lord.

The Epistle.   Act. xi. [v. 27 to end.]   Acts xii. [v. 1—3.]
The Gospel.   Math. xx. [v. 20—28.]

Saint Bartholomewe.

Non nobis domine.   Psalm cxv.

The Collect.

O ALMIGHTY and everlasting God, which hast given grace to thy apostle Bartholomewe truly to believe and to preach thy word : grant, we beseech thee, unto thy church, both to love that he believed, and to preach that he taught : through Christ our Lord.

The Epistle.   Acts v. [v. 12—16.]
The Gospel.   Luc. xxii.[7] [v. 24—30.]

¶ Saint Mathewe.

Laudate Dominum omnes gentes.   Psalm cxvii.

The Collect.

ALMIGHTY God, which by thy blessed Son didst call Mathewe from the receipt of custom to be an Apostle and Evangelist : Grant us grace to forsake all covetous desires and inordinate love of riches, and to follow thy said Son Jesus Christ : who liveth and reigneth, &c.

The Epistle.   2 Cor. iv. [v. 1—6.]
The Gospel.   Math. ix.[8] [v. 9—13.]

[5 Psalm xlviii. Oswen : but Ps. cxlviii. is given.]
[6 all the, Oswen.]
[7 Luke xx. Grafton, 1 and C ; but the same Gospel is given.]
[8 Luke xix. Grafton, 2 ; but the same Gospel is given.]

¶ Saint Michael and all Angels.

¶ At the Communion.
Laudate pueri. Psalm cxiii.

The Collect.

EVERLASTING God, which hast ordained and constituted the services of all Angels and men in a wonderful order: mercifully grant, that they which alway do thee service in heaven, may by thy appointment succour and defend us in earth: through Jesus Christ our Lord, &c.

The Epistle. Apoca. xii. [v. 7—12.]
The Gospel. Math. xviii. [v. 1—10.]

¶ Saint Luke Evangelist.

Super flumina. Psalm cxxxvii.[1]

The Collect.

ALMIGHTY God, which calledst Luke the physician, whose praise is in the gospel, to be a physician of the soul: it may please thee by the wholesome medicines of his doctrine, to heal all the diseases of our souls: through thy Son Jesus Christ our Lord.

The Epistle. 2 Tim. iv. [v. 5.—15.]
The Gospel. Luc. x. [v. 1—7.]

¶ Symon and Jude Apostles.

Laudate dominum. Psalm cl.

The Collect.

ALMIGHTY GOD, which hast builded the congregation upon the foundation of the Apostles aud prophets, Jesu Christ himself being the head corner-stone: grant us so to be joined together in unity of spirit by their doctrine, that we may be made an holy temple acceptable to thee: through Jesu Christ our Lord.

The Epistle. Jude 1 [—8.]
The Gospel. John xv. [v. 17 to end.]

[[1] Psal. cxxxii. Grafton, 1, 2 and C; but Ps. cxxxvii. is given.]

¶ All Saints.

Proper Lessons at Matins.

The first lesson, Sapi. iii. *unto,* "Blessed is rather the Barren."
The second lesson, Hebre. xi. xii. "Saints by faith subdued," *unto,* "If ye endure chastising."

At the Communion.
Cantate Domino. Psalm cxlix.[2]

The Collect.

ALMIGHTY God, which hast knit together thy elect in one communion and fellowship in the mystical body of thy Son Christ our Lord; grant us grace so to follow thy holy Saints in all virtues, and godly living, that we may come to those unspeakable[3] joys, which thou hast prepared for all them that unfeignedly love thee; through Jesus Christ.

The Epistle. Apoca. vii. [v. 2—12.]
The Gospel. Math. v. [v. 1—12.]

¶ Proper Lessons at Evensong.

The first lesson, Sapi. v. *unto,* "His jealousy also."
The second lesson, Apoc. xix. *unto,* "And I saw an angel stand."

[2 Psal. xlix. Oswen; but Ps. cxlix. is given.]
[3 inspeakable, Grafton, 2, C and Oswen.]

THE
SUPPER OF THE LORD,
AND
THE HOLY COMMUNION,
COMMONLY CALLED THE MASS.

¶ SO many as intend to be partakers of the holy Communion, shall signify their names to the Curate over night, or else in the morning, afore the beginning of Matins[1], or immediately after.

¶ And if any of those be an open and notorious evil liver, so that the congregation by him is offended, or have done any wrong to his neighbours by word or deed: The Curate shall call him, and advertise him, in any wise not to[2] presume to the Lord's table, until he have openly declared himself to have truly repented, and amended his former naughty life: that the congregation may thereby be satisfied, which afore were offended: and that he have recompensed the parties, whom he hath done wrong unto, or at the least be in full purpose so to do, as soon as he conveniently may.

¶ The same order shall the Curate use, with those betwixt whom he perceiveth malice and hatred to reign, not suffering them to be partakers of the Lord's table, until he know them to be reconciled. And if one of the parties so at variance be content to forgive from the bottom of his heart all that the other hath trespassed against him, and to make amends for that he himself hath offended: and the other party will not be persuaded to a godly unity, but remain still in his frowardness and malice: The Minister in that case ought to admit the penitent person to the holy Communion, and not him that is obstinate.

¶ Upon the day, and at the time appointed for the ministration of the holy Communion, the Priest that shall execute the holy[3] ministry, shall put upon him the vesture appointed for that ministration, that is to say: a white Albe plain, with a vestment or Cope. And where there be many Priests or Deacons, there so many shall be ready to help the Priest, in the ministration, as shall be requisite: And shall have upon them likewise the vestures appointed for their ministry, that is to say, Albes with tunicles. Then shall the Clerks sing in English for the office, or Introit, (as they call it,) a Psalm appointed for that day.

[¹ of the matins, Grafton, C.]   [² to, omitted by Grafton, 1, 2, and C.]
[³ holy, omitted by Grafton, C.]

The priest standing humbly afore the midst of the Altar, shall say the Lord's prayer, with this Collect.

ALMIGHTY God, unto whom all hearts be open, and all desires known, and from whom no secrets are hid: cleanse the thoughts of our hearts, by the inspiration of thy Holy Spirit: that we may perfectly love thee, and worthily magnify thy holy name: through Christ our Lord. Amen.

Then shall he say a Psalm appointed for the introit: which Psalm ended, the Priest shall say, or else the Clerks shall sing,

iii. Lord have mercy upon us.
iii. Christ have mercy upon us.
iii. Lord have mercy upon us.

Then the Priest standing at God's board shall begin,

Glory be to God on high.

The Clerks. And in earth peace, good will towards men.

We praise thee, we bless thee, we worship thee, we glorify thee, we give thanks to thee for thy great glory, O Lord GOD, heavenly King, God the Father Almighty.

O[4] Lord the only begotten Son Jesu Christ, O Lord GOD, Lamb of GOD, Son of the Father, that takest away the sins of the world, have mercy upon us: thou that takest away the sins of the world, receive our prayer.

Thou that sittest at the right hand of God the Father, have mercy upon us: For thou only art holy, thou only art the Lord. Thou only, O Christ, with the Holy Ghost, art most high in the glory of God the Father. Amen.

Then the priest shall turn him to the people and say,

The Lord be with you.

The Answer. And with thy spirit.

The[5] *Priest.* Let us pray.

Then shall follow the Collect of the day, with one of these two Collects following, for the King.

Priest[6]. Let us pray.

ALMIGHTY God, whose kingdom is everlasting, and power infinite, have mercy upon the whole congregation, and so

[4 O, omitted by Grafton, 1, and C.]
[5 *The*, omitted by Grafton, C.]
[6 *Priest*, Let us pray, omitted by Grafton, C.]

rule the heart of thy chosen servant Edward the sixth, our king and governor, that he (knowing whose minister he is) may above all things, seek thy honour and glory, and that we his subjects (duly considering whose authority he hath) may faithfully serve, honour, and humbly obey him, in thee, and for thee, according to thy blessed word and ordinance: through Jesus Christ our Lord, who with thee, and the Holy Ghost, liveth and reigneth, ever one God, world without end. Amen.

ALMIGHTY and everlasting GOD, we be taught by thy holy word, that the hearts of Kings are in thy rule and governance, and that thou dost dispose, and turn them as it seemeth best to thy godly wisdom: We humbly beseech thee so[1] to dispose and govern the heart of Edward the sixth, thy servant, our King and governor, that in all his thoughts, words, and works, he may ever seek thy honour and glory, and study to preserve thy people committed to his charge, in wealth, peace, and godliness: Grant this, O merciful Father, for thy dear Son's sake, Jesus Christ our Lord. Amen.

The Collects ended, the priest, or he that is appointed, shall read the Epistle, in a place assigned for the purpose, saying,

The Epistle of Saint Paul, written in the   Chapter of   to the

The Minister then shall read the Epistle. Immediately after the Epistle ended, the priest, or one appointed to read the Gospel, shall say,

The holy Gospel, written in the   Chapter of

The Clerks and people shall answer,

Glory be to thee, O Lord.

The Priest or Deacon then shall read the Gospel: After the Gospel ended, the Priest shall begin,

I BELIEVE in one God.

The Clerks shall sing the rest.

The Father almighty, maker of heaven and earth, and of all things visible, and invisible: And in one Lord Jesu Christ, the only begotten Son of God, begotten of his Father before all worlds, God of GOD, light of light, very God of very God, begotten, not made, being of one substance with the Father,

[1 so, omitted by Oswen.]

by whom all things were made, who for us men, and for our salvation, came down from heaven, and was incarnate by the Holy Ghost of the Virgin Mary, and was made man, and was crucified also for us under Pontius Pilate, he suffered and was buried, and the third day he arose again according to the scriptures, and ascended into heaven, and sitteth at the right hand of the Father: and he shall come again with glory, to judge both the quick and the dead.

And I believe in the Holy Ghost, the Lord and giver of life, who proceedeth from the Father and the Son, who with the Father and the Son together, is worshipped and glorified, who spake by the prophets. And I believe one Catholic and Apostolic Church. I acknowledge one Baptism, for the remission of sins. And I look for the resurrection of the dead: and the life of the world to come. Amen.

¶ After the Creed ended, shall follow the Sermon or Homily, or some portion of one of the Homilies, as they shall be hereafter divided: wherein if the people be not exhorted to the worthy receiving of the holy Sacrament of the body and blood of our Saviour Christ, then shall the Curate give this exhortation, to those that be minded to receive the same.

DEARLY beloved in the Lord, ye that mind to come to the holy Communion of the body and blood of our Saviour Christ, must consider what St Paul writeth to the Corinthians, how he exhorteth all persons diligently to try and examine themselves, before they presume to eat of that bread and drink of that cup: for as the benefit is great, if with a truly penitent heart, and lively faith, we receive that holy Sacrament; (for then we spiritually eat[2] the flesh of Christ, and drink his blood, then we dwell in Christ and Christ in us, we be made one with Christ, and Christ with us;) so is the danger great, if we receive the same unworthily; for then we become guilty of the body and blood of Christ our Saviour, we eat and drink our own damnation, not considering the Lord's body. We kindle God's wrath over us, we provoke him to plague us with divers diseases, and sundry kinds of death. Therefore if any here be a blasphemer, advouterer[3], or be in malice, or envy, or in any other grievous crime (except he be truly sorry therefore, and earnestly minded to

[2 eat of, Oswen.]   [3 advouterer: adulterer. ED.]

leave the same vices, and do trust himself to be reconciled to Almighty God, and in charity with all the world), let him bewail his sins, and not come to that holy table; lest after the taking of that most blessed bread, the devil enter into him, as he did into Judas, to fill him full of all iniquity, and bring him to destruction, both of body and soul. Judge therefore yourselves (brethren) that ye be not judged of the Lord. Let your mind[1] be without desire to sin, repent you truly for your sins past, have an earnest and lively faith in Christ our Saviour, be in perfect charity with all men; so shall ye be meet partakers of those holy mysteries. And above all things: ye must give most humble and hearty thanks to God the Father, the Son, and the Holy Ghost, for the redemption of the world by the death and passion of our Saviour Christ, both God and man, who did humble himself even to the death upon the cross, for us miserable sinners, which lay in darkness and shadow of death, that he might make us the children of God, and exalt us to everlasting life. And to the end that we should alway remember the exceeding love of our Master, and only Saviour Jesu Christ, thus dying for us, and the innumerable benefits, which (by his precious blood-shedding) he hath obtained to us, he hath left in those holy mysteries, as a pledge of his love, and a continual remembrance of the same, his own blessed body, and precious blood, for us to feed upon spiritually, to our endless comfort and consolation. To him therefore, with the Father [2] and the Holy Ghost, let us give (as we are most bounden) continual thanks, submitting ourselves wholly to his holy will and pleasure, and studying[3] to serve him in true holiness and righteouness, all the days of our life. Amen.

¶ In Cathedral churches or other places, where there is daily Communion, it shall be sufficient to read this exhortation above written, once in a month. And in parish churches, upon the week days it may be left unsaid.

¶ And if upon the Sunday or holyday, the people be negligent to come to the Communion: Then shall the Priest earnestly exhort

[1 minds, Oswen.]
[2 "and the Holy Ghost, let us give (as we are most bounden)" is repeated twice, with a pen drawn through, Grafton, C.]
[3 study, Grafton, 1 and C.]

his parishioners, to dispose themselves to the receiving of the holy communion more diligently, saying these or like words unto them.

DEAR friends, and you especially upon whose souls I have cure and charge, on   next, I do intend by God's grace, to offer to all such as shall be godly disposed, the most comfortable Sacrament of the body and blood of Christ, to be taken of them in the remembrance of his most fruitful and glorious Passion: by the which passion we have obtained remission of our sins, and be made partakers of the kingdom of heaven, whereof[4] we be assured and ascertained, if we come to the said Sacrament with hearty repentance for our offences, stedfast faith in God's mercy, and earnest mind to obey God's will, and to offend no more. Wherefore our duty is to come to these holy mysteries, with most hearty thanks to be given to Almighty GOD for his infinite mercy and benefits given and bestowed upon us his unworthy servants, for whom he hath not only given his body to death, and shed his blood, but also doth vouchsafe in a Sacrament and mystery to give us his said body and blood to feed upon spiritually. The which Sacrament being so divine and holy a thing, and so comfortable to them which receive it worthily, and so dangerous to them that will presume to take the same unworthily: My duty is to exhort you in the mean season, to consider the greatness of the thing, and to search and examine your own consciences, and that not lightly nor after the manner of dissimulers with GOD: but as they which should come to a most Godly and heavenly banquet, not to come but in the marriage garment required of God in scripture; that you may (so much as[5] lieth in you) be found worthy to come to such a table. The ways and means thereto is,

First, that you be truly repentant[6] of your former evil life, and that you confess with an unfeigned heart to Almighty God your sins and unkindness towards his Majesty committed, either by will, word, or deed, infirmity or ignorance: and that with inward sorrow and tears you bewail your offences, and require of Almighty God mercy and pardon, promising to him (from the bottom of your hearts)

[4 wherefore, Grafton, 1.]   [5 a lieth, Whitchurch, June.]
[6 repentance, Grafton, 2.]

the amendment of your former life. And amongst[1] all others, I am commanded of God, especially to move and exhort you to reconcile yourselves to your neighbours[2], whom you have offended, or who hath offended you, putting out of your hearts all hatred and malice against them, and to be in love and charity with all the world, and to forgive other as you would that God should forgive you. And if any man have done wrong to any other, let him make satisfaction, and due restitution of all lands and goods, wrongfully taken away or withholden, before he come to God's board, or at the least be in full mind and purpose so to do, as soon as he is able; or else let him not come to this holy table, thinking to deceive God, who seeth all men's hearts. For neither the absolution of the priest can any thing avail them, nor the receiving of this holy sacrament doth any thing but increase their damnation. And if there be any of you, whose conscience is troubled and grieved in any thing, lacking comfort or counsel, let him come to me, or to some other discreet and learned priest, taught in the law of God, and confess and open his sin and grief secretly, that he may receive such ghostly counsel, advice, and comfort, that his conscience may be relieved, and that of us (as of the ministers of GOD and of the church) he may receive comfort and absolution, to the satisfaction of his mind, and avoiding of all scruple and doubtfulness: requiring such as shall be satisfied with a general confession, not to be offended with them that do use, to their further satisfying, the auricular and secret confession to the priest; nor those also which think needful or convenient, for the quietness of their own consciences, particularly to open their sins to the priest, to be offended with them that are satisfied with their humble confession to GOD, and the general confession to the church. But in all things to follow and keep the rule of charity, and every man to be satisfied with his own conscience, not judging other men's minds or consciences; where as he hath no warrant of God's word to the same.

¶ Then shall follow for the Offertory one or more of these Sentences of holy scripture, to be sung whiles the people do offer, or else one of them to be said by the minister, immediately afore the offering.

[1 among, Grafton, 2.]   [2 neighbour, Grafton, 2.]

LET your light so shine before men, that they may see your good works, and glorify your Father which is in heaven. *Mat.* v.

Lay not up for yourselves treasure upon the earth, where the rust and moth doth corrupt, and where thieves break through and steal: But lay up for yourselves treasures[3] in heaven, where neither rust nor moth doth corrupt, and where thieves do not break through nor steal. *Mat.* vi.

Whatsoever you would that men should do unto you, even so do you unto them: for this is the law and the Prophets. *Math.* vii.

Not every one that saith unto me, Lord, Lord, shall enter into the kingdom of heaven, but he that doeth the will of my Father which is in heaven. *Mat.* vii.

Zachee stood forth, and said unto the Lord, Behold, Lord, the half of my goods I give to the poor, and if I have done any wrong to any man, I restore fourfold. *Luc.* xix.

Who goeth a warfare at any time at his own cost? Who planteth a vineyard, and eateth not of the fruit thereof? Or who feedeth a flock, and eateth not of the milk of the flock? 1 *Cor.* ix.

If we have sown unto you spiritual things, is it a great matter if we shall reap your worldly things? 1 *Cor.* ix.

Do ye not know, that they which minister about holy things, live of the sacrifice? They which wait of the altar are partakers with the altar? Even so hath the Lord also ordained: that they which preach the Gospel, should live of the Gospel. 1 *Cor.* ix.

He which soweth little, shall reap little, and he that soweth plenteously, shall reap plenteously. Let every man do according as he is disposed in his heart; not grudgingly, or of necessity; for God loveth a cheerful giver. 2 *Cor.* ix.

Let him that is taught in the word, minister unto him that teacheth, in all good things. Be not deceived; GOD is not mocked. For whatsoever a man soweth, that shall he reap. *Gala.* vi.

While we have time, let us do good unto all men, and specially unto them, which are of the household of faith. *Gala.* vi.

Godliness is great riches, if a man be contented with

[[3] treasure, Grafton, 1, 2, C, and Oswen.]

that he hath: For we brought nothing into the world, neither may[1] we carry any thing out. 1 *Timo.* vi.

Charge them which are rich in this world, that they be ready to give, and glad to distribute, laying up in store[2] for themselves a good foundation, against the time to come, that they may attain eternal life. 1 *Timo.* vi.

GOD is not unrighteous, that he[3] will forget your works and labour, that proceedeth of love, which love ye have shewed for his name's sake, which have ministered unto[4] the saints, and yet do minister. *Hebre.* vi.

To do good, and to distribute, forget not, for with such sacrifices God is pleased. *Hebre.* xiii.

Whoso hath this world's good, and seeth his brother have need, and shutteth up his compassion from him, how dwelleth the love of God in him? 1 *John* iii.

Give alms of thy goods, and turn never thy face from any poor man, and then the face of the Lord shall not be turned away from thee. *Toby* iv.

Be merciful after thy power: if thou hast much, give plenteously; if thou hast little, do thy diligence gladly to give of that little: for so gatherest thou thyself a good reward in the day of necessity. *Toby* iv.

He that hath pity upon the poor lendeth unto the Lord; and look, what he layeth out, it shall be paid him again. *Prov.*[5] xix.

Blessed be the man that provideth for the sick and needy; the Lord shall deliver him, in the time of trouble. *Psalm* xli.

Where there be Clerks, they shall sing one, or many of the sentences above written, according to the length and shortness of the time, that the people be offering.

In the mean time, whiles the Clerks do sing the Offertory, so many as are[6] disposed, shall offer to[7] the poor men's box every one according to his ability and charitable mind. And at the offering days appointed, every man and woman shall pay to the Curate the due and accustomed offerings.

[[1] can, Grafton, C.]   [[2] in store, omitted by Grafton, 1, 2, and C.]
[[3] ye, Oswen.]   [[4] to, Grafton, 1, 2 and C.]
[[5] This and the following reference are inverted by mistake in Grafton, C.]
[[6] be, Grafton, C.]   [[7] unto the, Grafton, C.]

Then so many as shall be partakers of the holy Communion, shall tarry still in the quire, or in some convenient place nigh the quire, the men on the one side, and the women on the other side. All other (that mind not to receive the said holy Communion) shall depart out of the quire, except the ministers and Clerks.

Then shall the minister take so much Bread and Wine, as shall suffice for the persons appointed to receive the holy Communion, laying the bread upon the corporas[8], or else in the paten, or in some other comely thing prepared for that purpose: And putting the wine into the Chalice, or else in some fair or convenient cup, prepared for that use (if the chalice will not serve), putting thereto a little pure and clean water: And setting both the bread and wine upon the Altar: Then the Priest shall say,

The Lord be with you.
Answer. And with thy spirit.
Priest. Lift up your hearts.
Answer. We lift them up unto the Lord.
Priest. Let us give thanks to our Lord God.
Answer. It is meet and right so to do.
The[9] *Priest.* It is very meet, right, and our bounden duty, that we should at all times, and in all places, give thanks to thee, O Lord, holy Father, almighty everlasting God.

¶ Here shall follow the proper preface, according to the time (if there be any specially appointed,) or else immediately shall follow,

Therefore with angels, &c[10].

PROPER PREFACES.

¶ *Upon Christmas Day.*

BECAUSE thou didst give Jesus Christ, thine only Son, to be born as this day for us, who by the operation of the Holy Ghost was made very man, of the substance of the Virgin Mary his mother, and that without spot of sin, to make us clean from all sin. Therefore &c.

[8 corporas, a cloth used at the communion table. ED.]
[9 The, omitted, Grafton, C.]   [10 &c. omitted, Grafton, C.]

¶ *Upon Easter Day.*

BUT chiefly are we bound to praise thee, for the glorious resurrection of thy Son Jesus Christ, our Lord; for he is the very Paschal Lamb, which was offered for us, and hath taken away the sin of the world, who by his death hath destroyed death, and by his rising to life again hath restored to us everlasting life. Therefore &c.

¶ *Upon the Ascension Day.*

THROUGH thy most dear beloved Son, Jesus Christ our Lord, who after his most glorious resurrection manifestly appeared to all his disciples, and in their sight ascended up into heaven, to prepare a place for us, that where he is, thither might we also ascend, and reign with him in glory. Therefore &c.

¶ *Upon Whitsunday.*

THROUGH Jesus Christ our Lord, according to whose most true promise, the Holy Ghost came down this day from heaven, with a sudden great sound, as it had been a mighty wind, in the likeness of fiery tongues, lighting upon the Apostles, to teach them, and to lead them to all truth, giving them both the gift of divers languages, and also boldness with fervent zeal, constantly to preach the Gospel unto all nations, whereby we are brought out of darkness and error, into the clear light and true knowledge of thee, and of thy Son Jesus Christ. Therefore &c.

¶ *Upon the feast of the Trinity.*

IT is very meet, right, and our bounden duty, that we should at all times, and in all places, give thanks to thee, O Lord almighty, everlasting God, which art one God, one Lord, not one only person, but three persons in one substance: For that which we believe of the glory of the Father, the same we believe of the Son, and of the Holy Ghost, without any difference, or inequality: whom the angels &c.[1]

[[1] &c. omitted, Grafton, C.]

After which preface shall follow immediately,

Therefore with Angels and Archangels, and with all the holy company of heaven, we laud and magnify thy glorious name, evermore praising thee, and saying,

¶ Holy, holy, holy, Lord God of Hosts: heaven and earth are full of thy glory: Osannah in the highest. Blessed is he that cometh in the name of the Lord: Glory to thee, O Lord, in the highest.

This the Clerks shall also sing.

¶ When the Clerks have done singing, then shall the Priest, or Deacon, turn him to the people, and say,

Let us pray for the whole state of Christ's church.

¶ Then the Priest, turning him to the Altar, shall say or sing, plainly and distinctly, this prayer following:

ALMIGHTY and everliving God, which by thy holy apostle hast taught us to make prayers and supplications, and to give thanks for all men: We humbly beseech thee most mercifully to receive these our prayers, which we offer unto thy divine Majesty, beseeching thee to inspire continually the universal church with the spirit of truth, unity, and concord: And grant that all they that do confess thy holy name, may agree in the truth of thy holy word, and live in unity and godly love. Specially we beseech thee to save and defend thy servant Edward our King, that under him we may be Godly and quietly governed. And grant unto his whole council, and to all that be put in authority under him, that they may truly and indifferently minister justice, to the punishment of wickedness and vice, and to the maintenance of God's true religion and virtue. Give grace (O heavenly Father) to all Bishops, Pastors, and Curates, that they may both by their life and doctrine set forth thy true and lively word, and rightly and duly administer thy holy Sacraments: and to all thy people give thy heavenly grace, that with meek heart and due reverence they may hear and receive thy holy word, truly serving thee in holiness and righteousness all the days of their life. And we most humbly beseech thee of thy goodness (O Lord) to comfort and succour all them, which in this transitory life be in trouble, sorrow, need, sickness, or any other adversity. And especially we commend unto thy merciful goodness this congregation which is here assembled in thy name, to celebrate the commemoration of the most glorious death of thy Son: And here we do give unto thee most high praise, and hearty thanks, for the wonderful grace and virtue, declared in all thy saints, from the beginning of the world: And chiefly in the glorious and most blessed virgin Mary, mother of thy Son Jesu Christ our Lord and God, and in the holy Patriarchs, Prophets, Apostles and Martyrs, whose examples (O Lord) and stedfastness in thy faith, and keeping thy holy commandments, grant us to follow. We commend unto thy mercy (O Lord) all other thy servants, which are departed hence from us, with the sign of faith, and now do rest in the sleep of peace: Grant unto them, we beseech thee, thy mercy, and everlasting peace, and that, at the day of the general resurrection, we and all they which be of the mystical body of thy Son, may altogether be set on his right hand, and hear that his most joyful voice: Come unto me, O ye that be blessed of my Father, and possess the kingdom, which is prepared for you from the beginning of the world: grant this, O Father, for Jesus Christ's sake, our only Mediator and Advocate.

O God heavenly Father, which of thy tender mercy didst give thine only Son Jesu[1] Christ, to suffer death upon the cross for our redemption, who made there (by his one oblation, once offered) a full, perfect, and sufficient sacrifice, oblation, and satisfaction, for the sins of the whole world, and did institute, and in his holy Gospel command us to celebrate, a perpetual memory of that his precious death, until his coming again: Hear us (O merciful Father) we beseech thee; and with thy Holy Spirit and word vouchsafe to bl✠ess and sanc✠tify these thy gifts, and creatures of bread and wine, that they may be unto us the body and blood of thy most dearly beloved Son Jesus Christ.

Here the Priest must take the bread into his hands. Who, in the same night that he was betrayed, took bread, and when he had blessed, and given thanks, he brake it, and gave it to his disciples, saying: Take, eat, this is my body which is given for you: do this in remembrance of me.

[1 Jesus, Grafton, 2.]

THE COMMUNION. 89

Likewise after supper he took the cup, and when he had given thanks, he gave it to them, saying: Drink ye all of this, for this is my blood of the new Testament, which is shed for you and for many, for remission of sins: Do this as oft as you shall drink it, in remembrance of me.

<small>Here the Priest shall take the cup into his hands.</small>

These words before rehearsed are to be said, turning still to the Altar, without any elevation, or shewing the Sacrament to the people.

WHEREFORE, O Lord and heavenly Father, according to the Institution of thy dearly beloved Son, our Saviour Jesu Christ, we thy humble servants do celebrate, and make here before thy divine Majesty, with these thy holy gifts, the memorial which thy Son hath willed us to make: having in remembrance his blessed passion, mighty resurrection, and glorious ascension, rendering unto thee most hearty thanks, for the innumerable benefits procured unto us by the same, entirely desiring thy fatherly goodness, mercifully to accept this our Sacrifice of praise and thanksgiving: most humbly beseeching thee to grant, that by the merits and death of thy Son Jesus Christ, and through faith in his blood, we and all thy whole church may obtain remission of our sins, and all other benefits of his passion. And here we offer and present unto thee (O Lord) ourself, our souls, and bodies, to be a reasonable, holy, and lively sacrifice unto thee: humbly beseeching thee, that whosoever shall be partakers[2] of this holy Communion, may worthily receive the most precious body and blood of thy Son Jesus Christ, and be fulfilled with thy grace and heavenly benediction, and made one body with thy Son Jesus Christ, that he may dwell in them, and they in him. And although we be unworthy (through our manifold sins) to offer unto thee any Sacrifice: Yet we beseech thee to accept this our bounden duty and service, and command these our prayers and supplications, by the ministry of thy holy Angels, to be brought up into thy holy Tabernacle before the sight of thy divine majesty; not weighing our merits, but pardoning our offences, through Christ our Lord; by whom, and with whom, in the unity of the Holy Ghost,

[[2] partaker, Grafton, 1.]

all honour and glory be unto thee, O Father Almighty, world without end. Amen.

Let us pray.

As our Saviour Christ hath commanded and taught us, we are bold to say. Our Father, which art in heaven, hallowed be thy name. Thy Kingdom come. Thy will be done in earth, as it is in heaven. Give us this day our daily bread. And forgive us our trespasses, as we forgive them that trespass against us. And lead us not into temptation.

The Answer. But deliver us from evil. Amen[1].

Then shall the Priest say,

The peace of the Lord be alway with you.
The Clerks. And with thy spirit.
The Priest. Christ our paschal Lamb is offered up for us, once for all, when he bare our sins on his body upon the cross; for he is the very Lamb of God, that taketh away the sins of the world: wherefore let us keep a joyful and holy feast with the Lord.

Here the Priest shall turn him toward those that come to the holy Communion, and shall say,

You that do truly and earnestly repent you of your sins to Almighty God, and be in love and charity with your neighbours, and intend to lead a new life, following the commandments of God, and walking from henceforth in his holy ways: draw near and take this holy Sacrament to your comfort, make your humble confession to Almighty God, and to his holy church here gathered together in his name, meekly kneeling upon your knees.

Then shall this general Confession be made, in the name of all those that are minded to receive the holy Communion, either by one of them, or else by one of the ministers, or by the Priest himself, all kneeling humbly upon their knees.

ALMIGHTY GOD, Father of our Lord Jesus Christ, maker of all things, judge of all men, we knowledge and bewail our manifold sins and wickedness, which we from

[1 Amen, omitted by Oswen.]

time to time, most grievously have committed, by thought, word and deed, against thy divine majesty, provoking most justly thy wrath and indignation against us : we do earnestly repent, and be heartily sorry for these our misdoings : the remembrance of them is grievous unto us, the burden of them is intolerable : have mercy upon us, have mercy upon us, most merciful Father, for thy Son our Lord Jesus Christ's sake, forgive us all that is past, and grant that we may ever hereafter serve and please thee in newness of life, to the honour and glory of thy name : Through Jesus Christ our Lord.

Then shall the Priest stand up, and turning himself to the people, say thus:

ALMIGHTY GOD, our heavenly Father, who of his great mercy, hath promised forgiveness of sins to all them, which with hearty repentance and true faith turn unto him : have mercy upon you, pardon and deliver you from all your sins, confirm and strengthen[2] you in all goodness, and bring you to everlasting life : through Jesus Christ our Lord. Amen.

Then shall the Priest also say,

Hear what comfortable words our Saviour Christ saith, to all that truly turn to him.

Come unto me all that travail, and be heavy laden, and I shall refresh you. So God loved the world that he gave his only-begotten Son, to the end that all that believe in him, should not perish, but have life everlasting.

Hear also what Saint Paul saith.

This is a true saying, and worthy of all men to be received, that Jesus Christ came into this world to save sinners.

Hear also what Saint John saith.

If any man sin, we have an advocate with the Father, Jesus Christ the righteous, and he is the propitiation for our sins.

Then shall the Priest, turning him to God's board, kneel down, and say in the name of all them, that shall receive the Communion, this prayer following.

[2 strength, Grafton, 1, and Oswen.]

THE COMMUNION.

WE do not presume to come to this thy table (O merciful Lord) trusting in our own righteousness, but in thy manifold and great mercies: we be not worthy so much as to gather up the crumbs under thy table: but thou art the same Lord whose property is always to have mercy: Grant us therefore (gracious Lord) so to eat the flesh of thy dear Son Jesus[2] Christ, and to drink his blood in these holy Mysteries, that we may continually dwell in him, and he in us, that our sinful bodies may be made clean by his body, and our souls washed through his most precious blood. Amen.

¶ Then shall the Priest first receive the Communion in both kinds himself, and next deliver it to other Ministers, if any be there present, (that they may be ready to help the chief Minister,) and after to the people.

¶ And when he delivereth the Sacrament of the body of Christ, he shall say to every one these words:

The body of our Lord Jesus Christ which was given for thee, preserve thy body and soul unto everlasting life.

And the Minister delivering the Sacrament of the blood, and giving every one to drink once and no more, shall say,

The blood of our Lord Jesus Christ which was shed for thee, preserve thy body and soul unto everlasting life.

If there be a Deacon or other Priest, then shall he follow with the Chalice: and as the Priest ministereth the Sacrament of the body, so shall he (for more expedition) minister the Sacrament of the blood, in form before written.

In the communion time the Clerks shall sing,

ii. O Lamb of God, that takest away the sins of the world: have mercy upon us.

O Lamb of God, that takest away the sins of the world: grant us thy peace.

Beginning so soon as the Priest doth receive the holy Communion, and when the Communion is ended, then shall the Clerks sing the post-Communion.

¶ *Sentences of holy scripture, to be said or sung every day one, after the holy Communion, called the post-Communion.*

[¹ Jesu, Oswen.]

If any man will follow me, let him forsake himself, and take up his cross, and follow me. *Math.* xvi.²

Whosoever shall endure unto the end, he shall be saved. *Mar.* xiii.

Praised be the Lord God of Israel, for he hath visited and redeemed his people: therefore let us serve him all the days of our life, in holiness and righteousness accepted before him. *Luc.* i.

Happy are those servants, whom the Lord (when he cometh) shall find waking. *Luc.* xii.

Be ye ready, for the Son of man will come at an hour when ye think not. *Luc.* xii.

The servant that knoweth his master's will, and hath not prepared himself, neither hath done according to his will, shall be beaten with many stripes. *Luc.* xii.

The hour cometh, and now it is, when true worshippers shall worship the Father in spirit and truth. *John* iv.

Behold, thou art made whole, sin no more, lest any worse thing happen unto thee. *John* v.

If ye shall continue in my word, then are ye my very disciples, and ye shall know the truth, and the truth shall make you free. *John* viii.

While ye have light, believe on the light, that ye may be the children of light. *John* xii.

He that hath my commandments, and keepeth them, the same is he that loveth me. *John* xiv.

If any man love me, he will keep my word, and my Father will love him, and we will come unto him, and dwell with him. *John* xiv.

If ye shall bide in me, and my word shall abide in you, ye shall ask what ye will, and it shall be done to you. *John* xv.

Herein is my Father glorified, that ye bear much fruit, and³ become my disciples. *John* xv.

This is my commandment, that you love together, as I have loved you. *John* xv.

If God be on our side, who can be against us? which did not spare his own Son, but gave him for us all. *Roma.* viii.

Who shall lay any thing to the charge of God's chosen?

[² Oswen omits this and the next reference.]
[³ an, Whitchurche, June.]

it is GOD that justifieth; who is he[1] that can condemn? *Roma.* viii.

The night is past, and the day is at hand; let us therefore cast away the deeds of darkness, and put on the armour of light. *Rom.* xiii.

Christ Jesus is made of GOD, unto us, wisdom, and righteousness, and sanctifying, and redemption, that (according as it is written) He which rejoiceth should rejoice in the Lord. 1 *Corin.* i.

Know ye not that ye are the temple of GOD, and that the Spirit of GOD dwelleth in you? If any man defile the temple of GOD, him shall God destroy. 1 *Corin.* iii.

Ye are dearly bought; therefore glorify God in your bodies, and in your spirits, for they belong to God. 1 *Cor.* vi.

Be you followers of God as dear children, and walk in love, even as Christ loved us, and gave himself for us an offering and a Sacrifice of a sweet savour to God. *Ephes.* v.[2]

Then the Priest shall give thanks to God, in the name of all them that have communicated, turning him first to the people, and saying,

The Lord be with you.

The Answer. And with thy spirit.

The Priest. Let us pray.

ALMIGHTY and everliving[3] GOD, we most heartily thank thee, for that thou hast vouchsafed to feed us in these holy Mysteries, with the spiritual food of the most precious body and blood of thy Son our Saviour Jesus Christ, and hast assured us (duly receiving the same) of thy favour and goodness toward us, and that we be very members incorporate in thy mystical body, which is the blessed company of all faithful people, and heirs through hope of thy everlasting kingdom, by the merits of the most precious death and passion of thy dear Son. We therefore most humbly beseech thee, O heavenly Father, so to assist us with thy grace, that we may continue in that holy fellowship, and do all such good works, as thou hast prepared for us to walk in: through Jesus Christ our Lord, to whom, with thee and the Holy Ghost, be all honour and glory, world without end.

[[1] he, omitted, Grafton, C.]
[[2] Ephes. vi. Grafton, 1, 2, and C; but the same passage as above.]
[[3] everlasting, Grafton, 1, and C.]

Then the Priest turning him to the people, shall let them depart with this blessing:

The peace of GOD (which passeth all understanding) keep your hearts and minds in the knowledge and love of GOD, and of his Son Jesus Christ our Lord: And the blessing of God Almighty, the Father, the Son, and the Holy Ghost, be amongst you and remain with you alway.

Then the people shall answer,

Amen.

Where there are no clerks, there the Priest shall say all things appointed here for them to sing.

When the holy Communion is celebrate on the workday, or in private houses: Then may be omitted, the[4] Gloria in excelsis, the Creed, the Homily, and the exhortation, beginning,

Dearly beloved, &c.

¶ Collects to be said after the Offertory, when there is no Communion, every such day one.

ASSIST us mercifully, O Lord, in these our supplications and prayers, and dispose the way of thy servants toward the attainment of everlasting salvation: that among all the changes and chances of this mortal life, they may ever be defended by thy most gracious and ready help; through Christ our Lord. Amen.

O ALMIGHTY Lord and everliving GOD, vouchsafe, we beseech thee, to direct, sanctify, and govern, both our hearts and bodies, in the ways of thy laws, and in the works of thy commandments: that through thy most mighty protection, both here and ever, we may be preserved in body and soul: Through our Lord and Saviour Jesus Christ. Amen.

GRANT, we beseech thee, Almighty God, that the words which we have heard this day with our outward ears, may through thy grace be so grafted inwardly in our hearts, that they may bring forth in us the fruit of good living, to the honour and praise of thy name: Through Jesus Christ our Lord. Amen.

[4 the, omitted by Oswen.]

PREVENT us, O Lord, in all our doings, with thy most gracious favour, and further us with thy continual help, that in all our works begun, continued, and ended in thee, we may glorify thy holy name, and finally by thy mercy obtain everlasting life: Through, &c.[1]

ALMIGHTY God, the fountain of all wisdom, which knowest our necessities before we ask, and our ignorance in asking: we beseech thee to have compassion upon our infirmities, and those things, which for our unworthiness we dare not, and for our blindness we cannot ask, vouchsafe to give us for the worthiness of thy Son Jesu Christ our Lord. Amen.

ALMIGHTY God, which hast promised to hear the petitions of them that ask in thy Son's name, we beseech thee mercifully to incline thine ears to us that have made now our prayers and supplications unto thee: and grant that those things which we have faithfully asked according to thy will, may effectually be obtained to the relief of our necessity, and to the setting forth of thy glory: Through Jesus Christ our Lord.

¶ For rain.

O GOD heavenly Father, which by thy Son Jesu Christ hast promised to all them that seek thy kingdom, and the righteousness thereof, all things necessary to the bodily sustenance: send us, we beseech thee, in this our necessity, such moderate rain and showers, that we may receive the fruits of the earth, to our comfort and to thy honour; Through Jesus Christ our Lord.

For fair weather.

O LORD God, which for the sin of man, didst once drown all the world, except eight persons, and afterward of thy great mercy, didst promise never to destroy it so again: We humbly beseech thee, that although we for our iniquities have worthily deserved this plague of rain and waters, yet, upon our true repentance, thou wilt send us such weather whereby we may receive the fruits of the earth in due season, and

[[1] Jesus Christ our Lord, Grafton, 2.]

learn both by thy[2] punishment to amend our lives, and by the granting of our petition to give thee praise and glory: Through Jesu Christ our Lord.

¶ Upon Wednesdays and Fridays, the English Litany shall be said or sung in all places, after such form as is appointed by the king's majesty's Injunctions: Or as is or shall be otherwise appointed by his highness[3]. And though there be none to communicate with the Priest, yet these days (after the Litany ended) the Priest shall put upon him a plain Albe or surplice, with a cope, and say all things at the Altar (appointed to be said at the celebration of the Lord's supper,) until after the offertory. And then shall add one or two of the Collects aforewritten, as occasion shall serve, by his discretion. And then turning him to the people shall let them depart with the accustomed blessing.

And the same order shall be used all other days, whensoever the people be customably assembled to pray in the church, and none disposed to communicate with the Priest.

Likewise in Chapels annexed, and all other places, there shall be no celebration of the Lord's supper, except there be some to communicate with the Priest. And in such Chapels annexed where the people hath not been accustomed to pay any holy bread, there they must either make some charitable provision for the bearing of the charges of the Communion, or else (for receiving of the same) resort to their parish Church.

For avoiding[4] of all matters and occasion of dissension, it is meet that the bread prepared for the Communion be made, through all this realm, after one sort and fashion: that is to say, unleavened, and round, as it was afore, but without all[5] manner of print, and something more larger and thicker than it was, so that it may be aptly divided in divers pieces: and every one shall be divided in two pieces, at the least, or more, by the discretion of the minister, and so distributed. And men[6] must not think less to be received in part than in the whole, but in each of them the whole body of our Saviour Jesu Christ.

And forsomuch as the Pastors and Curates within this realm shall continually find at their costs and charges in their cures sufficient bread

[2 thy, omitted by Grafton, 2.]
[3 or as it shall otherwise be appointed by his highness, omitted, Grafton, C.]
[4 advoiding, Grafton, 1, and C.]
[5 any, Grafton, 1, C, and Oswen.]
[6 men, omitted by Grafton, 2.]

and wine for the holy Communion (as oft as their Parishioners shall be disposed for their spiritual comfort to receive the same) it is therefore ordered, that in recompence of such costs and charges, the Parishioners of every Parish shall offer every Sunday, at the time of the Offertory, the just valour[1] and price of the holy loaf (with all such money and other things as were wont to be offered with the same) to the use of their Pastors and Curates, and that in such order and course, as they were wont to find and pay the said holy loaf.

Also that the receiving of the Sacrament of the blessed body and blood of Christ, may be most agreeable to the institution thereof, and to the usage of the primitive Church: In all[2] Cathedral and Collegiate churches, there shall always some communicate with the Priest that ministereth. And that the same may be also observed every where abroad in the country: Some one at the least of that house in every parish, to whom by course, after the ordinance herein made, it appertaineth to offer for the charges of the Communion, or some other whom they shall provide to offer for them, shall receive the holy Communion with the priest: the which may be the better done, for that they know before, when their course[3] cometh, and may therefore dispose themselves to the worthy receiving of the Sacrament. And with him or them who doth so offer the charges of the Communion, all other, who be then Godly disposed thereunto, shall likewise receive the Communion. And by this means the Minister having always some to communicate with him, may accordingly solemnise so high and holy mysteries, with all the suffrages and due order appointed for the same. And the Priest on the week day shall forbear to celebrate the Communion, except he have some that will communicate with him.

Furthermore, every man and woman to be bound to hear and be at the divine service, in the Parish church where they be resident, and there with devout prayer, or Godly silence and meditation, to occupy themselves. There to pay their duties, to communicate once in the year at the least, and there to receive and take all other Sacraments and rites, in this book appointed. And[4] whosoever willingly, upon no just cause, doth absent themselves, or doth ungodly in the Parish church occupy themselves: upon proof thereof, by the Ecclesiastical laws of the Realm, to be excommunicate, or suffer other punishment, as shall to the Ecclesiastical judge (according to his discretion) seem convenient.

And although it be read in ancient writers, that the people, many

[1 value, Ed.]   [2 all, omitted by Oswen.]
[3 courses, Grafton, 1, and C.]
[4 From, "And whosoever," &c., to "seem convenient," is a distinct paragraph in Oswen.]

years past, received at the Priest's hands the Sacrament of the body of Christ in their own hands, and no commandment of Christ to the contrary: Yet forasmuch as they many times conveyed the same secretly away, kept it with them, and diversly abused it to superstition and wickedness: lest any such thing hereafter should be attempted, and that an uniformity might be used throughout the whole Realm, it is thought convenient the people commonly receive the Sacrament of Christ's body in their mouths, at the Priest's hand.

THE
LITANY AND SUFFRAGES.[1]

O GOD the Father of heaven : have mercy upon us miserable sinners.

O God the Father of heaven : have mercy upon us[2] miserable sinners.

O God the Son, Redeemer of the world : have mercy upon us miserable sinners.

O God the Son, Redeemer of the world : have mercy upon us miserable sinners.

O God the Holy Ghost, proceeding from the Father and the Son : have mercy upon us miserable sinners.

O God, the Holy Ghost, proceeding from the Father and the Son : have mercy upon us miserable sinners.

O holy, blessed, and glorious Trinity, three persons and one God : have mercy upon us miserable sinners.

O holy, blessed, and glorious Trinity, three persons and one God : have mercy upon us miserable sinners.

Remember not, Lord, our offences, nor the offences of our forefathers, neither take thou vengeance of our sins : spare us, good Lord, spare thy people, whom thou hast redeemed with thy most precious blood, and be not angry with us for ever.

Spare us, good Lord.

From all evil and mischief, from sin, from the crafts and assaults of the devil, from thy wrath, and from everlasting damnation :

Good Lord, deliver us.

From blindness of heart, from pride, vainglory, and

[1 The Litany and Suffrages were not printed in the March editions of Whitchurch and Grafton. These were added in a separate sheet at the end, but without date. Ed.]

[2 &c. for *miserable sinners*, in this and the three following responses, Grafton, 2.]

hypocrisy, from envy, hatred, and malice, and all uncharitableness :
Good Lord, deliver us.

From fornication, and all other [3] deadly sin, and from all the deceits of the world, the flesh, and the devil :
Good Lord, deliver us.

From lightning and tempest, from plague, pestilence, and famine, from battle and murther, and from sudden death :
Good Lord, deliver us.

From all sedition and privy conspiracy, from the tyranny of the bishop of Rome and all his detestable enormities, from all false doctrine and heresy, from hardness of heart, and contempt of thy word and commandment:
Good Lord, deliver us.

By the mystery of thy holy incarnation, by thy holy nativity and Circumcision, by thy Baptism, fasting, and temptation:
Good Lord, deliver us.

By thine agony and bloody sweat, by thy cross and passion, by thy precious death and burial, by thy glorious resurrection and ascension, by the coming of the Holy Ghost :
Good Lord, deliver us.

In all time of our tribulation, in all time of our wealth, in the hour of death, in the day of judgment :
Good Lord, deliver us.

We sinners do beseech thee to hear us (O Lord God) and that it may please thee to rule and govern thy holy Church universal in the right way:
We beseech thee to hear us, good Lord.

That it may please thee to keep Edward the vi., thy servant our king and governor :
We beseech thee to hear us, good Lord.

That it may please thee to rule his heart in thy faith, fear, and love, that he may always have affiance in thee, and ever seek thy honour and glory :
We beseech thee to hear us, good Lord.

That it may please thee to be his defender and keeper, giving him the victory over all his enemies :
We beseech thee to hear us, good Lord.

[[3] other, omitted by Grafton, 2.]

That it may please thee to illuminate all Bishops, pastors and ministers of the Church, with true knowledge and understanding of thy word, and that both by their preaching and living they may set it forth, and shew it accordingly:
We beseech thee to hear us, good Lord.

That it may please thee to endue the Lords of the council, and all the nobility, with grace, wisdom, and understanding:
We beseech thee to hear us, good Lord.

That it may please thee to bless and keep the magistrates, giving them grace to execute justice, and to maintain truth:
We beseech thee to hear us, good Lord.

That it may please thee to bless and keep all thy people:
We beseech thee to hear us, good Lord.

That it may please thee to give to all nations unity, peace, and concord:
We beseech thee to hear us, good Lord.

That it may please thee to give us an heart to love and dread thee, and diligently to live after thy commandments:
We beseech thee to hear us, good Lord.

That it may please thee to give all thy people increase of grace, to hear meekly thy word, and to receive it with pure affection, and to bring forth the fruits of the Spirit:
We beseech thee to hear us, good Lord.

That it may please thee to bring into the way of truth all such as have erred and are deceived:
We beseech thee to hear us, good Lord.

That it may please thee to strengthen such as do stand, and to comfort and help the weak-hearted, and to raise up them that fall, and finally to beat down Satan under our feet:
We beseech thee to hear us, good Lord.

That it may please thee to succour, help, and comfort all that be in danger, necessity, and tribulation:
We beseech thee to hear us, good Lord.

That it may please thee to preserve all that travel by land or by water, all women labouring of child, all sick persons, and young children, and to shew thy pity upon all prisoners and captives:
We beseech thee to hear us, good Lord.

THE LITANY AND SUFFRAGES. 103

That it may please thee to defend and provide for the fatherless children and widows, and all that be desolate and oppressed :
We beseech thee to hear us, good Lord.
That it may please thee to have mercy upon all men :
We beseech thee to hear us, good Lord.
That it may please thee to forgive our enemies, persecutors, and slanderers, and to turn their hearts :
We beseech thee to hear us, good Lord.
That it may please thee to give and preserve to our use the kindly fruits of the earth, so as in due time we may enjoy them :
We beseech thee to hear us, good Lord.
That it may please thee to give us true repentance; to forgive us all our sins, negligences, and ignorances, and to endue us with the grace of thy holy Spirit to amend our lives according to thy holy word :
We beseech thee to hear us, good Lord.
Son of God : we beseech thee to hear us.
Son of God : we beseech thee to hear us.
O Lamb of God, that takest away the sins of the world :
Grant us thy peace.
O Lamb of God, that takest away the sins of the world :
Have mercy upon us.
O Christ, hear us.
O Christ, hear us.
Lord, have mercy upon us.
Lord, have mercy upon us.
Christ, have mercy upon us.
Christ, have mercy upon us.
Lord, have mercy upon us.
Lord, have mercy upon us.
Our Father, which art in heaven. *With the residue of the Paternoster.*
And lead us not into temptation.
But deliver us from evil.[1]
The Versicle. O Lord, deal not with us after our sins.
The Answer. Neither reward us after our iniquities.

[¹ Amen, added in Whitchurch, June.]

Let us pray.

O GOD merciful Father, that despisest not the sighing of a contrite heart, nor the desire of such as be sorrowful, mercifully assist our prayers, that we make before thee in all our troubles and adversities, whensoever they oppress us: And graciously hear us, that those evils, which the craft and subtilty of the devil or man worketh against us, be brought to nought, and by the providence of thy goodness they may be dispersed, that we thy servants, being hurt by no persecutions, may evermore give thanks unto thee, in thy holy Church: through Jesu[1] Christ our Lord.

O Lord, arise, help us, and deliver us for thy name's sake.

O God, we have heard with our ears, and our fathers have declared unto us, the noble works that thou didst in their days, and in the old time before them.

O Lord, arise, help us, and deliver us, for thy honour.

Glory be to the Father, the Son, and to the Holy Ghost[2]: as it was in the beginning, is now, and ever shall be world without end. Amen.

From our enemies defend us, O Christ.

Graciously look upon our afflictions.

Pitifully behold the sorrows of our heart.

Mercifully forgive the sins of thy[3] people.

Favourably with mercy hear our prayers.

O Son of David, have mercy upon us.

Both now and ever vouchsafe to hear us, Christ.

Graciously hear us, O Christ.

Graciously hear us, O Lord Christ.

The Versicle. O Lord, let thy mercy be shewed upon us.

The Answer. As we do put our trust in thee.

Let us pray.

WE humbly beseech thee, O Father, mercifully to look upon our infirmities, and for the glory of thy name's sake, turn from us all those evils that we most righteously have

---

[[1] Jesus, Grafton, 2, and Oswen.]

[[2] The latter part of the Doxology is separated in Whitchurch, June.]

[[3] the people, Oswen.]

deserved; and grant that in all our troubles we may put our whole trust and confidence in thy mercy, and evermore serve thee in pureness of living, to thy honour and glory: through our only mediator and advocate Jesus Christ our Lord. Amen.

ALMIGHTY God, which hast given us grace at this time with one accord to make our common supplications unto thee, and dost promise, that when two or three be gathered in thy name, thou wilt grant their requests: fulfil now, O Lord, the desires and petitions of thy servants, as may be most expedient for them, granting us in this world knowledge of thy truth, and in the world to come life everlasting. Amen.

OF THE

ADMINISTRATION OF PUBLIC BAPTISM

TO BE USED IN THE CHURCH.

It appeareth by ancient writers, that the Sacrament of Baptism in the old time was not commonly ministered but at two times in the year, at Easter and Whitsuntide, at which times it was openly ministered in the presence of all the congregation: Which custom (now being grown out of use) although it cannot for many considerations be well restored again, yet it is thought good to follow the same as near as conveniently may be: Wherefore the people are to be admonished, that it is most convenient that Baptism should not be ministered but upon Sundays and other holy days, when the most number of people may come together. As well for that the congregation there present may testify the receiving of them, that be newly baptized, into the number of Christ's Church, as also because in the Baptism of Infants, every man present may be put in remembrance of his own profession made to God in his Baptism. For which cause also, it is expedient that Baptism be ministered in the English tongue. Nevertheless (if necessity so require) children ought at all times to be baptized, either at the church or else at home.

PUBLIC BAPTISM.

When there are children to be baptized upon the Sunday or holy day, the parents shall give knowledge over night or in the morning, afore the beginning of Matins, to the curate. And then the Godfathers, Godmothers, and people, with the children, must be ready at the church door, either immediately afore the last Canticle at Matins, or else immediately afore the last Canticle at Evensong, as the Curate by his discretion shall appoint. And then, standing there, the Priest shall ask whether the children be baptized or no. If they answer, No, then shall the Priest say thus.

DEAR[1] beloved, forasmuch as all men be conceived and born in sin, and that no man born in sin can enter into the kingdom of God (except he be regenerate and born anew of water and the Holy Ghost;) I beseech you to call upon God the Father through our Lord Jesus Christ, that of his bounteous mercy he will grant to these children that thing which by nature they cannot have, that is to say, they may be baptized with the Holy Ghost, and received into Christ's holy church, and be made lively members of the same.

Then the Priest shall say,

Let us pray.

ALMIGHTY and everlasting God, which of thy justice didst destroy by floods of water the whole world for sin, except eight persons, whom of thy mercy (the same time) thou didst save in the Ark: And when thou didst drown in the Red Sea wicked King Pharao, with all his army, yet (at the same time) thou didst lead thy people the children of Israel safely through the midst thereof: whereby thou didst figure the washing of thy holy baptism: and by the baptism of thy wellbeloved Son Jesus Christ, thou didst sanctify the flood Jordan, and all other waters to this mystical washing away of sin: we beseech thee (for thy infinite mercies) that thou wilt mercifully look upon these children, and sanctify them with thy Holy Ghost, that by this wholesome laver of

[1 Dearly, Oswen.]

regeneration, whatsoever sin is in them, may be washed clean away; that they, being delivered from thy wrath, may be received into the ark of Christ's Church, and so saved from perishing : and being fervent in spirit, steadfast in faith, joyful through hope, rooted in charity, may ever serve thee : And finally attain to everlasting life, with all thy holy and chosen people. This grant us, we beseech thee, for Jesus Christ's sake our Lord. Amen.

¶ Here shall the Priest ask what shall be the name of the child, and when the Godfathers and Godmothers have told the name, then he[1] shall make a cross upon the child's forehead and breast, saying,

¶ *N*. Receive the sign of the holy Cross, both in thy forehead, and in thy breast, in token that thou shalt not be ashamed to confess thy faith in Christ crucified, and manfully to fight under his banner against sin, the world, and the devil, and to continue his faithful soldier and servant unto thy life's end. Amen.

And this he shall do and say to as many children as be present to be baptized, one after another.

Let us pray.

ALMIGHTY and immortal God, the aid of all that need, the helper of all that flee to thee for succour, the life of them that believe, and the resurrection of the dead : we call upon thee for these infants, that they coming to thy holy baptism, may receive remission of their sins, by spiritual regeneration. Receive them (O Lord) as thou hast promised by thy well-beloved Son, saying: Ask, and you shall have: seek, and you shall find: knock, and it shall be opened unto you. So give now unto us that ask : let us that seek find : open thy gate unto us that knock : that these infants may enjoy the everlasting benediction of thy heavenly washing, and may come to the eternal kingdom which thou hast promised by Christ our Lord. Amen.

Then let the Priest looking upon the children, say,

I COMMAND thee, unclean spirit, in the name of the Father, of the Son, and of the Holy Ghost, that thou come out, and depart from these infants, whom our Lord Jesus

[[1] shall he, Grafton, 1, C, and Oswen.]

Christ hath vouchsafed to call to his holy Baptism, to be made members of his body, and of his holy congregation. Therefore, thou cursed spirit, remember thy sentence, remember thy judgment[2], remember the day to be at hand wherein thou shalt burn in fire everlasting, prepared for thee and thy Angels. And presume not hereafter to exercise any tyranny toward these infants, whom Christ hath bought with his precious blood, and by this his holy Baptism calleth[3] to be of his flock.

Then shall the Priest say,

The Lord be with you.

The People. And with thy spirit.

The Minister. ¶ Hear now the Gospel written by St Mark.

Mark x.[4] [v. 13—16.]

After the Gospel is read, the Minister shall make this brief exhortation upon the words of the Gospel.

FRIENDS, you[5] hear in this Gospel the words of our Saviour Christ, that he commanded the children to be brought unto him: how he blamed those that would have kept them from him: how he exhorteth[6] all men to follow their innocency. Ye perceive how by his outward gesture and deed he declared his good will toward them. For he embraced them in his arms, he laid his hands upon them, and blessed them. Doubt ye not therefore, but earnestly believe, that he will likewise favourably receive these present infants, that he will embrace them with the arms of his mercy, that he will give unto them the blessing of eternal life, and make them partakers of his everlasting kingdom. Wherefore we being thus persuaded of the good will of our heavenly Father toward these infants, declared by his Son Jesus Christ; and nothing doubting but that he favourably alloweth this charitable work of ours, in bringing these children to his holy baptism: let us faithfully and devoutly give thanks unto him; and say the prayer which the Lord himself taught. And in declaration of our faith, let us also recite the articles contained in our Creed.

[[2] judgments, Grafton, C.]   [[3] called, Grafton, C.]
[[4] Mark x., omitted by Grafton, 2, but the same Gospel is given.]
[[5] ye, Oswen.]   [[6] exhorted, Oswen.]

PUBLIC BAPTISM.

Here the Minister, with the Godfathers[1], Godmothers, and people present, shall say,

¶ Our Father, which art in heaven, hallowed be thy name, &c.[2]

And then shall[3] say openly,

I believe in God the Father Almighty, &c.

The Priest shall add also this prayer,

ALMIGHTY and everlasting God, heavenly Father, we give thee humble thanks, that thou hast vouchsafed to call us to knowledge of thy grace, and faith in thee: increase and confirm this faith in us evermore: Give thy Holy Spirit to these infants, that they may be born again, and be made heirs of everlasting salvation, through our Lord Jesus Christ: who liveth and reigneth with thee and the Holy Spirit, now and for ever. Amen.

Then let the Priest take one of the children by the right hand, the other being brought after him. And coming into the church toward the font, say,

THE Lord vouchsafe to receive you into his holy household, and to keep and govern you alway in the same, that you may have everlasting life. Amen.

Then standing at the font the Priest shall speak to the Godfathers and Godmothers on this wise.

Wellbeloved friends, ye have brought these children here to be baptized; ye have prayed that our Lord Jesus Christ would vouchsafe to receive them, to lay his hands upon them, to bless them, to release them of their sins, to give them the kingdom of heaven, and everlasting life. Ye have heard also that our Lord Jesus Christ hath promised in his gospel, to grant all these things that ye have prayed for: which promise he for his part will most surely keep and perform. Wherefore, after this promise made by Christ, these infants must also faithfully for their part promise by you that be their sureties, that they will forsake the devil and all his works, and con-

[1 godfathers and, Grafton, C.]
[2 &c., omitted by Oswen; be thy, &c., Grafton, 2; hallowed be, Grafton, C.]
[3 shall he say, Grafton, 2, and C.]

stantly believe God's holy word, and obediently keep his commandments.

Then shall the Priest demand of the child (which shall be first baptized) these questions following: first naming the child, and saying,

N. Dost thou forsake the devil and all his works?
Answer. I forsake them.
Minister. Dost thou forsake the vain pomp and glory of the world, with all the covetous desires of the same?
Answer. I forsake them.
Minister. Dost thou forsake the carnal desires of the flesh, so that thou wilt not follow nor be led by them?
Answer. I forsake them.
Minister. Dost thou believe in God the Father Almighty, Maker of heaven and earth?
Answer. I believe.
Minister. Dost thou believe in Jesus Christ his only begotten Son our Lord, and that he was conceived by the Holy Ghost, born of the virgin Mary, that he suffered under Poncius Pilate, was crucified, dead, and buried; that he went down into hell, and also did rise again the third day; that he ascended into heaven, and sitteth on the right hand of God the Father Almighty: And from thence shall come again at the end of the world, to judge the quick and the dead: Dost thou believe this?
Answer. I believe.
Minister. Dost thou believe in the Holy Ghost, the holy Catholic Church, the Communion of Saints, Remission of Sins, Resurrection of the flesh and everlasting life after death?
Answer. I believe.
Minister. What dost thou desire?
Answer. Baptism.
Minister. Wilt thou be baptized?
Answer. I will.

¶ Then the Priest shall take the child in his hands, and ask the name. And naming the child, shall dip it in the water thrice. First dipping the right side: Second, the left side: The[4] third time

[[4] The, omitted in Grafton, 2.]

dipping the face toward the font: so it be discreetly and warily done, saying,

¶ *N.* I baptize thee in the name of the Father, and of the Son, and of the Holy Ghost. Amen.

¶ And if the child be weak, it shall suffice to pour water upon it, saying the foresaid words. *N.* I baptize thee, &c.

Then the Godfathers and Godmothers shall take and lay their hands upon the child, and the minister shall put upon him his white vesture, commonly called the Chrisom; and say,

TAKE this white vesture for a token of the innocency, which by God's grace in this holy sacrament of baptism is given unto thee; and for a sign whereby thou art admonished, so long as thou livest, to give thyself to innocency of living, that, after this transitory life, thou mayest be partaker of the life everlasting. Amen.

Then the Priest shall anoint the infant upon the head, saying,

ALMIGHTY God, the Father of our Lord Jesus Christ, who hath regenerate thee by water and the Holy Ghost, and hath given unto thee remission of all thy sins: he vouchsafe to anoint thee with the unction of his Holy Spirit, and bring thee to the inheritance of everlasting life. Amen.

When there are many to be baptized, this order of demanding, baptizing, putting on the Chrisom, and anointing, shall be used severally with every child: those that be first baptized departing from the font, and remaining in some convenient place within the Church until all be baptized. At the last end, the Priest, calling the Godfathers and Godmothers together, shall say this short Exhortation following:

FORASMUCH as these children have promised by you to forsake the devil and all his works, to believe in God, and to serve him; you must remember, that it is your parts and duty to see that these infants be taught, so soon as they shall be able to learn, what a solemn vow, promise, and profession they have made by you. And that they may know these things the better, ye shall call upon them to hear sermons; and chiefly you shall provide that they may learn the Creed, the Lord's Prayer, and the Ten Commandments, in the English tongue, and all other things which a Christian man ought to know and believe to his soul's health : and that these children may be virtuously brought up to lead a godly and¹ Christian life ; remembering always, that baptism doth represent unto us, our profession, which is, to follow the example of our Saviour Christ, and to be made like unto him ; that as he died and rose again for us, so should we (which are baptized) die from sin, and rise again unto righteousness, continually mortifying all our evil and corrupt affections, and daily proceeding in all virtue and godliness of living.

¶ The Minister shall command that the Chrisoms be brought to the church, and delivered to the Priests after the accustomed manner, at the purification of the mother of every child; and that the children be brought to the Bishop to be confirmed of him, so soon as they can say in their vulgar tongue the Articles of the Faith, the Lord's Prayer, and the Ten Commandments, and be further instructed in the Catechism, set forth for that purpose, accordingly as it is there expressed.

And so let the congregation depart in the name of the Lord.

¶ Note, that if the number of children to be baptized, and multitude of people present, be so great that they cannot conveniently stand at the church door; then let them stand within the church, in some convenient place, nigh unto the church door; and there all things be said and done, appointed to be said and done at the church door.

[¹ and a, Grafton, 2.]

OF THEM THAT BE

BAPTIZED IN PRIVATE HOUSES

IN TIME OF NECESSITY.

¶ The Pastors and Curates shall oft admonish the people, that they defer not the baptism of infants any longer than the Sunday, or other holy day next after the child be born, unless upon a great and reasonable cause declared to the Curate and by him approved.

And also they shall warn them, that without great cause, and necessity they baptize not children at home in their houses. And when great need shall compel them so to do, that then they minister it on this fashion.

¶ First let them that be present call upon God for his grace, and say the Lord's prayer, if the time will suffer. And then one of them shall name the child, and dip him in the water, or pour water upon him, saying these words:

¶ *N.* I baptize thee in the name of the Father, and of the Son, and of the Holy Ghost. Amen.

And let them not doubt, but that[1] the child so baptized is lawfully and sufficiently baptized, and ought not to be baptized again, in the Church. But yet nevertheless, if the child which is after this sort baptized do afterward live, it is expedient that he[2] be brought into the Church, to the intent the Priest may examine and try whether the child be lawfully baptized or no. And if those that bring any child to the church do answer that he is already baptized: Then shall the Priest examine them further.

¶ By whom the child was baptized?

Who was present when the child was baptized?

Whether they called upon God for grace and succour in that necessity?

With what thing, or what matter, they did baptize the child?

With what words the child was baptized?

Whether they think the child to be lawfully and perfectly baptized?

[1 that, omitted by Grafton, 2.]　　[2 they, Grafton, 2, and C.]

And if the minister[3] shall prove by the answers of such as brought the child, that all things were done, as they ought to be: Then shall not he christen the child again, but shall receive him, as one of the flock of the[4] true christian people, saying thus.

I CERTIFY you, that in this case ye have done well, and according unto due order concerning the baptizing of this child, which being born in original sin, and in the wrath of God, is now by the laver of regeneration in Baptism made the child of God, and heir of everlasting life: for our Lord Jesus Christ doth not deny his grace and mercy unto such infants, but most lovingly doth call them unto him: as the holy gospel doth witness to our comfort on this wise.

Mark x. [v. 13—16.]

After the Gospel is read: the minister shall make this exhortation upon the words of the gospel.

FRIENDS, ye hear in this gospel the words of our Saviour Christ, that he commanded the children to be brought unto him, how he blamed those that would have kept them from him, how he exhorted all men to follow their innocency: ye perceive how by his outward gesture and deed he declared his good will toward them; for he embraced them in his arms, he laid his hands upon them, and blessed them. Doubt you not therefore, but earnestly believe, that he hath likewise favourably received this present infant, that he hath embraced him with the arms of his mercy, that he hath given unto him the blessing of eternal life, and made him partaker of his everlasting kingdom. Wherefore we being thus persuaded of the good will of our heavenly Father, declared by his Son Jesus Christ towards this infant: Let us faithfully and devoutly give thanks unto him, and say the prayer which the Lord himself taught; and in declaration of our faith, let us also recite the articles contained in our Creed.

Here the minister with the Godfathers and Godmothers shall say.

OUR Father which art in heaven, hallowed be thy name: let[5] thy kingdom come, &c.

[[3] ministers, Grafton, 1.]   [[4] the, omitted, Grafton, C.]
[[5] Let, omitted by Whitchurch, June, and Oswen. Let thy kingdom come, omitted by Grafton, 1, 2, and C.]

Then shall they say the Creed, and then the Priest shall demand the name of the child, which being by the Godfathers and Godmothers pronounced, the minister shall say,

¶ *N.* Dost thou forsake the devil and all his works?
Answer. I forsake them.
Minister. Dost thou forsake the vain pomp and glory of the world, with all the covetous desires of the same?
Answer. I forsake them.
Minister. Dost thou forsake the carnal desires of the flesh, so that thou wilt not follow and[1] be led by them?
Answer. I forsake them.
Minister. Dost thou believe in God the Father almighty, maker of heaven and earth?
Answer. I believe.
Minister. Dost thou believe in Jesus Christ his only-begotten Son our Lord, and that he was conceived by the Holy Ghost, born of the virgin Mary, that he suffered under Pontius Pilate, was crucified, dead, and buried, that he went down into hell, and also did arise[2] again the third day, that he ascended into heaven, and sitteth on the right hand of God the Father almighty, and from thence shall come again at the end of the world to judge the quick and the dead: dost thou believe thus?
Answer. I believe.
Minister. Dost thou believe in the Holy Ghost, the holy catholic Church, the Communion of Saints, Remission of sins, Resurrection of the flesh, and everlasting life after death?
Answer. I believe.

Then the minister shall put the white vesture, commonly called the Chrisom, upon the child, saying,

TAKE this white vesture for a token of the innocency, which by God's grace in the[3] holy sacrament of Baptism is given unto thee, and for a sign whereby thou art admonished so long as thou shalt live[4], to give thyself to innocency of living, that after this transitory life thou mayest be partaker of the life everlasting. Amen.

[1 nor, Grafton, 2.]   [2 rise, Grafton, C.]
[3 this, Grafton, 2.]   [4 livest, Grafton, 2.]

¶ Let us pray.

ALMIGHTY and everlasting God, heavenly Father, we give thee humble thanks that thou hast vouchsafed to call us to the knowledge of thy grace, and faith in thee: Increase and confirm this faith in us evermore: Give thy Holy Spirit to this infant, that he being born again, and being made heir of everlasting salvation through our Lord Jesus Christ, may continue thy servant, and attain thy promises[5], through the same our Lord Jesus Christ thy Son: who liveth and reigneth with thee in unity of the same Holy Spirit everlastingly. Amen.

Then shall the minister make this exhortation to the Godfathers and Godmothers:

FORASMUCH as this child hath promised by you to forsake the devil and all his works, to believe in God, and to serve him, you must remember that it is your parts and duty to see that this infant be taught, so soon as he shall be able to learn, what a solemn vow, promise, and profession he hath made by you: and that he may know these things the better, ye shall call upon him to hear sermons: and chiefly ye shall provide that he may learn the Creed, the Lord's prayer, and the ten commandments in the English tongue, and all other things which a christian man ought to know and believe to his soul's health, and that this child may be virtuously brought up to lead a godly and a christian life: remembering alway that Baptism doth represent unto us our profession, which is to follow the example of our Saviour Christ, and to be made like unto him, that as he died and rose again for us, so should we, which are baptized, die from sin, and rise again unto righteousness, continually mortifying all our evil and corrupt affections, and daily proceeding in all virtue and godliness of living.

&c. As in public Baptism.

¶ But if they which bring the infants to the church, do make an uncertain answer to the priest's questions, and say that they cannot tell what they thought, did, or said, in that great fear and trouble of mind (as oftentimes it chanceth): Then let the priest baptize him in form above written, concerning public Baptism, saying that

[[5] promise, Oswen.]

at the dipping of the child in the font he shall use this form of words.

IF thou be not baptized already, *N.* I baptize thee in the name of the Father, and of the Son, and of the Holy Ghost. Amen.

The water in the font shall be changed every month once at the least, and afore any child be baptized in the water so changed, the Priest shall say at the font these prayers following.

O MOST merciful God our Saviour Jesu Christ, who hast ordained the element of water for the regeneration of thy faithful people, upon whom, being baptized in the river of Jordan, the Holy Ghost came down in[1] likeness of a dove: Send down, we beseech thee, the same thy Holy Spirit to assist us, and to be present at this our invocation of thy holy name: Sanctify ✠ this fountain of baptism, thou that art the sanctifier of all things, that by the power of thy word all those that shall be baptized therein may be spiritually regenerated, and made the children of everlasting adoption. Amen.

O MERCIFUL God, grant that the old Adam, in them that shall be baptized in this fountain, may be so[2] buried, that the new man may be raised up again. Amen.

GRANT that all carnal affections may die in them; and that all things, belonging to the Spirit, may live and grow in them. Amen.

GRANT to all them which at this fountain forsake the devil and all his works: that they may have power and strength to have victory and to triumph against him, the world, and the flesh. Amen.

WHOSOEVER shall confess thee, O Lord: recognise him also in thy kingdom. Amen.

GRANT that all sin and vice here may be so extinct: that they never have power to reign in thy servants. Amen.

[1 in the, Whitchurch, June, Grafton, 1, 2, and Oswen.]
[2 so be, Whitchurch, June, Grafton, 2, C, and Oswen.]

GRANT that whosoever here shall begin to be of thy flock: may evermore continue in the same. Amen.

GRANT that all they which for thy sake in this life do deny and forsake themselves: may win and purchase thee, O Lord, which art everlasting treasure. Amen.

GRANT that whosoever is here dedicated to thee by our office and ministry: may also be endued with heavenly virtues, and everlastingly rewarded through thy mercy, O blessed Lord God, who dost live and govern all things world without end. Amen.

The Lord be with you.
Answer. And with thy spirit.

ALMIGHTY everliving[3] God, whose most dearly beloved Son Jesus Christ for the forgiveness of our sins did shed out of his most precious side both water and blood, and gave commandment to his disciples that they should go[4] teach all nations, and baptize them in the name of the Father, the Son, and the Holy Ghost: Regard, we beseech thee, the supplications of thy congregation, and grant that all thy servants which shall be baptized in this water, prepared for the ministration of thy holy sacrament, may receive the fulness of thy grace, and ever remain in the number of thy faithful and elect children, through Jesus[5] Christ our Lord.

[3] everlasting, Grafton, 2.]   [4] go and teach, Grafton, 2.]
[5] Jesu, Grafton, 2.]

CONFIRMATION,

WHEREIN IS CONTAINED A CATECHISM FOR CHILDREN.

To the end that confirmation may be ministered to the more edifying of such as shall receive it (according to St Paul's doctrine, who teacheth that all things should be done in the church to the edification of the same) it is thought good that none hereafter shall be confirmed, but such as can say in their mother tongue the articles of the faith, the Lord's prayer, and the ten commandments; and can also answer to such questions of this short Catechism, as the Bishop (or such as he shall appoint) shall by his discretion appose[1] them in. And this order is most convenient to be observed for divers considerations.

¶ First, because that when children come to the years of discretion, and have learned what their Godfathers and Godmothers promised for them in Baptism, they may then themselves with their own mouth, and with their own consent, openly before the church, ratify and confess the same, and also promise that by the grace of God they will evermore endeavour themselves faithfully to observe and keep such things, as they by their own mouth and confession have assented unto.

¶ Secondly, forasmuch as confirmation is ministered to them that be baptized, that by imposition of hands and prayer they may receive strength and defence against all temptations to sin, and the assautes of the world, and the devil: it is most meet to be ministered, when children come to that age, that partly by the frailty of their own flesh, partly by the assautes of the world and the devil, they begin to be in danger to fall into sin.

¶ Thirdly, for that it is agreeable with the usage of the church in times past, whereby[2] it was ordained, that Confirmation should be ministered to them that were of perfect age, that they being instructed in Christ's religion, should openly profess their own faith, and promise to be obedient unto the will of God.

[1 *appose:* to question, or examine. ED.]   [2 where, Grafton, 2.]

¶ And that no man shall think that any detriment shall come to children by deferring of their confirmation: he shall know for truth, that it is certain by God's word, that children being baptized (if they depart out of this life in their infancy) are undoubtedly saved.

A CATECHISM,

THAT IS TO SAY,

AN INSTRUCTION TO BE LEARNED OF EVERY CHILD, BEFORE HE BE BROUGHT TO BE CONFIRMED OF THE BISHOP.

Question. WHAT is your name?
Answer. N. or M.
Question. Who gave you this name?
Answer. My Godfathers and Godmothers in my Baptism, wherein I was made a member of Christ, the child of God, and an[3] inheritor of the kingdom of heaven.
Question. What did your Godfathers and Godmothers then for you?
Answer. They did promise and vow three things in my name. First, that I should forsake the devil and all his works and pomps, the vanities of the wicked world, and all the sinful lusts of the flesh. Secondly, that I should believe all the articles of the Christian faith. And thirdly, that I should keep God's holy will and commandments, and walk in the same all the days of my life.
Question. Dost thou not think that thou art bound to believe, and to do as they have promised for thee?
Answer. Yes verily. And by God's help so I will. And I heartily thank our heavenly Father, that he hath called me to this state of salvation, through Jesus Christ our Saviour. And I pray God to give me his[4] grace, that I may continue in the same unto my life's end.
Question. Rehearse the articles of thy belief.

[3 an, omitted by Grafton, 2.]   [4 the grace, Grafton, 2.]

Answer. I believe in God the Father Almighty, maker of heaven and earth. And in Jesus Christ his only Son our Lord. Which was conceived by the Holy Ghost, born of the virgin Mary. Suffered under Ponce Pilate, was crucified, dead, and buried, he descended into hell. The third day he rose again from the dead. He ascended into heaven, and sitteth on the right hand of God the Father almighty. From thence shall he come to judge the quick and the dead. I believe in the Holy Ghost. The holy catholic church. The communion of saints. The forgiveness of sins. The resurrection of the body. And the life everlasting. Amen.

Question. What dost thou chiefly learn in these articles of thy belief?

Answer. First, I learn to believe in God the Father, who hath made me and all the world.

Secondly, in God the Son, who hath redeemed me and all mankind.

Thirdly, in God the Holy Ghost, who sanctifieth me and all the elect people of God.

Question. You said that your Godfathers and Godmothers did promise for you that ye should keep God's commandments. Tell me how many there be.

Answer. Ten.

Question. Which be they?

Answer. Thou shalt have none other Gods but me.

II. Thou shalt not make to thyself any graven image, nor the likeness of any thing that is in heaven above, or in the earth beneath, nor in the water under the earth: thou shalt not bow down to them, nor worship them.

III. Thou shalt not take the name of the Lord thy God in vain.

IV. Remember that thou keep holy the Sabbath day.

V. Honour thy father and thy mother.

VI. Thou shalt do no murder.

VII. Thou shalt not commit adultery.

VIII. Thou shalt not steal.

IX. Thou shalt not bear false witness against thy neighbour.

X. Thou shalt not covet thy neighbour's wife, nor his servant, nor his maid, nor his ox, nor his ass, nor any thing that is his.

Question. What dost thou chiefly learn by these commandments?

Answer. I learn two things: my duty towards God, and my duty towards my neighbour.

Question. What is thy duty towards God?

Answer. My duty towards God is, to believe in him. To fear him. And to love him with all my heart, with all my mind, with all my soul, and[1] with all my strength. To worship him. To give him thanks. To put my whole trust in him. To call upon him. To honour his holy name and his word, and to serve him truly all the days of my life.

Question. What is thy duty towards thy neighbour?

Answer. My duty towards my neighbour is, to love him as myself. And to do to all men as I would they should do to me. To love, honour, and succour my father and mother. To honour and obey the king and his ministers. To submit myself to all my governors, teachers, spiritual pastors, and masters. To order myself lowly and reverently to all my betters. To hurt no body by word nor deed. To be true and just in all my dealing. To bear no malice nor hatred in my heart. To keep my hands from picking and stealing, and my tongue from evil speaking, lying, and slandering. To keep my body in temperance, soberness, and chastity. Not to covet nor desire other men's goods. But learn and labour truly to get my own living, and to do my duty in that state of life, unto which it shall please God to call me.

Question. My good son, know this, that thou art not able to do these things of thyself, nor to walk in the commandments of God and to serve him, without his special grace, which thou must learn at all times to call for by diligent prayer. Let me hear therefore if thou canst say the Lord's prayer.

Answer. Our Father which art in heaven, hallowed be thy name. Thy kingdom come. Thy will be done in earth as it is in heaven. Give us this day our daily bread. And forgive us our trespasses, as we forgive them that trespass against us. And lead us not into temptation, but deliver us from evil. Amen.

Question. What desirest thou of God in this prayer?

Answer. I desire my Lord God our heavenly Father,

[1 and, omitted by Grafton, 2.]

who is the giver of all goodness, to send his grace unto me, and to all people, that we may worship him, serve him, and obey him, as we ought to do. And I pray unto God, that he will send us all things that be needful both for our souls and bodies: And that he will be merciful unto us, and forgive us our sins: And that it will please him to save and defend us in all dangers ghostly and bodily: And that he will keep us from all sin and wickedness, and from our ghostly enemy, and from everlasting death. And this I trust he will do of his mercy and goodness, through our Lord Jesu Christ. And therefore I say, Amen. So be it.

¶ So soon as the children can say in their mother tongue the articles of the faith, the Lord's prayer, the ten commandments, and also can answer to such questions of this short Catechism as the Bishop (or such as he shall appoint) shall by his discretion appose them in: then shall they be brought to the Bishop by one that shall be his Godfather or Godmother, that every child may have a witness of his Confirmation.

¶ And the Bishop shall confirm them on this wise.

¶ CONFIRMATION.

Our help is in the name of the Lord.
Answer. Which hath made both heaven and earth.
Minister. Blessed is the name of the Lord.
Answer. Henceforth world without end.
Minister. The Lord be with you.
Answer. And with thy spirit.

Let us pray.

ALMIGHTY and everliving God, who hast vouchsafed to regenerate these thy servants of water and the Holy Ghost: And hast given unto them forgiveness of all their sins: Send down from heaven, we beseech thee, O Lord, upon them thy Holy Ghost the Comforter, with the manifold gifts of grace, the spirit of wisdom and understanding; the spirit of counsel and ghostly strength; the spirit of knowledge and true godliness; and fulfil them, O Lord, with the spirit of thy holy fear.
Answer. Amen.

CONFIRMATION.

Minister. Sign them, O Lord, and mark them to be thine for ever, by the virtue of thy holy cross and passion. Confirm and strength them with the inward unction of thy Holy Ghost, mercifully unto everlasting life. Amen.

Then the Bishop shall cross them in the forehead, and lay his hand upon their head[1], saying,

N. I sign thee with the sign of the cross, and lay my hand upon thee: In the name of the Father, and of the Son, and of the Holy Ghost. Amen.

And thus shall he do to every child one after another. And when he hath laid his hand upon every child, then shall he say.

The peace of the Lord abide with you.
Answer. And with thy spirit.

Then shall the Bishop say[2].

¶ Let us pray.

ALMIGHTY everliving[3] God, which makest us both to will and to do those things that be good and acceptable unto thy majesty: we make our humble supplications unto thee for these children, upon whom (after the example of thy holy apostles) we have laid our hands, to certify them (by this sign) of thy favour and gracious goodness toward them: let thy fatherly hand (we beseech thee) ever be over them, let thy Holy Spirit ever be with them, and so lead them in the knowledge and obedience of thy word, that in the end they may obtain the life everlasting, through our Lord Jesus Christ, who with thee and the Holy Ghost liveth and reigneth one God world without end. Amen.

Then shall the Bishop bless the children, thus saying.

The blessing of God Almighty, the Father, the Son, and the Holy Ghost, be upon you, and remain with you for ever. Amen.

[1 heads, Grafton, 2, and Oswen.]
[2 Then shall the bishop say, not in Grafton, C.]
[3 everlasting, Grafton, 2.]

The Curate of every parish once in six weeks at the least, upon warning by him given, shall upon some Sunday or holy day, half an hour before evensong, openly in the church instruct and examine so many children of his parish sent unto him, as the time will serve, and as he shall think convenient, in some part of this Catechism. And all fathers, mothers, masters, and dames, shall cause their children, servants, and prentices (which are not yet confirmed), to come to the church at the day appointed, and obediently hear and be ordered by the Curate, until such time as they have learned all that is here appointed for them to learn.

¶ And whensoever the Bishop shall give knowledge for children to be brought afore him to any convenient place, for their confirmation: Then shall the Curate of every parish either bring, or send in writing, the names of all those[1] children of his parish which can say the articles of their faith, the Lord's prayer, and the ten commandments. And also how many of them can answer to the other questions contained in this Catechism.

¶ And there shall none be admitted to the holy communion, until such time as he be confirmed.

[1 all the, Grafton, 2, and C.]

THE FORM OF

SOLEMNIZATION OF MATRIMONY.

¶ First the banns must be asked three several Sundays or holy days, in the service time, the people being present, after the accustomed manner.

And if the persons that would be married dwell in divers parishes, the banns must be asked in both parishes, and the Curate of the one parish shall not solemnize matrimony betwixt them, without a certificate of the banns being thrice asked, from the Curate of the other parish.

At the day appointed for Solemnization of Matrimony, the persons to be married shall come into the body of the Church, with their friends and neighbours. And there the priest shall thus say.

DEARLY beloved friends, we are gathered together here in the sight of God, and in the face of his congregation, to join together this man and this woman in holy matrimony, which is an honourable estate instituted of God in paradise, in the time of man's innocency, signifying unto us the mystical union that is betwixt Christ and his church : which holy estate Christ adorned and beautified with his presence, and first miracle that he wrought, in Cana of Galilee, and is commended of Saint Paul to be honourable among all men; and therefore is not to be enterprised, nor taken in hand unadvisedly, lightly, or wantonly, to satisfy men's carnal lusts and appetites, like brute beasts that have no understanding : but reverently, discreetly, advisedly, soberly, and in the fear of God : duly considering the causes for the which matrimony was ordained. One cause was the procreation of children, to be brought up in the fear and nurture of the Lord, and praise of God. Secondly it was ordained for a remedy against sin, and to avoid fornication, that such persons as be married, might live chastely in matrimony, and keep themselves undefiled members of Christ's body. Thirdly for the mutual society, help, and comfort, that the one ought to have of the other, both in prosperity and adversity. Into the which holy estate these two persons present come now to be joined. Therefore if any man can shew any just cause why they may not lawfully be joined so together: Let him now speak, or else hereafter for ever hold his peace.

And also speaking to the persons that shall be married, he shall say.

I require and charge you (as you will answer at the dreadful day of judgment, when the secrets of all hearts shall be disclosed) that if either of you do know any impediment, why ye may not be lawfully joined together in matrimony, that ye confess it. For be ye well assured, that so many as be coupled together otherwise than God's word doth allow, are not joined of God, neither is their matrimony lawful.

At which day of marriage if any man do allege any impediment why they may not be coupled together in matrimony; and will be bound, and sureties with him, to the parties, or else put in a caution to the full value of such charges as the persons to be married do sustain, to prove his allegation: then the Solemnization must be deferred, unto such time as the truth be tried. If no impediment be alleged, then shall the Curate say unto the man.

N. Wilt thou have this woman to thy wedded wife, to live together after God's ordinance in the holy estate of matrimony? Wilt thou love her, comfort her, honour, and keep her in sickness and in health? and forsaking all other keep thee only to her, so long as you both shall live?

The man shall answer,
I will.

Then shall the Priest say to[1] the woman.

N. Wilt thou have this man to thy wedded husband, to live together after God's ordinance, in the holy estate of matrimony? Wilt thou obey him, and serve him, love, honour, and keep him in sickness and in health? and forsaking all other keep thee only to him, so long as you both shall live?

The woman shall answer,
I will.

Then shall the Minister say,

Who giveth this woman to be married to this man?

[1 unto, Grafton, C.]

OF MATRIMONY.

And the minister receiving the woman at her father or friend's hands, shall cause the man to take the woman by the right hand, and so either to give their troth to other: The man first saying,

I *N*. take thee *N*. to my wedded wife, to have and to hold from this day forward, for better, for worse, for richer, for poorer, in sickness, and in health, to love, and to cherish, till death us depart: according to God's holy ordinance: And thereto I plight thee my troth.

Then shall they loose their hands, and the woman taking again the man by the right hand shall say,

I *N*. take thee *N*. to my wedded husband, to have and to hold from this day forward, for better, for worse, for richer, for poorer, in sickness, and in health, to love, cherish, and to obey, till death us depart: according to God's holy ordinance: And thereto I give thee my troth.

Then shall they again loose their hands, and the man shall give unto the woman a ring, and other tokens of spousage, as gold or silver, laying the same upon the book: And the Priest taking the ring shall deliver it unto the man, to put it upon the fourth finger of the woman's left hand. And the man taught by the priest, shall say,

¶ With this ring I thee wed: This gold and silver I thee give: with my body I thee worship: and with all my worldly goods I thee endow: In the name of the Father, and of the Son, and of the Holy Ghost. Amen.

Then the man leaving the ring upon the fourth finger of the woman's left hand, the minister shall say,

¶ Let us pray.

O ETERNAL God, creator and preserver of all mankind, giver of all spiritual grace, the author of everlasting life: send thy blessing upon these thy servants, this man and this woman, whom we bless in thy name, that as Isaac and Rebecca (after bracelets and jewels of gold given of the one to the other for tokens of their matrimony) lived faithfully together; so these persons may surely perform and keep the vow and covenant betwixt them made, whereof this ring given and received is a token and pledge: and may ever remain in perfect love and peace together: and live according to thy laws; through Jesus Christ our Lord. Amen.

[DOCUMENTS, EDW. VI.]

Then shall the Priest join their right hands together, and say,

¶ Those whom God hath joined together, let no man put asunder.

Then shall the minister speak unto the people.

FORASMUCH as *N.* and *N.* have consented together in holy wedlock, and have witnessed the same here before God and this company; and thereto have given and pledged their troth either to other, and have declared the same by giving and receiving gold and silver, and by joining of hands: I pronounce that they be man and wife together: In the name of the Father, of the Son, and of the Holy Ghost. Amen.

And the minister shall add this blessing.

¶ God the Father bless you. ✠ God the Son keep you: God the Holy Ghost lighten your understanding: The Lord mercifully with his favour look upon you, and so fill you with all spiritual benediction, and grace, that you may have remission of your sins in this life, and in the world to come life everlasting. Amen.

Then shall they go into the quire, and the ministers or clerks shall say or sing this Psalm following.

Beati omnes. Psalm cxxviii.

Glory be to the Father, &c.
As it was in the beginning[1], &c.

Or else this Psalm following.

Deus misereatur nostri.[2] Psalm lxvii.

The Psalm ended, and the man and woman kneeling afore the altar: the priest standing at the altar, and turning his face toward them, shall say,

Lord, have mercy upon us.
Answer. Christ, have mercy upon us.
Minister. Lord, have mercy upon us.

[1 After the Psalms in the occasional services follows the *Gloria Patri*, variously abbreviated in this and the following services, in the different copies: but the variations are unimportant. See Note 2, p. 29.]

[2 *nostri*, not in Grafton, C.]

¶ Our Father which art in heaven, &c.
And lead us not into temptation.
Answer. But deliver us from evil. Amen.
Minister. O Lord, save thy servant, and thy handmaid.
Answer. Which put their trust in thee.
Minister. O Lord, send them help from thy holy place.
Answer. And evermore defend them.
Minister. Be unto them a tower of strength[3].
Answer. From the face of their enemy.
Minister. O Lord, hear my prayer.
Answer. And let my cry come unto thee.
The Minister. Let us pray.

O GOD of Abraham, God of Isaac, God of Jacob, bless these thy servants, and sow the seed of eternal life in their minds, that whatsoever in thy holy word they shall profitably learn, they may in deed fulfil the same. Look, O Lord, mercifully upon them from heaven, and bless them: And as thou didst send thy Angel Raphael to Thobie and Sara, the daughter of Raguel, to their great comfort; so vouchsafe to send thy blessing upon these thy servants, that they obeying thy will, and alway being in safety under thy protection, may abide in thy love unto their lives' end: through Jesu Christ our Lord. Amen.

This prayer following shall be omitted where the woman is past child-birth.

O MERCIFUL Lord, and heavenly Father, by whose gracious gift mankind is increased: We beseech thee, assist with thy blessing these two persons, that they may both be fruitful in procreation of children; and also live together so long in godly love and honesty, that they may see their childer's children unto the third and fourth generation, unto thy[4] praise and honour: through Jesus Christ our Lord. Amen.

O God, which by thy mighty power hast made all things of nought, which also after other things set in order didst appoint that out of man (created after thine own image and similitude) woman should take her beginning: and, knitting

[[3] a tower of defence, Oswen.]   [[4] the, Grafton, C.]

them together, didst teach, that it should never be lawful to put asunder those, whom thou by matrimony hadst made one: O God, which hast consecrated the state of matrimony to such an excellent mystery, that in it is signified and represented the spiritual marriage and unity betwixt Christ and his church: Look mercifully upon these thy servants, that both this man may love his wife, according to thy word, (as Christ did love his spouse the church, who gave himself for it, loving and cherishing it even as his own flesh;) and also that this woman may be loving and amiable to her husband as Rachael, wise as Rebecca, faithful and obedient as Sara; and in all quietness, sobriety, and peace, be a follower of holy and godly matrons. O Lord, bless them both, and grant them to inherit thy[1] everlasting kingdom, through Jesus[2] Christ our Lord. Amen.

Then shall the Priest bless the man and the woman, saying,

ALMIGHTY God, which at the beginning did create our first parents Adam and Eve, and did sanctify and join them together in marriage: Pour upon you the riches of his grace, sanctify and ✠ bless you, that ye may please him both in body and soul, and live together in holy love unto your lives' end. Amen.

Then shall be said after the gospel a sermon, wherein ordinarily (so oft as there is any marriage) the office of man and wife shall be declared according to holy scripture. Or if there be no sermon, the minister shall read this that followeth.

ALL ye which be married, or which intend to take the holy estate of matrimony upon you: hear what holy scripture doth say, as touching the duty of husbands toward their wives, and wives toward their husbands.

Saint Paul (in his Epistle to the Ephesians the fifth chapter) doth give this commandment to all married men.

Ye husbands, love your wives, even as Christ loved the church, and hath given himself for it, to sanctify it, purging it in the fountain of water, through the word, that he might make it unto himself a glorious congregation, not having spot, or wrinkle, or any such thing; but that it should be holy and blameless. So men are bound to love their own wives as

[1 the, Grafton, C.]   [2 Jesu, Grafton, 1.]

their own bodies: he that loveth his own wife, loveth himself. For never did any man hate his own flesh, but nourisheth and cherisheth it, even as the Lord doth the congregation; for we are members of his body, of his flesh, and of his bones. For this cause shall a man leave father and mother, and shall be joined unto his wife, and they two shall be one flesh. This mystery is great, but I speak of Christ and of the congregation. Nevertheless, let every one of you so love his own wife, even as himself.

Likewise the same Saint Paul (writing to the Colossians) speaketh thus to all men that be married: Ye men, love your wives and be not bitter unto them. *Coloss.* iii.

Hear also what saint Peter the apostle of Christ, (which was himself a married man,) saith unto all men that are married. Ye husbands, dwell with your wives according to knowledge: giving honour unto the wife, as unto the weaker vessel, and as heirs together of the grace of life, so that your prayers be not hindered. 1 *Pet.* iii.

Hitherto ye have heard the duty of the husband toward the wife.

Now likewise, ye wives, hear and learn your duty toward your husbands, even as it is plainly set forth in holy scripture.

Saint Paul (in the forenamed Epistle to the Ephesians) teacheth you thus: Ye women submit yourselves unto your own husbands as unto the Lord: for the husband is the wife's head, even as Christ is the head of the church: And he also is the Saviour of the whole body. Therefore as the church, or congregation, is subject unto Christ; so likewise let the wives also be in subjection unto their own husbands in all things. And again he saith: Let the wife reverence her husband. *Ephes.* v. And in his Epistle to the Colossians Saint Paul giveth you this short lesson: Ye wives, submit yourselves unto your own husbands, as it is convenient in the Lord. *Coloss.* iii.

Saint Peter also doth instruct you very godly, thus saying: Let[3] wives be subject to their own husbands, so that if any obey not the word, they may be won without the word, by the conversation of the wives; while they behold your chaste conversation, coupled with fear: whose

[3 Let the, Grafton, 2.]

apparel let it not be outward, with broided hair, and trimming about with gold, either in putting on of gorgeous apparel: But let the hid man, which is in the heart, be without all corruption, so that the spirit be mild and quiet, which is a precious thing in the sight of God.
For after this manner (in the old time) did the
holy women, which trusted in God, apparel
themselves, being subject to their own
husbands: as Sara obeyed Abraham
calling him lord, whose daughters
ye are made, doing well and
being not dismayed
with any fear.
1 *Pet.* iii.

The new married persons (the same day of their marriage) must receive the holy communion.

THE ORDER FOR THE

VISITATION OF THE SICK,

AND THE COMMUNION OF THE SAME.

¶ The Priest entering into the sick person's house, shall say,

Peace be in this house, and to all that dwell in it.

When he cometh into the sick man's presence, he shall say this Psalm.
Domine exaudi. Psalm cxliii.

¶ With this anthem.

REMEMBER not, Lord, our iniquities, nor the iniquities of our forefathers. Spare us, good Lord, spare thy people, whom thou hast redeemed with thy most precious blood, and be not angry with us for ever.

Lord, have mercy upon us.
Christ, have mercy upon us.
Lord, have mercy upon us.
Our Father, which art in heaven, &c.
And lead us not into temptation.
Answer. But deliver us from evil. Amen.
The Minister. O Lord, save thy servant.
Answer. Which putteth his trust in thee.
Minister. Send him help from thy holy place.
Answer. And evermore mightily defend him.
Minister. Let the enemy have none advantage of him.
Answer. Nor the wicked approach to hurt him.
Minister. Be unto him, O Lord, a strong tower.
Answer. From the face of his enemy.
Minister. Lord, hear my prayer.
Answer. And let my cry come unto thee.

Minister. Let us pray.

O LORD, look down from heaven, behold, visit, and relieve this thy servant: Look upon him with the eyes of thy mercy, give him comfort, and sure confidence in thee: Defend him from the danger of the enemy, and keep him in perpetual peace, and safety: through Jesus Christ our Lord. Amen.

HEAR us, Almighty and most merciful God and Saviour: extend thy accustomed goodness to this thy servant, which is grieved with sickness: Visit him, O Lord, as thou didst visit Peter's wife's mother and the Captain's servant. And as thou preservedst Thobie and Sara by thy Angel from danger: So restore unto this sick person his former health, (if it be thy will,) or else give him grace so to take thy correction, that after this painful life ended, he may dwell with thee in life everlasting. Amen.

Then shall the Minister exhort the sick person after this form, or other like.

DEARLY beloved, know this, that Almighty God is the Lord over life, and death, and over all things to them pertaining, as youth, strength, health, age, weakness, and sickness. Wherefore, whatsoever your sickness is, know you certainly, that it is God's visitation. And for what cause soever this sickness is sent unto you; whether it be to try your patience for the example of other, and that your faith may be found, in the day of the Lord, laudable, glorious, and honourable, to the increase of glory, and endless felicity: or else it be sent unto you to correct and amend in you, whatsoever doth offend the eyes of our heavenly Father: know you certainly, that if you truly repent you of your sins, and bear your sickness patiently, trusting in God's mercy, for his dear Son Jesus Christ's sake, and render unto him humble thanks for his fatherly visitation, submitting yourself wholly to his will; it shall turn to your profit, and help you forward in the right way that leadeth unto everlasting life[*].

* If the person visited be very sick, then the Curate may end his exhortation at this place.

Take therefore in good worth[2] the chastement of the Lord: for whom the Lord loveth he chastiseth. Yea (as Saint Paul saith,) he scourgeth every son,

[1 If the person, &c. omitted by Grafton, 2.]
[2 good worth : as kindly intended.]

which he receiveth: if you endure chastisement, he offereth himself unto you as unto his own children. What son is he that the father chastiseth not? If ye be not under correction (whereof all the true children are partakers), then are ye bastards, and not children.

Therefore seeing that when our carnal fathers do correct us, we reverently obey them, shall we not now much rather be obedient to our spiritual Father, and so live? And they for a few days do chastise us after their own pleasure: but he doth chastise us for our profit, to the intent he may make us partakers of his holiness. These words, good brother, are God's words, and written in holy scripture for our comfort and instruction, that we should patiently and with thanksgiving bear our heavenly Father's correction, whensoever by any manner of adversity it shall please his gracious goodness to visit us. And there should be no greater comfort to christian persons, than to be made like unto Christ, by suffering patiently adversities, troubles, and sicknesses. For he himself went not up to joy, but first he suffered pain: he entered not into his glory, before he was crucified. So truly our way to eternal joy is to suffer here with Christ, and our door to enter into eternal life is gladly to die with Christ, that we may rise again from death, and dwell with him in everlasting life. Now therefore taking your sickness, which is thus profitable for you, patiently: I exhort you in the name of God, to remember the profession which you made unto God in your Baptism. And forasmuch as after this life there is account to be given unto the righteous Judge, of whom all must be judged without respect of persons: I require you to examine yourself and your state, both toward God and man, so that accusing and condemning yourself for your own faults, you may find mercy at our heavenly Father's hand, for Christ's sake, and not be accused and condemned in that fearful judgment. Therefore I shall shortly rehearse the articles of our faith, that ye may know whether you do believe as a christian man should believe, or no.

Here the minister shall rehearse the articles of the faith, saying thus.

DOST thou believe in God the Father Almighty?

And so forth, as it is in Baptism.

Then shall the minister examine whether he be in charity with all the world: Exhorting him to forgive from the bottom of his heart all persons that have offended him: and if he have offended other, to ask them forgiveness: and where he hath done injury or wrong to any man, that he make amends to his uttermost power. And if he have not afore disposed his goods, let him then make his will. (But men must be oft admonished that they set an order for their[1] temporal goods and lands when they be in health.) And also to declare his debts, what he oweth, and what is owing unto[2] him: for[3] discharging of his conscience, and quietness of his executors.* The minister may not forget nor omit to move the sick person (and that most earnestly) to liberality toward the poor.

* This may be done before the minister begin his prayers, as he shall see cause.

¶ Here shall the sick person make a special confession, if he feel his conscience troubled with any weighty matter. After which confession, the Priest shall absolve him after this form: and the same form of absolution shall be used in all private confessions.

OUR Lord Jesus Christ, who hath left power to his Church to absolve all sinners, which truly repent and believe in him, of his great mercy forgive thee thine offences: and by his authority committed to me, I absolve thee from all thy sins, in the name of the Father, and of[4] the Son, and of the Holy Ghost. Amen.

And then the Priest shall say the Collect following.

Let us pray.

O MOST merciful God, which according to the multitude of thy mercies dost so put away the sins of those which truly repent, that thou rememberest them no more: open thy eye of mercy upon this thy servant, who most earnestly desireth pardon and forgiveness: Renew in him, most loving Father, whatsoever hath been decayed by the fraud[5] and malice of the devil, or by his own carnal will, and frailness: preserve and continue this sick member in the unity of thy Church, consider his contrition, accept his tears, assuage his pain, as shall be seen to thee most expedient for him. And forasmuch

[1 they, Grafton, 1, and Oswen.]   [2 to, Grafton, C.]
[3 for, omitted by Oswen.]
[4 and the son, &c. Amen. The rest omitted by Grafton, 2. Grafton, C, has, and of the Son, and of the, &c. Amen.]
[5 defraud, Grafton, 2.]

as he putteth his full trust only in thy mercy: Impute not unto him his former sins, but take him unto thy favour: through the merits of thy most dearly beloved Son Jesus Christ. Amen.

Then the minister shall say this Psalm.
In te Domine speravi. Psalm lxxi[6].

Adding this Anthem.

O SAVIOUR of the world, save us, which by thy cross and precious blood hast redeemed us, help us we beseech thee, O God.

Then shall the minister say,

THE Almighty Lord, which is a most strong tower to all them that put their trust in him, to whom all things in heaven, in earth, and under[7] earth, do bow and obey: be now and evermore thy defence, and make thee know and feel, that there is no other name under heaven given to man, in whom and through whom thou mayest receive health and salvation, but only the name of our Lord Jesus Christ. Amen.

¶ If the sick person desire to be anointed, then shall the Priest anoint him upon the forehead or breast only, making the sign of the cross, saying thus,

As with this visible oil thy body outwardly is anointed: so our heavenly Father, Almighty God, grant of his infinite goodness, that thy soul inwardly may be anointed with the Holy Ghost, who is the Spirit of all strength, comfort, relief, and gladness: and vouchsafe for his great mercy (if it be his blessed will) to restore unto thee thy bodily health, and strength, to serve him; and send thee release of all thy pains, troubles, and diseases, both in body and mind. And howsoever his goodness (by his divine and unsearchable providence) shall dispose of thee: we, his unworthy ministers and servants, humbly beseech the eternal majesty to do with thee according to the multitude of his innumerable mercies, and to pardon thee all thy sins and offences, committed by all thy bodily senses, passions, and carnal affec-

[6 Psalm xxi. Grafton, 2; but Psalm lxxi. is given.]
[7 under the, Grafton, 2, and C.]

tions: who also vouchsafe mercifully to grant unto thee ghostly strength, by his Holy Spirit, to withstand and overcome all temptations and assaults of thine adversary, that in no wise he prevail against thee, but that thou mayest have perfect victory and triumph against the devil, sin, and death, through Christ our Lord: Who by his death hath overcomed[1] the prince of death, and with the Father and the Holy Ghost evermore liveth and reigneth God, world without end. Amen.

Usque quo, Domine? Psalm xiii.

[[1] overcome, Grafton, 2.]

THE COMMUNION OF THE SICK.

FORASMUCH as all mortal men be subject to many sudden perils, diseases, and sicknesses[a], and ever uncertain what time they shall depart out of this life: Therefore to the intent they may be always in a readiness to die, whensoever it shall please Almighty God to call them, the curates shall diligently from time to time, but specially in the plague time, exhort their parishioners to the oft receiving (in the church) of the holy Communion of the body and blood of our Saviour Christ: which if they do, they shall have no cause, in their sudden visitation, to be unquieted for lack of the same. But if the sick person be not able to come to the church, and yet is desirous to receive the Communion in his house, then he must give knowledge over night, or else early in the morning to the curate, signifying also how many be appointed to communicate with him. And if the same day there be a celebration of the holy Communion in the church, then shall the Priest reserve (at the open Communion) so much of the sacrament of the body and blood, as shall serve the sick person, and so many as shall communicate with him (if there be any); and so soon as he conveniently may, after the open Communion ended in the church, shall go and minister the same, first to those that are appointed to communicate with the sick (if there be any), and last of all to the sick person himself. But before the curate distribute the holy Communion, the appointed *general confession* must be made in the name of the communicants, the curate adding the *absolution with the comfortable sentences of scripture* following in the open Communion: and after the communion ended, the Collect.

ALMIGHTY and everliving God, we most heartily thank thee, &c.

¶ But if the day be not appointed for the open communion in the church, then (upon convenient warning given) the curate shall come and visit the sick person afore noon. And having a convenient place in the sick man's house (where he may reverently celebrate) with all things necessary for the same, and not being otherwise letted with the public service or any other just impediment; he shall there celebrate the holy communion after such form and sort as hereafter is appointed.

[a sickness, Grafton, 2, and C.]

The Celebration of the Holy Communion for the Sick.

O PRAISE the Lord, all ye nations, laud him, all ye people: for his merciful kindness is confirmed toward us, and the truth of the Lord endureth for ever.

Glory be to the Father[1], and to the Son, &c.

Lord, have mercy upon us. ⎫
Christ, have mercy upon us. ⎬ Without any more repetition.
Lord, have mercy upon us. ⎭

The Priest. The Lord be with you.
Answer. And with thy spirit.

Let us pray.

ALMIGHTY everliving God, maker of mankind, which dost correct those whom thou dost love, and chastisest every one whom thou dost receive: we beseech thee to have mercy upon this thy servant visited with thy hand, and to grant that he may take his sickness patiently, and recover his bodily health (if it be thy gracious will), and whensoever his soul shall depart from the body, it may without spot be presented unto thee: through Jesus Christ our Lord. Amen.

The Epistle. Heb. xii.

MY son, despise not the correction of the Lord, neither faint when thou art rebuked of him: for whom the Lord loveth, him he correcteth, yea and he scourgeth every son, whom he receiveth.

The Gospel. John v.

VERILY, verily I say unto you, He that heareth my word, and believeth on him that sent me, hath everlasting life, and shall not come unto damnation, but he passeth from death unto life.

The Preface. The Lord be with you.
Answer. And with thy spirit.
¶ Lift up your hearts, &c.

Unto the end of the Canon.

[1 The Father, &c. Oswen.]

THE COMMUNION OF THE SICK. 143

¶ At the time of the distribution of the holy sacrament, the priest shall first receive the Communion himself, and after minister to them that be appointed to communicate with the sick (if there be any), and then to the sick person. And the sick person shall always desire some, either of his own house, or else of his neighbours, to receive the holy Communion with him; for that shall be to him a singular great comfort, and of their part a great token of charity.

¶ And if there be more sick persons to be visited the same day that the curate doth celebrate in any sick man's house : then shall the curate (there) reserve so much of the sacrament of the body[2] and blood, as shall serve the other sick persons, and such as be appointed to communicate with them, (if there be any); and shall immediately carry it, and minister it unto them.

¶ But if any man either by reason of extremity of sickness, or for lack of warning given in due time to the curate, or by any other just impediment, do not receive the sacrament of Christ's body and blood; then the curate shall instruct him, that if he do truly repent him of his sins, and stedfastly believe that Jesus Christ hath suffered death upon the cross for him, and shed his blood for his redemption, earnestly remembering the benefits he hath thereby, and giving him hearty thanks therefore; he doth eat and drink spiritually the body and blood of our Saviour Christ, profitably to his soul's health, although he do not receive the sacrament with his mouth.

¶ When the sick person is visited and receiveth the holy Communion all at one time : then the priest for more expedition shall use this order at the visitation.

The Anthem.

Remember not, Lord, &c.

Lord, have mercy upon us.
Christ, have mercy upon us.
Lord, have mercy upon us.

¶ Our Father which art in heaven, &c.
And lead us not into temptation.
Answer. But deliver us from evil. Amen.

Let us pray.

O Lord[3], look down from heaven, &c.

With the first part of the exhortation and all other things unto the Psalm,

In thee, O Lord, have I put my trust, &c.

And if the sick desire to be anointed, then shall the priest use the appointed prayer without any Psalm.

[2 of Christ's body, Grafton, 2.]
[3 Lord, omitted by Grafton, 2, and C : also &c. omitted in Grafton, C.]

THE ORDER FOR THE

BURIAL OF THE DEAD.

The priest meeting the corpse at the church stile, shall say: Or else the priests and clerks shall sing, and so go either into the church, or towards[1] the grave.

I AM the resurrection and the life (saith the Lord): he that believeth in me, yea though he were dead, yet shall he live. And whosoever liveth and believeth in me, shall not die for ever. *John* xi.

I KNOW that my Redeemer liveth, and that I shall rise out of the earth in the last day, and shall be covered again with my skin, and shall see God in my flesh: yea and I myself shall behold him, not with other but with these same eyes. *Job* xix[2].

WE brought nothing into this world, neither may we carry any thing out of this world. The Lord giveth, and the Lord taketh away. Even as it pleaseth the Lord, so cometh things to pass: blessed be the name of the Lord. 1 *Tim.* vi. *Job* i.

When they come at the grave, whiles the corpse is made ready to be laid into the earth, the priest shall say, or else the priest and clerks shall sing.

MAN that is born of a woman, hath but a short time to live, and is full of misery: he cometh up and is cut down like a flower; he flieth as it were a shadow, and never continueth in one stay. *Job* ix. [xiv.]

¶ In the midst of life we be in death: of whom may we seek for succour, but of thee, O Lord, which for our sins justly art moved? Yet[3] O Lord God most holy, O Lord

[1 toward, Whitchurch, June.]
[2 John xix. Grafton, C; but a mistake.]
[3 "O Lord, which for our sins justly art moved? Yet," omitted in Grafton, C.]

most mighty, O holy and most merciful Saviour, deliver us not into the bitter pains of eternal death. Thou knowest, Lord, the secrets of our hearts: shut not up thy merciful eyes to our prayers: But spare us, Lord most holy, O God most mighty, O holy and merciful Saviour, thou most worthy Judge eternal, suffer us not at our last hour for any pains of death to fall from thee.

Then the priest casting earth upon the corpse, shall say,

I COMMEND thy soul to God the Father Almighty, and thy body to the ground, earth to earth, ashes to ashes, dust to dust, in sure and certain hope of resurrection to eternal life, through our Lord Jesus Christ, who shall change our vile body, that it may be like to his glorious body, according to the mighty working whereby he is able to subdue all things to himself.

Then shall be said or sung,

I HEARD a voice from heaven, saying unto me: Write, blessed are the dead which die in the Lord. Even so saith the Spirit, that they rest from their labours. *Apoc.* xiv.

Let us pray.

WE commend into thy hands of mercy, most merciful Father, the soul of this our brother departed, *N.* And his body we commit to the earth, beseeching thine infinite goodness, to give us grace to live in thy fear and love, and to die in thy favour: that when the judgment shall come which thou hast committed to thy well beloved Son, both this our brother, and we, may be found acceptable in thy sight, and receive that blessing, which thy well beloved Son shall then pronounce to all that love and fear thee, saying, Come, ye blessed children of my Father: Receive the kingdom prepared for you before the beginning of the world. Grant this, merciful Father, for the honour of Jesu Christ our only Saviour, Mediator, and Advocate. Amen.

This prayer shall also be added.

ALMIGHTY God, we give thee hearty thanks for this thy servant, whom thou hast delivered from the miseries of this wretched world, from the body of death and all temptation; and, as we trust, hast brought his soul, which he committed into thy holy hands, into sure consolation and rest: Grant, we beseech thee, that at the day of judgment his soul and all the souls of thy elect, departed out of this life, may with us, and we with them, fully receive thy promises, and be made perfit[1] altogether, thorough the glorious resurrection of thy Son Jesus Christ our Lord.

These psalms with other suffrages following are to be said in the church, either before or after the burial of the corpse.

Dilexi quoniam. Psalm cxvi.[2]

Domine probasti. Psalm cxxxix.[3]

Lauda anima mea. Psalm cxlvi.[4]

Then shall follow this lesson, taken out of the fifteenth chapter to the Corinthians, the first Epistle. [v. 20 to end.]

The lesson ended, then shall the Priest say,

Lord, have mercy upon us.
Christ, have mercy upon us.
Lord, have mercy upon us.
¶ Our Father which art in heaven, &c.
And lead us not into temptation.
Answer. But deliver us from evil. Amen.
Priest. Enter not (O Lord) into judgment with thy servant.
Answer. For in thy sight no living creature shall be justified.
Priest. From the gates of hell.
Answer. Deliver their souls, O Lord.
Priest. I believe to see the goodness of the Lord.
Answer. In the land of the living.
Priest. O Lord, graciously hear my prayer.
Answer. And let my cry come unto thee.

[1 parfite, Grafton, C.]
[2 Psalm clxxvi. Grafton, 2; but Psalm cxvi. is given.]
[3 The order of this and the next Psalm is inverted, in Grafton, 2, C, and Oswen. This is noticed in the margin of all these copies, thus: "Note that this Psalm is to be said after the other that followeth."—]
[4 Psalm cxvi. Grafton, 2; but Psalm cxlvi. is given.]

BURIAL OF THE DEAD. 147

Let us pray.

O LORD, with whom do live the spirits of them that be dead: and in whom the souls of them that be elected, after they be delivered from the burden of the flesh, be in joy and felicity: Grant unto this thy servant, that the sins which he committed in this world be not imputed unto him, but that he, escaping the gates of hell, and pains of eternal darkness, may ever dwell in the region of light, with Abraham, Isaac, and Jacob, in the place where is no weeping, sorrow, nor heaviness; and when that dreadful day of the general resurrection shall come, make him to rise also with the just and righteous, and receive this body again to glory, then made pure and incorruptible: set him on the right hand of thy Son Jesus Christ, among thy holy and elect, that then he may hear with them these most sweet and comfortable words: Come to me, ye blessed of my Father, possess the kingdom which hath been prepared for you from the beginning of the world: Grant this, we beseech thee, O merciful Father, through Jesus Christ our Mediator and Redeemer. Amen.

The Celebration of the Holy Communion when there is a Burial of the Dead.

Quemadmodum. Psalm xlii.

Collect[5].

O MERCIFUL God the Father of our Lord Jesu Christ, who is the resurrection and the life: In whom whosoever believeth shall live, though he die: and whosoever liveth, and believeth in him, shall not die eternally: who also hath taught us (by his holy apostle Paul) not to be sorry as men without hope for them that sleep in him: We meekly beseech thee (O Father) to raise us from the death of sin unto the life of righteousness, that when we shall depart this life, we may sleep in him (as our hope is this our brother

[5 *The Collect*, Grafton and Oswen.]

doth), and at the general resurrection in the last day both we and this our brother departed, receiving again our bodies, and rising again in thy most gracious favour, may with all thine elect Saints obtain eternal joy. Grant this, O Lord God, by the means of our Advocate Jesus Christ: which with thee and the Holy Ghost, liveth and reigneth one God for ever. Amen.

The Epistle. 1 Thess. iv. [v. 13 to end.]
¶ *The Gospel.* John vi. [v. 37 to 40.]

THE ORDER OF THE
PURIFICATION OF WOMEN.

The woman shall come into the church, and there shall kneel down in some convenient place, nigh unto the quire door: and the Priest standing by her shall say these words, or such like, as the case shall require.

FORASMUCH as it hath pleased Almighty God of his goodness to give you safe deliverance, and your child baptism, and hath preserved you in the great danger of childbirth: ye shall therefore give hearty thanks unto God, and pray.

Then shall the Priest say this Psalm.

Levavi oculos. Psalm[1] cxxi.

Lord, have mercy upon us.
Christ, have mercy upon us.
Lord, have mercy upon us.
¶ Our Father which art in heaven, &c.
And lead us not into temptation.
Answer. But deliver us from evil. Amen.
Priest. O Lord, save this woman thy servant.
Answer. Which putteth her trust in thee.
Priest. Be thou to her a strong tower.
Answer. From the face of her enemy.
Priest. Lord[2], hear our prayer.
Answer. And let our cry come to thee.

Priest. ¶ Let us pray.

O ALMIGHTY God, which hast delivered this woman thy servant from the great pain and peril of childbirth: Grant, we beseech thee (most merciful Father), that she through thy help may both faithfully live, and walk in her vocation according to thy will in this life present; and also may be partaker of everlasting glory in the life to come: through Jesus Christ our Lord. Amen.

The woman that is purified, must offer her chrisom, and other accustomed offerings. And if there be a Communion, it is convenient that she receive the holy Communion.

[1 Psal. xxi. Grafton, 2; but Psal. cxxi. is given.]
[2 O Lord, Oswen, and Grafton, C.]

THE FIRST DAY OF LENT

COMMONLY CALLED

ASH-WEDNESDAY.

¶ After Matins ended, the people being called together by the ringing of a bell, and assembled in the church, the English Litany shall be said after the accustomed manner[1]: which ended, the Priest shall go into the pulpit, and say thus:

BRETHREN, in the primitive church there was a godly discipline, that at the beginning of Lent such persons as were notorious sinners, were put to open penance[2], and punished in this world, that their souls might be saved in the day of the Lord; and that other, admonished by their example, might be more afraid to offend. In the stead whereof, until the said discipline may be restored again, (which thing is much to be wished,) it is thought good, that at this time (in your presence) should be read the general sentences of God's cursing against impenitent sinners, gathered out of the xxviith chapter of Deuteronomy, and other places of scripture: and that ye should answer to every sentence, Amen. To the intent that you, being admonished of the great indignation of God against sinners, may the rather be called to earnest and true repentance, and may walk more warily in these dangerous days, fleeing[3] from such vices, for the which ye affirm with your own mouths the curse of God to be due.

¶ CURSED is the man that maketh any carved or molten image, an abomination to the Lord, the work of the hands of the craftsman, and putteth it in a secret place to worship it.

And the people shall answer, and say,
Amen.

[1 For, "after the accustomed manner," we find, "in such wise as in the end of this book is set forth, and in the accustomed places appointed by the King's Injunctions," Grafton, C.]
[2 put to open penance, omitted in Grafton, C.]
[3 flying, Grafton, 2, and Oswen.]

Minister. Cursed is he that curseth his father, and mother.

Answer. Amen.

Minister. Cursed is he that removeth away the mark of his neighbour's land.

Answer. Amen.

Minister. Cursed is he that maketh the blind to go out of his way.

Answer. Amen.

Minister. Cursed is he that letteth in judgment the right of the stranger, of them that be fatherless, and of widows.

Answer. Amen.

Minister. Cursed is he that smiteth his neighbour secretly.

Answer. Amen.

Minister. Cursed is he that lieth with his neighbour's wife.

Answer. Amen.

Minister. Cursed is he that taketh reward to slay the soul of innocent blood.

Answer. Amen.

Minister. Cursed is he that putteth his trust in man, and taketh man for his defence, and in his heart goeth from the Lord.

Answer. Amen.

Minister. Cursed are the unmerciful, the fornicators and advouterers, the covetous persons, the worshippers of images, slanderers, drunkards, and extortioners.

Answer. Amen.

The Minister. Now seeing that all they be accursed (as the prophet David beareth witness) which do err and go astray from the commandments of God, let us (remembering the dreadful judgment hanging over our heads, and being always at hand) return unto our Lord God, with all contrition and meekness of heart, bewailing and lamenting our sinful life, knowledging and confessing our offences, and seeking to bring forth worthy fruits of penance. For even now is the axe put unto the root of the trees, so that every tree which bringeth not forth good fruit, is hewn down and cast

Psal. cxviii.[4]

Mat. iii.

[[4] Psal. cxvii. Oswen.]

into the fire. It is a fearful thing to fall into the hands of the living God: he shall pour down rain upon the sinners, snares, fire and brimstone, storm and tempest: this shall be their portion to drink. For lo, the Lord is coming[1] out of his place, to visit the wickedness of such as dwell upon the earth. But who may abide the day of his coming? Who shall be able to endure when he appeareth? His fan is in his hand, and he will purge his floor, and gather his wheat into the barn, but he will burn the chaff with unquenchable fire. The day of the Lord cometh as a thief upon the night; and when men shall say peace, and all things are safe, then shall sudden destruction come upon them, as sorrow cometh upon a woman travailing with child, and they shall not escape: then shall appear the wrath of God in the day of vengeance, which obstinate sinners, through the stubbornness of their heart, have heaped unto themself, which despised the goodness, patience and longsufferance of God, when he called them continually to repentance. Then shall they call upon me (saith the Lord), but I will not hear: they shall seek me early, but they shall not find me, and that because they hated knowledge, and received not the fear of the Lord, but abhorred my counsel and despised my correction: then shall it be too late to knock, when the door shall be shut, and too late to cry for mercy, when it is the time of justice. O terrible voice of most just judgment, which shall be pronounced upon them, when it shall be said unto them, Go ye cursed into the fire everlasting, which is prepared for the devil and his angels. Therefore, brethren, take we heed betime, while the day of salvation lasteth, for the night cometh when none can work: but let us, while we have the light, believe in the light, and walk as the children of the light, that we be not cast into the utter darkness, where is weeping and gnashing of teeth. Let us not abuse the goodness of God, which calleth us mercifully to amendment, and of his endless pity promiseth us forgiveness of that which is past, if (with a whole mind and a true heart) we return unto him: for though our sins be red[5] as scarlet, they shall be as white as snow; and[6]

[[1] come, Grafton, 1, 2, and C.] [[2] Mal. xxv. Grafton, C; but mistake.]
[[3] 1 Thess. v. omitted, Grafton, 1.] [[4] 1 Cor. vi. Whitchurch, June.]
[[5] as red as, Grafton, C.] [[6] and, omitted, Grafton, C.]

though they be like purple, yet shall they be as white as wool. Turn you clean (saith the Lord) from all your wicked- Esech. xvii ness, and your sin shall not be your destruction. Cast away from you all your ungodliness that ye have done, make you new hearts, and a new spirit: wherefore will ye die, O ye house of Israel, seeing I have no pleasure in the death of him that dieth? saith the Lord God. Turn you then, and you shall live. Although we have sinned, yet have we an Advocate with the Father, Jesus Christ the righteous, and 1 John ii. he it is that obtaineth grace for our sins; for he was wounded for our offences, and smitten for our wickedness: let us Esai. iii. therefore return unto him, who is the merciful receiver of all true penitent sinners, assuring ourself that he is ready to receive us, and most willing to pardon us, if we come to him with faithful repentance: if we will submit ourselves unto him, and from henceforth walk in his ways: if we will take his easy yoke and light burden upon us to follow him Math. xi. in lowliness, patience, and charity, and be ordered by the governance of his holy Spirit, seeking always his glory, and serving him duly in our vocation with thanksgiving. This if we do, Christ will deliver us from the curse of the law, and from the extreme malediction which shall light upon them that shall be set on the left hand: and he will set us on his right hand, and give us the blessed benediction of his Father, commanding us to take possession Math. xxv. of his glorious kingdom; unto the which he vouchsafe to bring us all, for his infinite mercy. Amen.

¶ Then shall they all kneel upon their knees: and the Priest and clerks kneeling (where they are accustomed to say the Litany) shall say this psalm.

Miserere mei Deus. Psalm li.

¶ Lord, have mercy upon us.
¶ Christ, have mercy upon us.
¶ Lord, have mercy upon us.

Our Father which art in heaven, &c.
And lead us not into temptation.
Answer. But deliver us from evil. Amen.
Minister. O Lord save thy servants.
Answer. Which put their trust in thee.

[⁷ Esech. xviii. Grafton, 2, C, and Oswen.]

Minister. Send unto them help from above.
Answer. And evermore mightily defend them.
Minister. Help us, O God our Saviour.
Answer. And for the glory of thy name's sake deliver us, be merciful unto us sinners for thy name's sake.
Minister. O Lord, hear my prayer.
Answer. And let my cry come to thee,

Let us pray.

O LORD, we beseech thee mercifully hear our prayers, and spare all those which confess their sins to thee, that they whose consciences by sin are accused, by thy merciful pardon may be absolved, through Christ our Lord. Amen.

O MOST mighty God and merciful Father, which hast compassion of all men, and hatest nothing that thou hast made: which wouldest not the death of a sinner, but that he should rather turn from sin and be saved: mercifully forgive us our trespasses, receive and comfort us, which be grieved and wearied with the burden of our sin. Thy property is to have mercy, to thee only it appertaineth to forgive sins: spare us therefore, good Lord, spare thy people whom thou hast redeemed. Enter not into judgment with thy servants, which be vile earth, and miserable sinners: But so turn thy ire from us, which meekly knowledge our vileness, and truly repent us of our faults: so make haste to help us in this world, that we may ever live with thee in the world to come: through Jesus Christ our Lord. Amen.

Then shall this anthem be said or sung.

TURN thou us, good Lord, and so shall we be turned: be favourable (O Lord) be favourable to thy people, which turn to thee in weeping, fasting and praying: for thou art a merciful God, full of compassion, long suffering, and of a great piety[1]. Thou sparest when we deserve punishment, and in thy wrath thinkest upon mercy. Spare thy people, good Lord, spare them, and let not thine[2] heritage be brought to confusion: Hear us (O Lord) for thy mercy is great, and after the multitude of thy mercies look upon us.

[[1] pity, Grafton, 2, C, and Oswen.]   [[2] thy, Grafton, 1.]

OF CEREMONIES,
WHY SOME BE ABOLISHED AND SOME RETAINED.

Of such ceremonies as be used in the Church, and have had their beginning by the institution of man: Some at the first were of godly intent and purpose devised, and yet at[3] length turned to vanity and superstition: Some entered into the Church by undiscreet devotion, and such a zeal as was without knowledge; and for[4] because they were winked at in the beginning, they grew daily to more and more abuses, which not only for their unprofitableness, but also because they have much blinded the people, and obscured the glory of God, are worthy to be cut away, and clean rejected. Other there be, which although they have been devised by man, yet it is thought good to reserve them still, as well for a decent order in the Church (for the which they were first devised), as because they pertain to edification, whereunto all things done in the Church (as the Apostle teacheth) ought to be referred. And although the keeping or omitting of a ceremony (in itself considered) is but a small thing: yet the wilful and contemptuous transgression, and breaking of a common order, and discipline, is no small offence before God. Let all things be done among you (saith Saint Paul) in a seemly and due order. The appointment of the[5] which order pertaineth not to private men: Therefore no man ought to take in hand, nor presume to appoint or alter any public or common order in Christ's Church, except he be lawfully called and authorized thereunto. And whereas, in this our time, the minds of men be so diverse, that some think it a great matter of conscience to depart from a piece of the least of their ceremonies (they be so addicted to their old customs), and again on the other side, some be so new fangle that they would innovate all thing, and so do despise the old that nothing can like them, but that is new: It was thought expedient not so much to have respect how to please and satisfy either of these parties, as how to please God, and profit them both. And yet lest any man should be offended (whom good reason might satisfy), here be certain causes

[3 at the, Grafton, 2.]   [4 for, omitted by Oswen.]
[5 the, omitted, Grafton, C.]

rendered why some of the accustomed ceremonies be put away, and some be retained and kept still.

Some are put away, because the great excess and multitude of them hath so increased in these latter days, that the burden of them was intolerable: whereof St Augustine in his time complained, that they were grown to such a number, that the state of Christian people was in worse case (concerning that matter) than were the Jews. And he counselled that such yoke and burden should be taken away, as time would serve quietly to do it. But what would St Augustine have said, if he had seen the ceremonies of late days used among us, whereunto the multitude used in his time was not to be compared? This our excessive multitude of ceremonies was so great, and many of them so dark, that they did more confound and darken, than declare and set forth Christ's benefits unto us. And besides this, Christ's Gospel is not a ceremonial law (as much of Moses' law was); but it is a religion to serve God, not in bondage of the figure or shadow, but in the freedom of spirit, being content only with those ceremonies which do serve to a decent order and godly discipline, and such as be apt to stir up the dull mind of man, to the remembrance of his duty to God, by some notable and special signification, whereby he might be edified.

¶ Furthermore, the most weighty cause of the abolishment of certain ceremonies was, that they were so far abused, partly by the superstitious blindness of the rude and unlearned, and partly by the unsatiable avarice of such as sought more their own lucre than the glory of God; that the abuses could not well be taken away, the thing remaining still. But now as concerning those persons, which peradventure will be offended for that some of the old ceremonies are retained still: if they consider, that without some ceremonies it is not possible to keep any order or quiet discipline in the church, they shall easily perceive just cause to reform their judgments. And if they think much that any of the old do remain, and would rather have all devised anew: then such men (granting some ceremonies convenient to be had), surely where the old may be well used, there they cannot reasonably reprove the old (only for their age) without bewraying of their own folly. For in such a case they ought rather to have reverence unto them for their antiquity, if they will declare themselves to be more studious of unity and concord, than of innovations and newfangleness, which (as much as may be with the true setting forth of Christ's religion) is always to be eschewed. Furthermore, such shall have no just cause with the ceremonies reserved to be offended: for as those be taken away which were most abused, and did burden men's consciences without any cause; so the other that remain are retained for a discipline and order, which (upon just causes) may be altered and changed, and therefore are not to be esteemed equal with God's law. And moreover they be neither dark nor dumb ceremonies, but are so set forth that every man may understand what they do mean, and to what use they do serve. So that it is not like that they, in time to come, should be abused as the other have been. And in these all[1] our doings we condemn no other nations, nor prescribe any thing, but to our own people only. For we think it convenient that every country should use such ceremonies, as they shall think best to the setting forth of God's honour and glory, and to the reducing of the people to a most perfect and godly living, without error or superstition; and that they should put away other things, which from time to time they perceive[2] to be most abused, as in men's ordinances it often chanceth diversely in diverse countries.

Certain Notes for the more plain explication and decent ministration of things contained in this book.

IN the saying or singing of Matins and Evensong, Baptizing and Burying, the minister, in parish churches and chapels annexed to the same, shall use a Surplice. And in all Cathedral churches and Colleges, the Archdeacons, Deans, Provosts, Masters, Prebendaries, and Fellows, being graduates, may use in the quire, beside their Surplices, such hood as pertaineth to their several degrees, which they have taken in any university within this realm. But in all other places, every minister shall be at liberty to use any surplice or no. It is also seemly that graduates, when they do preach, shall[3] use such hoods as pertaineth to their several degrees.

¶ And whensoever the Bishop shall celebrate the holy communion in the church, or execute any other public ministration, he shall have upon him, beside his rochette, a Surplice or albe, and a cope or vestment, and also his pastoral staff in his hand, or else borne or holden by his chaplain.

¶ As touching kneeling, crossing, holding up of hands, knocking upon the breast, and other gestures, they may be used or left, as every man's devotion serveth, without blame[4].

[1 all, omitted by Grafton, 2.] [2 perceived, Grafton, 2.]
[3 should, Grafton, 1, and C.] [4 without blame, omitted by Oswen.]

¶ Also upon Christmas day, Easter day, the Ascension Day, Whit-Sunday, and the feast of the Trinity, may be used any part of holy scripture hereafter to be certainly limited and appointed, in the stead[1] of the Litany.

¶ If there be a sermon, or for other great cause, the Curate by his discretion may leave out the Litany, Gloria in Excelsis, the Creed, the[2] Homily, and the Exhortation to the Communion.

FINIS.

Imprinted at London in
Fletestrete, at the signe of the Sunne ouer against the conduyte, by EdVVarde VVhitchurche. The fourth daye of Maye[3], the yeare of our Lorde, 1549.

[4]The Kinges Maiestie, by
the aduyse of his moste deare uncle the Lord Protector and other his highnes Counsell, streightly chargeth and commaundeth, that no maner of person do[5] sell this present booke unbounde, aboue the price of ii. shyllynges & ii[6]. pence the piece[7]. And the same bounde in paste or in boordes[8], not aboue the price of three[9] shyllynges and viii. pence the piece.

GOD SAUE THE KING.

[1 instead, Oswen.]   [2 the, omitted, Grafton, C.]
[3 7th day of March, Grafton, 1; xvi day of June, Whitchurch, June; Mense Junii, Grafton; 30th day of July, Oswen.]
[4 "The King's Majesty," &c., not in Grafton, 1; it is placed before the colophon, Grafton, 2.]
[5 shall, Grafton, 2.]   [6 six, Oswen.]
[7 the piece, omitted by Grafton, 2.]
[8 covered with calves' leather, Whitchurch; in calves' leather, Grafton, 2; both omitted in Oswen.]
[9 four shillings, Whitchurch, June, Grafton, and Oswen.]

THE
FORM AND MANNER

OF

MAKING AND CONSECRATING

OF

ARCHBISHOPS, BISHOPS,

PRIESTS AND DEACONS.

ANNO DOMINI M.D.XLIX.

The forme

and maner of makyng

and consecratyng of

Archebishoppes

Bishoppes

Priestes

and

Deacons

M.D.XLIX.

THE PREFACE.

It is evident unto all men, diligently reading holy scripture, and ancient authors, that from the Apostles' time there hath been these orders of Ministers in Christ's church; Bishops, Priests, and Deacons: which Offices were evermore had in such reverent estimation, that no man by his own private authority might presume to execute any of them, except he were first called, tried, examined, and known to have such qualities as were requisite for the same; and also, by public prayer, with imposition of hands, approved, and admitted thereunto. And therefore, to the intent these orders should be continued, and reverently used, and esteemed, in this Church of England, it is requisite, that no man (not being at this present Bishop, Priest, nor Deacon) shall execute any of them, except he be called, tried, examined, and admitted, according to the form hereafter following. And none shall be admitted a Deacon, except he be twenty-one years of age at the least. And every man which is to be admitted a Priest, shall be full twenty-four years old. And every man, which is to be consecrated a Bishop, shall be fully thirty years of age. And the Bishop knowing, either by himself, or by sufficient testimony, any person to be a man of virtuous conversation, and without crime, and after examination and trial, finding him learned in the Latin tongue, and sufficiently instructed in holy scripture, may, upon a Sunday or holyday, in the face of the church, admit him a Deacon, in such manner and form, as hereafter followeth.

THE

FORM AND MANNER

OF

ORDERING OF DEACONS.

¶ First, when the day appointed by the Bishop is come, there shall be an exhortation, declaring the duty and office of such as come to be admitted Ministers, how necessary such orders are in the church of Christ, and also, how the people ought to esteem them in their vocation.

¶ After the exhortation ended, the Archdeacon, or his deputy, shall present such as come to be admitted, to the Bishop; every one of them, that are presented, having upon him a plain Albe: and the Archdeacon, or his deputy, shall say these words.

REVEREND Father in GOD, I present unto you these persons present, to be admitted Deacons.

¶ *The Bishop.* Take heed that the persons whom ye present unto us, be apt and meet, for their learning, and Godly conversation, to exercise their ministry duly, to the honour of God, and edifying of his Church.

The Archdeacon shall answer.

I have inquired of them, and also examined them, and think them so to be.

¶ And then the Bishop shall say unto the people,

BRETHREN, if there be any of you, who knoweth any impediment, or notable crime, in any of these persons presented to be ordered Deacons, for the which he ought not to be admitted to the same, let him come forth, in the name of God, and shew what the crime, or impediment is.

¶ And if any great crime or impediment be objected, the Bishop shall surcease from ordering that person, until such time as the party accused shall try himself clear of that crime.

Then the Bishop, commending such as shall be found meet to be ordered, to the prayers of the congregation, with the Clerks, and people present, shall say or sing the Litany as followeth.

THE ORDERING OF DEACONS.

The Litany and Suffrages.

O GOD the Father of heaven : have mercy upon us miserable sinners.

O God the Father of heaven : have mercy upon us miserable sinners.

O God the Son, Redeemer of the world : have mercy upon us miserable sinners.

O God the Son, Redeemer of the world : have mercy upon us miserable sinners.

O God the Holy Ghost, proceeding from the Father and the Son : have mercy upon us miserable sinners.

O God the Holy Ghost, proceeding from the Father and the Son : have mercy upon us miserable sinners.

O holy, blessed, and glorious Trinity, three persons and one God : have mercy upon us miserable sinners.

O holy, blessed, and glorious Trinity, three persons and one God : have mercy upon us miserable sinners.

Remember not, Lord, our offences, nor the offences of our forefathers, neither take thou vengeance of our sins : spare us, good Lord, spare thy people, whom thou hast redeemed with thy most precious blood, and be not angry with us for ever.

Spare us, good Lord.

From all evil and mischief, from sin, from the crafts and assaults of the devil, from thy wrath, and from everlasting damnation.

Good Lord, deliver us.

From blindness of heart, from pride, vainglory, and hypocrisy, from envy, hatred, and malice, and all uncharitableness.

Good Lord, deliver us.

From fornication, and all deadly sin; and from all the deceits of the world, the flesh, and the devil.

Good Lord, deliver us.

From Lightning and Tempest, from Plague, Pestilence, and Famine, from Battle and murther, and from sudden death.

Good Lord, deliver us.

From all sedition and privy conspiracy, from the tyranny of the Bishop of Rome, and all his detestable enormities,

11—2

from all false doctrine and heresy, from hardness of heart, and contempt of thy word and commandment.

Good Lord, deliver us.

By the mystery of thy holy incarnation, by thy holy nativity and Circumcision, by thy baptism, fasting, and temptation.

Good Lord, deliver us.

By thine agony and bloody sweat, by thy Cross and passion, by thy precious death and burial, by thy glorious resurrection and ascension, by the coming of the Holy Ghost.

Good Lord, deliver us.

In all time of our tribulation, in all time of our wealth, in the hour of death, in the day of judgment.

Good Lord, deliver us.

We sinners do beseech thee to hear us (O Lord God), and that it may please thee to rule and govern thy holy church universal in the right way.

We beseech thee to hear us, good Lord.

That it may please thee, to keep EDWARD the VI. thy servant, our King and governor.

We beseech thee to hear us, good Lord.

That it may please thee, to rule his heart in thy faith, fear and love, that he may always have affiance in thee, and ever seek thy honour and glory.

We beseech thee to hear us, good Lord.

That it may please thee, to be his defender and keeper, giving him the victory over all his enemies.

We beseech thee to hear us, good Lord.

That it may please thee, to illuminate all Bishops, Pastors, and ministers of the church, with true knowledge, and understanding of thy word, and that both by their preaching and living they may set it forth, and shew it accordingly.

We beseech thee to hear us, good Lord.

That it may please thee, to bless these men, and send thy grace upon them, that they may duly execute the office, now to be committed unto them, to the edifying of thy Church, and to thy honour, praise, and glory.

We beseech thee to hear us, good Lord.

That it may please thee, to endue the lords of the

THE ORDERING OF DEACONS.

council, and all the nobility, with grace, wisdom, and understanding.

We beseech thee to hear us, good Lord.

That it may please thee, to bless and keep the Magistrates, giving them grace to execute justice, and to maintain truth.

We beseech thee to hear us, good Lord.

That it may please thee, to bless and keep all thy people.

We beseech thee to hear us, good Lord.

That it may please thee, to give to all nations unity, peace, and concord.

We beseech thee to hear us, good Lord.

That it may please thee, to give us an heart, to love and dread thee, and diligently to live after thy commandments.

We beseech thee to hear us, good Lord.

That it may please thee, to give all thy people increase of grace, to hear meekly thy word, and to receive it with pure affection, and to bring forth the fruits of the Spirit.

We beseech thee to hear us, good Lord.

That it may please thee, to bring into the way of truth all such as have erred and are deceived.

We beseech thee to hear us, good Lord.

That it may please thee, to strengthen such as do stand, and to comfort and help the weak-hearted, and to raise them up that fall, and finally to beat down Sathan under our feet.

We beseech thee to hear us, good Lord.

That it may please thee, to succour, help and comfort, all that be in danger, necessity and tribulation.

We beseech thee to hear us, good Lord.

That it may please thee, to preserve all that travel by land, or by water, all women labouring of child, all sick persons, and young children, and to shew thy pity upon all prisoners and captives.

We beseech thee to hear us, good Lord.

That it may please thee, to defend and provide for the fatherless children and widows, and all that be desolate and oppressed.

We beseech thee to hear us, good Lord.

That it may please thee, to have mercy upon all men.

We beseech thee to hear us, good Lord.

That it may please thee, to forgive our enemies, persecutors, and slanderers, and to turn their hearts.

We beseech thee to hear us, good Lord.

That it may please thee, to give and preserve to our use the kindly fruits of the earth, so as in due time we may enjoy them.

We beseech thee to hear us, good Lord.

That it may please thee, to give us true repentance, to forgive us all our sins, negligences, and ignorances, and to endue us with the grace of thy holy Spirit to amend our lives, according to thy holy word.

We beseech thee to hear us, good Lord.

Son of GOD : we beseech thee to hear us.

Son of God : we beseech thee to hear us.

O Lamb of God, that takest away the sins of the world.

Grant us thy peace.

O Lamb of God, that takest away the sins of the world.

Have mercy upon us.

O Christ, hear us.

O Christ, hear us.

Lord, have mercy upon us.

Lord, have mercy upon us.

Christ, have mercy upon us.

Christ, have mercy upon us.

Lord, have mercy upon us.

Lord, have mercy upon us.

Our Father, which art in heaven,

With the residue of the *Pater Noster.*

And lead us not into temptation.

But deliver us from evil.

The Versicle. O Lord, deal not with us after our sins.

The Answer. *Neither reward us after our iniquities.*

Let us pray.

O GOD merciful Father, that despisest not the sighing of a contrite heart, nor the desire of such as be sorrowful, mercifully assist our prayers that we make before thee, in all our troubles and adversities, whensoever they oppress us : and graciously hear us, that those evils, which the craft and subtilty of the Devil, or man, worketh against us, be brought to nought, and by the providence of thy goodness they may be dispersed, that we thy servants, being hurt by no persecutions, may evermore give thanks unto thee, in thy holy Church : Through Jesu Christ our Lord.

O Lord, arise, help us, and deliver us, for thy name's sake.

O God, we have heard with our ears, and our fathers have declared unto us, the noble works, that thou didst in their days, and in the old time before them.

O Lord, arise, help us, and deliver us, for thine honour.

Glory be to the Father, the Son, and to the Holy Ghost : as it was in the beginning, is now, and ever shall be, world without end. Amen.

From our enemies defend us, O Christ.

Graciously look upon our afflictions.

Pitifully behold the dolor of our heart.

Mercifully forgive the sins of thy people.

Favourably with mercy hear our prayers.

O Son of David, have mercy upon us.

Both now and ever vouchsafe to hear us, O Christ.

Graciously hear us, O Christ.

Graciously hear us, O Lord Christ.

¶ *The Versicle.* O Lord, let thy mercy be shewed upon us.

The Answer. As we do put our trust in thee.

¶ Let us pray.

WE humbly beseech thee, O Father, mercifully to look upon our infirmities, and for the glory of thy name's sake, turn from us all those evils, that we most righteously have deserved : And grant that in all our troubles we may put our whole trust and confidence in thy mercy, and evermore serve thee, in pureness of living, to thy honour and glory, through our only mediator and advocate Jesus Christ our Lord. Amen.

ALMIGHTY God, which hast given us grace at this time with one accord to make our supplications unto thee; and dost promise, that when two or three be gathered in thy name, thou wilt grant their requests : fulfil now, O Lord, the desires and petitions of thy servants, as may be most expedient for them, granting us in this world knowledge of thy truth, and in the world to come life everlasting. Amen.

ALMIGHTY God, which by thy divine providence hast appointed diverse Orders of ministers in the church, and didst inspire thine holy Apostles to choose unto this Order of Deacons thy first Martyr saint Stephin, with other: mercifully behold these thy servants, now called to the like Office and ministration: replenish them so with the truth of thy doctrine, and innocency of life, that, both by word and good example, they may faithfully serve thee in this Office, to the glory of thy name, and profit of the congregation, through the merits of our Saviour Jesu Christ, who liveth and reigneth with thee, and the Holy Ghost, now and ever. Amen.

Then shall be sung or said, the Commnnion of the day, saving the Epistle shall be read out of Timothy, as followeth. 1 Tim. iii. [ver. 8, to end.]

Or else this, out of the sixth of the Acts. [ver. 2—7.]

¶ And before the Gospel, the Bishop sitting in a Chair, shall cause the Oath of the King's Supremacy, and against the usurped power and authority of the Bishop of Rome, to be ministered unto every of them, that are to be ordered.

¶ The Oath of the *King's Supremacy*.

I FROM henceforth shall utterly renounce, refuse, relinquish, and forsake the Bishop of Rome, and his authority, power, and jurisdiction. And I shall never consent nor agree, that the bishop of Rome shall practise, exercise, or have, any manner of authority, jurisdiction, or power within this realm, or any other the king's dominions, but shall resist the same at all times, to the uttermost of my power. And I, from henceforth will accept, repute, and take the King's Majesty to be the only supreme head in earth, of the church of England: And to my cunning, wit, and uttermost of my power, without guile, fraud, or other undue mean, I will observe, keep, maintain and defend, the whole effects and contents of all and singular acts and statutes made, and to be made within this realm, in derogation, extirpation, and extinguishment of the Bishop of Rome, and his authority, and all other acts and statutes, made or to be made, in reformation and corroboration of the King's power, of the supreme head in earth, of the church of England: and this I will do against all manner of persons, of what estate, dignity or degree, or condition they be, and in no wise do nor attempt, nor to my power suffer to be done or attempted, directly, or indirectly, any thing or things, privily or apertly, to the let, hinderance, damage or derogation thereof, or any part thereof, by any manner of means, or for any manner of pretence. And in case any other be made, or hath been made, by me, to any person or persons, in maintenance, defence, or favour of the Bishop of Rome, or his authority, jurisdiction, or power, I repute the same as vain and annihilate, so help me GOD, all saints and the holy Evangelist.

Then shall the Bishop examine every one of them, that are to be ordered, in the presence of the people, after this manner following.

Do you trust that you are inwardly moved by the Holy Ghost to take upon you this Office and ministration, to serve GOD, for the promoting of his glory, and the edifying of his people?

Answer. I trust so.

The Bishop. Do ye think, that ye truly be called, according to the will of our Lord Jesus Christ, and the due order of this realm to the ministry of the church?

Answer. I think so.

The Bishop. Do ye unfeignedly believe all the Canonical scriptures, of the old and new Testament?

Answer. I do believe.

The Bishop. Will you diligently read the same unto the people assembled in the church where you shall be appointed to serve?

Answer. I will.

The Bishop. It pertaineth to the office of a Deacon to assist the Priest in divine service, and specially when he ministereth the holy Communion, and help him in the distribution thereof, and to read holy scriptures and Homilies in the congregation, and instruct the youth in the Catechism, and also to baptize and preach if he be commanded by the Bishop. And furthermore, it is his office to search for the sick, poor, and impotent people of the parish, and to intimate their estates, names, and places where they dwell to the Curate, that by his exhortation they may be relieved by the parish or other convenient alms: will you do this gladly and willingly?

Answer. I will so do by the help of God.

The Bishop. Will you apply all your diligence to frame and fashion your own lives, and the lives of all your family according to the doctrine of Christ, and to make both yourselves and them, as much as in you lieth, wholesome examples of the flock of Christ?

Answer. I will so do, the Lord being my helper.

The Bishop. Will you reverently obey your ordinary and other chief Ministers of the Church, and them to whom the government and charge is committed over you, following with a glad mind and will their godly admonitions?

Answer. I will thus endeavour myself, the Lord being my helper.

¶ Then the Bishop laying his hands severally upon the head of every one of them, shall say.

Take thou authority to execute the office of a Deacon in the Church of God committed unto thee: in the name of the Father, the Son, and the Holy Ghost. Amen.

Then shall the Bishop deliver to every one of them the new Testament, saying.

Take thou authority to read the Gospel in the Church of God, and to preach the same, if thou be thereunto ordinarily commanded.

Then one of them, appointed by the Bishop, putting on a tunicle, shall read the Gospel of that day.

Then shall the Bishop proceed to the Communion, and all that be ordered, shall tarry and receive the holy communion the same day with the Bishop.

The Communion ended, after the last collect and immediately before the benediction, shall be said this Collect following.

ALMIGHTY God, giver of all good things, which of thy great goodness hast vouchsafed to accept and take these thy servants unto the office of Deacons in thy church: make them, we beseech thee, O Lord, to be modest, humble, and constant in their ministration, and to have a ready will to

THE ORDERING OF DEACONS.

observe all spiritual discipline, that they having always the testimony of a good conscience, and continuing ever stable and strong in thy Son Christ, may so well use themselves in this inferior office, that they may be found worthy to be called unto the higher ministries in thy Church, through the same thy Son our Saviour Christ, to whom be glory and honour world without end. Amen.

¶ And here it must be shewed unto the Deacon, that he must continue in that office of a Deacon the space of a whole year at the least (except for reasonable causes it be otherwise seen to his ordinary) to the intent he may be perfect, and well expert in the things appertaining to the Ecclesiastical administration, in executing whereof if he be found faithful and diligent, he may be admitted by his diocesan to the order of Priesthood.

THE FORM
OF
ORDERING PRIESTS.

When the exhortation is ended, then shall be sung, for the Introit to the Communion, this Psalm.
Expectans expectavi Dominum. Psalm xl.
Or else this Psalm.
Memento Domine David. Psalm cxxxii.
Or else this Psalm.
Laudate nomen Domini. Psalm cxxxv.

Then shall be read for the Epistle this out of the xx. Chapter of the Acts of the Apostles. [ver. 17—35.]

Or else this third Chapter of the first Epistle to Timothy. [ver. 1 to end.]

After this shall be read for the Gospel a piece of the last Chapter of Matthew, as followeth. [Matt. xxviii. ver. 18 to end.]

Or else this that followeth, of the x. Chapter of John. [ver. 1—16.]
Or else this, of the xx. chapter of John. [ver. 19—23.]
When the Gospel is ended, then shall be said or sung.

COME Holy Ghost eternal God,
proceeding from above,
Both from the Father and the Son,
the God of peace and love:
Visit our minds, and into us
thy heavenly grace inspire,
That in all truth and Godliness
we may have true desire.

Thou art the very comforter,
in all woe and distress,
The heavenly gift of God most high,
which no tongue can express,
The fountain and the lively spring
of joy celestial,
The fire so bright, the love so clear,
and unction spiritual.

Thou in thy gifts art manifold,
whereby Christ's Church doth stand,
In faithful hearts writing thy law,
the finger of God's hand:
According to thy promise made,
thou givest speech of grace,
That through thy help, the praise of God
may sound in every place.

O Holy Ghost, into our wits
send down thy heavenly light,
Kindle our hearts with fervent love,
to serve God day and night,
Strength and stablish all our weakness,
so feeble and so frail,
That neither flesh, the world, nor devil,
against us do prevail.

Put back our enemy far from us,
and grant us to obtain
Peace in our hearts with God and man,
without grudge or disdain.
And grant, O Lord, that thou being
our leader and our guide,
We may eschew the snares of sin,
and from thee never slide.

To us such plenty of thy grace,
good Lord, grant, we thee pray,
That thou Lord mayest be our comfort,
at the last dreadful day.
Of all strife and dissension,
O Lord, dissolve the bands,
And make the knots of peace and love
throughout all Christian lands.

Grant us, O Lord, through thee to know
the Father most of might,
That of his dear beloved Son
we may attain the sight:

And that with perfit faith also
we may acknowledge thee,
The Spirit of them both, alway
one God in persons three.

Laud and praise be to the Father,
and to the Son equal,
And to the Holy Spirit also,
one God coeternal:
And pray we that the only Son
vouchsafe his Spirit to send
To all that do profess his name,
unto the world's end.
Amen.

And then the Archdeacon shall present unto the Bishop all them that shall receive the order of Priesthood that day, every one of them having upon him a plain Albe: The Archdeacon saying.

REVEREND father in God, I present unto you these persons present, to be admitted to the Order of Priesthood, *cum interrogatione et responsione, ut in Ordine Diaconatus.*

And then the Bishop shall say to the people.

GOOD people, these be they whom we purpose, God willing, to receive this day unto the holy office of Priesthood. For after due examination, we find not the contrary, but that they be lawfully called to their function and ministry, and that they be persons meet for the same. But yet if there be any of you, which knoweth any impediment, or notable crime in any of them, for the which he ought not to be received to this holy ministry, now in the name of God declare the same.

¶ *And if any great crime or impediment be objected, &c. ut supra in Ordine Diaconatus usque ad finem Litaniæ cum hac Collecta.*

ALMIGHTY God, giver of all good things, which by thy Holy Spirit hast appointed diverse orders of Ministers in thy church: mercifully behold these thy servants, now called to the Office of Priesthood, and replenish them so with the truth of thy doctrine, and innocency of life, that both by word and good example they may faithfully serve thee in this office, to the glory of thy name, and profit of the congregation, through the merits of our Saviour Jesu Christ, who liveth and reigneth, with thee and the Holy Ghost, world without end. Amen.

¶ Then the Bishop shall minister unto every of them the oath, concerning the King's Supremacy, as it is set out in the Order of Deacons. And that done, he shall say unto them, which are appointed to receive the said Office, as hereafter followeth.

You have heard, brethren, as well in your private examination, as in the exhortation, and in the holy lessons taken out of the Gospel, and of the writings of the Apostles, of what dignity, and of how great importance this office is, (whereunto ye be called). And now we exhort you, in the name of our Lord Jesus Christ, to have in remembrance, into how high a dignity, and to how chargeable an office ye be called, that is to say, to be the Messengers, the Watchmen, the Pastors, and the Stewards of the Lord, to teach, to premonish, to feed, and provide for the Lord's family: to seek for Christ's Sheep, that be dispersed abroad, and for his children, which be in the midst of this naughty world, to be saved through Christ for ever. Have always therefore printed in your remembrance, how great a treasure is committed to your charge: for they be the Sheep of Christ, which he bought with his death, and for whom he shed his blood. The Church and congregation, whom you must serve, is his spouse and his body. And if it shall chance the same Church, or any member thereof, to take any hurt or hinderance by reason of your negligence, ye know the greatness of the fault, and also of the horrible punishment which will ensue. Wherefore, consider with yourselves the end of your ministry, towards the children of God, toward the spouse and body of Christ, and see that you never cease your labour, your care and diligence, until you have done all that lieth in you, according to your bounden duty, to bring all such as are, or shall be committed to your charge, unto that agreement in faith, and knowledge of God, and to that ripeness, and perfectness of age in Christ, that there be no place left among them, either for error in religion, or for viciousness in life.

Then forasmuch as your office is both of so great excellency, and of so great difficulty, ye see with how great care and study ye ought to apply yourselves, as well that you may shew yourselves kind to that Lord, who hath placed you in so high a dignity, as also to beware, that neither you yourselves offend, neither be occasion that other offend. Howbeit, ye cannot have a mind and a will thereto of yourselves, for that power and ability is given of God alone. Therefore ye see how ye ought and have need, earnestly to pray for his Holy Spirit. And seeing that ye cannot, by any other means, compass the doing of so weighty a work, pertaining to the salvation of man, but with doctrine and exhortation, taken out of holy Scripture, and with a life agreeable unto the same, ye perceive how studious ye ought to be in reading and learning the holy scriptures, and in framing the manners, both of yourselves, and of them that specially pertain unto you, according to the rule of the same scriptures. And for this selfsame cause, ye see how you ought to forsake and set aside (as much as you may) all worldly cares and studies.

We have a good hope, that you have well weighed and pondered these things with yourselves, long before this time, and that you have clearly determined, by God's grace, to give yourselves wholly to this vocation, whereunto it hath pleased God to call you, so that (as much as lieth in you) you apply yourselves wholly to this one thing, and draw all your cares and studies this way, and to this end: And that you will continually pray for the heavenly assistance of the Holy Ghost, from God the Father, by the mediation of our only Mediator and Saviour Jesus Christ, that by daily reading and weighing of the scriptures ye may wax riper and stronger in your Ministry: and that ye may so endeavour yourselves, from time to time, to sanctify the lives of you and yours, and to fashion them, after the rule and doctrine of Christ, and that ye may be wholesome and godly examples and patterns, for the rest of the congregation to follow: and that this present congregation of Christ, here assembled, may also understand your minds and wills, in these things.

¶ And that this your promise shall more move you to do your duties, ye shall answer plainly to these things, which we in the name of the Congregation shall demand of you, touching the same.

Do you think in your heart, that you be truly called,

according to the will of our Lord Jesus Christ, and the order of this Church of England, to the ministry of Priesthood?

Answer. I think it.

The Bishop. Be you persuaded that the holy scriptures contain sufficiently all doctrine, required of necessity for eternal salvation, through faith in Jesu Christ? And are you determined with the said scriptures to instruct the people committed to your charge, and to teach nothing, as required of necessity to eternal salvation, but that you shall be persuaded, may be concluded, and proved by the scripture?

Answer. I am so persuaded, and have so determined by God's grace.

The Bishop. Will you then give your faithful diligence always, so to minister the doctrine, and Sacraments, and the discipline of Christ, as the Lord hath commanded, and as this realm hath received the same, according to the commandments of God, so that ye may teach the people committed to your cure and charge with all diligence to keep and observe the same?

Answer. I will so do, by the help of the Lord.

The Bishop. Will you be ready with all faithful diligence to banish and drive away all erroneous and strange doctrines contrary to God's word, and to use both public and private monitions and exhortations, as well to the sick as to the whole, within your cures, as need shall require and occasion be given?

Answer. I will, the Lord being my helper.

The Bishop. Will you be diligent in prayers and in reading of the holy scriptures, and in such studies as help to the knowledge of the same, laying aside the study of the world and the flesh?

Answer. I will endeavour myself so to do, the Lord being my helper.

The Bishop. Will you be diligent to frame and fashion your own selves and your families according to the doctrine of Christ, and to make both yourselves and them (as much as in you lieth) wholesome examples and spectacles to the flock of Christ?

Answer. I will so apply myself, the Lord being my helper.

The Bishop. Will you maintain and set forwards (as much as lieth in you) quietness, peace, and love amongst all Christian people, and specially amongst them that are or shall be committed to your charge?

Answer. I will so do, the Lord being my helper.

The Bishop. Will you reverently obey your ordinary, and other chief ministers, unto whom the government and charge is committed over you, following with a glad mind and will their godly admonition, and submitting yourselves to their godly judgments?

Answer. I will so do, the Lord being my helper.

¶ Then shall the Bishop say,

ALMIGHTY God, who hath given you this will to do all these things, grant also unto you strength and power to perform the same, that he may accomplish his work which he hath begun in you, until the time he shall come at the latter day to judge the quick and the dead.

¶ After this the congregation shall be desired secretly in their prayers to make humble supplications to God for the foresaid things, for the which prayers there shall be a certain space kept in silence.

That done, the Bishop shall pray in this wise.

The Lord be with you.
Answer. And with thy spirit.

¶ Let us pray.

ALMIGHTY God and heavenly Father, which of thy infinite love and goodness towards us, hast given to us thy only and most dear beloved Son Jesus Christ, to be our redeemer and author of everlasting life: who after he had made perfect our redemption by his death, and was ascended into heaven, sent abroad into the world his Apostles, Prophets, Evangelists, Doctors, and Pastors, by whose labour and ministry he gathered together a great flock in all the parts of the world, to set forth the eternal praise of thy holy name: For these so great benefits of thy eternal goodness, and for that thou hast vouchsafed to call these thy servants here present to the same office and ministry of the salvation of mankind, we render unto thee most hearty thanks, we worship and praise thee; and we humbly beseech thee by the same thy Son, to grant unto all us which either here or elsewhere call upon thy name, that we may shew ourselves thankful to thee for these and all other thy benefits, and that we may daily increase and go forwards in the knowledge and faith of thee, and thy Son, by the Holy Spirit. So that as well by these thy ministers, as by them to whom they shall be appointed ministers, thy holy name may be always glorified, and thy blessed kingdom enlarged: through the same thy Son our Lord Jesus Christ, which liveth and reigneth with thee in the unity of the same Holy Spirit world without end. Amen.

¶ When this prayer is done, the Bishop with the Priests present shall lay their hands severally upon the head of every one that receiveth orders. The receivers humbly kneeling upon their knees, and the Bishop saying:

RECEIVE the Holy Ghost: whose sins thou dost forgive, they are forgiven: and whose sins thou dost retain, they are retained: and be thou a faithful dispenser of the word of God, and of his holy sacraments. In the name of the Father, and of the Son, and of the Holy Ghost. Amen.

The Bishop shall deliver to every one of them the Bible in the one hand, and the Chalice or cup with the bread, in the other hand, and say.

TAKE thou authority to preach the word of God, and to minister the holy Sacraments in this Congregation.

¶ When this is done, the Congregation shall sing the Creed, and also they shall go to the Communion, which all they that receive orders shall take together, and remain in the same place where the hands were laid upon them, until such time as they have received the Communion.

¶ The Communion being done, after the last Collect, and immediately before the benediction, shall be said this Collect:

MOST merciful Father, we beseech thee, so to send upon these thy Servants thy heavenly blessing, that they may be clad about with all justice, and that thy word spoken by their mouths may have such success, that it may never be spoken in vain. Grant also that we may have grace to hear and receive the same as thy most holy word and the mean of our salvation, that in all our words and deeds we may seek thy glory and the increase of thy kingdom, through Jesus Christ our Lord. Amen.

¶ If the orders of Deacon and Priesthood be given both upon one day, then shall the Psalm for the Introit and other things at the holy Communion be used as they are appointed at the ordering of Priests. Saving that for the Epistle, the whole iii. chapter of the first to Timothy shall be read, as it is set out before in the order of Priests. And immediately after the Epistle, the Deacons shall be ordered. And it shall suffice the Litany to be said once.

THE

FORM OF CONSECRATING

OF AN

ARCHBISHOP OR BISHOP.

The Psalm for the Introit at the Communion, as at the Ordering of Priests.

The Epistle. 1 Tim. iii. [1—7.]

THIS is a true saying, If a man desire the office of a Bishop, he desireth an honest work. A Bishop therefore must be blameless, the husband of one wife, diligent, sober, discreet, a keeper of hospitality, apt to teach, not given to overmuch wine, no fighter, not greedy of filthy lucre, but gentle, abhorring fighting, abhorring covetousness, one that ruleth well his own house; one that hath children in subjection with all reverence. For if a man cannot rule his own house, how shall he care for the congregation of God? he may not be a young scholar, lest he swell, and fall into the judgment of the evil speaker. He must also have a good report of them which are without, lest he fall into rebuke and snare of the evil speaker.

The Gospel. [John xxi. 15—17.]

JESUS said to Simon Peter, Simon Johanna, lovest thou me more than these? He said unto him, Yea, Lord, thou knowest that I love thee. He said unto him, Feed my lambs. He said to him again the second time: Simon Johanna, lovest thou me? He said unto him, Yea, Lord, thou knowest that I love thee. He said unto him, Feed my sheep. He said unto him the third time, Simon Johanna, lovest thou me? Peter was sorry because he said unto him the third time, Lovest thou me? and he said unto him: Lord, thou knowest all things, thou knowest that I love thee. Jesus said unto him, Feed my sheep.

¶ Or else out of the x. Chapter of John, as before in the order of Priests.

¶ After the Gospel and Credo ended, first the elected Bishop, having upon him a surplice and a cope, shall be presented by two Bishops (being also in surplices and copes, and having their pastoral staves in their hands) unto the Archbishop of the Province, or to some other Bishop appointed by his commission: the Bishops that present, saying:

MOST reverend Father in God, we present unto you this godly and well learned man to be consecrated Bishop.

¶ And then the King's mandate to the Archbishop for the consecration shall be read. And the oath touching the knowledging of the King's supremacy shall be ministered to the person elected, as it is set out in the order of Deacons. And then shall be ministered also the Oath of due obedience unto the Archbishop as followeth.

¶ *The Oath of due obedience to the Archbishop.*

IN the name of GOD, Amen. I, *N*. chosen Bishop of the church and see of *N*. do profess and promise all due reverence and obedience to the Archbishop and to the Metropolitical church of *N*. and to their successors, so help me God and his holy Gospel.

¶ Then the Archbishop shall move the congregation present to pray, saying thus to them.

BRETHREN, it is written in the Gospel of Saint Luke, that our Saviour Christ continued the whole night in prayer or ever that he did choose and send forth his xii. Apostles. It is written also in the Acts of the Apostles, that the disciples which were at Antioch did fast and pray or ever they laid hands upon or sent forth Paul and Barnabas. Let us therefore, following the example of our Saviour Christ and his Apostles, first fall to prayer or that we admit and send forth this person presented unto us, to the work whereunto we trust the Holy Ghost hath called him.

¶ And then shall be said the Litany as afore in the order of Deacons. And after this place: That it may please thee to illuminate all Bishops &c. he shall say.

THAT it may please thee to bless this our brother elected, and to send thy grace upon him, that he may duly

THE ORDERING OF BISHOPS.

execute the office whereunto he is called, to the edifying of thy church, and to the honour, praise and glory of thy name.

Answer. We beseech thee to hear us, good Lord.

Concluding the Litany in the end with this prayer:

ALMIGHTY God, giver of all good things, which by thy Holy Spirit hast appointed divers orders of Ministers in thy Church: mercifully behold this thy servant now called to the work and ministry of a Bishop, and replenish him so with the truth of thy doctrine and innocency of life, that both by word and deed he may faithfully serve thee in this office, to the glory of thy name, and profit of thy congregation: through the merits of our Saviour Jesu Christ, who liveth and reigneth with thee and the Holy Ghost, world without end. Amen.

Then the Archbishop sitting in a chair, shall say this to him that is to be consecrated.

BROTHER, forasmuch as holy Scripture and the old Canons commandeth that we should not be hasty in laying on hands and admitting of any person to the government of the congregation of Christ, which he hath purchased with no less price than the effusion of his own blood, afore that I admit you to this administration whereunto ye are called, I will examine you in certain articles, to the end the Congregation present may have a trial and bear witness how ye be minded to behave yourself in the church of God.

Are you persuaded that you be truly called to this ministration according to the will of our Lord Jesus Christ and the order of this realm?

Answer. I am so persuaded.

The Archbishop. Are you persuaded that the holy Scriptures contain sufficiently all doctrine required of necessity for eternal salvation through the faith in Jesu Christ? And are you determined with the same holy Scriptures to instruct the people committed to your charge, and to teach or maintain nothing, as required of necessity to eternal salvation, but that you shall be persuaded may be concluded and proved by the same?

Answer. I am so persuaded and determined by God's grace.

The Archbishop. Will you then faithfully exercise yourself in the said holy Scriptures, and call upon God by prayer for the true understanding of the same, so as ye may be able by them to teach and exhort with wholesome doctrine, and to withstand and convince the gainsayers?

Answer. I will so do, by the help of God.

The Archbishop. Be you ready with all faithful diligence to banish and drive away all erroneous and strange doctrine contrary to God's word, and both privately and openly to call upon and encourage other to the same?

Answer. I am ready, the Lord being my helper.

The Archbishop. Will you deny all ungodliness, and worldly lusts, and live soberly, righteously, and Godly in this world, that you may shew yourself in all things an example of good works unto other, that the adversary may be ashamed, having nothing to lay against you?

Answer. I will so do, the Lord being my helper.

The Archbishop. Will you maintain and set forward (as much as shall lie in you) quietness, peace, and love, among all men? And such as be unquiet, disobedient, and criminous within your diocese, correct and punish, according to such authority, as ye have by God's word, and as to you shall be committed, by the ordinance of this realm?

Answer. I will so do, by the help of God.

The Archbishop. Will you shew yourself gentle, and be merciful for Christ's sake, to poor and needy people, and to all strangers destitute of help?

Answer. I will so shew myself by God's grace.

The Archbishop. Almighty God our heavenly Father, who hath given you a good will to do all these things, grant also unto you strength and power, to perform the same, that he accomplishing in you the good work which he hath begun, ye may be found perfect, and irreprehensible at the latter day, through Jesu Christ our Lord. Amen.

Then shall be sung or said, *Come Holy Ghost,* &c. as it is set out in the Order of Priests.

That ended, the Archbishop shall say,

The Lord be with you.
Answer. And with thy spirit.

THE ORDERING OF BISHOPS.

¶ Let us pray.

ALMIGHTY God and most merciful Father, which of thy infinite goodness, hast given to us thy only and most dear beloved Son Jesus Christ, to be our redeemer and author of everlasting life, who after that he had made perfect our redemption by his death, and was ascended into heaven, poured down his gifts abundantly upon men, making some Apostles, some Prophets, some Evangelists, some Pastors and Doctors, to the edifying and making perfect of his congregation: Grant, we beseech thee, to this thy servant such grace, that he may be evermore ready to spread abroad thy Gospel, and glad tidings of reconcilement to God, and to use the authority given unto him, not to destroy, but to save, not to hurt, but to help, so that he as a faithful and a wise servant, giving to thy family meat in due season, may at the last day be received into joy, through Jesu Christ our Lord, who with thee and the Holy Ghost liveth and reigneth one God, world without end Amen.

Then the Archbishop and Bishops present shall lay their hands upon the head of the elect Bishop, the Archbishop saying.

TAKE the Holy Ghost, and remember that thou stir up the grace of God, which is in thee, by imposition of hands: for God hath not given us the spirit of fear, but of power, and love, and of soberness.

Then the Archbishop shall lay the Bible upon his neck, saying.

GIVE heed unto reading, exhortation and doctrine, think upon those things contained in this book, be diligent in them, that the increase coming thereby may be manifest unto all men. Take heed unto thyself, and unto teaching, and be diligent in doing them, for by doing this thou shalt save thyself and them that hear thee, through Jesus Christ our Lord.

Then shall the Archbishop put into his hand the pastoral staff, saying:

BE to the flock of Christ a shepherd, not a wolf, feed them, devour them not, hold up the weak, heal the sick, bind together the broken, bring again the outcasts, seek the lost: Be so merciful, that you be not too remiss, so minister discipline, that ye forget not mercy, that when the chief Shepherd shall come, ye may receive the immarcessible Crown of glory, through Jesus Christ our Lord.

¶ Then the Archbishop shall proceed to the Communion, with whom the new consecrated Bishop shall also communicate. And after the last Collect, immediately afore the benediction, shall be said this prayer:

MOST merciful Father, we beseech thee to send down upon this thy Servant thy heavenly blessing, and so endue him with thy Holy Spirit, that he preaching thy word, may not only be earnest to reprove, beseech, and rebuke with all patience and Doctrine, but also may be to such as believe an wholesome example in word, in conversation, in love, in faith, in chastity, and purity, that faithfully fulfilling his course, at the latter day he may receive the crown of righteousness, laid up by the Lord, the righteous Judge, who liveth and reigneth, one God with the Father and Holy Ghost, world without end. Amen.

RICHARDVS GRAFTON
typographus Regius
excudebat.

Mense Martii
A.M.D.XLIX
Cum priuilegio ad imprimendum solum.

[The copy of this edition, which has been followed, is in the Archiepiscopal Library, Lambeth, MS. No. 885.]

THE BOOK OF COMMON PRAYER,

AND

ADMINISTRATION OF THE SACRAMENTS,

AND OTHER

RITES AND CEREMONIES

IN THE

CHURCH OF ENGLAND.

1552.

✠ The Boke of

common prayer, and ad-
miniſtracion of the
Sacramentes,
and other
rites
and Ceremonies in
the Churche of
Englande.

ℂ *Londini, in officina Ed-*
vvardi Whytchurche.

℃ Cum priuilegio ad ImPrimendum Solum.

Anno. 1552.

[The copy of this, the second edition of Whitchurch, which has been followed, is in the British Museum, 468. a. 7.]

The Boke of
common prayer, and ad=
miniſtracion of the
Sacramentes,
and other
rites
and Ceremonies in
the Churche of
Englande.

¶ *Londini, in officina Edo-*
vardi Whytchurche.

¶ Cum priuilegio ad ImPrimendum Solum.

Anno. 1552.

[*The colophon of this edition is as follows.*]

¶ Imprinted at London in Fleteſtrete at the Signe
of the Sunne ouer agaynſte the conduite by Edvvarde
Whitchurche.

M.D.L.II

Cum priuilegio ad imprimendum solum.

[The copy of this, the first edition of Whitchurch, which has been collated, is in the possession of Lea Wilson, Esq., Norwood, Surrey.]

The Boke of
common praier, and ad=
miniſtracion of the
Sacramentes,
and other
rites
and Cere=
monies in the
Churche
of
Englande.

Londini, in officina Ri-
chardi Graftoni:

Regij Impreſſoris.

Cum priuilegio ad impri-
mendum solum.

Anno. 1552.

[*The colophon of this edition is as follows.*]

RICHARDVS GRAF-
tonus, typographus Regius excudebat.

Menſe Auguſti.

Anno. Domini. 1552.

Cum priuilegio ad impri-
mendum ſolum.

[The copy of this, the first edition of Grafton, which has been also collated, is in the Archiepiscopal Library, Lambeth, xxiv. 5. 24.]

The Boke of
common praier, and ad-
miniftracion of the
Sacramentes,
and other
Rites
and Cere-
monies in the
Churche
of
Englande.

*Londini, in officina Richardi Graftoni:
Regij imprefforis.*

Cum priuilegio ad imprimendum solum.

Anno, 1552.

[*The colophon of this edition is as follows.*]

RICHARDVS GRAF-
tonus, *Typographus Regius excudebat.*
Menfe Augufti.
Anno Domini. 1552.
Cum Priuilegio ad Imprimendum solum.

[The copy of this, the second edition of Grafton, which has been also collated, is in the British Museum, 468. b. 6.]

THE CONTENTS OF THIS BOOK.

1. A PREFACE.
2. Of Ceremonies, why some be abolished, and some retained.
3. The order how the Psalter is appointed to be read.
4. The Table for the order of the Psalms to be said at Morning and Evening prayer.
5. The order how the rest of holy Scripture is appointed to be read.
6. Proper Psalms and Lessons at Morning and Evening Prayer, for certain feasts and days.
7. An Almanack.
8. The Table and Kalendar for Psalms and Lessons, with necessary Rules appertaining to the same.
9. The order for Morning prayer and Evening prayer, throughout the year.
10. The Litany.
11. The Collects, Epistles, and Gospels, to be used at the ministration of the holy Communion, throughout the year.
12. The order of the ministration of the holy Communion.
13. Baptism both public and private.
14. Confirmation, where also is a Catechism for children.
15. Matrimony.
16. Visitation of the sick.
17. The Communion of the sick.
18. Burial.
19. The Thanks giving of women after child birth.
20. A Commination against sinners, with certain prayers to be used divers times in the year.
21. The form and manner of making and consecrating of Bishops, Priests, and Deacons.

[1 "An Act for the Uniformity of Common Prayer," is the first article in the Contents of Grafton, 2; but the Act itself is given in the same order as in this copy: and in Grafton, 1, it is given at the end of the volume, after the Colophon.]

THE PREFACE.[2]

There was never any thing by the wit of man so well devised, or so sure established, which (in continuance of time) hath not been corrupted: as (among other things) it may plainly appear by the common prayers in the Church, commonly called divine service; the first original and ground whereof if a man would search out by the ancient fathers, he shall find that the same was not ordained but of a good purpose, and for a great advancement of godliness. For they so ordered the matter, that all the whole Bible (or the greatest part thereof) should be read over once in the year: intending thereby, that the Clergy, and specially such as were ministers of the congregation, should (by often reading and meditation of God's word) be stirred up to godliness themselves, and be more able also to exhort other by wholesome doctrine, and to confute them that were adversaries to the truth; and further, that the people (by daily hearing of holy scripture read in the Church) should continually profit more and more in the knowledge of God, and be the more inflamed with the love of his true religion. But these many years passed, this godly and decent order of the ancient fathers hath been so altered, broken, and neglected, by planting in uncertain stories[3], Legends, Responds, Verses, vain repetitions, Commemorations, and Synodals, that commonly when any book of the Bible was begun, before three or four chapters were read out, all the rest were unread. And in this sort the book of Esay was begun in Advent, and the book of Genesis in Septuagesima: but they were only begun, and never read through. After a like sort were other books of holy scripture used. And moreover, whereas saint Paul would have such language spoken to the people in the Church, as they might understand, and have profit

[2 In Whitchurch, 1. the Kalendar and Act for Uniformity are placed before the Preface; in this copy they are after the Almanack for nineteen years.]

[3 See note 2, page 17.]

[DOCUMENTS, EDW. VI.]

by hearing the same, the service in this Church of England (these many years) hath been read in Latin to the people, which they understood not: so that they have heard with their ears only, and their hearts, spirit, and mind, have not been edified thereby. And furthermore, notwithstanding that the ancient fathers have divided the Psalms into seven portions, whereof every one was called a Nocturn; now of late time, a few of them have been daily said (and oft repeated) and the rest utterly omitted. Moreover, the number and hardness of the rules, called the Pie[1], and the manifold changings of the service, was the cause, that to turn the book only was so hard and intricate a matter, that many times there was more business to find out what should be read, than to read it when it was found out.

These inconveniences therefore considered, here is set forth such an order, whereby the same shall be redressed. And for a readiness in this matter, here is drawn out a kalendar for that purpose, which is plain and easy to be understanden, wherein (so much as may be) the reading of holy scriptures is so set forth, that all things shall be done in order, without breaking one piece thereof from another. For this cause be cut off Anthems, Responds, Invitatories[2], and such like things, as did break the continual course of the reading of the scripture. Yet because there is no remedy, but that of necessity there must be some rules, therefore certain rules are here set forth, which as they be few in number, so they be plain and easy to be understanden. So that here you have an order for prayer (as touching the reading of holy scripture) much agreeable to the mind and purpose of the old fathers, and a great deal more profitable and commodious, than that which of late was used. It is more profitable, because here are left out many things, whereof some be untrue, some uncertain, some vain and superstitious, and is ordained nothing to be read, but the very pure word of God, the holy scriptures, or that which is evidently grounded upon the same, and that in such a language and order, as is most easy and plain for the understanding, both of the readers and hearers. It is also more commodious, both for the shortness thereof, and for

[[1] See note 1, page 18.]
[[2] See note 2, page 18.]

the plainness of the order, and for that the rules be few and easy. Furthermore, by this order, the curates shall need none other books for their public service, but this book, and the Bible: by the means whereof, the people shall not be at so great charge for books, as in time past they have been.

And where heretofore there hath been great diversity in saying and singing in Churches within this realm, some following Salisbury use, some Hereford use, some the use of Bangor, some of York, and some of Lincoln: Now from henceforth, all the whole realm shall have but one use. And if any would judge this way more painful, because that all things must be read upon the book, whereas before, by the reason of so often repetition, they could say many things by heart, if those men will weigh their labour with the profit and knowledge, which daily they shall obtain by reading upon the book, they will not refuse the pain, in consideration of the great profit that shall ensue thereof.

And forasmuch as nothing can almost be so plainly set forth, but doubts may rise in the use and practising of the same: To appease all such diversity (if any arise), and for the resolution of all doubts concerning the manner how to understand, do, and execute the things contained in this book; the parties that so doubt, or diversly take any thing, shall alway resort to the Bishop of the Diocese, who by his discretion shall take order for the quieting and appeasing of the same: so that the same order be not contrary to any thing contained in this book. And if the Bishop of the Diocese be in any doubt, then may he send for the resolution thereof unto the Archbishop.

Though it be appointed in the afore written Preface, that all things shall be read and sung in the Church in the English tongue, to the end that the congregation may be thereby edified; yet it is not meant, but when men say Morning and Evening prayer privately, they may say the same in any language that they themselves do understand.

And all Priests and Deacons shall be bound to say

daily the Morning and Evening prayer, either privately or openly, except they be letted by preaching, studying of divinity, or by some other urgent cause.

And the Curate that ministereth in every Parish Church or Chapel, being at home, and not being otherwise reasonably letted, shall say the same in the Parish Church or Chapel where he ministereth, and shall toll a bell thereto, a convenient time before he begin, that such as be disposed may come to hear God's word, and to pray with him.

OF CEREMONIES,

WHY SOME BE ABOLISHED, AND SOME RETAINED.

Of such ceremonies as be used in the church, and have had their beginning by the institution of man: some at the first were of Godly intent and purpose devised, and yet at length turned to vanity and superstition: some entered into the church by undiscreet devotion, and such a zeal as was without knowledge, and for because they were winked at in the beginning, they grew daily to more and more abuses; which not only for their unprofitableness, but also because they have much blinded the people, and obscured the glory of God, are worthy to be cut away, and clean rejected. Other there be, which although they have been devised by man, yet it is thought good to reserve them still, as well for a decent order in the church (for the which they were first devised) as because they pertain to edification; whereunto all things done in the church (as the Apostle teacheth) ought to be referred. And although the keeping or omitting of a ceremony (in itself considered) is but a small thing: yet the wilful and contemptuous transgression and breaking of a common order and discipline is no small offence before God.

Let all things be done among you (saith S. Paul) in a seemly and due order. The appointment of the which order pertaineth not to private men: therefore no man ought to take in hand, nor[1] presume to appoint or alter any public or common order in Christ's church, except he be lawfully called and authorized thereunto.

And whereas in this our time, the minds of men are so diverse, that some think it a great matter of conscience to depart from a piece of the least of their ceremonies (they be so addicted to their old customs:) and again on the other side, some be so new fangled, that they would innovate all thing, and so do despise the old, that nothing can like them, but that is new: it was thought expedient, not so much to have respect, how to please and satisfy either of these

[1 or presume, Grafton, 2.]

parties, as how to please God, and profit them both. And yet lest any man should be offended (whom good reason might satisfy) here be certain causes rendered, why some of the accustomed ceremonies be put away, and some retained and kept still.

Some are put away, because the great excess and multitude of them hath so increased in these latter days, that the burthen of them was intolerable; whereof S. Augustine in his time complained, that they were grown to such a number, that the state of Christian people was in worse case (concerning that matter) than were the Jews. And he counselled that such yoke and burthen should be taken away, as time would serve quietly to do it.

But what would S. Augustine have said, if he had seen the ceremonies of late days used among us? whereunto the multitude used in his time was not to be compared. This our excessive multitude of ceremonies was so great, and many of them so dark, that they did more confound, and darken, than declare and set forth Christ's benefits unto us.

And besides this, Christ's gospel is not a ceremonial law (as much of Moses' law was) but it is a religion to serve God, not in bondage of the figure or shadow, but in the freedom of spirit, being content only with those ceremonies, which do serve to a decent order and godly discipline, and such as be apt to stir up the dull mind of man, to the remembrance of his duty to God, by some notable and special signification, whereby he might be edified.

Furthermore, the most weighty cause of the abolishment of certain ceremonies was, that they were so far abused, partly by the superstitious blindness of the rude and unlearned, and partly by the unsatiable avarice of such as sought more their own lucre, than the glory of God; that the abuses could not well be taken away, the thing remaining still. But now as concerning those persons, which peradventure will be offended, for that some of the old ceremonies are retained still: if they consider that without some ceremonies it is not possible to keep any order or quiet discipline in the church, they shall easily perceive just cause to reform their judgments. And if they think much, that any of the old do remain, and would rather have all devised anew: Then such men granting some ceremonies convenient to be had, surely where

OF CEREMONIES.

the old may be well used, there they cannot reasonably reprove the old only for their age, without bewraying of their own folly. For in such a case, they ought rather to have reverence unto them for their antiquity, if they will declare themselves to be more studious of unity and concord, than of innovations and newfangleness, which (as much as may be with the true setting forth of Christ's Religion) is always to be eschewed. Furthermore, such shall have no just cause with the ceremonies reserved to be offended. For as those be taken away, which were most abused, and did burthen men's consciences without any cause: so the other that remain are retained for a discipline and order, which (upon just causes) may be altered and changed, and therefore are not to be esteemed equal with God's law. And moreover, they be neither dark nor dumb ceremonies; but are so set forth, that every man may understand what they do mean, and to what use they do serve. So that it is not like that they in time to come should be abused as the other have been. And in these our doings we condemn no other nations, nor prescribe any thing, but to our own people only. For we think it convenient that every country should use such ceremonies, as they shall think best to the setting forth of God's honour or glory, and to the reducing of the people to a most perfect and godly living, without error or superstition: and that they should put away other things, which from time to time they perceive to be most abused, as in men's ordinances it often chanceth diversely in diverse countries.

THE
TABLE AND KALENDAR,

EXPRESSING THE

ORDER OF THE PSALMS AND LESSONS,

TO BE SAID AT THE

MORNING AND EVENING PRAYER

THROUGHOUT THE YEAR,

EXCEPT CERTAIN PROPER FEASTS, AS THE RULES FOLLOWING MORE PLAINLY DECLARE.

¶ The order how the Psalter is appointed to be read.

THE Psalter shall be read through once every month. And because that some Months be longer than some other be, it is thought good to make them even by this means.

To every Month shall be appointed (as concerning this purpose) just xxx days.

And because January and March hath one day above the said number, and February, which is placed between them both, hath only xxviii days: February shall borrow of either of the Months (of January and March) one day. And so the Psalter which shall be read in February, must begin the last day of January, and end the first day of March.

And whereas May, July, August, October and December, have[1] xxxi days apiece: it is ordered that the same Psalms shall be read the last day of the said Months, which were read the day before. So that the Psalter may begin again the first day of the next Months[2] ensuing.

Now to know what Psalms shall be read every day, look in the Kalendar the number that is appointed for the Psalms, and then find the same number in this table, and upon that number shall you see, what Psalms shall be said at Morning and Evening Prayer.

And where the cxixth Psalm is divided into xxii portions, and is over long to be read at one time: it is so ordered,

[¹ hath, Grafton, 2.]   [² month, Grafton, 2.]

that at one time shall not be read above four or five of the said portions, as you shall perceive to be noted in this Table following.

And here is also to be noted, that in this table, and in all other parts of the Service, where any Psalms are appointed, the number is expressed after the great English Bible, which from the ixth Psalm unto the cxlviiith Psalm (following the division of the Hebrues) doth vary in numbers from the common Latin translation.

The Table for the Order of the Psalms, to be said at Morning and Evening prayer.

	¶ Morning Prayer.	¶ Evening Prayer.
i.	1, 2, 3, 4, 5.	6, 7, 8.
ii.	9, 10, 11.	12, 13, 14.
iii.	15, 16, 17.	18.
iv.	19, 20, 21.	22, 23.
v.	24, 25, 26.	27, 28, 29.
vi.	30, 31.	32, 33, 34.
vii.	35, 36.	37.
viii.	38, 39, 40.	41, 42, 43.
ix.	44, 45, 46.	47, 48, 49.
x.	50, 51, 52.	53, 54, 55.
xi.	56, 57, 58.	59, 60, 61.
xii.	62, 63, 64.	65, 66, 67.
xiii.	68.	69, 70.
xiv.	71, 72.	73, 74.
xv.	75, 76, 77.	78.
xvi.	79, 80, 81.	82, 83, 84, 85.
xvii.	86, 87, 88.	89.
xviii.	90, 91, 92.	93, 94.
xix.	96, 97.	98, 99, 100, 101.
xx.	102, 103.	104.
xxi.	105.	106.
xxii.	107.	108, 109.
xxiii.	110, 111, 112, 113.	114, 115.
xxiv.	116, 117, 118.	119, Inde. 4.
xxv.	Inde. 5.	Inde. 4.
xxvi.	Inde. 5.	Inde. 4.
xxvii.	120, 121, 122, 123, 124, 125.	126, 127, 128, 129, 130, 131.
xxviii.	132, 133, 134, 135.	136, 137, 138.
xxix.	139, 140, 141.	142, 143.
xxx.	144, 145, 146.	147, 148, 149, 150.

The Order how the rest of holy scripture (beside the Psalter) is appointed to be read.

The Old Testament is appointed for the first Lessons at Morning and Evening prayer, and shall be read through, every year once, except certain books and chapters, which be least edifying, and might best be spared, and therefore be left unread.

The New Testament is appointed for the second Lessons at Morning and Evening prayer, and shall be read over orderly every year thrice, beside the Epistles and Gospels: except the Apocalypse, out of the which there be only certain Lessons appointed, upon divers proper feasts.

And to know what Lessons shall be read every day: find the day of the Month in the Kalendar following: and there ye shall perceive the books and chapters, that shall be read for the Lessons, both at Morning and Evening prayer.

And here is to be noted, that whensoever there be any proper Psalms or[1] Lessons, appointed for any feast, moveable or unmoveable: then the Psalms and Lessons, appointed in the Kalendar, shall be omitted for that time.

Ye must note also that the Collect, Epistle, and Gospel, appointed for the Sunday, shall serve all the week after, except there fall some feast that hath his proper.

This is also to be noted, concerning the Leap years, that the xxvth day of February, which in Leap year is counted for two days, shall in those two days alter neither Psalm nor Lesson: but the same Psalms and Lessons, which be said the first day, shall also serve for the second day.

Also, wheresoever the beginning of any Lesson, Epistle, or Gospel is not expressed, there ye must begin at the beginning of the chapter.

And wheresoever is not expressed how far shall be read, there shall you read to the end of the chapter.

[[1] Psalms and Lessons, Grafton, 2.]

PROPER PSALMS AND LESSONS,

FOR DIVERS FEASTS AND DAYS, AT MORNING AND EVENING PRAYER.

On Christmas day at Morning prayer.

Psalms xix. xlv. lxxxv. The first Lesson. Esay. ix. The ii. Lesson. Luk. ii. *unto* And unto men a good will.

At Evening prayer.

Psalms lxxxix. cx. cxxxii. The first Lesson. Esa. vii. God spake once again to Achas. &c., *unto the end.* The second Lesson. Tit. iii. The kindness and love. &c. *unto* foolish questions.

On Saint Stephen's day, at Morning prayer.

The second Lesson. Acts. vi. and vii. Stephen full of faith and power, *unto* And when forty years were. &c.

At Evening prayer.

The second Lesson. Acts. vii. And when forty years were expired, there appeared unto Moses. &c. *unto* Stephen full of the Holy Ghost.

On Saint John the Evangelist's day, at Morning prayer.

The second Lesson. Apocalyps i. The whole Chapter.

At Evening prayer.

The second Lesson. Apocalyps. xxii.

On the Innocents' day, at Morning prayer.

The first Lesson. Jeremie. xxxi. *unto* Moreover I heard Ephraim.

On the Circumcision day, at Morning prayer.

The first Lesson. Genesis. xvii. The second Lesson. Roma. ii.

At Evening prayer.

The first Lesson. Deut. x. And now Israel. &c. The second Lesson. Colos. ii.

On the Epiphany, at Morning prayer.

The first Lesson. Esay. lx.
The second Lesson. Luke iii. And it fortuned, &c.

At Evening prayer.

The first Lesson. Esay. xlix. The second Lesson. John. ii. After this he went down to Capernaum.

On Wednesday before Easter, at Evening[1] prayer.
The first Lesson. Ozee. xiii. xiv.

On Thursday before Easter, at Morning[2] prayer.
The first Lesson. Daniel. ix.

At Evening prayer.
The first Lesson. Jeremie. xxxi.

On Good Friday, at Morning prayer.
The first Lesson. Genesis. xxii.

At Evening prayer.
The first Lesson. Esay. liii.

On Easter Even, at Morning prayer.
The first Lesson. Zachary. ix.

On Easter day, at Morning prayer.
Psalms ii. lvii. cxi. The first Lesson. Exodi. xii. The second Lesson. Ro. vi.

At Evening prayer.
Psalms cxiii. cxiv. cvxiii.[3] The second Lesson. Act. ii.

On Monday in Easter week, at Morning prayer.
The second Lesson. Math. xxviii.

At Evening prayer.
The second Lesson. Acts. iii.

On Tuesday in Easter week, at Morning prayer.
The second Lesson. Luke xxiv. *unto* And behold two of them.

At Evening prayer.
The second Lesson. 1 Corin. xv.

On the Ascension day, at Morning prayer.
Psalms viii. xv. xxi. The ii. Lesson. John. xiv.

At Evening prayer.
Psalms xxiv. lxviii. cviii. The ii. Lesson. Ephe. iv.

[1 Morning Prayer, Grafton, 2.]
[2 Evening Prayer, Grafton, 2.]
[3 Misprint in this copy for cxviii. as in the other copies.]

On Whitsunday, at Morning prayer.

Psalms xlviii. lxvii.[4] The second Lesson. Act. x. Then Peter opened his. &c.

At Evening prayer.

Psalms civ. cxlv. The second Lesson. Act. xix. It fortuned when Apollo went to Corinthum, &c. *unto* After these things.

¶ On Trinity Sunday, at Morning prayer.

The first Lesson. Gene. xviii. The second Lesson. Math. iii.

Conversion of Saint Paul, at Morning prayer.

The second Lesson. Acts. xxii. *unto* They heard him.

At Evening prayer.

The second Lesson. Acts. xxvi.

Saint Barnabie's day, at Morning prayer.

The second Lesson. Acts. xiv.

At Evening prayer.

The second Lesson. Acts. xv. *unto* After certain days.

St John Baptist's day, at Morning prayer.

The first Lesson. Malachi. iii. The second Lesson. Math. iii.

At Evening prayer.

The first Lesson. Malachi. iv. The second Lesson. Math. xiv. *unto* When Jesus heard.

Saint Peter's day, at Morning prayer.

The second Lesson. Acts. iii.

At Evening prayer.

The second Lesson. Acts. iv.

All Saints' day at Morning prayer.

The first Lesson. Sapien. iii. *unto* Blessed is rather the barren. The second Lesson. Hebr. xi. xii. Saints by faith subdued. *unto* If you endure chastising.

At Evening prayer.

The first Lesson. Sapience. v. *unto* His jealousy also. The second Lesson. Apocalyps xix. *unto* And I saw an angel stand.

[[4] Psalm xlvii. Whitchurch, 1, and Grafton, 1.]

An Almanack for Nineteen Years.

The year of our Lord.	The Golden Number.	The Epact.	The Cycle of the Sun.	Dominical letter.	Easter day.
1552	14	4	21	C. B.	17 April.
1553	15	15	22	A.	2 April.
1554	16	26	23	G.	25 March.
1555	17	7	24	F.	14 April.
1556	18	18	25	E. D.	5 April.
1557	19	29 [1]	26	C.	18 April.
1558	1	11	27	B.	10 April.
1559	2	22	28	A.	26 March.
1560	3	3	1	G. F.	14 April.
1561	4	14	2	E.	6 April.[2]
1562	5	25	3	D.	
1563	6	26	4	C.	
1564	7	17	5	B. A.	
1565	8	28	6	G.	
1566	9	9	7	F.	
1567	10	20	8	E.	
1568	11	1	9	D. C.	
1569	12	12	10	B.	
1570	13	23	11	A.	

[1 49 for 29, Grafton, 2, but the type is not quite clear.]
[2 This column is continued in Grafton, 2, to the year 1570, as follows: 22 March; 11 April; 3 April; 22 April; 7 April; 30 March; 8 March; 10 April; 26 March.]

JANUARY hath XXXI DAYS.

			Psalms.	MORNING PRAYER.		EVENING PRAYER.	
				1 *Less.*	2 *Less.*	1 *Less.*	2 *Less.*
3	A	Kalend. Circumcision.	1	Gene. 17	Roma. 2	Deut. 10	Colos. 2
	b	4 No.	2	Gene. 1	Math. 1	Gene. 2	Roma. 1
11	c	3 No.	3	3	2	4	2
	d	Prid. No.	4	5	3	6	3
19	e	Nonas.	5	7	4	8	4
8	f	8 Id. Epiphanie.	6	Esai. 60	Luke. 3	Esai. 49	John. 2
	g	7 Id.	7	Gen. 9	Math. 5	Gen. 11	Roma. 5
16	A	6 Id.	8	12	6	13	6
5	b	5 Id.	9	14	7	15	7
	c	4 Id.	10	16	8	17	8
13	d	3 Id. Sol in aqua.[1]	11	18	9	19	9
2	e	Prid. Id.	12	20	10	21	10
	f	Idus.	13	22	11	23	11
10	g	19 kl. Februarii.	14	24	12	25	12
	A	18 kl.	15	26	13	27	13
18	b	17 kl. Term begi.	16	28	14	29	14
7	c	16 kl.	17	30	15	31	15
	d	15 kl.	18	32	16	33	16
15	e	14 kl.	19	34	17	35	1 Cor. 1
4	f	13 kl.	20	36	18	37	2
12	A	12 kl.	21	39	19	39	3
1	b	11 kl.	22	40	20	41	4
	c	10 kl.	23	42	21	43	5
9	d	9 kl.	24	44	22	45	6
	e	8 kl. Con. Paul.	25	46	Act. 22	47	Acts.26
17	f	7 kl.	26	48	Math. 23	49	1 Corin.7
6	g	6 kl.	27	50	24	Exod. 1	8
	A	5 kl.	28	Exod. 2	25	3	9
14	b	4 kl.	29	4	26	5	10
3	c	3 kl.	30	6	27	7	11
		Prid. kl.	1	8	28	9	12

[10 d. 3 Id. Sol. i aqua, Whitchurch, 1; but 10 is a misprint. In this Kalendar we notice not, because unimportant, the slight abbreviations of some of the words, which are various in the different copies : for example, Whitchurch, 1, has February and Genesis, where Whitchurch, 2, has Februarii and Gene.]

207

FEBRUARY hath XXVIII DAYS.

			Psalms.	MORNING PRAYER.		EVENING PRAYER.	
				1 *Less.*	2 *Less.*	1 *Less.*	2 *Less.*
11	d	Kalend.	2	Exodi. 10	Mark. 1	Exodi. 11	Cor. 13
	e	4 No.[2] Puri. Mary.	3	12	2	13	14
19	f	3 No.	4	14	3	15	15
8	g	Prid. No.	5	16	4	17	16
	A	Nonas.	6	18	5	19	2Corin.1
16	b	8 Id.	7	20	6	21	2
5	c	7 Id.	8	22	7	23	3
	d	6 Id.	9	24	8	32	4
13	e	5 Id.	10	33	9	34	5
2	f	4 Id. Sol in Pisces.	11	35	10	40	6
10	A	3 Id.	12	Lev. 18	11	Lev. 19	7
	A	Prid. Id.[3]	13	20	12	Num.10	8
	b	Idus.	14	Nume. 11	13	12	9
18	c	16 kl. March.	15	13	14	14	10
7	d	15 kl.	16	15	15	16	11
	e	14 kl.	17	17	16	18	12
15	f	13 kl.	18	19	Luk. di. 1	20	13
4	g	12 kl.	19	21	di. 1	22	Galath.1
	A	11 kl.	20	23	2	24	2
12	b	10 kl.	21	25	3	26	
1	c	9 kl.	22	27	4	28	4
	d	8 kl.	23	29	5	30	5
9	e	7 kl.	24	31	6	32	6
	f	6 kl. S. Mathias.	25	33	7	34	Ephesi.1
17	g	5 kl.	26	35	8	36	2
6	A	4 kl.	27	Deut. 1	9	Deut. 2	3
	b	3 kl.	28	3	10	4	4
14	c	Prid. kl.	29	5	11	6	5

[[2] No. omitted by Grafton, 2, and the red letter slightly displaced.]
[[3] 10 A Prid. Id. Terme ende, Grafton, 2.]

MARCH HATH XXXI DAYS.

			Psalms.	MORNING PRAYER.		EVENING PRAYER.	
				1 Less.	2 Less.	1 Less.	2 Less.
3	d	Kalend.	30	Deu. 7	Luk. 12	Deu. 8	Ephe. 6
	e	6 No.	1	9	13	10	Philip. 1
11	f	5 No.	2	11	14	12	2
	g	4 No.	3	13	15	14	3
19	A	3 No.	4	15	16	16	4
8	b	Prid. No.	5	17	17	18	Colos. 1
	c	Nonas.	6	19	18	20	2
16	d	8 Id.	7	21	19	22	3
5	e	7 Id.	8	23	20	24	4
	f	6 Id.	9	25	21	26	1 Thessa. 1
13	g	5 Id. Equinoctium.	10	27	22	28	2
2	A	4 Id. Sol in ariete.	11	29	23	30	3
	b	3 Id.	12	31	24	32	4
10	c	Prid. Id.	13	33	John. 1	34	5
	d	Idus.	14	Josue. 1	2	Josue. 2	2 Thessa. 1
18	e	17 kl. Aprilis.	15	3	3	4	2
7	f	16 kl.	16	4	4	5	3
	g	15 kl.	17	5	5	6	1 Timo. 1
15	A	14 kl.	18	6	6	7	2, 3
4	b	13 kl.	19	7	7	8	4
	c	12 kl.	20	8	8	9	5
12	d	11 kl.	21	9	9	10	6
1	e	10 kl.	22	10	10	11	2 Timo. 1
	f	9 kl.	23	12	11	20	2
9	g	8 kl. Annunciation.	24	21	12	22	3
	A	7 kl.	25	23	13	24	4
17	b	6 kl.	26	Judic. 1	14	Judic. 2	Titus. 1
6	c	5 kl.	27	3	15	4	2, 3
	d	4 kl.	28	5	16	6	Philem. 1
14	e	3 kl.	29	7	17	8	Hebre. 1
3	f	Prid. kl.	30	9	18	10	2

[¹ In Whitchurch, 1, there is a variation from the other copies, the numeral 8 being not black letter, but Roman. This occurs in a few other places.]

APRIL HATH XXX DAYS.

			Psalms.	MORNING PRAYER.		EVENING PRAYER.	
				1 Less.	2 Less.	1 Less.	2 Less.
11	g	Kalend.	1	Judic. 11	John. 19	Judi. 12	Hebre. 3
	A	4 No.	2	13	20	14	4
	b	3 No.	3	15	21	16	5
19	c	Prid. No.	4	17	Actes. 1	18	6
8	d	Nonas.	5	19	2	20	7
16	e	8 Id.	6	21	3	Ruth. 1	8
5	f	7 Id.	7	Ruth. 2	4	3	9
	g	6 Id.	8	4	5	2 Regum. 2	10
13	A	5 Id.	9	1 Regum. 2	6	5	11
2	b	4 Id.	10	4	7	7	12
	c	3 Id.	11	6	8	9	13
10	d	Prid. Id. Sol. in tauro.	12	8	9	11	Jacobi. 1
	e	Idus.	13	10	10	13	2
18	f	18 kl. Maii.	14	12	11	15	3
7	g	17 kl.	15	14	12	17	4
15	A	16 kl.	16	16	13	19	1 Petri. 1
4	b	15 kl.	17	18	14	21	2
	c	14 kl.	18	20	15	23	3
12	d	13 kl.	19	22	16	25	4
1	e	12 kl.	20	24	17	27	5
	f	11 kl.	21	26	18	29	2 Petri. 1
9	A	10 kl.	22	28	19	31	2
	b	9 kl. S. George.	23	30	20	1 Reg. 2	3
17	c	8 kl.	24	2 Reg. 1	21	4	1 John. 1
6	d	7 kl. Mark Euan.	25	3	22	6	2
	e	6 kl.	26	5	23	8	3
14	f	5 kl.	27	7	24	10	4
3	g	4 kl.	28	9	25	12	5
	A	3 kl.	29	11	26	14	2, 3 Joh.
		Prid. kl.	30	13	27		

209

MAY HATH XXXI DAYS.

Psalms.				MORNING PRAYER.		EVENING PRAYER.	
				1 Less.	2 Less.	1 Less.	2 Less.
11	b		Kalend. Philip & Ja.	1		2 Re. 16	Judas.1
	c		6 No.	2 Re. 15	Act. 8	18	Roma.1
19	d		5 No.	17	28	20	2
8	e		4 No.	19	Math. 1	22	3
	f		3 No.	21	2	24	4
16	g		Prid. No.	23	3		5
5	A		Nonas.	3 Regum.1	4	3 Reg. 1	6
	b		8 Id.	2	5	2	7
13	c		7 Id.	3	6	4	8
2	d		6 Id.	5	7	9	9
	e		5 Id. Sol in Ge	9	8	10	10
10	f		4 Id.	11	9	12	11
	g		3 Id.	13	10	14	12
18	A		Prid. Id.	15	11	16	13
7	b		Idus.	17	12	18	14
	c		17 kl. Junii,	19	13	20	15
15	d		16 kl.	21	14	22	16
4	e		15 kl.	4 Re. 1	15	4 Re. 2	1 Cor.1
	f		14 kl.	3	16	6	2
12	g		13 kl.	5	17	8	3
1	A		12 kl.	7	18	10	4
	b		11 kl.	9	19	12	5
9	c		10 kl.	11	20	14	6
	d		9 kl.	13	21	16	7
17	e		8 kl.	15	22	18	8
6	f		7 kl.	17	23	20	9
	g		6 kl.	19	24	22	10
14	A		5 kl.	21	25	24	11
3	b		4 kl.	23	26	25	12
	c		3 kl.	25	27	1 Esdr. 2	13
11	d		Prid. kl.	[2] 30	28	4	14
				3	Mark. 1		

[1 7 b dus. Grafton, 2. The I omitted.]
[2 Some one has written 1 after 30 in Whitchurch, 1.]

JUNE HATH XXXI[1] DAYS.

Psalms.				MORNING PRAYER.		EVENING PRAYER.	
				1 Less.	2 Less.	1 Less.	2 Less.
19	e		Kalend.	1	Mark.2	1 Esdr. 5	1 Cor. 15
8	f		4 No.	2	3	6	16
	g		3 No.	3	4	7	2 Corin.1
16	A		Prid. No.	4	5	8	2
5	b		Nonas.	5	6	10	3
	c		8 Id.	6 2 Esdr. 1	7	3	4
13	d		7 Id.[2]	4	8	5	5
2	e		6 Id.	6	9	8	6
	f		5 Id.	9	10	13	7
10	g		4 Id.[3]	10 Hester.1	11	Hester. 2	8
	A		3 Id.	11	Act. 14	4	Acts. 15
18	b		Prid. Id.	12 5	Mar. 12	6	2 Corin.9
7	c		Idus. Sol in can.	13	13	8	10
	d		18 kl. Julii.	14 9	14	Job. 1	11
15	e		17 kl.	15 Job. 2	15	3	12
4	f		16 kl.	16 4	16	5	13
	g		15 kl. Term begin.	17 6	Luke. 1	7	Galat. 1
12	A		14 kl.	18 8	2	9	2
1	b		13 kl.	19 10	3	11	3
	c		12 kl.	20 12	4	13	4
9	d		11 kl.	21 14	5	15	5
	e		10 kl.	22 16	6	17, 18	
17	f		9 kl.	23 19	7	20	Ephesi.1
6	g		8 kl. John Baptist.	24 Mal. 3	Math. 3	Mal. 4	Math. 14
	A		7 kl.	25 Job. 21	Luke. 8	Job. 22[4]	Ephesi.2
14	b		6 kl.	26 23	9	24. 25	3
3	c		5 kl.	27 26. 27	10	28	4
	d		4 kl.	28 29	11	30	5
11	e		3 kl. S. Peter ap.	29 31	Acts. 3	32	Acts. 4
	f		Prid. kl.	30 33	Luke. 12	34	Ephesi.6

[1 Misprint for XXX., as in the other copies.]
[2 4 d 7 Id. Whitchurch, 1.] [3 A 3 Id. Barnabe. Ap. Grafton, 2.]
[4 22 and 25,-not in black letter, but Rouan, Whitchurch, 1.]

[DOCUMENTS, EDW. VI.]

JULY HATH XXXI DAYS.

				Psalms.	1 Less.	2 Less.	1 Less.	2 Less.
						MORNING PRAYER.	EVENING PRAYER.	
19	g		Kalend.	1	Job 35	Luk. 13	Job 36[1]	Philip. 1
8	A	6 No.		2	37	14	38	2
	b	5 No.		3	39	15	40	3
16	c	4 No.		4	41	16	42	4
5	d	3 No.	Prid. No. Term end.	5	Prouer.1	17	Prouer.2	Collos. 1
	e	Prid. No.	Dog days.	6	4	18	4	2
13	f	Nonas.		7	5	19	6	3
2	g	8 Id.		8	7	20	8	
	A	7 Id.		9	9	21	10	1 Thes. 1
10	b	6 Id.		10	11	22	12	2
	c	5 Id.		11	13	23	14	3
18	d	4 Id.		12	15	24	16	4
7	e	3 Id.		13	17	John. 1	18	5
	f	Prid. Id.	Sol in Leo.	14	19	2	20	2 Thes. 1
15	g	Idus.		15	21	3	22	2
4	A	17 kl.	Augustii.	16	23	4	24	1 Timo.1
	b	16 kl.		17	25	5	26	2. 3
12	c	15 kl.		18	27	6	28	4
1	d	14 kl.		19	29	7	30	5
	e	13 kl.		20	31	8	Eccle. 1	6
9	f	12 kl.		21	Eccles. 2	9	3	2 Timo.1
	g	11 kl.		22	4	10	5	2
17	A	10 kl.		23	6	11	7	3
6	b	9 kl.		24	8	12	9	4
	c	8 kl.	James apo.	25	10	13	11	Titus. 1
14	d	7 kl.		26	12	14	Jerem. 1	2. 3
3	e	6 kl.		27	Jerem. 2	15	3	Phile. 1
	f	5 kl.		28	4	16	5	Hebre. 1
11	A	4 kl.		29	6	17	7	2
	A	3 kl.		30	8	18	9	3
19	b	Prid. kl.		2 30	10	19	11	

[1 36 not in black letter, but Roman, Whitchurch, 1.]
[2 Some one has written 1 after 30, in Grafton, 1.]

AUGUST HATH XXXI DAYS.

				Psalms.	1 Less.	2 Less.	1 Less.	2 Less.
						MORNING PRAYER.	EVENING PRAYER.	
8	c	Kalend.	Lammas.	1	Jere. 12	John. 20	Jere. 13	Hebr. 4
16	d	4 No.		2	14	21	15	5
5	e	3 No.		3	16	Actes. 1	17	6
	f	Prid. No.		4	18	2	19	7
13	g	Nonas.		5	20	3	21	8
2	A	8 Id.		6	22	4	23	9
	b	7 Id.		7	24	5	25	10
10	c	6 Id.		8	26	6	27	11
	d	5 Id.		9	28	7	29	12
18	e	4 Id.	S. Laurence.	10	30	8	31	13
7	f	3 Id.		11	32	9	33	Jacobi.1
	g	Prid. Id.		12	34	10	35	2
15	A	Idus.		13	36	11	37	3
4	b	19 kl.	Septembris.	14	38	12	39	4
	c	18 kl.	Sol in virgo.	15	40	13	41	5
12	d	17 kl.		16	42	14	43	1 Peter.1
1	e	16 kl.		17	44	15	45. 46	2
	f	15 kl.		18	47	16	48	3
9	g	14 kl.		19	49	17	50	4
	A	13 kl.		20	51	18	52	5
17	b	12 kl.		21	Lamen.1	19	Lamen. 2	2Peter. 1
6	c	11 kl.		22	3	20	4	2
	d	10 kl.		23	5	21	Ezech. 2	3
14	e	9 kl.	Bartho. apo.	24	Ezech. 3	22	6	1 John.1
3	f	8 kl.		25	7	23	13	2
	g	7 kl.		26	14	24	18	3
11	A	6 kl.		27	33	25	34	4
	b	5 kl.		28	Daniel.1	26	Danie. 2	5
19	c	4 kl.		29	3	27	4	2. 3 Joh.
8	d	3 kl.		30	5	28	6	Jude 1
	e	Prid. kl.			7	Math. 1	8	Roma. 1

SEPTEMBER HATH XXX DAYS.

			MORNING PRAYER.		EVENING PRAYER.	
		Psalms.	1 Less.	2 Less.	1 Less.	2 Less.
16	f	Kalend.	1 Danie. 9	Math. 2	Danie.10	Roma. 2
5	g	4 No.	2	11	3	12	3
	A	3 No.	3	13	4	14	4
13	b	Prid. No.	4 Ozee. 1	5	Oze.2.3[1]	5
2	c	Nonas. Dog days end.	5	6	5, 6	6
	d	8 Id.	6	7	8	7
10	e	7 Id.	7	9	10	8
	f	6 Id.	8	11	12	9
18	A	5 Id.	9 Joel. 1	13	14	10
7	b	4 Id.	10	3	Joel. 2	11
	c	3 Id.	11 Amos. 2	11	Amos. 1	12
15	d	Prid. Id.	12	13	3	13
4	e	Idus.	13	14	5	14
12	f	18 kl. Octobris.	14 Amos. 4	15	7	15
1	g	17 kl. Sol in Libra.	15	6	16	9	16
	A	16 kl.	16 Abdias. 1	17	Jonas. 1	1 Corin.1
9	b	15 kl.	17 Joh.[2]2.3	18	4	2
	c	14 kl.	18 Miche. 1	19	Miche. 2	3
17	d	13 kl.	19	3	20	4	4
6	e	12 kl.[3]	20	5	21	6	5
	f	11 kl. S. Mathew.	21	7	22	Naum.1	6
14	g	10 kl.	22 Naum. 2	23	3	7
3	A	9 kl.[4]	23 Abacu. 1	24	Abacu. 2	8
	b	8 kl.	24	3	25	Soph. 1	9
11	c	7 kl.	25 Soph. 2	26	3	10
	d	6 kl.	26 Agge. 1	27	Agge. 2	11
19	e	5 kl.	27 Zacha. 1	28	Zac. 2. 3	12
8	f	4 kl.	28	4. 5	Mark. 1	8	13
	g	3 kl. S. Michael.	29	7	2	10	14
16		Prid. kl.	30	9	3		15

[1] 2 and 3, not black letter, but Roman, in Whitchurch, 1.]
[2] misprint for Jon.]
[3] 13 g 9 kl. Grafton, 2.]
[4] 16 d 12 kl. Grafton, 2.]

OCTOBER HATH XXXI DAYS.

			MORNING PRAYER.		EVENING PRAYER.	
		Psalms.	1 Less.	2 Less.	1 Less.	2 Less.
16	A	Kalend.	1 Zacha.11	Mar. 4	Zach. 12	1 Cori.16
5	b	6 No.	2	13	5	14	2 Corin.1
13	c	5 No.	3 Malac. 1	6	Mala. 2	2
2	d	4 No.	4	3	7	4	3
	e	3 No.	5 Tobi. 1	8	Tobi. 2	4
10	f	Prid. No.	6	3	9	4	5
	g	Nonas.	7	5	10	6	6
18	A	8 Id.	8	7	11	8	7
7	b	7 Id. Term begin.	9	9	12	10	8
	c	6 Id.	10	11	13	12	9
15	d	5 Id.	11	13	14	14	10
4	e	4 Id.	12 Judith.1	15	Judit. 2	11
	f	3 Id.	13	3	16	4	12
12	g	Prid. Id. Sol in scor.	14	5	Luke.di.6	6	13
	A	Idus.[1]	15	7	di. 1	8	Galat. 1
	b	17 kl. Nouembris.	16	9	2	10	2
9	c	16 kl.	17	11	3	12	3
	d	15 kl. Luke Euan.	18	13	4	14	4
17	e	14 kl.	19	15	5	16	5
6	f	13 kl.	20 Sapie. 1	6	Sapi. 2	6
14	A	11 kl.	21	3	5	4	Ephes. 1
3	b	10 kl.	22	5	7	6	2
	c	9 kl.	23	7	9	8	3
11	d	8 kl.	24	9	11	10	4
	e	7 kl.	25	11	13	12	5
19	f	6 kl.	26	13	15	14	6
8	g	5 kl. Simon. & Jude.	27	15	17	16	Philip. 1
	A	4 kl.	28	17	19	18	2
16	b	3 kl.	29 Eccles. 2	Eccles. 1	3
5	c	Prid. kl.	30				4	Colossi.1

[1 A Idus, in the other copies.]

NOVEMBER hath XXX DAYS.

			Psalms.	1 Less.	2 Less.	1 Less.	2 Less.
						MORNING PRAYER.	EVENING PRAYER.
13	d	Kalend. All Saints.	1	Sap. 3	He.11.12	Sap. 5	Apoc. 19
2	e	4 No.	2	Eccle. 6	Lu. 18	Eccle. 7	Colos. 2
	f	3 No.	3	8	19	9	3
10	g	Prid. No.	4	10	20	11	1 Thess.1
	A	Nonas.	5	12	21	13	2
18	b	8 Id.	6	14	22	15	3
7	c	7 Id.	7	16	23	17	4
	d	6 Id.	8	18	24	19	5
15	e	5 Id.	9	20	John. 1	21	2 Thess. 1
4	f	4 Id.	10	22	2	23	2
	A	3 Id.	11	24	3	25	3
12	b	Prid. Id.	12	26	4	27	1 Timo.1
1	c	Idus. Sol in Sa.	13	28	5	29	2, 3
	d	18 kl. Decembre.	14	30	6	31	4
9	e	17 kl.	15	32	7	33	5
	f	16 kl.	16	34	8	35	6
17	g	15 kl.	17	36	9	37	2 Timo.1
6	A	14 kl.	18	38	10	39	2
	b	13 kl.	19	40	11	41	3
14	c	12 kl.	20	42	12	43	4
3	d	11 kl.	21	44	13	45	Titus. 1
	e	10 kl.	22	46	14	47	2, 3
11	f	9 kl. S. Clement.	23	48	15	49	Phile. 1
	g	7 kl.[2]	24	50	16	51	Hebre. 1
19	A	6 kl.	25	Baruc. 1	17	Baruc. 2	2
8	b	5 kl.	26	3	18	4	3
	c	4 kl. Term end.	27	5	19	6	4
16	d	3 kl.	28	Esai. 1	20	Esai. 2	5
5	e	Prid. kl. Andrew ap.	29	3	21	4	6
			30	5	Actes. 1	6	

[[1] f 8 kl.; Grafton, 2, the 11 omitted.]
[[2] 19 g 7 kl. Grafton, 2; the 19 transposed from the next line below.]

212

DECEMBER hath XXXI DAYS.

			Psalms.	1 Less.	2 Less.	1 Less.	2 Less.
						MORNING PRAYER.	EVENING PRAYER.
	f	Kalend.	1	Esai. 7	Actes. 2	Esai. 8	Hebr. 7
13	g	4 No.	2	9	3	10	8
2	f	3 No.	3	11	4	12	9
10	b	Prid. No.	4	13	5	14	10
	c	Nonas.	5	15	6	16	11
18	d	8 Id.	6	17	6. 7	18	12
7	e	7 Id.	7	19	6. 7	20, 21	13
	f	6 Id.	8	22	8	23	Jacob. 1
15	g	5 Id.	9	24	9	25	2
4	A	4 Id.	10	26	10	27	3
	b	3 Id.	11	28	11	29	4
12	c	Prid. Id. Sol in[1] Sa.	12	30	12	31	5
1	d	Idus.	13	32	13	33	1 Pet. 1
	e	19 kl. Januarii.	14	34	14	35	2
9	f	18 kl.	15	36	15	37	3
	g	17 kl.	16	38	16	39	4
17	A	16 kl.	17	40	17	41	5
6	b	15 kl.	18	42	18	43	2 Pet. 1
	c	14 kl.	19	44	19	45	2
14	d	13 kl.	20	46	20	47	3
3	e	12 kl. Thomas apo.	21	48	21	49	1 John 1
	f	11 kl.	22	50	22	51	2
11	g	10 kl.	23	52	23	53	3
	A	9 kl.	24	54	24	55	4
19	b	8 kl. Christmas.	25	Esai. 9	Luk. 22	Esai. 7	Titus. 3[2]
8	c	7 kl. S. Stephen.	26	56	Act. 6. 7	57	Act. 1
	d	6 kl. S. John.	27	58	Apoca.1	59	Apoc. 22
16	e	5 kl. Innocentes.	28	Jer. 31	Act. 25	60	1 John. 5
5	f	4 kl.	29	Esai. 61	26	62	2 John. 1
	g	3 kl.	30	63	27	64	3 John. 1
13	A	Prid. kl.		65	28	66 [3]	Jude. 1

[[1] For Ca. or Capr. as in the other copies, but variously abbreviated.]
[[2] 3, not in black letter, but Roman, Whitchurch, 1.] [[3] 65, Grafton, 2.]

[1]AN ACT FOR THE
UNIFORMITY OF COMMON PRAYER,
AND
ADMINISTRATION OF THE SACRAMENTS.

WHERE there hath been a very Godly order set forth by authority of Parliament, for common prayer and administration of the Sacraments, to be used in the mother tongue within this Church of England, agreeable to the word of God, and the primitive Church, very comfortable to all good people, desiring to live in Christian conversation, and most profitable to the state of this realm; upon the which the mercy, favour, and blessing of Almighty God is in no wise so readily and plenteously poured, as by common prayers, due using of the Sacraments, and often preaching of the Gospel, with the devotion of the hearers: And yet this notwithstanding, a great number of people, in divers parts of this realm, following their own sensuality, and living either without knowledge or due fear of God, do wilfully, and damnably before Almighty God, abstain and refuse to come to their parish Churches and other places, where common prayer, administration of the Sacraments, and preaching of the word of God is used, upon the Sundays and other days, ordained to be holy days.

For reformation hereof, be it enacted by the King our sovereign Lord, with the assent of the Lords and commons, in this present Parliament assembled, and by the authority of the same, that from, and after the feast of All Saints next coming, all and every person, and persons, inhabiting within this realm, or any other the King's majesty's dominions, shall diligently and faithfully (having no lawful or reasonable excuse to be absent) endeavour themselves to resort to their Parish Church, or Chapel accustomed, or upon reasonable let thereof, to some usual place, where common prayer and such service of God shall be used in such time of let, upon every

[1 This Act is inserted after the colophon in Grafton, 1.]

Sunday, and other days, ordained, and used to be kept as holy days, and then, and there to abide, orderly and soberly, during the time of the common prayer, preachings, or other service of God, there to be used and ministered, upon pain of punishment by the censures of the Church.

And for the due execution hereof, the King's most excellent majesty, the lords temporal, and all the commons in this present Parliament assembled, doth in God's name earnestly require and charge all the Archbishops, Bishops, and other Ordinaries, that they shall endeavour themselves to the uttermost[1] of their knowledges, that the due and true execution hereof may be had throughout their dioceses and charges, as they will answer before God, for such evils and plagues, wherewith Almighty God may justly punish his people, for neglecting this good and wholesome law.

And for their authority in this behalf, be it further likewise enacted by the authority aforesaid, that all and singular the same Archbishops, Bishops, and all other their officers, exercising Ecclesiastical jurisdiction, as well in place exempt, as not exempt, within their dioceses, shall have full power and authority by this act, to reform, correct, and punish, by censures of the Church, all and singular persons which shall offend within any their jurisdictions or dioceses, after the said feast of All Saints next coming, against this act and statute, any other law, statute, privilege, liberty, or provision heretofore made, had, or suffered, to the contrary notwithstanding.

And because there hath arisen in the use and exercise of the foresaid common service in the Church heretofore set forth, divers doubts for the fashion and manner of the ministration of the same, rather by the curiosity of the minister and mistakers, than of any other worthy cause: therefore as well for the more plain and manifest explanation hereof, as for the more perfection of the said order of common service, in some places where it is necessary to make the same prayer and fashion of service more earnest and fit to stir christian people to the true honouring of Almighty God: The king's most excellent majesty, with the assent of the lords and commons in this present Parliament assembled, and by the authority of the same, hath caused the

[1 outermost, Grafton, 2.]

foresaid order of common service, entitled, *The book of common prayer*, to be faithfully and godly perused, explained, and made fully perfect: and by the foresaid authority, hath annexed and joined it, so explained and perfected, to this present statute, adding also a form and manner of making and consecrating of Archbishops, Bishops, Priests, and Deacons, to be of like force, authority, and value, as the same like foresaid book, entitled, *The book of common prayer*, was before: and to be accepted, received, used and esteemed in like sort and manner, and with the same clauses of provisions and exceptions, to all intents, constructions and purposes, as by the act of Parliament made in the second year of the King's majesty's reign was ordained, limited, expressed, and appointed for the uniformity of service, and administration of the Sacraments throughout the realm, upon such several pains, as in the said act of Parliament is expressed. And the said former act to stand in full force and strength, to all intents and constructions, and to be applied, practised, and put in use, to, and for the establishing the book of common prayer, now explained and hereunto annexed: and also the said form of making of Archbishops, Bishops, Priests, and Deacons, hereunto annexed, as it was for the former book.

And by the authority aforesaid it is now further enacted, that if any manner of person, or persons, inhabiting, and being within this realm, or any other the King's majesty's dominions, shall after the said feast of All Saints, willingly, and wittingly, hear, and be present at any other manner, or form of common prayer, of administration of the Sacraments, of making of ministers in the Churches, or of any other rites contained in the book annexed to this act, than is mentioned and set forth in the said book, or that is contrary to the form of sundry provisions and exceptions, contained in the foresaid former statute, and shall be thereof convicted, according to the laws of this realm, before the Justices of Assize, Justices of Oyer, and Determiner, Justices of peace in their Sessions, or any of them, by the verdict of twelve men, or by his, or their own confession, or otherwise, shall for the first offence suffer imprisonment, for six months, without bail, or mainprise: and for the second offence, being likewise convicted, (as is above said,) imprisonment for one whole year: and for the third offence, in like manner, imprisonment during his, or their lives. And for the more knowledge to be given hereof, and better observation of this law: Be it enacted by the authority aforesaid, that all and singular Curates shall upon one Sunday every quarter of the year, during one whole year, next following the foresaid feast of All Saints, next coming, read this present Act in the Church, at the time of the most assembly: and likewise once in every year following, at the same time, declaring unto the people by the authority of the Scripture, how the mercy and goodness of God hath in all ages been shewed to his people, in their necessities and extremities, by means of hearty and faithful prayers made to Almighty God, specially[1] where people be gathered together with one faith and mind, to offer up their hearts by prayer, as the best sacrifices that Christian men can yield.

[1 especially, Grafton, 2.]

THE ORDER

WHERE

MORNING AND EVENING PRAYER

SHALL BE USED AND SAID.

¶ The morning and evening prayer shall be used in such place of the Church, Chapel or Chancel, and the Minister shall so turn him, as the people may best hear. And if there be any controversy therein, the matter shall be referred to the ordinary, and he or his deputy shall appoint the place, and the chancels shall remain, as they have done in times past.

And here is to be noted, that the Minister at the time of the communion, and at all other times in his ministration, shall use neither Alb, Vestment, nor Cope: but being Archbishop, or Bishop, he shall have and wear a rochet: and being a priest or Deacon, he shall have and wear a surplice only.

AN

ORDER FOR MORNING PRAYER

DAILY THROUGHOUT THE YEAR.

At the beginning both of morning prayer, and likewise of evening prayer, the Minister shall read with a loud voice some one of these sentences of the scriptures that follow. And then he shall say that, which is written after the said sentences.

AT what time soever a sinner doth repent him of his sin Ezechie.xviii. from the bottom of his heart: I will put all his wickedness out of my remembrance, saith the Lord.

I do know mine own wickedness, and my sin is alway[2] Psalm. li. against me.

Turn thy face away from our sins (O Lord) and blot Psalm. li. out all our offences.

A sorrowful spirit is a sacrifice to God: despise not Psalm. li. (O Lord) humble and contrite hearts.

Rent[3] your hearts, and not your garments, and turn to Joel ii.

[2 always, Grafton, 2.]   [3 Rend, Grafton, 2.]

the Lord your God: because he is gentle and merciful, he is patient and of much mercy, and such a one that is sorry for your afflictions.

<small>Danie. ix.</small> To thee, O Lord God, belongeth mercy and forgiveness: for we have gone away from thee, and have not hearkened to thy voice, whereby we might walk in thy laws, which thou hast appointed for us.

<small>Jerem. ii.</small> Correct us, O Lord, and yet in thy judgment, not in thy fury, lest we should be consumed and brought to nothing.

<small>Math. iii.</small> Amend your lives, for the kingdom of God is at hand.

<small>Luke xv.</small> I will go to my father and say to him: Father, I have sinned against heaven, and against thee, I am no more worthy to be called thy son.

<small>Psa. cxlii.[1]</small> Enter not into judgment with thy servants, O Lord, for no flesh is righteous in thy sight.

<small>1 John i.</small> If we say that we have no sin, we deceive ourselves, and there is no truth in us.

DEARLY beloved brethren, the scripture moveth us in sundry places, to acknowledge and confess our manifold sins and wickedness, and that we should not dissemble nor cloke them before the face of Almighty God our heavenly Father, but confess them with an humble, lowly, penitent and obedient heart : to the end that we may obtain forgiveness of the same by his infinite goodness and mercy. And although we ought at all times humbly to knowledge our sins before God: yet ought we most chiefly so to do, when we assemble and meet together, to render thanks for the great benefits that we have received at his hands, to set forth his most worthy praise, to hear his most holy word, and to ask those things which be requisite and necessary, as well for the body as the soul. Wherefore I pray and beseech you, as many as be here present, to accompany me with a pure heart and humble voice, unto the throne of the heavenly grace, saying after me.

¶ A general confession, to be said of the whole congregation after the Minister, kneeling.

ALMIGHTY and most merciful Father, we have erred and strayed from thy ways, like lost sheep. We have followed too

[[1] Psal. clxii. Grafton, 2, but same scripture.]

much the devices and desires of our own hearts. We have offended against thy holy laws. We have left undone those things which we ought to have done, and we have done those things which we ought not to have done, and there is no health in us : but thou, O Lord, have mercy upon us miserable offenders. Spare thou them, O God, which confess their faults. Restore thou them that be penitent, according to thy promises declared unto mankind, in Christ Jesu our Lord. And grant, O most merciful Father, for his sake, that we may hereafter live a godly, righteous, and sober life, to the glory of thy holy name. Amen.

The absolution[2] to be pronounced by the Minister alone.

ALMIGHTY God, the Father of our Lord Jesus Christ, which desireth not the death of a sinner, but rather that he may turn from his wickedness and live : and hath given power and commandment to his ministers, to declare and pronounce to his people, being penitent, the absolution and remission of their sins : he pardoneth and absolveth[3] all them which truly repent, and unfeignedly believe his holy Gospel. Wherefore we beseech him to grant us true repentance and his holy Spirit, that those things may please him, which we do at this present, and that the rest of our life hereafter may be pure and holy : so that at the last we may come to his eternal joy, through Jesus Christ our Lord.

¶ *The people shall answer.*

Amen.

¶ *Then shall the Minister begin the Lord's prayer with a loud voice.*

OUR Father which art in heaven, hallowed be thy Name. Thy kingdom come. Thy will be done in earth as it is in heaven. Give us this day our daily bread. And forgive us our trespasses, as we forgive them that trespass against us. And lead us not into temptation. But deliver us from evil. Amen.

¶ *Then likewise he shall say.*

O Lord, open thou our lips.

Answer. And our mouth shall shew forth thy praise.

[2 obsolution, Grafton, 2.]   [3 obsolveth, Grafton, 2.]

Priest. O God, make speed to save us.
Answer. O Lord, make haste to help us.
Priest. Glory be to the Father, and to the Son, and to the Holy Ghost.
As it was in the beginning, is now, and ever shall be : world without end. Amen.
Praise ye the Lord.

¶ Then shall be said or sung this Psalm following.

[Psalm xcv.[1]]

¶ Then shall follow certain Psalms in order, as they be[2] appointed in a Table, made for that purpose: except there be proper Psalms appointed for that day. And at the end of every Psalm throughout the year, and likewise in the end of *Benedictus, Benedicite, Magnificat,* and *Nunc dimittis,* shall be repeated:

Glory be to the Father, and to the Son, &c.

¶ Then shall be read two Lessons distinctly with a loud voice, that the people may hear. The first of the old Testament, the second of the new. Like as they be appointed by the Kalendar, except there be proper Lessons assigned for that day: the Minister that readeth the Lesson, standing and turning him so, as he may best be heard of all such as be present. And before every Lesson, the Minister shall say thus: The first, second, third, or fourth Chapter of Genesis or Exodus, Matthew, Mark, or other like, as is appointed in the Kalendar. And in the end of every Chapter, he shall say:

Here endeth such a Chapter of such a Book.

And (to the end the people may the better hear) in such places where they do sing, there shall the Lessons be sung in a plain tune, after the manner of distinct reading: and likewise the Epistle and Gospel.

¶ After the first Lesson shall follow *Te deum Laudamus,* in English, daily through the whole year.

Te Deum.

We praise thee, O God : we knowledge thee to be the Lord.

All the earth doth worship thee, the Father everlasting.

To thee all Angels cry aloud, the heavens and all the powers therein.

[[1] After the Psalms follows the Gloria Patri; sometimes abbreviated and sometimes at length : but variously in the editions collated.]

[[2] been, Grafton, 2.]

To thee Cherubin and Seraphin, continually do cry.
Holy, holy, holy, Lord God of Sabaoth.
Heaven and earth are full of the Majesty of thy glory.
The glorious company of the Apostles, praise thee.
The goodly fellowship of the prophets, praise thee.
The noble army of Martyrs, praise thee.
The holy Church throughout all the world, doth knowledge thee.
The Father, of an infinite Majesty.
Thy honourable, true, and only Son.
Also the Holy Ghost, the Comforter.
Thou art the King of Glory, O Christ.
Thou art the everlasting Son of the Father.
When thou tookest upon thee to deliver man, thou didst not abhor the virgin's womb.
When thou hadst overcomed[3] the sharpness of death, thou didst open the kingdom of heaven to all believers.
Thou sittest on the right hand of God, in the glory of the Father.
We believe that thou shalt come to be our judge.
We therefore pray thee, help thy servants, whom thou hast redeemed with thy precious blood.
Make them to be numbered with thy saints, in glory everlasting.
O Lord, save thy people : and bless thine heritage.
Govern them and lift them up for ever.
Day by day we magnify thee.
And we worship thy name, ever world without end.
Vouchsafe, O Lord, to keep us this day without sin.
O Lord have mercy upon us : have mercy upon us.[4]
O Lord, let thy mercy lighten upon us : as our trust is in thee.
O Lord, in thee have I trusted : let me never be confounded.

¶ Or this Canticle, *Benedicite omnia opera Domini Domino.*

O ALL ye works of the Lord, bless ye the Lord : praise him and magnify him for ever.

[3 overcome, Grafton, 1 and 2.]
[4 A few words of this and the following Canticle are in MS ; a corner of the leaf having been repaired. After "Or this Canticle, &c." Whitchurch, 1, has *Benedicite.*]

O ye Angels of the Lord, bless ye the Lord : praise ye him and magnify him for ever.

O ye heavens, bless ye the Lord : praise him and magnify him for ever.

O ye waters that be above the firmament, bless ye the Lord : praise him and magnify him for ever.

O all ye powers of the Lord, bless ye the Lord : praise him and magnify him for ever.

O ye Sun, and Moon, bless ye the Lord : praise him and magnify him for ever.

O ye stars of heaven, bless ye the Lord : praise him and magnify him for ever.

O ye showers and dew, bless ye the Lord : praise him and magnify him for ever.

O ye winds of God, bless ye the Lord : praise him and magnify him for ever.

O ye fire and heat, bless ye the Lord : praise him and magnify him for ever.

O ye winter and summer, bless ye the Lord : praise him and magnify him for ever.

O ye dews and frosts, bless ye the Lord : praise him and magnify him for ever.

O ye frost and cold, bless ye the Lord : praise him and magnify him for ever.

O ye ice and snow, bless ye the Lord : praise him and magnify him for ever.

O ye nights and days, bless ye the Lord : praise him and magnify him for ever.

O ye light and darkness, bless ye the Lord : praise him and magnify him for ever.

O ye lightnings and clouds, bless ye the Lord : praise him and magnify him for ever.

O let the earth bless the Lord : yea, let it praise him and magnify him for ever.

O ye mountains and hills, bless ye the Lord : praise him, and magnify him for ever.

O all ye green things upon the earth, bless ye the Lord : praise him and magnify him for ever.

O ye wells, bless ye the Lord : praise him, and magnify him for ever.

O ye seas and floods, bless ye the Lord : praise him and magnify him for ever.

O ye whales and all that move in the waters, bless ye the Lord : praise him and magnify him for ever.

O ye fowls of the air, bless ye the Lord : praise him and magnify him for ever.

O all ye beasts and cattle, bless ye the Lord : praise him and magnify him for ever.

O ye children of men, bless ye the Lord : praise him and magnify him for ever.

O let Israel bless the Lord : praise him and magnify him for ever.

O ye priests of the Lord, bless ye the Lord : praise him and magnify him for ever.

O ye servants of the Lord, bless ye the Lord : praise him and magnify him for ever.

O ye spirits and souls of the righteous, bless ye the Lord : praise him and magnify him for ever.

O ye holy and humble men of heart, bless ye the Lord : praise him and magnify him for ever.

O Ananias, Azarias, and Misael, bless ye the Lord : praise him and magnify him for ever.

Glory be to the Father, and to the Son : and to the Holy Ghost.

As it was in the beginning, is now, and ever[1] shall be : world without end. Amen.

¶ And after the second Lesson shall be used and said, *Benedictus*, in English as followeth.

Benedictus.

BLESSED be the Lord God of Israel : for he hath visited and redeemed his people.

And hath raised up a mighty salvation for us : in the house of his servant David.

As he spake by the mouth of his holy Prophets : which have been since the world began.

That we should be saved from our enemies : and from the hands of all that hate us.

To perform the mercy promised to our forefathers : and to remember his holy covenant.

[[1] is now, and ever, &c., Grafton, 2.]

To perform the oath which he sware to our forefather Abraham : that he would give us.

That we being delivered out of the hands of our enemies : might serve him without fear.

In holiness and righteousness before him : all the days of our life.

And thou, child, shalt be called the Prophet of the highest : for thou shalt go before the face of the Lord; to prepare his ways.

To give knowledge of salvation unto his people : for the remission of their sins.

Through the tender mercy of our God : whereby the day-spring from an[1] high hath visited us.

To give light to them that sit in darkness, and in the shadow of death : and to guide our feet into the way of peace.

Glory be to the Father, and to the Son : and to the Holy Ghost.

As it was in the beginning, is now, and ever shall be : world without end. Amen.

¶ Or else this Psalm[2].

Jubilate Deo. Psalm c.

¶ Then shall be said the *Creed*, by the Minister and the people, standing.

I BELIEVE in God the Father almighty, maker of heaven and earth. And in Jesus Christ his only Son our Lord, which was conceived by the Holy Ghost, born of the virgin Mary : suffered under Ponce Pilate, was crucified, dead and buried, he descended into hell. The third day he rose again from the dead. He ascended into heaven, and sitteth on the right hand of God the Father almighty. From thence shall he[3] come to judge the quick and the dead. I believe in the Holy Ghost. The holy catholic Church. The communion of Saints. The forgiveness of sins. The resurrection of the body. And the life everlasting. Amen.

¶ And after that, these prayers following, as well at evening prayer as at morning prayer : all devoutly kneeling. The Minister first pronouncing with a loud voice.

[1 on, Grafton, 2.]   [2 Or the c. Psalm, Jubilate, Grafton, 1 and 2.]
[3 he shall, Grafton, 2.]

The Lord be with you.
Answer. And with thy spirit.
The Minister. Let us pray.
Lord, have mercy upon us.
Christ, have mercy upon us.
Lord, have mercy upon us.

¶ Then the Minister, Clerks and people, shall say the Lord's prayer in English, with a loud voice.

¶ Our Father which art, &c.

¶ Then the Minister standing up shall say.

O Lord, shew thy mercy upon us.
Answer. And grant us thy salvation.
Priest. O Lord, save the King.
Answer. And mercifully hear us, when we call upon thee.
Priest. Endue thy ministers with righteousness.
Answer. And make thy chosen people joyful.
Priest. O Lord, save thy people.
Answer. And bless thine inheritance.
Priest. Give peace in our time, O Lord.
Answer. Because there is none other that fighteth for us, but only thou, O God.
Priest. O God, make clean our hearts within us.
Answer. And take not thine[1] holy Spirit from us.

¶ Then shall follow three Collects. The first of the day, which shall be the same that is appointed at the Communion. The second for peace. The third for Grace to live well. And the two last Collects shall never alter, but daily be said at morning prayer, throughout all the year as followeth.

¶ *The second Collect for Peace.*

O GOD, which art author of peace, and lover of concord, in knowledge of whom standeth our eternal life, whose service is perfect freedom, defend us thy humble servants in all assaults of our enemies, that we surely trusting in thy defence, may not fear the power of any adversaries: through the might of Jesu Christ our Lord. Amen.

[⁴ thy, Grafton, 2.]

¶ *The third Collect for Grace.*

O LORD our heavenly Father, almighty and everlasting God, which hast safely brought us to the beginning of this day, defend us in the same with thy mighty power, and grant that this day we fall into no sin, neither run into any kind of danger: but that all our doings may be ordered by thy governance, to do always that is righteous in thy sight: through Jesus Christ our Lord. Amen.

AN
ORDER FOR EVENING PRAYER
THROUGHOUT THE YEAR.

¶ *The Priest shall say,*
Our Father which, &c.
Then likewise he shall say.
O Lord, open thou our lips.
Answer. And our mouth shall shew forth thy praise.
Priest. O God, make speed to save us.
Answer. Lord, make haste to help us.
Priest. Glory be to the Father, and to the Son, and to the Holy Ghost.
As it was in the beginning, is now, and ever shall be : world without end. Amen.
Praise ye the Lord.

Then Psalms in order as they be appointed in the Table for Psalms, except there be proper Psalms appointed for that day. Then a Lesson of the old Testament as is appointed likewise in the Kalendar, except there be proper lessons appointed for that day. After that, *Magnificat,* in English as followeth.

Magnificat[1].
My soul doth magnify the Lord :
And my spirit hath rejoiced in God my Saviour.
For he hath regarded the lowliness of his handmaiden :
For behold from henceforth all generations shall call me blessed.
For he that is mighty, hath magnified me : and holy is his name.
And his mercy is on them that fear him : throughout all generations.
He hath shewed strength with his arm : he hath scattered the proud, in the imagination of their hearts.

[[1] the reference Luke i. is omitted in this copy, and Grafton, 1.]

He hath put down the mighty from their seat : and hath exalted the humble and meek.

He hath filled the hungry with good things : and the rich he hath sent empty away.

He remembering his mercy, hath holpen his servant Israel: as he promised to our forefathers, Abraham and his seed for ever.

Glory[1] be to the Father, &c.

As it was in the, &c.

¶ Or else[2] this Psalm.

Cantate Domino. Psalm xcviii.

Then a Lesson of the new Testament. And after that *Nunc dimittis* in English, as followeth.

LORD, now lettest thou thy servant depart in peace : according to thy word.

For mine eyes have seen : thy salvation,

Which thou hast prepared : before the face of all people.

To be a light to lighten the Gentiles : and to be the glory of thy people Israel.

Glory be to the Father[3], &c. As it was in the, &c.

¶ Or else this Psalm[4].

Deus misereatur. Psalm lxvii[5].

¶ Then shall follow the Creed, with other prayers as is before appointed at morning prayer after *Benedictus.* And with three Collects : First of the Day : the second of Peace : Third for Aid against all perils, as hereafter followeth : which two last Collects shall be daily said at evening prayer without alteration.

The second Collect at Evening prayer.

O GOD, from whom all holy desires, all good counsels, and all just works do proceed : give unto thy servants that

[[1] The *Gloria Patri,* at full length in Grafton, 1 and 2.]

[[2] or the xcviii. Ps., *Cantate Domino canticum novum,* Grafton, 2 ; to which is added, *quia mirabilia fecit,* Grafton, 1 ; but the Psalm in English omitted.]

[[3] Gloria Patri, at full length in Grafton, 2.]

[[4] Or this Psalm, *Deus misereatur nostri,* in English, Grafton, 1 and 2.]

[[5] The reference Ps. lxvii. omitted by Grafton, 1 and 2.]

peace, which the world cannot give: that both our hearts may be set to obey thy commandments, and also that by thee we being defended from the fear of our enemies, may pass our time in rest and quietness, through the merits of Jesus Christ our Saviour. Amen.

The third Collect, for aid against all perils.

LIGHTEN our darkness we beseech thee, O Lord, and by thy great mercy defend us from all perils and dangers of this night, for the love of thy only Son our Saviour Jesus Christ. Amen.

¶ In the feasts of Christmas, the Epiphany, Saint Mathie, Easter, the Ascension, Pentecost, Saint John Baptist, Saint James, Saint Bartholomew, Saint Mathew, Saint Symon and Jude, Saint Andrew, and Trinity Sunday: shall be sung or said immediately after *Benedictus*, this Confession of our Christian Faith.

[6]

WHOSOEVER will be saved : before all things it is necessary that he hold the catholic faith.

Which faith except every one do keep holy and undefiled : without doubt he shall perish everlastingly.

And the catholic faith is this : That we worship one God in Trinity, and Trinity in unity.

Neither confounding the persons : nor dividing the substance.

For there is one person of the Father, another of the Son : and another of the Holy Ghost.

But the Godhead of the Father, of the Son, and of the Holy Ghost is all one : the glory equal, the majesty co-eternal.

Such as the Father is, such is the Son : and such is the Holy Ghost.

The Father uncreate, the Son uncreate : and the Holy Ghost uncreate.

The Father incomprehensible, the Son incomprehensible : and the Holy Ghost incomprehensible.

The Father eternal, the Son eternal : and the Holy Ghost eternal.

[6 Quicunque vult, &c., in Grafton, 2, and in Grafton, 1, omitting &c.]

And yet they are not three eternals : but one eternal.

As also there be not three incomprehensibles, nor three uncreated : but one uncreated, and one incomprehensible.

So likewise the Father is almighty, the Son almighty : and the Holy Ghost almighty.

And yet they[1] are not three almighties : but one almighty.

So the Father is God, the Son is God : and the Holy Ghost is God.

And yet are they not three Gods : but one God.

So likewise the Father is Lord, the Son Lord : and the Holy Ghost Lord.

And yet not three Lords : but one Lord.

For like as we be compelled by the Christian verity : to acknowledge every person by himself, to be God and Lord.

So are we forbidden by the Catholic religion : to say there be three Gods, or three Lords.

The Father is made of none : neither created nor begotten.

The Son is of the Father alone : not made nor created, but begotten.

The Holy Ghost is of the Father and of the Son : neither made, nor created, nor begotten, but proceeding.

So there is one Father, not three Fathers, one Son, not three Sons : one Holy Ghost, not three Holy Ghosts.

And in this Trinity, none is afore or after other : none is greater, nor less than another[2].

But the whole three persons : be co-eternal together and co-equal.

So that in all things, as is aforesaid : the unity in Trinity, and the Trinity in unity, is to be worshipped.

He therefore that will be saved : must thus think of the Trinity.

Furthermore, it is necessary to everlasting salvation : that he also believe rightly in the incarnation of our Lord Jesu Christ.

For the right faith is, that we believe and confess : that our Lord Jesus Christ, the Son of God, is God and man.

God of the substance of the Father, begotten before the worlds : and man of the substance of his mother, born in the world.

[[1] are they not, Grafton, 1 ; are there not, Grafton, 2.]
[[2] other, Grafton, 2.]

Perfect God, and perfect man : of a reasonable soul, and human flesh subsisting.

Equal to the Father, as touching his Godhead : and inferior to the Father, touching his manhood.

Who although he be God and man : yet he is not two, but one Christ.

One, not by conversion of the Godhead into flesh : but by taking of the manhood into God.

One altogether, not by confusion of substance : but by unity of person.

For as the reasonable soul and flesh is[3] one man : so God and man is[4] one Christ.

Who suffered for our salvation : descended into hell, rose again the third day from the dead.

He ascended into heaven, he sitteth on the right hand of the Father, God almighty : from whence he shall come to judge the quick and the dead.

At whose coming all men shall rise again with their bodies : and shall give account for their own works.

And they that have done good, shall go into life everlasting : and they that have done evil, into everlasting fire.

This is the Catholic faith : which except a man believe faithfully, he cannot be saved.

Glory be to the Father, and to the Son : and to the Holy Ghost.

As it was in the beginning, is now, and ever shall be : world without end. Amen.

¶ *Thus endeth the order of Morning and Evening prayer, through the whole Year.*

[3 is but, Grafton, 2.]   [4 is but, Grafton, 2.]

HERE FOLLOWETH THE

LITANY

TO BE USED

UPON SUNDAYS, WEDNESDAYS, AND FRIDAYS,

AND AT OTHER TIMES, WHEN IT SHALL BE COMMANDED
BY THE ORDINARY.

O GOD the Father of heaven : have mercy upon us miserable sinners.

O God the Father of heaven[1] : *have mercy upon us miserable sinners.*

O God the Son, Redeemer of the world : have mercy upon us miserable sinners.

O God the Son, Redeemer of the world : have mercy upon us miserable sinners.

O God the Holy Ghost, proceeding from the Father and the Son : have mercy upon us miserable sinners.

O God the Holy Ghost, proceeding from the Father and the Son : have mercy upon us miserable sinners.

O holy, blessed, and glorious Trinity, three persons and one God : have mercy upon us miserable sinners.

O holy, blessed, and glorious Trinity, three persons and one God : have mercy upon us miserable sinners.

Remember not, Lord, our offences, nor the offences of our forefathers, neither take thou vengeance of our sins : spare us, good Lord, spare thy people whom thou hast redeemed with thy most precious blood, and be not angry with us for ever.

Spare us, good Lord.

From all evil and mischief, from sin, from the crafts and assaults of the devil, from thy wrath, and from everlasting damnation.

Good Lord, deliver us.

From all blindness of heart, from pride, vain-glory and hypocrisy, from envy, hatred and malice, and all uncharitableness.

Good Lord, deliver us.

[[1] "O God the Father of heaven, &c." Grafton, 2: similarly the three following responses are abridged.]

THE LITANY. 233

From fornication and all other deadly sin, and from all the deceits of the world, the flesh and the devil.

Good Lord, deliver us.

From lightnings and tempests, from plague, pestilence and famine, from battle and murther, and from sudden death.

Good Lord, deliver us.

From all sedition and privy conspiracy, from the tyranny of the Bishop of Rome, and all his detestable enormities, from all false doctrine and heresy, from hardness of heart, and contempt of thy word and commandment.

Good Lord, deliver us.

By the mystery of thy holy incarnation, by thy holy nativity and circumcision, by thy baptism, fasting, and temptation.

Good Lord, deliver us.

By thine agony and bloody sweat, by thy cross and passion, by thy precious death and burial, by thy glorious resurrection and ascension, and by the coming of the Holy Ghost.

Good Lord, deliver us.

In all time of our tribulation, in all time of our wealth, in the hour of death, and in the day of judgment.

Good Lord, deliver us.

We sinners do beseech thee to hear us, O Lord God, and that it may please thee to rule and govern thy holy church universally in the right way.

We beseech thee to hear us, good Lord.

That it may please thee to keep Edward the sixth thy servant, our King and governor.

We beseech thee to hear us, good Lord.

That it may please thee to rule his heart in thy faith, fear and love, that he may always have affiance in thee, and ever seek thy honour and glory.

We beseech thee to hear us, good Lord.

That it may please thee to be his defender and keeper, giving him the victory over all his enemies.

We beseech thee to hear us, good Lord.

That it may please thee to illuminate all Bishops, Pastors, and ministers of the Church, with true knowledge and understanding of thy word: and that both by their preaching and living they may set it forth and shew it accordingly.

We beseech thee to hear us, good Lord.

That it may please thee to endue the Lords of the council, and all the nobility, with grace, wisdom, and understanding.

We beseech thee to hear us, good Lord.

That it may please thee to bless and keep the Magistrates, giving them grace to execute justice, and to maintain truth.

We beseech thee to hear us, good Lord.

That it may please thee to bless and keep all thy people.

We beseech thee to hear us, good Lord.

That it may please thee to give to all nations unity, peace and concord.

We beseech thee to hear us, good Lord.

That it may please thee to give us an heart to love and dread thee, and diligently to live after thy commandments.

We beseech thee to hear us, good Lord.

That it may please thee to give all thy people increase of grace, to hear meekly thy word, and to receive it with pure affection, and to bring forth the fruits of the Spirit.

We beseech thee to hear us, good Lord.

That it may please thee to bring into the way of truth all such as have erred and are[1] deceived.

We beseech thee to hear us, good Lord.

That it may please thee to strengthen such as do stand, and to comfort and help the weak hearted, and to raise them up that fall, and finally to beat down Satan[2] under our feet.

We beseech thee to hear us, good Lord.

That it may please thee to succour, help and comfort, all that be in danger, necessity, and tribulation.

We beseech thee to hear us, good Lord.

That it may please thee to preserve all that travel by land or by water, all women labouring of child, all sick persons and young children, and to shew thy pity upon all prisoners and captives.

We beseech thee to hear us, good Lord.

That it may please thee to defend and provide for the fatherless children and widows, and all that be desolate and oppressed.

We beseech thee to hear us, good Lord.

[[1] be, Grafton, 2.]   [[2] Sathan, Grafton, 2.]

That it may please thee to have mercy upon all men.
We beseech thee to hear us, good Lord.
That it may please thee to forgive our enemies, persecutors and slanderers, and to turn their hearts.
We beseech thee to hear us, good Lord.
That it may please thee to give and preserve to our use the kindly fruits of the earth, so as in due time we may enjoy them.
We beseech thee to hear us, good Lord.
That it may please thee to give us true repentance, to forgive us all our sins, negligences, and ignorances, and to endue us with the grace of thy holy Spirit, to amend our lives according to thy holy word.
We beseech thee to hear us, good Lord.
Son of God : we beseech thee to hear us.
Son of God : we beseech thee to hear us.
O Lamb of God, that takest away the sins of the world:
Grant us thy peace.
O Lamb of God, that takest away the sins of the world:
Have mercy upon us.
O Christ, hear us.
O Christ, hear us.
Lord, have mercy upon us.
Lord, have mercy upon us.
Christ, have mercy upon us.
Christ, have mercy upon us.
Lord, have mercy upon us.
Lord, have mercy upon us.
Our Father, which art in heaven, &c.
And lead us not into temptation.
But deliver us from evil[3].
The Versicle. O Lord, deal not with us after our sins.
The Answer. Neither reward us after our iniquities.

Let us pray.

O GOD merciful Father, that despisest not the sighing of a contrite heart, nor the desire of such as be sorrowful : mercifully assist our prayers that we make before thee in all our troubles and adversities, whensoever they oppress us. And graciously hear us, that those evils, which the craft and

[[3] evil, Amen, Grafton, 2.]

subtilty of the devil or man worketh against us, be brought to nought, and by the providence of thy goodness they may be dispersed, that we thy servants being hurt by no persecutions, may evermore give thanks unto[1] thee in thy holy Church, through Jesu[2] Christ our Lord.

O Lord, arise, help us, and deliver us for thy name's sake.

O GOD, we have heard with our ears, and our fathers have declared unto us, the noble works that thou didst in their days, and in the old time before them.

O Lord arise, help us, and deliver us for thine honour.

Glory be to the Father, and to the Son, and to the Holy Ghost : as it was in the beginning, is now, and ever shall be : world without end. Amen.

From our enemies defend us, O Christ.

Graciously look upon our afflictions.

Pitifully behold the sorrows of our heart.

Mercifully forgive the sins of thy people.

Favourably with mercy hear our prayers.

O Son of David, have mercy upon us.

Both now and ever vouchsafe to hear us, O Christ.

Graciously hear us, O Christ, Graciously hear us, O Lord Christ.

The Versicle. O Lord, let thy mercy be shewed upon us.

The Answer. As we do put our trust in thee.

Let us pray.

WE humbly beseech thee, O Father, mercifully to look upon our infirmities; and for the glory of thy name's sake turn from us all those evils that we most righteously have deserved : and grant that in all our troubles we may put our whole trust and confidence in thy mercy, and evermore serve thee in holiness and pureness of living, to thy honour and glory : Through our only mediator and advocate Jesus Christ our Lord. Amen.

For rain, if the time require.

O GOD, heavenly Father, which by thy Son Jesu[3] Christ hast promised to all them that seek thy kingdom and the

[[1] to, Grafton, 2.]   [[2] Jesus, Grafton, 2.]
[[3] Jesus, Grafton, 1.]

righteousness thereof, all things necessary to their bodily sustenance: send us, we beseech thee, in this our necessity, such moderate rain and showers, that we may receive the fruits of the earth to our comfort, and to thy honour: through Jesus Christ our Lord. Amen.

¶ *For fair weather.*

O LORD God, which for the sin of man didst once drown all the world, except eight persons, and afterward of thy great mercy didst promise never to destroy it so again: we humbly beseech thee, that although we for our iniquities have worthily deserved this plague of rain and waters, yet upon our true repentance thou wilt send us such weather whereby we may receive the fruits of the earth in due season, and learn both by thy punishment to amend our lives, and for thy clemency to give thee praise and glory: through Jesus[4] Christ our Lord. Amen.

¶ *In the time of dearth and famine.*

O GOD heavenly Father, whose gift it is that the rain doth fall, the earth is fruitful, beasts increase, and fishes do multiply: behold, we beseech thee, the afflictions of thy people, and grant that the scarcity and dearth (which we do now most justly suffer for our iniquity) may through thy goodness be mercifully turned into cheapness and plenty, for the love of Jesu Christ our Lord: to whom with thee and the Holy Ghost. &c.[5]

¶ *Or thus.*

O GOD merciful Father, which, in the time of Heliseus the Prophet, didst suddenly turn in Samaria great scarcity and dearth into plenty and cheapness, and extreme famine into abundance of victual: Have pity upon us, that now be punished for our sins with like adversity, increase the fruits of the earth by thy heavenly benediction: And grant, that we receiving thy bountiful liberality, may use the same to thy glory, our comfort, and relief of our needy neighbours: through Jesu[6] Christ our Lord. Amen.

[4 Jesu, Grafton, 2.]   [5 &c. Amen, Grafton, 2.]
[6 Jesus, Grafton, 1.]

In the time of War.

O ALMIGHTY God, king of all kings, and governor of all things, whose power no creature is able to resist, to whom it belongeth justly to punish sinners, and to be merciful to them that truly repent: save and deliver us (we humbly beseech thee) from the hands of our enemies: abate their pride, assuage their malice, and confound their devices, that we being armed with thy defence, may be preserved evermore from all perils to glorify thee, which art the only giver of all victory, through the merits of thy only Son Jesu Christ our Lord.[1]

¶ *In the time of any common plague or sickness.*

O ALMIGHTY God, which in thy wrath, in the time of king David, didst slay with the plague of pestilence lx[2] and ten thousand, and yet remembering thy mercy didst save the rest: have pity upon us miserable sinners, that now are visited with great sickness and mortality, that like as thou didst then command thy[3] angel to cease from punishing, so it may now please thee to withdraw from us this plague and grievous sickness, through Jesu[4] Christ our Lord.[5]

¶ And the Litany shall ever end with this Collect following:

ALMIGHTY God, which hast given us grace at this time with one accord to make our common supplications unto thee, and dost promise that when two or three be gathered in thy name, thou wilt grant their requests: fulfil now, O Lord, the desires and petitions of thy servants, as may be most expedient for them, granting us in this world knowledge of thy truth, and in the world to come life everlasting. Amen.

[1 Amen, Grafton, 2.]   [2 threescore, Grafton, 2.]
[3 thine, Grafton, 2.]   [4 Jesus, Grafton, 2.]
[5 Amen, Grafton, 2.]

THE
COLLECTS, EPISTLES AND GOSPELS,

TO BE USED AT THE CELEBRATION OF THE LORD'S SUPPER AND HOLY COMMUNION THROUGH THE YEAR.

¶ *The first Sunday of Advent.*

The Collect.

ALMIGHTY God, give us grace that we may cast away the works of darkness, and put upon us the armour of light, now in the time of this mortal life, in the which thy Son Jesus Christ came to visit us in great humility; that in the last day, when he shall come again in his glorious majesty to judge both the quick and the dead, we may rise to the life immortal through him: who liveth and reigneth with thee and the Holy Ghost, now and ever. Amen.

The Epistle. Ro. xiii. [v. 8 to end.]
The Gospel. Mat. xxi. [v. 1—13.]

¶ *The second Sunday*[6].

The Collect.

BLESSED Lord, which hast caused all holy scriptures to be written for our learning: grant us that we may in such wise hear them, read, mark, learn, and inwardly digest them, that by patience and comfort of thy holy word, we may embrace and ever hold fast the blessed hope of everlasting life, which thou hast given us in our Saviour Jesus Christ.[7]

The Epistle. Rom. xv. [v. 4—13.]
The Gospel. Luk. xxi. [v. 25—33.]

[6 In Advent, is added to the running title of Grafton, 1 and 2.]
[7 Amen, Grafton, 2.]

¶ *The third Sunday.*

The Collect.

LORD, we beseech thee give ear to our prayers, and by thy gracious visitation lighten the darkness of our heart, by our Lord Jesus Christ.[1]

The Epistle. 1 Cor. iv. [v. 1—5.]
The Gospel. Math. xi. [v. 2—10.]

¶ *The fourth Sunday.*

The Collect.

LORD, raise up (we pray thee) thy power, and come among us, and with great might succour us: that whereas (through our sins and wickedness) we be sore let and hindered, thy bountiful grace and mercy, (through the satisfaction of thy Son our Lord,) may speedily deliver us: to whom with thee and the Holy Ghost be honour and glory world without end.[1]

The Epistle. Phili. iv. [v. 4—7.]
The Gospel. John i. [v. 19—28.]

¶ *Christmas Day*[2].

The Collect.

ALMIGHTY God, which hast given us thy only-begotten Son to take our nature upon him, and this day to be born of a pure virgin: Grant that we being regenerate and made thy children by adoption and grace, may daily be renewed by thy holy Spirit, through the same our Lord Jesus Christ: who liveth and reigneth with. &c. Amen.[3]

The Epistle. Hebre. i. [v. 1—12.]
The Gospel. John i. [v. 1—14.]

¶ *Saint Stephin's day.*

The Collect.

GRANT us, O Lord, to learn to love our enemies by the example of thy martyr Saint Stephin, who prayed for his persecutors to thee: which livest and. &c.[4]

[1 Amen, Grafton, 2.]
[2 On Christmas Day, Grafton, 2.]
[3 with thee and the Holy Ghost, now and ever, Amen, Grafton, 2.]
[4 persecutors: to thee which livest and reignest, &c. Grafton, 2.]

¶ Then shall follow a [5] Collect of the Nativity, which shall be said continually unto new year's day.

The Epistle. Actes vii. [v. 55 to end.]
The Gospel. Mathew xxiii. [v. 34 to end.]

¶ Saint John Evangelist's day.
The Collect.

MERCIFUL Lord, we beseech thee to cast thy bright beams of light upon thy Church: that it being lightened by the doctrine of thy blessed Apostle and Evangelist John, may attain to thy everlasting gifts, through Jesus Christ our Lord. Amen.

The Epistle. 1 John i. [v. 1 to end.]
The Gospel. John xxi. [v. 19 to end.]

¶ The Innocents' day.
The Collect.

ALMIGHTY God, whose praise this day the young innocents thy witnesses hath confessed, and shewed forth, not in speaking, but in dying: mortify and kill all vices in us, that in our conversation our life may express thy faith, which with our tongues we do confess: through Jesus Christ our Lord.

The Epistle. Apo. xiv. [v. 1—5.]
The Gospel. Math. ii. [v. 13—18.]

¶ The Sunday after Christmas day.
The Collect.

ALMIGHTY God, which hast given us. &c.[6] As upon Christmas day.

The Epistle. Gala. iv. [v. 1—7.]
The Gospel. Math. i. [v. 1 to end.]

¶ The Circumcision of Christ.
The Collect.

ALMIGHTY God, which madest thy blessed Son to be circumcised and obedient to the law for man: grant us the true circumcision of the spirit, that our hearts and all our[7]

[5 The Collect, Grafton, 2.]   [6 Given at length in Grafton, 2.]
[7 our, omitted in Grafton, 2.]

members being mortified from all worldly and carnal lusts, may in all things obey thy blessed will: through the same thy Son Jesus Christ our Lord.

The Epistle. Rom. iv. [v. 8—14.]
The Gospel. Luke ii. [v. 15—21.]

If there be a Sunday between the Epiphany, and the Circumcision, then shall be used the same Collect, Epistle and Gospel, at the Communion, which was used upon the day of Circumcision.

¶ *The Epiphany.*

The Collect.

O GOD, which by the leading of a star didst manifest thy only begotten Son to the Gentiles: Mercifully grant, that we which know thee now by faith, may after this life have the fruition of thy glorious Godhead, through Christ our Lord.

The Epistle. Ephe. iii. [v. 1—12.]
The Gospel. Math. ii. [v. 1—12.]

¶ *The first Sunday after the Epiphany.*

The Collect.

LORD, we beseech thee mercifully to receive the prayers of thy people which call upon thee : and grant that they may both perceive and know what things they ought to do, and also have grace and power, faithfully to fulfil the same, through Jesus Christ our Lord.[1]

The Epistle. Rom. xii. [v. 1—5.]
The Gospel. Luke ii. [v. 42 to end.]

The second Sunday after the Epiphany.

The Collect.

ALMIGHTY and everlasting God, which dost govern all things in heaven and earth: mercifully hear the supplications of thy people, and grant us thy peace all the days of our life.

The Epistle. Rom. xii. [v. 6—16.]
The Gospel. John ii.[2] [v. 1—11.]

[[1] Amen, Grafton, 2.]
[[2] John iii., Grafton, 1; but the same Gospel.]

The third Sunday.
The Collect.
ALMIGHTY and everlasting God, mercifully look upon our infirmities: and in all our dangers and necessities stretch forth thy right hand to help and defend us, through Christ our Lord.

The Epistle. Rom. xii. [v. 16 to end.]
The Gospel. Mat. viii. [v. 1—13.]

¶ The fourth Sunday.
The Collect.
GOD, which knowest us to be set in the midst of so many and great dangers, that for man's frailness we cannot always stand uprightly: Grant to us the health of body and soul, that all those things which we suffer for sin, by thy help we may well pass and overcome: through Christ our Lord.

The Epistle. Ro. xiii. [v. 1—7.]
The Gospel. Mat. viii. [v. 23 to end.]

¶ The fifth Sunday.
The Collect.
LORD, we beseech thee to keep thy Church and household continually in thy true religion: that they which do lean only upon hope of thy heavenly grace, may evermore be defended by thy mighty power: through Christ our Lord.

The Epistle. Colo. iii. [v. 12—17.]
The Gospel. Mat. xiii. [v. 24—30.]

The vi. Sunday (if there be so many) shall have the same[3] Collect, Epistle, and Gospel, that was upon the fifth Sunday.

¶ The Sunday called Septuagesima.
The Collect.
O LORD, we beseech thee favourably to hear the prayers of thy people, that we which are justly punished for our offences, may be mercifully delivered by thy goodness, for

[[3] the same Psalm, Collect, &c., Grafton, 1.]

the glory of thy name, through Jesu[1] Christ our Saviour: who liveth and reigneth world without end.[2]

The Epistle. 1 Cor. ix. [v. 24 to end.]
The Gospel. Math. xx. [v. 1—16.]

¶ *The Sunday called Sexagesima.*

The Collect.

LORD GOD, which seest that we put not our trust in any thing that we do: mercifully grant, that by thy power we may be defended against all adversity, through Jesus Christ our Lord.

The Epistle. 2 Co. xi. [v. 19—31.]
The Gospel. Luk. viii. [v. 4—15.]

The Sunday called Quinquagesima.

The Collect.

O LORD, which dost teach us, that all our doings without charity are nothing worth: send thy Holy Ghost, and pour in our hearts that most excellent gift of charity, the very bond of peace and all virtues, without the which whosoever liveth, is counted dead before thee: Grant this for thy only Son Jesus Christ's sake.

The Epistle. 1 Cor. xiii. [v. 1 to end.]
The Gospel. Luk. xviii.[3] [v. 31 to end.]

¶ *The first day of Lent.*

The Collect.

ALMIGHTY and everlasting God, which hatest nothing that thou hast made, and dost forgive the sins of all them that be penitent: Create and make in us new and contrite hearts, that we worthily lamenting our sins, and knowledging our wretchedness, may obtain of thee, the God of all mercy, perfect remission and forgiveness, through Jesus Christ.

The Epistle. Joel ii. [v. 12—17.]
The Gospel. Math. vi. [v. 16—21.]

[[1] Jesus, Grafton, 2.] [[2] who liveth and reigneth. &c., Grafton, 2.]
[[3] Luke xvii. Whitchurch, 1 ; but the same Gospel.]

¶ *The first Sunday in Lent.*
The Collect.
O LORD, which for our sake didst fast forty days, and forty nights: Give us grace to use such abstinence, that our flesh being subdued to the spirit, we may ever obey thy godly monitions[4], in righteousness and true holiness, to thy honour and glory: which livest and reignest. &c.

The Epistle. 2 Cor. vi. [v. 1—10.]
The Gospel. Math. iv. [v. 1—11.]

¶ *The second Sunday.*[5]
The Collect.
ALMIGHTY God, which dost see that we have no power of ourselves to help ourselves: keep thou us both outwardly in our bodies, and inwardly in our souls, that we may be defended from all adversities which may happen to the body, and from all evil thoughts which may assault and hurt the soul: through Jesus Christ. &c.

The Epistle. 1 Thess. iv. [v. 1—8.]
The Gospel. Math. xv. [v. 21—28.]

¶ *The third Sunday.*
The Collect.
WE beseech thee, almighty God, look upon the hearty desires of thy humble servants: and stretch forth the right hand of thy majesty, to be our defence against all our enemies: through Jesus Christ our Lord.

The Epistle. Ephesi. v. [v. 1—14.]
The Gospel. Luke xi. [v. 14—28.]

¶ *The fourth Sunday.*
The Collect.
GRANT, we beseech thee, almighty GOD, that we which for our evil deeds are worthily punished, by the comfort of thy grace may mercifully be relieved: through our Lord Jesus Christ.

The Epistle. Gala. iv. [v. 21 to end.]
The Gospel. John vi. [v. 1—14.]

[4 motions, Whitchurch, 1; and Grafton, 2.]
[5 *In Lent,* added to the running title in Grafton, 2.]

¶ The fifth Sunday.

The Collect.

WE beseech thee, almighty God, mercifully to look upon thy people: that by thy great goodness they may be governed and preserved evermore both in body and soul, through Jesus Christ our Lord.

The Epistle. Hebre. ix. [v. 11—15.]
The Gospel. John viii. [v. 46 to end.]

¶ The Sunday next before Easter.

The Collect.

ALMIGHTY and everlasting God, which of thy tender love towards man, hast sent our Saviour Jesus Christ to take upon him our flesh, and to suffer death upon the cross, that all mankind should follow the example of his great humility: mercifully grant, that we both follow the example of his patience, and be made partakers of his resurrection: through the same Jesus Christ our Lord.

The Epistle. Philip. ii. [v. 5—11.]
The Gospel. Ma. xxvi. [v. 1 to end.] [xxvii. v. 1—56.]

¶ Monday before Easter.

The Epistle. Esai. lxiii. [v. 1 to end.]
The Gospel. Mar. xiv. [v. 1 to end.]

¶ Tuesday before Easter.

The Epistle. Esai. l. [v. 5 to end.]
The Gospel. Mat.[1] xv. [v. 1 to end.]

¶ Wednesday before Easter.

The Epistle. Hebr. ix. [v. 16 to end.]
The Gospel. Luk. xxii. [v. 1 to end.]

¶ Thursday before Easter.

The Epistle. 1 Cor. xi.[2] [v. 17 to end.]
The Gospel. Lu. xxiii. [v. 1 to end.]

[[1] Mar. xv., Grafton, 1 and 2; but the same Gospel.]
[[2] The reference 1 Cor. xi. is omitted, Grafton, 1.]

¶ On Good Friday.

The Collects.

ALMIGHTY God, we beseech thee graciously to behold this thy family, for the which our Lord Jesus Christ was contented to be betrayed, and given up into the hands of wicked men, and to suffer death upon the cross: who liveth and reigneth.[3] &c.

ALMIGHTY and everlasting God, by whose Spirit the whole body of the Church is governed and sanctified: receive our supplications and prayers, which we offer before thee for all estates of men in thy holy congregation, that every member of the same in his vocation and ministry may truly and godly serve thee: through our Lord Jesus Christ.

MERCIFUL God, who hast made all men, and hatest nothing that thou hast made, nor wouldest the death of a sinner, but rather that he should be converted and live: have mercy upon all Jews, Turks, Infidels, and Heretics, and take from them all ignorance, hardness of heart, and contempt of thy word. And so fetch them home, blessed Lord, to thy flock, that they may be saved among the remnant of the true Israelites, and be made one fold, under one shepherd Jesus Christ our Lord: who liveth[4] and reigneth. &c.

The Epistle. Hebre. x. [v. 1—25.]
The Gospel. John xviii. [v. 1 to end.] [xix. v. 1 to end.]

¶ Easter Even.

The Epistle. 1 Petr. iii. [v. 17 to end.]
The Gospel. Mathew xxvii. [v. 57 to end.]

¶ Easter day.

¶ At Morning prayer, instead of the Psalm, O come let us. &c. These Anthems shall be sung or said.

CHRIST rising again from the dead, now dieth not. Death from henceforth hath no power upon him. For in that he died, he died but once to put away sin: but in that he liveth, he liveth unto God. And so likewise, count[5] yourselves dead unto sin, but living unto God in Christ Jesus our Lord.

[[3] with thee, and the Holy Ghost now and ever, &c., Grafton, 2.]
[[4] who liveth. &c., Grafton, 2.]   [[5] account, Grafton, 2.]

CHRIST is risen again the firstfruits of them that sleep: for seeing that by man came death, by man also cometh the resurrection of the dead. For as by Adam all men do die, so by Christ all men shall be restored to life.

The Collect.

ALMIGHTY God, which through thy only begotten Son Jesus Christ hast overcome death, and opened unto us the gate of everlasting life: we humbly beseech thee, that as by thy special grace preventing us thou dost put in our minds good desires; so by thy continual help we may bring the same to good effect, through Jesus Christ our Lord: who[1] liveth and reigneth. &c.

The Epistle. Colo. iii. [v. 1—7.]
The Gospel. John xx. [v. 1—10.]

¶ *Monday in Easter Week.*

The Collect.

ALMIGHTY God, which through thy only begotten Son Jesus Christ hast overcome death, and opened unto us the gate of everlasting life: we humbly beseech thee, that as by thy special grace preventing us thou dost put in our minds good desires; so by thy continual help we may bring the same to good effect, through Jesus Christ our Lord: who[1] liveth and reigneth. &c.

The Epistle. Acts x. [v. 34—43.]
The Gospel. Lu. xxiv. [v. 13—35.]

¶ *Tuesday in Easter Week.*

The Collect.

ALMIGHTY Father, which hast given thy only Son to die for our sins, and to rise again for our justification: Grant us so to put away the leaven of malice and wickedness, that we may alway serve thee in pureness of living and truth: through Jesus Christ our Lord.

The Epistle. Act. xiii. [v. 26—41.]
The Gospel. Lu. xxiv. [v. 36—48.]

[[1] who, &c., Grafton, 2.]

¶ *The first Sunday after Easter.*

The Collect.

ALMIGHTY God. &c. *As at the Communion on Easter day.*

The Epistle. 1 John v. [v. 4—12.]
The Gospel. John xx. [v. 19—23.]

¶ *The second Sunday after Easter.*[2]

The Collect.

ALMIGHTY God, which hast given thy holy Son to be unto us both a sacrifice for sin, and also an example of godly life: Give us the grace that we may always most thankfully receive that his inestimable benefit, and also daily endeavour ourselves to follow the blessed steps of his most holy life.

The Epistle. 1 Peter ii. [v. 19 to end.]
The Gospel. John x. [v. 11—16.]

¶ *The third Sunday.*

The Collect.

ALMIGHTY God, which shewest to all men that be in error the light of thy truth, to the intent that they may return into the way of righteousness: Grant unto all them that be admitted into the fellowship of Christ's religion, that they may eschew those things that be contrary to their profession, and follow all such things as be agreeable to the same: through our Lord Jesus Christ.

The Epistle. 1 Peter ii. [v. 11—17.]
The Gospel. John xvi. [v. 16—22.]

¶ *The fourth Sunday.*

The Collect.

ALMIGHTY God, which dost make the minds of all faithful men to be of one will: Grant unto thy people, that they may love the thing which thou commandest, and desire that which thou dost promise: that among the sundry and manifold changes of the world, our hearts may surely there be fixed,

[[2] after Easter, omitted in Grafton, 2.]

where as true joys are to be found: Through Christ[1] our Lord.

The Epistle. James i. [v. 17—21.]
The Gospel. John xvi. [v. 5—14.]

¶ *The fifth Sunday.*
The Collect.

LORD, from whom all good things do come: grant us thy humble servants, that by thy holy inspiration we may think those things that be good, and by thy merciful guiding may perform the same[2]: through our Lord Jesus Christ.

The Epistle. James i. [v. 22 to end.]
The Gospel. John xvi. [v. 23 to end.]

The[3] *Ascension day.*
The Collect.

GRANT, we beseech thee, almighty God, that like as we do believe thy only begotten Son our Lord to have ascended into the heavens: so we may also in heart and mind thither ascend, and with him continually dwell.

The Epistle. Acts i. [v. 1—11.]
The Gospel. Mar.[4] xvi. [v. 14 to end.]

¶ *The Sunday after the Ascension day.*
The Collect.

O GOD, the King of glory, which hast exalted thine only Son, Jesus Christ, with great triumph unto thy kingdom in heaven: we beseech thee leave us not comfortless, but send to us thine Holy Ghost to comfort us, and exalt us unto[5] the same place, whither our Saviour Christ is gone before: who liveth and reigneth. &c.

The Epistle. 1 Pete. iv. [v. 7—11.]
The Gospel. John xv. [v. 26, 27.] [xvi. v. 1—4.]

[1 through Christ, &c. Grafton, 2.]
[2 the same, omitted, Grafton, 2.]
[3 The, omitted by Grafton, 2.]
[4 Mar. xvii. Grafton, 2, and omitted, Grafton, 1; but the same Gospel is given in all the copies.]
[5 to, Grafton, 2.]

Whitsunday.

The Collect.

GOD, which as upon this day hast taught the hearts of thy faithful people, by the sending to them the light of thy Holy Spirit: Grant us by the same Spirit to have a right judgment in all things, and evermore to rejoice in his holy comfort, through the merits of Christ Jesu our Saviour: who liveth and reigneth with thee in the unity of the same Spirit, one God world without end.

The Epistle. Acts ii. [v. 1—11.]
The Gospel. John xiv. [v. 15—31.]

¶ Monday in Whitsun week.

The Collect.
¶ GOD, which[6]. &c. (*As upon Whitsunday.*)

The Epistle. Acts x.[7] [v. 34 to end.]
The Gospel. John iii. [v. 16—21.]

¶ The Tuesday after Whitsunday.

The Collect.
GOD, which. &c. (*As upon Whitsunday.*)

The Epistle. Act. viii. [v. 14—17.]
The Gospel. John x. [v. 1—10.]

¶ Trinity Sunday.

The Collect.

ALMIGHTY and everlasting God, which hast given unto us thy servants grace by the confession of a true faith to acknowledge the glory of the eternal Trinity, and in the power of the divine Majesty to worship the Unity: we beseech thee that through the stedfastness of this faith we may evermore be defended from all adversity, which livest and reignest, one God world without end. Amen.

The Epistle. Apoc. iv. [v. 1 to end.]
The Gospel. John iii. [v. 1—15.]

[6 which has given. &c., Grafton, 2.]
[7 Acts iv. Grafton, 2; but the same Epistle.]

¶ The first Sunday after Trinity Sunday.

The Collect.

GOD the strength of all them that trust in thee, mercifully accept our prayers: and because the weakness of our mortal nature can do no good thing without thee, grant us the help of thy grace, that in keeping of thy commandments we may please thee both in will and deed: through Jesus Christ our Lord.

The Epistle. 1 Joh. iv. [v. 7 to end.]
The Gospel. Luk. xvi. [v. 19 to end.]

¶ The second Sunday.

The Collect.

LORD, make us to have a perpetual fear and love of thy holy name: for thou never failest to help and govern them, whom thou dost bring up in thy stedfast love: Grant this. &c.

The Epistle. 1 John iii. [v. 13 to end.]
The Gospel. Luk. xiv. [v. 16—24.]

¶ The third Sunday.

The Collect.

LORD, we beseech thee mercifully to hear us, and unto whom thou hast given an hearty desire to pray: grant that by thy mighty aid we may be defended: through Jesus Christ our Lord.

The Epistle. 1 Petri[1] v. [v. 5—11.]
The Gospel. Luke xv. [v. 1—10.]

¶ The fourth Sunday.

The Collect.

GOD, the Protector of all that trust in thee, without whom nothing is strong, nothing is holy: increase and multiply upon us thy mercy, that thou being our ruler and guide, we may so pass through things temporal, that we finally lose

[[1] Rom. viii. Grafton, 2; but the same Epistle.]

not the things eternal: grant this, heavenly Father, for Jesu Christ's sake our Lord.

The Epistle. Rom. viii. [v. 18—23.]
The Gospel. Luke vi. [v. 36—42.]

¶ *The fifth Sunday.*

The Collect.

GRANT, Lord, we beseech thee, that the course of this world may be so peaceably ordered by thy governance, that thy congregation may joyfully serve thee in all godly quietness: through Jesus Christ our Lord.

The Epistle. 1 Petr. iii. [v. 8—15.]
The Gospel. Luke v. [v. 1—11.]

¶ *The sixth Sunday.*

The Collect.

GOD, which hast prepared to them that love thee, such good things as pass all man's understanding: Pour into our hearts such love toward thee, that we loving thee in all things, may obtain thy promises, which exceed all that we can desire: through Jesus Christ our Lord.

The Epistle. Rom. vi. [v. 3—11.]
The Gospel. Math. v. [v. 20—26.]

The seventh Sunday.

The Collect.

LORD of all power and might, which art the author and giver of all good things: graff in our hearts the love of thy name, increase in us true religion, nourish us with all goodness, and of thy great mercy keep us in the same: Through Jesus Christ our Lord.

The Epistle. Rom. vi. [v. 19 to end.]
The Gospel. Mar. viii. [v. 1—9.]

¶ *The eighth Sunday.*

The Collect.

GOD, whose providence is never deceived: we humbly beseech thee, that thou wilt put away from us all hurtful things, and give those things which be profitable for us: Through Jesus Christ our Lord.

The Epistle. Rom. viii.[1] [v. 12—17.]
The Gospel. Mat. vii. [v. 15—21.]

¶ *The ninth Sunday.*

The Collect.

GRANT to us, Lord, we beseech thee, the spirit to think and do always such things as be rightful: that we, which cannot be without thee, may by thee be able to live according to thy will: Through Jesu[2] Christ our Lord.

The Epistle. [1 Cor. x.[3] v. 1—13.]
The Gospel. Luke xvi. [v. 1—9.]

¶ *The tenth Sunday.*

The Collect.

LET thy merciful ears, O Lord, be open to the prayers of thy humble servants: and that they may obtain their petitions, make them to ask such things as shall please thee: through Jesus Christ our Lord.

The Epistle. 1 Cor. xii. [v. 1—11.]
The Gospel. Luk. xix. [v. 41—47.]

The eleventh Sunday.

The Collect.

GOD, which declarest[4] thy almighty power, most chiefly in shewing mercy and pity: Give unto us abundantly thy grace, that we running to thy promises, may be made partakers of thy heavenly treasure: through Jesus Christ our Lord.

The Epistle. 1 Cor. xv. [v. 1—11.]
The Gospel. Lu. xviii. [v. 9—14.]

[[1] 1 Pete. v. Grafton, 2; but the same Epistle.]
[[2] Jesus, Grafton, 2.]
[[3] The reference, 1 Cor. x., omitted by Whitchurch, 2; but not by Grafton, 2.]
[[4] declared, Grafton, 2.]

The twelfth Sunday.

The Collect

ALMIGHTY and everlasting God, which art always more ready to hear than we to pray: and art wont to give more than either we desire or deserve: Pour down upon us the abundance of thy mercy, forgiving us those things whereof our conscience is afraid, and giving unto us that, that our prayer dare not presume to ask: through Jesus Christ our Lord.

The Epistle. 2 Cor. iii. [v. 4—9.]
The Gospel. Mar. vii. [v. 31 to end.]

The thirteenth Sunday.

The Collect.

ALMIGHTY and merciful God, of whose only gift it cometh, that thy faithful people do unto thee true and laudable service: grant, we beseech thee, that we may so run to thy heavenly promises, that we fail not finally to attain the same: Through Jesus Christ our Lord.

The Epistle. Galat. iii. [v. 16—22.]
The Gospel. Luke x. [v. 23—37.]

The fourteenth Sunday.

The Collect.

ALMIGHTY and everlasting God, give unto us the increase of faith, hope, and charity, and, that we may obtain that which thou dost promise, make us to love that which thou dost command, through Jesus[5] Christ our Lord.

The Epistle. Galat. v. [v. 16—24.]
The Gospel. Lu. xvii. [v. 11—19.]

The fifteenth Sunday.

The Collect.

KEEP, we beseech thee, O Lord, thy Church with thy

[5 Jesu, Grafton, 2.]

perpetual mercy, and because the frailty of man, without thee, cannot but fall: keep us ever by thy help, and lead us to all things profitable to our salvation: through Jesus Christ our Lord. Amen.

The Epistle. Galat. vi. [v. 11 to end.]
The Gospel. Math. vi. [v. 24 to end.]

The sixteenth Sunday.
The Collect.

LORD, we beseech thee, let thy continual pity cleanse and defend thy congregation: and because it cannot continue in safety without thy succour, preserve it evermore by thy help and goodness: through Jesus Christ our Lord.

The Epistle. Ephe. iii. [v. 13 to end.]
The Gospel. Luke vii. [v. 11—17.]

¶ *The seventeenth Sunday.*
The Collect.

LORD, we pray thee that thy grace may always prevent and follow us, and make us continually to be given to all good works: through Jesu[1] Christ our Lord.

The Epistle. Ephe. iv. [v. 1—6.]
The Gospel. Lu. xiv. [v. 1—11.]

¶ *The eighteenth Sunday.*
The Collect.

LORD, we beseech thee, grant thy people grace to avoid the infections of the devil, and with pure heart and mind to follow thee, the only God: through Jesus Christ our Lord.

The Epistle. 1 Corin. i.[2] [v. 4—8.]
The Gospel. Mat. xxii. [v. 34 to end.]

¶ *The nineteenth Sunday.*
The Collect.

O GOD, forasmuch as without thee we are not able to

[1 Jesus, Grafton, 2.]
[2 The reference, 1 Cor. i., omitted by Grafton, 2; but same Epistle is given.]

please thee: Grant that the working of thy mercy may in all things direct and rule our hearts: Through Jesus Christ our Lord.

The Epistle. Ephe. iv. [v. 17 to end.]
The Gospel. Math. ix. [v. 1—8.]

¶ *The twentieth Sunday.*
The Collect.

ALMIGHTY and merciful God, of thy bountiful goodness keep us from all things that may hurt us: that we being ready both in body and soul, may with free hearts accomplish those things, that thou wouldest have done: Through Jesus Christ our Lord.

The Epistle. Ephesi. v. [v. 15—21.]
The Gospel. Mat. xxii. [v. 1—14.]

¶ *The twenty-first Sunday.*
The Collect.

GRANT, we beseech thee, merciful Lord, to thy faithful people pardon and peace, that they may be cleansed from all their sins, and serve thee with a quiet mind: Through Jesus Christ our Lord.

The Epistle. Ephes. vi. [v. 10—20.]
The Gospel. John iv. [v. 46 to end.]

¶ *The twenty-second Sunday.*
The Collect.

LORD, we beseech thee to keep thy household the Church in continual godliness: that through thy protection, it may be free from all adversities, and devoutly given to serve thee in good works, to the glory of thy name: Through Jesus Christ our Lord.

The Epistle. Philip. i. [v. 3—11.]
The Gospel. Mathew xviii. [v. 21 to end.]

¶ *The twenty-third Sunday.*
The Collect.

GOD our refuge and strength, which art the author of all godliness, be ready to hear the devout prayers of the[3]

[[3] thy, Grafton, 2.]

Church: and grant that those things which we ask faithfully, we may obtain effectually: through Jesu Christ our Lord.

The Epistle. Philip. iii. [v. 17 to end.]
The Gospel. Mat. xxii. [v. 15—22.]

¶ *The twenty-fourth Sunday.*

The Collect.

LORD, we beseech thee, assoil[1] thy people from their offences: that through thy bountiful goodness, we may be delivered from the bands of all those sins, which by our frailty we have committed: Grant this. &c.[2]

The Epistle. Colossi. i. [v. 3—12.]
The Gospel. Math. ix. [v. 18—26.]

¶ *The twenty-fifth Sunday.*

The Collect.

STIR up, we beseech thee, O Lord, the wills of thy faithful people: that they plenteously bringing forth the fruit of good works, may of thee be plenteously rewarded: through Jesus Christ our Lord.[3]

The Epistle. Jer. xxiii. [v. 5—8.]
The Gospel. John vi. [v. 5—14.]

¶ If there be any more Sundays before Advent Sunday, to supply the same shall be taken the service of some of those Sundays that were omitted between the Epiphany and Septuagesima.

¶ *Saint Andrew's Day.*

The Collect.

ALMIGHTY God, which didst give such grace unto thy holy apostle Saint Andrew, that he readily obeyed the calling of thy Son Jesus Christ, and followed him without delay: Grant unto us all, that we being called by thy holy word, may forthwith give over ourselves, obediently to follow thy holy commandments: through the same Jesus Christ our Lord.

The Epistle. Roma. x. [v. 9 to end.]
The Gospel. Mat. iv. [v. 18—22.]

[1 to release, to absolve.]   [2 Amen, Grafton, 2.]
[3 Amen, Grafton, 2.]

¶ Saint Thomas the Apostle.

The Collect.

ALMIGHTY everliving God, which for the more confirmation of the faith, didst suffer thy holy Apostle Thomas to be doubtful in thy Son's resurrection: grant us so perfectly, and without all doubt to believe in thy Son Jesus Christ, that our faith in thy sight never be reproved: hear us, O Lord, through the same Jesus Christ: to whom with thee and the Holy Ghost[4] be all honour, &c.

The Epistle. Ephe. ii. [v. 19 to end.]
The Gospel. John xx. [v. 24 to end.]

¶ The Conversion of Saint Paul.

The Collect.

GOD, which hast taught all the world, through the preaching of thy blessed Apostle Saint Paul: grant, we beseech thee, that we which have his wonderful conversion in remembrance, may follow and fulfil thy holy doctrine that he taught: through Jesu Christ our Lord.[5]

The Epistle. Act. ix.[6] [v. 1—22.]
The Gospel. Mat. xix. [v. 27 to end.]

¶ The Purification of Saint Mary the virgin.

The Collect.

ALMIGHTY and everlasting God, we humbly beseech thy Majesty, that as thy only begotten Son was this day presented in the Temple, in substance of our flesh; so grant that we may be presented unto thee with pure and clear minds: By Jesus Christ our Lord.

The Epistle.

¶ The same that is appointed for the Sunday.

The Gospel. Luke ii. [v. 22—27.]

[4 Holy Ghost, &c., Grafton, 2.]
[5 Amen, Grafton, 2.]
[6 Acts i., Grafton, 2; but Acts ix. given.]

Saint Mathie's day.

The Collect.

ALMIGHTY God, which in the place of the traitor Judas didst choose thy faithful servant Mathie to be of the number of thy twelve Apostles: Grant that thy church, being alway preserved from false Apostles, may be ordered and guided by faithful and true pastors: Through Jesus Christ our Lord.

The Epistle. Act. i. [v. 15 to end.]
The Gospel. Math. xi. [v. 25 to end.]

The Annunciation of the virgin Mary.

The Collect.

WE beseech thee, Lord, pour thy grace into our hearts, that as we have known Christ thy Son's incarnation, by the message of an Angel; so by his cross and passion, we may be brought unto the glory of his resurrection: Through the same Christ our Lord.

The Epistle. Esai. vii. [v. 10—15.]
The Gospel.[1] [Luke i. v. 26—38.]

¶ Saint Mark's Day.

The Collect.

ALMIGHTY God, which hast instructed thy holy Church, with the heavenly doctrine of thy Evangelist Saint Mark: give us grace so to be established by thy holy gospel, that we be not, like children, carried away with every blast of vain doctrine: Through Jesus Christ our Lord.

The Epistle. Ephe. iv. [v. 7—16.]
The Gospel. John. xv. [v. 1—11.]

Saint Philip and James.

The Collect.

ALMIGHTY God, whom truly to know is everlasting life: grant us perfectly to know thy Son Jesus Christ, to be the

---

[1] The reference, Luke i., omitted only in Whitchurch, 2; but the same Gospel in all the copies.]

way, the truth, and the life, as thou hast taught Saint Philip, and other the apostles: Through Jesus Christ our Lord.

The Epistle. James. i. [v. 1—12.]
The Gospel. John. xiv. [v. 1—14.]

¶ *Saint Barnabe Apostle.*

The Collect.

LORD almighty, which hast endued thy holy Apostle Barnabas, with singular gifts of thy Holy Ghost: let us not be destitute of thy manifold gifts, nor yet of grace, to use them alway to thy honour and glory: Through Jesus Christ our Lord.

The Epistle. Act. xi. [v. 22 to end.]
The Gospel. John. xv. [v. 12—16.]

¶ *Saint John Baptist.*

The Collect.

ALMIGHTY God, by whose providence thy servant John Baptist was wonderfully born, and sent to prepare the way of thy Son our Saviour by preaching of penance: make us so to follow his doctrine and holy life, that we may truly repent, according to his preaching, and after his example constantly[2] speak the truth, boldly rebuke vice, and patiently suffer for the truth's sake: through Jesus Christ our Lord.

The Epistle. Esay. xl. [v. 1—11.]
The Gospel. Luke. i. [v. 57 to end.]

¶ *Saint Peter's Day.*

The Collect.

ALMIGHTY God, which by thy Son Jesus Christ hast given to thy Apostle Saint Peter many excellent gifts, and commandest[3] him earnestly to feed thy flock: make, we be-

[2 constantly to, Grafton, 2.]
[3 commandedst, Whitchurch, 1, and Grafton, 2.]

seech thee, all Bishops and Pastors diligently to preach thy holy word, and the people obediently to follow the same, that they may receive the crown of everlasting glory: through Jesus Christ our Lord.

The Epistle. Acts xii. [v. 1—11.]
The Gospel. Mat. xvi. [v. 13—19.]

¶ *Saint James the Apostle.*

The Collect.

GRANT, O merciful God, that as thy[1] holy Apostle Saint[2] James, leaving his father and all that he had, without delay, was obedient unto the calling of thy Son Jesus Christ, and followed him: So we, forsaking all worldly and carnal affections, may be evermore[3] ready to follow thy commandments: through Jesu Christ our Lord.

The Epistle. Acts xi.[4] [v. 27 to end.] [xii. v. 1—3.]
The Gospel. Math. xx. [v. 20—28.]

Saint Bartholomew.

The Collect.

O ALMIGHTY and everlasting God, which hast given grace to thy Apostle Bartholomew truly to believe and to preach thy word: grant, we beseech thee, unto thy church, both to love that he believed, and to preach that he taught: through Christ our Lord.

The Epistle. Acts v. [v. 12—16.]
The Gospel. Luke xxii. [v. 24—30.]

¶ *Saint Mathew.*

The Collect.

ALMIGHTY God, which by thy blessed Son didst call Mathew from the receipt of custom to be an Apostle and Evangelist: Grant us grace to forsake all covetous desires, and inordinate love of riches, and to follow thy said Son Jesus Christ: who liveth and reigneth. &c.

[1 thine, Grafton, 1.]   [2 Saint, omitted, Grafton, 1.]
[3 evermore be, Grafton, 2.]
[4 The references, Acts xi. and xii., are given in Grafton, 2.]

The Epistle. 2 Cor. iv. [v. 1—6.]
The Gospel. Math. ix. [v. 9—13.]

¶ Saint Michael and all Angels.

The Collect.

EVERLASTING God, which hast ordained and constituted the services of all Angels and men in a wonderful order: mercifully grant, that they which alway do thee service in heaven, may by thy appointment succour and defend us in earth: through Jesus Christ our Lord. &c.

The Epistle. Apoc. xii. [v. 7—12.]
The Gospel. Mat. xviii. [v. 1—10.]

¶ Saint Luke the Evangelist.

The Collect.

ALMIGHTY God, which calledst Luke the physician, whose praise is in the gospel, to be a physician of the soul: it may please thee by the wholesome medicines of his doctrine to heal all the diseases of our souls: through thy Son Jesu Christ our Lord.

The Epistle. 2⁵ Tim. iv. [v. 5—15.]
The Gospel. Luke x. [v. 1—7.]

¶ Simon and Jude Apostles.

The Collect.

ALMIGHTY GOD, which hast builded thy congregation upon the foundation of the Apostles and Prophets, Jesu Christ himself being the head corner stone: grant us so to be joined together in unity of spirit by their doctrine, that we may be made an holy temple acceptable to thee: through Jesu Christ our Lord[6].

The Epistle. Jude i. [v. 1—8.]
The Gospel. John xv. [v. 17 to end.]

[5 1 Tim. iv., Grafton, 1; but same Epistle.]
[6 Amen, Grafton, 2.]

¶ *All Saints.*

The Collect.

ALMIGHTY God, which hast knit together thy elect in one communion and fellowship, in the mystical body of thy Son Christ our Lord: grant us grace so to follow thy holy Saints in all virtues, and godly living, that we may come to those inspeakable joys, which thou hast prepared for them that unfeignedly love thee: Through Jesus Christ, our Lord. Amen.

The Epistle. Apoc. vii. [v. 2—12.]
The Gospel. Math. v. [v. 1—12.]

THE ORDER FOR THE ADMINISTRATION
OF THE
LORD'S SUPPER
OR
HOLY COMMUNION.

SO many as intend to be partakers of the holy Communion, shall signify their names to the Curate over night, or else in the morning, afore the beginning of morning prayer, or immediately after.

And if any of those be an open and notorious evil liver, so that the congregation by him is offended, or have done any wrong to his neighbours, by word or deed: The Curate having knowledge thereof, shall call him, and advertise him, in any wise not to presume to the Lord's Table, until he have openly declared himself to have truly repented, and amended his former naughty life, that the congregation may thereby be satisfied, which afore were offended: and that he have recompensed the parties, whom he hath done wrong unto, or at the least declare himself to be in full purpose so to do, as soon as he conveniently may.

¶ The same order shall the Curate use with those, betwixt whom he perceiveth malice and hatred to reign, not suffering them to be partakers of the LORD'S table, until he know them to be reconciled. And if one of the parties so at variance be content to forgive, from the bottom of his heart, all that the other hath trespassed against him, and to make amends for that he himself hath offended: and the other party will not be persuaded to a godly unity, but remain still in his frowardness and malice: The Minister in that case ought to admit the penitent person to the holy Communion, and not him that is obstinate.

¶ The Table having at the Communion time a fair white linen cloth upon it, shall stand in the body of the Church, or in the chancel, where Morning prayer and Evening prayer be appointed to be said. And the Priest standing at the north side of the Table, shall say the Lord's prayer, with this Collect following.

ALMIGHTY God, unto whom all hearts be open, all desires known, and from whom no secrets are hid: cleanse the thoughts of our hearts by the inspiration of thy Holy Spirit, that we may perfectly love thee, and worthily magnify thy holy name: through Christ our Lord. Amen.

¶ Then shall the Priest rehearse distinctly all the Ten Commandments: and the people kneeling, shall after every Commandment ask God's mercy for their transgression of the same, after this sort.

Minister. God spake these words, and said: I am the Lord thy God. Thou shalt have none other Gods but me.

People. Lord, have mercy upon us, and incline our hearts to keep this law.

Minister. Thou shalt not make to thyself any graven image, nor the likeness of any thing that is in heaven above, or in the earth beneath, nor[1] in the water under the earth. Thou shalt not bow down to them, nor worship them: for I the Lord thy God am a jealous God, and visit the sin of the fathers upon the children, unto the third and fourth generation of them that hate me, and shew mercy unto thousands in them that love me and keep my commandments.

People. Lord, have mercy upon us, and incline our hearts to keep this law.

Minister. Thou shalt not take the name of the Lord thy God in vain: for the Lord will not hold him guiltless that taketh his name in vain.

People. Lord, have mercy upon us, and incline our. &c.

Minister. Remember that thou keep holy the Sabbath day. Six days shalt thou labour and do all that thou hast to do, but the seventh day is the sabbath of the Lord thy God. In it thou shalt do no manner of work, thou and thy son and thy daughter, thy man servant, and thy maidservant, thy cattle, and the stranger that is within thy gates: for in six days the Lord made heaven and earth, the sea, and all that in them is, and rested the seventh day. Wherefore the Lord blessed the seventh day, and hallowed it.

People. Lord, have mercy upon us, and incline our. &c.

Minister. Honour thy father and thy mother, that thy days may be long in the land which the Lord thy God giveth thee.

[1 or, Grafton, 2.]

People. Lord, have mercy upon us, and incline our. &c.
Minister. Thou shalt do no[2] murther.
People. Lord, have mercy upon us, and incline[3] our. &c.
Minister. Thou shalt not commit adultery.
People. Lord, have mercy upon us, and incline our. &c.
Minister. Thou shalt not steal.
People. Lord, have mercy upon us[4], and incline our. &c.
Minister. Thou shalt not bear false witness against thy neighbour.
People. Lord, have mercy upon us, and incline our hearts to keep this law.
Minister. Thou shalt not covet thy neighbour's house. Thou shalt not covet thy neighbour's wife, nor his servant, nor his maid, nor his ox, nor his ass, nor any thing that is his.
People. Lord, have mercy upon us, and write all these thy laws in our hearts we beseech thee.

¶ Then shall follow the Collect of the day, with one of these two Collects following for the king: the Priest standing up and saying.

¶ Let us pray.   Priest.

ALMIGHTY God, whose kingdom is everlasting, and power infinite: have mercy upon the whole congregation, and so rule the heart of thy chosen servant Edward the sixth, our king and governor, that he (knowing whose minister he is) may above all things seek thy honour and glory: and that we his subjects (duly considering whose authority he hath) may faithfully serve, honour, and humbly obey him, in thee, and for thee, according to thy blessed word and ordinance: Through Jesus Christ our Lord, who with thee, and the Holy Ghost, liveth, and reigneth ever one God, world without end. Amen.

ALMIGHTY and everlasting God, we be taught by thy holy word, that the hearts of kings are in thy rule and governance, and that thou dost dispose, and turn them as it seemeth best to thy godly wisdom: we humbly beseech thee, so to dispose and govern the heart of Edward the sixth, thy

[2] not do, Grafton, 2.]
[3] incline, &c., in this and the two following responses, Grafton, 1 and 2.]
[4] have mercy upon us, &c., Grafton, 2.]

servant, our king and governor, that in all his thoughts, words, and works, he may ever seek thy honour and glory, and study to preserve thy people committed to his charge, in wealth, peace, and godliness. Grant this, O merciful Father, for thy dear Son's sake Jesus Christ our Lord. Amen.

¶ Immediately after the Collects, the Priest shall read the Epistle, beginning thus.

¶ The Epistle written in the. Chapter of.

And the Epistle ended, he shall say the Gospel, beginning thus.

The Gospel, written in the. Chapter of.

And the Epistle and Gospel being ended, shall be said the Creed.

I BELIEVE in one God, the Father almighty, maker of heaven and earth, and of all things visible, and invisible: And in one Lord Jesu Christ, the only begotten Son of God, begotten of his Father before all worlds: God of Gods[1], light of light, very God of very God: begotten[2], not made, being of one substance with the Father, by whom all things were made: who for us men and for our salvation, came down from heaven, and was incarnate by the Holy Ghost, of the virgin Mary, and was made man: and was crucified also for us, under Pontius Pilate. He suffered and was buried, and the third day he arose again according to the scriptures: and ascended into heaven, and sitteth at the right hand of the Father. And he shall come again with glory, to judge both the quick and the dead: Whose kingdom shall have none end. And I believe in the Holy Ghost, the Lord and giver of life, who proceedeth from the Father and the Son, who with the Father and the Son together, is worshipped and glorified, who spake by the Prophets. And I believe one Catholic and Apostolic church. I acknowledge one Baptism, for the remission of sins. And I look for the resurrection of the dead, and the life of the world to come. Amen.

After the Creed, if there be no sermon, shall follow one of the homilies already set forth, or hereafter to be set forth by common authority.

[1 God of God, Whitchurch, 1, and Grafton, 2: and in Whitchurch, 2, the *s* is blotted out by a pen.]

[2 gotten, Grafton, 2.]

After such sermon, homily, or exhortation, the Curate shall declare unto the people whether there be any holy days or fasting days the week following: and earnestly exhort them to remember the poor, saying one or more of these Sentences following, as he thinketh most convenient by his discretion.

LET your light so shine before men, that they may see your good works, and glorify your Father which is in heaven. *Math.* v.

Lay not up for yourselves treasure upon the earth, where the rust and moth doth corrupt, and where thieves break through and steal: But lay up for yourselves treasures in heaven, where neither rust nor moth doth corrupt, and where thieves do not break through and steal. *Math.* vi.

Whatsoever you would that men should do unto you, even so do unto them: for this is the law and the Prophets. *Math.* vii.

Not every one that saith unto me, Lord, Lord, shall enter into the kingdom of heaven: but he that doeth the will of my Father which is in heaven. *Math.* vii.

Zache stood forth, and said unto the Lord: Behold, Lord, the half of my goods I give to the poor, and if I have done any wrong to any man, I restore fourfold. *Luk.* xix.

Who goeth a warfare at any time of his own cost? who planteth a vineyard, and eateth not of the fruit thereof? Or who feedeth a flock, and eateth not of the milk of the flock? 1 *Cor.* ix.

If we have sown unto you spiritual things, is it a great matter, if we shall reap your worldly things? 1 *Cor.* ix.

Do ye not know, that they which minister about holy things, live of the sacrifice? They which wait of the altar, are partakers with the altar? Even so hath the Lord also ordained, that they which preach the gospel, should live of the gospel. 1 *Cor.* ix.

He which soweth little shall reap little, and he that soweth plenteously shall reap plenteously. Let every man do according as he is disposed in his heart, not grudging,[3] or of necessity: for God loveth a cheerful giver. 2 *Cor.* ix.

Let him that is taught in the word, minister unto him that teacheth, in all good things. Be not deceived, God is not mocked: for whatsoever a man soweth, that shall he reap. *Gal.* vi.

[[3] grudgingly, Grafton, 2.]

While we have time, let us do good unto all men, and specially unto them, which are of the household of faith. *Gala.* vi.

Godliness is great riches, if a man be contented[1] with that he hath : for we brought nothing into the world, neither may we carry any thing out. 1 *Tim.* vi.

Charge them which are rich in this world, that they be ready to give, and glad to distribute : laying up in store for themselves a good foundation against the time to come, that they may attain eternal life. 1 *Tim.* vi.

God is not unrighteous, that he will forget your works and labour that proceedeth of love : which love ye have shewed for his name's sake, which have ministered unto saints, and yet do minister. *Hebr.* vi.

To do good, and to distribute, forget not : for with such sacrifices God is pleased. *Hebr.* xiii.

Whoso hath this world's good, and seeth his brother have need, and shutteth up his compassion from him, how dwelleth the love of God in him? 1 *Joh.* iii.

Give alms of thy goods, and turn never thy face from any poor man, and then the face of the Lord shall not be turned away from thee. *Tob.* iv.

Be merciful after thy power. If thou hast much, give plenteously : If thou hast little, do thy diligence gladly to give of that little: for so gatherest thou thyself a good reward in the day of necessity. *Tob.* iv.

He that hath pity upon the poor, lendeth unto the Lord : and look what he layeth out, it shall be paid him again. *Pro.* xix.

Blessed be the man that provideth for the sick and needy, the Lord shall deliver him in the time of trouble. *Psal.* lxi.

¶ Then shall the Church wardens, or some other by them appointed, gather the devotion of the people, and put the same into the poor men's box : and upon the offering days appointed, every man and woman shall pay to the Curate the due and accustomed offerings : after which done, the Priest shall say.

Let us pray for the whole state[2] of Christ's Church militant here in earth.

ALMIGHTY and everliving God, which by thy holy Apostle hast taught us to make prayers and supplications, and to give thanks for all men : we humbly beseech thee most mercifully

[[1] content, Grafton, 2.]   [[2] estate, Grafton, 2.]

to accept our *alms, and to receive these our prayers which we offer unto thy divine Majesty: beseeching thee to inspire continually the universal church with the spirit of truth, unity and concord: and grant that all they that do confess thy holy name, may agree in the truth of thy holy word, and live in unity and godly love. We beseech thee also to save and defend all Christian Kings, Princes, and governors, and specially thy servant, Edward our King, that under him we may be godly and quietly governed: and grant unto his whole council, and to all that be put in authority under him, that they may truly and indifferently minister justice, to the punishment of wickedness and vice, and to the maintenance of God's true religion and virtue. Give grace (O heavenly Father) to all Bishops, Pastors and Curates, that they may both by their life and doctrine set forth thy true and [4] lively word, and rightly and duly administer thy holy Sacraments: and to all thy people give thy heavenly grace, and especially to this congregation here present, that with meek heart and due reverence they may hear and receive thy holy word, truly serving thee in holiness and righteousness all the days of their life. And we most humbly beseech thee of thy goodness (O Lord) to comfort and succour all them which in this transitory life be in trouble, sorrow, need, sickness, or any other adversity: Grant this, O Father, for Jesus Christ's sake, our only mediator and advocate. Amen.

* If there be none [3] alms given unto the poor, then shall the words of accepting our alms be left out unsaid.

Then shall follow this exhortation at certain times when the Curate shall see the people negligent to come to the holy Communion.

WE be come together at this time, dearly beloved brethren, to feed at the Lord's supper, unto the which in God's behalf I bid you all that be here present, and beseech you for the Lord Jesus Christ's sake, that ye will not refuse to come thereto, being so lovingly called and bidden of God himself. Ye know how grievous and unkind a thing it is, when a man hath prepared a rich feast, decked his table with all kind of provision, so that there lacketh nothing but the guests to sit down: and yet they which be called, without any cause most unthankfully refuse to come. Which of

[3 no, Grafton, 2.]   [4 and, omitted, Grafton, 2.]

you, in such a case, would not be moved? Who would not think a great injury and wrong done unto him? Wherefore, most dearly beloved in Christ, take ye good heed, lest ye withdrawing yourselves from this holy supper, provoke God's indignation against you. It is an easy matter for a man to say, I will not communicate, because I am otherwise letted with worldly business: but such excuses be not so easily accepted and allowed before God. If any man say, I am a grievous sinner, and therefore am afraid to come: wherefore then do you[1] not repent and amend? When God calleth you, be you not ashamed to say you[1] will not come? When you should return to God, will you excuse yourself and say that you be not ready? Consider earnestly with yourselves how little such feigned excuses shall avail before God. They that refused the feast in the gospel, because they had bought a farm, or would try their yokes of oxen, or because they were married, were not so excused, but counted unworthy of the heavenly feast. I for my part am here present, and according unto[2] mine office, I bid you in the name of God, I call you in Christ's behalf, I exhort you, as you love your own salvation, that ye will be partakers of this holy Communion. And as the Son of God did vouchsafe to yield up his soul by death upon the Cross for your health: even so it is your duty to receive the Communion together in the remembrance of his death, as he himself commanded. Now if you will in no wise thus do, consider with yourselves how great injury you[1] do unto God, and how sore punishment hangeth over your heads for the same. And whereas ye offend God so sore in refusing this holy Banquet, I admonish, exhort, and beseech you, that unto this unkindness ye will not add any more. Which thing ye[3] shall do, if ye stand by as gazers and lookers on[4] them that do communicate, and be no partakers of the same yourselves. For what thing can this be accounted else, than a further contempt and unkindness unto God. Truly it is a great unthankfulness to say nay when ye be called: but the fault is much greater when men stand by, and yet will neither eat nor drink this holy Communion with other. I pray you what

[[1] ye, Grafton, 2.]   [[2] to, Grafton, 1 and 2.]
[[3] you, Grafton, 2.]   [[4] of, Grafton, 2.]

THE COMMUNION.

can this be else, but even to have the mysteries of Christ in derision? It is said unto all: Take ye and eat. Take and drink ye all of this: do this in remembrance of me. With what face then, or with what countenance shall ye hear these words? What will this be else but a neglecting, a despising, and mocking of the Testament of Christ? Wherefore, rather than you should so do, depart you hence and give place to them that be godly disposed. But when you depart, I beseech you, ponder with yourselves from whom you[5] depart: ye depart from the Lord's table, ye depart from your brethren, and from the banquet of most heavenly food. These things if ye earnestly consider, ye shall by God's grace return to a better mind, for the obtaining whereof, we shall make our humble petitions while we shall receive the holy Communion.

¶ And sometime shall be said this also, at the discretion of the Curate.

DEARLY beloved, forasmuch as our duty is to render to Almighty God our heavenly Father most hearty thanks, for that he hath given his Son our Saviour Jesus Christ, not only to die for us, but also to be our spiritual food and sustenance, as it is declared unto us, as well by God's word as by the holy Sacraments of his blessed body and blood, the which being so comfortable a thing to them which receive it worthily, and so dangerous to them that will presume to receive it unworthily: My duty is to exhort you to consider the dignity of the holy mystery, and the great peril of the unworthy receiving thereof, and so to search and examine your own consciences, as you should come holy and clean to a most Godly and heavenly feast: so that in no wise you come but in the marriage garment, required of God in holy scripture; and so come and be received, as worthy partakers of such a heavenly table. The way and means thereto is: First to examine your lives and conversation by the rule of God's commandments, and whereinsoever ye shall perceive yourselves to have offended, either by will, word, or deed, there bewail your own sinful lives, confess yourselves to almighty God with full purpose of amendment of life. And if ye shall perceive your of-

[5 ye, Grafton, 2.]

fences to be such, as be not only against God, but also against your neighbours: then ye shall reconcile yourselves unto them, ready to make restitution and satisfaction, according to the uttermost of your powers, for all injuries and wrongs done by you to any other: and likewise being ready to forgive other that have offended you, as you would have forgiveness of your offences at God's hand: for otherwise the receiving of the holy Communion doth nothing else, but increase your damnation. And because it is requisite that no man should come to the holy Communion but with a full trust in God's mercy, and with a quiet conscience: therefore if there be any of you which by the means afore said cannot quiet his own conscience, but requireth further comfort or counsel; then let him come to me, or some other discreet and learned minister of God's word, and open his grief, that he may receive such ghostly counsel, advice, and comfort, as his conscience may be relieved; and that by the ministry of God's word he may receive comfort and the benefit of absolution, to the quieting of his conscience, and avoiding of all scruple and doubtfulness.

Then shall the Priest say this exhortation.

DEARLY beloved in the Lord: ye that mind to come to the holy Communion of the body and blood of our Saviour Christ, must consider what S. Paul writeth to[1] the Corinthians, how he exhorteth all persons diligently to try and examine themselves, before they presume to eat of that bread, and drink of that cup: for as the benefit is great, if with a truly penitent heart and lively faith we receive that holy Sacrament, (for then we spiritually eat the flesh of Christ, and drink his blood, then we dwell in Christ and Christ in us, we be one with Christ, and Christ with us;) so is the danger great, if we receive the same unworthily. For then we be guilty of the body and blood of Christ our Saviour. We eat and drink our own damnation, not considering the Lord's body. We kindle God's wrath against us, we provoke him to plague us with divers diseases, and sundry kinds of death. Therefore, if any of you be a blasphemer of God, an hinderer or slanderer of his word, an adulterer, or be in malice or envy, or in any other grievous crime, bewail your sins, and come not to this holy Table, lest after

[[1] writeth unto, Grafton, 2.]

the taking of that holy Sacrament, the devil enter into you, as he entered into Judas, and fill you full of all iniquities, and bring you to destruction, both of body and soul. Judge therefore yourselves, brethren, that ye be not judged of the Lord. Repent you truly for your sins past, have a lively and stedfast faith in Christ our Saviour. Amend your lives, and be in perfect charity with all men: so shall ye be meet partakers of those holy mysteries. And above all things, ye must give most humble and hearty thanks to God the Father, the Son, and the Holy Ghost, for the redemption of the world by the death and passion of our Saviour Christ, both God and man: who did humble himself, even to the death upon the Cross, for us miserable sinners, which lay in darkness and shadow of death, that he might make us the children of God, and exalt us to everlasting life. And to the end that we should alway remember the exceeding great love of our Master and only Saviour Jesu Christ, thus dying for us, and the innumerable benefits (which by his precious blood shedding he hath obtained to us,) he hath instituted and ordained holy mysteries, as pledges of his love, and continual remembrance of his death, to our great and endless comfort. To him therefore with the Father and the Holy Ghost, let us give (as we are most bounden) continual thanks: submitting ourselves wholly to his holy will and pleasure, and studying to serve him in true holiness and righteousness all the days of our life. Amen.

¶ Then shall the Priest say to them that come to receive the holy Communion.

You that do truly and earnestly repent you of your sins, and be in love and charity with your neighbours, and intend to lead a new life, following the commandments of God, and walking from henceforth in his holy ways: Draw near, and take this holy Sacrament to your comfort: make your humble confession to almighty God before this congregation here gathered together in his holy name, meekly kneeling upon your knees.

¶ Then shall this general confession be made, in the name of all those that are minded to receive the holy Communion, either by one of them, or else by one of the ministers, or by the Priest himself, all kneeling humbly upon their knees.

ALMIGHTY God, Father of our Lord Jesus Christ, Maker of all things, Judge of all men, We knowledge[1] and bewail our manifold sins and wickedness, which we from time to time most grievously have committed, by thought, word and deed, against thy divine Majesty; provoking most justly thy wrath and indignation against us: we do earnestly repent, and be heartily sorry for these our misdoings: the remembrance of them is grievous unto us, the burthen of them is intolerable: have mercy upon us, have mercy upon us, most merciful Father, for thy Son our Lord Jesus Christ's sake: forgive us all that is past, and grant that we may ever hereafter serve and please thee, in newness of life, to the honour and glory of thy name: Through Jesus Christ our Lord.

Then shall the Priest or the Bishop (being present) stand up, and turning himself to the people, say[2] thus.

ALMIGHTY God our heavenly Father, who of his great mercy hath promised forgiveness of sins to all them, which with hearty repentance and true faith turn unto[3] him: have mercy upon you, pardon and deliver you from all your sins, confirm and strength[4] you in all goodness, and bring you to everlasting life: through Jesus Christ our Lord. Amen.

Then shall the Priest also say.

Hear what comfortable words our Saviour Christ saith, to all that truly turn to him.

COME unto me, all that travail and be heavy laden, and I shall refresh you. So God loved the world, that he gave his only begotten Son, to the end that all that believe in him should not perish, but have life everlasting.

Hear also what saint Paul sayeth.

This is a true saying, and worthy of all men to be received, that Jesus Christ came into the world to save sinners.

Hear also what Saint John sayeth.

If any man sin, we have an advocate with the Father, Jesus Christ the righteous, and he is the propitiation for our sins.

[1 acknowledge, Grafton, 2.]   [2 shall say, Grafton, 2.]
[3 to, Grafton, 2.]   [4 strengthen, Grafton, 2.]

THE COMMUNION. 277

¶ *After the which, the Priest shall proceed, saying.*

Lift up your hearts.
Answer. We lift them up unto the Lord.
Priest. Let us give thanks unto our Lord God.
Answer. It is meet and right so to do.
Priest. It is very meet, right, and our bounden duty, that we should at all times, and in all places, give thanks unto thee, O Lord holy Father, almighty everlasting God.

¶ Here shall follow the proper Preface,[5] according to the time, if there be any specially appointed: or else immediately shall follow: Therefore with Angels. &c.

PROPER PREFACES.

¶ *Upon Christmas day, and seven days after.*

BECAUSE thou didst give Jesus Christ, thine only Son, to be born as this day for us, who, by the operation of the Holy Ghost, was made very man, of the substance of the Virgin Mary his mother, and that without spot of sin, to make us clean from all sin. Therefore.[6] &c.

Upon Easter day, and seven days after.

BUT chiefly are we bound to praise thee, for the glorious resurrection of thy Son Jesus Christ our Lord, for he is the very Paschal lamb, which was offered for us, and hath taken away the sin of the world, who by his death hath destroyed death, and by his rising to life again hath restored to us everlasting life. Therefore. &c.

¶ *Upon the Ascension day, and seven days after.*

THROUGH thy most dear beloved Son, Jesus Christ our Lord: who after his most glorious resurrection manifestly appeared to all his Apostles, and in their sight ascended up into heaven, to prepare a place for us, that where he is, thither might we also ascend, and reign with him in glory. Therefore with.[7] &c.

[5 Prefaces, Grafton, 2.]
[6 Therefore with Angels, &c.: the same in the three next responses, Grafton, 2.]
[7 Therefore with Angels, &c., Grafton, 1.]

THE COMMUNION.

¶ *Upon Whitsunday, and six days after.*

THROUGH Jesus[1] Christ our Lord, according to whose most true promise, the Holy Ghost came down this day from heaven, with a sudden great sound, as it had been a mighty wind, in the likeness of fiery tongues, lighting upon the Apostles, to teach them, and to lead them to all truth, giving them both the gift of divers languages, and also boldness with fervent zeal, constantly to preach the gospel unto all nations, whereby we are brought out of darkness and error into the clear light and true knowledge of thee, and of thy Son Jesus Christ. Therefore with. &c.

Upon the feast of Trinity only.

IT is very meet, right, and our bounden duty, that we should at all times, and in all places, give thanks to thee, O Lord, almighty and everlasting God, which art one God, one Lord, not one only person, but three persons in one substance: for that which we believe of the glory of the Father, the same we believe of the Son, and of the Holy Ghost, without any difference or inequality. Therefore[2] with. &c.

After which preface, shall follow immediately.

¶ Therefore with Angels and Archangels, and with all the company of heaven, we laud and magnify thy glorious name, evermore praising thee, and saying:

Holy, holy, holy, Lord God of hosts: heaven and earth are full of thy glory: glory be to thee, O Lord most high.

Then shall the Priest, kneeling down at God's board, say in the name of all them that shall receive the Communion, this prayer following.

WE do not presume to come to this thy table (O merciful Lord) trusting in our own righteousness, but in thy manifold and great mercies: we be not worthy so much as to gather up the crumbs under thy table: but thou art the same Lord, whose property is always to have mercy: grant us therefore (gracious Lord) so to eat the

[[1] Jesu, Grafton, 2.]   [[2] Therefore, &c., Grafton, 2.]

flesh of thy dear Son Jesus Christ, and to drink his blood, that our sinful bodies may be made clean by his body, and our souls washed through his most precious blood, and that we may evermore dwell in him, and he in us. Amen.³

Then the Priest standing up shall say, as followeth.

ALMIGHTY God our heavenly Father, which of thy tender mercy didst give thine only Son Jesus Christ, to suffer death upon the cross for our redemption, who made there (by his one oblation of himself once offered) a full, perfect and sufficient sacrifice, oblation, and satisfaction for the sins of the whole world, and did institute, and in his holy Gospel command us to continue, a perpetual memory of that his precious death, until his coming again: Hear us, O merciful Father, we beseech thee: and grant that we receiving these thy creatures of bread and wine, according to thy Son our Saviour Jesu Christ's holy institution, in remembrance of his death and passion, may be partakers of his most blessed body and blood: who, in the same night that he was betrayed, took bread, and when he had given thanks, he brake it, and gave it to his disciples, saying: Take, eat, this is my body which is given for you. Do this in remembrance of me. Likewise after supper he took the cup, and when he had given thanks, he gave it to them, saying: Drink ye all of this, for this is my blood of the new Testament, which is shed for you and for many, for remission of sins: do this as oft as ye shall drink it in remembrance of me.

¶ Then shall the minister first receive the Communion in both kinds himself, and next deliver it to other ministers, if any be there present (that they may help the chief minister), and after to the people in their hands kneeling. And when he delivereth the bread, he shall say.

Take and eat this, in remembrance that Christ died for thee, and feed on him in thy heart by faith, with thanksgiving.

¶ And the minister that delivereth the cup, shall say.

Drink this in remembrance that Christ's blood was shed for thee, and be thankful.

[³ Amen, omitted in Grafton, 2.]

¶ Then shall the Priest say the Lord's prayer, the people repeating after him every petition.

¶ After shall be said as followeth.

O LORD and heavenly Father, we, thy humble servants, entirely desire thy fatherly goodness, mercifully to accept this our sacrifice of praise and thanksgiving: most humbly beseeching thee to grant, that by the merits and death of thy Son Jesus Christ, and through faith in his blood, we and all thy whole church may obtain remission of our sins, and all other benefits of his passion. And here we offer and present unto thee, O Lord, ourselves, our souls and bodies, to be a reasonable, holy, and lively sacrifice unto thee: humbly beseeching thee, that all we which be partakers of this holy Communion, may be fulfilled with thy grace and heavenly benediction. And although we be unworthy, through our manifold sins, to offer unto thee any sacrifice: yet we beseech thee to accept this our bounden duty and service, not weighing our merits, but pardoning our offences, through Jesus Christ our Lord: by whom and with whom, in the unity of the Holy Ghost, all honour and glory be unto thee, O Father Almighty, world without end. Amen.

¶ Or this.

ALMIGHTY and everliving God, we most heartily thank thee, for that thou dost vouchsafe to feed us, which have duly received these holy mysteries, with the spiritual food of the most precious body and blood of thy Son our Saviour Jesus Christ, and dost assure us thereby of thy favour and goodness toward us, and that we be very members incorporate in thy mystical body, which is the blessed company of all faithful people, and be also heirs through hope of thy everlasting kingdom, by the merits of the most precious death and passion of thy dear Son: we now most humbly beseech thee, O heavenly Father, so to assist us with thy grace, that we may continue in that holy fellowship, and do all such good works as thou hast prepared for us to walk in, through Jesus Christ our Lord: to whom, with thee and the Holy Ghost, be all honour and glory, world without end. Amen.

¶ Then shall be said or sung,

GLORY be to God on high. And in earth peace, good will towards men. We praise thee, we bless thee, we worship

THE COMMUNION.

thee, we glorify thee, we give thanks to thee, for thy great glory. O Lord God heavenly king, God the Father almighty. O Lord, the only begotten Son Jesu Christ: O Lord God, Lamb of God, Son of the Father, that takest away the sins of the world, have mercy upon us: Thou that takest away the sins of the world, have mercy upon us. Thou that takest away the sins of the world, receive our prayer. Thou that sittest at the right hand of God the Father, have mercy upon us. For thou only art holy: Thou only art the Lord. Thou only, O Christ, with the Holy Ghost, art most high in the glory of God the Father. Amen.

Then the Priest or the Bishop, if he be present, shall let them depart with this blessing.

THE peace of God, which passeth all understanding, keep your hearts and minds in the knowledge and love of God, and of his Son Jesu Christ our Lord: and the blessing of God almighty, the Father, the Son, and the Holy Ghost, be amongst[1] you, and remain with you always. Amen.

Collects to be said after the Offertory, when there is no Communion, every such day one. And the same may be said also as often as occasion shall serve, after the Collects, either of Morning and Evening prayer, Communion, or Litany, by the discretion of the minister.

ASSIST us mercifully, O Lord, in these our supplications and prayers, and dispose the way of thy servants toward the attainment of everlasting salvation: that among all the changes and chances of this mortal life, they may ever be defended by thy most gracious and ready help: through Christ our Lord. Amen.

O ALMIGHTY Lord and everliving God, vouchsafe, we beseech thee, to direct, sanctify and govern both our hearts and bodies, in the ways of thy laws, and in the works of thy commandments: that through thy most mighty protection, both here and ever, we may be preserved in body and soul: through our Lord and Saviour Jesus Christ. Amen.

GRANT, we beseech thee, Almighty God, that the words which we have heard this day, with our outward ears, may through thy grace be so grafted inwardly in our hearts, that

[1 among, Grafton, 2.]

they may bring forth in us the fruit of good living, to the honour and praise of thy name: through Jesus Christ our Lord. Amen.

PREVENT us, O Lord, in all our doings, with thy most gracious favour, and further us with thy continual help, that in all our works begun, continued, and ended in thee, we may glorify thy holy name, and finally by thy mercy obtain everlasting life: through Jesus Christ our Lord. Amen.

ALMIGHTY God, the fountain of all wisdom, which knowest our necessities before we ask, and our ignorance in asking: we beseech thee to have compassion upon our infirmities, and those things which for our unworthiness we dare not, and for our blindness we cannot ask, vouchsafe to give us for the worthiness of thy Son Jesus Christ our Lord. Amen.

ALMIGHTY God, which hast promised to hear the petitions of them that ask in thy Son's name: we beseech thee mercifully to incline thine ears to us that have made now our prayers and supplications unto thee; and grant that those things which we[1] faithfully asked according to thy will, may effectually be obtained, to the relief of our necessity, and to the setting forth of thy glory: through Jesus Christ our Lord. Amen.

¶ Upon the holy days, if there be no Communion, shall be said all that is appointed at the Communion, until the end of the Homily, concluding with the general prayer, for the whole state[2] of Christ's church militant here in earth: and one or more of these Collects before rehearsed, as occasion shall serve.

¶ And there shall be no celebration of the Lord's Supper, except there be a good number to communicate with the Priest, according to his discretion.

¶ And if there be not above twenty persons in the Parish, of discretion to receive the Communion: yet there shall be no Communion, except four, or three at the least communicate with the Priest. And in Cathedral and Collegiate churches, where be many Priests and Deacons, they shall all receive the Communion with the minister every Sunday at the least, except they have a reasonable cause to the contrary.

¶ And to take away the superstition, which any person hath, or might

[[1] we have, Grafton, 1 and 2.]   [[2] estate, Grafton, 2.]

have in the bread and wine, it shall suffice that the bread be such, as is usual to be eaten at the table with other meats, but the best and purest wheat bread, that conveniently may be gotten. And if any of the bread or wine remain, the Curate shall have it to his own use.

¶ The bread and wine for the Communion shall be provided by the Curate, and the churchwardens, at the charges of the Parish, and the Parish shall be discharged of such sums of money, or other duties, which hitherto they have paid for the same, by order of their houses every Sunday.

¶ And note, that every Parishioner shall communicate, at the least three times in the year: of which, Easter to be one: and shall also receive the Sacraments, and other rites, according to the order in[3] this book appointed. And yearly at Easter, every Parishioner shall reckon with his Parson, Vicar, or Curate, or his, or their deputy or deputies, and pay to them or him all ecclesiastical duties, accustomably due, then and at that time to be paid.

[4]Although no order can be so perfectly devised, but it may be of some, either for their ignorance and infirmity, or else of malice and obstinacy, misconstrued, depraved, and interpreted in a wrong part: And yet because brotherly charity willeth, that so much as conveniently may be, offences should be taken away: therefore we willing to do the same. Whereas it is ordained in the book of common prayer, in the administration of the Lord's Supper, that the Communicants kneeling should receive the holy Communion: which thing being well meant, for a signification of the humble and grateful acknowledging of the benefits of Christ, given unto the worthy receiver, and to avoid the profanation and disorder, which about the holy Communion might else ensue: lest yet the same kneeling might be thought or taken otherwise, we do declare that it is not meant thereby, that any adoration is done, or ought to be done, either unto the sacramental bread or wine there bodily received, or to any real and essential presence there being of Christ's natural flesh and blood. For as concerning the sacramental bread and wine, they remain still in their very natural substances, and therefore may not be adored, for that were Idolatry to be abhorred of all faithful Christians. And as concerning the natural body and blood of our Saviour Christ, they are in heaven and not here. For it is against the truth of Christ's true natural body, to be in more places than in one at one time.

[3 order of, Grafton, 2.]
[4 This paragraph is fourth in order in Grafton, 2. It is printed on a separate leaf in other copies, and, as is evident from the signatures, was added afterwards. In Grafton, 1, the leaf is pasted in after the copy was bound; and several copies are without it.]

THE

MINISTRATION OF BAPTISM

TO BE USED IN THE CHURCH.

It appeareth by ancient writers, that the Sacrament of Baptism in the old time was not commonly ministered, but at two times in the year: at Easter, and Whitsuntide. At which times it was openly ministered, in the presence of all the congregation. Which custom (now being grown out of use) although it can not for many considerations be well restored again, yet it is thought good to follow the same as near as conveniently may be: wherefore the people are to be admonished, that it is most convenient that Baptism should not be ministered but upon Sundays, and other holy days, when the most number of people may come together, as well for that the congregation there present may testify the receiving of them that be newly baptized into the number of Christ's Church, as also because in the Baptism of infants every man present may be put in remembrance of his own profession made to God in his Baptism.

For which cause also, it is expedient that Baptism be ministered in the English tongue.

Nevertheless (if necessity so require) children may at all times be baptized at home.

PUBLIC BAPTISM.

¶ When there are children to be baptized upon the Sunday, or holy day, the Parents shall give knowledge over night, or in the morning, afore the beginning of Morning prayer to the Curate. And then the Godfathers, Godmothers, and people, with the children, must be ready at the Font, either immediately after the last lesson at Morning prayer, or else immediately after the last lesson at Evening prayer, as the Curate by his discretion shall appoint. And then standing there, the Priest shall ask whether the children be baptized or no. If they answer, no: then shall the Priest say thus.

DEARLY beloved, forasmuch as all men be conceived and born in sin, and that our Saviour Christ saith, none can enter into the kingdom of God, except he be regenerate, and born anew of water, and the Holy Ghost: I beseech you to call upon God the Father, through our Lord Jesus Christ, that of his bounteous mercy, he will grant to these children, that thing which by nature they cannot have, that they may be baptized with water and the Holy Ghost, and received into Christ's holy church, and be made lively members of the same.

Then the Priest shall say.

¶ Let us pray.

ALMIGHTY and everlasting God, which of thy great mercy didst save Noe and his family in the Ark, from perishing by water: and also didst safely lead the children of Israel, thy people, through the Red Sea, figuring thereby thy holy Baptism; and by the Baptism of thy wellbeloved Son Jesus Christ, didst sanctify the flood Jordan, and all other waters, to the mystical washing away of sin: We beseech thee for thy infinite mercies, that thou wilt mercifully look upon these children, sanctify them and wash them with thy Holy Ghost, that they being delivered from thy wrath, may be received into the Ark of Christ's church, and being stedfast in faith, joyful through hope, and rooted in charity, may so pass the waves of this troublesome world, that finally they may come to the land of everlasting life, there to reign with thee, world without end: through Jesus Christ our Lord. Amen.

ALMIGHTY and immortal God, the aid of all that need, the helper of all that flee to thee for succour, the life of them that believe, and the resurrection of the dead: We call upon thee for these infants, that they coming to thy holy Baptism, may receive remission of their sins by spiritual regeneration. Receive them, O Lord, as thou hast promised by thy wellbeloved Son, saying: Ask and you shall have, seek and you shall find, knock and it shall be opened unto you. So give now unto us that ask. Let us that seek find. Open the[1] gate unto us that knock, that these infants may enjoy the everlasting benediction of thy heavenly washing, and may come to the eternal kingdom, which thou hast promised by Christ our Lord. Amen.

¶ Then shall the Priest say: Hear the words of the Gospel, written by Saint Mark in the tenth Chapter.

AT a certain time they brought children to Christ that he should touch them, and his disciples rebuked those that brought them. But when Jesus saw it, he was displeased, and said unto them: Suffer little children to come unto me, and forbid them not; for to such belongeth the kingdom of God. Verily I say unto you: whosoever doth not receive the kingdom of God, as a little child, he shall not enter therein. And when he had taken them up in his arms, he put his hands upon them, and blessed them. *Mark* x.

After the Gospel is read, the Minister shall make this brief exhortation upon the words of the Gospel.

FRIENDS, you[2] hear in this Gospel the words of our Saviour Christ, that he commanded the children to be brought unto him: how he blamed those that would have kept them from him: how he exhorteth[3] all men to follow their innocency. You[4] perceive how by his outward gesture and deed he declared his good-will toward them. For he embraced them in his arms, he laid his hands upon them, and blessed them. Doubt not ye[5] therefore, but earnestly believe, that he will likewise favourably receive these present infants, that he

[1 open thy, Grafton, 2.]   [2 ye hear, Grafton, 2.]
[3 exhorted, Grafton, 2.]   [4 ye perceive, Grafton, 2.]
[5 you, Grafton, 2.]

will embrace them with the arms of his mercy, that he will give unto them the blessing of eternal life, and make them partakers of his everlasting kingdom. Wherefore we being thus persuaded of the good-will of our heavenly Father, toward[6] these infants declared by his Son Jesus Christ, and nothing doubting but that he favourably alloweth this charitable work of ours, in bringing these children to his holy Baptism: Let us faithfully and devoutly give thanks unto him, and say.

ALMIGHTY and everlasting God, heavenly Father, we give thee humble thanks, that thou hast vouchsafed[7] to call us to the knowledge of thy grace and faith in thee: increase this knowledge, and confirm this faith in us evermore. Give thy holy Spirit to these infants, that they may be born again, and be made heirs of everlasting salvation, through our Lord Jesus Christ: who liveth and reigneth with thee and the Holy Spirit, now and for ever. Amen.

¶ Then the Priest shall speak unto the Godfathers and Godmothers, on this wise.

WELLBELOVED friends, ye have brought these children here to be baptized; ye have prayed that our Lord Jesus Christ would vouchsafe to receive them, to lay his hands upon them, to bless them, to release them of their sins, to give them the kingdom of heaven, and everlasting life. Ye have heard also that our Lord Jesus Christ hath promised in his Gospel to grant all these things that ye have prayed for: which promise he for his part will most surely keep and perform. Wherefore after this promise made by Christ, these infants must also faithfully for their part promise by you that be their sureties, that they will forsake the devil and all his works, and constantly believe God's holy word, and obediently keep his commandments.

¶ Then shall the Priest demand of the Godfathers and Godmothers these questions following[8].

DOST thou forsake the devil and all his works, the vain pomp and glory of the world, with all[9] covetous desires of

[6] towards, Grafton, 2.]   [7] vouchsafe, Grafton, 2.]
[8] following, omitted by Grafton, 2.]   [9] all the, Grafton, 2.]

the same, the[1] carnal desires of the flesh, so that thou wilt not follow, nor be led by them?

Answer. I forsake them all.

Minister. Dost thou believe in God the Father almighty, maker of heaven and earth? and in Jesus Christ his only-begotten Son our Lord, and that he was conceived by the Holy Ghost, born of the virgin Mary, that he suffered under Poncius Pilate, was crucified, dead, and buried, that he went down into hell, and also did rise again the third day, that he ascended into heaven, and sitteth at the right hand of God the Father almighty, and from thence shall come again at the end of the world, to judge the quick and the dead?

And dost thou believe in the Holy Ghost, the holy Catholic Church, the Communion of Saints, the remission of sins, the resurrection of the flesh, and everlasting life after death?

Answer. All this I steadfastly believe.

Minister. Wilt thou be baptized in this faith?

Answer. That is my desire.

Then shall the Priest say.

O MERCIFUL God, grant that the old Adam in these children may be so buried, that the new man may be raised up in them. Amen.

Grant that all carnal affections may die in them, and that all things belonging to the Spirit may live and grow in them. Amen.

Grant that they may have power and strength to have victory and to triumph against the devil, the world and the flesh. Amen.

Grant that whosoever is here dedicated to thee by our office and ministry, may also be endued with heavenly virtues, and everlastingly rewarded through thy mercy, O blessed Lord God, who dost live and govern all things world without end. Amen.

ALMIGHTY everliving God, whose most dearly beloved Son Jesus Christ, for the forgiveness of our sins, did shed out of his most precious side both water and blood, and gave

[[1] and the, Grafton, 2.]

commandment to his disciples that they should go teach all nations, and baptize them in the name of the Father, the Son, and of the Holy Ghost: Regard, we beseech thee, the supplications of thy congregation, and grant that all thy servants which shall be baptized in this water, may receive the fulness of thy grace, and ever remain in the number of thy faithful and elect children, through Jesus Christ our Lord. Amen.

¶ Then the Priest shall take the child in his hands, and ask the name; and naming the child, shall dip it in the water, so it be discreetly and warily done, saying.

¶ *N.* I baptize thee in the name of the Father, and of the Son, and of the Holy Ghost. Amen.

And if the child be weak, it shall suffice to pour water upon it, saying the foresaid words.

N. I baptize thee in the name of the Father, and of the Son, and of the Holy Ghost. Amen.

Then the Priest shall make a cross upon the child's forehead, saying.

WE receive this child into the congregation of Christ's flock, and do sign him with the sign of the cross, in token that hereafter he shall not be ashamed to confess the faith of Christ crucified, and manfully to fight under his banner against sin, the world, and the devil, and to continue Christ's faithful soldier and servant unto his life's end. Amen.

Then shall the Priest say.

SEEING now, dearly beloved brethren, that these children be regenerate and grafted into the body of Christ's congregation: let us give thanks unto God for these benefits, and with one accord make our prayers unto almighty God, that they may lead the rest of their life according to this beginning.

Then shall be said.

¶ Our Father which[2] art in heaven. &c.

Then shall the Priest say.

WE yield thee hearty thanks, most merciful Father, that

[[2] Our Father which, &c., Grafton, 2.]

it hath pleased thee to regenerate this infant with thy Holy Spirit, to receive him for thy[1] own child by adoption, and to incorporate him into thy holy congregation. And humbly we beseech thee to grant that he, being dead unto sin, and living unto righteousness, and being buried with Christ in his death, may crucify the old man, and utterly abolish the whole body of sin: that as he is made partaker of the death of thy Son, so he may be partaker of his resurrection: so that finally, with the residue of thy holy congregation, he may be inheritor of thine everlasting kingdom: through Christ our Lord. Amen.

¶ At the last end, the Priest calling the Godfathers and Godmothers together, shall say this short exhortation following.

FORASMUCH as these children have promised by you to forsake the Devil and all his works, to believe in God, and to serve him, you must remember that it is your parts and duties to see that these infants be taught so soon as they shall be able to learn what a solemn vow, promise, and profession, they have made by you. And that they may know these things the better, ye shall call upon them to hear sermons. And chiefly ye shall provide that they may learn the Creed, the Lord's prayer, and the ten Commandments in the English tongue, and all other things which a Christian man ought to know and believe, to his soul's health: and that these children may be virtuously brought up, to lead a godly and Christian life: remembering alway[2] that Baptism doth represent unto us our profession, which is to follow the example of our Saviour Christ, and to be made like unto him; that as he died and rose again for us, so should we which are baptized, die from sin, and rise again unto righteousness, continually mortifying all our evil and corrupt affections, and daily proceeding in all virtue, and godliness of living.

¶ The Minister shall command that the children be brought to the Bishop to be confirmed of him, so soon as they can say in their vulgar tongue the articles of the faith, the Lord's prayer, and the x. Commandments, and be further instructed in the Catechism set forth for that purpose, accordingly as it is there expressed.

[[1] thine, Grafton, 2.]   [[2] always, Grafton, 1 and 2.]

OF THEM THAT BE

BAPTIZED IN PRIVATE HOUSES,

IN TIME OF NECESSITY.

¶ The Pastors and Curates shall oft admonish the people, that they defer not the Baptism of infants any longer than the Sunday, or other holy day next after the child be born, unless upon a great and reasonable cause declared to the Curate, and by him approved.
And also they shall warn them, that without great cause and necessity, they baptize not children at home in their houses. And when great need shall compel them so to do, that then they minister it on this fashion.
First, let them that be present call upon God for his grace, and say the Lord's prayer, if the time will suffer. And then one of them shall name the child, and dip him in the water, or pour water upon him, saying these words.

¶ *N*. I baptize thee in the name of the Father, and of the Son, and of the Holy Ghost. Amen.

And let them not doubt, but that the child so baptized, is lawfully and sufficiently baptized, and ought not to be baptized again in the Church. But yet nevertheless, if the child which is after this sort baptized, do afterward live: it is expedient that he be brought into the church, to the intent the Priest may examine and try, whether the child be lawfully baptized or no. And if those that bring any child to the church do answer that he is already baptized, then shall the Priest examine them further.

¶ By whom the child was baptized?
Who was present when the child was baptized?
Whether they called upon God for grace and succour in that necessity?
With what thing, or what matter they did baptize the child?
With what words the child was baptized?
Whether they think the child to be lawfully and perfectly baptized?

And if the Minister shall prove by the answers of such as brought the child, that all things were done as they ought to be: Then shall not he christen the child again, but shall receive him, as one of the flock of the true Christian people, saying thus.

I CERTIFY you, that in this case ye have done well, and according unto due order concerning the baptizing of this child, which being born in original sin and in the wrath of God, is now by the laver of regeneration in Baptism received into the number of the children of God, and heirs of everlasting life: for our Lord Jesus Christ doth not deny his grace and mercy unto such infants, but most lovingly doth call them unto him, as the holy Gospel doth witness to our comfort, on this wise.

AT[1] a certain time they brought children unto Christ that he should touch them, and his disciples rebuked those that brought them. But when Jesus saw it, he was displeased, and said unto them: Suffer little children to come unto me, and forbid them not, for to such belongeth the kingdom of God. Verily I say unto you, whosoever doth not receive the kingdom of God as a little child, he shall not enter therein. And when he had taken them up in his arms, he put his hands upon them and blessed them. *Mark* x.

¶ After the Gospel is read, the Minister shall make this exhortation upon the words of the Gospel.

FRIENDS, you[2] hear in this Gospel the words of our Saviour Christ, that he commanded the children to be brought unto him: how he blamed those that would have kept them from him: how he exhorted all men to follow their innocency. Ye perceive how by his outward gesture and deed he declared his good-will toward them. For he embraced them in his arms, he laid his hands upon them, and blessed them. Doubt ye not[3] therefore, but earnestly believe, that he hath likewise favourably received this present infant, that he hath embraced him with the arms of his mercy, that he hath given unto him the blessing of eternal life, and made him partaker of his everlasting kingdom. Wherefore we being thus persuaded of the good-will of our

[[1] This paragraph is headed, The Gospel, by Grafton, 2.]
[[2] ye, Grafton, 2.]
[[3] doubt not you, Grafton, 2.]

heavenly Father, declared by his Son Jesus Christ towards this infant: Let us faithfully and devoutly give thanks unto him, and say the prayer which the Lord himself taught; and in declaration of our faith, let us recite the articles contained in our Creed.

Here the Minister with the Godfathers and Godmothers shall say.

OUR Father, which[4] art in heaven. &c.

¶ Then shall the Priest demand the name of the child, which being by the Godfathers and Godmothers pronounced, the Minister shall say.

Dost thou in the name of this child forsake the Devil and all his works, the vain pomp and glory of the world, with all the covetous desires of the same, the carnal desires of the flesh, and not to follow, and be led by them?

Answer. I forsake them all.

Minister. Dost thou in the name of this child profess this faith, to believe in God the Father almighty, maker of heaven and earth: And in Jesus Christ his only-begotten Son our Lord: and that he was conceived by the Holy Ghost, born of the virgin Mary, that he suffered under Poncius Pilate, was crucified, dead and buried: that he went down into hell, and also did rise again the third day: that he ascended into heaven, and sitteth at the right hand of God the Father almighty: and from thence he shall come again at the end of the world, to judge the quick and the dead?

And do you in his name believe in the Holy Ghost. The holy Catholic Church. The Communion of saints. The remission of sins. Resurrection, and everlasting life after death?

Answer. All this I stedfastly believe.

¶ Let us pray.

ALMIGHTY and everlasting God, heavenly Father, we give thee humble thanks, for that thou hast vouchsafed[5] to call us to the knowledge of thy grace and faith in thee: increase this knowledge and confirm this faith in us evermore. Give thy holy Spirit to this infant, that he being born again,

[4 Our Father, which, &c., Grafton, 2.]
[5 vouchsafe, Grafton, 2.]

and being made heir of everlasting salvation, through our Lord Jesus Christ, may continue thy servant, and attain thy promise, through the same our Lord Jesus Christ thy Son : who liveth and reigneth with thee in the unity of the same Holy Spirit everlastingly. Amen.

Then shall the Minister make this exhortation to the Godfathers, and Godmothers.

FORASMUCH as this child hath promised by you to forsake the devil and all his works, to believe in God, and to serve him : you must remember that it is your part and duty to see that this infant be taught so soon as he shall be able to learn, what a solemn vow, promise, and profession he hath made by you. And that he may know these things the better, ye shall call upon him to hear sermons : And chiefly ye shall provide that he may learn the Creed, the Lord's prayer, and the ten Commandments in the English tongue, and all other things which a Christian man ought to know and believe, to his soul's health : and that this child may be virtuously brought up, to lead a godly and a Christian life : remembering alway that Baptism doth represent unto us our profession, which is to follow the example of our Saviour Christ, and be made like unto him; that as he died and rose again for us, so should we which are baptized, die from sin, and rise again unto righteousness, continually mortifying all our evil and corrupt affections, and daily proceeding in all virtue, and godliness of living.

¶ *And so forth, as in Public Baptism.*

¶ *But if they which bring the infants to the Church, do make an uncertain answer to the Priest's questions, and say that they cannot tell what they thought, did, or said in that great fear, and trouble of mind (as oftentimes it chanceth), then let the Priest baptize him in form above written concerning Public Baptism, saving that at the dipping of the Child in the Font, he shall use this form of words.*

IF thou be not baptized already. *N.* I baptize thee in the name of the Father, and of the Son, and of the Holy Ghost. Amen.

CONFIRMATION

WHEREIN IS CONTAINED A CATECHISM FOR CHILDREN.

To the end that Confirmation may be ministered to the more edifying of such as shall receive it (according unto[1] Saint Paul's doctrine, who teacheth that all things should be done in the Church to the edification of the same) it is thought good that none hereafter shall be confirmed, but such as can say in their mother tongue the articles of the faith, the Lord's prayer, and the x. commandments: and can also answer to such questions of this short Catechism, as the Bishop (or such as he shall appoint) shall by his discretion appose them in. And this order is most convenient to be observed for divers considerations.

First, because that when children come to the years of discretion, and have learned what their Godfathers and Godmothers promised for them in baptism, they may then themselves with their own mouth, and with their own consent, openly before the Church, ratify and confirm the same: and also promise that, by the grace of God, they will evermore endeavour themselves faithfully to observe and keep such things, as they by their own mouth and confession have assented unto.

Secondly, forasmuch as Confirmation is ministered to them that be baptized, that by imposition of hands and prayer they may receive strength and defence against all temptations to sin, and the assaults of the world, and the Devil: it is most meet to be ministered when children come to that age, that partly by the frailty of their own flesh, partly by the assaults of the world and the Devil, they begin to be in danger to fall into sundry kinds of sin.

Thirdly, for that it is agreeable with the usage of the Church in times past, whereby it was ordained that Confirmation should be ministered to them that were of perfect age, that they, being instructed in Christ's religion, should openly profess their own faith, and promise to be obedient unto the will of God.

And that no man shall think that any detriment shall come to children by deferring of their Confirmation, he shall know for truth, that it is certain by God's word, that children being baptized have all things necessary for their salvation, and be undoubtedly saved.

[1 according to, Grafton, 1.]

A CATECHISM,

THAT IS TO SAY,

AN INSTRUCTION TO BE LEARNED OF EVERY CHILD, BEFORE HE BE BROUGHT TO BE CONFIRMED OF THE BISHOP.

Question. WHAT is your name?
Answer. N. or M.
Question. Who gave you this name?
Answer. My Godfathers and Godmothers in my baptism, wherein I was made a member of Christ, the child of God, and an inheritor of the kingdom of heaven.
Question. What did your Godfathers and Godmothers then for you?
Answer. They did promise and vow three things in my name. First, that I should forsake the devil and all his works and pomps, the vanities of the wicked world, and all the sinful lusts of the flesh. Secondly, that I should believe all the articles of the Christian faith. And thirdly, that I should keep God's holy will and commandments, and walk in the same all the days of my life.
Question. Dost thou not think that thou art bound to believe and to do as they have promised for thee?
Answer. Yes verily. And by God's help so I will. And I heartily thank our heavenly Father, that he hath called me to this state of salvation, through Jesus Christ our Saviour. And I pray God to give me his grace, that I may continue in the same unto my life's end.
Question. Rehearse the articles of thy belief.
Answer. I believe in God the Father almighty, maker of heaven and of earth. And in Jesus Christ his only Son our Lord. Which was conceived of the Holy Ghost, born of the virgin Mary. Suffered under Ponce Pilate, was crucified, dead and buried, he descended into hell. The third day he rose again from the dead. He ascended into heaven, and sitteth at the right hand of God the Father Almighty. From thence he shall come to judge the quick and the dead. I

believe in the Holy Ghost. The holy Catholic Church. The communion of saints. The forgiveness of sins. The resurrection of the body. And the life everlasting. Amen.

Question. What dost thou chiefly learn in these articles of thy belief?

Answer. First, I learn to believe in God the Father, who hath made me and all the world.

Secondly, in God the Son, who hath redeemed me and all mankind.

Thirdly, in God the Holy Ghost, who sanctifieth me and all the elect people of God.

Question. You said that your Godfathers and Godmothers did promise for you that you should keep God's commandments. Tell me how many there be?

Answer. Ten.

Question. Which be they?

Answer. The same which God spake in the xx. Chapter of Exodus, saying: I am the Lord thy God which have brought thee out of the land of Egypt, out of the house of bondage.

I. Thou shalt have none other gods but me.

II. Thou shalt not make to thyself any graven image nor the likeness of any thing that is in heaven above, or in the earth beneath, nor in the water under the earth: thou shalt not bow down to them, nor worship them. For I the Lord thy God am a jealous God, and visit the sins of the fathers upon the children, unto the third and fourth generation of them that hate me, and shew mercy unto thousands in them that love me, and keep my commandments.

III. Thou shalt not take the name of the Lord thy God in vain: for the Lord will not hold him guiltless that taketh his name in vain.

IV. Remember thou keep holy the Sabbath day. Six days shalt thou labour and do all that thou hast to do: but the seventh day is the Sabbath of the Lord thy God. In it thou shalt do no manner of work, thou, and thy son and thy daughter, thy man servant, and thy maid servant, thy cattle, and the stranger that is within thy gates: for in six days the Lord made heaven and earth, the sea, and all that in them is, and rested the seventh day. Wherefore the Lord blessed the seventh day, and hallowed it.

V. Honour thy father and thy mother, that thy days may be long in the land which the Lord thy God giveth thee.

VI. Thou shalt do no murther.

VII. Thou shalt not commit adultery.

VIII. Thou shalt not steal.

IX. Thou shalt not bear false witness against thy neighbour.

X. Thou shalt not covet thy neighbour's house, thou shalt not covet thy neighbour's wife, nor his servant, nor his maid, nor his ox, nor his ass, nor any thing that is his.

Question. What dost thou chiefly learn by these commandments?

Answer. I learn two things. My duty towards God, and my duty towards[1] my neighbour.

Question. What is thy duty towards God?

Answer. My duty towards God is, to believe in him; to fear him, and to love him with all my heart, with all my mind, with all my soul, and with all my strength. To worship him. To give him thanks. To put my whole trust in him. To call upon him. To honour his holy name and his word, and to serve him truly all the days of my life.

Question. What is thy duty towards[1] thy neighbour?

Answer. My duty towards my neighbour is, to love him as myself. And to do to all men as I would they should do unto me. To love, honour and succour my father and mother. To honour and obey the king and his ministers. To submit myself to all my governors, teachers, spiritual Pastors and masters. To order myself lowly and reverently to all my betters. To hurt no body by word nor deed. To be true and just in all my dealing. To bear no malice nor hatred in my heart. To keep my hands from picking and stealing, and my tongue from evil speaking, lying and slandering. To keep my body in temperance, soberness, and chastity. Not to covet nor desire other men's goods. But learn and labour truly to get mine own living, and to do my duty in that state of life, unto which it shall please God to call me.

Question. My good child, know this, that thou art not able to do these things of thyself, nor to walk in the com-

[1 toward, Grafton, 2.]

mandments of God, and to serve him, without his special grace, which thou must learn at all times to call for by diligent prayer. Let me hear therefore if thou canst say the Lord's Prayer.

Answer. Our Father, which art in heaven, hallowed be thy name. Thy kingdom come. Thy will be done in earth, as it is in heaven. Give us this day our daily bread. And forgive us our trespasses, as we forgive them that trespass against us. And lead us not into temptation. But deliver us from evil. Amen.

Question. What desirest thou of God in this prayer?

Answer. I desire my Lord God our heavenly Father, who is the giver of all goodness, to send his grace unto me and to all people, that we may worship him, serve him, and obey him as we ought to do. And I pray unto God, that he will send us all things that be needful both for our souls and bodies. And that he will be merciful unto us, and forgive us our sins: and that it will please him to save and defend us in all dangers ghostly and bodily. And that he will keep us from all sin and wickedness, and from our ghostly enemy, and from everlasting death. And this[2] I trust he will do of his mercy and goodness, through our Lord Jesu Christ. And therefore I say, Amen. So be it.

So soon as the children can say in their mother tongue, the articles of the faith, the Lord's prayer, the x. Commandments: and also can answer to such questions[3] of this short Catechism, as the Bishop (or such as he shall appoint) shall by his discretion appose them in: then shall they be brought to the Bishop by one that shall be his Godfather, or Godmother, that every child may have a witness of his Confirmation.

¶ And the Bishop shall confirm them on this wise.

¶ CONFIRMATION.

Our help is in the name of the Lord.
Answer. Which hath made both heaven and earth.
Minister. Blessed is the name of the Lord.
Answer. Henceforth world without end.
Minister. Lord, hear our prayer.
Answer. And let our cry come to thee.

[2 thus, Grafton, 2.]   [3 question, Grafton, 2.]

CONFIRMATION.

Let us pray.

ALMIGHTY and everliving God, who[1] hast vouchsafed[2] to regenerate these thy servants by water and the Holy Ghost, and hast given unto them forgiveness of all their sins: strengthen them, we beseech thee, O Lord, with the Holy Ghost the Comforter, and daily increase in them thy manifold gifts of grace: the spirit of wisdom and understanding, the spirit of counsel and ghostly strength, the spirit of knowledge and true godliness: and fulfil them, O Lord, with the spirit of thy holy fear. Amen.

Then the Bishop shall lay his hand upon every child severally, saying.

Defend, O Lord, this child with thy heavenly grace, that he may continue thine for ever, and daily increase in thy Holy Spirit more and more, until he come unto thy everlasting kingdom. Amen.

Then shall the Bishop say[3].

ALMIGHTY everliving God, which makest us both to will, and to do those things that be good and acceptable unto thy Majesty: we make our humble supplications unto thee for these children, upon whom (after the example of thy holy Apostles) we have laid our hands, to certify them (by this sign) of thy favour, and gracious goodness toward them: let thy fatherly hand, we beseech thee, ever be over them: let thy Holy Spirit ever be with them; and so lead them in the knowledge and obedience of thy word, that in the end they may obtain the everlasting life, through our Lord Jesus Christ: who with thee and the Holy Ghost liveth and reigneth one God, world without end. Amen.

Then the Bishop shall bless the children, thus saying.

The blessing of God Almighty, the Father, the Son, and the Holy Ghost, be upon you, and remain with you for ever. Amen.

The Curate of every Parish, or some other at his appointment, shall diligently upon Sundays, and holy days half an hour before Evensong[4], openly in the Church instruct and examine so many

[[1] which, Grafton, 2.]   [[2] vouchedsafe, Grafton, 2.]
[[3] Bishop say. Let us pray, Grafton, 1 and 2.]
[[4] Evening prayer, Grafton, 2.]

children of his parish sent unto him, as the time will serve, and as he shall think convenient, in some part of this Catechism.

And all Fathers, Mothers, Masters, and Dames, shall cause their children, servants, and prentices (which have not learned their Catechism) to come to the church at the time appointed, and obediently to hear, and be ordered by the Curate, until such time as they have learned all that is here appointed for them to learn. And whensoever the Bishop shall give knowledge for children to be brought afore him to any convenient place, for their Confirmation: Then shall the Curate of every parish either bring or send in writing the names of all those children of his parish, which can say the Articles of their faith, the Lord's prayer, and the x. Commandments: and also how many of them can answer to the other questions contained in this Catechism.

And there shall none be admitted to the holy Communion, until such time as he can say the Catechism, and be confirmed.

THE FORM OF

SOLEMNIZATION OF MATRIMONY.

First the banns must be asked three several Sundays or holy days, in the time of service[1], the people being present after the accustomed manner.
And if the persons that would be married dwell in divers Parishes, the banns must be asked in both Parishes, and the Curate of the one Parish shall not solemnize Matrimony betwixt them, without a certificate of the banns being thrice asked from the Curate of the other Parish. At the day appointed for Solemnization of Matrimony, the persons to be married shall come into the body of the church, with their friends and neighbours. And there the Priest shall thus say.

DEARLY beloved friends, we are gathered together here in the sight of God, and in the face of his congregation, to join together this man and this woman in holy matrimony, which is an honourable estate instituted of God in Paradise, in the time of man's innocency, signifying unto us the mystical union, that is betwixt Christ and his Church: which holy estate Christ adorned and beautified with his presence and first miracle that he wrought in Cana of Galilee, and is commended of Saint Paul to be honourable among all men, and therefore is not to be enterprised nor taken in hand unadvisedly, lightly or wantonly, to satisfy men's carnal lusts and appetites, like brute beasts that have no understanding; but reverently, discreetly, advisedly, soberly, and in the fear of God: Duly considering the causes for which Matrimony was ordained. One was the procreation of children, to be brought up in the fear and nurture of the Lord, and praise of God. Secondly, it was ordained for a remedy against sin, and to avoid fornication, that such persons as have not the gift of continence, might marry, and keep themselves undefiled members of Christ's body. Thirdly, for the mutual society, help and comfort, that the one ought to have of the other, both in prosperity and adversity. Into

[[1] in the service time, Grafton, 1.]
[[2] for the which, Grafton, 2.]

the which holy estate these two persons present come now to be joined. Therefore, if any man can shew any just cause, why they may not lawfully be joined together: let him now speak, or else hereafter for ever hold his peace.

And also speaking to the persons that shall be married, he shall say.

I require and charge you (as you will answer at the dreadful day of judgment, when the secrets of all hearts shall be disclosed) that if either of you do know any impediment why ye may not be lawfully joined together in Matrimony, that ye confess it. For be ye well assured, that so many as be coupled together otherwise than God's word doth allow, are not joined together by God, neither is their Matrimony lawful.

At which day of marriage if any man do allege and declare any impediment why they may not be coupled together in Matrimony, by God's law or the laws of this Realm: and will be bound, and sufficient sureties with him, to the parties, or else put in a caution to the full value of such charges as the persons to be married doth[3] sustain to prove his allegation: then the Solemnization must be deferred unto such time as the truth be tried. If no impediment be alleged, then shall the Curate say unto the man.

N. Wilt thou have this woman to thy wedded wife, to live together after God's ordinance in the holy estate of Matrimony? Wilt thou love her, comfort her, honour, and keep her, in sickness and in health, and forsaking all other keep thee only to her, so long as you both shall live?

The man shall answer.

I will.

Then shall the Priest say to the woman.

N. Wilt thou have this man to thy wedded husband, to live together after God's ordinance in the holy estate of Matrimony? Wilt thou obey him and serve him, love, honour and keep him, in sickness and in health, and forsaking all other keep thee only unto[4] him, so long as you both shall live?

The woman shall answer.

I will.

[3 do, Grafton, 2.]   [4 to him, Grafton, 2.]

Then shall the Minister say.

Who giveth this woman to be married unto this man?

And the Minister receiving the woman at her father or friend's hands, shall cause the man to take the woman by the right hand, and so either to give their troth to other. The man first saying.

I *N.* take thee *N.* to my wedded wife, to have and to hold from this day forward, for better, for worse, for richer, for poorer, in sickness and in health, to love and to cherish, till death us depart, according to God's holy ordinance: And thereto I plight thee my troth.

Then shall they loose their hands, and the woman taking again the man by the right hand shall say.

I *N.* take thee *N.* to my wedded husband, to have and to hold from this day forward, for better, for worse, for richer, for poorer, in sickness and in health, to love, cherish, and to obey, till death us depart, according to God's holy ordinance: And thereto I give thee my troth.

Then shall they again loose their hands, and the man shall give unto the woman a ring, laying the same upon the book with the accustomed duty to the Priest and Clerk. And the Priest taking the ring, shall deliver it unto the man to put it upon the fourth finger of the woman's left hand. And the man taught by the Priest, shall say.

With this ring I thee wed: with my body I thee worship: and with all my worldly goods I thee endow. In the name of the Father, and of the Son, and of the Holy Ghost. Amen.

Then the man leaving the ring upon the fourth finger of the woman's left hand, the Minister shall say.

¶ Let us pray.

O ETERNAL God, creator and preserver of all mankind, giver of all spiritual grace, the author of everlasting life: Send thy blessing upon these thy servants, this man and this woman, whom we bless in thy name, that as Isaac and Rebecca lived faithfully together, so these persons may surely perform and keep the vow and covenant betwixt them made, whereof this ring given and received is a token and pledge, and may ever remain in perfect love and peace together, and live according[1] unto thy laws: through Jesus Christ our Lord. Amen.

Then shall the Priest join their right hands together and say.

Those whom God hath joined together, let no man put asunder.

Then shall the Minister speak unto the people.

FORASMUCH as *N.* and *N.* have consented together in holy wedlock, and have witnessed the same before God and this company, and thereto have given and pledged their troth either to other, and have declared the same by giving and receiving of a ring, and by joining of hands: I pronounce that they be man and wife together. In the name of the Father, of the Son, and of the Holy Ghost. Amen.

And the Minister shall add this blessing.

God the Father, God the Son, God the Holy Ghost, bless, preserve, and keep you: the Lord mercifully with his favour look upon you, and so fill you with all spiritual benediction and grace, that you may so live together in this life, that in the world to come you may have life everlasting. Amen.

Then the Ministers or Clerks, going to the Lord's table, shall say or sing this Psalm following.

Beati omnes. Psalm cxxviii.

BLESSED are all they that fear the Lord : and walk in his ways.

For thou shalt eat the labour of thy hands ; O well is thee, and happy shalt thou be.

Thy wife shall be as the fruitful vine : upon the walls of thy house.

Thy children like the olive branches : round about thy table.

Lo, thus shall the man be blessed : that feareth the Lord.

[1 according to, Grafton, 1.]

The Lord from out of Sion shall bless thee : that thou shalt see Hierusalem in prosperity all thy life long.

Yea, that thou shalt see thy children's children : and peace upon Israel.

Glory be to the Father, &c.

As it was in the, &c.

Or else this Psalm following.

Deus misereatur.   Psalm lxvii.

GOD be merciful unto us, and bless us : and shew us the light of his countenance, and be merciful unto us.

That thy way may be known upon the earth : thy saving health among all nations.

Let the people praise thee, O God : yea, let all the people praise thee.

O let the nations rejoice and be glad : for thou shalt judge the flock[1] righteously, and govern the nations upon the earth.

Let the people praise thee, O God : let all the people praise thee.

Then shall the earth bring forth her increase : and God, even our God, shall give us his blessing.

God shall bless us, and all the ends of the world shall fear him.

Glory be to the Father, &c.

As it was in the, &c.

¶ The Psalm ended, and the man and the woman kneeling afore the Lord's table : the Priest standing at the table, and turning his face toward them, shall say.

Lord, have mercy upon us.
Answer. Christ, have mercy upon us.
Minister. Lord, have mercy upon us.
¶ Our Father, which art[2] in heaven, &c.
And lead us not into temptation.
Answer. But deliver us from evil. Amen.

[1 folk, Grafton, 2.]   [2 which art, &c. Grafton, 2.]

Minister. O Lord, save thy servant, and thy handmaid;
Answer. Which put their trust in thee.
Minister. O Lord, send them help from thy holy place.
Answer. And evermore defend them.
Minister. Be unto them a tower of strength.
Answer. From the face of their enemy.
Minister. O Lord, hear our prayer.
Answer. And let our cry come unto thee.

The Minister.

O God of Abraham, God of Isaac, God of Jacob, bless these thy servants, and sow the seed of eternal life in their minds, that whatsoever in thy holy word they shall profitably learn, they may in deed fulfil the same. Look, O Lord, mercifully upon them from heaven, and bless them. And as thou didst send thy blessing upon Abraham and Sara to their great comfort: so vouchsafe to send thy blessing upon these thy servants, that they obeying thy will, and alway being in safety under thy protection, may abide in thy love unto their lives' end: through Jesu Christ our Lord. Amen.

This prayer next following shall be omitted, where the woman is past child birth.

O merciful Lord and heavenly Father, by whose gracious gift mankind is increased: we beseech thee assist with thy blessing these two persons, that they may both be fruitful in procreation of children, and also live together so long in godly love and honesty, that they may see their children's[3] children, unto the third and fourth generation, unto thy praise and honour: through Jesus Christ our Lord. Amen.

O God, which by thy mighty power hast made all things of nought, which also after other things set in order didst appoint that out of man (created after thine own image and similitude) woman should take her beginning: and knitting them together, didst teach that it should never be lawful to put asunder those, whom thou by matrimony hadst made one: O God, which hast consecrated the state of matrimony

[3 childer's children, Grafton, 2.]

to such an excellent mystery, that in it is signified and represented the spiritual marriage and unity betwixt Christ and his church: Look mercifully upon these thy servants, that both this man may love his wife, according to thy word (as Christ did love his spouse the church, who gave himself for it, loving and cherishing it even as his own flesh;) and also that this woman may be loving and amiable to her husband, as Rachel, wise as Rebecca, faithful and obedient as Sara, and in all quietness, sobriety and peace, be a follower of holy and godly matrons: O Lord, bless them both, and grant them to inherit thy everlasting kingdom: through Jesus Christ our Lord. Amen.

Then shall the Priest say,

ALMIGHTY God, which at the beginning did create our first parents Adam and Eve, and did sanctify and join them together in marriage: pour upon you the riches of his grace, sanctify and bless you, that ye may please him both in body and soul, and live together in holy love, unto your lives' end. Amen.

Then shall begin the Communion, and after the Gospel shall be said a sermon, wherein ordinarily (so oft as there is any marriage) the office of a man and wife shall be declared, according to holy scripture: or if there be no sermon, the Minister shall read this that followeth.

ALL ye which be married, or which intend to take the holy estate of matrimony upon you: hear what holy scripture doth say, as touching the duty of husbands toward their wives, and wives toward their husbands. Saint Paul (in his Epistle to the Ephesians the fifth chapter) doth give this commandment to all married men.

Ye husbands, love your wives, even as Christ loved the church, and hath given himself for it, to sanctify it, purging it in the fountain of water, through thy[1] word, that he might make it unto himself a glorious congregation, not having spot or wrinkle, or any such thing, but that it should be holy and blameless. So men are bound to love their own wives as their own bodies. He that loveth his own wife, loveth himself. For never did any man hate his

[[1] the word, Grafton, 2.]

own flesh, but nourisheth and cherisheth it, even as the Lord doth the congregation: for we are members of his body, of his flesh, and of his bones.

For this cause shall a man leave father and mother, and shall be joined unto his wife, and they two shall be one flesh. This mystery is great, but I speak of Christ and of the congregation. Nevertheless, let every one of you so love his own wife, even as himself.

Likewise the same Saint Paul (writing to the Colossians) speaketh thus to all men that be married. Ye men love your wives, and be not bitter unto them. *Colo.* iv.

Hear also what Saint Peter the apostle of Christ, which was himself a married man, saith unto all men that are married. Ye husbands, dwell with your wives according to knowledge: giving honour unto the wife as unto the weaker vessel, and as heirs together of the grace of life, so that your prayers be not hindered. 1 *Petri.* iii.

Hitherto ye have heard the duty of the husband toward the wife:

Now likewise ye wives hear and learn your duty towards[2] your husbands, even as it is plainly set forth in holy scripture.

Saint Paul (in the forenamed Epistle to the Ephesians) teacheth you thus: Ye women, submit yourselves unto your own husbands as unto the Lord: for the husband is the wife's head, even as Christ is the head of the Church. And he is also the Saviour of the whole body. Therefore as the Church or congregation is subject unto Christ: so likewise let the wives also be in subjection unto their own husbands in all things. And again he saith, Let the wife reverence her husband. Ephesi. v. And (in his Epistle to the Colossians) Saint Paul giveth you this short lesson. Ye wives submit yourselves unto your own husbands, as it is convenient in the Lord. *Colo.* iii.

Saint Peter also doth instruct you very godly, thus saying: Let wives be subject to their own husbands, so that if any obey not the word, they may be won without the word, by the conversation of the wives, while they behold your chaste conversation coupled with fear: whose apparel let it not be outward, with broided hair and trimming about with gold,

[2 toward, Grafton, 2.]

either in putting on of gorgeous apparel: but let the hid man which is in the heart, be without all corruption, so that the spirit be mild and quiet, which is a precious thing in the sight of God. For after this manner (in the old time) did the holy women which trusted in God apparel themselves, being subject to their own husbands: as Sara obeyed Abraham, calling him lord, whose daughters ye are made, doing well, and being not dismayed with any fear. 1 *Petri.* iii.[1]

The new married persons (the same day of their marriage) must receive the holy Communion.

[[1] 1 Pet. iv. Grafton, 2; but the same scripture.]

THE ORDER FOR THE
VISITATION OF THE SICK.

¶ *The Priest entering into the sick person's house, shall say.*

Peace be in this house, and to all that dwell in it.

When he cometh into the sick man's presence, he shall say kneeling down.

REMEMBER not, Lord, our iniquities, nor the iniquities of our forefathers. Spare us, good Lord, spare thy people, whom thou hast redeemed with thy most precious blood, and be not angry with us for ever.

Lord, have mercy upon us.
Christ, have mercy upon us.
Lord, have mercy upon us.
Our Father, which art in heaven, &c.
And lead us not into temptation.
Answer. But deliver us from evil. Amen.
Minister. O Lord, save thy servant.
Answer. Which putteth his trust in thee.
Minister. Send him help from thy holy place.
Answer. And evermore mightily defend him.
Minister. Let the enemy have none advantage of him.
Answer. Nor the wicked approach to hurt him.
Minister. Be unto him, O Lord, a strong tower,
Answer. From the face of his enemy.
Minister. Lord, hear our prayers.
Answer. And let our cry come unto thee.

Minister.

O LORD, look down from heaven, behold, visit, and relieve this thy servant: Look upon him with the eyes of thy mercy, give him comfort, and sure confidence in thee: Defend him from the danger of the enemy, and keep him in perpetual peace and safety: through Jesus Christ our Lord. Amen.

HEAR us, almighty and most merciful God and Saviour. Extend thy accustomed goodness to this thy servant which is grieved with sickness: Visit him, O Lord, as thou didst visit Peter's wife's mother and the Captain's servant. So visit and restore unto this sick person his former health (if it be thy will), or else give him grace so to take thy visitation, that after this painful life ended, he may dwell with thee in life everlasting. Amen.

Then shall the Minister exhort the sick person after this form or other like.

DEARLY beloved, know this: that almighty God is the Lord of life and death, and over all things to them pertaining, as youth, strength, health, age, weakness, and sickness. Wherefore, whatsoever your sickness is, know you certainly, that it is God's visitation. And for what cause soever this sickness is sent unto you: whether it be to try your patience for the example of other, and that your faith may be found in the day of the Lord laudable, glorious, and honourable, to the increase of glory, and endless felicity; or else it be sent unto you to correct and amend in you whatsoever doth offend the eyes of our heavenly Father: know you certainly, that if you truly repent you of your sins, and bear your sickness patiently, trusting in God's mercy for his dear Son Jesus Christ's sake, and render unto him humble thanks for his fatherly visitation, submitting yourself wholly to his will; it shall turn to your profit, and help you forward in the right way that leadeth unto everlasting life.

If the person visited be very sick, then the Curate may end his exhortation in this place.[1]

¶ TAKE therefore in good worth the chastement of the Lord: For whom the Lord loveth, he chastiseth. Yea (as Saint Paul saith) he scourgeth every son which he receiveth: if you endure chastisement, he offereth himself unto you as unto his own children. What son is he that the father chastiseth not? If ye be not under correction (whereof all true children are partakers) then are ye bastards and not children. Therefore, seeing that when our carnal fathers do

[1 This is put in the margin, in Grafton, 2, without a break in what follows.]

correct us, we reverently obey them: shall we not now much rather be obedient to our spiritual Father, and so live? And they for a few days do chastise[2] us after their own pleasure, but he doth chastise us for our profit, to the intent he may make us partakers of his holiness. These words, good brother, are God's words, and written in holy scripture for our comfort and instruction, that we should patiently and with thanksgiving bear our heavenly Father's correction, whensoever by any manner of adversity it shall please his gracious goodness to visit us. And there should be no greater comfort to Christian persons, than to be made like unto Christ by suffering patiently adversities, troubles, and sicknesses. For he himself went not up to joy, but first he suffered pain: he entered not into his glory, before he was crucified. So truly our way to eternal joy is to suffer here with Christ, and our door to enter into eternal life is gladly to die with Christ, that we may rise again from death, and dwell with him in everlasting life. Now therefore taking your sickness, which is thus profitable for you, patiently: I exhort you in the name of God, to remember the profession which you made unto God in your Baptism. And forasmuch as after this life there is account to be given unto the righteous Judge, of whom all must be judged without respect of persons: I require you to examine yourself, and your state, both toward God and man: so that accusing and condemning yourself for your own faults, you may find mercy at our heavenly Father's hand for Christ's sake, and not be accused and condemned in that fearful judgment. Therefore I shall shortly rehearse the articles of our faith, that ye may know whether you do believe, as a Christian man should, or no.

¶ Here the Minister shall rehearse the articles of the faith, saying thus,

Dost thou believe in God the Father Almighty?

¶ And so forth, as it is in Baptism.

¶ Then shall the Minister examine whether he be in charity with all the world: Exhorting him to forgive from the bottom of his heart all persons that have offended him; and if he have offended other, to ask them forgiveness: And where he hath done injury or wrong to any man, that he make amends to the uttermost of his power.

[[2] chasten, Grafton, 2.]

⁋ And if he have not afore disposed his goods, let him then make his will. But men must be oft admonished that they set an order for their temporal goods and lands, when they be in health. And also declare his debts, what he oweth, and what is owing unto him, for discharging of his conscience, and quietness of his executors.

¶ These words before rehearsed, may be said before the Minister begin his prayer, as he shall see cause.¹

¶ The Minister may not forget, nor omit to move the sick person, (and that most earnestly) to liberality toward the poor.

¶ Here shall the sick person make a special confession, if he feel his conscience troubled with any weighty matter. After which confession the Priest shall absolve him after this sort.

OUR Lord Jesus Christ, who hath left power to his Church to absolve all sinners, which truly repent and believe in him, of his great mercy forgive thee² thine offences: and by his authority committed to me, I absolve thee from all thy sins, in the name of the Father, and of the Son³, and of the Holy Ghost. Amen.

¶ And then the Priest shall say the Collect following.

¶ Let us pray.

O MOST merciful God, which according to the multitude of thy mercies dost so put away the sins of those which truly repent, that thou rememberest them no more: open thy eye of mercy upon this thy servant, who most earnestly desireth pardon and forgiveness. Renew in him, most loving Father, whatsoever hath been decayed by the fraud and malice of the devil, or by his own carnal will and frailness: preserve and continue this sick member in the unity of thy church, consider his contrition, accept his tears, assuage his pain, as shall be seen to thee most expedient for him. And forasmuch as he putteth his full trust only in thy mercy, impute not unto him his former sins, but take him unto⁴ thy favour: through the merits of thy most dearly beloved Son Jesus Christ. Amen.

[¹ This may be done before the Minister begin his prayers, as he shall see cause, Grafton, 2, in the margin.]

[² thee, omitted, Grafton, 2.]

[³ the Son, &c., Amen, Grafton, 2; the Son and &c., Amen, Grafton, 1.]

[⁴ to thy favour, Grafton, 2.]

THE VISITATION OF THE SICK.

Then the Minister shall say this Psalm.
In te Domine speravi. Psalm xxi.

¶ Adding this.

O SAVIOUR of the world, save us, which by thy cross and precious blood hast redeemed us, help us, we beseech thee, O God.

Then shall the Minister say.

THE Almighty Lord, which is a most strong tower to all them that put their trust in him, to whom all things in heaven, in earth, and under[5] earth, do bow and obey: be now and evermore thy defence, and make thee know and feel, that there is no other name under heaven given to man, in whom, and through whom, thou mayest receive health and salvation, but only the name of our Lord Jesus Christ. Amen.

[[5] under the earth, Grafton, 2.]

THE

COMMUNION OF THE SICK.

FORASMUCH as all mortal men be subject to many sudden perils, diseases and sicknesses, and ever uncertain what time they shall depart out of this life: Therefore, to the intent they may be always in a readiness to die, whensoever it shall please Almighty God to call them, the Curates shall diligently from time to time, but specially in the plague time, exhort their parishioners, to the oft receiving in the church of the holy communion of the body and blood of our Saviour Christ. Which if they do, they shall have no cause in their sudden visitation to be unquieted for lack of the same: but if the sick person be not able to come to the church, and yet is desirous to receive the communion in his house, then he must give knowledge over night, or else early in the morning to the Curate, signifying also how many be appointed to communicate with him. And having a convenient place in the sick man's house, where the Curate may reverently minister, and a good number to receive the communion with the sick person, with all things necessary for the same, he shall there minister the holy communion.

The Collect.

ALMIGHTY everliving God, Maker of mankind, which dost correct those whom thou dost love, and chastisest every one whom thou dost receive: we beseech thee to have mercy upon this thy servant visited with thy hand, and to grant that he may take his sickness patiently, and recover his bodily health (if it be thy gracious will), and whensoever his soul shall depart from the body, it may be without spot presented unto thee: through Jesus Christ our Lord. Amen.[1]

The Epistle. Hebr. xii.

MY son, despise not the correction of the Lord, neither faint when thou art rebuked of him: For whom the Lord loveth, him he correcteth, yea and he scourgeth every son, whom he receiveth.

The Gospel. John v.

VERILY, verily I say unto you, he that heareth my word, and believeth on him that sent me, hath everlasting life, and shall not come unto damnation, but he passeth from death unto life.

[[1] Amen, omitted, Grafton, 2.]

THE COMMUNION OF THE SICK.

At the time of the distribution of the holy Sacrament, the Priest shall first receive the communion himself, and after minister unto them that be appointed to communicate with the sick.

But if any man, either by reason of extremity of sickness, or for lack of warning in due time to the Curate, or for lack of company to receive with him, or by any other just impediment, do not receive the Sacrament of Christ's body and blood: then the Curate shall instruct him, that if he do truly repent him of his sins, and stedfastly believe that Jesus Christ hath suffered death upon the cross for him, and shed his blood for his redemption, earnestly remembering the benefits he hath thereby, and giving him hearty thanks therefore, he doth eat and drink the body and blood of our Saviour Christ, profitably [2] to his soul's health, although he do not receive the Sacrament with his mouth.

When the sick person is visited, and receiveth the holy communion all at one time, then the priest for more expedition, shall cut off the form of the visitation at the Psalm, *In thee, O Lord, have I put my trust,* and go straight to the communion.

In the time of plague, sweat, or such other like contagious times of sicknesses or diseases, when none of the parish[3] or neighbours can be gotten to communicate with the sick in their houses, for fear of the infection, upon special request of the diseased, the minister may alonly communicate with him.

[2 profitable, Grafton, 2.]   [3 Paroche, Grafton, 2.]

THE ORDER FOR THE

BURIAL OF THE DEAD.

The Priest meeting the corpse at the Church stile, shall say: Or else the priests and clerks shall sing, and so go either unto the church, or towards the grave.

I AM the resurrection and the life, saith the Lord: he that believeth in me, yea though he were dead, yet shall he live. And whosoever liveth and believeth in me, shall not die for ever. *John* xi.

I KNOW that my Redeemer liveth, and that I shall rise out of the earth in the last day, and shall be covered again with my skin, and shall see God in my flesh: yea, and I myself shall behold him, not with other, but with these same eyes. *Job* xix.

WE brought nothing into this world, neither may we carry any thing out of this world. 1 *Tim.* vi. The Lord giveth, and the Lord taketh away. Even as it hath pleased the Lord, so cometh things to pass: blessed be the name of the Lord. *Job* i.

When they come at[1] the grave, whiles the corpse is made ready to be laid into the earth, the Priest shall say, or the Priest and clerks shall sing.

MAN that is born of a woman hath but a short time to live, and is full of misery: he cometh up and is cut down like a flower, he flieth as it were a shadow, and never continueth in one stay. *Job* ix.[2] In the midst of life we be in death: of whom may we seek for succour but of thee, O Lord, which for our sins justly art displeased? Yet, O Lord God most holy, O Lord most mighty, O holy and most merciful Saviour, deliver us not into the bitter pains of eternal death. Thou knowest, Lord, the secrets of our hearts, shut not up thy merciful eyes to our prayers: But spare us, Lord

[[1] come to, Grafton, 2.]
[[2] Job xix. Grafton, 1; but the same scripture.]

most holy, O God most mighty, O holy and merciful Saviour, thou most worthy Judge eternal, suffer us not at our last hour for any pains of death to fall from thee.

Then while the earth shall be cast upon the body, by some standing ₒby, the Priest shall say.

FORASMUCH as it hath pleased almighty God of his great mercy to take unto himself the soul of our dear brother here departed: we therefore commit his body to the ground, earth to earth, ashes to ashes, dust to dust, in sure and certain hope of resurrection to eternal life, through our Lord Jesus Christ: who shall change our vile body that it may be like to his glorious body, according to the mighty working whereby he is able to subdue all things to himself.

¶ Then shall be said or sung.

I HEARD a voice from heaven, saying unto me, Write: from henceforth, blessed are the dead which die in the Lord. Even so saith the Spirit, that they rest from their labours.

Then shall follow this lesson, taken out of the xv. Chapter to the Corinthians, the first Epistle—[v. 20 to end.]

The lesson ended, the Priest shall say.

Lord, have mercy upon us.
Christ, have mercy upon us.
Lord, have mercy upon us.
¶ Our Father which art in heaven, &c.
And lead us not into temptation.
Answer. But deliver us from evil. Amen.

The Priest. ALMIGHTY God, with whom do live the spirits of them that depart hence in the Lord, and in whom the souls of them that be elected, after they be delivered from the burden[3] of the flesh, be in joy and felicity: We give thee hearty thanks, for that it hath pleased thee to deliver this *N.* our brother out of the miseries of this sinful world: beseeching thee, that it may please thee of thy gracious goodness, shortly to accomplish the number of thine elect, and to haste thy kingdom, that we with this our

[a burthen, Grafton, 1 and 2.]

brother, and all other departed in the true faith of thy holy name, may have our perfect consummation and bliss, both in body and soul, in thy eternal and everlasting glory. Amen.

The Collect.

O MERCIFUL God, the Father of our Lord Jesus Christ, who is the resurrection and the life, in whom whosoever believeth, shall live though he die; and whosoever liveth and believeth in him, shall not die eternally : who also taught us (by his holy apostle Paul) not to be sorry, as men without hope, for them that sleep in him : We meekly beseech thee (O Father) to raise us from the death of sin unto the life of righteousness, that when we shall depart this life, we may rest in him, as our hope is this our brother doth; and that at the general resurrection in the last day, we may be found acceptable in thy sight, and receive that blessing which thy wellbeloved Son shall then pronounce to all that love and fear thee, saying: Come, ye blessed children of my Father, receive the kingdom prepared for you from the beginning of the world. Grant this we beseech thee, O merciful Father, through Jesus Christ our Mediator and Redeemer. Amen.

THE THANKSGIVING OF WOMEN AFTER CHILD BIRTH,

COMMONLY CALLED

THE CHURCHING OF WOMEN.

The woman shall come into the church, and there shall kneel down in some convenient place, nigh unto the place where the table standeth: and the Priest standing by her, shall say these words, or such like as the case shall require.

FORASMUCH as it hath pleased almighty God of his goodness to give you safe deliverance, and hath preserved you in the great danger of child birth: ye shall therefore give hearty thanks unto God, and pray.

Then shall the Priest say this Psalm.

[Psalm cxxi.]

I HAVE lifted up mine eyes unto the hills: from whence cometh my help.

My help cometh even from the Lord: which hath made heaven and earth.

He will not suffer thy foot to be moved: and he that keepeth thee will not sleep.

Behold, he that keepeth Israel: shall neither slumber nor sleep.

The Lord himself is thy keeper: the Lord is thy defence upon thy right hand.

So that the Sun shall not burn thee by day: neither the Moon by night.

The Lord shall preserve thee from all evil: yea, it is even he that shall keep thy soul.

The Lord shall preserve thy going out, and thy coming in: from this time forth for evermore.

Glory be to the Father, and to the Son, and to, &c.

As it was in the beginning, is now, and ever, &c.

 Lord, have mercy upon us.
 Christ, have mercy upon us.
 Lord, have mercy upon us.

[DOCUMENTS, EDW. VI.]

¶ Our Father, which,[1] &c.
And lead us not into temptation.
Answer. But deliver us from evil. Amen.
Priest. O Lord, save this woman thy servant.
Answer. Which putteth her trust in thee.
Priest. Be thou to her a strong tower,
Answer. From the face of her enemy.
Priest. Lord, hear our prayer.
Answer. And let our cry come unto thee.

Priest. ¶ Let us pray.

O ALMIGHTY God, which hast delivered this woman thy servant from the great pain and peril of child birth: Grant, we beseech thee, most merciful Father, that she through thy help may both faithfully live and walk in her vocation, according to thy will in this life present; and also may be partaker of everlasting glory in the life to come, through Jesus Christ our Lord. Amen.

The woman that cometh to give her thanks, must offer accustomed offerings: and if there be a Communion, it is convenient that she receive the holy Communion.

[[1] which art, &c. Grafton, 2.]

A

COMMINATION AGAINST SINNERS,

WITH CERTAIN

PRAYERS TO BE USED DIVERS TIMES IN THE YEAR.

¶ After Morning prayer, the people being called together by the ringing of a bell, and assembled in the Church, the English Litany shall be said, after the accustomed manner: which ended, the Priest shall go into the pulpit and say thus.

BRETHREN, in the primitive church there was a Godly discipline, that at the beginning of Lent such persons as were notorious sinners, were put to open penance, and punished in this world, that their souls might be saved in the day of the Lord; and that others[2], admonished by their example, might be more afraid to offend. In the stead whereof, until the said discipline may be restored again (which thing is much to be wished), it is thought good, that at this time (in your presence) should be read the general sentences of God's cursing against impenitent sinners, gathered out of the xxvii. Chapter of Deuteronomy, and other places of scripture; and that ye should answer to every sentence, Amen. To the intent that you, being admonished of the great indignation of God against sinners, may the rather be called to earnest and true repentance, and may walk more warily in these dangerous days, fleeing[3] from such vices, for the which ye affirm with your own mouths the curse of God to be due.

CURSED is the man that maketh any carved or molten Image, an abomination to the Lord, the work of the hands of the craftsman, and putteth it in a secret place to worship it.

And the people shall answer and say.
Amen.

Minister. Cursed is he that curseth his father and mother.
Answer. Amen.

[2 other, Grafton, 1.]   [3 flying, Grafton, 2.]

Minister. Cursed is he that removeth away the mark of his neighbour's land.

Answer. Amen.

Minister. Cursed is he that maketh the blind to go out of his way.

Answer. Amen.

Minister. Cursed is he that letteth in judgment the right of the stranger, of them that be fatherless, and of widows.

Answer. Amen.

Minister. Cursed is he that smiteth his neighbour secretly.

Answer. Amen.

Minister. Cursed is he that lieth with his neighbour's wife.

Answer. Amen.

Minister. Cursed is he that taketh reward to slay the soul of innocent blood.

Answer. Amen.

Minister. Cursed is he that putteth his trust in man, and taketh man for his defence, and in his heart goeth from the Lord.

Answer. Amen.

Minister. Cursed are the unmerciful, the fornicators, and adulterers, and the covetous persons, the worshippers of images, slanderers, drunkards, and extortioners.

Answer. Amen.

The Minister. Now, seeing that all they be accursed (as the prophet David beareth witness) which do err and go astray from the commandments of God: let us (remembering the dreadful judgment hanging over our heads, and being always at hand) return unto our Lord God, with all contrition and meekness of heart, bewailing and lamenting our sinful life, knowledging and confessing our offences, and seeking to bring forth worthy fruits of penance. For now is the axe put unto the root of the trees, so that every tree which bringeth not forth good fruit, is hewn down, and cast into the fire. It is a fearful thing to fall into the hands of the living God: he shall pour down rain upon the sinners, snares, fire and brimstone, storm and tempest: this shall be their portion to drink. For lo, the Lord is coming out of his place, to visit the wickedness of such as dwell upon the earth. But who may abide the day of his coming? Who shall be able to endure when he appeareth? His fan is in his hand, and Mat. iii. he will purge his floor, and gather his wheat into the barn: but he will burn the chaff with unquenchable fire. The day of the Lord cometh as a thief upon the night, and when men shall say peace, and all things are safe, then shall sud- 1 Thes. v. denly destruction come upon them, as sorrow cometh upon a woman travailing with child, and they shall not escape: then shall appear the wrath of God in the day of vengeance, which obstinate sinners, through the stubbornness of their heart, have heaped unto themself, which despised the goodness, Rom. ii. patience, and long sufferance of God, when he called them continually to repentance. Then shall they call upon me, Prove. i. saith the Lord, but I will not hear: they shall seek me early, but they shall not find me, and that because they hated knowledge, and received not the fear of the Lord, but abhorred my counsel, and despised my correction: then shall it be too late to knock, when the door shall be shut, and too late to cry for mercy, when it is the time of justice. O terrible voice of most just judgment, which shall be pronounced upon them, when it shall be said unto them: Go, ye cursed, Mat. xxv. into the fire everlasting, which is prepared for the devil and his Angels. Therefore, brethren, take we heed betime[1], while 2 Cor. vi. the day of salvation lasteth, for the night cometh when none can work: but let us, while we have the light, believe in John ix. the light, and walk as the children of the light, that we be not cast into the utter darkness where is weeping and gnashing of teeth. Let us not abuse the goodness of God, which Mat. xxv. calleth us mercifully to amendment, and of his endless pity promiseth[2] us forgiveness of that which is past, if (with a whole mind and true heart) we return unto him: for though our Esai. i. sins be red as scarlet, they shall be as white as snow; and though they be like purple, yet shall they be as white as wool. Turn you clean (saith the Lord) from all your wick- Ezechiel xxviii. edness, and your sin shall not be your destruction. Cast away from you all your ungodliness that ye have done, make you new hearts, and a new spirit: wherefore will ye die, O ye house of Israel? Seeing that I have no pleasure in the death of him that dieth, saith the Lord God. Turn you then and you shall live. Although we have sinned, yet have we 1 John ii.

[[1] by time, Whitchurch, 1, and Grafton, 2.]
[[2] promised, Grafton, 2.]

an advocate with the Father, Jesus Christ the righteous : and he it is that obtaineth grace for our sins; for he was wounded for our offences, and smitten for our wickedness. Let us therefore return unto him, who is the merciful receiver of all true penitent sinners, assuring ourself, that he is ready to receive us, and most willing to pardon us, if we come to him with faithful repentance; if we will submit ourselves unto him, and from henceforth walk in his ways; if we will take his easy yoke and light burden upon us, to follow him in lowliness, patience, and charity, and be ordered by the governance of his Holy Spirit, seeking always his glory, and serving him duly in our vocation, with thanksgiving. This if we do, Christ will deliver us from the curse of the law, and from the extreme malediction, which shall light upon them, that shall be set on the left hand: and he will set us on his right hand, and give us the blessed benediction of his Father, commanding us to take possession of his glorious kingdom, unto the which he vouchsafe to bring us all, for his infinite mercy. Amen.

Then shall they all kneel upon their knees: and the Priests and Clerks kneeling (where they are accustomed to say the Litany,) shall say this Psalm.

Miserere mei Deus. Psalm li.

Lord, have mercy upon us.
Christ, have mercy upon us.
Lord, have mercy upon us.

¶ Our Father, which art in heaven, &c.
And lead us not into temptation.
Answer. But deliver us from evil. Amen.
Minister. O Lord, save thy servants.
Answer. Which put their trust in thee.
Minister. Send unto them help from above.
Answer. And evermore mightily defend them.
Minister. Help us, O God our Saviour.
Answer. And for the glory of thy name's sake deliver us, be merciful unto us sinners, for thy name's sake.
Minister. O Lord, hear our prayers.
Answer. And let our cry come unto thee.

Let us pray.

O LORD, we beseech thee mercifully hear our prayers, and spare all those which confess their sins to thee: that they (whose consciences by sin are accused) by thy merciful pardon may be absolved: Through Christ our Lord. Amen.

O MOST mighty God and merciful Father, which hast compassion of all men, and hatest nothing that thou hast made: which wouldest not the death of a sinner, but that he should rather turn from sin, and be saved: mercifully forgive us our trespasses, receive and comfort us, which be grieved and wearied with the burthen[1] of our sin. Thy property is to have mercy; to thee only it appertaineth to forgive sins: spare us therefore, good Lord, spare thy people whom thou hast redeemed. Enter not into judgment with thy servants, which be vile earth, and miserable sinners: but so turn thy[2] ire from us, which meekly knowledge our vileness, and truly repent us of our faults; so make haste[3] to help us in this world, that we may ever live with thee, in the world to come: through Jesus Christ our Lord. Amen.

¶ Then shall the people say this that followeth, after the Minister.

TURN thou us, O good Lord, and so shall we be turned: be favourable (O Lord) be favourable to thy people, which turn to thee in weeping, fasting and praying: for thou art a merciful God, full of compassion, long suffering, and of a great pity. Thou sparest when we deserve punishment, and in thy wrath thinkest upon mercy. Spare thy people, good Lord, spare them, and let not thy heritage be brought to confusion: hear us (O Lord) for thy mercy is great, and after the multitude of thy mercies look upon us.

[1 burden, Grafton, 2.]   [2 thine ire, Grafton, 2.]
[3 haste help, Grafton, 2.]

THE

FORM AND MANNER

OF

MAKING AND CONSECRATING

BISHOPS, PRIESTS, AND DEACONS.

ANNO DOMINI M.D.LII.

The fourme

and maner of makynge

and confecratynge, Bif-

choppes, Prieftes,

and Deacons.

¶ *Anno*[1] *Domini*
M.D.L.II.

[[1] *Anno a falutifero Virginis partu.*
1552. Grafton, 2.]

THE PREFACE.

It is evident unto all men, diligently reading holy Scripture, and ancient authors, that from the Apostles' time there hath been these orders of Ministers in Christ's church: Bishops, Priests, and Deacons: which offices were evermore had in such reverent estimation, that no man by his own private authority might presume to execute any of them, except he were first called, tried, examined, and known to have such qualities, as were requisite for the same; and also by public prayer, with imposition of hands, approved and admitted thereunto. And therefore to the intent these orders should be continued, and reverently used and esteemed in this Church of England: it is requisite, that no man (not being at this present Bishop, Priest, nor Deacon) shall execute any of them, except he be called, tried, examined, and admitted, according to the form hereafter following. And none shall be admitted a Deacon, except he be xxi. years of age at the least. And every man, which is to be admitted a Priest, shall be full xxiv. years old. And every man, which is to be consecrated a Bishop, shall be fully thirty years of age. And the Bishop knowing, either by himself, or by sufficient testimony, any person to be a man of virtuous conversation, and without crime, and after examination and trial, finding him learned in the Latin tongue, and sufficiently instructed in holy Scripture, may upon a Sunday or holy day, in the face of the church admit him a Deacon, in such manner and form, as hereafter followeth.

THE FORM AND MANNER

OF

ORDERING OF DEACONS.

First, when the day appointed by the Bishop is come, there shall be an exhortation declaring the duty and office of such as come to be admitted Ministers, how necessary such Orders are in the Church of Christ, and also how the people ought to esteem them in their vocation.

¶ After the Exhortation ended, the Archdeacon, or his deputy, shall present such as come to the Bishop to be admitted, saying these words.

REVEREND Father in GOD, I present unto you these persons present, to be admitted Deacons.

¶ *The Bishop.* Take heed that the persons whom ye present unto us, be apt and meet, for their learning and godly conversation, to exercise their ministry duly, to the honour of GOD, and edifying of his Church.

The Archdeacon shall answer.

I have inquired of them, and also examined them, and think them so to be.

¶ And then the Bishop shall say unto the people.

BRETHREN, if there be any of you, who knoweth any impediment, or notable crime, in any of these persons presented to be ordered Deacons, for the which he ought not to be admitted to the same, let him come forth in the name of GOD, and shew what the crime or impediment is.

¶ And if any great crime or impediment be objected, the Bishop shall surcease from ordering that person, until such time as the party accused shall try himself clear of that crime.

¶ Then the Bishop, commending such as shall be found meet to be ordered to the prayers of the congregation, with the Clerks and people present, shall say or sing the Litany as followeth with the prayers.

THE LITANY AND SUFFRAGES.

O God the Father of heaven : have mercy upon us miserable sinners.

¶ *O God the Father of heaven*[1] *: have mercy upon us miserable sinners.*

O God the Son, Redeemer of the world : have mercy upon us miserable sinners.

¶ *O God the Son, Redeemer of the world : have mercy upon us miserable sinners.*

O God, the Holy Ghost, proceeding from the Father and the Son : have mercy upon us miserable sinners.

¶ *O God the Holy Ghost, proceeding from the Father and the Son : have mercy upon us miserable sinners.*

O holy, blessed, and glorious Trinity, three Persons and one God : have mercy upon us miserable sinners.

¶ *O holy, blessed, and glorious Trinity, three Persons and one God : have mercy upon us miserable sinners.*

Remember not, Lord, our offences, nor the offences of our forefathers, neither take thou vengeance of our sins : spare us, good Lord, spare thy people, whom thou hast redeemed with thy most precious blood, and be not angry with us for ever.

Spare us, good Lord.

From all evil and mischief, from sin, from the crafts and assaults of the devil, from thy wrath, and from everlasting damnation.

Good Lord, deliver us.

From all blindness of heart, from pride, vainglory, and hypocrisy, from envy, hatred, and malice, and all uncharitableness.

Good Lord, deliver us.

From fornication, and all other deadly sin, and from all the deceits of the world, the flesh, and the devil.

Good Lord, deliver us.

From lightnings and tempests, from plague, pestilence, and famine, from battle and murther, and from sudden death.

Good Lord, deliver us.

[[1] O God the "Father of heaven," &c. Grafton, 2. In like manner the three following responses are abridged.]

From all sedition and privy conspiracy, from the tyranny of the Bishop of Rome, and all his detestable enormities, from all false doctrine and heresy, from hardness of heart, and contempt of thy word and commandment.

Good Lord, deliver us.

By the mystery of thy holy incarnation, by thy holy nativity and circumcision, by thy baptism, fasting, and temptation.

Good Lord, deliver us.

By thine agony and bloody sweat, by thy cross and passion, by thy precious death and burial, by thy glorious resurrection and ascension, and by the coming of the Holy Ghost.

Good Lord, deliver us.

In all time of our tribulation, in all time of our wealth, in the hour of death, and in the day of judgment.

Good Lord, deliver us.

We sinners do beseech thee to hear us (O Lord God) and that it may please thee to rule and govern thy holy Church universally, in the right way.

We beseech thee to hear us, good Lord.

That it may please thee, to keep Edward the Sixth thy servant, our King and governor.

We beseech thee to hear us, good Lord.

That it may please thee, to rule his heart in thy faith, fear and love, that he may always have affiance in thee, and ever seek thy honour and glory.

We beseech thee to hear us, good Lord.

That it may please thee, to be his defender and keeper, giving him the victory over all his enemies.

We beseech thee to hear us, good Lord.

That it may please thee, to illuminate all Bishops, Pastors, and Ministers of the Church, with true knowledge and understanding of thy word, and that both by their preaching and living, they may set it forth, and shew it accordingly.

We beseech thee to hear us, good Lord.

That it may please thee, to bless these men, and send thy grace upon them, that they may duly execute the office now to be committed unto them, to the edifying of thy Church, and to thy honour, praise and glory.

We beseech thee to hear us, good Lord.

That it may please thee, to endue the Lords of the Council, and all the nobility with grace, wisdom, and understanding.
We beseech thee to hear us, good Lord.

That it may please thee, to bless and keep the Magistrates, giving them grace to execute justice, and to maintain truth.
We beseech thee to hear us, good Lord.

That it may please thee, to bless and keep all thy people.
We beseech thee to hear us, good Lord.

That it may please thee, to give to all nations unity, peace, and concord.
We beseech thee to hear us, good Lord.

That it may please thee to give us an heart, to love and dread thee, and diligently to live after thy commandments.
We beseech thee to hear us, good Lord.

That it may please thee to give all thy people increase of grace, to hear meekly thy word, and to receive it with pure affection, and to bring forth the fruits of the Spirit.
We beseech thee to hear us, good Lord.

That it may please thee, to bring into the way of truth all such as have erred, and are[1] deceived.
We beseech thee to hear us, good Lord.

That it may please thee, to strengthen such as do stand, and to comfort, and help the weak hearted, and to raise them up that fall, and finally to beat down Sathan under our feet.
We beseech thee to hear us, good Lord.

That it may please thee, to succour, help, and comfort all that be in danger, necessity, and tribulation.
We beseech thee to hear us, good Lord.

That it may please thee, to preserve all that travel by land or by water, all women labouring of child, all sick persons, and young children, and to shew thy pity upon all prisoners and captives.
We beseech thee to hear us, good Lord.

That it may please thee, to defend and provide for the fatherless children and widows, and all that be desolate and oppressed.
We beseech thee to hear us, good Lord.

That it may please thee, to have mercy upon all men.
We beseech thee to hear us, good Lord.

[1 be, Grafton, 2.]

That it may please thee, to forgive our enemies, persecutors, and slanderers, and to turn their hearts.

We beseech thee to hear us, good Lord.

That it may please thee, to give and preserve to our use the kindly fruits of the earth, so as in due time we may enjoy them.

We beseech thee to hear us, good Lord.

That it may please thee, to give us true repentance, to forgive us all our sins, negligences and ignorances, and to endue us with the grace of thy holy Spirit, to amend our lives according to thy holy word.

We beseech thee to hear us, good Lord.

Son of God, we beseech thee to hear us.

Son of God: we beseech thee to hear us.

O Lamb of God, that takest away the sins of the world.

Grant us thy peace.

O Lamb of God, that takest away the sins of the world.

Have mercy upon us.

O Christ, hear us.

O Christ, hear us.

Lord, have mercy upon us.

Lord, have mercy upon us.

Christ, have mercy upon us.

Christ, have mercy upon us.

Lord, have mercy upon us.

Lord, have mercy upon us.

¶ Our Father, which art in heaven. &c.

And lead us not into temptation.

But deliver us from evil.

The Versicle. O Lord, deal not with us after our sins.

The Answer. Neither reward us after our iniquities.

Let us pray.

O GOD merciful Father, that despisest not the sighing of a contrite heart, nor the desire of such as be sorrowful; mercifully assist our prayers, that we make before thee, in all our troubles and adversities, whensoever they oppress us: and graciously hear us, that those evils, which the craft and subtilty of the devil, or man worketh against us, be brought to nought, and by the providence of thy goodness they may be dispersed, that we thy servants, being hurt by no persecutions, may evermore give thanks unto[1] thee, in thy holy Church, through Jesu[2] Christ our Lord.

O Lord, arise, help us, and deliver us, for thy name's sake.

O GOD, we have heard with our ears, and our fathers have declared unto us, the noble works, that thou didst in their days, and in the old time before them.

O Lord, arise, help us, and deliver us for thy honour.

Glory be to the Father, and to the Son, and to the Holy Ghost. As it was in the beginning, is now, and ever shall be: world without end. Amen.
From our enemies defend us, O Christ.
Graciously look upon our afflictions.
Pitifully behold the sorrows of our heart.
Mercifully forgive the sins of thy people.
Favourably with mercy hear our prayers.
O Son of David, have mercy upon us.
Both now and ever vouchsafe to hear us, O Christ.
Graciously hear us, O Christ, Graciously hear us, O Lord Christ.
The Versicle. O Lord, let thy mercy be shewed upon us.
The Answer. As we do put our trust in thee.

Let us pray.

WE humbly beseech thee, O Father, mercifully to look upon our infirmities, and for the glory of thy name's sake, turn from us all those evils, that we most righteously have deserved: And grant that in all our troubles we may put our whole trust and confidence in thy mercy, and evermore serve thee in holiness and pureness of living to thy honour and glory: through our only mediator and advocate Jesus Christ our Lord. Amen.

ALMIGHTY God, which hast given us grace at this time with one accord, to make our common supplications unto thee,

[1 to thee, Grafton, 2.]
[2 Jesus, Grafton, 2.]

and dost promise that when two or three be gathered in thy name, thou wilt grant their requests: fulfil now, O Lord, the desires and petitions of thy servants, as may be most expedient for them, granting us in this world knowledge of thy truth, and in the world to come life everlasting. Amen.

Then shall be said also this that followeth.

ALMIGHTY God, which by thy divine providence hast appointed diverse orders of ministers in the Church: and didst inspire thine holy Apostles to choose unto this order of Deacons the first Martyr saint Stephin, with other: mercifully behold these thy servants, now called to the like office and administration: replenish them so with the truth of thy doctrine, and innocency of life, that both by word and good example they may faithfully serve thee in this office, to the glory of thy name, and profit of the congregation, through the merits of our Saviour Jesu Christ: who liveth and reigneth with thee, and the Holy Ghost, now and ever. Amen.

Then shall be sung or said the Communion of the day, saving the Epistle shall be read out of Timothy, as followeth.

[1 Tim. iii. v. 8 to end.]
Or else this, out of the sixth of the Acts.
[vi. 2—7.]

¶ And before the Gospel, the Bishop sitting in a chair, shall cause the Oath of the King's supremacy, and[1] against the usurped power and authority of the Bishop of Rome, to be ministered unto every of them that are to be ordered.

¶ *The Oath of the King's Supremacy.*

I FROM henceforth shall utterly renounce, refuse, relinquish, and forsake the Bishop of Rome, and his authority, power, and jurisdiction. And I shall never consent nor agree, that the Bishop of Rome shall practise, exercise, or have any manner of authority, jurisdiction, or power within this realm, or any other the King's dominions, but shall resist the same at all times, to the uttermost of my power. And I

[1 and, omitted in Grafton, 2.]

from henceforth will accept, repute and take the King's Majesty, to be the only Supreme head in earth, of the Church of England: And to my cunning, wit, and uttermost of my power, without guile, fraud, or other undue mean, I will observe, keep, maintain and defend, the whole effects and contents of all and singular acts and Statutes made, and to be made within this realm, in derogation, extirpation, and extinguishment of the Bishop[2] of Rome and his authority, and all other Acts and Statutes, made or to be made, in confirmation and corroboration of the King's power, of the supreme head in earth, of the Church of England: and this I will do[3] against all manner of persons, of what estate, dignity or degree, or condition they be, and in no wise do nor attempt, nor to my power suffer to be done or attempted, directly or indirectly, any thing or things, privily or apertly, to the let, hinderance, damage, or derogation thereof, or any part thereof, by any manner of means, or for any manner of pretence. And in case any oath be made, or hath been made by me to any person or persons, in maintenance, defence, or favour of the Bishop of Rome, or his authority, jurisdiction, or power, I repute the same, as vain and annihilate: so help me God through Jesus Christ.

¶ Then shall the Bishop examine every one of them that are to be ordered, in the presence of the people, after this manner following.

Do you trust that you are inwardly moved by the Holy Ghost, to take upon you this office and ministration, to serve God, for the promoting of his glory, and the edifying of his people?

Answer. I trust so.

The Bishop. Do ye think that ye truly be called according to the will of our Lord Jesus Christ, and the due order of this realm, to the ministry of the church?

Answer. I think so.

The Bishop. Do ye unfeignedly believe all the Canonical scriptures of the old and new Testament?

Answer. I do believe.

The Bishop. Will you diligently read the same unto

[² B. of Rome, Grafton, 2.]   [³ will I do, Grafton, 2.]

the people assembled in the Church, where you shall be appointed to serve?

Answer. I will.

The Bishop. It pertaineth to the office of a Deacon in the Church where he shall be appointed, to assist the Priest in divine service, and specially when he ministereth the holy Communion, and to help him in distribution thereof, and to read holy scriptures and Homilies in the congregation, and to instruct the youth in the Catechism, to baptize and to preach if he be admitted thereto by the Bishop. And furthermore, it is his office, where provision is so made, to search for the sick, poor, and impotent people of the parish, and to intimate their estates, names and places where they dwell, to the Curate, that by his exhortation they may be relieved by the parish, or other convenient alms : will you do this gladly and willingly?

Answer. I will so do by the help of God.

The Bishop. Will you apply all your diligence to frame and fashion your own lives, and the lives of all your family according to the doctrine of Christ, and to make both yourselves and them, as much as in you lieth, wholesome examples of the flock of Christ?

Answer. I will so do, the Lord being my helper.

The Bishop. Will you reverently obey your ordinary, and other chief Ministers of the Church, and them to whom the government and charge is committed over you, following with a glad mind and will their godly admonitions?

Answer. I will thus endeavour myself, the Lord being my helper.

Then the Bishop laying his hands severally upon the head of every of them, shall say.

TAKE thou authority to execute the office of a Deacon in the Church of God committed unto thee : in the name of the Father, the Son, and the Holy Ghost. Amen.

Then shall the Bishop deliver to every one of them the new Testament, saying.

TAKE thou authority to read the Gospel in the Church of God, and to preach the same, if thou be thereunto ordinarily commanded.

THE ORDERING OF DEACONS.

Then one of them appointed by the Bishop, shall read the Gospel of that day.

Then shall the Bishop proceed to the Communion, and all that be ordered shall tarry and receive the holy Communion the same day with the Bishop.

The Communion ended, after the last Collect and immediately before the benediction, shall be said this Collect following.

1

ALMIGHTY God, giver of all good things, which of thy great goodness hast vouchsafed to accept, and take these thy servants unto the Office of Deacons in thy church, make them, we beseech thee, O Lord, to be modest, humble, and constant in their ministration, to have a ready will to observe all spiritual discipline, that they having always the testimony of a good conscience, and continuing ever stable and strong in thy Son Christ, may so well use themselves in this inferior office, that they may be found worthy to be called unto the higher ministries in thy Church: through the same thy Son our Saviour Christ, to whom be glory, and honour, world without end. Amen.

¶ And here it must be shewed unto the Deacon, that he must continue in that office of a Deacon, the space of an[2] whole year at the least (except for reasonable causes it be otherwise seen to his Ordinary) to the intent he may be perfect, and well expert in the things appertaining to the Ecclesiastical administration, in executing whereof, if he be found faithful and diligent, he may be admitted by his Diocesan to the order of Priesthood.

[[1] Here two leaves of this copy are supplied from another; but in the four copies collated there is only one various reading, that marked 2, on this page.]

[[2] a whole year, in the other copies.]

¶ THE FORM
OF
ORDERING PRIESTS.

When the exhortation is ended, then shall follow the Communion. And for the Epistle shall be read out of the twentieth Chapter of the Acts of the Apostles as followeth. [v. 17—35.]

¶ Or else this third Chapter, of the first Epistle to Timothy. 1 Timo. iii. [v. 1 to end.]

After this shall be read for the Gospel, a piece of the last Chapter of Mathew, as followeth. Mat. xxviii. [20 to end.]

¶ Or else this that followeth, of the x. Chapter of John. [v. 1—16.]

Or else this, of the xx. Chapter of John. [v. 19—23.]

When the Gospel is ended, then shall be said or sung.

COME, Holy Ghost, eternal God, proceeding from above:
Both from the Father and the Son, the God of peace and love.
Visit our minds, and into us thy heavenly grace inspire:
That in all truth and godliness we may have true desire.
Thou art the very Comforter, in all woe and distress:
The heavenly gift of God most high, which no tongue can express.
The fountain and the lively spring of joy celestial:
The fire so bright, the love so clear, and Unction spiritual.
Thou in thy gifts art manifold, whereby Christ's Church doth stand:
In faithful hearts writing thy [1] law, the finger of God's hand.
According to thy promise made, thou givest speech of grace:
That through thy help the praise of God may sound in every place.

[¹ the law, Grafton, 2.]

O Holy Ghost, into our wits send down thine heavenly light:
Kindle our hearts with fervent love, to serve God day and night.
Strength and stablish all our weakness, so feeble and so frail:
That neither flesh, the world nor devil, against us do prevail.
Put back our enemy far from us, and grant us to obtain
Peace in our hearts with God and man, without grudge or disdain.
And grant, O Lord, that thou being our leader and our guide,
We may eschew the snares of sin, and from thee never slide.
To us such plenty of thy grace, good Lord, grant, we thee pray,
That thou mayest be our comforter[2] at the last dreadful day.
Of all strife and dissension, O LORD, dissolve the bands:
And make the knots of peace and love, throughout all Christian lands.
Grant us, O Lord, through thee to know the Father most of might:
That of his dear beloved Son we may attain the sight.
And that with perfect faith also, we may acknowledge thee,
The Spirit of them both alway, one God in persons three.
Laud and praise be to the Father, and to the Son equal;
And to the Holy Spirit also, one God coeternal.
And pray we that the only Son vouchsafe his Spirit to send
To all that do profess his name, unto the world's end. Amen.

And then the Archdeacon shall present unto the Bishop all them that shall receive the order of Priesthood that day. The Archdeacon saying.

REVEREND father in God, I present unto you these persons present, to be admitted to the order of Priesthood. *Cum interrogatione et responsione, ut in Ordine Diaconatus.*

[[2] comfort, Grafton, 2.]

And then the Bishop shall say to the people,

GOOD people, these be they whom we purpose, God willing, to receive this day unto the holy office of Priesthood. For after due examination, we find not the contrary but that they be lawfully called to their function and ministry, and that they be persons meet for the same: but yet if there be any of you which knoweth any impediment, or notable crime in any of them, for the which he ought not to be received into this holy ministry; now in the name of God declare the same.

And if any great crime or impediment be objected. &c. Ut supra in Ordine Diaconatus usque ad finem Litaniæ cum hac Collecta.

ALMIGHTY GOD, giver of all good things, which by thy Holy Spirit hast appointed diverse orders of Ministers in thy church, mercifully behold these thy servants, now called to the office of Priesthood, and replenish them so with the truth of thy doctrine, and innocency of life, that both by word and good example they may faithfully serve thee in this office, to the glory of thy name, and profit of the congregation, through the merits of our Saviour Jesu Christ: who liveth and reigneth with thee, and the Holy Ghost, world without end. Amen.

Then the Bishop shall minister unto every of them the oath, concerning the king's Supremacy, as it is set out in the order of Deacons. And that done, he shall say unto them which are appointed to receive the said office, as hereafter followeth.

YOU have heard, brethren, as well in your private examination, as in the exhortation, and in the holy lessons taken out of the Gospel, and of the writings of the Apostles, of what dignity, and of how great importance this office is (whereunto ye be called). And now we exhort you, in the name of our Lord Jesus Christ, to have in remembrance, into how high a dignity, and to how chargeable an office ye be called; that is to say, to be the messengers, the watchmen, the Pastors, and the stewards of the LORD: to teach, to premonish, to feed, and provide for the LORD'S family: to seek for Christ's sheep that be dispersed abroad, and for his children which be in the midst of this naughty world, to be saved through Christ for ever. Have always therefore printed in your remembrance, how great a treasure is committed to your charge: for they be the sheep of Christ, which he bought with his death, and for whom he shed his blood. The church and congregation whom you must serve, is his spouse and his body. And if it shall chance the same church, or any member thereof, to take any hurt or hinderance, by reason of your negligence, ye know the greatness of the fault, and also of the horrible punishment which will ensue. Wherefore, consider with yourselves the end of your ministry, towards the children of God, toward the spouse and body of Christ; and see that you never cease your labour, your care and diligence, until you have done all that lieth in you, according to your bounden duty, to bring all such as are, or shall be committed to your charge, unto that agreement in faith, and knowledge of God, and to that ripeness, and perfectness of age in Christ, that there be no place left among them, either for error in religion, or for viciousness in life.

Then, forasmuch as your office is both of so great excellency, and of so great difficulty, ye see with how great care and study ye ought to apply yourselves, as well that you may shew yourselves kind to that Lord, who hath placed you in so high a dignity, as also to beware, that neither you yourselves offend, neither be occasion that other offend. Howbeit, ye can not have a mind and a will thereto of yourselves; for that power and ability is given of God alone. Therefore ye see how ye ought, and have need, earnestly to pray for his Holy Spirit. And seeing that you cannot by any other means compass the doing of so weighty a work pertaining to the salvation of man, but with doctrine and exhortation, taken out of holy scripture, and with a life agreeable unto the same; ye perceive how studious ye ought to be in reading and in learning the holy scriptures, and in framing the manners, both of yourselves, and of them that specially pertain unto you, according to the rule of the same scriptures. And for this self-same cause, ye see how you ought to forsake and set aside (as much as you may) all worldly cares and studies.

We have a good hope, that you have well weighed and pondered these things with yourselves, long before this time, and that you have clearly determined, by God's grace, to give yourselves wholly to this vocation, whereunto it hath pleased God to call you, so that (as much as lieth in you) you apply yourselves wholly to this one thing, and draw all your cares and studies this way, and to this end. And that you will continually pray for the heavenly assistance of the Holy Ghost, from GOD the Father, by the mediation of our only Mediator and Saviour Jesus Christ, that by daily reading and weighing of the scriptures, ye may wax riper and stronger in your ministry. And that ye[1] may so endeavour yourselves from time to time to sanctify the lives of you and yours, and to fashion them after the rule and doctrine of Christ: And that ye may be wholesome and Godly examples and patterns, for the rest of the congregation to follow. And that this present congregation of Christ here assembled, may also understand your minds and wills in these things: and that this your promise shall more move you to do your duties, ye shall answer plainly to these things, which we in the name of the congregation shall demand of you, touching the same.

Do you think in your heart that you be truly called according to the will of our Lord Jesus Christ, and the order of this Church of England, to the ministry of Priesthood?

Answer. I think it.

The Bishop. Be you persuaded that the holy scriptures contain sufficiently all doctrine required of necessity for eternal salvation, through faith in Jesu Christ? And are you determined with the said scriptures to instruct the people committed to your charge, and to teach nothing, (as required of necessity to eternal salvation) but that you shall be persuaded may be concluded, and proved by the scripture?

Answer. I am so persuaded, and have so determined by God's grace.

The Bishop. Will you then give your faithful diligence always, so to minister the doctrine and Sacraments, and the discipline of Christ, as the Lord hath commanded, and as this realm hath received the same, according to the commandments of God, so that you may teach the people committed to your cure and charge, with all diligence to keep and observe the same?

Answer. I will so do, by the help of the Lord.

[[1] you, Grafton, 2.]

The Bishop. Will you be ready with all faithful diligence to banish and drive away all erroneous and strange doctrines, contrary to God's word, and to use both public and private monitions and exhortations, as well to the sick as to the whole, within your cures, as need shall require and occasion be given?

Answer. I will, the Lord being my helper.

The Bishop. Will you be diligent in prayers, and in reading of the holy scriptures, and in such studies as help to the knowledge of the same, laying aside the study of the world and the flesh?

Answer. I will endeavour myself so to do, the Lord being my helper.

The Bishop. Will you be diligent to frame and fashion your own selves, and your families, according to the doctrine of Christ, and to make both yourselves and them (as much as in you lieth) wholesome examples and spectacles to the flock of Christ?

Answer. I will so apply myself, the Lord being my helper.

The Bishop. Will you maintain and set forwards (as much as lieth in you) quietness, peace, and love amongst all christian people; and specially among[2] them that are, or shall be committed to your charge?

Answer. I will so do, the Lord being my helper.

The Bishop. Will you reverently obey your ordinary, and other chief ministers, unto whom the government and charge is committed over you, following with a glad mind and will their godly admonition, and submitting yourselves to their godly judgments?

Answer. I will so do, the Lord being my helper.

[3]

Then shall the Bishop say.

ALMIGHTY God, who hath given you this will to do all these things: grant also unto you strength and power to perform the same, that he may accomplish his work which he hath begun in you, until the time he shall come at the latter day, to judge the quick and the dead.

[[2] amongst, Grafton, 1 and 2.]

[[3] Here four leaves are supplied in Grafton, 1, from another copy: from, "I will so do, the Lord being my helper," to "strangers destitute of help," at the bottom of page 352.]

After this, the congregation shall be desired, secretly in their prayers, to make humble supplications to God for the foresaid things: for the, which prayers, there shall be a certain space kept in silence.

That done, the Bishop shall pray in this wise.

¶ Let us pray.

ALMIGHTY God and heavenly Father, which, of thy infinite love and goodness towards us, hast given to us thy only and most dear beloved Son Jesus Christ, to be our redeemer and author of everlasting life: who after he had made perfect our redemption by his death, and was ascended into heaven, sent abroad into the world his Apostles, Prophets, Evangelists, Doctors, and Pastors, by whose labour and ministry he gathered together a great flock in all the parts of the world, to set forth the eternal praise of thy holy name: For these so great benefits of thy eternal goodness, and for that thou hast vouchsafed to call these thy servants here present to the same office and ministry of the salvation of mankind, we render unto thee most hearty thanks, we worship and praise thee, and we humbly beseech thee by the same thy Son, to grant unto all us which either here, or elsewhere call upon thy name, that we may shew ourselves thankful to thee, for these and all other the [1] benefits, and that we may daily increase and go forwards in the knowledge and faith of thee, and thy Son, by the Holy Spirit. So that as well by these thy ministers, as by them to whom they shall be appointed ministers, thy holy name may be always glorified, and thy blessed kingdom enlarged, through the same thy Son our Lord Jesus Christ: which liveth and reigneth with thee, in the unity of the same Holy Spirit, world without end. Amen.

¶ When this prayer is done, the Bishop with the Priests present shall lay their hands severally upon the head of every one that receiveth orders: the receivers humbly kneeling upon their knees, and the Bishop saying.

RECEIVE the Holy Ghost: whose sins thou dost forgive, they are forgiven: and whose sins thou dost retain, they are retained: and be thou a faithful dispenser of the word of God, and of his holy Sacraments. In the name of the Father, and of the Son, and of the Holy Ghost. Amen.

[1 thy benefits, in the other copies.]

THE ORDERING OF PRIESTS. 349

¶ The Bishop shall deliver to every one of them the Bible in his hand, saying.

TAKE thou authority to preach the word of God, and to minister the holy Sacraments in this congregation, where thou shalt be so appointed.

¶ When this is done, the congregation shall sing the *Creed*, and also they shall go to the Communion: which all they that receive orders shall take together, and remain in the same place where the hands were laid upon them, until such time as they have received the Communion.

¶ The Communion being done, after the last Collect, and immediately before the benediction, shall be said this Collect.

MOST merciful Father, we beseech thee so to send upon these thy servants thy heavenly blessing, that they may be clad about with all justice, and that thy word spoken by their mouths may have such success, that it may never be spoken in vain. Grant also that we may have grace to hear, and receive the same as thy most holy word, and the mean of our salvation, that in all our words and deeds we may seek thy glory, and the increase of thy kingdom, through Jesus Christ our Lord. Amen.

¶ And if the Orders of Deacon and Priesthood, be given both upon one day: then shall all things at the holy Communion be used as they are appointed at the ordering of Priests. Saving that for the Epistle, the whole third Chapter of the first to Timothy shall be read as it is set out before in the order of Priests. And immediately after the Epistle, the Deacons shall be ordered. And it shall suffice, the Litany to be said once.

THE

FORM OF CONSECRATING

OF AN

ARCHBISHOP OR BISHOP[1].

¶ At the Communion.[2]
The Epistle. [1 Tim. iii.[3] v. 1—7.]
The Gospel. John iv.[4] [v. 15—17.]

¶ Or else out of the tenth Chapter of John, as before in the order of Priests.

¶ After the gospel and *Credo* ended, first the elected Bishop shall be presented by two Bishops unto the Archbishop of that Province, or to some other Bishop appointed by his commission: The Bishops that present him, saying.

MOST reverend father in God, we present unto you this godly and well learned man, to be consecrated Bishop.

¶ Then shall the Archbishop demand the King's *mandate* for the consecration, and cause it to be read. And the oath touching the knowledge of the king's supremacy, shall be ministered to the person elected, as it is set out in the order of Deacons. And then shall be ministered also the oath of due obedience unto the Archbishop, as followeth.

¶ *The Oath of due Obedience to the Archbishop.*

IN the name of God, Amen. I, *N.* chosen Bishop of the Church and see of *N.* do profess and promise all due reverence and obedience to the Archbishop, and to the Metropolitical church of *N.* and to their successors: so help me God, through Jesus Christ.

¶ This oath shall not be made at the consecration of an Archbishop.
¶ Then the Archbishop shall move the congregation present to pray: saying thus to them.

[1 The form of Consecrating an Archbishop or Bishop, is the running title to the end, in Grafton, 2.]
[2 The Epistle, at the Communion, Grafton, 2.]
[3 the reference, 1 Tim. iii., is given in Grafton, 2.]
[4 Misprint here and in the other copies, except Grafton, 2, for xxi.]

CONSECRATION OF BISHOPS. 351

BRETHREN, it is written in the gospel of Saint Luke, that our Saviour Christ continued the whole night in prayer, or ever that he did choose and send forth his twelve apostles. It is written also in the Acts of the Apostles, that the disciples which were at Antioch did fast and pray, or ever they laid hands upon, or sent forth Paul and Barnabas. Let us therefore, following the example of our Saviour Christ and his Apostles, first fall to prayer, or that we admit and send forth this person presented unto us, to the work whereunto we trust the Holy Ghost hath called him.

¶ And then shall be said the Litany, as afore in the order of Deacons. And after this place: That it may please thee to illuminate all Bishops. &c. he shall say.

THAT it may please thee to bless this our brother elected, and to send thy grace upon him, that he may duly execute the office whereunto he is called, to the edifying of thy church, and to the honour, praise, and glory of thy name.

Answer. We beseech thee to hear us, good Lord.

¶ Concluding the Litany in the end, with this prayer.

ALMIGHTY GOD, giver of all good things, which by thy Holy Spirit hast appointed diverse orders of ministers in thy church: mercifully behold this thy servant, now called to the work and ministry of a Bishop, and replenish him so with the truth of thy doctrine, and innocency of life, that both by word and deed, he may faithfully serve thee in this office, to the glory of thy name, and profit of thy congregation: Through the merits of our Saviour Jesu Christ, who liveth and reigneth with thee and the Holy Ghost, world without end. Amen.

¶ Then the Archbishop sitting in a chair, shall say this to him that is to be consecrated.

BROTHER, forasmuch as holy scripture and the old Canons commandeth, that we should not be hasty in laying on hands, and admitting of any person to the government of the congregation of Christ, which he hath purchased with no less price than the effusion of his own blood: afore that I admit you to this administration whereunto ye are called, I will examine you in certain articles, to the end the congregation present may have a trial and bear witness how ye be minded to behave yourself in the church of God. Are you persuaded that you be truly called to this ministration, according to the will of our Lord Jesus Christ, and the order of this realm?

Answer. I am so persuaded.

The Archbishop. Are you persuaded that the holy scriptures contain sufficiently all doctrine, required of necessity for eternal salvation, through the faith in Jesu Christ? And are you determined with the same holy scriptures to instruct the people committed to your charge, and to teach or maintain nothing, as required of necessity to eternal salvation, but that you shall be persuaded may be concluded, and proved by the same?

Answer. I am so persuaded and determined by God's grace.

The Archbishop. Will you then faithfully exercise yourself in the said holy scriptures, and call upon God by prayer for the true understanding of the same, so as ye may be able by them to teach and exhort with wholesome doctrine, and to withstand and convince the gainsayers?

Answer. I will so do, by the help of God.

The Archbishop. Be you ready with all faithful diligence to banish and drive away all erroneous and strange doctrine contrary to God's word, and both privately and openly to call upon, and encourage other to the same?

Answer. I am ready, the Lord being my helper.

The Archbishop. Will you deny all ungodliness and worldly lusts, and live soberly, righteously, and godly in this world, that you may shew yourself in all things an example of good works unto other, that the adversary may be ashamed having nothing to lay against you?

Answer. I will so do, the Lord being my helper.

The Archbishop. Will you maintain and set forward (as much as shall lie in you) quietness, peace, and love, among all men? And such as be unquiet, disobedient and criminous within your Diocese, correct and punish according to such authority as ye have by God's word, and as to you shall be committed by the ordinance of this realm?

Answer. I will so do, by the help of God.

The Archbishop. Will you shew yourself gentle, and be merciful for Christ's sake to poor and needy people, and to all strangers destitute of help?

Answer. I will so shew myself by God's help.

The Archbishop. Almighty God our heavenly Father, who hath given you a good will to do all these things: grant also unto you strength and power to perform the same, that he accomplishing in you the good work which he hath begun, ye may be found perfect, and irreprehensible at the latter day: through Jesu Christ our Lord. Amen.

Then shall be sung or said, Come Holy Ghost. &c. as it is set out in the Order of Priests.

That ended, the Archbishop shall say.

Lord, hear our prayer.

Answer. And let our cry come unto thee.

¶ Let us pray.

ALMIGHTY God and most merciful Father, which of thy infinite goodness hast given to us thy only and most dear beloved Son Jesus Christ to be our redeemer and author of everlasting life: who after that he had made perfect our redemption by his death, and was ascended into heaven, poured down his gifts abundantly upon men, making some Apostles, some Prophets, some Evangelists, some Pastors and Doctors, to the edifying and making perfect of his congregation: grant, we beseech thee, to this thy servant, such grace that he may evermore be ready to spread abroad thy gospel, and glad tidings of reconcilement to God, and to use the authority given unto him, not to destroy, but to save; not to hurt, but to help; so that he as a wise and a faithful servant, giving to thy family meat in due season, may at the last day be received into joy, through Jesu Christ our Lord: who with thee, and the Holy Ghost, liveth and reigneth one God, world without end. Amen.

¶ Then the Archbishop and Bishops present shall lay their hands upon the head of the elected Bishop, the Archbishop saying.

TAKE the Holy Ghost, and remember that thou stir up the grace of God, which is in thee, by imposition of hands: for God hath not given us the spirit of fear, but of power, and love, and of soberness.

¶ Then the Archbishop shall deliver him the Bible, saying.

GIVE heed unto reading, exhortation and doctrine. Think upon these things contained in this book, be dili-

[DOCUMENTS, EDW. VI.]

gent in them, that the increase[1] coming thereby may be manifest unto all men. Take heed unto thyself, and unto teaching, and be diligent in doing them: for by doing this, thou shalt save thyself, and them that hear thee: be to the flock of Christ a shepherd, not a wolf: feed them, devour them not: hold up the weak, heal the sick, bind together the broken, bring again the outcasts, seek the lost. Be so merciful, that you be not too remiss: so minister discipline, that you forget not mercy: that when the chief Shepherd shall come, ye may receive the immarcessible[2] crown of glory, through Jesus Christ our Lord. Amen.

Then the Archbishop shall proceed to the Communion, with whom the new consecrated Bishop, with other, shall also communicate. And after the last Collect, immediately before the benediction, shall be said this prayer.

MOST merciful Father, we beseech thee to send down upon this thy servant thy heavenly blessing, and so endue him with thy Holy Spirit, that he preaching thy word, may not only be earnest to reprove, beseech, and rebuke with all patience and doctrine, but also may be to such as believe an wholesome example in word, in conversation, in love, in faith, in chastity, and purity: that faithfully fulfilling his course, at the latter day he may receive the crown of righteousness, laid up by the Lord, the righteous judge: who liveth and reigneth, one God with the Father and the Holy Ghost, world without end. Amen.

☾ Imprinted at London in Fleteſtrete at the ſig
of the Sunne ouer agaynſte the conduite by Edvvarde
Whitchurche.
M.D.LII.
Cum priuilegio ad imprimendum ſolum.

[1 increasing, Grafton, 2.]
[2 immarcessible, or immarcescible, unfading.]

¶ This booke is truely and diligently imprynted.

¶ The prices thereof.

THE Imprinter to sell this Booke in Queres for two shillynges and sixe pence, and not aboue, bound in Parchement, or forell, for three shillynges and iiii. pence and not aboue: And bounde in Lether, in Paper Boordes or Claspes, for foure shillynges, and not aboue. And at the next impression, the imprinter leauyng out the fourme of makyng and consecratyng of Archebishoppes, Bishoppes, Priestes, and Deacons, shal sel the saied booke in queres, for twoo shillynges, and not aboue, and bounde in forelle for twoo shillynges and eight pence, and not aboue. And bounde in lether, in paste bordes or claspes, for three shillynges and foure pence, and not aboue.

THE PRIMER:

OR

BOOK OF PRIVATE PRAYER,

NEEDFUL TO BE USED OF

ALL CHRISTIANS.

AUTHORISED AND SET FORTH BY ORDER OF

KING EDWARD VI.

1553.

A Prymmer or
boke of priuate prayer nedeful to be vsed of al faythfull Christianes, Whiche boke is auctorysed and set fourth by the Kinges maiestie, to be taughte, learned, redde and used of al hys louynge subiectes.

Continue in prayer.
Rom. 12.

Londini ex officina Vvilhelmi Seres typographi.

Cum priuilegio ad imprimendum solum.
1553.

[The copy of this edition, which has been followed, is in the Bodleian Library, Oxford; Douce, B.B. 41.]

An EXTRACT *of the King's Majesty's Privilege.*

EDWARD the VI. by the grace of God King of England, France, and of Ireland, &c.

To all Printers, Stationers, Book sellers, and to all other our officers and subjects these our letters hearing or seeing, we do you to understand, that of our grace especial certain science and mere motion, we have granted and given privilege, and by these presents do grant and give privilege and license to our wellbeloved subject William Seres and to his assigns, to print or cause to be printed all manner of books of private prayers, called and usually taken and reputed for Primers, both in great volumes and little, which are and shall be set forth agreeable and according to the book of common prayers established by us in our high court of Parliament, any other privilege or license to the contrary notwithstanding. And furthermore our mind and pleasure is, that the same William Seres and his assigns, shall and may have the only printing from time to time of the said primers aforesaid in all kind of volumes. Straitly forbidding by these presents all and singular our subjects, as well Printers, and Book sellers as all other persons whatsoever they be, to print, utter or sell, or cause to be printed, uttered or sold, within this our Realm or any other our dominions any other sorts or impressions of primers or daily prayers but only such as shall be printed by the same William Seres or his assigns, according to the true meaning of this our present license and privilege upon pain, that every offender therein shall forfeit to our use all such sorts of primers wheresoever they be found. Wherefore we will and command all our officers and subjects, as they tender our favour, and will avoid our displeasure, that they and every of them, if need require, do aid, and assist the said William Seres and his assigns in the due execution of this our license. In witness whereof, we have caused these our letters to be made patents. Witnesseth our self. At Westminster, the sixth day of March, the seventh year of our reign.

GOD SAVE THE KING.

THE
ORDER OF THE KALENDAR.

1 FIRST you shall have the golden number or prime printed with red ink, and it is marked in the top of the
2 page with this red letter. *P.* Then in the next row downward you shall see the days of the month set out in ciphers,
3 and marked in the top of the page with the letter. *D.* After that followeth the row of hours of the change of the moon
4 signified above with the letter. *H.* And then orderly shall you find the row of minutes of the change of the moon noted
5 above with the letter. *M.* After that in order followeth the row of Sunday letters marked above with the letter. *L.*
6 Further, in *January* and *February* you shall find a row of black primes, whereby you may easily find the moveable Sunday called *Septuagesima*, marked in the top of the page
7 with the letter. *S.* Then in *February* and *March*, shall in order follow another row of black primes for the finding out of the Sunday called *Quadragesima*, marked in the top of the
8 page with the letter. *Q.* Also in *March* and *April* doth follow another row of black primes for the finding out of the feast of *Easter*, marked in the top of the page with the letter
9 *E.* Then in *April* and *May* orderly followeth another row of black primes for the finding out of the feast of the *Ascension of Christ*, which is noted in the top of the page with an
10 *A.* After that in order is set another row of black primes beginning on the ninth day of *May*, and ending upon the sixth day of *June*, whereby you may easily find out the feast of *Pentecost*, noted in the top of the page with a black. *P.*
11 Then orderly followeth the *Saints' days*. And finally by
12 the margent towards the right side is set forth, what hour or quarter of the hour the *Sun* shall set every week in the whole year, which row is marked in the top of the page with this red letters. *S.S.*

    A Rule teaching you to find out for ever the five moveable feasts which are: *Septuagesima, Quadragesima, Easter, the Ascension of Christ,* and *Pentecost.*

    Under the mark of every one of the said feasts, which is noted with a letter in the top of the page in that row of

THE ORDER OF THE CALENDAR. 361

black primes seek out the prime of that year, and on the next Sunday immediately following shall be the said moveable feast. But if it be the *Ascension day*, then is it the next *Thursday*, immediately following the said prime of that year.

A Rule, enduring for ever, which teacheth to find out verily the *Prime* or *Golden Number* for the year present.

Mark the number of the present year of our Lord, and put one unto it. And then divide it by nineteen, and that number that remaineth is the Prime for all that year. But if nothing remain after the division made, then nineteen must be the Prime for that year.

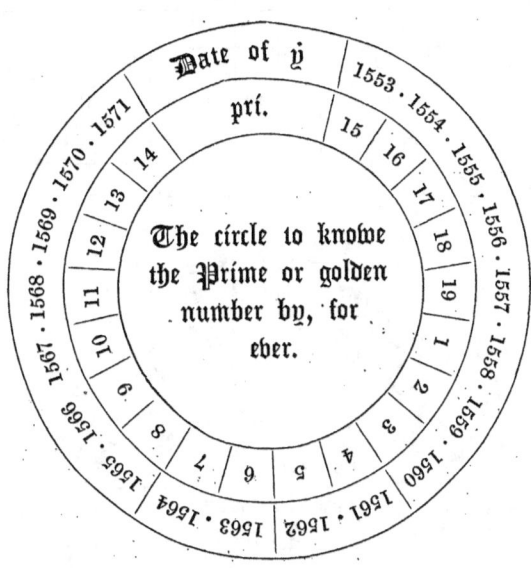

Here followeth a rule teaching you to find out the Sunday's letter for every year present for ever.

Add the number of nine to the number of the present year of our Lord, and divide the whole number by twenty-eight. And look what number remaineth after the division is made, and seek that number in this table beneath: and the letter right under that number is the Sunday's letter for that present year. But if there be two letters directly under the number, then is it *Leap year*, and then the first letter beneath the said number must serve for the *Sunday* letter, from the beginning of *January* unto the feast of *S. Mathie*. And the other letter beneath it must be the Sunday letter from the said feast of *S. Mathie* till the end of that year. But when the division is made, if there remain nothing, then shall A be the Sunday letter for that year.

The Table for the Sunday Letter.

22	23	24	25	26	27	28	1	2	3	4	5	6	7
A	G	F	E	C	B	A	G	E	D	C	B	G	F
			D				F				A		
8	9	10	11	12	13	14	15	16	17	18	19	20	21
E	D	B	A	G	F	D	C	B	A	F	E	D	C
-	C				E			G					B

And then begin the whole table again. &c.

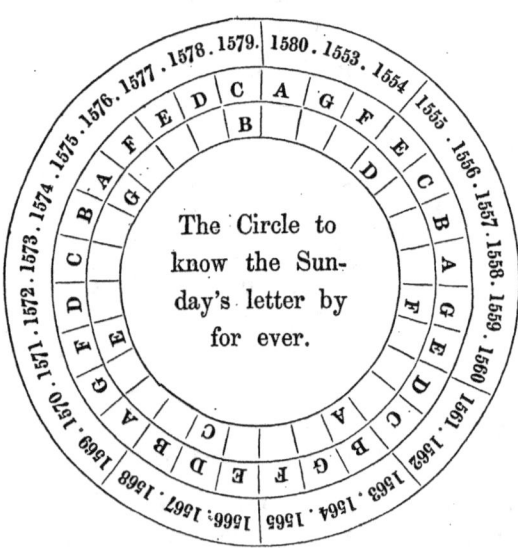

THE ORDER OF THE CALENDAR. 363

A Rule to know at what hour and quarter after the hour the Sun setteth.

In the row of setting of the Sun, which is noted in the top of the page with the red letters *SS.* the ciphers signify the quarters after the hour of the setting of the Sun.

¶ A Rule to know at what hour or quarter of the hour the Sun riseth.

Mark the hour of the setting of the Sun, and reckon how many hours it is from the setting unto twelve of the clock, and at so many hours after midnight the Sun riseth. And when the quarters go after the hours at the setting, you must reckon them before at the sun rising.

¶ To know the change of the Moon in every month.

First in every month seek out the golden number or Prime of the year present (for in this kalendar the prime is alway set upon the change day), and then proceed and go right forward to the day in the second row, and so right forth to the hour in the third row, and from thence straight to the place of minutes, that is in the fourth row, and so right forth to the letter that sheweth the day of the week, and so shall you rightly judge of the change of the Moon, both touching the day of the week, the day of the month, the hour of the day, and the minute of the hour.

But here you must understand, that after this kalendar (which is set out after the *Astronomer supputation* or reckoning) the moon never changeth before, but ever at or after noon, so many hours and minutes as ye find upon the same day against which your prime standeth. And so this rule serveth but for this and such like *kalendar*.

Note here also, that this *kalendar* for the change of the moon with the hours and minutes for the same will serve, not only for this present year, which is the year from Christ's incarnation 1553. but also for fifteen years hereafter to come. And then in the sixteenth year for to come if you will withdraw from every change fifty minutes, that is, half an hour, and twenty minutes, that which remaineth shall shew you the day, hour and minute of the change, and so to continue for nineteen years longer. And so ever in the twentieth year withdraw from all the changes half an hour and twenty minutes, which is fifty minutes, and so will this rule serve for ever.

Moreover, note ye well and mark upon what day the Prime standeth, for the moon shall change upon the same day just at noon, if there be in the place of hours and minutes no significative figures, but only round ciphers, as 0.h.0.m. As for example, when 8 is prime, the moon shall change the second day of *March* just at noon. But when there be any significative figures in the places of hours and minutes, then shall the moon change so many hours and minutes as they do shew, after noon of the same day whereupon your Prime standeth.

As in this example: In this present year of our Lord 1553, is 15. the Prime, which Prime I find upon the tenth day of *June*. And there I find also 15 in the place of hours, and 40 in the place of minutes. And therefore I say, that in *June*, the moon shall change fifteen hours and forty minutes after noon upon the said tenth day of June, that is to say, upon the eleventh day before noon half an hour and ten minutes after three of the clock.

¶ A brief declaration when every Term beginneth and endeth.

¶ Be it known that Easter Term beginneth always the eighteenth day after Easter reckoning Easter Day for one; and endeth the Monday next after the Ascension Day.

¶ Trinity Term beginneth alway the Friday next after Trinity Sunday, and endeth the twenty-eighth day of June.

¶ Michaelmas Term beginneth the ninth or tenth day of October, and endeth the twenty-eighth or twenty-ninth day of November.

¶ Hilary Term beginneth the twenty-third or twenty-fourth day of January, and endeth the twelfth or thirteenth day of February.

¶ In Easter Term on the Ascension Day; in Trinity Term on the Nativity of St John Baptist; in Michaelmas Term on the Feast of All Saints; in Hilary Term on the Feast of the purification of our Lady; the king's judges at Westminster do not use to sit in judgment, nor upon any Sundays.

JANUARY hath XXXI DAYS.

P	D	H	M	L	S	Saints' days.	SS
	1			A		Circumcision.	
8	2	3	0	b			
16	3	11	25	c		. . . . . .	3 °
5	4	21	21	d			
	5			e			
13	6	10	56	f		Epiphanie.	
	7			g			
2	8	20	0	A		Luciani.	
	9			b			
10	10	12	30	c			
	11			d		Sol in aquario	4.
18		3	11				
7	12			e			
		10	10				
15	13	19	40	f		Hylarii.	
	14			g		Felicis.	
4	15	15	0	A		Mauri.	
	16			b		Marcelli.	
12	17	9	57	c	16	Sulpitii.	
	18			d	5	Septuagesima pristi.	4 °
1	19	17	0	e		Wlstani.	
	20			f	13	Fabiani.	
9	21	3	10	g	2	Agnetis.	
17	22	14	0	A		Vincentii.	
6	23	20	50	b	10		
	24			c			
14	25	8	50	d	18	Conversion of S. Paul.	
3	26	15	0	e	7	. . . .	4 °
	27			f		Juliani.	
11	28	8	0	g	15	Agnetis.	
	29			A	4		
19	30	1	0	b		Batildis.	
8	31	12	20	c	12		

FEBRUARY hath XXVIII DAYS.

P	D	H	M	L	S	Q	Saints' days.	SS
16	1	20	30	d	1		Fish. Brigiddæ[1].	
	2			e			Puri. of ma.	4 °
5	3	11	0	f	9		Blasti.	
	4			g				
13	5	4	30	A	17		Agathæ[1].	
	6			b	6		Vedasti.	
2	7	14	0	c		16		
	8			d	14	5		
10	9	3	5	e	3			
		15	20					
18	10			f		13	Sol in pis. Scolasti.	5.
7		20	5					
	11			g	11	2		
15	12	7	40	A				
	13			b	19	10		
4	14	9	0	c	8		Valentini.	
	15			d	18			
12	16	5	0	e	7		Julianæ.	
	17			f			. . . . . .	5 °.
1	18	6	0	g	15			
9	19	14	10	A	4			
17	20	23	40	b				
	21			c	12			
6	22	9	50	d	1		Cathedra. S. Petri.	
	23			e			Fish.	
14	24	0	15	f	9		S. Mathias apo.	5 °
3	25	9	0	g			In the leap year this letter	
	26			A	17		f must be twice reckoned.	
11	27	0	20	b	6			
19	28	14	0	c				

MARCH hath XXXI DAYS.

P	D	H	M	L	Q	E]	Saints' days.	SS
	1			d	14		Dauid.	
8	2	0	0	e	3		Ceddæ.	
16	3	7	40	f				
	4			g	11		. . . . .	5 °.
5	5	4	0	A				
13	6	22	19	b	19			
	7			c	8		Perpetuæ.	
2	8	4	0	d				
10	9	15	6	e				
	10			f				
18	11	1	17	g			Æquinoctium.	
7	12	7	6	A			Sol in Arie. Grego. 6.	
15	13	20	40	b				
	14			c				
	15			d				
4	16	3	0	e				
12	17	21	40	f			Patricii.	
	18			g			Edwardi Regis.	
1	19	17	0	A				
	20			b			Cuthberti.	6. °
9	21	0	0	c	16		Benedicti.	
17	22	8	30	d	5		First Easter.	
6	23	0	0	e				
14	24	16	40	f	13		Fish.	
	25			g	2		Annunciatyon of Mary.	
	26			A				
3	27	1	0	b	10			
11	28	14	10	c				6. °
	29			d	18			
19	30	1	0	e	7			
8	31	7	0	f				

[1 In this and similar cases the old form Brigidde, &c. occurs in the copy.]

APRIL hath XXX DAYS.

P	D	H	M	L	E	A	Saints' days.	SS
16	1	18	20	g	15			
	2			A	4			
5	3	20	0	b			Ricardi.	6. °
	4			c	12		Ambrosii.	
13	5	15	30	d	1			
2	6	17	0	e				
	7			f	9			
10	8	0	9	g				
18	9	9	40	A	17			
7	10	18	7	b	6			
	11			c			Sol in Tauro.	
15	12	10	30	d	14			
	13			e	3			
4	14	19	0	f			Tiburci.	
	15			g	11			
12	16	12	0	A				
	17			b	19			

	1	18	2	0	c	8		
	9	19	7	15	d		Alphegi.	7. °
	17	20	17	10	e			
	6	21	13	50	f			
		22			g			
	14	23	8	40	A		S. George.	
		24			b			
	3	25	14	0	c		S. Mark Euange.	
		26			d			
	11	27	0	7	e		. . . . 7. °	
	19	28	10	0	f		Vitalis.	
	8	29	16	0	g	16		
		30			A	5	The first of the Ascen.	

MAY hath XXXI DAYS.

P	D	H	M	L	A	P	Saints' days.	SS
16	1	5	40	b			S. Philip & James.	
	2			c	13			
5	3	12	0	d	2		Inuentio crucis.	
	4			e			7. °	
13	5	6	30	f	10			
2	6	2	0	g			Johannis ante port. Lati.	
10	7	8	10	A	18		Johannis beuerlaci.	
18	8	17	3	b	7			
	9			c		16		
7	10	6	8	d	15	5	First Penteco. Gordi.	
	11			e	4		Sol in gemine.	
15	12	0	50	f		13	Nerii.	8.
	13			g	12	2		
4	14	9	0	A	1			
12	15	23	40	b		10		
	16			c	9			
1	17	9	0	d		18		

9	18	15	0	e	17	7		
	19			f		6	Dunstani	8. °
17	20	2	40	g		15		
6	21	4	46	A	14	4		
	22			b	3			
14	23	0	0	c		12		
	24			d	11	1		
3	25	1	0	e			Aldelmi.	
11	26	8	15	f	19	9	Augu. anglo. leg.	8. °
10	27	17	0	g	8			
	28			A		17	Germani.	
8	29	2	5	b		6		
16	30	18	0	c				
	31			d		14	Petronillæ.	

JUNE hath XXX DAYS.

P	D	H	M	L	P	Saints' days.	SS
	1			e	3	Nichomedis.	
5	2	3	0	f		Marcellini.	
13	3	19	0	g	11	Uttermost. Ascen.	
2	4	9	0	A			
10	5	15	5	b	19	Bonifacii.	8 ° °
	6			c	8		
18	7	0	40	d			
7	8	18	20	e		Medardi.	
	9			f		Edmundi epyscopi.	
15	10	15	40	g		Barnabæ.	
	11			A		Basilidis.	
4	12	21	0	b		Sol in can. Utter. Pente, 9.	
	13			c		Basilii epyscopi.	
12	14	9	0	d		Viti.	
1	15	16	0	e		Ricardi.	
	16			f			
9	17	22	40	g			

17	18	12	40	A	Marci.	
6	19	19	30	b	Geruasii.	
	20			c	Edwardi Regis.	
14	21	13	40	d		8. ° °
	22			e	Albani.	
3	23	9	0	f	Fish. Etheldred.	
11	24	15	11	g	S. Johan. Baptistæ.	
	25			A		
19	26	11	0	b	Johannis and Pauli.	
8	27	13	3	c		
	28			d	Fish. Leonis.	
16	29	7	40	e	S. Peter apostle.	8. °
	30			f	Commemoratio. S. Pauli apo.	

367

JULY hath XXXI DAYS.

P	D	H	M	L	Saints' days.	SS
5	1	16	0	g		
	2			A	Visitatio Mariæ.	
13	3	6	30	b		
2		16	0			
	4			c	Martini.	
10	5	0	0	d		
18	6	9	13	e		
	7			f	Dog days begin.	8. ○
7	8	9	30	g	Becket Traitor.	
	9			A		
15	10	6	30	b	Septem Fratrum.	
	11			c	Benedicti.	
4	12	7	0	d		
12	13	17	0	e		
1	14	23	0	f	Sol in Leo.	
	15			g	Swithuni.	
9	16	8	40	A	Osmundi.	
	17			b	Kenelmi.	
17	18	1	0	c	Arnulphi.	
6	19	10	3	d		
	20			e	Margaretæ.	
14	21	3	0	f	Praxedis.	
3	22	16	0	g	Magdalene.	7. ○ °
	23			A	Apolinaris.	
11	24	0	0	b	Fish. Christinæ.	
19	25	7	0	c	S. James Apostle.	
	26			d	Annæ.	
8	27	2	17	e	Septem dormientum.	
16	28	22	50	f	Samsonis.	
	29			g	Felicis.	
	30			A	Abdon.	7. °
5	31	4	0	b	Germani.	

AUGUST hath XXXI DAYS.

P	D	H	M	L	Saints' days.	SS
13	1	16	13	c	Lammas day.	
2		23	0			
	2			d	Stephani.	
10	3	6	20	e	Inuentio Stephani.	
18	4	20	0	f		
	5			g	Oswoldi.	
	6			A	Transfiguratio Christi.	
7	7	1	0	b	Jesus day.	7. ○
15	8	21	6	c	Cyriaci.	
	9			d	Romani.	
4	10	17	0	e	S. Laurence.	
	11			f	Tibertii.	
12	12	0	30	g		
1	13	9	20	A	Ypoliti.	
9	14	20	40	b	Eusebii.	[7.
	15			c	Sol in Virgine. Assumptio ma.	
17	16	17	13	d		
	17			e		
6	18	0	35	f	Agapeti.	
14	19	0	35	g	Magni.	
	20			A		
3	21	0	0	b		
11	22	6	0	c		6 ° °
	23			d	Fish. Timothei.	
19	24	1	0	e	S. Bartholomewe Apostle.	
8	25	18	0	f		
	26			g		
16	27	14	40	A	Ruphi.	
	28			b	Augustini Episcopi.	
5	29	16	0	c	Beheading Joh. ba.	6 °
	30			d	Felicis.	
13	31	1	16	e	Cuthbergæ.	
2		8	0			

SEPTEMBER hath XXX DAYS.

P	D	H	M	L	Saints' days.	SS
10	1	17	8	f	Egidii.	
	2			g		
18	3	9	40	A		
	4			b	Cuthberti.	
7	5	17	6	c	Dog days end. Ber.	6. ○
	6			d		
15	7	11	40	e		
	8			f	Nativitas Mariæ.	
4	9	1	0	g	Gorgonii.	
12	10	8	30	A		
1	11	21	0	b	Prothi.	
	12			c		
9	13	11	23	d	Sol in libra.	6.
	14			e	Exaltatio crucis.	
17	15	7	43	f		
6	16	14	10	g	Edithæ.	
	17			A	Lamberti.	
14	18	2	0	b		
3	19	8	0	c		
11	20	16	0	d	Fish.	5 ° °
	21			e	S. Mathewe Apostle.	
19	22	5	0	f	Mauritii.	
	23			g	Teclæ.	
8	24	11	6	A		
	25			b	Firmini.	
16	26	7	3	c	Cypriani.	
	27			d	Cosmæ.	
5	28	2	0	e		5. °
13	29	19	16	f	S. Michael Archangel.	
2		10	15			
	30			g	S. Hierome.	

OCTOBER hath XXXI DAYS.

P	D	H	M	L	Saints' days.	SS
10	1	6	50	A	Remigii.	
	2			b	Leodegarii.	
18	3	1	40	c		
	4			d	Francisci.	
7	5	9	11	e		
	6			f	Fidis.	5. ○
15	7	1	8	g	Marci.	
4	8	10	0	A		
12	9	17	55	b	Dionisii.	
	10			c	Gerionis.	
1	11	12	0	d	Nicasii.	
	12			e		5.
9	13	4	43	f	Edwardi Regis.	
	14			g	Sol in Scorp. Calixti.	
17	15	1	40	A	Wulfranni.	
6	16	3	0	b	Michaelis de monte.	
14	17	12	30	c	Etheldredæ.	
3	18	19	0	d	Luke Euangelist.	
	19			e	Frideswidæ.	
11	20	4	16	f		
	21			g	Vndecim milium virg. 4. ⦂○
19	22	11	0	A		
	23			b	Romani.	
8	24	5	6	c		
16	25	23	5	d	Crispini et Crispiniani.	
	26			e		
5	27	12	0	f	Fish.	
13	28	19	40	g	Symon and Jude Apostles.
2	29	9	40	A		4. ⦂
	30			b		
10	31	0	0	c	Quintini. Fish.	

NOVEMBER hath XXX DAYS.

P	D	H	M	L	Saints' days.	SS
18	1	20	0	d	All Saints. .	
	2			e		
	3			f	Wenefrida.	
7	4	0	0	g		4. ○
15	5	13	40	A		
4	6	21	0	b	Leonardi.	
	7			c		
12	8	5	19	d	Quatuor coronatorum.	
	9			e	Theodori.	
1	10	6	0	f		
	11			g	Martini.	
9	12	0	0	A	Sol in Sagitta.	
17	13	19	40	b	Brictii.	4.
6	14	14	40	c	Erkenwaldi.	
14	15	22	40	d	Machuti.	
	16			e	Edmundi Archiepiscopi.	
3	17	7	0	f	Hugonis.	
11	18	19	30	g		
	19			A		
	20			b	Edmundi Regis.	
19	21	6	0	c		3. ⦂○
	22			d	Ceciliæ.	
8	23	0	0	e	Clementis.	
16	24	13	50	f	Grisogoni.	
5	25	20	0	g	Katherinæ.	
	26			A	Lini.	
13	27	6	20	b		
2	28	1	0	c		
10	29	18	11	d	Fish. Saturnini.	3. ⦂
	30			e	S. Andrewe Apostle.	

DECEMBER hath XXXI DAYS.

P	D	H	M	L	Saints' days.	SS
18	1	15	11	f		
	2			g		
7	3	14	6	A		
	4			b	Osmundi.	
15	5	1	0	c		
4	6	7	0	d	Nicolai.	
12	7	19	2	e		
	8			f	Conceptio Mariæ.	
	9			g		
1	10	1	0	A		
9	11	18	25	b		
	12			c	Sol in Capricor.	
17	13	12	30	d	Lucia.	
6	14	1	30	e		
14	15	8	50	f		
3	16	23	0	g		
	17			A		
11	18	13	17	b		
	19			c		
	20			d	Fish.	3. ○.
19	21	8	40	e	S. Thomas Apostle.	
8	22	14	5	f		
	23			g		
16	24	2	30	A	Fish.	
5	25	9	0	b	Christmas.	
13	26	18	30	c	S. Stephen.	
2	27	20	0	d	S. John Evangelist.	3. ⦂
	28			e	Innocentes.	
10	29	14	0	f		
	30			g		
18	31	9	40	A	Sylvestri.	

A CATECHISM,

THAT IS TO SAY,

AN INSTRUCTION TO BE LEARNED OF EVERY CHILD, BEFORE HE BE BROUGHT TO BE CONFIRMED OF THE BISHOP.

Question. WHAT is your name?
Answer. N. or M.
Question. Who gave you this name?
Answer. My Godfathers and Godmothers in my Baptism, wherein I was made a member of Christ, the child of God, and an inheritor of the kingdom of heaven.
Question. What did your Godfathers and Godmothers then for you?
Answer. They did promise and vow three things in my name.

i. First, that I should forsake the Devil and all his works and pomps, the vanities of the wicked world, and all the sinful lusts of the flesh.

ii. Secondly, that I should believe all the articles of the christian faith.

iii. And thirdly, that I should keep God's holy will and commandments, and walk in the same all the days of my life.

Question. Dost thou not think that thou art bound to believe and to do as they have promised for thee?
Answer. Yes, verily. And by God's help so I will. And I heartily thank our heavenly Father, that he hath called me to this state of salvation, through Jesus Christ our Saviour. And I pray God to give me grace; that I may continue in the same unto my life's end.

Question. Rehearse the articles of thy belief.
Answer. I believe in God the Father Almighty, maker of heaven and earth. And in Jesus Christ his only Son our Lord, which was conceived by the Holy Ghost, born of the virgin Mary. Suffered under Ponce Pilate, was crucified, dead and buried, he descended into hell. The third day he rose again from the dead. He ascended into heaven, and sitteth on the right hand of God the Father almighty. From thence shall

he come to judge the quick and the dead. I believe in the Holy Ghost. The holy catholic church. The communion of saints. The forgiveness of sins. The resurrection of the body. And the life everlasting. Amen.

Question. What dost thou chiefly learn in these articles of thy belief?

Answer. i. First, I learn to believe in God the Father, who hath made me and all the world.

ii. Secondly, in God the Son, who hath redeemed me, and all mankind.

iii. Thirdly, in God the Holy Ghost, who sanctifieth me and all the elect people of God.

Question. You said, that your Godfathers and Godmothers did promise for you that you should keep God's commandments. Tell me how many there be.

Answer. Ten.

Question. Which be they?

Answer. The same which God spake in the twentieth chapter of Exodus, saying: I am the Lord thy God, which have brought thee out of the land of Egypt, out of the house of bondage.

I. Thou shalt have none other Gods but me.

II. Thou shalt not make to thyself any graven image, nor the likeness of anything that is in heaven above, or in the earth beneath, nor in the water under the earth: thou shalt not bow down to them nor worship them. For I the Lord thy God am a jealous God, and visit the sins of the fathers upon the children, unto the third and fourth generation of them that hate me, and shew mercy unto thousands in them that love me, and keep my commandments.

III. Thou shalt not take the name of the Lord thy God in vain: for the Lord will not hold him guiltless that taketh his name in vain.

IV. Remember that thou keep holy the Sabbath day. Six days shalt thou labour, and do all that thou hast to do: But the seventh day is the Sabbath of the Lord thy God. In it shalt thou do no manner of work, thou, and thy son and thy daughter, thy man servant, and thy maid servant, thy cattle, and the stranger that is within thy gates: for in six days the Lord made heaven and earth, the sea, and all that in them is, and rested the seventh day.

Wherefore the Lord blessed the seventh day, and hallowed it.

V. Honour thy father and thy mother, that thy days may be long in the land which the Lord thy God giveth thee.

VI. Thou shalt do no murder.

VII. Thou shalt not commit adultery.

VIII. Thou shalt not steal.

IX. Thou shalt not bear false witness against thy neighbour.

X. Thou shalt not covet thy neighbour's house, thou shalt not covet thy neighbour's wife, nor his servant, nor his maid, nor his ox, nor his ass, nor anything that is his.

Question. What dost thou chiefly learn by these commandments?

Answer. I learn two things, my duty towards God, and my duty towards my neighbour.

Question. What is thy duty towards God?

Answer. My duty towards God is, to believe in him, to fear him, and to love him with all my heart, with all my mind, with all my soul, and with all my strength. To worship him. To give him thanks. To put my whole trust in him. To call upon him. To honour his holy name and his word, and to serve him truly all the days of my life.

Question. What is thy duty towards thy neighbour?

Answer. My duty toward my neighbour is, to love him as myself. And to do to all men as I would they should do unto me. To love, honour, and succour my father and mother. To honour and obey the king and his ministers. To submit myself to all my governors, teachers, spiritual Pastors and Masters. To order myself lowly and reverently to all my betters. To hurt nobody by word nor deed. To be true and just in all my dealing: To bear no malice nor hatred in my heart. To keep my hands from picking and stealing, and my tongue from evil speaking, lying, and slandering. To keep my body in temperance, soberness, and chastity. Not to covet nor desire other men's goods[1]. But learn and labour truly to get mine own living, and to do my duty in that state of life, unto the which it shall please God to call me.

[1 goodnes, in the original.]

Question. My good child, know this, that thou art not able to do these things of thyself, nor to walk in the commandments of God, and to serve him without his special grace, which thou must learn at all times to call for by diligent prayer. Let me hear therefore if thou canst say the Lord's prayer.

Answer. Our Father which art in heaven, hallowed be thy name. Thy kingdom come. Thy will be done in earth as it is in heaven. Give us this day our daily bread. And forgive us our trespasses, as we forgive them that trespass against us. And lead us not into temptation. But deliver us from evil. Amen.

Question. What desirest thou of God in this prayer?

Answer. I desire my Lord God our heavenly Father, who is the giver of all goodness, to send his grace unto me and to all people, that we may worship, serve him, and obey him, as we ought to do. And I pray unto God, that he will send us all things that be needful both for our souls and bodies. And that he will be merciful unto us, and forgive us our sins: and that it will please him to save and defend us in all dangers ghostly and bodily. And that he will keep us from all sin and wickedness, and from our ghostly enemy, and from everlasting death. And this I trust he will do of his mercy and goodness, through our Lord Jesus Christ. And therefore I say: Amen. So be it.

GRACES TO BE SAID BEFORE DINNER AND SUPPER.

¶ *Grace before dinner.*

THE eyes of all things do look up and trust in thee, O Lord, thou givest them meat in due season. Thou dost open thine hand, and fillest with thy blessing every living thing. Good Lord, bless us, and all thy gifts which we receive of thy bounteous liberality, through Jesus Christ our Lord. Amen.

¶ The King of eternal glory make us partakers of thy heavenly table. Amen.

¶ God is charity, and he that dwelleth in charity dwelleth in God, and God in him. God grant us all to dwell in him. Amen.

¶ Grace after dinner.

THE God of peace and love vouchsafe alway to dwell with us, and thou, Lord, have mercy upon us. Glory, honour and praise be to thee, O God, which hast fed us from our tender age, and givest sustenance to every living thing: replenish our hearts with joy and gladness, that we alway having sufficient may be rich and plentiful in all good works, through our Lord Jesu Christ. Amen.

Grace after supper.

BLESSED is God in all his gifts, and holy in all his works. Our help is in the name of the Lord, who hath made both heaven and earth. Blessed be the name of our Lord. From henceforth, world without end.

Most mighty Lord and merciful Father, we yield thee hearty thanks for our bodily sustenance, requiring also most entirely thy gracious goodness, so to feed us with the food of thy heavenly grace, that we may worthily glorify thy holy name in this life, and after be partakers of the life everlasting, through our Lord Jesus Christ. Amen.

¶ Lord, save thy Church, our King and Realm, and send us peace in Christ. Amen.

Another Grace before meat.

AT the beginning of this refection, let us reverently and earnestly call to our remembrance the holy scripture which saith : Whether we eat or drink, or whatsoever we do else, let us do it to the laud and praise of God. _{1 Cor. 10.}

Answer. Laud, praise, and glory be unto God, now and evermore. So be it.

¶ Thanks after meat.

FORASMUCH as you have well refreshed your bodies, remember the lamentable afflictions and miseries of many thousands of your neighbours and brethren in Christ visited by the hand of God, some with mortal plagues and diseases, some with imprisonment, some with extreme poverty and necessity, that either they cannot, or they have not to feed on as you have done. Remember therefore how much and how deeply ye are bound to the goodness of almighty God, for your health, wealth, liberty, and many other his benefits given unto you.

Answer. ¶ Praise and thanks be to God now and always, for these and all other his gracious gifts, of his goodness, so mercifully, lovingly and abundantly shewed unto us. Amen.

Grace before supper.

CHRIST, which at his last supper promised his body to be crucified, and his precious blood to be shed for our sins, bless us and our supper. Amen.

Thanks after dinner or supper.

ALL ye whom God hath here refreshed with his sufficient repast, remember your poor and needy brethren, of the which some lay in the streets sore sick, naked, and cold, some be hungry and so dry, that they would be glad of the least draught of your drink, and of the smallest paring of your bread: they be your own flesh and brethren in Christ, bought as dearly with his precious blood as ye were, but yet our Lord hath dealt more easily with you than with them, and more sharply with them than with you: relieve them therefore to your power, and give to God all glory, honor and praise for ever and ever. Amen.

Grace before dinner.

ALL that is and shall be set upon the board
Be that same sanctified, by the Lord's word.
   Our Father, which art, &c.

Thanks after dinner.

WE give thee thanks, O Father almighty,
For thy graces and benefits manifold,
Which thou hast poured on us abundantly:
Of thy tender kindness that can not be told
Grant us thy sonnes, that we may be bold
For Christ Jesus' sake to come to the sweet dinner
Where nother shall be hunger, thirst nor cold,
But all joy and mirth for ever and ever. Amen.

Grace before supper.

He that is King of glory, and Lord over all,
Bring us to the supper of the life eternall.
   Our Father, which art, &c.

Thanks after supper.

O LAMB of God, Christ, which takest away
The sins of the world, and cleansest all thing,
We give thanks, that us sinners this day
Hast saved us, kept us, and given us feeding.
Grant us, we beseech thee, at our ending
Clean remission, and that in perfect love
We may depart hence, full of thy blessing,
And rest in Abraham's bosom above. Amen.

Grace before meat.

PRAY we to God the almighty Lord,
That sendeth food to beasts and men,
To send his blessing on this board
To feed us now and ever. Amen.

Thanks after meat.

BLESSED be the Father celestial,
Who hath fed us with his material bread;
Beseeching him likewise to feed the soul
And grant us his kingdom when we be dead.

Before thou pray.

I. FIRST examine thine own conscience with what kind of temptation or sin thou art most encumbered withal, and pray earnestly unto God for remedies therefore. Asking of him all things needful both for soul and body, privately for thine own self, and thy family, and generally for all the christian congregation. If any of you lack wisdom (that is, any gift of grace), let him ask of God which giveth to all men indifferently, and casteth no man in the teeth, and it shall be given him, etc. [James i.]

II. Secondarily, upon consideration of thine own lack, and the common lack of the congregation. Remember that God commandeth thee by prayer to call upon him for remedy, aid, and help, saying, Ask, seek, knock, watch and pray, call upon me (saith God) in the day of tribulation. [Matt. vii. Mark xiii. Ps. l.]

III. Thirdly, consider that God doth not only command thee to pray, but also promiseth graciously to hear and grant all thine honest, lawful, and Godly requests and petitions, saying: Ask, and ye shall have, knock and it shall be opened unto you. Every one that asketh hath, &c. Call upon me, saith God, in the day of trouble and I will deliver thee.

IV. Fourthly, thou must steadfastly believe God's promises, and trust undoubtedly, that both he can and will perform them. Ask in faith (saith Saint James), nothing doubting; for why shouldest thou doubt, seeing that the holy scripture testifieth of God, that he is faithful, just, and true in all his words and promises, saying, The Lord is faithful in all his words. He will ever be mindful of his covenant. The truth of the Lord endureth for ever.

V. Fifthly, thou must ask of God all thy petitions and requests for his mercy and truth sake, for Christ Jesus' sake, and in his blessed and holy name. Save me, O God, (saith David,) for thy name's sake. No man cometh unto the Father but by me, saith Christ. Verily, verily, I say unto you, whatsoever you shall ask the Father in my name, he will give it you. Mark, that he saith, in my name.

VI. Sixthly, thou must ask all bodily, worldly and corruptible things pertaining to this transitory life, as bodily health, wealth, strength, beauty, honor, lands, riches, offices, promotions, and such like; all such things (I say) thou must ever ask of God with these conditions. If it be thy will, O Lord, if it stand with thine honor and glory: if it be for my soul's health, profit and commodity: if not, thy will be done and not mine. All these things your heavenly Father knoweth what you have need of before ye ask of him. With this condition prayed Christ, saying: Father, if it be possible, let this cup pass from me: nevertheless, not as I will, but as thou wilt, &c. With like condition prayed David for his return in his exile.

VII. Seventhly, thou must appoint God no certain time of gratifying thy requests, but utterly commit that to his godly will and pleasure, which knoweth best what time of granting thy requests is most commodious and profitable for thee. Hereof thou hast a goodly example in Judith.

VIII. Finally, thou must in any wise take heed when thou prayest, that thou be in love and charity with all men, or else all these aforesaid things profit nothing at all. For like as a surgeon cannot heal perfectly a wound so long as any iron remaineth in it: even so cannot prayer profit so long as the mind is cankered and defiled with guile, fraud, deceit, rancour, hatred, malice, and such other like wretchedness: for brotherly reconciliation must needs go before prayer. As Christ saith: If thou offerest thy gift at the altar, and Matt. v. there rememberest that thy brother hath ought against thee, leave there thine offering before the altar, and go thy way first, and be reconciled to thy brother, and then come and offer thy gift.

Prepare thyself therefore to prayer with the eight aforesaid considerations, and being adorned and garnished with faith, hope, charity, meekness, soberness, equity, pity, and godliness, go to in Christ's name, and pray unto God with all diligence.

And that, thy prayer may be more effectuous, let it be joined always with temperate fasting and charitable alms to thy needy neighbour according to the godly counsel of the good man Tobias: Prayer is good with fasting and alms. Tobi. xii.

And in thy faithful prayers remember Thomas Cottesforde the preparer of this preparative.

Summa.

Pray because
1. Thou hast need.
2. God commands thee.
3. Of God's promises.
4. Pray in faith of God's promise.
5. Ask all things in Christ's name.
6. Ask worldly and temporal things conditionally.
7. Appoint God no time but abide his pleasure.
8. In any wise pray in charity.
9. Ask things pertaining to thy salvation, remission of sin and life everlasting, without condition.

¶ For these hath God certainly promised to all them that Ps. lxxxvii. with a true faithful and obedient heart doth come unto him in earnest and continual prayer.

A Prayer, containing in it all the aforesaid preparative unto prayer.

O GRACIOUS Lord and most merciful Father, which hast from the beginning of mine age hitherto delivered me from innumerable perils and dangers, both of soul and body, I most heartily thank thee. And yet, forasmuch as I feel in myself so many faults and imperfections, such readiness to evil, and such frowardness and slackness to do good, I quake and tremble for fear of thy fierce wrath and strait judgment. But when I consider with myself that thou commandest me by prayer to crave of thee all things necessary for soul and body, I conceive a little hope of recovery of that that I stand need of. And to tell you the truth, it fully comforteth me and maketh me not a little joyful, when I remember, that not only thou O Father, commandest me to pray, but also of thine exceeding great mercy promisest graciously to hear my lamentable suit, and mercifully to grant to me my lawful and needful requests. And my faith, confidence and sure trust is, that thou art true and just in all thy words and promises, and both can and wilt perform them, and grant me mine honest petitions. Howbeit, for all that, I will not presume to ask them in mine own name, neither for mine own merit or deserving, but for Christ Jesus' sake, and in his blessed and holy name, and for thy mercy and truth's sake. But touching all those things that pertain to this my corruptible body and transitory life, I humbly beseech thy fatherly goodness to grant me them so far forth as they agree unto thy holy will, pleasure, honor, and glory, and to my most furtherance, profit and commodity. Nevertheless I beseech thee, good Lord, grant me them, not at such time as I fancy to be best; but at such time as shall be seen most meet to thy Godly majesty, unto whose tuition I fully and wholly commit both me and all mine. Moreover, seeing that thou regardest no prayer unless it be done in love and charity, I humbly beseech thy gracious goodness, that I may alway pray in charity, receive my petitions and requests in charity, use all thy gracious gifts and benefits in charity, and lead all my whole life and conversation in charity. And finally I heartily pray thee, that I may daily through the assistance of thy holy Spirit more and more mortify all my carnal desires and filthy affections. And vouchsafe to prosper both me and mine, and all the christian congregation in all our honest and godly affairs: increase also thy gracious gifts in us, and confirm us and establish us so in grace, that we may go forward in all goodness. Grant this, most merciful Father, for Jesus Christ's sake, our only mediator and advocate. So be it.

At thine uprising in the morning, say,

I ENTER into this day, to do all things, in the name of the Father, and of the Son, and of the Holy Ghost. So be it.

Add this prayer following.

AFTER due examination of my former life, with an humble and contrite heart, with a sorrowful and repentant spirit, I sue unto thee, most merciful Father, beseeching thee of mercy and forgiveness of all mine offences, which in this night, or at any time heretofore I have committed against thy godly will and pleasure, by any manner of uncleanness of soul or body that I have fallen into by the illusion of the devil or else by frailty of mine own flesh, trespassing against thy godly majesty, either in thought, consent, delectation, word or deed. And I most heartily thank thee, that thou hast vouchsafe to preserve me this night from sudden death, and all other mischief, that any person, man or woman hath been stricken withal by thy permission and sufferance, knowing of a surety, that the selfsame or such like had worthily light on my head also, haddest not thou defended me and preserved me. And now I beseech thee, blessed Father, that thou wilt vouchsafe to have a merciful eye unto me this day, support me and sustain me, bear me up and save me, that I fall not into the danger of thy displeasure through breaking of thy commandments. Give me grace to walk warily among the innumerable snares of our mortal enemies, the devil, the world and the flesh, and in all things to be circumspect and prudent, and diligently to consider beforehand, what I shall speak, and what I shall go about to do, that all my whole life, thought, words, and works be so ordered, that in all mine enterprises thine honour, laud and glory, the edifying of mine own soul in virtue, and the profit of my christian brethren may be only sought for and intended; through the gracious mediation[1] of Jesus Christ our Lord and only advocate. So be it.

Going to thy rest, say.

I LAY me down to rest, in the name of the Father, and of the Son, and of the Holy Ghost. So be it.

[[1] meditation, in the original.]

Add this prayer following.

O MOST gracious Lord and merciful Father, I thy sinful creature and most unworthy child, prostrate in my heart before thine high majesty, most humbly beseech thee of mercy and forgiveness of all my sin and iniquity, that I have this day committed against thee. Yea, and ever sith the time that I was conceived in my mother's womb, unto this present instant, and specially in this, &c. (Here call to thy remembrance what heinous offence thou hast committed that chiefly grudgeth thy conscience.) And most heartily I thank thee, that thou hast preserved me hitherto from all such offences, as I have not fallen in, and whereinto any other person through his own fault and thy sufferance hath fallen, into the which I also without doubt should have fallen, hadst not thou with thy grace prevented me, saved me, supported me, and sustained me. That I have fallen many ways, my great fault and blame it is, for the which in most humble wise I ask mercy and forgiveness of thee. That thou hast preserved me, thy great goodness, mercy and grace it is, for the which, with all mine heart, I thank thee. And now I beseech thee, most merciful Father, that thou wilt no more be angry with me, neither henceforth forsake me, but that thou wilt continually not only assist, fortify and strength me against the assaults of the devil, but also be my succour and defence in this night and always to my life's end against all sin and iniquity. And that thou wilt vouchsafe also of thy abundant bountifulness, (if it be thy will,) to refresh my brittle body so with convenient rest this night, that I may the more readily, freshly and promptly with all diligence serve thee to-morrow, according to that state that thou hast set me in and called me unto, so that all my life may please thee, and through thine assistance be so ordered and governed, that after this vain and transitory life I may attain the life everlasting. Through Jesus Christ our Lord. So be it.

A Prayer for the Morning.

O MERCIFUL Lord God, heavenly Father, I render most high lauds, praise, and thanks unto thee, that thou hast preserved me both at this night and all the time and days of my life hitherto under thy protection, and hast suffered me to live until this present hour. And I beseech thee heartily thou wilt vouchsafe to receive me this day and the residue of my whole life from henceforth, unto thy tuition, ruling and governing me with thy holy Spirit, that all manner of darkness of misbelief, infidelity, and carnal lusts and affections may be utterly chased and driven out of my heart, and that I may be justified and saved both body and soul, through a right and perfect faith, and so walk in the light of thy most Godly truth, to thy glory and praise, and to the profit and furtherance[1] of my neighbour, through Jesus Christ our Lord and Saviour. Amen.

A Prayer to be said at night going to bed.

O MERCIFUL Lord God, heavenly Father, whether we sleep or wake, live or die, we are always thine. Wherefore I beseech thee heartily, that thou wilt vouchsafe to take care and charge of me, and not to suffer me to perish in the works of darkness, but to kindle the light of thy countenance in my heart, that thy Godly knowledge may daily increase in me, through a right and pure faith, and that I may always be found to walk and live after thy will and pleasure; through Jesus Christ our Lord and Saviour. Amen.

[[1] fordraunce, original.]

AN

ORDER OF PRIVATE PRAYER

FOR

MORNING AND EVENING

EVERY DAY IN THE WEEK, AND SO THROUGHOUT THE WHOLE YEAR.

AT the beginning of morning and evening private prayer, thou shalt daily read, meditate, weigh and deeply consider one of these sentences of holy scripture that follow. And then from the bottom of thine heart add the confession of thy sins and the prayer following.

Sentences of holy scripture.

Ezech. xviii.   IF the ungodly will turn away from all his sins that he hath done, and keep all my commandments. and do the thing that is equal and right, doubtless he shall live and not die. As for all his sins that he did before, they shall not be thought upon: but in his righteousness that he hath done, he shall live. For I have no pleasure in the death of a sinner, saith the Lord God, but rather that he convert and live. Wherefore be converted, and turn you clean from all your wickedness, so shall there no sin do you harm.

Zach. i.   Turn you unto me, saith the Lord of Hosts, and I will turn me unto you.

Luke xiii.   Except ye repent, ye shall all perish, (saith Christ.)

Luke xv.   ¶ There shall be joy in the presence of the angels of God over one sinner that repenteth.

Math. iii.   ¶ Amend your lives, for the kingdom of God is at hand.

Psal. li.   ¶ A sorrowful spirit is a sacrifice to God: despise not, O God, humble and contrite hearts.

Esay lv.   ¶ Let the ungodly man forsake his own ways, and the unrighteous his own imaginations, and turn again unto the Lord, so shall he be merciful unto him, and to our God, for he is ready to forgive.

Joel ii.   ¶ Turn you unto me (saith the Lord) with all your hearts, with fasting, weeping and mourning. Rent your hearts and not your clothes.' Turn you unto the Lord your God, for he is gracious and merciful, long suffering, and of great compassion, and ready to pardon wickedness.

¶ Make no tarrying to turn unto the Lord, and put not off from day to day: for suddenly shall his wrath come, and in time of vengeance he shall destroy thee. *Eccle. v.*

¶ Turn us, O God our Saviour, and let thine anger cease from us. Convert thou me, and I shall be converted, for thou art my Lord God. *Psal. lxxxv Jere. xxxi.*

¶ If we knowledge our sins, God is faithful and just to forgive us our sins, and to cleanse us from all unrighteousness. *1 John i*

A Confession of sins.

ALMIGHTY and most merciful Father, I have erred and strayed from thy ways, like a lost sheep; I have followed too much the devices and desires of mine own heart. I have offended against thy holy laws. I have left undone those things which I ought to have done, and I have done those things which I ought not to have done, and there is no health in me: But thou, O Lord, have mercy upon me, miserable offender, spare thou me, O God, which confess my faults, restore thou me, that am penitent, according to thy promises declared unto mankind, in Christ Jesu our Lord. And grant, O most merciful Father, for his sake, that I may hereafter live a Godly, righteous and sober life, to the glory of thy holy name. Amen.

Add to this confession this Prayer.

ALMIGHTY God, the Father of our Lord Jesus Christ, which desirest not the death of a sinner, but rather that he may turn from his wickedness and live: and hast given power and commandment to thy ministers, to declare and pronounce to thy people, being penitent, the absolution and remission of their sins, and pardonest and absolvest them which truly repent, and unfeignedly believe thy holy gospel: I beseech thee to grant me true repentance, and thy holy Spirit, that those things may please thee, which I do at this present, and that the rest of my life hereafter, may be pure and holy, so that at the last I may come to thy eternal joy, Through Jesus Christ our Lord. Amen.

THE BEGINNING OF MORNING PRAYER.

Morning prayer for Sunday.

OUR Father, which art in heaven, hallowed be thy name. Thy kingdom come. Thy will be done in earth, as it is in heaven. Give us this day our daily bread. And forgive us our trespasses, as we forgive them that trespass against us. And lead us not into temptation. But deliver us from evil. Amen.

¶ Then say,

O Lord, open thou my lips.
And my mouth shall shew forth thy praise.
O God, make speed to help me.
O Lord, make haste to save me.
Glory be to the Father, and to the Son, and to the Holy Ghost.
As it was in the beginning, is now, and ever shall be, world without end. Amen.

¶ Praise we the Lord.

Venite. Psalm xcv.

O COME, let us sing unto the Lord : let us heartily rejoice in the strength of our salvation.

Let us come before his presence with thanksgiving : and shew ourself glad in him with psalms.

For the Lord is a great God : and a great king above all Gods.

In his hands are all the corners of the earth : and the strength of the hills is his also.

The sea is his, and he made it : and his hands prepared the dry land.

O come, let us worship and fall down : and kneel before the Lord our maker.

For he is (the Lord) our God : and we are the people of his pasture, and the sheep of his hands.

To-day if ye will hear his voice, harden not your hearts : as in the provocation, and as in the day of temptation in the wilderness.

When your fathers tempted me : proved me, and saw my works.

Forty years long was I grieved with this generation, and said : It is a people that do err in their hearts, for they have not known my ways.

Unto whom I sware in my wrath : that they should not enter into my rest.

Glory be to the Father, and to the Son : and to the Holy Ghost.

As it was in the beginning, is now, and ever shall be : world without end. Amen.

Beatus Vir. Psalm i.

BLESSED is that man that hath not walked in the counsel of the ungodly :

Nor stand in the way of sinners, and hath not sit in the seat of the scornful.

But his delight is in the law of the Lord : And in his law will exercise himself day and night.

And he shall be like a tree planted by the water side : That will bring forth his fruit in due season.

His leaf also shall not wither : And look whatsoever he doeth it shall prosper.

As for the ungodly, it is not so with them : But they are like the chaff, which the wind scattereth away (from the face of the earth.)

Therefore the ungodly shall not be able to stand in the judgment : Neither the sinners in the congregation of the righteous.

But the Lord knoweth the way of the righteous : And the way of the ungodly shall perish.

Domine, quid multiplicati. Psalm iii.

LORD, how are they increased that trouble me : Many are they that rise up against me.

Many one there be that say of my soul : There is no help for him in (his) God.

But thou, O Lord, art my defender : Thou art my worship, and the lifter up of my head.

I did call upon the Lord with my voice : And he heard me out of his holy hill.

I lay me down and slept : and rose up again, for the Lord sustained me.

I will not be afraid for ten thousand of people : That have set themself against me round about.

Up Lord, and help me, O my God : For thou smitest all mine enemies upon the cheek bone, thou hast broken the teeth of the ungodly.

Salvation belongeth unto the Lord : and thy blessing is upon the people.

¶ The fourth Psalm.

Cum invocarem. Psalm iv.

HEAR me when I call, O God of my righteousness : Thou hast set me at liberty when I was in trouble; have mercy upon me, and hearken unto my prayer.

O ye sons of men, how long will ye blaspheme mine honour : and have such pleasure in vanity, and seek after leasing?

Know this also, that the Lord hath chosen to himself the man that is godly : when I call upon the Lord he will hear me.

Stand in awe and sin not : commune[1] with your own heart, and in your chamber, and be still.

Offer the sacrifice of righteousness : and put your trust in the Lord.

There be many that will say : Who will shew us any good? Lord, lift thou up : the light of thy countenance upon us.

Thou hast put gladness in my heart : since the time that their corn and wine (and oil) increased.

I will lay me down in peace, and take my rest : for it is thou Lord only, that makest me dwell in safety.

Glory be to the Father, and to the Son, and to the Holy Ghost.

As it was in the beginning, is now, and ever shall be world without end. Amen.

The First Lesson out of Exodus xx.

REMEMBER that thou keep holy the Sabbath day. Six days shalt thou labour and do all that thou hast to do. But the seventh day is the Sabbath of the Lord thy God,

[1 comen, original.]

in it shalt thou do no manner of work, thou and thy son and thy daughter, thy man servant, and thy maid servant, thy cattle, and the stranger that is within thy gates; for in six days the Lord made heaven and earth, the sea, and all that in them is, and rested the seventh day. Wherefore the Lord blessed the seventh day and hallowed it.

¶ Thus endeth the first lesson taken out of the twenty chapter of Exodus.

Te Deum Laudamus.

WE praise thee, O God we knowledge thee to be the Lord.

All the earth doth worship thee the Father everlasting.

To thee all angels cry aloud, the heavens and all the powers therein.

To thee Cherubim and Seraphim, continually do cry.

Holy, holy, holy, Lord God of Sabaoth.

Heaven and earth are full of the Majesty of thy glory.

The glorious company of Apostles praise thee.

The goodly fellowship of the Prophets praise thee.

The noble army of Martyrs, praise thee.

The holy church, throughout all the world doth knowledge thee.

The Father of an infinite majesty.

Thy honourable, true, and only Son.

Also the Holy Ghost the Comforter.

Thou art the king of glory, O Christ.

Thou art the everlasting Son of the Father.

When thou tookest upon thee to deliver man : thou didst not abhor the virgin's womb.

When thou hadst overcome the sharpness of death : thou didst open the kingdom of heaven to all believers.

Thou sittest on the right hand of God : in the glory of the Father.

We believe that thou shalt come to be our judge.

We therefore pray thee, help thy servants : whom thou hast redeemed with thy precious blood.

Make them to be numbered with thy saints : in glory everlasting.

O Lord, save thy people : and bless thine heritage.

Govern them and lift them up for ever.

Day by day we magnify thee.

And we worship thy name ever world without end.

Vouchsafe, O Lord, to keep us this day without sin.

O Lord, have mercy upon us : have mercy upon us.

O Lord, let thy mercy lighten upon us : as our trust is in thee.

O Lord, in thee have I trusted : let me never be confounded.

¶ Or this canticle.

Benedicite.

O ALL ye works of the Lord, bless ye the Lord : praise him and magnify him for ever.

O ye angels of the Lord, bless ye the Lord : praise ye him and magnify him for ever.

O ye heavens, bless ye the Lord : praise him and magnify him for ever.

O ye waters that be above the firmament, bless ye the Lord : praise him and magnify him for ever.

O all ye powers of the Lord, bless ye the Lord : praise him and magnify him for ever.

O ye sun and moon, bless ye the Lord : praise him and magnify him for ever.

O ye stars of heaven, bless ye the Lord : praise him and magnify him for ever.

O ye showers and dew, bless ye the Lord : praise him and magnify him for ever.

O ye winds of God, bless ye the Lord : praise him and magnify him for ever.

O ye fire and heat, bless ye the Lord : praise him and magnify him for ever.

O ye winter and summer, bless ye the Lord : praise him and magnify him for ever.

O ye dews and frosts, bless ye the Lord : praise him and magnify him for ever.

O ye frost and cold, bless ye the Lord : praise him and magnify him for ever.

O ye ice and snow, bless ye the Lord : praise him and magnify him for ever.

O ye nights and days, bless ye the Lord : praise him and magnify him for ever.

O ye light and darkness, bless ye the Lord : praise him and magnify him for ever.

O ye lightnings and clouds, bless ye the Lord : praise him and magnify him for ever.

O let the earth bless the Lord : yea, let it praise him and magnify him for ever.

O ye mountains and hills, bless ye the Lord : praise him and magnify him for ever.

O all ye green things upon the earth, bless ye the Lord : praise him and magnify him for ever.

O ye wells, bless ye the Lord : praise him and magnify him for ever.

O ye seas and floods, bless ye the Lord : praise him and magnify him for ever.

O ye whales and all that move in the waters, bless ye the Lord : praise him and magnify him for ever.

O all ye fowls of the air, bless ye the Lord : praise him and magnify him for ever.

O all ye beasts and cattle, bless ye the Lord : praise him and magnify him for ever.

O ye children of men, bless ye the Lord : praise him and magnify him for ever.

O let Israel bless the Lord : praise him and magnify him for ever.

O ye priests of the Lord, bless ye the Lord : praise him and magnify him for ever.

O ye servants of the Lord, bless ye the Lord : praise him and magnify him for ever.

O ye spirits and souls of the righteous, bless ye the Lord : praise him and magnify him for ever.

O ye holy and humble men of heart, bless ye the Lord : praise him and magnify him for ever.

O Ananias, Azarias, and Misael, bless ye the Lord : praise him and magnify him for ever.

Glory be to the Father, and to the Son : and to the Holy Ghost.

As it was in the beginning, is now, and ever shall be : world without end. Amen.

¶ The Second Lesson taken out of the fifth chapter of the Gospel of Saint Matthew.

WHEN Jesus saw the people, he went up into a mountain, Math. v. and when he was set, his disciples came to him : And after that he had opened his mouth, he taught them, saying: Blessed are the poor in spirit, for theirs is the kingdom of heaven. Blessed are they that mourn, for they shall receive comfort. Blessed are the meek: for they shall receive the inheritance of the earth. Blessed are they which hunger and thirst after righteousness: for they shall be satisfied. Blessed are the merciful: for they shall obtain mercy. Blessed are the pure in heart: for they shall see God. Blessed are the peace makers: for they shall be called the children of God. Blessed are they which suffer persecution for righteousness sake: for theirs is the kingdom of heaven. Blessed are ye, when men revile you, and persecute you, and shall falsely say all manner of evil saying against you for my sake. Rejoice and be glad; for great is your reward in heaven. For so persecuted they the prophets, which were before you. Ye are the salt of the earth. But if the salt have lost the saltness, what shall be seasoned therewith? It is thenceforth good for nothing, but to be cast out, and to be trodden down of men. Ye are the light of the world. A city that is set on an hill cannot be hid, neither do men light a candle, and put it under a bushel, but on a candlestick, and it giveth light unto all that are in the house. Let your light so shine before men, that they may see your good works, and glorify your Father which is in heaven.

¶ Thus endeth the second lesson, taken out of the fifth chapter of the Gospel of S. Matthew.

Benedictus. Luke i.

BLESSED be the Lord God of Israel : for he hath visited and redeemed his people.

And hath raised a mighty salvation for us : in the house of his servant David.

As he spake by the mouth of his holy prophets : which have been since the world began.

That we should be saved from our enemies : and from the hands of all that hate us.

To perform the mercy promised to our forefathers : and to remember his holy covenant.

To perform the oath which he sware to our forefather Abraham : that he would give us.

That we being delivered out of the hands of our enemies : might serve him without fear.

In holiness and righteousness before him : all the days of our life.

And thou, child, shall be called the Prophet of the Highest : for thou shall go before the face of the Lord, to prepare his ways.

To give knowledge of salvation unto his people for the remission of their sins.

Through the tender mercy of our God : whereby the day-spring from on high hath visited us.

To give light to them that sit in darkness, and in the shadow of death : and to guide our feet into the ways of peace.

Glory be to the Father, and to the Son, and to the Holy Ghost.

As it was in the beginning, is now, and ever shall be : world without end. Amen.

Or else this Psalm.

Jubilate Deo. Psalm c.

O BE joyful in the Lord, (all ye lands:) serve the Lord with gladness, and come before his presence with a song.

Be ye sure that the Lord he is God : it is he that hath made us, and not we ourselves, we are his people and the sheep of his pasture.

O go your way into his gates with thanksgiving, and into his courts with praise : be thankful unto him, and speak good of his name.

For the Lord is gracious, his mercy is everlasting : and his truth endureth from generation to generation.

Glory be to the Father, and to the Son, and to the Holy Ghost.

As it was in the beginning, is now, and ever shall be : world without end. Amen.

¶ *The Creed.*

I BELIEVE in God the Father almighty, maker of heaven and earth. And in Jesus Christ his only Son our Lord. Which was conceived by the Holy Ghost, born of the virgin Mary. Suffered under Ponce Pilate, was crucified, dead and buried, he descended into hell. The third day he rose again from the dead. He ascended into heaven, and sitteth on the right hand of God the Father almighty. From thence shall he come to judge the quick and the dead. I believe in the Holy Ghost: the holy catholic Church. The communion of Saints. The forgiveness of sins. The resurrection of the body, and the life everlasting. Amen.

Then kneeling devoutly say.

Lord, have mercy upon us.
Christ, have mercy upon us.
Lord, have mercy upon us.

Our Father, which art, &c.

O Lord, shew thy mercy upon us.
And grant us thy salvation.
O Lord, save the King.
And mercifully hear us, when we call upon thee.
Endue thy ministers with righteousness.
And make thy chosen people joyful.
O Lord, save thy people.
And bless thine inheritance.
Give peace in our time, O God.
Because there is none other that fighteth for us, but only thou, O God.
O God, make clean our hearts within us.
And take not thy holy Spirit from us.

¶ Then say the Collect that pertaineth unto that Sunday, which Collect also shall serve for the first Collect all the whole week following.

The second Collect for Peace.

O GOD, which art Author of peace, and lover of concord, in whom standeth our eternal life, whose service is perfect freedom, defend us thy humble servants, in all assaults of our enemies, that we surely trusting in thy defence, may not fear the power of any adversaries: through the might of Jesus Christ our Lord. Amen.

For Grace.

O LORD our heavenly Father, almighty and everlasting God, which hast safely brought us to the beginning of this day: Defend us in the same with thy mighty power, and grant that this day we fall into no sin, neither run into any kind of danger : But that all our doings may be ordered by thy governance, to do always that is righteous in thy sight : through Jesus Christ our Lord. Amen.

The fourth Collect for the King.

O LORD Jesu Christ, most high, most mighty King of Kings, Lord of Lords, the only ruler of all princes, the very Son of God, on whose right hand sitting, dost from thy throne behold all the dwellers upon earth; with most lowly hearts we beseech thee, vouchsafe with favourable regard to behold our most gracious sovereign Lord King Edward the Sixth, and so replenish him with the grace of thy holy Spirit, that he may alway incline to thy will and walk in thy way. Keep him far from ignorance, but through thy gracious gift let prudence and godly knowledge alway abound in his royal heart. So instruct him, O Lord Jesu, reigning upon us in earth, that his noble grace may alway obey thy godly majesty in fear and dread; endue him plentifully with heavenly gifts, grant him in health long to live, heap glory and honour upon him, glad him with the joy of thy countenance, so strength him that he may vanquish and overcome all his and our foes, and be dread and feared of all the enemies of this realm, and finally after this life that he may attain everlasting joy and felicity. Amen.

Here followeth the Litany.

O GOD the Father of heaven, have mercy upon us miserable sinners.

O God the Father of heaven, have mercy upon us miserable sinners.

O God the Son redeemer of the world, have mercy upon us miserable sinners.

O God the Son redeemer of the world, have mercy upon us miserable sinners.

O God the Holy Ghost proceeding from the Father and the Son, have mercy upon us miserable sinners.

O God the Holy Ghost proceeding from the Father and the Son, have mercy upon us miserable sinners.

O holy, blessed, and glorious Trinity, three persons and one God : have mercy upon us miserable sinners.

O holy, blessed, and glorious Trinity, three persons and one GOD : have mercy upon us miserable sinners.

Remember not, Lord, our offences, nor the offences of our forefathers, neither take thou vengeance of our sins : spare us, good Lord, spare thy people whom thou hast redeemed with thy most precious blood, and be not angry with us for ever.

Spare us, good Lord.

From all evil and mischief, from sin, from the crafts and assaults of the devil, from thy wrath, and from everlasting damnation.

Good Lord, deliver us.

From all blindness of heart, from pride, vain glory and hypocrisy, from envy, hatred and malice, and all uncharitableness.

Good Lord, deliver us.

From all fornication and all other deadly sin, and from all the deceits of the world, the flesh and the devil.

Good Lord, deliver us.

From lightnings and tempests, from plague, pestilence and famine, from battle and murder, and from sudden death.

Good Lord, deliver us.

From all sedition and privy conspiracy, from the tyranny of the Bishop of Rome, and all his detestable enormities, from all false doctrine and heresy, from hardness of heart, and contempt of thy word and commandments.

Good Lord, deliver us.

By the mystery of thy holy incarnation, by thy holy nativity and circumcision, by thy baptism, fasting, and temptation.

Good Lord, deliver us.

By thine agony and bloody sweat, by thy cross and passion, by thy precious death and burial, by thy glorious resurrection and ascension, and by the coming of the Holy Ghost.

Good Lord, deliver us.

In all time of our tribulation, in all time of our wealth, in the hour of death, and in the day of judgment.

Good Lord, deliver us.

We sinners do beseech thee to hear us (O Lord God), and that it may please thee to rule and govern thy holy Church universally in the right way.

We beseech thee to hear us, good Lord.

That it may please thee to keep Edward the sixth thy servant, our king and governor.
We beseech thee to hear us, good Lord.
That it may please thee to rule his heart in thy faith, fear and love, that he may have always affiance in thee, and ever seek thy honour and glory.
We beseech thee to hear us, good Lord.
That it may please thee to be his defender and keeper, giving him the victory over all his enemies.
We beseech thee to hear us, good Lord.
That it may please thee to illuminate all Bishops, Pastors, and Ministers of the Church, with true knowledge and understanding of thy word: and that both by their preaching and living they may set it forth and shew it accordingly.
We beseech thee to hear us, good Lord.
That it may please thee to endue the Lords of the council, and all the nobility, with grace, wisdom, and understanding.
We beseech thee to hear us, good Lord.
That it may please thee to bless and keep the Magistrates, giving them grace to execute justice, and to maintain truth.
We beseech thee to hear us, good Lord.
That it may please thee to bless and keep all thy people.
We beseech thee to hear us, good Lord.
That it may please thee to give to all nations unity, peace, and concord.
We beseech thee to hear us, good Lord.
That it may please thee to give us an heart to love and dread thee, and diligently to live after thy commandments.
We beseech thee to hear us, good Lord.
That it may please thee to give all thy people increase of grace, to hear meekly thy word, and to receive it with pure affection, and to bring forth the fruits of the Spirit.
We beseech thee to hear us, good Lord.
That it may please thee to bring into the way of truth all such as have erred and are deceived.
We beseech thee to hear us, good Lord.
That it may please thee to strengthen such as do stand, and to comfort and help the weak hearted, and to raise them up that fall, and finally to beat down Satan under our feet.
We beseech thee to hear us, good Lord.

That it may please thee to succour, help, and comfort, all that be in danger, necessity, and tribulation.
We beseech thee to hear us, good Lord.

That it may please thee to preserve all that travel by land or by water, all women labouring of child, all sick persons and young children, and to shew thy pity upon all prisoners and captives.
We beseech thee to hear us, good Lord.

That it may please thee to defend and provide for the fatherless children and widows, and all that be desolate and oppressed.
We beseech thee to hear us, good Lord.

That it may please thee to have mercy upon all men.
We beseech thee to hear us, good Lord.

That it may please thee to forgive our enemies, persecutors, and slanderers, and to turn their hearts.
We beseech thee to hear us, good Lord.

That it may please thee to give and preserve to our use the kindly fruits of the earth, so as in due time we may enjoy them.
We beseech thee to hear us, good Lord.

That it may please thee to give us true repentance, to forgive us all our sins, negligences, and ignorances, and to endue us with the grace of thy holy Spirit to amend our lives according to thy holy word.
We beseech thee to hear us, good Lord.

Son of God : we beseech thee to hear us.
Son of God : we beseech thee to hear us.

O Lamb of God, that takest away the sins of the world :
Grant us thy peace.

O Lamb of God, that takest away the sins of the world :
Have mercy upon us.

O Christ, hear us.
O Christ, hear us.

Lord, have mercy upon us.
Lord, have mercy upon us.

Christ, have mercy upon us.
Christ, have mercy upon us.

Lord, have mercy upon us.
Lord, have mercy upon us.

Our Father, which art, &c.
And lead us not into temptation.
But deliver us from evil. Amen.

O Lord, deal not with us after our sins.
Neither reward us after our iniquities.

Let us pray.

O GOD, merciful Father, that despisest not the sighing of a contrite heart, nor the desire of such as be sorrowful: mercifully assist our prayers that we make before thee, in all our troubles and adversities, whensoever they oppress us. And graciously hear us, that those evils, which the craft and subtilty of the devil or man worketh against us, be brought to nought, and by the providence of thy goodness they may be dispersed, that we thy servants being hurt by no persecution, may evermore give thanks unto thee in thy holy church, through Jesus Christ our Lord.

O Lord, arise, help us, and deliver us for thy Name's sake.

O God, we have heard with our ears, and our fathers have declared unto us, the noble works that thou didst in their days, and in the old time before them.

O Lord, arise, help us, and deliver us for thine honour.

Glory be to the Father, and to the Son, and to the Holy Ghost.

As it was in the beginning, is now, and ever shall be, world without end. Amen.

From our enemies defend us, O Christ.
Graciously look upon our afflictions.
Pitifully behold the sorrows of our heart.
Mercifully forgive the sins of thy people.
Favourably with mercy hear our prayers.
O Son of David, have mercy upon us.
Both now and ever vouchsafe to hear us, O Christ.
Graciously hear us, O Christ, Graciously hear us, O Lord Christ.

The Versicle. O Lord, let thy mercy be shewed upon us
The Answer. As we do put our trust in thee.

¶ Let us pray.

WE humbly beseech thee, O Father, mercifully to look upon our infirmities, and for the glory of thy name's sake turn from us all those evils, that we most righteously have deserved: and grant that in all our troubles we may put our whole trust and confidence in thy mercy, and evermore serve thee in holiness and pureness of living, to thy honour and glory: through our only mediator and advocate, Jesus Christ our Lord. Amen.

For rain, if the time require.

O GOD, heavenly Father, which by thy Son Jesus Christ hast promised to all them that seek thy kingdom and the righteousness thereof, all things necessary to their bodily sustenance: send us, we beseech thee, in this our necessity, such moderate rain and showers, that we may receive the fruits of the earth to our comfort, and to thy honour: through Jesus Christ our Lord. Amen.

¶ *For fair weather.*

O LORD God, which for the sin of man didst once drown all the world, except eight persons, and afterward of thy great mercy didst promise never to destroy it so again: we humbly beseech thee, that although we for our iniquities have worthily deserved this plague of rain and waters, yet upon our true repentance thou wilt send us such weather, whereby we may receive the fruits of the earth in due season, and learn both by thy punishment to amend our lives, and for thy clemency to give thee praise and glory, through Jesus Christ our Lord. Amen.

¶ *In the time of dearth and famine.*

O GOD, heavenly Father, whose gift it is that the rain doth fall, the earth is fruitful, beasts increase, and fishes do multiply: Behold, we beseech thee, the afflictions of thy people, and grant, that the scarcity and dearth (which we do now most justly suffer for our iniquity) may through thy goodness be mercifully turned into cheapness and plenty, for the love of Jesu Christ our Lord: to whom with thee and the Holy Ghost, &c. Amen.

¶ *Or thus.*

O GOD, merciful Father, which, in the time of Heliseus the Prophet, didst suddenly turn in Samaria great scarcity and dearth into plenty and cheapness, and extreme famine into abundance of victual: have pity upon us, that now be punished for our sins with like adversity; increase the fruits of the earth by thy heavenly benediction; and grant, that we receiving thy bountiful liberality, may use the same to thy glory, our comfort, and relief of our needy neighbours, through Jesus Christ our Lord. Amen.

In the time of war.

O ALMIGHTY God, king of all kings, and governor of all things, whose power no creature is able to resist, to whom it belongeth justly to punish sinners, and to be merciful to them that truly repent: save and deliver us (we humbly beseech thee) from the hands of our enemies; abate their pride, asswage their malice, and confound their devices, that we being armed with thy defence, may be preserved evermore from all perils to glorify thee, which art the only giver of all victory: through the merits of thy only Son Jesus Christ our Lord. Amen.

¶ *In the time of any common plague or sickness.*

O ALMIGHTY God: which in thy wrath, in the time of king David, didst slay with the plague of pestilence three score and ten thousand, and yet remembering thy mercy didst save the rest: have pity upon us miserable sinners, that now are visited with great sickness and mortality, that like as thou didst then command thine Angel to cease from punishing, so it may now please thee to withdraw from us this plague and grievous sickness, through Jesu Christ our Lord. Amen.

¶ *For one that is sore sick.*

HEAR us, Almighty and most merciful God, and Saviour, extend thy accustomed goodness to thy servant, N. which is grieved with sickness: visit him, O Lord, as thou didst visit Peter's wife's mother, and the captain's servant. So visit and restore unto this sick person his former health (if it be thy will), or else give him grace, so to take thy visitation, that after this painful life ended, he may dwell with thee in life everlasting. Amen.

Other general Collects.

ASSIST us mercifully, O Lord, in these our supplications and prayers, and dispose the way of thy servants toward the attainment of everlasting salvation: That among all the changes of this mortal life, they may ever be defended by thy most gracious and ready help: through Christ our Lord.

O ALMIGHTY Lord and everliving God, vouchsafe, we beseech thee, to direct, sanctify and govern both our hearts and bodies, in the ways of thy laws, and in the works of thy commandments, that through thy most mighty protection, both here and ever, we may be preserved in body and soul, through our Lord and Saviour, Jesus Christ. Amen.

After the Sermon or Homily.

GRANT, we beseech thee, Almighty God, that the words which we have heard this day with our outward ears, may through thy grace be so grafted inwardly in our hearts, that they may bring forth in us the fruit of good living, to the honour and praise of thy name, through Jesus Christ our Lord. Amen.

PREVENT us, O Lord, in all our doings with thy most gracious favour, and further us with thy continual help, that in all our works begun, continued, and ended in thee, we may glorify thy holy name, and finally by thy mercy obtain everlasting life, through Jesus Christ our Lord. Amen.

ALMIGHTY God, the fountain of all wisdom, which knowest our necessities before we ask, and our ignorance in asking, we beseech thee to have compassion upon our infirmities, and those things which for our unworthiness we dare not, and for our blindness we cannot ask, vouchsafe to give us for the worthiness of thy Son Jesus Christ our Lord. Amen.

ALMIGHTY God, the fountain of all wisdom, which hast promised to hear the petitions of them that ask in thy Son's name: We beseech thee mercifully to incline thine ears to us, that have made now our prayers and supplications unto thee: And grant that these things which we faithfully asked according to thy will, may effectually be obtained, to the relief of our necessity and to the setting forth of thy glory, through Jesus Christ our Lord. Amen.

¶ The Litany shall ever end with this Collect following.

ALMIGHTY God, which hast given us grace at this time with one accord to make our common supplications unto thee, and dost promise, that when two or three be gathered in thy name, thou wilt grant their requests, fulfil now, O Lord, the desires and petitions of thy servants, as may be most expedient for them, granting us in this world knowledge of thy truth, and in the world to come life everlasting. Amen.

[Evening Prayer for Sunday.]

¶ As before morning prayer, even so before evening prayer, begin with a sentence, and add thereunto the confession of sins and the prayer following, and then say.

Our Father, which art, &c.
O God, make speed to save me.
O Lord, make haste to help me.
Glory be to the Father, and to the Son, and to the Holy Ghost.
As it was in the beginning, is now, and ever shall be, world without end. Amen.
Praise we the Lord.

Confitebor tibi. Psalm ix.

I WILL give thanks unto the Lord, with my whole heart: secretly among the faithful, and in the congregation.
The works of the Lord are great : sought out of all them that have pleasure therein.

[DOCUMENTS, EDW. VI.]

His work is worthy to be praised and had in honour : and his righteousness endureth for ever.

The merciful and gracious Lord hath so done his marvellous works : that they ought to be had in remembrance.

He hath given meat unto them that fear him : he shall ever be mindful of his covenant.

He hath shewed his people the power of his works : that he may give them the heritage of the heathen.

The works of his hands are verity and judgment : all his commandments are true.

They stand fast for ever and ever : and are done in truth and equity.

He hath sent redemption unto his people : he hath commanded his covenant for ever, holy and reverent is his name.

The fear of the Lord is the beginning of wisdom : a good understanding have all they that do thereafter, the praise of it endureth for ever.

Glory be to the Father, &c.

As it was in the beginning, &c.

Beatus Vir. Psalm cxii.

BLESSED is the man that feareth the Lord : he hath great delight in his commandments.

His seed shall be mighty upon earth : the generation of the faithful shall be blessed.

Riches and plenteousness shall be in his house : and his righteousness endureth for ever.

Unto the godly there ariseth up light in darkness : he is merciful, loving and righteous.

A good man is merciful and lendeth : and will guide his words with discretion.

For he shall never be moved : and the righteous shall be had in an everlasting remembrance.

He will not be afraid for any evil tidings : for his heart standeth fast, and believeth in the Lord.

His heart is stablished and will not shrink : until he see his desire upon his enemies.

He hath dispersed abroad, and given to the poor : and his righteousness remaineth for ever, his horn shall be exalted with honour.

The ungodly shall see it, and it shall grieve him : he shall gnash with his teeth, and consume away; the desire of the ungodly shall perish.

Glory be to the Father, and to the Son, and to the Holy Ghost.

As it was in the beginning, is now, and ever shall be, world without end. Amen.

¶ The first lesson, taken out of the first chapter of the Proverbs.

WISDOM crieth without, and putteth forth her voice in the streets. She calleth before the congregation in the open gates, and sheweth her words through the city, saying: O ye children, how long will the scorners delight in scorning? and the unwise be enemies unto knowledge? O turn you unto my correction: Lo, I will express my mind unto you, and make you understand my words. Seeing then that I have called, and ye refuse it, I have stretched out my hand, and no man regarded it, but all my counsels have ye despised, and set my correction at nought: Therefore shall I also laugh in your destruction, and mock you, when the thing that ye fear cometh upon you, even when the thing that ye be afraid of falleth in suddenly like a storm, and your misery like a tempest: yea, when trouble and heaviness cometh upon you. Then they shall seek me early, but they shall not find me: and that because they hated knowledge, and received not the fear of the Lord, but abhorred my counsel, and despised my correction.

¶ Here endeth the first Lesson, taken out of the first Chapter of the Proverbs.

Magnificat. Luke i.

My soul doth magnify the Lord.

And my spirit hath rejoiced in God my Saviour.

For he hath regarded the lowliness of his handmaiden.

For behold, from henceforth all generations shall call me blessed.

For he that is mighty hath magnified me : and holy is his name.

And his mercy is on them that fear him : throughout all generations.

He hath shewed strength with his arm : he hath scattered the proud in the imagination of their hearts.

He hath put down the mighty from their seat : and hath exalted the humble and meek.

He hath filled the hungry with good things : and the rich he hath sent empty away.

He remembering his mercy, hath holpen his servant Israel: as he promised to our forefathers, Abraham and his seed for ever.

Glory be to the Father, and to the Son : and to the Holy Ghost.

As it was in the beginning, is now, and ever shall be : world without end. Amen.

Or else this Psalm.

Cantate. Psalm xcviii.

O SING unto the Lord a new song : for he hath done marvellous things.

With his own right hand, and his holy arm : hath he gotten himself the victory.

The Lord declared his salvation : his righteousness hath he openly shewed in the sight of the heathen.

He hath remembered his mercy and truth toward the house of Israel : and all the ends of the world have seen the salvation of our God.

Shew yourself joyful unto the Lord, all ye lands : sing, rejoice and give thanks.

Praise the Lord upon the harp : sing to the harp with a psalm of thanksgiving.

With trumpets also and shawms : O shew yourselves joyful before the Lord the king.

Let the sea make a noise and all that therein is : the round world, and they that dwell therein.

Let the floods clap their hands, and let the hills be joyful together before the Lord : for he is come to judge the earth.

With righteousness shall he judge the world : and the people with equity.

Glory be to the Father, and to the Son : and to the Holy Ghost.

As it was in the beginning, is now, and ever shall be : world without end. Amen.

¶ The second lesson, taken out of the twelfth chapter to the Romans.

I BESEECH you, brethren, by the mercifulness of God, Rom. xii. that ye make your bodies a quick sacrifice, holy and acceptable unto God; which is your reasonable serving of God: and fashion not yourselves like unto this world: but be ye changed in your shape by the renewing of your mind, that ye may prove what thing that good, and acceptable, and perfect will of God is. For I say (through the grace that unto me given is) to every man among you, that no man stand high in his own conceit, more than it becometh him to esteem of himself: but so judge of himself that he be gentle and sober, according as God hath dealt to every man the measure of faith. For as we have many members in one body, and all members have not one office; so we being many are one body in Christ, and every man among ourselves one another's members.

¶ Thus endeth the second lesson, taken out of the twelfth chapter of the Epistle to the Romans.

Nunc dimittis. Luke ii.

LORD, now lettest thou thy servant depart in peace: according to thy word.

For mine eyes have seen : thy salvation,

Which thou hast prepared : before the face of all people;

To be a light for to light the Gentiles : and to be the glory of thy people Israel.

Glory be to the Father, and to the Son : and to the Holy Ghost.

As it was in the beginning, is now, and ever shall be : world without end. Amen.

Or else this Psalm.

Deus misereatur nostri. Psalm lxvii.

GOD be merciful unto us, and bless us : and shew us the light of his countenance, and be merciful unto us.

That thy way may be known upon earth : thy saving health among all nations.

Let the people praise thee, O God : yea, let all the people praise thee.

O let the nations rejoice and be glad : for thou shalt judge the folk righteously, and govern the nations upon earth.

Let the people praise thee, O God : let all the people praise thee.

Then shall the earth bring forth her increase : and God, even our own God, shall give us his blessing.

God shall bless us : and all the ends of the world shall fear him.

Glory be to the Father, and to the Son, &c.

As it was in the beginning, is now, and, &c.

¶ Then say the Creed, with other Suffrages, as is before appointed at Morning Prayer after *Benedictus,* adding the Sunday Collect, and these two that follow.

¶ *For Peace.*

O GOD, from whom all holy desires, all good counsels, and all just works do proceed, give unto thy servants that peace, which the world cannot give: that both our hearts may be set to obey thy commandments, and also that by thee we being defended from the fear of our enemies, may pass our time in rest and quietness, through the merits of Jesus Christ our Saviour. Amen.

¶ *For Aid against all Perils.*

LIGHTEN our darkness, we beseech thee, O Lord, and by thy great mercy defend us from all perils and dangers of this night, for the love of thy only Son, our Saviour Jesus Christ.

¶ *A prayer for the King.*

MOST merciful Father, all we thy servants by duty, and children by grace, do beseech thee most humbly to preserve Edward the sixth, thy son and servant, and our King and governor : Sow in him, good Lord, such seed of virtue now in his young age, that many years this realm may enjoy much fruit of this thy blessing in him, through Jesus Christ our Lord. Amen.

THE peace of God, which passeth all understanding, keep our hearts and minds in the knowledge and love of God, and of his Son Jesus Christ our Lord. And the blessing of God Almighty, the Father, the Son, and the Holy Ghost, be among us, and remain with us always. Amen.

Thus endeth the Morning and Evening Prayer for the Sunday. And the same order shall ye keep every day in the week in all points, except only psalms and lessons, which shall be proper for every day in the week, as shall appear by the order of this book following.

Our Father, which art, &c.

Then say,

O Lord, open thou my lips, &c.

And so forth, &c.

¶ *Psalms for Morning Prayer on Monday.*

Verba mea auribus. Psalm v.

PONDER my words, O Lord : consider my meditation.

O hearken thou unto the voice of my calling, my King and my God : for unto thee will I make my prayer.

My voice shalt thou hear betimes, O Lord : early in the morning will I direct my prayer unto thee, and will look up.

For thou art the God that hath no pleasure in wickedness : neither shall any evil dwell with thee.

Such as be foolish, shall not stand in thy sight : for thou hatest all them that work vanity.

Thou shalt destroy them that speak leasing : the Lord will abhor both the bloodthirsty and deceitful man.

But as for me, I will come into thy house, even upon the multitude of thy mercy : and in thy fear will I worship toward thy holy temple.

Lead me, O Lord, in thy righteousness, because of my enemies : make thy way plain before my face.

For there is no faithfulness in his mouth : their inward parts are very wickedness.

Their throat is an open sepulchre : they flatter with their tongue.

Destroy thou them, O God, let them perish through their own imaginations: cast them out in the multitude of their ungodliness, for they have rebelled against thee.

And let all them that put their trust in thee, rejoice: they shall ever be giving of thanks, because thou defendest them : they that love thy name shall be joyful in thee.

For thou, Lord, wilt give thy blessing unto the righteous : and with thy favourable kindness wilt thou defend him, as with a shield.

Glory be to the Father, and to the Son : and to the Holy Ghost.

As it was in the beginning, is now, and &c.

Domine dominus noster. Psal. viii.

O LORD our governor, how excellent is thy name in all the world : thou that hast set thy glory above the heavens.

Out of the mouth of very babes and sucklings hast thou ordained strength because of thine enemies : that thou mightest still the enemy and the avenger.

For I will consider thy heavens, even the work of thy fingers : the moon and the stars which thou hast ordained.

What is man that art mindful of him : and the son of man, that thou visitest him? thou madest him lower than the angels, to crown him with glory and worship.

Thou makest him to have dominion of the works of thy hands : and thou hast put all things in subjection under his feet.

All sheep and oxen : yea, and the beasts of the field.

The fowls of the air, and the fishes of the sea : and whatsoever walketh through the paths of the seas.

O Lord our governor : how excellent is thy name in all the world.

Glory be to the Father, and to the Son : and to the Holy Ghost.

As it was in the beginning, is now, and ever shall be : world without end. Amen.

In Domino confido. Psal. xi.

IN the Lord put I my trust : how say ye then to my soul, that she should flee as a bird to the hill ?

For lo, the ungodly bend their bow : and make ready their arrows within the quiver, that they may privily shoot at them, which are true of heart.

For the foundations will be cast down : and what hath the righteous done?

The Lord is in his holy temple : the Lord's seat is in heaven.

His eyes consider the poor : and his eyelids trieth the children of men.

The Lord alloweth the righteous : but the ungodly and him that delighteth in wickedness, doth his soul abhor.

Upon the ungodly he shall rain snares, fire and brimstone, storm and tempest : this shall be their portion to drink.

For the righteous Lord loveth righteousness : his countenance will behold the thing that is just.

Glory be to the Father, and to the Son : and to the Holy Ghost.

As it was in the beginning, is now, and ever shall be : world without end. Amen.

¶ The first lesson, taken out of the sixth chapter of the Proverbs.

Go to the emmet, (thou sluggard,) consider her ways, and learn to be wise. She hath no guide, nor overseer, nor ruler. Yet in the summer she provideth her meat, and gathereth her food together in the harvest. How long wilt thou sleep, thou sluggish man? When wilt thou arise out of thy sleep? Yea, sleep on still a little, slumber a little. Fold thine hands together a little, that thou mayest sleep: so shall poverty come unto thee, as one that travelleth by the way, and necessity, like a weaponed man. But if thou be not slothful, thy harvest shall come as a springing well, and poverty shall fly far from thee. Prov. vi. 13; xxiv. 30.

Thus endeth the first lesson, out of the sixth of the Proverbs.

We praise thee, O Lord, &c.

The second lesson, taken out of the sixth chapter of Matthew.

No man can serve two masters : for either he shall hate the one, and love the other, or else lean to the one, and despise the other : Ye cannot serve God and mammon. Therefore I say unto you, be not careful for your life what Math. vi.

ye shall eat or drink, nor yet for your body what raiment ye shall put on. Is not the life more worth than meat? and the body more of value than raiment? Behold the fowls of the air; for they sow not, neither do they reap, nor carry into the barns: and your heavenly father feedeth them: are ye not much better than they? Which of you, (by taking careful thought,) can add one cubit unto his stature? And why care you for raiment? Consider the lilies of the field, how they grow. They labour not, neither do they spin; and yet I say unto you, that even Salomon, in all his royalty, was not arrayed like one of these. Wherefore, if God so clothe the grass of the field, which (though it stand to day) is to morrow cast into the furnace: shall he not much more do the same for you, O ye of little faith? Therefore take no thought, saying, what shall we eat, or what shall we drink, or wherewith shall we be clothed? After all these things do the Gentiles seek: for your heavenly Father knoweth, that ye have need of all these things. But rather seek ye first the kingdom of God, and the righteousness thereof, and all these things shall be ministered unto you. Care not for to morrow, for the morrow day shall care for itself: sufficient unto the day is the travail thereof.

¶ Thus endeth the second lesson, taken out of the sixth chapter of Matthew.

Blessed be the Lord God of Israel, &c.

Evening Prayer for Monday.

Our Father, which art, &c.
O Lord, open thou my lips, &c.
O God, make speed to save me.
O Lord, make haste to help me.
Glory be to the Father, and to the Son: and to the Holy Ghost.
As it was in the beginning, is now, and ever shall be: world without end. Amen.

Beati immaculati. Psalm cxix.

BLESSED are those that be undefiled in the way : and walk in the law of the Lord.

Blessed are they that keep his testimonies : and seek him with their whole heart.

For they which do no wickedness : walk in his ways.

Thou hast charged, that we shall diligently keep thy commandments.

O that my ways were made so direct : that I might keep thy statutes.

So shall I not be confounded : while I have respect unto all thy commandments.

I will thank thee with an unfeigned heart : when I shall have learned the judgments of thy righteousness.

I will keep thy ceremonies : O forsake me not utterly.

Glory be to the Father, and to the Son, and to the Holy Ghost.

As it was in the beginning, is now, and ever shall be world without end. Amen.

WHEREWITHAL shall a young man cleanse his way : even by ruling himself after thy word.

With my whole heart have I sought thee : O let me not go wrong out of thy commandments.

Thy words have I hid within mine heart : that I should not sin against thee.

Blessed art thou, O Lord : O teach me thy statutes.

With my lips have I been telling : of all the judgments of thy mouth.

I have had as great delight in the way of thy testimonies : as in all manner of riches.

I will talk of thy commandments : and have respect unto thy ways.

My delight shall be in thy statutes : and I will not forget thy word.

Glory be to the Father, and to the Son, and to the Holy Ghost.

As it was in the beginning, is now, and ever shall be world without end. Amen.

¶ The first lesson, taken out of the second chapter of Ecclesiasticus.

<small>Eccle. ii.</small>

<small>Sapi. iii.
Pro. xvii.</small>

MY son, if thou wilt come into the service of God, stand fast in righteousness and fear, and arm thy soul to temptation: settle thy heart, be patient, bow down thine ears, receive the words of understanding: and shrink not away when thou art enticed, hold thee fast upon God, join thyself unto him, suffer that thy life may increase at the last, whatsoever happeneth unto thee receive it, suffer in heaviness, and be patient in thy trouble; for like as gold and silver are tried in the fire, even so are acceptable men in the furnace of adversity. Believe in God, and he shall help thee, order thy way aright, and put thy trust in him, hold fast his fear and grow therein. O ye that fear the Lord, take sure hold of his mercy: shrink not away from him, that ye fall not. O ye that fear the Lord, believe him, and your reward shall not be empty. O ye that fear the Lord, put your trust in him, and many shall come unto you for pleasure. O ye that fear the Lord, set your love upon him, and your hearts shall be lightened. Consider the old generation of men, O ye children, and mark them well : was there ever any one confounded, that put his trust in the Lord? who ever continued in his fear and was forsaken? or whom did he ever despise, that called faithfully upon him? For God is gracious and merciful, he forgiveth sins in the time of trouble, and is a defender of all them that seek him in truth.

¶ Thus endeth the first lesson out of Ecclesiasticus, the second chapter.

My soul doth magnify, &c.

¶ The second lesson, taken out of the twelfth chapter to the Romans.

LET him that hath an office wait on his office. Let him that teacheth take heed to his doctrine. Let him that exhorteth, give attendance to his exhortation. If any man give, let him do it with singleness; let him that ruleth, do it with diligence. If any man shew mercy, let him do it with cheerfulness. Let love be without dissimulation. Hate that which is evil, and cleave unto that which is good. Be kind one to another with brotherly love. In giving honour, go one before another. Be not slothful in the business which ye have in hand, be fervent in the spirit. Apply yourselves to the time. Rejoice in hope. Be patient in tribulation. Continue in prayer. Distribute unto the necessity of the saints. Be ready to harbour.

¶ Thus endeth the second lesson out of the twelfth chapter of the Romans.

Lord, now lettest thou, &c.

Our Father, which art, &c.
O God, make speed to save me.
O Lord, make haste to help me.
Glory be to the Father, and to the Son, and to the Holy Ghost.
As it was in the beginning, is now, and ever shall be world without end. Amen.

Domine quis habitabit. Psalm xv.

LORD, who shall dwell in thy tabernacle : who shall rest upon thy holy hill?

Even he that leadeth an uncorrupt life : and doth the thing which is right, and speaketh the truth from his heart.

He that hath used no deceit in his tongue : nor done evil to his neighbours, and hath not slandered his neighbours.

He that setteth not by himself, but is lowly in his own eyes : and maketh much of them that fear the Lord.

He that sweareth unto his neighbour, and disappointeth him not : though it were to his own hindrance.

He that hath not given his money upon usury : nor taken reward against the innocent.

Whoso doth these things : shall never fall.

Glory be to the Father, and to the Son, and to the Holy Ghost.

As it was in the beginning, is now, and ever shall be world without end. Amen.

Dominus regit me. Psalm xxiii.

THE Lord is my shepherd : therefore can I lack nothing.

He shall feed me in a green pasture : and lead me forth beside the waters of comfort.

He shall convert my soul : and bring me forth in the paths of righteousness, for his name's sake.

Yea, though I walk through the valley of the shadow of death : I will fear no evil ; for thou art with me, thy rod and thy staff comfort me.

Thou shalt prepare a table before me, against them that trouble me : thou hast anointed my head with oil, and my cup shall be full.

But (thy) loving kindness and mercy shall follow me all the days of my life : and I will dwell in the house of the Lord for ever.

Glory be to the Father, &c.

As it was in the beginning, &c.

¶ The first lesson out of the fifth of Jeremy.

Look through Jerusalem, behold and see : Seek through her streets also within, if he can find one man, that doeth equal and right, or that laboureth to be faithful. And I shall spare him, saith the Lord : for though they can say, the Lord liveth, yet do they swear to deceive : Whereas thou, O Lord, lookest only upon faith and truth. Thou hast scourged them, but they took no repentance : Thou hast corrected them for amendment, but they refused thy correction. They made their faces harder than a stone, and would not amend.

Thus endeth the first lesson out of the fifth chapter of Jeremy.

We praise thee, &c.

¶ The second lesson out of the eleventh chapter of Matthew.

Math. xi.

Then began Jesus to upbraid the cities, which most of his miracles were done in, because they repented not of their sins. Woe unto thee, Chorasin : Woe unto thee, Bethsaida : for if the miracles, which were shewed in you, had been done in the city of Tyre or Sidon, they had repented of their sins long agone in sackcloth and ashes. Nevertheless, I say unto you: it shall be easier for Tyre and Sidon at the day of judgment, than for you. And thou, Capernaum, which art lift up unto heaven, shalt be brought down to hell. For if the miracles which have been done in thee, had been shewed in Zodoma, they had remained until this day. Nevertheless, I say unto you, that it shall be easier for the land of Zodom in the day of judgment, than for thee.

Thus endeth the second lesson out of the eleventh chapter of Matthew.

Blessed be the Lord God, &c.
Our Father, which art, &c.
O God, make speed to save me.
O Lord, make haste to help me.
Glory be to the Father, and to the Son, and to the Holy Ghost.
As it was in the beginning, is now, and ever shall be world without end. Amen.

Ad Dominum cum tribularer. Psalm cxx.

WHEN I was in trouble I called upon the Lord, and he heard me.

Deliver my soul, (O Lord,) from lying lips : and from a deceitful tongue.

What reward shall be given or done unto thee, thou false tongue? even mighty and sharp arrows, with hot burning coals.

Woe is me, that I am constrained to dwell with Mesech : and to have mine habitation among the tents of Cedar.

My soul hath long dwelt among them that be enemies unto peace.

I labour for peace, but when I speak unto them thereof: they make them ready to battle.

Glory be to the Father, and to the Son, and to the Holy Ghost.
As it was in the beginning, is now, and ever shall be world without end. Amen.

Levavi oculos meos. Psalm cxxi.

I WILL lift up mine eyes unto the hills: from whence cometh my help.

My help cometh even from the Lord : which hath made heaven and earth.

He will not suffer thy foot to be moved : and he that keepeth thee will not sleep.

Behold, he that keepeth Israel : shall neither slumber nor sleep.

The Lord himself is thy keeper : the Lord is thy defence upon thy right hand.

So that the sun shall not burn thee by day : neither the moon by night.

The Lord shall preserve thee from all evil : yea, it is even he that shall keep thy soul.

The Lord shall preserve thy going out and thy coming in : from this time forth for evermore.

Glory be to the Father, and to the Son : and to the Holy Ghost.

As it was in the beginning, is now, and ever shall be : world without end. Amen.

¶ *The first lesson, taken out of the fifth chapter of Ecclesiastes.*

HE that loveth money will never be satisfied with money : and whoso delighteth in riches shall have no profit thereof. Is not this also a vain thing? Where as many riches are, there are many also that spend them away. And what pleasure more hath he that possesseth them, saving that he may look upon them with his eyes? A labouring man sleepeth sweetly, whether it be little or much that he eateth : but the abundance of the rich will not suffer him to sleep. Yet is there a sore plague, which I have seen under the sun, (Namely,) Riches kept to the hurt of him that hath them in possession, for ofttimes they perish with his great misery and trouble : and if he have a child, it getteth nothing. Like as he came naked out of his mother's womb, so goeth he thither again; and carrieth nothing away with him of all his labour.

Thus endeth the first lesson, taken out of the first chapter of Ecclesiastes.

My soul doth magnify, &c.

¶ *The second lesson, taken out of the sixth chapter of the first epistle of St Paul to Timothy.*

1 Tim. vi.
Eccle. xxix.
Hebr. xiii.
Job i.
Eccle. v.

GODLINESS is great riches, if a man be content with that he hath : for we brought nothing into the world, neither may we carry anything out. But when we have food and raiment, we must therewith be content. They that will be rich fall into temptation and snares of the (devil) and into many foolish and noisome lusts, which drown men into perdition and destruction. For covetousness of money is the root of all evil: which while some lusted after, they erred from the faith, and tangled themselves with many sorrows. But thou, man of God, flee such things. Follow righteousness, godliness, faith, love, patience, meekness, fight the good fight of faith: lay hand on eternal life, whereunto thou art also called, and hast professed a good profession before many witnesses.

¶ Thus endeth the second lesson, &c

Lord, now lettest thou thy servant, &c.

As on Sunday evening prayer.

Morning Prayer for Wednesday.

Our Father, which art, &c.
O Lord, open thou my lips.
And my mouth shall shew forth thy praise.
O God, make speed to save me.
O Lord, make haste to help me.
Glory be to the Father, &c.
As it was in the, &c.

Ad te Domine. Psalm xxv.

UNTO thee, (O Lord,) will I lift up my soul; my God, I have put my trust in thee: O let me not be confounded, neither let mine enemies triumph over me.

For all they that hope in thee shall not be ashamed: but such as transgress without a cause shall be put to confusion.

Shew me thy ways, O Lord: and teach me thy paths.

Lead me forth in thy truth, and learn me, for thou art the God of my salvation: in thee hath been my hope all the day long.

Call to remembrance, O Lord, thy tender mercies: and thy loving kindness, which have been ever of old.

O remember not the sins and offences of my youth: but according unto thy mercy think thou upon me, (O Lord,) for thy goodness.

[DOCUMENTS, EDW. VI.]

Gracious and righteous is the Lord : therefore will he teach sinners in the way.

Them that be meek shall he guide in judgment : and such as be gentle, them shall he learn his way.

All the paths of the Lord are mercy and truth : unto such as keep his covenant and his testimonies.

For thy name's sake, O Lord : be merciful unto my sin, for it is great.

What man is he that feareth the Lord? him shall he teach in the way that he shall choose.

His soul shall dwell at ease : and his seed shall inherit the land.

The secrets of the Lord is among them that fear him : and he will shew them his covenant.

Mine eyes are ever looking unto the Lord : for he shall pluck my feet out of the net.

Turn thee unto me, and have mercy upon me : for I am desolate and in misery.

The sorrows of mine heart are enlarged : O bring thou me out of my troubles.

Look upon mine adversity and misery : and forgive me all my sin.

Consider mine enemies how many they are : and they that bear a tyrannous hate against me.

O keep my soul and deliver me : let me not be confounded, for I have put my trust in thee.

Let perfectness and righteous dealing wait upon me : for my hope hath been in thee. Deliver Israel, O God, out of all his troubles.

Glory be to the Father, and to the Son : and to the Holy Ghost.

As it was in the beginning, is now, and ever shall be : world without end. Amen.

Dominus Illuminatio. Psalm xxvii.

THE Lord is my light and my salvation : whom then shall I fear? The Lord is the strength of my life, of whom then shall I be afraid?

When the wicked, (even mine enemies and my foes,) came upon me to eat up my flesh, they stumbled and fell.

Though an host of men were laid against me, yet shall

not my heart be afraid : and though there rose up war against me, yet will I put my trust in him.

One thing have I desired of the Lord, which I will require : even that I may dwell in the house of the Lord all the days of my life, to behold the fair beauty of the Lord, and to visit his temple.

For in the time of trouble he shall hide me in his Tabernacle : yea, in the secret place of his dwelling shall he hide me, and set me up upon a rock of stone.

And now shall he lift up my head : above mine enemies round about me.

Therefore will I offer in his dwelling an oblation with great gladness : I will sing and speak praises unto the Lord.

Hearken unto my voice, O Lord, when I cry unto thee : have mercy upon me, and hear me.

My heart hath talked of thee, seek ye my face : thy face, Lord, will I seek.

O hide not thou thy face from me : nor cast thy servant away in displeasure.

Thou hast been my succour : leave me not, neither forsake me, O God of my salvation.

When my father and mother forsake me : the Lord taketh me up.

Teach me thy way, O Lord : and lead me the right way, because of mine enemies.

Deliver me not over into the will of mine adversaries : for there are false witnesses risen up against me, and such as speak wrong.

I should utterly have fainted : but that I believe verily to see the goodness of the Lord, in the land of the living.

O tarry thou the Lord's leisure : be strong, and he shall comfort thine heart, and put thou thy trust in the Lord.

Glory be to the Father, &c.

As it was in the beginning, &c.

Lesson for Morning Prayer on Wednesday.

The first lesson, taken out of the eleventh chapter of the Proverbs.

A FALSE balance is an abomination unto the Lord : But a true weight pleaseth him. Where pride is, there is shame

Pro. xi.

also and confusion. But where as is lowliness, there is wisdom. The innocent dealing of the just shall lead them: but the unfaithfulness of the despisers shall be their own destruction. Riches help not in the day of vengeance. But righteousness delivereth from death. The righteousness of the innocent ordereth his way: but the ungodly shall fall in his own wickedness. The righteousness of the just shall deliver them: but the despisers shall be taken in their own ungodliness.

Thus endeth the first lesson, taken out of the eleventh chapter of the Proverbs.

We praise thee, O God, &c.

The second lesson.

Matth. v. I SAY unto you, (saith Christ,) Except your righteousness exceed the righteousness of the Scribes and Pharisees, ye cannot enter into the kingdom of heaven. Ye have heard that it was said unto them of the old time: Thou shalt not kill, whosoever killeth shall be in danger of judgment. But I say unto you: that whosoever is angry with his brother (unadvisedly) shall be in danger of judgment. And whosoever sayeth unto his brother, Racha, shall be in danger of a council. But whosoever sayeth, Thou fool, shall be in danger of hell fire. Therefore, if thou offerest thy gift at the altar, and there rememberest that thy brother hath ought against thee: Leave there thine offering before the altar, and go thy way first, and be reconciled to thy brother, and then come and offer thy gift.

Thus endeth, &c.

Blessed be the Lord God of Israel, &c.

Psalms for Evening Prayer, on Wednesday.

Our Father, which art, &c.
O Lord, open thou my lips, &c.
O God, make speed to save me.
O Lord, make haste to help me.
Glory be to the Father, &c.
As it was in the beginning, is now, &c.

Letatus sum in. Psalm cxxii.

I WAS glad when they said unto me : we will go into the house of the Lord.

Our feet shall stand in thy gates : O Jerusalem.

Jerusalem is builded as a city : that is at unity in itself.

For thither the tribes go up, even the tribes of the Lord : to testify unto Israel, to give thanks unto the name of the Lord.

For there is the seat of judgment : even the seat of the house of David.

O pray for the peace of Jerusalem : they shall prosper that love thee.

Peace be within thy walls : and plenteousness within thy palaces.

For my brethren and companions' sakes : I will wish thee prosperity.

Yea, because of the house of the Lord our God : I will seek to do thee good.

Glory to the Father, &c.

As it was in the, &c.

Ad te levavi oculos meos. Psalm cxxiii.

UNTO thee lift I up mine eyes : O thou that dwellest in the heavens.

Behold, even as the eyes of servants look unto the hands of their masters, and as the eyes of a maiden unto the hand of her mistress : even so our eyes wait upon the Lord our God, until he have mercy upon us.

Have mercy upon us, O Lord, have mercy upon us : for we are utterly despised.

Our soul is filled with the scornful reproof of the wealthy : and with the despitefulness of the proud.

Glory be to the Father, &c.

As it was in the, &c.

The first lesson, taken out of the third chapter of Ecclesiasticus.

THE children of wisdom are a congregation of the righteous, and their exercise is obedience and love. Hear me, your Father, (O my dear children,) and do thereafter that ye may be safe : For the Lord will have the father honoured of the children, and look what a mother com- Eccle. iii.

mandeth her children to do, he will have it kept. Whoso honoureth his father, his sins shall be forgiven him: And he that honoureth his mother, is like one that gathereth treasure together. Whoso honoureth his father, shall have joy of his own children: and when he maketh his prayer, he shall be heard.

He that honoureth his father shall have a long life. And he that is obedient for the Lord's sake, his mother shall have joy of him. He that feareth the Lord honoureth his father and mother, and doeth them service, as it were unto the Lord himself. Honour thy father in deed, in word, and in all patience, that thou mayest have his blessing.

Thus endeth, &c.

My soul doth magnify, &c.

The second lesson, taken out of the sixth chapter to the Ephesians.

Ephes. vi. CHILDREN, obey your fathers and mothers in the Lord, for that is right. Honour thy father and mother (the same is the first commandment in the promise), that thou mayest prosper, and live long on the earth. Ye fathers, move not your children to wrath: but bring them up through the doctrine and correction of the Lord. Ye servants, obey them that are your bodily masters with fear and trembling, even with the singleness of your heart, as unto Christ: not doing service unto the eye, as they that go about to please men; but as the servants of Christ, doing the will of God from the heart with good will, serving the Lord, and not men, knowing this, that whatsoever good thing any man doeth, the same shall he receive again of God, whether he be bond or free. And ye masters, do even the same things unto them, putting away threatenings: Knowing that your master also is in heaven: Neither is there any respect of person with him.

Thus endeth, &c.

Lord, now lettest thou thy, &c.
As on Sunday.

Psalms for Morning Prayer on Thursday.

Our Father, which art, &c.
O Lord, open thou my lips.
And my mouth shall shew forth thy praise.

O God, make speed to save me.
O Lord, make haste to help me.
Glory be to the Father, &c.
As it was in the beginning, is now, &c.

Exaltabo te. Psalm xxx.

I WILL magnify thee, O Lord, for thou hast set me up : and not made my foes to triumph over me.

O Lord my God, I cried unto thee and thou hast healed me.

Thou, Lord, hast brought my soul out of hell : thou hast kept my life from them that go down to the pit.

Sing praises unto the Lord, (O ye saints of his :) and give thanks unto him, for a remembrance of his holiness.

For his wrath endureth but the twinkling of an eye, and in his pleasure is life : heaviness may endure for a night, but joy cometh in the morning.

And in my prosperity I said, I shall never be removed : thou, Lord, of thy goodness hadst made my hill so strong.

Thou didst turn thy face (from me :) and I was troubled.

Then cried I unto thee, O Lord : and gat me unto my Lord right humbly.

What profit is there in my blood : when I go down to the pit?

Shall the dust give thanks unto thee : or shall it declare thy truth?

Hear, O Lord, and have mercy upon me : Lord, be thou my helper.

Thou hast turned my heaviness into joy : thou hast put off my sackcloth, and garded[1] me with gladness.

Therefore shall every good man sing of thy praise without ceasing : O my God, I will give thanks unto thee for ever.

Glory be to the Father, &c.
As it was in the beginning, &c.

Benedicam Dominum. Psalm xxxiv.

I WILL alway give thanks unto the Lord : his praise shall ever be in my mouth.

My soul shall make her boast in the Lord : the humble shall hear thereof and be glad.

[[1] garded : decked or adorned. But perhaps, *girded*.]

O praise the Lord with me, and let us magnify his name together.

I sought the Lord, and he heard me : yea, he delivered me out of all my fear.

They had an eye unto him and were lightened : and their faces were not ashamed.

Lo, the poor crieth, and the Lord heareth him : yea, and saveth him out of all his troubles.

The angel of the Lord tarrieth round about them that fear him : and delivereth them.

O taste and see how gracious the Lord is : blessed is the man that trusteth in him.

O fear the Lord ye that be his saints : for they that fear him, lack nothing.

The lions do lack, and suffer hunger : but they which seek the Lord, shall want no manner of thing that is good.

Come ye children, and hearken unto me : I will teach you the fear of the Lord.

What man is he that lusteth to live, and would fain see good days? keep thy tongue from evil, and thy lips that they speak no guile.

Eschew evil and do good : seek peace and ensue it.

The eyes of the Lord are over the righteous : and his ears are open unto their prayers.

The countenance of the Lord is against them that do evil : to root out the remembrance of them from off the earth.

The righteous cry, and the Lord heareth them : and delivereth them out of all their troubles.

The Lord is nigh unto them that are of a contrite heart : and will save such as be of an humble spirit.

Great are the troubles of the righteous : but the Lord delivereth him out of all.

He keepeth all his bones : so that not one of them is broken.

But misfortune shall slay the ungodly : and they that hate the righteous, shall be desolate.

The Lord delivereth the souls of his servants : and all they that put their trust in him, shall not be destitute.

Glory be to the Father, &c.

As it was in the beginning, &c.

Lessons for Morning Prayer on Thursday.

The first lesson, taken out of the twenty-third chapter of Ecclesiasticus.

LET not thy mouth be accustomed with swearing, for in it there are many falls. Let not the name of God be continually in thy mouth: for like as a servant which is oft punished cannot be without some sore; even so whatsoever he be that sweareth and nameth God shall not be clean purged from sin. A man that useth much swearing shall be filled with wickedness, and the plague shall never go from his house. If he beguile his brother, his fault shall be upon him. If he knowledge not his sin, he maketh a double offence: and if he swear in vain, he shall not be found righteous, for his house shall be full of plagues. The words of the swearer bringeth death. God grant that it be not found in the house of Jacob. But they that fear God eschew all such and not lie weltering in sin. *Eccle. xxiii.*

Thus endeth, &c.

We praise thee, O Lord, &c.

The second Lesson taken out of the fifth chapter of Saint Matthew.

YE have heard, how it was said to them of old time: thou shalt not forswear thyself. But shalt perform unto the Lord those things that thou swearest. But I say unto you: swear not. Swear not at all, neither by heaven, for it is God's seat, nor by the earth, for it is his footstool: neither by Jerusalem, for it is the city of the great King: neither shalt thou swear by thy head, because thou canst not make one hair white or black. But your communication shall be, yea, yea; nay, nay; for whatsoever is added than these, it cometh of evil.

Thus endeth the second lesson, &c.

Blessed be the Lord God of Israel, &c.

And so as morning prayer endeth on Sunday.

Psalms for Evening Prayer on Thursday.

Our Father, which art, &c.
O God, make speed to save me.
O Lord, make haste to help me.
Glory be to the Father, &c.
As it was in the beginning, is now, &c.

Nisi Dominus. Psalm cxxvii.

EXCEPT the Lord build the house : their labour is but lost that build it.

Except the Lord keep the city : the watchman waketh but in vain.

It is but lost labour that ye haste to rise up early, and so late take rest : and eat the bread of carefulness, for so he giveth his beloved sleep.

Lo, children, and the fruit of thy womb : are an heritage and gift, that cometh of the Lord.

Like as the arrows in the hand of the giant : even so are the young children.

Happy is the man that hath his quiver full of them : they shall not be ashamed when they speak with their enemies in the gate.

Glory be to the Father, &c.

As it was in the, &c.

Beati omnes. Psalm cxxviii.

BLESSED are all they that fear the Lord : and walk in his ways.

For thou shalt eat the labours of thine hands : O well is thee, and happy shalt thou be.

Thy wife shall be as the fruitful vine : upon the walls of thine house.

Thy children like the olive branches : round about thy table.

Lo, thus shall the man be blessed : that feareth the Lord.

The Lord from out of Sion shall so bless thee : that thou shall see Hierusalem in prosperity all thy life long.

Yea, that thou shalt see thy childer's children : and peace upon Israel.

Glory be to the Father, &c.

As it was in the beginning, &c.

Lessons for Evening Prayer on Thursday.

The first lesson, taken out of the twenty-fourth chapter of the Proverbs.

LAY no privy wait wickedly upon the house of the righteous, and disquiet not his resting place. For a just man falleth seven times, and riseth up again; but the ungodly falleth to wickedness. Rejoice not at the fall of thine enemy: and let not thine heart be glad when he stumbleth. Lest the Lord (when he seeth it) be angry, and turn his wrath from him unto thee. Let not thy wrath and jealousy move thee, to follow the wicked and ungodly. And why? the wicked have nothing to hope for, and the candle of the ungodly shall be put out. My son, fear thou the Lord and the King, and keep no company with the seditious persons: For their destruction shall come suddenly, and who knoweth the fall of them both (?)

Thus endeth, &c.

My soul doth magnify, &c.

The second lesson. Rom. xiii.

LET every soul submit himself unto the authority of the higher powers. For there is no power but of God. The powers that be, are ordained of God. Whosoever therefore resisteth power, resisteth the ordinance of God. But they that resist, shall receive to themself damnation. For rulers are not fearful to them that do good, but to them that do evil. Wilt thou be without fear of the power? do well then: and so shalt thou be praised of the same, for he is the minister of God for thy wealth. But if thou do that which is evil, then fear, for he beareth not the sword for nought: For he is the minister of God, to take vengeance of him that doeth evil. Wherefore, ye must needs obey, not only for fear of vengeance, but also because of conscience. And even for this cause pay ye tribute. For they are God's ministers serving for the same purpose. Give to every man therefore his duty; tribute, to whom tribute belongeth: custom, to whom custom is due: fear, to whom fear belongeth: honour, to whom honour pertaineth.

Thus endeth the second, &c.

Lord, now lettest thou thy servant, &c.

As on Sunday Evening prayer.

Psalms for Morning Prayer on Friday.

Our Father, which art, &c.
O Lord, open thou my lips.
And my mouth shall shew forth thy praise.

O God, make speed to save me :
O Lord, make haste to help me.

Glory be to the Father, and to the Son, and to the Holy Ghost.

As it was in the beginning, is now, and ever shall be, world without end. Amen.

Noli æmulari. Psalm xxxvii.

Fret not thyself because of the ungodly : Neither be thou envious against the evil doers.

For they shall soon be cut down like grass : and be withered even as the green herb.

Put thou thy trust in the Lord, and be doing good : dwell in the land, and verily thou shalt be fed.

Delight thou in the Lord : and he shall give thee thy heart's desire.

Commit thy way unto the Lord, and put thy trust in him : and he shall bring it to pass.

He shall make thy righteousness as clear as the light : and thy just dealing as the noon day.

Hold thee still in the Lord, and abide patiently upon him : but grieve not thyself at him, whose way doth prosper, against the man that doeth after evil counsels.

Leave off from wrath, and let go displeasure : fret not thyself, else shalt thou be moved to do evil.

Wicked doers shall be rooted out : and they that patiently abide the Lord, those shall inherit the land.

Yet a little while, and the ungodly shall be clean gone : thou shalt look after his place, and he shall be away.

But the meek spirited shall possess the earth : and shall be refreshed in the multitude of peace.

The ungodly seeketh counsel against the just : and gnasheth upon him with his teeth.

The Lord shall laugh him to scorn : for he hath seen, that his day is coming.

The ungodly have drawn out the sword, and have bended their bow : to cast down the poor and needy, and to slay such as be of a right conversation.

Their sword shall go through their own heart : and their bow shall be broken.

A small thing that the righteous hath : is better than great riches of the ungodly.

For the arms of the ungodly shall be broken : and the Lord upholdeth the righteous.

The Lord knoweth the days of the godly : and their inheritance shall endure for ever.

They shall not be confounded in the perilous time : and in the days of dearth they shall have enough.

As for the ungodly, they shall perish, and the enemies of the Lord shall consume as the fat of lambs : yea, even as the smoke shall they consume away.

The ungodly borroweth and payeth not again : but the righteous is merciful and liberal.

Such as be blessed of God, shall possess the land : and they that be cursed of him shall be rooted out.

The Lord ordereth a good man's going : and maketh his way acceptable to himself.

Though he fall, he shall not be cast away : for the Lord upholdeth him with his hand.

I have been young, and now am old : and yet saw I never the righteous forsaken, nor his seed begging their bread.

The righteous is ever merciful and lendeth : and his seed is blessed.

Fly from evil, and do the thing that is good : and dwell for evermore.

For the Lord loveth the thing that is right : he forsaketh not his that be godly ; but they are preserved for ever.

(The righteous shall be punished :) as for the seed of the ungodly, it shall be rooted out.

The righteous shall inherit the land : and dwell therein for ever.

The mouth of the righteous is exercised in wisdom : and his tongue will be talking of judgment.

The law of his God is in his heart : and his goings shall not slide.

The ungodly seeth the righteous : and seeketh occasion to slay him.

The Lord will not leave him in his hand, nor condemn him when he is judged.

Hope thou in the Lord, and keep his way, and he shall

promote thee : that thou shall possess the land, when the ungodly shall perish, thou shalt see it.

I myself have seen the ungodly in great power, and flourishing like a green bay tree.

And I went by, and lo, he was gone : I sought him, but his place could no where be found.

Keep innocency, and take heed unto the thing that is right : for that shall bring a man peace at the last.

As for the transgressors, they shall perish together : and the end of the ungodly is, they shall be rooted out at the last.

But the salvation of the righteous cometh of the Lord : which is also their strength in the time of trouble.

And the Lord shall stand by them, and save them : He shall deliver them from the ungodly, and shall save them, because they put their trust in him.

Glory be to the Father, &c.

As it was in the, &c.

Lessons for Morning Prayer on Friday.

The first lesson, taken out of the twenty-first chapter of Ecclesiasticus.

MY son, if thou hast sinned, do it no more. But pray for thy fore-sins, that they may be forgiven thee. Fly from sin, even as from a serpent : for if thou comest nigh to her, she will bite thee. The teeth thereof are as the teeth of a lion, to slay the souls of men. The wickedness of man is a sharp two-edged sword, which maketh such wounds that they cannot be healed. Strife and wrongeous dealing shall waste away a man's goods, and through pride a rich house shall be brought to nought. Thus the riches of the proud shall be rooted out. From the mouth of the poor his prayer shall be heard, and the revenging of him shall hastily come. Whoso hateth to be reformed, it is a token of an ungodly person. But he that feareth God will remember himself.

Thus endeth the first lesson, &c.

We praise thee, O God, &c.

¶ The second lesson, taken out of the third chapter of John.

John iii.

GOD so loved the world, that he gave his only begotten Son, that whosoever believeth in him should not perish, but have everlasting life. For God sent not his Son into the world to condemn the world, but that the world through him might be saved. He that believeth on him is not condemned. But he that believeth not is condemned already; because he hath not believed in the name of the only begotten Son of God. And this is the condemnation, that light is come into world, and men loved darkness more than light, because their deeds were evil. For every one that evil-doeth, hateth the light; neither loveth the light, lest his deeds should be reproved. But he that doeth truth, cometh to the light, that his deeds may be known, how that they are wrought in God.

Thus endeth the second lesson, &c.

Blessed be the Lord God of Israel, &c.

Psalms for Evening Prayer on Friday.

Our Father, which art, &c.
O God, make speed to save me.
O Lord, make haste to help me.
Glory be to the Father, &c.
As it was in the beginning, is now, &c.

De profundis clamavi. Psalm cxxx.

OUT of the deep have I called unto thee, O Lord : Lord hear my voice.

O let thine ears consider well : the voice of my complaint.

If thou Lord, wilt be extreme to mark what is done amiss : O Lord, who may abide it?

For there is mercy with thee : therefore shalt thou be feared.

I look for the Lord, my soul doth wait for him : in his word is my trust.

My soul flieth unto the Lord, before the morning watch : (I say) before the morning watch.

O Israel, trust in the Lord, for with the Lord there is mercy : and with him is plenteous redemption.

And he shall redeem Israel : from all his sins.

Glory be to the Father, &c.
As it was in the beginning, &c.

Ecce quam bonum. Psalm cxxxiii.

BEHOLD, how good and joyful a thing it is : brethren to dwell together in unity.

It is like the precious ointment upon the head, that ran down even to the beard : even unto Aaron's beard, and went down to the skirts of his clothing.

Like as the dew of Hermon : which fell upon the hill of Sion.

For there the Lord promised his blessing : and life for evermore.

Glory be to the Father, &c.

As it was in the, &c.

Lessons for Evening Prayer on Friday.

The first lesson, taken out of the thirty-fifth chapter of Ecclesiasticus.

Eccl. xxxv. THE Lord heareth the oppressed, he despiseth not the desire of the fatherless, nor the widow, when she poureth out her prayer before him. Doth not God see the tears that run down the cheeks of the widow? Or heareth he not the complaint, over such as make her to weep? Whoso serveth God after his pleasure shall be accepted, and his prayer reacheth unto the clouds: till she come nigh, she will not be comforted, nor go her way, till the highest God have respect unto her. Give true sentence and perform the judgment. And the Lord will not be slack in coming nor tarry long; till he have smitten in sunder the backs of the unmerciful, and avenged himself of the heathen.

Thus endeth, &c.

My soul doth magnify, &c.

The second lesson, taken out of the sixth chapter to the Ephesians.

Ephe. vi. FINALLY, my brethren, be strong through the Lord, and through the power of his might: put on all the armour of God, that ye may stand against the assaults of the devil: for we wrestle not against blood and flesh; but against rule, and against power, against worldly rulers, even governors of the darkness of this world, against spiritual craftiness in heavenly things. Wherefore take unto you the whole armour of God, that ye may be able to resist in the evil day, and stand perfect in all things. Stand therefore, and your loins gird with the truth, having on the breastplate of righteousness, and having shoes on your feet, that ye may be prepared for the gospel of peace. Above all, take to you the shield of faith, wherewith ye may quench all the fiery darts of the wicked. And take the helmet of salvation, and the sword of the Spirit, which is the word of God. And pray always with all manner of prayer and supplication in the spirit: and watch thereunto with all instance.

Thus endeth, &c.

Lord, now lettest thou thy servant, &c.

Psalms for Morning Prayer on Saturday.

Our Father, which art, &c.
O Lord, open thou my lips.
And my mouth shall shew forth thy praise.
O God, make speed to save me.
O Lord, make haste to help me.
Glory be to the Father, and to the Son, and to the Holy Ghost.
As it was in the beginning, is now, and ever shall be world without end. Amen.

Quid gloriaris in malitia. Psalm lii.

WHY boasteth thou thyself, thou tyrant : that thou canst do mischief?

Whereas the goodness of God : endureth yet daily.

Thy tongue imagineth wickedness : and with lies thou cuttest like a sharp razor.

Thou hast loved ungraciousness more than goodness : and to talk of lies more than righteousness.

Thou hast loved to speak all words that may do hurt : O thou false tongue.

Therefore shall God destroy thee for ever : he shall take thee and pluck thee out of thy dwelling, and root thee out of the land of the living.

The righteous also shall see this, and fear : and shall laugh him to scorn.

Lo, this is the man that took not God for his strength :

[DOCUMENTS, EDW. VI.]

but trusted unto the multitude of his riches, and strengthened himself in his wickedness.

As for me, I am like a green olive tree in the house of God : my trust is in the tender mercy of God, for ever and ever.

I will alway give thanks unto thee, for that thou hast done : and I will hope in thy name, for thy saints like it well.

Glory be to the Father, and to the Son, and to the Holy Ghost.

As it was in the beginning, is now, and ever shall be, &c.

Nonne Deo subjecta. Psalm lxii.

My soul truly waiteth still upon God : for of him cometh my salvation.

He verily is my strength and my salvation : he is my defence, so that I shall not greatly fall.

How long will ye imagine mischief against every man? Ye shall be slain all the sort of you: yea, as a tottering wall shall ye be, and like a broken hedge.

Their device is only how to put him out whom God will exalt : their delight is in lies, they give good words with their mouth, but curse with their heart.

Nevertheless, my soul, wait thou still upon God : for my hope is in him.

He truly is my strength, and my salvation : he is my defence, so that I shall not fall.

In God is my health and my glory : the rock of my might, and in God is my trust.

O put your trust in him alway, (ye people :) pour out your hearts before him, for God is our hope.

As for the children of men, they are but vain : the children of men are deceitful upon the weights, they are altogether lighter than vanity itself.

O trust not in wrong and robbery, give not yourselves unto vanity : if riches increase, set not your heart upon them.

God spake once, and twice : I have also heard the same, that power belongeth unto God.

And that thou, Lord, art merciful : for thou rewardest every man according to his work.

Glory be to the Father, &c.

As it was in the beginning, &c.

Lessons for Morning Prayer on Saturday.

The first lesson, taken out of the twenty-eighth chapter of Ecclesiasticus.

HE that seeketh vengeance shall find vengeance of the Lord, which shall surely keep his sins. Forgive thy neighbour the hurt that he hath done to thee, and so shall thy sins be forgiven thee also, when thou prayest. A man that beareth hatred against another, how dare he desire forgiveness of God? He that sheweth no mercy to man which is like himself, how dare he ask forgiveness of his sins? If he that is but flesh beareth hatred, and keepeth it, who will entreat for his sins? Remember the end, and let enmity pass, which seeketh death and destruction, and abide thou in the commandments. Remember the commandments, so shalt not thou be rigorous over thy neighbour. Think upon the covenant of the highest, and forgive thy neighbour's ignorance. *Eccle. xxviii.*

Thus endeth, &c.

We praise thee, O God, &c.

The second lesson, taken out of the thirteenth chapter of Mark.

TAKE heed, watch and pray, for ye know not when the time is. As a man which is gone into a strange country, and hath left his house, and given his substance to his servants, and to every man his work, and commanded the Porter to watch: Watch ye therefore; for ye know not when the master of the house will come, at even or at midnight, whether at the cock-crowing, or in the dawning: Lest if he come suddenly, he find you sleeping. And that I say unto you, I say unto you all, watch. *Mark xiii.*

Thus endeth, &c.

Blessed be the Lord God of Israel, &c.

Psalms for Evening Prayer on Saturday.

Our Father, which art, &c.
O God, make speed to save me.
O Lord, make haste to help me.
Glory be to the Father, and to the Son: and to the Holy Ghost.
As it was in the beginning, is now, &c.

Voce mea ad Dominum. Psalm cxlii.

I CRIED unto the Lord with my voice : yea, even unto the Lord did I make my supplication.

I poured out my complaints before him : and shewed him of my trouble.

When my spirit was in heaviness, thou knewest my path : in the way wherein I walked have they privily laid a snare for me.

I looked also upon my right hand : and see, there was no man that would know me.

I had no place to flee unto : and no man cared for my soul.

I cried unto thee, O Lord, and said : Thou art my hope and my portion in the land of the living.

Consider my complaint : for I am brought very low.

O deliver me from my persecutors : for they are too strong for me.

Bring my soul out of prison, that I may give thanks unto thy name : which thing if thou wilt grant me, then shall the righteous resort unto my company.

Glory be to the Father, &c.

As it was, &c.

Exaltabo te Deus. Psalm cxlv.

I WILL magnify thee, O God, my king : and I will praise thy name for ever and ever.

Every day will I give thanks unto thee : and praise thy name for ever and ever.

Great is the Lord, and marvellous, worthy to be praised : there is no end of his greatness.

One generation shall praise thy works unto another : and declare thy power.

As for me, I will be talking of thy worship : thy glory, thy praise, and wondrous works.

So that men shall speak of the might of thy marvellous acts : and I will also tell of thy greatness.

The memorial of thine abundant kindness shall be shewed : and men shall sing of thy righteousness.

The Lord is gracious and merciful : long-suffering and of great goodness.

The Lord is loving unto every man : and his mercy is over all his works.

All thy works praise thee, O Lord : and thy saints give thanks unto thee.

They shew the glory of thy kingdom : and talk of thy power.

That thy power, thy glory, and mightiness of thy kingdom : might be known unto men.

Thy kingdom is an everlasting kingdom : and thy dominion endureth throughout all ages.

The Lord upholdeth all such as fall : and lifteth up all those that be down.

The eyes of all wait upon thee, O Lord : and thou givest them their meat in due season.

Thou openest thine hand : and fillest all things living with plenteousness.

The Lord is righteous in all his ways : and holy in all his works.

The Lord is nigh unto all them that call upon him : yea, all such as call upon him faithfully.

He will fulfil the desire of them that fear him : he also will hear their cry, and will help them.

The Lord preserveth all them that love him : but scattereth abroad all the ungodly.

My mouth shall speak the praise of the Lord : and let all flesh give thanks unto his holy name for ever and ever.

Glory be to the Father, and to the Son, and to the Holy Ghost.

As it was in the beginning, is now, and ever shall be world without end. Amen.

The first lesson, taken out of the seventh chapter of Ecclesiasticus.

Lessons for evening[1] prayer on Saturday.

FEAR the Lord with all thy soul, and honour his ministers. Love thy Maker with all thy strength, and forsake not his servants. Fear the Lord with all thy soul, and honour his priests. Give them their portion of the first-fruits, and increase of the earth, like as it is commanded thee : and reconcile thyself of thy negligence with the little flock : Eccle. vii.

[[1] morning, in the original.]

give them the shoulders, and their appointed offerings and firstlings: Reach thine hand unto the poor that God may bless thee with plenteousness. Be liberal unto all men living, yet let not but do good even unto them that are dead. Let not them that weep be without comfort, but mourn with such as mourn. Let it not grieve thee to visit the sick; for that shall make thee to be beloved: whatsoever thou takest in hand, remember the end, and thou shalt never do amiss.

Thus endeth, &c.

My soul doth magnify, &c.

The second lesson, taken out of the ninth chapter of the first Epistle to the Corinthians.

WHO goeth a warfare at any time at his own cost? Who planteth a vineyard, and eateth not of the fruit thereof? Or who feedeth a flock, and eateth not of the milk of the flock? Say I these things after the manner of men? Sayeth not the law the same also? For it is written in the law of Moses, Thou shalt not muzzle the mouth of the ox that treadeth out the corn. Doth God take thought for oxen? Saith he it not altogether for our sakes? For our sakes no doubt this is written: that he which eareth, should ear in hope, and that he which thresheth in hope should be partaker of his hope. If we sow unto you spiritual things, is it a great thing if we reap your bodily things? If other be partakers of this power over you, wherefore are not we rather? Nevertheless, we have not used this power, but suffer all things, lest we should hinder the gospel of Christ. Do ye not know, how that they which minister about holy things, live of the sacrifice? They which wait of the temple, are partakers of the temple. Even so also did the Lord ordain, that they which preach the gospel should live of the gospel.

Thus endeth, &c.

Lord, now lettest thou thy, &c.

As on Sunday Evening prayer.

(Margin notes: Deut. xxv. 1 Timo. v.; Acts xx.)

THE COLLECTS

FOR

SUNDAYS AND HOLY DAYS THROUGHOUT ALL THE YEAR.

¶ *The first Sunday of Advent.*

ALMIGHTY God, give us grace that we may cast away the works of darkness, and put upon us the armour of light, now in the time of this mortal life (in the which thy Son Jesus Christ came to visit us in great humility), that in the last day, when he shall come again in his glorious majesty to judge both the quick and the dead, we may rise to the life immortal through him: who liveth and reigneth with thee and the Holy Ghost now and ever. Amen.

¶ *The second Sunday.*

BLESSED Lord, which hast caused all holy Scriptures to be written for our learning: grant us that we may in such wise hear them, read, mark, learn, and inwardly digest them, that by patience and comfort of thy holy word, we may embrace and ever hold fast the blessed hope of everlasting life, which thou hast given us in our Saviour Jesus Christ. Amen.

The third Sunday.

LORD, we beseech thee to hear to our prayers, and by thy gracious visitation lighten the darkness of our heart, by our Lord Jesus Christ. Amen.

The fourth Sunday.

LORD, raise up (we pray thee) thy power, and come among us, and with great might succour us: that whereas (through our sins and wickedness) we be sore let and hindered, thy bountiful grace and mercy, through the satisfaction of thy Son our Lord, may speedily deliver us: To whom, with thee and the Holy Ghost, be honour and glory, world without end. Amen.

Christmas Day.

ALMIGHTY God, which hast given us thy only begotten Son to take our nature upon him, and this day to be born of a pure virgin: grant that we being regenerate, and made thy children by adoption and grace, may daily be renewed by thy Holy Spirit, through the same our Lord Jesus Christ: who liveth and reigneth with thee, and the Holy Ghost, now and ever. Amen.

¶ Saint Stephen's Day.

GRANT us, O Lord, to learn to love our enemies by the example of thy martyr Saint Stephen, who prayed for his persecutors to thee: which livest and reignest. &c.

¶ Saint John Evangelist's Day.

MERCIFUL Lord, we beseech thee, to cast thy bright beams of light upon thy church: That it being lightened by the doctrine of thy blessed Apostle and Evangelist John, may attain to thy everlasting gifts: Through Jesus Christ our Lord. Amen.

The Innocents' Day.

ALMIGHTY God, whose praise this day the young Innocents thy witnesses hath confessed and shewed forth, not in speaking, but in dying: mortify and kill all vices in us, that in our conversation our life may express thy faith, which with our tongues we do confess: through Jesus Christ our Lord.

The Sunday after Christmas Day.

ALMIGHTY God, which hast given us, &c.
As upon Christmas Day.

The Circumcision of Christ.

ALMIGHTY God, which madest thy blessed Son to be circumcised and obedient to the law for man: grant us the circumcision of the Spirit, that our hearts and all our members, being mortified from all worldly and carnal lusts, may in all things obey thy blessed will: through the same thy Son Jesus Christ our Lord.

The Epiphany.

O GOD, which by the leading of a star didst manifest thy only begotten Son to the Gentiles: Mercifully grant that we, which knowledge thee now by faith, may after this life have the fruition of thy glorious Godhead, through Christ our Lord. Amen.

The first Sunday after the Epiphany.

LORD, we beseech thee mercifully to receive the prayers of thy people, which call upon thee: And grant that they may both perceive and know what things they ought to do, and also have grace and power faithfully to fulfil the same, through Jesus Christ our Lord. Amen.

¶ The second Sunday after the Epiphany.

ALMIGHTY and everlasting God, which dost govern all things in heaven and earth: mercifully hear the supplications of thy people, and grant us thy peace all the days of our life.

The third Sunday.

ALMIGHTY and everlasting God, mercifully look upon our infirmities: and in all our dangers and necessities stretch forth thy right hand to help and defend us, through Jesus Christ our Lord. Amen.

The fourth Sunday.

GOD, which knowest us to be set in the midst of so many and great dangers, that for man's frailness we cannot always stand uprightly: grant to us the health of body and soul, that all those things which we suffer for sin, by thy help we may well pass and overcome: through Christ our Lord. Amen.

The fifth Sunday.

LORD, we beseech thee to keep thy church and household continually in thy true religion: that they which do lean only upon hope of thy heavenly grace, may evermore be defended by thy mighty power: through Christ our Lord. Amen.

The sixth Sunday.

O LORD, we beseech thee favourably to hear the prayers of thy people, that we which are justly punished for our offences, may be mercifully delivered by thy goodness, for the glory of thy name: through Jesus Christ our Saviour, who liveth and reigneth with thee and the Holy Ghost, ever one God, world without end. Amen.

The seventh Sunday.

LORD God, which seest that we put not our trust in any thing that we do: Mercifully grant, that by thy power we may be defended against all adversity: through Jesus Christ our Lord. Amen.

The eighth Sunday.

O LORD, which dost teach us, that all our doings without charity are nothing worth: Send thy Holy Ghost, and pour in our hearts that most excellent gift of charity, the very bond of peace and all virtues, without the which whosoever liveth is counted dead before thee: Grant this for thy only Son Jesus Christ's sake. Amen.

The first day in Lent.

ALMIGHTY and everlasting God, which hatest nothing that thou hast made, and dost forgive the sins of all them that be penitent: Create and make in us new and contrite hearts, that we worthily lamenting our sins, and knowledging our wretchedness, may obtain of thee, the God of all mercy, perfect remission and forgiveness through Jesus Christ.

The first Sunday in Lent.

O LORD, which for our sake didst fast forty days and forty nights: Give us grace to use such abstinence, that our flesh being subdued to the spirit, we may ever obey thy godly motions, in righteousness and true holiness, to thy honour and glory: which livest and reignest with the Father and the Holy Ghost ever one God world without end. Amen.

The second Sunday.

ALMIGHTY God, which dost see that we have no power of ourselves to help ourselves: keep thou us both outwardly in our bodies, and inwardly in our souls, that we may be defended from all adversities which may happen to the body, and from all evil thoughts which may assault and hurt the soul: through Jesus Christ our Lord.

¶ The third Sunday.

WE beseech thee, Almighty God, look upon the hearty desires of thy humble servants: and stretch forth the right hand of thy majesty, to be our defence against all our enemies: through Jesus Christ our Lord. Amen.

The fourth Sunday.

GRANT, we beseech thee, Almighty God, that we which for our evil deeds are worthily punished, by the comfort of thy grace may mercifully be relieved through our Lord Jesus Christ. Amen.

¶ The fifth Sunday.

WE beseech thee Almighty God, mercifully to look upon thy people: that by thy great goodness they may be governed and preserved evermore both in body and soul: through Jesus Christ our Lord.

¶ The sixth Sunday.

ALMIGHTY and everlasting God, which of thy tender love towards man, hast sent our Saviour Jesus Christ to take upon him our flesh, and to suffer death upon the cross, that all mankind should follow the example of his great humility: Mercifully grant that we both follow the example of his patience, and be made partakers of his resurrection: through the same Jesus Christ our Lord. Amen.

¶ On Good Friday.

ALMIGHTY God, we beseech thee graciously to behold this thy family, for the which our Lord Jesus Christ was contented to be betrayed, and given up into the hands of wicked men, and to suffer death upon the cross: Who liveth and reigneth with thee and the Holy Ghost ever one God world without end. Amen.

Easter Day.

¶ At Morning Prayer instead of the Psalm, O come let us sing, &c. say these anthems following.

CHRIST rising again from the dead, now dieth not, death from hence forth hath no power upon him. For in that he died, he died but once to put away sin. But in that he liveth, he liveth unto God. And so likewise, count yourselves dead unto sin, but living unto God in Christ Jesus our Lord.

Christ is risen again the first-fruits of them that sleep: for seeing that by man came death, by man also cometh the resurrection of the dead. For as by Adam all men do die, so by Christ all men shall be restored to life.

Easter Day.

ALMIGHTY God, which through thy only begotten Son Jesus Christ hast overcome death, and opened unto us the gate of everlasting life: We humbly beseech thee, that as by thy special grace preventing us, thou dost put in our minds good desires; so by thy continual help, we may bring the same to good effect, through Jesus Christ our Lord: Who liveth and reigneth with thee and the Holy Ghost, ever one God, world without end. Amen.

Monday in Easter Week.

ALMIGHTY Father, which hast given thy only Son to die for our sins, and to rise again for our justification: grant us so to put away the leaven of malice and all kind of wickedness, that we may alway serve thee in pureness of living and truth: Through Jesus Christ our Lord. Amen.

Tuesday in Easter Week.

ALMIGHTY Father, which hast, &c.
    As on Monday.

The first Sunday after Easter.

ALMIGHTY God, &c.
    As on Easter Day.

¶ The second Sunday after Easter.

ALMIGHTY God, which hast given thy holy Son to be unto us both a sacrifice for sin, and also an example of godly life: give us the grace that we may always most thankfully receive that his inestimable benefit, and also daily endeavour ourselves to follow the blessed steps of his most holy life. Amen.

The third Sunday.

ALMIGHTY God, which shewest to all men that be in error the light of thy truth, to the intent that they may return into the way of righteousness: Grant unto all them that be admitted into the fellowship of Christ's religion, that they may eschew those things that be contrary to their profession, and follow such things as be agreeable to the same: Through our Lord Jesus Christ. Amen.

The fourth Sunday.

ALMIGHTY God, which dost make the minds of all faithful men to be of one will: Grant unto thy people, that they may love the thing which thou commandest, and desire that which thou dost promise: that among the sundry and manifold changes of the world, our hearts may surely there be fixed, where as true joys are to be found: Through Christ our Lord.

The fifth Sunday.

LORD, from whom all good things do come: grant us thy humble servants, that by thy holy inspiration we may think those things that be good, and by thy merciful guiding may perform the same; through our Lord Jesus Christ.

The Ascension Day.

GRANT, we beseech thee, Almighty God, that like as we do believe thy only begotten Son our Lord to have ascended into the heavens: so we may also in heart and mind thither ascend, and with him continually dwell. Amen.

The Sunday after the Ascension Day.

O GOD the King of glory, which hast exalted thine only Son, Jesus Christ, with great triumph unto thy kingdom in heaven: We beseech thee, leave us not comfortless, but send to us thine Holy Ghost to comfort us, and exalt us unto the same place, whither our Saviour Christ is gone before: Who liveth and reigneth with thee and the Holy Ghost, one God, for ever and ever. Amen.

Whitsunday.

GOD, which as upon this day hast taught the hearts of thy faithful people, by the sending to them the light of thy Holy Spirit: Grant us by the same Spirit to have a right judgment in all things, and evermore to rejoice in his holy comfort, through the merits of Christ Jesu our Saviour: Who liveth and reigneth with thee in the unity of the same Spirit, one God, world without end. Amen.

The same collect serveth all the whole week.

Trinity Sunday.

ALMIGHTY and everlasting God, which hast given unto us thy servants grace by the confession of a true faith to acknowledge the glory of the eternal Trinity, and in the power of thy divine majesty to worship the unity: We beseech thee, that through the stedfastness of this faith we may evermore be defended from all adversity, which livest and reignest one God, world without end. Amen.

¶ *The first Sunday after Trinity Sunday.*

GOD, the strength of all them that trust in thee, mercifully accept our prayers. And because the weakness of our mortal nature can do no good thing without thee: grant us the help of thy grace, that in keeping of thy commandments we may please thee both in will and deed: through Jesus Christ our Lord.

The second Sunday.

LORD, make us to have a perpetual fear and love of thy holy name: for thou never failest to help and govern them, whom thou dost bring up in thy stedfast love. Grant this, most merciful, &c.

The third Sunday.

LORD, we beseech thee mercifully to hear us, and unto whom thou hast given an hearty desire to pray: grant that by thy mighty aid we may be defended, through Jesus Christ our Lord. Amen.

¶ The fourth Sunday.

GOD, the protector of all that trust in thee, without whom nothing is strong, nothing is holy: increase and multiply upon us thy mercy; that, thou being our ruler and guide, we may so pass through things temporal, that we finally lose not the things eternal: grant this, heavenly Father, for Jesus Christ's sake our Lord. Amen.

¶ The fifth Sunday.

GRANT, Lord, we beseech thee, that the course of this world may be so peaceably ordered by thy governance, that thy congregation may joyfully serve thee in all godly quietness: through Jesus Christ our Lord. Amen.

¶ The sixth Sunday.

GOD, which hast prepared to them that love thee such good things as pass all man's understanding: Pour into our hearts such love towards thee, that we loving thee in all things, may obtain thy promises which exceed all that we can desire: Through Jesus Christ our Lord. Amen.

¶ The seventh Sunday.

LORD of all power and might, which art the author and giver of all good things: Graff in our hearts the love of thy name, increase in us true religion, nourish us with all goodness, and of thy great mercy keep us in the same: Through Jesus Christ our Lord. Amen.

¶ The eighth Sunday.

GOD, whose providence is never deceived: we humbly beseech thee, that thou wilt put away from us all hurtful things, and give those things which be profitable for us: through Jesus Christ our Lord. Amen.

¶ *The ninth Sunday.*

Grant to us, Lord, we beseech thee, the spirit to think and do always such things as be rightful: that we which cannot be without thee, may by thee be able to live according to thy will. Through Jesus Christ our Lord. Amen.

¶ *The tenth Sunday.*

Let thy merciful ears, O Lord, be open to the prayers of thy humble servants: and that they may obtain their petitions, make them to ask such things as shall please thee; through Jesus Christ our Lord.

¶ *The eleventh Sunday.*

God, which declarest thy Almighty power, most chiefly in shewing mercy and pity: Give unto us abundantly thy grace, that we running to thy promises, may be made partakers of thy heavenly treasure: through Jesu Christ our Lord.

¶ *The twelfth Sunday.*

Almighty and everlasting God, which art always more ready to hear than we to pray: and art wont to give more than either we desire or deserve: Pour down upon us the abundance of thy mercy, forgiving us those things whereof our consciences are afraid, and giving unto us that, that our prayer dare not presume to ask: Through Jesus Christ our Lord.

¶ *The thirteenth Sunday.*

Almighty and merciful God, of whose only gift it cometh, that thy faithful people do unto thee true and laudable service: grant, we beseech thee, that we may so run unto thy heavenly promises, that we fail not finally to attain the same: Through Jesus Christ our Lord. Amen.

The fourteenth Sunday.

Almighty and everlasting God, give unto us the increase of faith, hope, and charity; and that we may obtain that which thou dost promise, make us to love that which thou dost command: Through Jesus Christ our Lord. Amen.

The fifteenth Sunday.

KEEP, we beseech thee, O Lord, thy church with thy perpetual mercy; and because the frailty of man without thee cannot but fall, keep us ever by thy help, and lead us to all things profitable to our salvation: through Jesus Christ our Lord. Amen.

The sixteenth Sunday.

LORD, we beseech thee, let thy continual pity cleanse and defend thy congregation, and because it cannot continue in safety without thy succour, preserve it evermore by thy help and goodness: through Jesus Christ our Lord. Amen.

The seventeenth Sunday.

LORD, we pray thee that thy grace may always prevent and follow us, and make us continually to be given to all good works: through Jesus Christ our Lord. Amen.

The eighteenth Sunday.

LORD, we beseech thee, grant thy people grace to avoid the infections of the devil, and with pure heart and mind to follow thee, the only God: Through Jesus Christ our Lord.

The nineteenth Sunday.

O GOD, forasmuch as without thee, we are not able to please thee: grant that the working of thy mercy may in all things direct and rule our hearts: Through Jesus Christ our Lord. Amen.

The twentieth Sunday.

ALMIGHTY and merciful God, of thy bountiful goodness keep us from all things that may hurt us: that we being ready both in body and soul, may with free hearts accomplish those things that thou wouldest have done: Through Jesus Christ our Lord.

The twenty-first Sunday.

GRANT, we beseech thee, merciful Lord, to thy faithful people pardon and peace, that they may be cleansed from all their sins, and serve thee with a quiet mind: Through Jesus Christ our Lord. Amen.

[DOCUMENTS, EDW. VI.]

The twenty-second Sunday.

LORD, we beseech thee to keep thy household, the church, in continual godliness, that through thy protection it may be free from all adversities, and devoutly given to serve thee in good works, to the glory of thy name: through Jesus Christ our Lord. Amen.

The twenty-third Sunday.

GOD, our refuge and strength, which art the author of all godliness, be ready to hear the devout prayers of the church. And grant that those things which we ask faithfully, we may obtain effectually: through Jesus Christ our Lord. Amen.

¶ The twenty-fourth Sunday.

LORD, we beseech thee, assoil thy people from their offences: that through thy bountiful goodness we may be delivered from the bonds[1] of all those sins, which by our frailty we have committed: grant this, most merciful Father, for Christ Jesus' sake, our Saviour and only Mediator. Amen.

¶ The twenty-fifth Sunday.

STIR up, we beseech thee, O Lord, the wills of thy faithful people: that they, plenteously bringing forth the fruit of good works, may of thee be plenteously rewarded: through Jesus Christ our Lord. Amen.

Collects on Saints' days.

¶ Saint Andrew's day.

ALMIGHTY God, which didst give such grace unto thy holy apostle Saint Andrew, that he readily obeyed the calling of thy Son Jesus Christ, and followed him without delay: Grant unto us all, that we being called by thy holy word may forthwith give over ourselves obediently to follow thy holy commandments: through the same Jesus Christ our Lord.

Saint Thomas the Apostle.

ALMIGHTY and everlasting God, which for the more confirmation of the faith didst suffer thy holy apostle Thomas to be doubtful in thy Son's resurrection, grant us so perfectly

[[1] boundes, in original.]

and without all doubt to believe in thy Son Jesus Christ, that our faith in thy sight never be reproved. Hear us, O Lord, through the same Jesus Christ: to whom with thee and the Holy Ghost be all honour and glory for ever and ever.

¶ *The Conversion of Saint Paul.*

GOD, which hast taught all the world, through the preaching of thy blessed Apostle Saint Paul: Grant, we beseech thee, that we which have his wonderful conversion in remembrance, may follow and fulfil thy holy doctrine that he taught: through Jesu Christ our Lord.

The Purification of Saint Mary the virgin.

ALMIGHTY and everlasting God, we humbly beseech thy Majesty, that as thy only begotten Son was this day presented in the temple, in substance of our flesh: so grant that we may be presented unto thee with pure and clear minds by Jesus Christ our Lord. Amen.

Saint Mathias' day.

ALMIGHTY God, which in the place of the traitor Judas didst choose thy faithful servant Mathie to be of the number of thy twelve Apostles: Grant that thy church, being alway preserved from false apostles, may be ordered and guided by faithful and true pastors: through Jesus Christ our Lord.

The Annunciation of the virgin Mary.

WE beseech thee, Lord, pour thy grace into our hearts, that as we have known Christ thy Son's incarnation by the message of an Angel; so by his cross and passion we may be brought unto the glory of his resurrection: through the same Christ our Lord.

Saint Mark's day.

ALMIGHTY God, which hast instructed thy holy church with the holy doctrine of thy Evangelist Saint Mark: Give us grace so to be established by thy holy Gospel, that we be not like children carried away with every blast of vain doctrine. Grant this through Jesus Christ our Lord.

Saint Philip and James.

ALMIGHTY God, whom truly to know is everlasting life: grant us perfectly to know thy Son Jesus Christ to be the way, the truth, and the life, as thou hast taught Saint Philip, and other the Apostles: through Jesus Christ our Lord.

Saint Barnabe Apostle.

LORD Almighty, which hast endued thy holy apostle Barnabas with singular gifts of thy holy Ghost: let us not be destitute of thy manifold gifts, nor yet of grace, to use them alway to thy honour and glory: through Jesus Christ our Lord. Amen.

Saint John Baptist.

ALMIGHTY God, by whose providence thy servant John Baptist was wonderfully born, and sent to prepare the way of thy Son our Saviour, by preaching of penance: make us so to follow his doctrine and holy life, that we may truly repent according to his preaching, and after his example constantly speak the truth, boldly rebuke vice, and patiently suffer for the truth's sake: through Jesus Christ our Lord.

Saint Peter's day.

ALMIGHTY God, which by thy Son Jesus Christ hast given to thy apostle Saint Peter many excellent gifts, and commandedst him earnestly to feed thy flock: Make, we beseech thee, all bishops and pastors diligently to preach thy holy word, and the people obediently to follow the same, that they may receive the crown of everlasting glory: through Jesus Christ our Lord.

Saint James the Apostle.

GRANT, O merciful God, that as thy holy apostle Saint James, leaving his father and all that he had, without delay, was obedient unto the calling of thy Son Jesus Christ, and followed him; so we, forsaking all worldly and carnal affections, may be evermore ready to follow thy commandments; through Jesus Christ our Lord.

Saint Bartholomew.

O ALMIGHTY and everlasting God, which hast given grace to thy apostle Bartholomew truly to believe and to preach thy word : grant, we beseech thee, unto thy church both to love that he believed, and to preach that he taught: through Jesus Christ our Lord.

Saint Matthew.

ALMIGHTY God, which by thy blessed Son didst call Matthew from the receipt of custom to be an apostle and evangelist: Grant us grace to forsake all covetous desires and inordinate love of riches, and to follow thy said Son, Jesus Christ: who liveth and reigneth with thee and the holy Ghost, one God, world without end. Amen.

Saint Michael and all Angels.

EVERLASTING God, which hast ordained and constituted the services of all Angels and men in a wonderful order: mercifully grant, that they which alway do thee service in heaven, may by thy appointment succour and defend us in earth : through Jesus Christ our Lord.

Saint Luke the Evangelist.

ALMIGHTY God, which calledst Luke the physician, whose praise is in the gospel, to be a physician of the soul : it may please thee by the wholesome medicines of his holy doctrine to heal all the diseases of our souls : through thy Son Jesus Christ our Lord.

Simon and Jude, Apostles.

ALMIGHTY God, which hast builded thy congregation upon the foundation of the Apostles and Prophets, Jesus Christ himself being the head corner stone : grant us so to be joined together in unity of spirit by their doctrine, that we may be made an holy temple acceptable to thee : through Jesus Christ our Lord.

All Saints.

ALMIGHTY God, which hast knit together thy elect in one communion and fellowship, in the mystical body of thy

Son Christ our Lord: grant us so to follow thy holy Saints in all virtues, and godly living, that we may come to those inspeakable joys which thou hast prepared for them that unfeignedly love thee: through Jesus Christ our Lord.

SUNDRY GODLY PRAYERS FOR DIVERS PURPOSES.

For the King.

ALMIGHTY God, whose kingdom is everlasting and power infinite, have mercy upon the whole congregation, and so rule the heart of thy chosen servant Edward the sixth, our king and governor, that he, knowing whose minister he is, may above all things seek thine honour and glory; and that we his subjects, duly considering whose authority he hath, may faithfully serve, honour, and humbly obey him in thee, and for thee, according to thy blessed word and ordinance: through Jesus Christ our Lord, who with thee and the Holy Ghost liveth and reigneth, ever one God, world without end. Amen.

Another for the King.

ALMIGHTY and everlasting God, we be taught by thy holy word, that the hearts of kings are in thy rule and governance, and that thou dost dispose and turn them as it seemeth best to thy godly wisdom: We humbly beseech thee so to dispose and govern the heart of Edward the sixth, thy servant our king and governor, that in all his thoughts, words and works, he may ever seek thy honour and glory, and study to preserve thy people committed to his charge in wealth, in peace, and godliness: Grant this, O merciful Father, for thy dear Son's sake, Jesus Christ our Lord. Amen.

For the King.

O ALMIGHTY God, King of kings, and Lord of lords, which by thy divine ordinance hast appointed temporal rulers to govern thy people according to equity and justice, and to live among them as a loving father among his natural children, for the advancement of the good, and punishment of the evil; we most humbly beseech thee favourably to behold Edward the sixth thy servant, our king and governor, and to breathe into his heart, through thy holy Spirit, the wisdom that is ever about the throne of thy majesty, whereby he may be provoked, moved, and stirred, to love, fear, and serve thee, to seek thy glory, to banish idolatry, superstition, and hypocrisy out of this realm, and unfeignedly to advance thy holy and pure religion among us his subjects, unto the example of other foreign nations. O Lord, defend him from his enemies, send him a long and prosperous life among us, and give him grace not only in his own person godly and justly to rule, but also to appoint such magistrates under him, as may be likewise affected both towards thy holy word, and also toward the commonwealth; that we his subjects, living under his dominion in all godliness, peace, and wealth, may pass the time of this our short pilgrimage in thy fear and service, unto the glory of thy blessed name, which alone is worthy all honour for ever and ever. Amen.

For the King's Council.

IT is written, O most mighty and everlasting King, that where many are that give good counsel, there goeth it well Prov. xi. with the common people, there are all things conserved in a good and seemly order, there doth the public wealth flourish with the abundance of all good things. It may please therefore, O Lord, which hast the heart of all rulers in thy hand, and directest their counsels unto what end it is thy good pleasure, mercifully to assist all those which are of the king's Prov. xxi. most honourable council, and to give them thy holy Spirit to be their president, ruler, and governor, that in all their assemblies they may ever set before their eyes thy most high and princelike majesty, the fear of thy name, the accomplishment of thy commandments; and alway remember that they are servants appointed for the wealth and commodity of the king and his people, executing true judgment indifferently towards all the king's subjects through justice and mercy, being void of all covetousness, that whatsoever they attempt privately or openly, may turn to the glory of thy blessed name, to the setting forth of thy holy word, to the advancement of the king's honour, to the profit of the commons, to the destruction of vice, and to the commendation of virtue. Give them grace (O most merciful Father) so with one mind in all godly and virtuous things, that they ruling righteously, and we living obediently, may all together, with quiet hearts and free consciences, praise and magnify thee our Lord God for ever and ever. Amen.

¶ *For Judges.*

O God, thou most righteous Judge, which commandest by thy holy word such to be chosen judges over thy people, as be of approved conversation, wise and learned in thy holy laws, and fear thee their Lord God, and such as both are true themselves, and also love truth, and hate covetousness; we beseech thee to send us such judges, as thy holy sacred scriptures do paint, and set forth unto us; and so to rule their hearts with thy holy Spirit, that in their judgments they admit no false accusations, have no respect of persons, neither to be desirous of gifts, which make wise men blind, and corrupt the causes of the righteous; nor yet give sentence with the ungodly for bribes, and so condemn the innocent and shed righteous blood; but that they having alway thy fear before their eyes, and knowing that they execute the judgment not of man, but of their Lord God, may hear indifferently all matters; judge according to equity and justice, deliver the oppressed from the power of the violent, be favourable to the stranger, defend the fatherless and widow, plead the cause of the righteous, help the poor, advance virtue, suppress vice, and in all both their words and works so behave themselves, as though they should straightways appear before the righteous throne of thy majesty, and render accounts of their doings: grant this, most merciful Father, for thy dear Son's sake, Jesus Christ our Lord. Amen.

For Bishops, spiritual Pastors, and Ministers of God's word.

O Lord Jesu Christ, most true Pastor, Shepherd and Herdman of our souls, we most humbly beseech thee mercifully to behold thy poor and scattered flock, whom thou hast purchased with thy most precious blood, and to send them such shepherds as both can and will diligently seek up the lost sheep, lovingly lay them on their shoulders, and faithfully bring them home again to the sheepfold. Take away from us, O Lord, all such wicked ministers as deface thy glory, corrupt thy blessed word, despise thy flock, and feed themselves, and not thy sheep. And in their rooms vouchsafe to place good bishops, learned preachers, faithful teachers, godly ministers, and diligent flock-feeders, even such as have a fervent and unfeigned zeal toward the setting forth of thy glory, health of thy people. Endue them with thy holy Spirit, that they may be faithful, wise, and discreet servants, _{Math. xxiv.} _{Luke xxi.} giving thy household meat in due season. Give them that thy wisdom, which no man is able to resist, wherewith also they may be both able to exhort with wholesome doctrine, _{Tit. i.} and also to convict and overcome them that speak against it. Finally, grant, we pray thee, most merciful Saviour, that in all things they may so behave themselves according to thy blessed will and commandment, that when thou, the most high Bishop and chief Shepherd, shalt appear, they may receive the uncorruptible crown of glory. Amen.

For Gentle men.

ALBEIT whatsoever is born of flesh is flesh, and all that _{John iii.} _{Gen. iii.} we receive of our natural parents is earth, dust, ashes and _{Eccles. vii. x.} corruption, so that no child of Adam hath any cause to boast himself of his birth and blood, seeing we have all one flesh and one blood, begotten in sin, conceived in uncleanness, and _{Psal. li.} _{Eph. ii.} born by nature the children of wrath; yet forasmuch as some for their wisdom, godliness, virtue, valiantness, strength, eloquence, learning and policy, be advanced above the common sort of people unto dignities and temporal promotions, as men worthy to have superiority in a christian commonwealth, and by this means have obtained among the people a more noble and worthy name: We most entirely beseech thee, from whom alone cometh the true nobility to so many as are born of thee and made thy sons through faith, whether they be rich or _{Gal. iii.} poor, noble or unnoble, to give a good spirit to our superiors, that as they be called gentle men in name, so they may shew themselves in all their doings gentle, courteous, loving, pitiful and liberal unto their inferiors; living among them as natural fathers among their children, not polling, pilling, and oppressing them, but favouring, helping, and cherishing them:

not destroyers, but fathers of the commonalty: not enemies to the poor, but aiders, helpers, and comforters of them: that when thou shalt call them from this vale of wretchedness, they afore shewing gentleness to the common people, may receive gentleness again at thy merciful hand, even everlasting life, through Jesus Christ our Lord. Amen.

For Landlords.

Psal. xxiv.

Psal. cxv.

THE earth is thine, (O Lord,) and all that is contained therein; notwithstanding thou hast given the possession thereof unto the children of men, to pass over the time of their short pilgrimage in this vale of misery: We heartily pray thee, to send thy holy Spirit into the hearts of them that possess the grounds, pastures, and dwelling places of the earth, that they, remembering themselves to be thy tenants, may not rack and stretch out the rents of their houses and lands, nor yet take unreasonable fines and incomes after the manner of covetous worldlings, but so let them out to other, that the inhabitants thereof may both be able to pay the rents, and also honestly to live, to nourish their families, and to relieve the poor: give

1 Pet. ii.
Heb. xiii.

them grace also to consider, that they are but strangers and pilgrims in this world, having here no dwelling place, but seeking one to come; that they, remembering the short continuance of their life, may be content with that that is sufficient, and

Esa. v.

not join house to house, nor couple land to land, to the impoverishment of other, but so behave themselves in letting out their tenements, lands, and pastures, that after this life they may be received into everlasting dwelling places: through Jesus Christ our Lord. Amen.

For Merchants.

ALMIGHTY God, maker and disposer of all things, which hast placed thy creatures necessary for the use of men in divers lands and sundry countries, yea, and that unto this end, that all kinds of men should be knit together in unity and love, seeing we have all need one of another's help, one country of another country's commodity, one realm of another realm's gifts and fruits: We beseech thee to preserve and keep all such as travel either by land or sea, for the getting of things that be necessary for the wealth of the realms or countries where they dwell, and not to bring in vain trifles and unprofitable merchandise to the enticing and impoverishing the commonwealth. Give them (gracious Lord) safe passage both in their going and coming, that they having prosperous journeys may shew themselves thankful to thee, and beneficial to their neighbours, and so occupy their merchandise without fraud, guile, or deceit, that the commonwealth may prosper and flourish with the abundance of worldly things through their godly and righteous travails, unto the glory of thy name. Amen.

For Lawyers.

WE know, O Lord, that the law is good, if a man use it 1 Tim. i. lawfully, given of thee as a singular gift unto the children of men for maintenance of godly orders, for putting away of iniquity and wrongs, for restoring of men unto their right, for the advancement of virtue, and punishment of vice: we most heartily pray thee, which art the lawgiver, which alone is able to save and to destroy, from whom also cometh all wisdom, and prudence, and knowledge, so to rule through the governance of thy holy Spirit the hearts of Lawyers, that they with discretion and indifferency hearing men's causes being in controversy, and weighing them justly and truly according to the truth and equity of the law, may without partiality both faithfully give counsel, and also indifferently pronounce of all such causes as be brought unto them, and by no means suffer themselves to be corrupted with bribes and gifts, which Eccles. xx. Deut. xvii. blind the eyes of the wise and subvert true judgment: but grant them to walk so uprightly in all men's matters, that they seeking with godly travails a quietness among men in this world, may after their departure from this troublous vale of misery enjoy everlasting rest and quietness in thy heavenly mansion, through Jesus Christ our Lord. Amen.

For Labourers and men of occupations.

As the bird is born to fly, so is man born to labour: for Job v. thou, O Lord, hast commanded by thy holy word, that man Gen. iii. Psal. cxxviii. shall eat his bread in the labour of his hands and in the sweat of his face: yea, thou hast given commandment that 2 Thess. iii. 1 Thess. iv. if any man will not labour, the same should not eat. Thou requirest of us also, that we withdraw ourselves from every brother that walketh inordinately, and giveth not his mind unto labour; so that thy godly pleasure is, that no man be idle, but every man labour according to his vocation and calling: we most humbly beseech thee, to grave in the hearts of all labourers and workmen a willing disposition to travail for their living according to thy word, and to bless the labourer's pains, and travails of all such as either till the earth, or exercise any other handicraft; that they studying to be quiet and to meddle with their own business, and to work with their own hand, and through thy blessing en- *James i.* joying the fruits of their labours, may knowledge thee, the giver of all good things, and glorify thy holy name. Amen.

For Rich Men.

Prov. x.
Matt. xiii.
Mark iv. x.
Luke viii.
xviii.
Matt. ix.
1 Tim. vi.
Eccles. x.

ALBEIT, O Lord, thou art the giver of all good things, and through thy blessing men become rich, that are godly and justly rich; yet are we taught in thy divine scriptures, that riches and the cares of worldly things smother and choke up thy holy word, and that it is more easy for a gable rope to go through the eye of a needle, than a rich man to enter into the kingdom of heaven: again, that they which will be rich fall into temptation, and snares, and into many foolish and noisome lusts, which whelm men into perdition and destruction, (for covetousness is the root of all evil.) We therefore, perceiving by thy blessed word so many incommodities, yea, pestilences of man's salvation to accompany riches, most entirely beseech thee, to bless such as thou hast made rich with a good, humble, loving, and free mind, that they, remembering themselves to be thy dispensers and stewards, may not set their minds upon the deceitful treasures of this world, which are more brittle than glass, and more *Abacuk ii.* vain than smoke, nor yet heap up thick clay against themselves, but liberally and cheerfully bestow part of such goods, *Luke xvi.* as thou hast committed unto them, upon their poor neigh-
Matt. v.
1 Tim. vi. bours, make them friends of this wicked mammon, be merciful to the needy, be rich in good works, and ready to give and distribute to the necessity of the saints, laying up in store for themselves a good foundation against the time to come, that they may obtain everlasting life: through Jesus Christ thy Son and our Lord. Amen.

For poor people.

As riches, so likewise poverty is thy gift, O Lord. And as thou hast made some rich to despise the worldly goods, so hast thou appointed some to be poor, that they may receive thy benefits at the rich men's hands. And as the godly rich are well beloved of thee, so in like manner are the poor, if they bear the cross of poverty patiently, and thankfully; for good and evil, life and death, poverty and riches are of thee, O Lord: we therefore most humbly pray thee, to give a good spirit to all such as it hath pleased thee to burthen with the yoke of poverty, that they may with a patient and thankful heart walk in their state, like to that poor Lazar of whom we read in the gospel of thy well beloved Son, which chosed rather patiently and godly to die, than unjustly or by force to get any man's goods; and by no means envy, murmur, or grudge[1] against such as it hath pleased thee to endue with more abundance of worldly goods: but knowing their state, although never so humble and base, to be of thee their Lord God, and that thou wilt not forsake them in this their great need, but send them things necessary for their poor life, may continually praise thee, and hope for better things in the world to come, through thy Son Jesus Christ our Lord. Amen.

Eccles. xi.

Eccles. xi.

Luke xvi.

The prayer of a true subject.

As it is thy godly appointment, O Lord God, that some should bear rule in this world, to see thy glory set forth, and the common peace kept: so it is thy pleasure again, that some should be subjects and inferiors to other in their vocation, although before thee there is no respect of persons. And forasmuch it is thy godly will and pleasure to appoint and set me in the number of subjects, I beseech thee to give me a faithful and obedient heart unto the high powers, that there may be found in me no disobedience, no unfaithfulness, no treason, no falsehood, no dissimulation, no insurrection, no commotion, no conspiracy, nor any kind of rebellion, in word or in deed, against the civil magistrates, but all faithfulness, obedience, quietness, subjection, humility, and whatsoever else becometh a subject; that I,

[1 grutche, in original.]

living here in all lowness of mind, may at the last day, through thy favour, be lifted up into everlasting glory, where thou, most merciful Father, with thy Son and the Holy Ghost livest and reignest very God, for ever and ever. Amen.

For Fathers and Mothers.

Psal. xii. 8.

THE fruit of the womb and the multitude of children is thy gift and blessing, O Lord God, given to this end, that they may live to thy glory, and the commodity of their neighbour. Forasmuch therefore, as thou of thy goodness hast given me children, I beseech thee give me also grace to train them up even from their cradles in thy nurture and doctrine, in thy holy laws and blessed ordinances, that from their very young age they may know thee, believe in thee, fear, love, and obey thee, and diligently walk in thy commandments all the days of their life, unto the praise of thy glorious name : through Jesus Christ our Lord. Amen.

Of Children.

Exod. xx.

THOU hast given a commandment in thy law, O heavenly Father, that children should honour their fathers and mothers. I most humbly beseech thee therefore to breathe thy holy Spirit into my breast, that I may reverence and honour my father and mother not only with outward gestures of my body, but also with the unfeigned affection of my heart, love them, obey them, pray for them, help them, and do for them, both in word and deed, whatsoever lieth in my power, that thou seeing my unfeigned hearty good-will toward my parents, mayest become my loving heavenly Father, and number me among those thy children, whom from everlasting thou hast appointed to be heirs of thy glorious kingdom : through thy well beloved Son Jesus Christ our Lord. Amen.

Of Masters.

Eph. vi.
Col. iii.

THY commandment is by thine holy apostle, O most merciful Lord Christ, that masters should entreat their servants gently, putting away threatenings, and doing that unto them which is just and equal, forasmuch as we also have a master in heaven, with whom there is no respect of persons : Grant, I most heartily pray thee, that I may so order my servants, that I attempt no unrighteousness against them; but that I may so use my rule and authority over them, that I may alway remember that thou art the common Lord of all, and we all thy servants: again, that I may not forget, that we be all brethren, having one Father, which is in heaven, and look for one glorious kingdom, where thou, with the Father and Holy Ghost, livest and reignest true and everlasting God for ever. Amen.

Of Servants.

O LORD Jesu Christ, we are commanded by thy blessed apostles, that we should honour and obey our bodily masters in fear and trembling, not only if they be good and courteous, but also though they be froward, and serve them, not unto the eye as men-pleasers, but with singleness of heart, not churlishly answering them again, nor picking, stealing, or conveying away any part of their goods, unjustly, but shewing all good faithfulness unto our masters, as though we served God and not men: Grant me grace, I most humbly beseech thee, so to serve my master and my superiors, that there may be found no fault in me, but that I, behaving myself uprightly, justly, faithfully, and truly in my vocation, may do worship to the doctrine of thee my God and Saviour in all things. Amen. *Eph.* vi. *Col.* ii. *Tit.* iii. *1 Pet.* ii.

Of Maids.

THERE is nothing that becometh a maid better than silence, shamefacedness, and chastity of both body and mind. For these things being once lost, she is no more a maid, but a strumpet in the sight of God, howsoever she disguiseth herself and dissembleth with the world: I therefore most humbly beseech thee, O merciful Father, from whom cometh every good and perfect gift, and without whom we are able to do nothing, that thou wilt so order my tongue and dispose my talk, that I speak nothing but that become my state, age, and person, neither that I delight to hear any talk that might in any point move me to lewdness, seeing that evil words corrupt good manners. Give me also such shamefacedness[1] as may pluck me away from the delectation either of thinking, speaking, hearing, seeing, or doing evil, that my whole de-

[[1] shamefastness, in original.]

light may be in virtue, in godliness, in eschewing idleness, in giving myself continually to some godly exercise, but above all things in thinking and speaking of thee, in reading thy blessed word and heavenly law, which is a lantern to my feet, and a light to my paths. Moreover suffer neither my mind to be defiled with evil thoughts, nor my body to be corrupted with any kind of uncleanness; but give me grace so to order myself in eschewing idleness and wanton wicked company, that my mind being free from evil affects, and my body clear from all uncleanness, I may be found a meet temple for the Holy Ghost to inhabit, and if it be thy good pleasure hereafter to call me unto the honourable state of matrimony, that I may bring also unto my husband a pure and undefiled body, and so live with him in thy fear, unto the praise and glory of thy blessed name. Amen.

Of Single Men.

1 Thess. iv.

LORD, thou hast commanded by thy holy apostle, that we should abstain from fornication, and that every one of us should know how to keep his vessel, that is to say, his body, in holiness and honour, and not in the lust of concupiscence, as do the heathen, which know not God. I beseech thee, give me grace to behave myself according to this thy holy commandment: that in this time of my single life, I defile not my body with whoredom or any other uncleanness; but so order myself with all honesty and pureness of life, that I may glorify thee, my Lord God, both in body and spirit. Amen.

Of Husbands.

FORASMUCH, O heavenly Father, as thou hast called me from the single life unto the holy state of honourable wedlock, which is thy good and blessed ordinance for all them to live in, that have not the gift of continence, and hast given me a woman to wife, that I living with her in thy fear may avoid all uncleanness: I most heartily pray thee, give me grace to live with her according to thy godly pleasure. Kill in me all filthy and fleshly lusts. Suffer me not to delight in any strange flesh, but to content myself only with her love, to love her as Christ loved the congregation, to cherish her as I would cherish mine own body, to provide for her according to my ability, to instruct her with the knowledge of thy blessed word, quietly and peaceably to live with her, and to agree together in such perfect concord and unity, as is found among many members in one body, seeing now that we also are no more two, but one flesh; that other, seeing our godly and quiet conversation, may hereby be provoked to forsake their filthy living, and to embrace the holy state of honourable wedlock, unto the glory and praise of thy holy name. Amen.

Of Wives.

O Lord, forasmuch as thou of thy fatherly goodness hast vouchedsafe to keep me from my tender age unto this present, and hast now called me from my single life unto the holy state of honourable wedlock, that I living therein might, according to thine ordinance, bring forth children unto thy glory : Give me grace, I most entirely beseech thee, to walk worthy of my vocation, to knowledge my husband to be my head, to be subject unto him, to learn thy blessed word of him, to reverence him, to obey him, to please him, to be ruled by him, peaceably and quietly to live with him, to wear such apparel as is meet for my degree, and by no means to delight in costly jewels and proud gallant vestures, but alway to use such clothing as become a sober Christian woman, circumspectly and warily to look unto my household, that nothing perish through my negligence, and always have a diligent eye that no dishonesty, no wickedness, no ungodliness be committed in my house, but in it all things be ordered according to thy holy will, which art worthy all honour, glory, and praise, for ever and ever. Amen.

Of Householders.

To have children and servants is thy blessing, O Lord, but not to order them according to thy word deserveth thy dreadful curse : Grant therefore, that as thou hast blessed me with an household, so I may diligently watch, that nothing be committed of the same that might offend thy fatherly goodness, and be an occasion of turning thy blessing into cursing; but that so many as thou hast committed to my charge, may eschew all vice, embrace all virtue, live in thy fear, call upon thy holy name, learn thy blessed commandments, hear thy holy word, and avoiding idleness, diligently exercise themselves every one in his office, according to their vocation and calling, unto the glory of thy most honourable name. Amen.

Of all Christians.

ALBEIT, O heavenly Father, all we that unfeignedly profess thy holy religion, and faithfully call on thy blessed name, are thy sons and heirs of everlasting glory: yet as all the members of a body have not one office, so likewise we being many, and making one body (whereof thy dearly beloved Son is the head), have not all one gift, neither are we all called to one office, but as it hath pleased thee to distribute, so receive we: We therefore most humbly pray thee to send the spirit of love with concord among us, that without any disorder or debate every one of us may be content with our calling, quietly live in the same, study to do good unto all men by the true and diligent exercise thereof, without too much seeking of our own private gain, and so order our life in all points according to thy godly will, that by well doing we may stop the mouths of such foolish and ignorant people as report us to be evil doers, and cause them through our good works to glorify thee our Lord God in the day of visitation. Amen.

A prayer meet for all men, and to be said at all times.

MOST merciful Father, grant me to covet with an ardent mind those things which may please thee, to search them wisely, to know them truly, and to fulfil them perfectly, to the laud and glory of thy name. Order my living so that I may do that which thou requirest of me, and give me grace that I may know it, and have will and power to do it, and that I may obtain those things which be most convenient for my soul. Gracious Lord, make my way sure and straight to thee, so that I fall not between prosperity and adversity; but that in prosperous things I may give thee thanks, and in adversity be patient, so that I be not lift up with the one, nor oppressed with the other: and that I may rejoice in nothing but that which moveth me to thee, nor to be sorry for nothing, but for those things which draw me from thee, desiring to please nobody, nor fearing to [dis-][1] please any besides thee. Most loving Father, let all worldly things be vile unto me for thee, and be thou my most special comfort above all. Let me not be merry with the joy that is without thee. And let me desire nothing besides thee. Let all labour delight me which is for thee, and let all the rest weary me which is not in thee. Make to lift up my heart oftentimes to thee; and when I fall, make me to think on thee, and be sorry with a steadfast purpose of amendment. Loving Lord, make me humble without feigning: merry without lightness: sad without mistrust: sober without dulness: true without doubleness: fearing thee, without desperation: trusting in thee, without presumption: telling my neighbours their faults meekly, without dissimulation: teaching them with words and examples, without any mockings: obedient without arguing: patient, without grudging: and pure without corruption. Give me also, I beseech thee, a waking spirit, that no curious thought withdraw me from thee. Let it be so strong, that no filthy affection draw me backward: so stable, that no tribulation break it. Grant me also to know thee: diligent to seek a godly conversation to please thee, and finally, hope to embrace thee, for the precious blood sake of that immaculate lamb, our only Saviour Jesu Christ: To whom with thee, O Father, and the Holy Ghost, three persons and one God, be all honour and glory, world without end. Amen.

General Prayers to be said.

¶ For the grace and favour of God.

WHOSOEVER liveth without thy grace and favour, O most gracious and favourable Lord, although for a time he walloweth in all kind of fleshly pleasures, and abound with so much worldly riches, yet is he nothing else but the wretched bond-slave of Satan, and the vile dunghill of sin. All his pleasure is extreme poison, all his wealth is nothing but plain beggary. For what felicity can there be, where thy grace and favour wanteth? But where thy grace and favour is present (though the devil roar, the world rage, the flesh swell) there is true blessedness, unfeigned pleasure and

[[1] dis, omitted in original.]

continual wealth. Pour down therefore thy heavenly grace and fatherly favour upon us, that we, being assured of thy favourable goodness towards us, may rejoice and glory in thee, and have merry hearts whensoever we be most assailed with any kind of adversity, be it poverty or sickness, loss of friends or persecution for thy name's sake, to whom be glory for ever. Amen.

For the gift of the Holy Ghost.

So frail is our nature, so vile is our flesh, so lewd is our heart, so corrupt are our affects, so wicked are all our thoughts even from our childhood upwards, that of ourselves we can neither think, breathe, speak, or do anything that is praiseworthy in thy sight, O heavenly Father: yea, except thou dost assist us with thy merciful goodness, all things are so far out of frame in us, that we see nothing present in ourselves but thy heavy displeasure and eternal damnation. Vouchsafe therefore, O sweet Father, to send thy Holy Spirit unto us, which may make us new creatures, put away from us all fleshly lusts, fill our hearts with new affects and spiritual motions, and so altogether renew us, both in body and soul, through his godly inspiration, that we may die unto old Adam, and live unto thee in newness of life, serving thee our Lord God in holiness and righteousness all the days of our life. Amen.

For the true knowledge of ourselves.

It is written in thy holy gospel, most loving Saviour, that thou camest into this world not to call the righteous, that is, such as justify themselves, but sinners unto repentance. Suffer me not therefore, O Lord, to be in the number of those justiciaries, which boasting their own righteousness, their own works, and merits, despise that righteousness that cometh by faith, which alone is allowable before thee. Give me grace to knowledge mine own self as I am, even the son of wrath by nature, a wretched sinner, and an unprofitable servant, and wholly to depend on thy merciful goodness with a strong and unshaken faith, that in this world thou mayest continually call me unto true repentance, seeing I continually sin, and in the world to come bring me unto everlasting glory. Amen.

For a pure and clean Heart.

THE heart of man naturally is lewd and unsearchable through the multitude of sins, which as in a stinking dunghill lie buried in it, insomuch that no man is able to say, My heart is clean, and I am clear from sin. Remove from me therefore, O heavenly Father, my lewd, stony, stubborn, stinking, and unfaithful heart. Create in me a clean heart, free from all noisome and ungodly thoughts. Breathe into my heart by thy Holy Spirit godly and spiritual motions, that out of the good treasure of the heart I may bring forth good things unto the praise and glory of thy name. Amen.

For a quiet Conscience.

THE wicked is like a raging sea which is never in quiet, neither is there any peace to the ungodly; but such as love thy law, O Lord, they have plenty of peace, they have quiet minds and contented consciences, which is the greatest treasure under the sun, given of thee to so many as seek it at thy hand with true faith and continual prayer. Give me, O Lord, that joyful jewel, even a quiet mind and a contented conscience, that I being free from the damnable accusations of Sathan, from the crafty persuasions of the world, from the subtle enticements of the flesh, from the heavy curse of the law, and fully persuaded of thy merciful goodness toward me through faith in thy Son Christ Jesu, may quietly serve thee both bodily and ghostly, in holiness and righteousness all the days of my life. Amen.

For Faith.

FORASMUCH as nothing pleaseth thee, that is done without Faith, appear it before the blind world never so beautiful and commendable, but is counted in thy sight sinful and damnable, yea, the self sin and damnation; this is most humbly to desire thee, O Father, for Christ's sake, to breathe into my heart by thy Holy Spirit this most precious and singular gift of Faith, which worketh by Charity; whereby also we are justified, and received into thy favour: that I truly believing in thee, and fully persuaded of the truth of thy holy word, may be made thy son and inheritor of everlasting glory, through Jesu Christ our Lord. Amen.

For Charity.

THY cognizance and badge, whereby thy disciples are known, O Lord and Saviour Jesu Christ, is Charity or love, which cometh out of a pure heart, and a good conscience, and of faith unfeigned. I pray thee, therefore, give me this Christian love and perfect charity, that I may love thee my Lord God with all my heart, with all my mind, with all my soul, and with all my strengths, doing alway of very love that only, which is pleasant in thy sight; again, that I may love my neighbour and christian brother as myself, wishing as well to him as to myself, and ready at all times to do for him whatsoever lieth in my power, that when we all shall stand before thy dreadful judging-place, I being known by thy badge, may be numbered among thy disciples, and so through thy mercy receive the reward of eternal glory. Amen.

For Patience.

WHEN thou livedst in this world, O LORD Christ, thou shewedst thyself a mere mirror of perfect patience, suffering quietly not only the spiteful words, but also cruel deeds of thy most cruel enemies, forgiving them and praying for them, which most tyrantlike handled thee. Give me grace, O most meek and loving Lamb of God, to follow this thy patience, quietly to bear the slanderous words of mine adversaries, patiently to suffer the cruel deeds of mine enemies, to forgive them, to pray for them, yea, to do good for them, and by no means to about once to avenge myself, but rather give place unto wrath, seeing that vengeance is thine, and thou wilt reward; seeing also that thou helpest them to their right that suffer wrong; that I thus patiently suffering all evils may afterward reign with thee in glory. Amen.

For Humility.

WHAT have we, O heavenly Father, that we have not received? Every good gift, and every perfect gift is from above, and cometh down from thee, which art the Father of lights. Seeing then all that we have is thine, whether it pertain to the body or to the soul, how can we be proud, and to boast ourselves of that which is none of our own; seeing also that as to give, so also to take away again thou art able and wilt, whensoever thy gifts be abused, and thou not knowledged to be the giver of them? Take therefore away from me all pride and haughtiness of mind, graff in me true humility, that I may knowledge thee the giver of all good things, be thankful unto thee for them, and use them unto thy glory and the profit of my neighbour. Grant also that all my glory and rejoicing may be in no earthly creatures, but in thee alone, which dost mercy, equity, and righteousness upon earth. To thee alone be all glory. Amen.

For Mercifulness.

THY dearly beloved Son in his holy gospel exhorteth us to be merciful, even as thou our heavenly Father art merciful, and promisest that if we be merciful to other, we shall obtain mercy of thee, which art the Father of mercies, and God of all consolation. Grant therefore that, forasmuch as thou art our father, and we thy children, we may resemble thee in all our life and conversation; and that as thou art beneficial and liberal, not only to the good, but also to the evil, so we likewise may shew ourselves merciful, gentle, and liberal to so many as have need of our help, that at the dreadful day of doom we may be found in the number of those merciful, whom thou shalt appoint by thy only begotten Son to go into everlasting life, to whom with thee, and the Holy Ghost, be all honour and praise. Amen.

For true Godliness.

IN thy law, O thou Maker of heaven and earth, thou hast appointed us a way to walk in, and hast commanded that we should turn neither on the right hand, nor on the left, but do according to thy good will and pleasure, without adding of our own good intents and fleshly imaginations. As thou hast commanded, so give me grace, good Lord, to do. Let me neither follow mine own will, nor the fancies of other men; neither let me be beguiled with the vizor of old customs, long usages, fathers' decrees, ancient laws, nor any other thing that fighteth with thy holy ordinances and blessed commandments; but faithfully believe and steadfastly confess that to be the true godliness which is learned in thy holy Bible, and according unto that to order my[1] life, unto the praise of thy holy name. Amen.

For the true understanding of God's word.

O LORD, as thou alone art the Author of the holy scriptures, so likewise can no man, although he be never so wise, politic and learned, understand them, except he be taught by thy Holy Spirit, which alone is the Schoolmaster to lead the faithful into all truth. Vouchsafe therefore, I most humbly beseech thee, to breathe into my heart thy blessed Spirit, which may renew the senses of my mind, open my wits, reveal unto me the true understanding of thy holy mysteries, and plant in me such a certain and infallible knowledge of thy truth, that no subtle persuasion of man's wisdom may pluck me from thy truth, but that, as I have learned the true understanding of thy blessed will, so I may remain in the same continually, come life, come death, unto the glory of thy blessed name. Amen.

For a life agreeable to our knowledge.

As I have prayed unto thee, O heavenly Father, to be taught the true understanding of thy blessed word by thy Holy Spirit, so I most entirely beseech thee to give me grace to lead a life agreeable to my knowledge. Suffer me not to be of the number of them, which profess that they know God with their mouth, but deny him with their deeds. Let me not be like unto that son which said unto his father, that he would labour in his vineyard, and yet laboured nothing at all, but went abroad loitering idly. Make me rather like unto that good and fruitful land, which yieldeth again her seed with great increase, that men seeing my good works, may glorify thee, my heavenly Father. Amen.

For the health of the Body.

I FEEL in myself, O merciful Saviour, how grievous a prison this my body is unto my soul, which continually wisheth to be loosed out of this vile carcase and to come unto thee,

[[1] In the copy *thy*.]

seeing it hath here no rest, but is at every hour vexed with the filthy lusts of the flesh, with the wicked assaults of the devil and the world, and is never at quiet, but alway in danger to be overcome of her enemies, were it not preserved of thy goodness by the mystery and service-doing of thy holy Angels. Notwithstanding, O most loving Lord, forasmuch as it is thy good pleasure that my body and soul shall still remain here together as yet in this vale of misery, I beseech thee to preserve my soul from all vice, and my body from all sickness, that I enjoying through thy benefit the health both of body and soul, may be the more able to serve thee, and my neighbour, in such works as are acceptable in thy sight. Amen.

For a good name.

NOTHING become the professor of thy name better, O heavenly Father, than so to behave himself according to his profession, that he may be well reported of them that be of the household of faith. Yea, such sincerity and pureness of life ought to be in them which profess thy holy name, that the very adversaries of thy truth should be ashamed once to mutter against them. Give me grace therefore, I most entirely desire thee, so to frame my life according to the rule of thy blessed word, that I may give no occasion to speak evil of me, but rather so live in my vocation, that I may be an example to other to live godly and virtuously, unto the honour and praise of thy glorious name. Amen.

For a competent living.

ALTHOUGH I doubt not of thy fatherly provision for this my poor and needy life, yet forasmuch as thou hast both commanded and taught me by thy dear Son to pray unto thee for things necessary for this my life, I am bold at this present to come unto thy divine majesty, most humbly beseeching thee, that as thou hast given me life, so thou wilt give me meat and drink to sustain the same: again, as thou hast given me a body, so thou wilt give me clothes to cover it, that I having sufficient for my living, may the more freely and with the quieter mind apply myself unto thy service and honour. Amen.

For a patient and thankful heart in sickness.

WHOM thou lovest, O Lord, him dost thou chasten, yea, every son that thou receivest, thou scourgest, and in so doing thou offerest thyself unto him, as a father unto his son. For what son is whom the father chasteneth not? Grant therefore, I most heartily pray thee, that whensoever thou layest thy cross on me, and visitest me with thy loving scourge of sickness, I may by no means strive against thy fatherly pleasure, but patiently and thankfully abide thy chastisement, ever being persuaded, that it is for the health both of my body and soul, and that by this means thou workest my salvation, subduest the flesh unto the spirit, and makest me a new creature, that I may hereafter serve thee the more freely, and continue in thy fear unto my life's end. Amen.

For strength against the devil, the world, and the flesh.

O LORD God, the devil goeth about like a roaring lion, seeking whom he may devour. The flesh lusteth against the spirit. The world persuadeth unto vanities that we may forget thee our Lord God, and so for ever be damned. Thus are we miserably on every side besieged of cruel and unrestful enemies, and like at every moment to perish, if we be not defended with thy godly power against their tyranny. I therefore, poor and wretched sinner, despairing of my own strength, which indeed is none, most heartily pray thee to endue me with strength from above, that I may be able, through thy help, with strong faith to resist Sathan, with fervent prayer to mortify the raging lusts of the flesh, with continual meditation of thy holy law to avoid the foolish vanities and transitory pleasures of this wicked world, that I through thy grace being set at liberty from the power of mine enemies, may live and serve thee in holiness and righteousness all the days of my life. Amen.

For the help of God's holy Angels.

AN infinite number of wicked Angels are there, O Lord Christ, which without ceasing seek my destruction. Against this exceeding great multitude of evil spirits send thou me thy blessed and heavenly Angels, which may pitch their tents round about me, and so deliver me from their tyranny. Thou, O God, hast devoured hell, and overcome the prince of darkness with all his ministers: yea, and that not for thyself, but for them that believe in thee. Suffer me not therefore to be overcome of Sathan, nor of his servants, but rather let me triumph over them, that I through strong faith and the help of thy blessed Angels having the victory of the hellish army, may with a joyful heart say: Death, where is thy sting? Hell, where is thy victory? And so for ever and ever magnify thy holy name. Amen.

For the glory of heaven.

THE joys, O Lord, which thou hast prepared for them that love thee, no eye hath seen, no ear hath heard, neither is any heart able to think. But as the joys are great and unspeakable, so are there few that do enjoy them: for strait is the gate, and narrow is the way, which leadeth unto life, and few there be that find it. Notwithstanding, O heavenly Father, thou hast a little flock to whom it is thy pleasure to give the glorious kingdom of heaven. There is a certain number of sheep, that hear thy voice, whom no man is able to pluck out of thy hand, which shall never perish, to whom also thou shalt give eternal life. Make me therefore, O Lord, of that number, whom thou from everlasting hast predestinate to be saved, whose names also are written in the book of life. Pluck me out of the company of the stinking goats, which shall stand on thy left hand and be damned, and place me among those thy sheep, which shall stand on thy right hand and be saved. Grant me this, O merciful Father, for thy dear Son's sake, Jesus Christ our Lord. So shall I, enjoying this singular benefit at thy hand, and being placed in thy glorious kingdom, sing perpetual praises to thy godly majesty, which livest and reignest with thy dearly beloved Son, and the Holy Ghost, one true and everlasting God, world without end. Amen.

¶ *A Thanksgiving unto God for all his benefits.*

THY benefits toward me, O most loving Father, are so great and infinite, whether I have respect unto my body or unto my soul, that I find not in myself how to recompense any part of thine unspeakable goodness toward me. But thou, which needest none of my goods, knowing our beggary, yea, our nothing, requirest of us for a recompence of thy kindness only the sacrifice of praise and thanksgiving. O Lord and merciful Father, what worthy thanks am I, poor and wretched sinner, able to give thee? Notwithstanding trusting on thy mercy and favourable kindness, I offer unto thee in the name of Christ the sacrifice of praise, ever thanking thee most heartily for all thy benefits, which thou hast bestowed upon me thine unprofitable servant from the beginning of my life unto this present hour, most humbly beseeching thee to continue thy loving kindness toward me, and to give me grace so to walk worthy of this thy fatherly goodness, that when thou shalt call me out of this careful life, I may enjoy that most singular and last benefit, which is everlasting glory, through Jesus Christ our Lord, to whom with thee and the Holy Ghost be all honour and praise for ever and ever. Amen.

A Prayer necessary to be said at all times.

O BOUNTIFUL Jesu, O sweet Saviour, O Christ the Son of God, have pity upon me, mercifully hear me, and despise not my prayers. Thou hast created me of nothing, thou hast redeemed me from the bondage of sin, death, and hell, neither with gold or silver, but with thy most precious body once offered upon the Cross, and thine own blood shed once for all, for my ransom: therefore cast me not away whom thou by thy great wisdom hast made; despise me not, whom thou hast redeemed with such a precious treasure: nor let my wickedness destroy that which thy goodness hath builded. Now whiles I live, O Jesu, have mercy on me; for if I die out of thy favour, it will be too late afterward to call for thy mercy: whiles I have time to repent, look upon me with thy merciful eyes, as thou didst vouchsafe to look upon Peter thine Apostle, that I may bewail my sinful life, and obtain thy favour, and die therein. I acknowledge, that if thou shouldest deal with me according to very justice, I have deserved everlasting death. Therefore I appeal to thy high throne of mercy, trusting to obtain God's favour, not for my merits, but for thy merits, O Jesu, who hast given thyself an acceptable sacrifice to thy Father to please his wrath, and to bring all sinners truly repenting and amending their evil life into his favour again. Accept me, O Lord, among the number of them that shall be saved, forgive my sins, give me grace to lead a godly and innocent life, grant me thy heavenly wisdom, inspire my heart with faith, hope, and charity, give me grace to be humble in prosperity, patient in adversity, obedient unto my rulers, faithful unto them that trust me, dealing truly with all men, to live chastely in wedlock, to abhor adultery, fornication, and all uncleanness, to do good after my power unto all men, to hurt no man, that thy name may be glorified in me during this present life, and that I afterward may obtain everlasting life, through thy mercy and the merits of thy passion. Amen.

A Prayer of Jeremy. Jeremy xxxi.

O LORD, thou hast correct me, and thy chastening have I received as an untamed calf. Convert thou me, and I shall be converted: for thou art my Lord God: yea, as soon as thou turnest me, I shall reform myself: and when I understand I shall smite upon my thigh, for verily I have committed shameful things: oh let my youth bear his reproof and confusion. Amen.

A Prayer when we are punished of God for our sins or trial.

O LORD, thou art righteous, and all thy judgments are true: Yea, all thy ways are mercy, faithfulness, and judgment. And now, O Lord, be mindful of me, and take no vengeance of my sins, neither remember the misdeeds of mine elders. For we have not been obedient unto thy commandments. Therefore are we spoiled, brought into captivity, into death, into derision and shame unto all nations, among whom thou scattered us. And now, O Lord, thy judgments are great, for we have not done according to thy commandments, neither have walked innocently before thee: and now, O Lord, deal with me according to thy will, and command my spirit to be received in peace; for more expedient were it for me to die than to live.

A Prayer of Jeremy. Jeremy xvii.

HEAL me, O Lord, and I shall be whole: Save thou me, and I shall be saved: for thou art my praise. Behold, these men say unto me, Where is the word of the Lord? let it now come: whereas I nevertheless, leading the flock in thy ways, have compelled none by violence, for I never desired any man's death: this knowest thou well, my words also were right before thee: be not terrible unto me, O Lord, for thou art he in whom I hope when I am in peril. Let my persecutors be confounded, but not me: let them be defrauded, and not me. Thou shalt bring upon them the time of their plague, and shalt destroy them right sore. Amen.

The Blessing and Thanksgiving that Toby the elder thanked God with, at the end of his life. Toby xiii. a.

GREAT art thou, Lord God, for evermore, and thy kingdom world without end: for thou scourgest and healest: thou leadest unto hell, and bringest out again, and there is none that may escape thy hand. O give thanks unto the Lord, ye children of Israel, and praise him in the sight of the heathen; for among the heathen, which know him not, hath he scattered you, to the intent that ye should shew forth his miraculous works, and cause them for to know that there is none other God Almighty but he. He hath chastened us for our misdeeds, and for his own mercies' sake shall he save us. Consider then how he hath dealt with you, and praise him with fear and dread, and magnify the everlasting King in your works. I will praise him even in the land of my captivity, for he hath shewed his majesty unto us a sinful people. Turn you therefore, O ye sinners, and do righteousness before God, and be ye sure that he will shew his mercy upon you. As for me and my soul, we will rejoice in God. O praise the Lord, all ye his chosen, hold the days of gladness, and be thankful unto him.

A Prayer of Salomon, for sufficing of livelihood. Prov. xxx. a.

Two things I require of thee, that thou wilt not deny me before I die: remove from me vanity and lies. Give me neither poverty nor riches, only grant me a necessary living: lest if I be too full, I deny thee and say, What fellow is the Lord? and lest I, being constrained through poverty, fall into stealing, and forswear the name of my God.

A Prayer of Nehemias before God, for the sins of the People. 2 Esdras i. a.

Lord God of heaven, thou great and terrible God, thou that keepest covenant and mercy for them that love thee, and observe thy commandments: Let thine ears mark, I beseech thee, and let thine eyes be open, that thou mayest hear the prayer of thy servant, which I pray now before thee day and night for the children of Israel thy servants, and knowledge the sins of the children of Israel, which we have committed against thee. And I and my father's house have sinned also: we have been corrupt unto thee, in that we have not kept the commandments, laws, and statutes which thou commandest thy servant Moses. Yet call to mind the word that thou commandest thy servant Moses, and saidst: If ye transgress, then will I cast you abroad among the nations; but if ye turn unto me, and keep my commandments, and do them, though ye were cast out unto the utmost part of heaven, yet will I gather you from thence, even unto the place that I have chosen for my name, to dwell there. They are thy servants and thy people, whom thou hast delivered through thy great power and mighty hand. O Lord, let thine ears mark the prayer of thy servant, and the prayer of thy servants whose desire is to fear thy name. Amen.

A Prayer for Sin, which Jeremy teacheth the Israelites to say. Jeremy iii. e.

Lo, we turn unto thee, we are thine, for thou art the Lord our God. The hills fall, and the pride of the mountains: but the salvation of Israel standeth only upon God our Lord. Confusion hath devoured our fathers' labour from our youth up: yea, their sheep and bullocks, their sons and daughters. So do we also sleep in our confusion, and shame covereth us: for we and our fathers from our youth up, unto this day, have sinned against the Lord our God, and have not obeyed the voice of the Lord our God. Amen.

A Prayer in prosperity.

Most merciful Father, which hast of thy gracious mercy, without my deserving, endued me abundantly with many gracious gifts, both spiritually and bodily, and hast hitherto preserved me from innumerable perils and dangers, both of soul and body, and hast at this present bestowed upon me bodily health, wealth, and abundance of worldly substance, I most heartily thank thee: beseeching thee most humbly, so to illuminate my mind that I may in all things be thankful unto thee for thy great benefits, and also during my life may freely bestow thy gracious gifts, to the glorifying of thy holy name, the advancement of thy honour, and profit of my neighbour. Grant this, most merciful Father, for thy Son Jesus Christ's sake, our only Saviour and Mediator. Amen.

A Prayer in adversity.

ALMIGHTY God, which for mine ingratitude and sinful life hast worthily punished me with much affliction and adversity, I most humbly beseech thee, to give me grace utterly to detest and abhor my former wretched and sinful life, and to study daily for the amendment of the same, and that I may fully be persuaded that this affliction hath not chanced to me by casualty or misfortune, but by thy foreknowledge, counsel, permission, and determinate pleasure, and that thou beatest me with this thy rod of fatherly correction, not to the intent to cast me clean out of thy favour, but because thou wouldst thereby nurture me and reclaim me to unfeigned repentance for my former life, to be more circumspect of godly life hereafter, to exercise my faith in thy godly promises, to try me whether I will be patient and constant in adversity, to make me abhor the vain pleasures of this life, and finally with fervent and continual desire to long for the life everlasting. Wherefore I most heartily pray thee, vouchsafe to increase and strengthen my faith, hope, charity and meekness, and that I may without murmur or grutch[1] patiently bear this thy fatherly chastisement, specially grant me that I may daily more and more increase in fervent love towards thee. For thy holy word saith, that to them that love God all things shall happen for the best, whether it be prosperity or adversity, health or sickness, life or death. In consideration whereof, I submit me wholly to thee, and fully surrender and resign all my will to thy most godly will and pleasure, which I nothing doubt shall end this mine affliction so as shall be most meetest and agreeable to thine honour and glory, and to my

[1 The old form of *grudge.*]

most perfect wealth and everlasting salvation, through Jesus' Christ, our only Saviour, Redeemer, Advocate, and Mediator. So be it.

A Prayer to be said when the sick person is joyful and glad to die.

O LORD Jesu Christ, I beseech thy mercy and goodness, that thou wilt strengthen and conduct my soul in the great journey which approacheth unto me. I believe that thou, for my sake, didst die and rise again, and that thou through thy mercy shalt forgive me all my sins, and that thou hast promised me everlasting life. Of this my belief, O Lord, shalt thou be witness with all thine elect. This shall also be my last will, in this faith, O Lord, do I die upon thine incomparable mercy. And if through pain or smart, impatience, or other temptation, I should or would shrink from this faith, O Lord, I beseech thee let me not stick in such unbelief and blasphemy, but strengthen and increase my faith, to the intent that sin, hell, and the devil may not hurt me. For thou art stronger and mightier than all they: to this do I stedfastly trust; Lord, let me not be confounded. Amen.

A Prayer.

LAUD, honour, and thanks be unto thee, most merciful Lord Jesu Christ, for thy holy incarnation, for thy pains and bitter passion, through the which I know that thou art my Redeemer and Saviour, and believe that thou hast overcome sin, hell, and the devil, so that they cannot hurt me: to this do I only trust, upon this do I build, upon this standeth all my hope, in this trust and confidence will I be found. Only, O Lord, be propitious and merciful unto me, even as I, according to thy faithful promises, do nothing doubt. O Lord, leave me not in this great distress, but deliver me from evil. Amen.

A Prayer for them that lie in extreme pangs of death.

O PITIFUL Physician and healer both of body and soul, Christ Jesu, vouchsafe to cast thy merciful eyes upon thy poor and sinful creature, *N. M.*, who lieth here captive, and

[DOCUMENTS, EDW. VI.]

bound with sickness, turning his weakness to thy glory, and to his health. And vouchsafe, good Lord, to send him patience and sufferance, that he may stedfastly continue to the end; and that he may, with a true, and perfect faith, fight manfully against all temptations of the devil, when he may no longer continue. So be it.

A general exhortation unto all men.

THOU shalt reprehend thy brother when he sinneth, lest his offence come over all men. Be ye all of one mind, one suffer with another, love as brethren, be pitiful, be courteous. Recompense not evil for evil, neither rebuke for rebuke, but contrariwise bless, and know that ye are called thereto, even that ye should be heirs of the blessing. For whoso listeth to live, and would fain see good days, let him refrain his tongue from evil, and his lips that they speak no guile. Let him eschew evil and do good. Let him seek peace and ensue it. For the eyes of the Lord are over the righteous, and his ears are open unto their prayers. But the face of the Lord beholdeth them that do evil.

The oration of Job in his most grievous adversity and loss of goods.

NAKED came I out of my mother's womb, and naked shall I turn again. The Lord gave, and the Lord hath taken away; as it hath pleased the Lord, so is it done: now blessed be the name of the Lord.

Exod. xxiii.
Acts xxiii. a.
Pro. xxiv. a.
and xx.
The rulers of the people shalt thou not blaspheme. Fear the Lord and the King, and keep no company with the slanderers, for their destruction shall come suddenly.

¶ Thanks be given unto God, Obedience unto our prince, And love to our neighbours.

FINIS.

THE TABLE.

THE CONTENTS

OF THIS

PRIMER OR BOOK OF PRIVATE PRAYER.

¶ Rules declaring the order of the Kalendar, and the right understanding of it.
¶ Rules to find the Prime, or golden number, and the Sunday's letter.
¶ A Kalendar declaring the day, hour, and minute of the changing of the moon.
¶ The Catechism with divers and sundry Graces.
¶ A Preparative unto prayer with a Prayer concerning the same.
¶ A Prayer to be said at the uprising in the morning.
¶ Another Prayer to be said at thy going to bed.
¶ An Order of private prayer for Morning and Evening.
¶ Sentences of holy scripture for an entrance to unfeigned repentance.
¶ A Confession of sins.
¶ A prayer containing the absolution of sin.
¶ Morning prayer on Sunday.
¶ The Litany with good prayers for many necessary things.
¶ Evening prayer on Sunday.
¶ A Rule for the order of prayer in the week days.
¶ Proper Psalms and Lessons for Morning and Evening prayer on Monday.
¶ Proper Psalms and Lessons for Morning and Evening prayer on Tuesday.
¶ Proper Psalms and Lessons for Morning and Evening prayer on Wednesday.

¶ Proper Psalms and Lessons for Morning and Evening prayer on Thursday.
¶ Proper Psalms and Lessons for Morning and Evening prayer on Friday.
¶ Proper Psalms and Lessons for Morning and Evening prayer on Saturday.
¶ Collects for Sundays and holy days through all the year.
¶ Sundry godly prayers for divers purposes.
¶ Three godly prayers for the King, our sovereign Lord.
¶ For the King's Council.
¶ For Judges.
¶ For Bishops, spiritual Pastors, and Ministers of God's word.
¶ For Gentlemen.
¶ For Landlords.
¶ For Merchants.
¶ For Lawyers.
¶ For Labourers and men of occupations.
¶ For Rich men.
¶ For Poor people.
¶ The prayer of a true subject.
¶ The prayer of Fathers and Mothers.
¶ The prayer of Children.
¶ A prayer of Masters.
¶ The prayer of Servants.
¶ The prayer of Maidens.
¶ A prayer of Single Men.
¶ The prayer of Husbands.
¶ The prayer of Wives.
¶ The prayer of Householders.

¶ A prayer to be said of all Christians.
¶ A prayer meet for all men and to be said at any time.
¶ General prayers to be said—
¶ For to obtain the grace and favour of God.
¶ For the gift of the Holy Ghost.
¶ For the true knowledge of ourselves.
¶ For a pure and clean heart.
¶ For a quiet conscience.
¶ For the gracious gift of true faith.
¶ For charity.
¶ For patience.
¶ For humility.
¶ For mercifulness.
¶ For true godliness.
¶ For the true understanding of God's word.
¶ For a life agreeable to our knowledge.
¶ For health of the body.
¶ For a good name.
¶ For a competent living.
¶ For a patient and thankful heart in sickness.
¶ For strength against the devil, the world, and the flesh.
¶ For the help of God's holy Angels.
¶ For the glory of heaven.
¶ A thanksgiving to God for all his benefits.
¶ A prayer necessary to be said at all times.
¶ A prayer of Jeremy. Jere. xxxi.
¶ A prayer when we are punished for our sins or trial.
¶ A prayer of Jeremy. Jere. xvii.
¶ The blessing and thanksgiving of Toby the elder, thanked God with at the end of his life. Toby xiii.
¶ A prayer of Salomon for sufficience of livelihood. Prov. xxx.
¶ A prayer of Nehemias before God for the people's sins. 2 Esdras i. a.
¶ A prayer for sin which Jeremy teacheth the Israelites to say. Jere. iii. e.
¶ A prayer in prosperity.
¶ A prayer in adversity.
¶ A prayer to be said when the sick person is joyful and glad to die.
¶ A prayer for sure trust in God.
¶ A prayer for them that lie in extreme pangs of death.
¶ A general exhortation unto all men.
¶ An oration of Job in his most grievous adversity.

FINIS.

¶ These bookes are to be solde, at the weste ende of Paules towarde Ludgate, at the sygne of the Hedgehogge.

A SHORT CATECHISM;

OR,

PLAIN INSTRUCTION,

CONTAINING

THE SUM OF CHRISTIAN LEARNING,

SET FORTH BY

THE KING'S MAJESTY'S AUTHORITY,

FOR ALL

SCHOOLMASTERS TO TEACH.

1553.

A SHORT

Catechisme, or playne in-
struction, conteynynge the
summe of Christian learninge, sett
fourth by the Kings maiesties
authoritie, for all Schole-
maisters to teache.

To thys Catechisme are
adioyned the Articles agreed upon by the Bishoppes and other learned and godly men, in the last conuocation
at London, in the yeare of our Lorde, M.
D.LII, for to roote out the discord of
ot opinions, and stablish the agre-
ment of trew religion: Like-
wyse publisshed by the
Kinges maiesties
authoritie.

1553.

Imprinted at London by Ihon
Day with the kinges most gracious licence
and priuiledge: Forbidding all other
to print the same Catechisme.

[The copy of this edition, which has been followed, is in the possession of the Right Honourable Thomas Grenville, London.]

¶ *The copy of the King's Majesty's letters Patents for the Printing of this and the little Catechism.*

EDWARD the sixth by the grace of God King of England, France and Ireland, Defender of the Faith, and of the church of England and also of Ireland in earth the supreme head.

TO all manner of Printers, Booksellers, and other our Officers, Ministers and Subjects greeting.

We do you to understand, that of our grace especial, we have granted and given privilege and licence, and by these presents do grant and give privilege and licence, to our wellbeloved subject John Daye, of our City of London Printer, unto his factors and assigns, to Print, or cause to be printed, as well this Catechism in English, which we have caused to be set forth for the better instruction of youth, to be taught in English Schools, as also an A. B. C. with the Brief Catechism, already printed, any other privilege to the contrary in anywise notwithstanding.

AND furthermore our pleasure is that the same John Day, his factors and assigns, shall and may have the only printing from time to time of the same Catechisms, in recompense of his industry pains and charges to be sustained in that behalf. ¶ Straitly forbidding by these presents all and singular our subjects, as well printers as booksellers, as all other persons within our Realms and dominions whatsoever they be, to print, or cause to be printed, within any our said dominions, these Catechisms aforesaid, or any of them, but only the said John Day, and his assigns, neither to buy any other sorts of impressions than such as shall be printed by the said John Day and his assigns, upon pain of our high displeasure, and that every offender therein shall forfeit to our use xl s. for every such catechism, so printed, or bought, contrary to the true meaning of this our present licence and privilege, over and besides all such catechisms to be forfeited to whomsoever shall sustain the charges and sue the said forfeiture in our behalf.

¶ Willing therefore and commanding all our officers and ministers as they tender our favour and will avoid our displeasure and indignation for the contrary, that they and every one of them (if need shall require) do aid and assist the foresaid John Day, his factors and assigns, in due exercising and execution of this our present licence and privilege with the effect according to the true meaning of the same. In witness whereof we caused these our letters to be made patents. Witness ourself at Westminster, the xxv. day of March, the vii. year of our Reign.

THE TABLE.

A.
Absent.
Christ governeth his church absent, 506.
How Christ is absent, and present in the world, 506.

Adam.
The names of Adam and Eve, 502.

Advoutry.
Advoutry, 498.

Ascension.
Christ's ascension, 506.
Our profit by Christ's ascension, 508.
Causes of Christ's ascension, 508.

B.
Baptism.
The ministration of baptism, 516.
The meaning of baptism, 517.

Bread.
The bread, 517.
Our daily bread, 521.
What bread meaneth, 521.
Daily bread or supernatural, 521.
Why we ask our bread to be daily, 521.

Brother.
The name of brethren, 524.

C.
Ceremonies.
Ceremonies of the law, 500.

Charity.
Charity, 524.
Degrees of charity, 525.

Children.
Children to be taught true religion, 495.

Church.
The church, 513.
Christ governeth his Church absent, 506.
The holy Church, 511.
Who be of Christ's church, 511.
Marks of the Church, 513.
Why the Church is called universal, 515.

Christ.
Christ's doings for our behoof, 509.
Christ an example of life unto us, 509.
Honour of Christ, 510.
Christ's benefits to us, 524.

Communion.
Communion of Saints, 514.

Contention.
The harms of contention, 522.

Covenant.
God's covenants, 503.
Our covenant with God: as we forgive, &c., 522.

Covetise.
Covetise of another's, 498.

Creed.
The Creed, 496, and 500.
Why the Creed is called a symbol, 496.

D.
Death.
Christ's death, 504.

Doom.
The day of doom, 511.

Epiousion.
Epiousion, 521.

E.

Eve.
The names of Adam and Eve, 502.

Example.
Christ an example of life unto us, 509.

F.

Faith.
Justification by faith, 512.
True faith and works inseparate, 513.
Faith the mouth of the soul, 517.
Faith in prayer, 523.

Father.
Why we call God father, 501.
What we gather of (our Father,) 519.

Feed.
How we feed upon Christ's body and blood, 517.

Forgiveness.
Forgiveness of trespasses, 521.
Charitable forgiveness one to another ceaseth brawls, 522.

G.

God.
What God is, 496.
One God, 497.
Taking the name of God, 497.
God is each where, 519.
God alway present to help us, 520.
Knowledge, desire, fear, and love of God, 524.

Godlessness.
Godlessness, 524.

Godly.
The bliss of the Godly, 525.

Good.
Good, not evil, to be rendered for evil, 522.

Gospel.
The law and the gospel, 496.

H.

Hallow.
How God's name is to be hallowed, 520.

Heaven.
What is meant by (which art in heaven,) 519.

Holy Ghost.
The Holy Ghost, 514.
Why the Holy Ghost is called holy, 514.
Wherein resteth the Holy Ghost's sanctification, 514.

Honour.
Honour of Christ, 510.

Hypocrisy.
Superstition and hypocrisy, 524.

I.

Ignorance.
Ignorance brought in by corruption of nature, 499.

Image.
Images, 497.
The image that man was made after, 502.
God's image defaced in man, 502.

Justification.
Causes of our justification, 512.
Justification by faith, 512.

K.

Key.
Keys to bind and loose, 513.

Kingdom.
Christ's kingdom not yet perfect, 520.
Christ's kingdom, 520.
Why this is added: (for thine is the kingdom,) 523.

L.

Law.
The law and the gospel, 496.
Laws of the first table, 497.

Laws of the second table, 497.
The sum of the law by Christ, 499.
Why the law was written in tables, 499.
None made righteous by the law, 500.
Why the law was given to one people, 500.
The moral law common to all, 500.

Life.
Honest frame of life, 523.

M.

Man.
The making of man, 501.
The image that man was made after, 502.
Man's fall, 502.

Measure.
Measure another by thyself, 524.

Mouth.
Faith the mouth of the soul, 517.

Murther.
Murther, 497.

N.

Nature.
The law of nature, 499 and 524.

O.

Original Sin.
Original sin, 503.

P.

Parents.
Honour of parents, 497.

Passion.
Christ's passion, 504.

Prayer.
Prayer, 518.
The Lord's prayer, 518.
Whether we may use any other prayer but the Pater noster, 518.
Nothing in the Lord's prayer hard to understand, 519.

Faith in prayer, 523.
What to be asked in prayer, 523.

Preacher.
Office of preachers, 518.

Presence.
Christ's bodily presence, 507.

Present.
How Christ is absent and present in the world, 506.
God alway present to help us, 520.

Profession.
All Christians should know their profession, 495.

Q.

Question.
Teaching by questions, 495.

R.

Redemption.
The means of redemption, 503.

Religion.
Children to be taught true religion, 495.
Christian religion, 495.
Parts of Christian religion, 496.

Resurrection.
Christ's resurrection, 504.
The resurrection of Christ necessary, 505.
The resurrection, 511.

Reward.
The reward of the godly and ungodly, 498.

Righteous.
None made righteous by the law, 500.

S.

Sabbath.
The Sabbath, 497 and 515.

Sacrament.
What sacraments are, 516.

Sanctification.
Wherein resteth the Holy Ghost's sanctification, 514.

Scripture.
The Scriptures preserved from the beginning, 496.

Seed.
The Seed of the woman, 503.

Serpent.
The Serpent's head, 503.

Service.
Parts of God's true inward service, 515.
Outward service of God, 516.

Sin.
Sins forgiven by Christ's death only, 500.

Sun.
Christ compared to the Sun, 507.

Spirit.
The Spirit sent down, 504.

Superstition.
Superstition and hypocrisy, 524.

Supper.
The use of the Lord's Supper, 516.
The meaning of the Lord's Supper, 517.

Symbol.
Why the Creed is called a Symbol, 496.

T.

Table.
Laws of the first table, 497.
Laws of the second table, 497.
Why the law was written in tables, 499.

Tentation.
Tentation, 522.

Theft.
Theft, 498.

V.

Vice.
Vices to be rooted out, that virtues may be planted in their place, 525.

Universal.
Why the church is called universal, 515.

W.

Weakness.
Our weakness, 522.

Will.
God's will be done, 521.

Wine.
The wine, 517.

Witness.
False witness, 498.

Work.
True faith and works unseparate, 513.

World.
The making and preservation of the world, 501.
The end of the world, 510.

¶ The end of the Table.

AN INJUNCTION

Given by the king our sovereign Lord his most excellent majesty to all schoolmasters and teachers of youth, within all his Grace's realm and dominions, for authorizing and establishing the use of this Catechism.

EDWARD the Sixth, by the grace of God king of England, France and Ireland: defender of the faith and of the church of England and also of Ireland in earth the Supreme head: To all Schoolmasters and teachers of youth.

¶ When there was presented unto us, to be perused, a short and plain order of Catechism written by a certain godly and learned man: we committed the debating, and diligent examination thereof, to certain Bishops, and other learned men, whose judgment we have in great estimation. And because it seemed agreeable with the scriptures, and the ordinances of our Realm, we thought it good, not only for that agreement to put it forth abroad to print; but also, for the plainness and shortness, to appoint it out for all Schoolmasters to teach: that the yet unskilful and young age, having the foundations laid, both of religion and good letters, may learn godliness together with wisdom; and have a rule for the rest of their life, what judgment they ought to have of God, to whom all our life is applied; and how they may please God, wherein we ought, with all the doings and duties of our life, to travail.

¶ We will therefore and command, both all and each of you, as ye tender our favour, and as ye mind to avoid the just punishment of transgressing our authority, that ye truly and diligently teach this Catechism in your schools, immediately after the other brief Catechism which we have already set forth: that young age, yet tender and wavering, being by authority of good lessons and instructions of true religion stablished, may have a great furtherance to the right worshipping of God, and good helps to live in all points according to duty. Wherewith being furnished, by better using due godliness toward God, the author of all things; obedience toward their King, the shepherd of the people; loving affection to the common weal, the general mother of all; they may seem not born for themselves, but be profitable and dutiful, toward God, their King, and their country.

¶ Given at Greenwich, the xx. of May, the vii. year of our reign.

THE
CATECHISM.

It is the duty of them all, whom Christ hath redeemed by his death, that they not only be servants to obey, but also children to inherit: so to know which is the true trade of life, and that God liketh, that they may be able to answer to every demand of religion, and to render account of their faith and profession. *All Christians should know their profession.*

And this is the plainest way of teaching, which not only in philosophy Socrates, but also in our religion Apollinarius, hath used: that both by certain questions, as it were by pointing, the ignorant might be instructed; and the skilful put in remembrance, that they forget not what they have learned. We therefore having regard to the profit, which we ought to seek in teaching of youth; and also to shortness, that in our whole schooling there should be nothing, either overflowing or wanting; have conveyed the whole sum into a dialogue, that the matter itself might be the plainer to perceive, and we the less stray in other matters beside the purpose. Thus then beginneth the Master to appose his Scholar. *Teaching by questions.*

Master. Sith I know (dear son) that it is a great part of my duty, not only to see that thou be instructed in good letters, but also earnestly and diligently to examine what sort of religion thou followest, in this thy tender age: I thought it best to oppose thee by certain questions, to the intent I may perfectly know, whether thou hast well or ill travailed therein. Now therefore tell me (my son) what religion that is which thou professest. *Children to be taught true religion.*

Scholar. That, good master, do I profess, which is the religion of the Lord Christ: which in the xi. of the Acts is called the christian religion. *Christian religion.*

Master. Dost thou then confess thyself to be a follower of christian godliness and religion, and a scholar of our Lord Christ?

Scholar. That forsooth do I confess, and plainly and boldly profess: yea, therein I account the whole sum of all my glory, as in the thing which is both of more honour, than that the slenderness of my wit may attain unto it; and also more approaching to God's majesty, than that I, by any feat of utterance, may easily express it.

Master. Tell me then (dear son) as exactly as thou canst, in what points thou thinkest that the sum of christian religion standeth.

<small>Parts of Christian religion.</small>

Scholar. In two points, that is to say: true faith in God, and assured persuasion conceived of all those things, which are contained in the holy scriptures; and in charity, which belongeth both to God and to our neighbour.

Master. That faith which is conceived by hearing and reading of the word, what doth it teach thee concerning God?

<small>What God is.</small>

Scholar. This doth it principally teach: that there is one certain nature, one substance, one ghost and heavenly mind, or rather an everlasting Spirit, without beginning or ending, which we call God: whom all the people of the world ought to worship, with sovereign honour, and the highest kind of reverence. Moreover out of the holy words of GOD, which by the prophets and the beloved of almighty God are in the holy books published, to the eternal glory of his name, I learn the law and the threatening thereof; then the promises and the gospel of God. These things, first written by Moses and other men of God, have been preserved whole and uncorrupted, even to our age: and since that, the chief articles of our faith have been gathered into a short abridgement, which is commonly called the Creed, or Symbol, of the Apostles.

<small>The law and the gospel.</small>

<small>The scriptures preserved from the beginning.</small>

<small>The Creed.</small>

Master. Why is this abridgement of the faith termed with the name of a symbol?

<small>Called a symbol.</small>

Scholar. A symbol is as much to say, as a sign, mark, privy token, or watchword, whereby the soldiers of one camp are known from their enemies. For this reason the abridgement of the faith, whereby the Christians are known from them that be no Christians, is rightly named a Symbol.

Master. First tell me somewhat, what thou thinkest of the law: and then afterward of the Creed or Symbol.

Scholar. I shall do (good master) with a good will as

you command me. The Lord God hath charged us by Moses, that we have none other God at all, but him; that is to say, that we take him alone for our one only God, our Maker and Saviour: that we reverence not, nor worship any portraiture or any image whatsoever, whether it be painted, carved, graven, or by any mean fashioned howsoever it be: that we take not the name of our Lord God in vain; that is, either in a matter of no weight or of no truth. Last of all this ought we to hold stedfastly and with devout conscience, that we keep holily and religiously the sabbath day; which was appointed out from the other for rest and service of God. *(Laws of the first table. One God. Images. Taking the name of God. The Sabbath.)*

Master. Very well. Now hast thou rehearsed unto me the laws of the first table: wherein is, in a sum, contained the knowledge and true service of God. Go forward and tell me, which be the duties of charity, and our love toward men.

Scholar. Do you ask me (master) what I think of the other part of the law, which is commonly called the second table? *(Laws of the second table.)*

Master. Thou sayest true, my son: that is it indeed that I would fain hear of.

Scholar. I will in few words dispatch it, as my simple wit will serve me. Moses hath knit it up in a short sum: that is, that with all loving affection we honour and reverence our father and mother; that we kill no man; that we commit no advoutry; that we steal nothing; that we bear false witness against none: last of all, that we covet nothing that is our neighbour's.

Master. How is that commandment, of the honouring father and mother, to be understanded?

Scholar. Honour of father and mother containeth love, fear, and reverence, yea, and it further standeth in obeying, succouring, defending, and nourishing them, if need require. It bindeth us also most humbly, and with most natural affection, to obey the magistrate, to reverence the ministers of the church, our schoolmasters, with all our elders, and betters. *(Honour of Parents.)*

Master. What is contained in that commandment, Do not kill? *(Murther.)*

Scholar. That we hate, wrong, or revile no man.

Moreover it commandeth us, that we love even our foes, do good to them that hate us, and that we pray for all prosperity and good hap to our very mortal enemies.

Master. The commandment of not committing advoutry, what thinkest thou it containeth?

Advoutry.   *Scholar.* Forsooth this commandment containeth many things; for it forbiddeth, not only to talk with another man's wife, or any other woman unchastely: but also to touch her, yea, or to cast an eye at her wantonly: or with lustful look to behold her: or by any unhonest mean to woo her: either ourselves, or any other in our behalf: finally, herein is debarred all kind of filthy and straying lust.

Master. What thinkest thou of the commandment, not to steal?

Theft.   *Scholar.* I shall shew you, as briefly as I have done the rest, if it please you to hear me. It commandeth us, to beguile no man: to occupy no unlawful wares: to envy no man his wealth: and to think nothing profitable, that either is not just, or differeth from right and honesty: briefly, rather willingly lose[1] that is thine own, than thou wrongfully take that is another's, and turn it to thine own commodity.

Master. How may that commandment be kept, of False witness. bearing no false witness?

Scholar. If we neither ourselves speak any false or vain lie: nor allow it in other, either by speech or silence, or by our present company. But we ought always to maintain truth, as place and time serveth.

Master. Now remaineth the last commandment, of not coveting any thing that is our neighbour's: what meaneth that?

Covetise of another's.   *Scholar.* This law doth generally forbid all sorts of evil lusts: and commandeth us to bridle and restrain all greedy unsatiable desire of our will, which holdeth not itself within the bounds of right and reason: and it willeth that each man be content with his estate. But whosoever coveteth more than right, with the loss of his neighbour, and wrong to another; he breaketh and bitterly looseth the bond of charity, and fellowship among men. Yea, and upon him The reward of (unless he amend) the Lord God, the most stern revenger of godly and ungodly. the breaking his law, shall execute most grievous punishment. On the other side, he that liveth according to the rule of

[1 leese, in the original.]

these laws, shall find both praise and bliss, and God also his merciful and bountiful good Lord.

Master. Thou hast shortly set out the ten commandments: Now then tell me, how all these things, that thou hast particularly declared, Christ hath in few words contained, setting forth unto us in a sum the whole pith of the law?

Scholar. Will you that I knit up in a brief abridgment all that belongeth both to God and to men?

Master. Yea.

Scholar. Christ saith thus: Thou shalt love the Lord, thy God, with all thy heart: with all thy soul: with all thy mind: and with all thy strength. This is the greatest commandment in the law. The other is like unto this: Thou shalt love thy neighbour as thyself. Upon these two commandments hang the whole law, and the Prophets. *[The sum of the law by Christ.]*

Master. I will now that thou tell me further, what law is that which thou speakest of; that which we call the law of nature? or some other besides? *[The law of nature.]*

Scholar. I remember, master, that I learned that of you long ago: that it was engraffed by God in the nature of man, while nature was yet sound and uncorrupted. But after the entrance of sin, although the wise were somewhat after a sort not utterly ignorant of that light of nature; yet was it by that time so hid from the greatest part of men, that they scant perceived any shadow thereof. *[Ignorance brought in by corruption of nature.]*

Master. What it the cause, that God willed it to be written out in tables; and that it should be privately appointed to one people alone?

Scholar. I will shew you. By original sin and evil custom, the image of God in man was so at the beginning darkened, and the judgment of nature so corrupted, that man himself doth not sufficiently understand, what difference is between honesty and dishonesty, right and wrong. The bountiful God therefore, minding to renew that image in us, first wrought this by the law written in tables, that we might know ourselves, and therein, as it were in a glass, behold the filth and spots of our soul, and stubborn hardness of a corrupted heart; that by this mean yet, acknowledging our sin, and perceiving the weakness of our flesh, and the wrath of God fiercely bent against us for sin, we might the more fervently long for our Saviour Christ Jesus; which by his *[Why the law was written in tables.]*

32—2

500 THE CATECHISM.

death and precious sprinkling of his blood hath cleansed and washed away our sins: pacified the wrath of the almighty Father: by the holy breath of his Spirit createth new hearts in us: and reneweth our minds after the image and likeness of their Creator, in true righteousness and holiness. Which thing neither the justice of the law, nor any sacrifices of Moses were able to perform. And that no man is made righteous by the law, it is evident: not only thereby, that the righteous liveth by faith; but also hereby, that no mortal man is able to fulfil all that the law of both the tables commandeth. For we have hindrances that strive against the law: as the weakness of the flesh: froward appetite, and lust naturally engendered. As for sacrifice, cleansings, washings, and other ceremonies of the law: they were but shadows, likenesses, images and figures of the true and everlasting sacrifice of Jesus Christ, done upon the cross; by the benefit whereof alone all the sins of all believers, even from the beginning of the world, are pardoned, by the only mercy of God, and by no desert of ours.

Master. I hear not yet, why Almighty God's will was to declare his secret pleasure to one people alone, which was the Israelites.

Scholar. Forsooth that had I almost forgotten. I suppose it was not done for this intent, as though the law of the x. commandments did not belong generally to all men; forasmuch as the Lord our God is not only the God of the Jews, but also of the Gentiles: but rather this was meant thereby, that the true Messias, which is our Christ, might be known at his coming into the world: who must needs have been born of that nation, and none other, for true performance of the promise. For the which cause, God's pleasure was to appoint out for himself one certain people, holy, sundered from the rest, and as it were peculiarly his own; that by this mean his divine word might be continually kept holy, pure, and uncorrupted.

Master. Hitherto thou hast well satisfied me, dear son. Now let us come to the Christian confession, which I will that thou plainly rehearse unto me.

Scholar. It shall be done. I believe in God, the Father almighty: maker of heaven and earth. And in Jesu Christ, his only Son, our Lord: which was conceived by the

Side notes: None made righteous by the law. Ceremonies of the law. Sins forgiven by Christ's death only. Why the law was given to one people. The moral law common to all. The Creed.

Holy Ghost: born of the virgin Mary: suffered under Ponce Pilate: was crucified: dead: and buried. He went down to hell: the third day he rose again from the dead. He went up to heaven: sitteth on the right hand of God the Father almighty: from thence shall he come, to judge the quick and the dead. I believe in the Holy Ghost. I believe the holy universal church: the communion of saints: the forgiveness of sins: the rising again of the flesh: and the life everlasting.

Master. All these (my son) thou hast rehearsed generally and shortly. Therefore thou shalt do well to set out largely all that thou hast spoken particularly; that I may plainly perceive what thy belief is concerning each of them. And first I would hear of the knowledge of God, afterward of the right serving of him.

Scholar. I will with a good will obey your pleasure (dear master) as far as my simple wit will suffer me. Above all things we must stedfastly believe and hold: that God almighty, the Father, in the beginning, and of nothing, made and fashioned this whole frame of the world, and all things whatsoever are contained therein: and that they all are made by the power of his word, that is of Jesu Christ the Son of God. Which thing is sufficiently approved by witness of scriptures. Moreover that, when he had thus shapen all creatures, he ruled, governed and saved them by his bounty and liberal hand: hath ministered, and yet also ministereth most largely all that is needful, for maintenance and preserving of our life: that we should so use them, as behoveth mindful and godly children. *[The making and preservation of the world.]*

Master. Why dost thou call God Father?

Scholar. For two causes: the one, for that he made us all at the beginning, and gave life unto us all: the other is more weighty, for that by his Holy Spirit and by faith he hath begotten us again: making us his children: giving us his kingdom and the inheritance of life everlasting, with Jesu Christ his own, true, and natural Son. *[Why we call God Father.]*

Master. Seeing then God hath created all other things to serve man: and made man to obey, honour, and glorify him: what canst thou say more of the beginning and making of man?

Scholar. Even that which Moses wrote: that God shaped the first man of clay: and put into him soul and life: then, *[The making of man.]*

that he cast Adam in a dead sleep, and brought forth a woman, whom he drew out of his side, to make her a companion with him of all his life and wealth. And therefore was man called Adam, because he took his beginning of the earth; and the woman called Eve, because she was appointed to be the mother of all living.

<small>The name of Adam and Eve.</small>

Master. What image is that, after the likeness whereof thou sayest that man was made?

Scholar. That is most absolute righteousness and perfect holiness: which most nearly belongeth to the very nature of God: and most clearly appeared in Christ, our new Adam. Of the which in us there scant are to be seen any sparkles.

<small>The image that man was made after.</small>

Master. What? are there scant to be seen?

Scholar. It is true forsooth: for they do not now so shine, as they did in the beginning, before man's fall: forasmuch as man by the darkness of sins, and mist of errors, hath corrupted the brightness of this image. In such sort hath God in his wrath wreaked him upon the sinful man.

<small>God's image defaced in man.</small>

Master. But I pray thee tell me, wherefore came it thus to pass?

Scholar. I will shew you. When the Lord God had made the frame of this world, he himself planted a garden, full of delight and pleasure, in a certain place eastward, and called it Eden: wherein, beside other passing fair trees, not far from the midst of the garden was there one specially called the tree of life, and another called the tree of knowledge of good and evil. Herein the Lord of his singular love placed man: and committed unto him the garden to dress, and look unto: giving him liberty to eat of the fruits of all the trees of paradise, except the fruit of the tree of knowledge of good and evil. The fruit of this tree if ever he tasted, he should without fail die for it. But Eve, deceived by the devil counterfeiting the shape of a serpent, gathered of the forbidden fruit: which was for the fairness to the eye to be desired: for the sweetness in taste to be reached at: and pleasant for the knowledge of good and evil: and she eat thereof, and gave unto her husband to eat of the same. For which doing they both immediately died; that is to say, were not only subject to the death of the body, but also lost the life of the soul, which is righteousness. And forthwith the image of God was defaced in them: and the most beautiful proportion of righteousness, holiness, truth, and knowledge of God, was confounded and in a manner utterly blotted out. There remained the earthly image, joined with unrighteousness, guile, fleshly mind, and deep ignorance of godly and heavenly things. Hereof grew the weakness of our flesh: hereof came this corruption, and disorder of lusts and affections: hereof came that pestilence: hereof came that seed and nourishment of sins wherewith mankind is infected, and it is called sin original. Moreover *Original sin.* thereby nature was so corrupted and overthrown, that unless the goodness and mercy of almighty God had holpen us by the medicine of grace, even as in body we are thrust down into all wretchedness of death, so must it needs have been, that all men of all sorts should be thrown into everlasting punishment and fire unquenchable.

Master. Oh the unthankfulness of men! But what hope had our first parents, and from thenceforth the rest, whereby they were relieved?

Scholar. When the Lord God had both with words *The means of redemption.* and deeds chastised Adam and Eve (for he thrust them both out of the garden with a most grievous reproach), he then cursed the serpent, threatening him, that the time should one day come, when the Seed of the woman should break his head. Afterward the Lord God stablished that same glorious and most bountiful promise: first with a covenant *God's covenants.* made between him and Abraham, by circumcision, and in Isaac his son: then again by Moses: last of all by the oracles of the noble prophets.

Master. What meaneth the serpent's head, and that Seed that God speaketh of?

Scholar. In the serpent's head lieth all his venom, and *The serpent's head.* the whole pith of his life and force. Therefore do I take the serpent's head to betoken the whole power and kingdom, or more truly the tyranny, of the old serpent the devil. The *The Seed of the woman.* Seed (as saint Paul doth plainly teach) is Jesus Christ, the Son of God, very God and very man: conceived of the Holy Ghost: engendered of the womb and substance of Mary, the blessed pure and undefiled maid: and was so born and fostered by her as other babes be, saving that he was most far from all infection of sin.

Master. All these foundations that thou hast laid are

most true. Now therefore let us go forward to those his doings, wherein lieth our salvation and conquest against that old serpent.

Scholar. It shall be done, good master. After that Christ Jesus had delivered in charge to his Apostles that most joyful and in all points heavenly doctrine, the gospel, which in Greek is called Euangelion, in English good tidings: and had as by sealing stablished the same with tokens, and miracles innumerable, whereof all his life was full: at length was he sore scourged: mocked with potting, scorning, and spitting in his face: last of all his hands and feet bored through with nails: and he fastened to a cross. Then he truly died, and was truly buried: that by his most sweet sacrifice he might pacify his Father's wrath against mankind; and subdue him by his death, who had the authority of death, which was the devil: forasmuch not only the living, but also the dead, were they in hell, or elsewhere, they all felt the power and force of this death: to whom lying in prison (as Peter saith) Christ preached, though dead in body, yet relived in Spirit. The third day after he uprose again, alive in body also: and with many notable proofs, the space of forty days, he abode among his disciples, eating and drinking with them. In whose sight he was conveyed away in a cloud, up into heaven, or rather above all heavens: where he now sitteth at the right hand of God the Father: being made Lord of all things, be they in heaven, or in earth: King of all kings: our everlasting and only high Bishop: our only attorney: only mediator, only peace-maker between God and men. Now since that he is entered into his glorious majesty; by sending down his Holy Spirit unto us (as he promised) he lighteneth our dark blindness: moveth, ruleth, teacheth, cleanseth, comforteth, and rejoiceth our minds: and so will he still continually do, till the end of the world.

Master. Well, I see thou hast touched the chief Articles of our religion, and hast set out, as in a short abridgment, the Creed, that thou didst rehearse. Now therefore I will demand thee questions of certain points.

Scholar. Do as shall please you, master: for ye may more perfectly instruct me in those things that I do not throughly understand: and put me in remembrance of that I have forgotten: and print in my mind deeper such things, as have not taken stedfast hold therein.

Master. Tell me then. If by his death we get pardon of our sins: was not that enough, but that he must also rise again from the dead?

Scholar. It was not enough, if ye have a respect either to him, or to us. For unless he had risen again, he should not be taken for the Son of God. For which cause also, while he hung upon the cross, they that saw him upbraided him and said: He hath saved other, but can not save himself: Let him now come down from the cross, and we will believe him. But now uprising from the dead to everlasting continuance of life, he hath shewed a much greater power of his Godhead, than if by coming down from the cross he had fled from the terrible pains of death. For to die is common to all men: but to loose the bonds of death, and by his own power to rise again, that properly belongeth to Jesus Christ, the only-begotten Son of God, the only author of life. Moreover it was necessary, that he should rise again with glory, that the sayings of David and other prophets of God might be fulfilled, which told before: that neither his body should see corruption: nor his soul be left in hell. As for us, we neither had been justified, nor had had any hope left to rise again, had not he risen again, as Paul doth in divers places plainly shew. For if he had remained in the prison of death, in grave: and been holden in corruption, as all men beside: how could we have hoped for safety by him which saved not himself? It was meet therefore, and needful, for the part that he had in hand: and for the chief stay of our safeguard: that Christ should first deliver himself from death, and afterward assure us of safety by his uprising again.

<small>The resurrection of Christ necessary.</small>

Master. Thou hast touched (my son) the chief cause of Christ's rising again. Now would I fain hear thy mind of his going up into heaven. What answer, thinkest thou, is to be made to them, that say, It had been better for him to tarry here with us, presently to rule and govern us? For, beside other divers causes, it is likely, that the love of the people toward their prince, specially being good and gracious, should grow the greater by his present company.

Scholar. All these things which he should do present,

Christ governeth his church absent. that is to say, if he were in company among us, he doth them absent. He ruleth, maintaineth, strengtheneth, defendeth, rebuketh, punisheth, correcteth: and performeth all such things as do become such a prince, or rather God himself. All those things (I say) performeth he, which belong either to our need or profit, honour or commodity. Beside this, *How Christ is absent and present in the world.* Christ is not so altogether absent from the world, as many do suppose. For albeit the substance of his body be taken up from us: yet is his Godhead perpetually present with us: although not subject to the sight of our eyes. For things that be not bodily, can not be perceived by any bodily mean. Who ever saw his own soul? No man. Yet what is there more present? or what to each man nearer, than his own soul? Spiritual things are not to be seen, but with the eye of the spirit. Therefore he that in earth will see the Godhead of Christ: let him open the eyes, not of his body, but of his mind, but of his faith: and he shall see him present, whom eye hath not seen: he shall see him present, and in the midst of them, wheresoever be two or three gathered together in his name: he shall see him present with us, even unto the end of the world. What said I? shall he see Christ present? Yea, he shall both see and feel him dwelling within himself: in such sort as he doth his own proper soul. For he dwelleth and abideth in the mind and heart of him which fasteneth all his trust in him.

Christ's ascension. *Master.* Very well: but our confession is that he is ascended up into heaven. Tell me therefore how that is to be understood.

Scholar. So use we commonly to say of him, that hath attained to any high degree or dignity: that he is ascended up, or advanced into some high room, some high place or state: because he hath changed his former case, and is become of more honour than the rest. In such case is Christ gone up, as he before came down. He came down from highest honour to deepest dishonour, even the dishonour and vile state of a servant, and of the cross. And likewise afterward he went up, from the deepest dishonour, to the highest honour, even that same honour, which he had before. His going up into heaven, yea, above all heavens, to the very royal throne of God, must needs be evident by most just reason, that his glory and majesty might in comparison agreeably answer to the proportion of his baseness and reproachful estate. This doth Paul teach us, in his writing to the Philippians: he became obedient even unto death: yea, the very death of the cross. Wherefore God hath both advanced him to the highest state of honour: and also given him a name above all names: that at the name of Jesus every knee should bow, of all things in heaven, earth and hell. But although he be already gone up into heaven: nevertheless by his nature of Godhead, and by his Spirit, he shall always be present in his church: even to the end of the world. Yet this proveth not that he is present among us in his body. For his Godhead hath one property: his manhood another. His manhood was create, his Godhead uncreate. His manhood is in some one place of heaven: his Godhead is in such sort eachwhere, that it filleth both heaven and earth. But to make this point plainer, by a similitude or comparing of like to like. There is nothing that doth trulier, like a shadow, express Christ, than the sun: for it is a fit image of the light and brightness of Christ. The sun doth alway keep the heaven: yet do we say that it is present also in the world: for without light there is nothing present, that is to say, nothing to be seen of any man: for the sun with his light fulfilleth all things. So Christ is lifted up above all heavens, that he may be present with all, and fully furnish all things, as S. Paul doth say. But as touching the bodily presence of Christ here in earth (if it be lawful to place in comparison great things with small), Christ's body is present to our faith: as the sun, when it is seen, is present to the eye: the body whereof, although it do not bodily touch the eye, nor be presently with it together here in earth, yet is it present to the sight, notwithstanding so large a distance of space between. So Christ's body, which at his glorious going up was conveyed from us: which hath left the world, and is gone unto his Father: is a great way absent from our mouth, even then when we receive with our mouth the holy sacrament of his body and blood. Yet is our faith in heaven: and beholdeth that Sun of righteousness: and is presently together with him in heaven, in such sort as the sight is in heaven with the body of the sun, or in earth the sun with the sight. And as the sun is present to all things by his light: so is Christ also in his Godhead. Yet neither

Christ's bodily presence.

Christ compared to the sun.

can from the body the light of the sun be sundered: nor from his immortal body the Godhead of Christ. We must therefore so say, that Christ's body is in some one place of heaven, and his Godhead every where: that we neither of his Godhead make a body: nor of his body a God.

Master. I see (my son) thou art not ignorant, after what sort Christ is rightly said to be from us in body, and with us in spirit. But this one thing would I know of thee: why Christ our Lord is thus conveyed away from the sight of our eyes; and what profit we take by his going up to heaven?

<small>Our profit by Christ's ascension.</small>
Scholar. The chief cause thereof was, to pluck out of us that false opinion, which sometime deceived the Apostles themselves: that Christ should in earth visibly reign, as other kings, and ruffling princes of the world. This error he minded to have utterly suppressed in us: and that we should think his kingdom to consist in higher things. Which <small>Causes of Christ's ascension.</small> thing he therefore thought fitter, because it was more for our commodity and profit, that some such kingdom should be set up, as the foundations thereof should rest upon our faith. Wherefore it was necessary that he should be conveyed away from us, past perceiving of all bodily sense: that by this mean our faith might be stirred up and exercised to consider his government and providence, whom no sight of bodily eyes can behold. And forasmuch as he is not king of some one country alone: but of heaven and earth: of quick and dead: it was most convenient that his kingdom should be otherwise governed, than our senses may attain unto. For else he should have been constrained, sometime to be carried up to heaven: sometime to be driven down to the earth: to remove sometime into one country, sometime into another: and like an earthly prince to be carried hither and thither, by divers change of chanceable affairs. For he could not be presently with all at once, unless his body were so turned into Godhead, that he might be in all or in many places together: as Eutyches, and certain like heretics held opinion. If it so were that he might be eachwhere present with all, at one very instant time: then were he not man, but a ghost: neither should he have had a true body, but a fantastical: whereof should have sprung forthwith a thousand errors: all which he hath dispatched

by carrying his body up whole to heaven. In the mean season he, remaining invisible, governeth his kingdom and commonweal, that is his church, with sovereign wisdom and power. It is for men to rule their commonweals by a certain civil policy of men: but for Christ and God, by a heavenly godlike order. But all that I have hitherto said containeth but a small parcel of the profit, that we take by the carrying up of Christ's body into heaven. For there are many more things, that here might be rehearsed, whereof large store of fruit is to be gathered. But specially this may not be left unspoken: that the benefits are such, and so great, which come unto us by the death, rising again, and going up of Christ, as no tongue either of men or angels is able to express. And that you may know my mind herein: I will rehearse certain of the chief: whereunto, as it were two principal points, the rest may be applied. I say therefore: that both by these and other doings of Christ, two commodities do grow unto us: the one, that all the things that ever he hath done, for our profit and behoof he hath done them: so that they be as well our own, if we will cleave thereunto with stedfast and lively faith, as if we had done them ourselves. He was nailed to the cross: we were also nailed with him: and in him our sins punished. He died: and was buried: we likewise with our sins are dead, and buried: and that in such sort, that all remembrance of our sins is utterly taken out of mind. He is risen again: and we are also risen again with him: that is, are so made partakers of his rising again and life, that from henceforth death hath no more rule over us. For the same Spirit is in us that raised up Jesus from the dead. Finally, as he is gone up into heavenly glory: so are we lifted up with him. Albeit that these things do not now appear: yet then shall they all be brought to light, when Christ, the light of the world, shall shew himself in his glory, in whom all our bliss is laid up in store. Moreover by his going up are granted us the gifts of the Holy Ghost: as Paul doth sufficiently witness (Ephe. iv.). The other commodity, which we take by the doings of Christ, is: that Christ is set for an example unto us, to frame our lives thereafter. If Christ hath been dead: if he hath been buried for sin: he was so but once. If he be risen again: if he be gone up to heaven: he is but

Christ's doings for our behoof.

Christ's example of life unto us.

once risen: but once gone up. From henceforth he dieth no more, but liveth with God: and reigneth in everlasting continuance of glory. So if we be dead: if we be buried to sin: how shall we hereafter live in the same? If we be risen again with Christ: if by stedfast hope we live now in heaven with him: heavenly and godly things, not earthly and frail, we ought to set our care upon. And even as heretofore we have borne the image of the earthly man: so from henceforward let us bear the image of the heavenly. As the Lord Christ never ceased to do us good, by bestowing upon us his Holy Spirit: by garnishing his church with so many notable gifts: and by perpetual praying to his Father for us: like reason ought to move us to aid our neighbour with all our endeavour: to maintain, as much as in us lieth, *Honor of Christ.* the bond of charity; and to honour Christ our Lord and Saviour, not with wicked traditions and cold devices of men, but with heavenly honour and spiritual in deed, most fit for us that give it, and him that shall receive it, even as he hath honoured and doth honour his Father. For he that honoureth him honoureth also the Father, of which he himself is a substantial witness.

Master. The end of the world holy scripture calleth the fulfilling and performance of the kingdom and mystery of Christ, and the renewing of all things. For (saith the Apostle Peter in his second Epistle the third chapter,) We look for a new heaven, and a new earth, according to the promise of God: wherein dwelleth righteousness. And it seemeth reason that corruption, unstedfast change, and sin, whereunto the whole world is subject, should at length have an end. Now by what way, and what fashion circumstances these things shall come to pass, I would fain hear thee tell.

The end of the world. *Scholar.* I will tell you as well as I can, according to the witness of the same Apostle. The heavens shall pass away like a storm: the elements shall melt away: the earth, and all the works therein, shall be consumed with fire: as though he should say: as gold is wont to be fined: so shall the whole world be purified with fire, and be brought to his full perfection. The lesser world, which is man, following the same, shall likewise be delivered from corruption and change. And so for man this greater world (which for his sake was first created) shall at length be renewed, and be clad with another hue, much more pleasant and beautiful.

Master. What then remaineth?

Scholar. The last and general doom. For Christ shall come: at whose voice all the dead shall rise again, perfect and sound both in body and soul. The whole world shall behold him, sitting in the Royal throne of his Majesty: and after the examination of every man's conscience, the last sentence shall be pronounced. Then the children of God shall be in perfect possession of that kingdom of freedom from death and of everlasting life, which was prepared for them before the foundations of the world were laid. And they shall reign with Christ for ever. But the ungodly that believed not, shall be thrown from thence into everlasting fire, appointed for the devil and his angels. *The day of doom.* *The resurrection.*

Master. Thou hast said enough of the again rising of the dead. Now remaineth, that thou speak of the holy church: whereof I would very fain hear thy opinion. *The holy church.*

Scholar. I will rehearse that in few words shortly: which the holy scriptures set out at large and plentifully. Afore that the Lord God had made the heaven and earth, he determined to have for himself a most beautiful kingdom and holy commonwealth. The apostles and the ancient fathers that wrote in Greek, called it Ecclesia, in English, a congregation or assembly: into the which he hath admitted an infinite number of men: that should all be subject to one king as their sovereign and only one head: him we call Christ, which is as much to say as anointed. For the high bishops, and kings among the Jews, (who in figure betokened Christ, whom the Lord anointed with his holy Spirit,) were wont by God's appointment at their consecration to have material oil poured on them. To the furnishing of this commonwealth belong all they, as many as do truly fear, honour and call upon God, wholly applying their mind to holy and godly living; and all those that putting all their hope and trust in him, do assuredly look for the bliss of everlasting life. But as many as are in this faith stedfast, were forechosen, predestinate, and appointed out to everlasting life, before the world was made. Witness hereof they have within in their hearts the Spirit of Christ, the author, earnest and unfailable pledge of their faith. Which faith only *Who be of Christ's church.*

is able to perceive the mysteries of God: only bringeth peace unto the heart: only taketh hold on the righteousness, that is in Christ Jesus.

Master. Doth then the Spirit alone and faith (sleep we never so soundly, or stand we never so reckless and slothful) so work all things for us, as without any help of our own to carry us idle up to heaven?

Scholar. I use (master) as you have taught me, to make a difference between the cause and the effects. The Causes of our justification. first, principal, and most perfect cause of our justifying and salvation, is the goodness and love of God: whereby he chose us for his, before he made the world. After that, God granteth us to be called by the preaching of the gospel of Jesus Christ, when the Spirit of the Lord is poured into us: by whose guiding and governance we be led to settle our trust in God: and hope for the performance of all his promises. With this choice is joined, as companion, the mortifying of the old man, that is of our affection and lust. From the same Spirit also cometh our sanctification: the love of God, and of our neighbour: justice: and uprightness of life: finally, to say all in sum, whatsoever is in us, or may be done of us, pure, honest, true and good, that altogether springeth out of this most pleasant root, from this most plentiful fountain, the goodness, love, choice and unchangeable purpose of God. He is the cause, the rest are the fruits and effects. Yet are also the goodness, choice and Spirit of God, and Christ himself, causes conjoined and coupled each with other: which may be reckoned among the principal causes of our salvation. As oft Justification by faith. therefore as we use to say, that we are made righteous and saved by only faith: it is meant thereby: that faith, or rather trust alone, doth lay hand upon, understand and perceive, our righteous-making to be given us of God freely; that is to say, by no deserts of our own, but by the free grace of the Almighty Father. Moreover faith doth engender in us the love of our neighbour, and such works as God is pleased withal. For if it be a lively and true faith, quickened by the Holy Ghost, she is the mother of all good saying and doing. By this short tale is it evident, whence, and by what means we attain to be made righteous. For not by the worthiness of our deservings were we heretofore chosen, or long ago saved: but by the only mercy of God, and pure grace of Christ our Lord, whereby we were in him made to those good works, that God hath appointed for us to walk in. And although good works cannot deserve to make us righteous before God: yet do they so cleave unto faith, that neither can faith be found without them, nor good works be any where without faith. True faith and works unseparate.

Master. I like very well this short declaration of faith and works: for Paul plainly teacheth the same. But canst thou yet further depaint me out that congregation, which thou callest a kingdom or commonweal of Christians; and so set it out before mine eyes, that it may severally and plainly be known asunder from each other fellowship of men?

Scholar. I will prove how well I can do it. Your pleasure is (master) as I take it, that I point ye out some certain congregation, that may be seen.

Master. That it is indeed: and so it shall be good for ye to do.

Scholar. That congregation is nothing else but a certain multitude of men: which, wheresoever they be, profess the pure and upright learning of Christ, and that in such sort, as it is faithfully set forth in the holy testament, by the evangelists and apostles: which in all points are governed and ruled by the laws and statutes of their king and high Bishop Christ, in the bond of charity: which use his holy mysteries, that are commonly called sacraments, with such pureness and simplicity (as touching their nature and substance) as the apostles of Christ used and left behind in writing. The marks therefore of this church are: first, pure preaching of the gospel: then brotherly love, out of which, as members of all one body, springeth good will of each to other: thirdly, upright and uncorrupted use of the Lord's sacraments, according to the ordinance of the gospel: last of all, brotherly correction, and excommunication, or banishing those out of the church, that will not amend their lives. This mark the holy fathers termed discipline. This is that same church, that is grounded upon the assured rock, Jesus Christ, and upon trust in him. This is that same church, which Paul calleth the pillar and upholding stay of truth. To this church belong the keys, wherewith heaven is locked and unlocked: for that is done by the ministration of the word: whereunto properly appertaineth the power to bind and loose; The church. Marks of the church. Keys to bind and loose.

to hold for guilty, and forgive sins. So that whosoever believeth the gospel preached in this church, he shall be saved: but whosoever believeth not, he shall be damned.

Master. Now would I fain hear thy belief of the Holy Ghost.

Scholar. I confess him to be the third person of the holy trinity: And sith he is equal with the Father and the Son, and of the very same nature, that he ought equally[1] to be worshipped with them both.

<small>The Holy Ghost.</small>

Master. Why is he called holy?

Scholar. Not only for his own holiness: but for that by him are made holy the chosen of God, and members of Christ. And therefore have the scriptures termed him the Spirit of sanctification or making holy.

<small>Why the Holy Ghost is called holy.</small>

Master. Wherein consisteth this sanctification?

Scholar. First, we be new gotten by his inward motion. And therefore said Christ, we must be new born of water, and of the Spirit. Then by his inspiration are we adopted, and as it were by choice made the children of God. For which cause he is not causeless called the Spirit of adoption. By his light are we enlightened, to understand God's mysteries. By his judgment are sins pardoned and retained. By his power is the flesh with her lusts kept down and tamed. By his pleasure are the manifold gifts dealt among the holy. Finally, by his means shall our mortal bodies be relieved. Therefore in the author of so great gifts we do not without a cause believe, honour, and call upon him.

<small>Wherein resteth the Holy Ghost's sanctification.</small>

Master. Well, thou hast now said sufficiently of the Holy Ghost. But this would I hear of thee: why it immediately followeth, that we believe the holy universal church and the communion of saints.

Scholar. These two things I have alway thought to be most fitly coupled together, Because the fellowships and incorporations of other men proceed and be governed by other means and policies: but the church, which is an assembly of men called to everlasting salvation, is both gathered together and governed by the Holy Ghost, of whom we even now made mention. Which thing, sith it can not be perceived by bodily sense or light of nature, is by right and

<small>Communion of Saints.</small>

[1 egally, in the original.]

for good reason here reckoned among things that are known by belief. And therefore this calling together of the faithful is called universal, because it is bound to no one special place. For God throughout all coasts of the world hath them that worship him: which, though they be far scattered asunder by divers distance of countries and dominions, yet are they members most nearly joined of that same body, whereof Christ is the head; and have one spirit, faith, sacraments, prayers, forgiveness of sins, and heavenly bliss, common among them all: and be so knit with the bond of love, that they endeavour themselves in nothing more, than each to help other, and to build together in Christ. *(Why the church is called universal. Communion of Saints.)*

Master. Seeing thou hast already spoken of the knowledge of God, and his members: I would also hear, what is the true service of God,

Scholar. First we must consider, that the right and true knowledge of God, is the principal and only foundation of God's service. The same knowledge fear doth foster and maintain, which in scriptures is called the beginning of wisdom. Faith and hope are the props and stays, whereupon lean all the rest that I have rehearsed. Furthermore charity, which we call love, is like an everlasting bond, by the strait knot whereof all other virtues be bound in one together, and their force increased. These be the inward parts of God's service, that is to say, which consist in the mind. *(Parts of God's true inward service.)*

Master. What hast thou to say of the Sabbath, or the holy day, which even now thou madest mention of, among the laws of the first table?

Scholar. Sabbath is as much to say, as rest. It was appointed for only honour and service of God: and it is a figure of that rest and quietness, which they have that believe in Christ. For our trust in Christ doth set our minds at liberty from all slavish fear of the law, sin, death and hell; assuring us in the mean season, that by him we please God, and that he hath made us his children and heirs of his kingdom: whereby there groweth in our hearts peace and true quietness of mind: which is a certain foretaste of the most blessed quiet, which we shall have in his kingdom. As for those things that are used to to done on the sabbath day, as ceremonies, and exercises in the service of God, they are tokens and witnesses of this assured trust. And meet it is, *(The Sabbath.)*

that faithful Christians, on such days as are appointed out for holy things, should lay aside unholy works, and give themselves earnestly to religion and serving of God.

Master. What be the parts of that outward serving God, which thou saidest even now did stand in certain bodily exercises; which are also tokens of the inward serving him?

Outward service of God.

Scholar. First, to teach, and hear the learning of the gospel: then the pure and natural use of the ceremonies and sacraments: last of all, prayer made unto God by Christ, and in the name of Christ, which without fail obtaineth the Holy Ghost, the most assured author of all true serving God, and upright religion.

Master. Tell me what thou callest sacraments.

What Sacraments are.

Scholar. They are certain customable reverent doings and ceremonies ordained by Christ; that by them he might put us in remembrance of his benefits, and we might declare our profession, that we be of the number of them, which are partakers of the same benefits, and which fasten all their affiance in him; that we are not ashamed of the name of Christ, or to be termed Christ's Scholars.

Master. Tell me (my son) how these two sacraments be ministered: baptism; and that which Paul calleth the supper of the Lord.

The ministration of Baptism.

Scholar. Him that believeth in Christ: professeth the Articles of the Christian religion: and mindeth to be baptized (I speak now of them that be grown to ripe years of discretion, sith for the young babes their parents' or the church's profession sufficeth), the minister dippeth in, or washeth with pure and clean water only, in the name of the Father, and of the Son, and of the Holy Ghost: and then commendeth him by prayer to God, into whose church he is now openly as it were enrolled, that it may please God to grant him his grace, whereby he may answer in belief and life agreeably to his profession.

Master. What is the use of the Lord's supper?

The use of the Lord's Supper.

Scholar. Even the very same, that was ordained by the Lord himself, Jesus Christ: which (as S. Paul saith) the same night, that he was betrayed, took bread: and when he had given thanks, brake it: and said, This is my body, which is broken for you: Do this in remembrance of me.

In like manner, when supper was ended, he gave them the cup, saying: This cup is the new testament in my blood. Do this, as oft as ye shall drink thereof, in the remembrance of me. This was the manner and order of the Lord's supper: which we ought to hold and keep; that the remembrance of so great a benefit, the passion and death of Christ, be alway kept in mind; that, after that the world is ended, he may come, and make us to sit with him at his own board.

Master. What doth baptism represent and set before our eyes?

Scholar. That we are by the Spirit of Christ new born, and cleansed from sin: that we be members and parts of his church, received into the communion of saints. For water signifieth the Spirit. Baptism is also a figure of our burial in Christ, and that we shall be raised up again with him in a new life, as I have before declared in Christ's resurrection. The meaning of Baptism.

Master. What declareth and betokeneth the supper unto us, which we solemnly use in the remembrance of the Lord?

Scholar. The Supper (as I have shewed a little before) is a certain thankful remembrance of the death of Christ: forasmuch as the bread representeth his body, betrayed to be crucified for us; the wine standeth in stead and place of his blood, plenteously shed for us. And even as by bread and wine our natural bodies are sustained and nourished: so by the body, that is the flesh and blood of Christ, the soul is fed through faith, and quickened to the heavenly and godly life. The meaning of the Lord's Supper. The bread. The wine.

Master. How come these things to pass?

Scholar. These things come to pass by a certain secret mean, and lively working of the Spirit: when we believe that Christ hath, once for all, given up his body and blood for us, to make a sacrifice and most pleasant offering to his heavenly Father; and also when we confess and acknowledge him our only Saviour, high Bishop, Mediator, and Redeemer: to whom is due all honour and glory. How we feed upon Christ's body and blood.

Master. All this thou dost well understand. For methinketh thy meaning is: that faith is the mouth of the soul, whereby we receive this heavenly meat, full both of salvation and immortality, dealt among us, by the means of the Holy Ghost. Now, sith we have entreated of the sacraments, pass forward to the other parts of God's service. Faith the mouth of the soul.

Scholar. I will do your commandment. There remain two things, belonging to the perfection of God's service. First, our Lord Jesus Christ's will was, that there should be teachers and evangelists, that is to say, preachers of the gospel: to this intent, that his voice might continually be heard sound in his church. He that coveteth (as all ought to covet) to bear the name of a Christian, may have no doubt, that he ought with most earnest affection and fervent desire endeavour himself to hear and soak into his mind the word of the Lord; not like the words of any man, but like (as it is indeed) the word of Almighty God. Secondarily, because all that is good, and that ought of a Christian to be desired, cometh unto us from God, and is by him granted: therefore of him we ought to require all things, and by thanksgiving acknowledge them all received of him. Which thing he so well liketh, that he esteemeth it instead of a passing pleasant sacrifice: as it is most evident by the witness of the prophets and apostles.

<small>Office of Preachers.</small>

<small>Prayer.</small>

Master. Hast thou any certain and appointed manner of praying?

<small>The Lord's prayer.</small>

Scholar. Yea forsooth: even the very same, that our Lord taught his disciples, and in them all other Christians. Who, being on a time required to teach them some sort of prayer, taught them this. When ye pray, quoth[1] he, say: Our Father which art in heaven, hallowed be thy name. Thy kingdom come. Thy will be done in earth as it is in heaven. Give us this day our daily bread, and forgive us our trespasses as we forgive them that trespass against us. And lead us not into temptation: But deliver us from evil. For thine is the kingdom, power and glory for ever. Amen.

Master. How thinkest thou? is it lawful for us to use any other words of prayer?

<small>Whether we may use any other prayer but the Pater noster.</small>

Scholar. Although in this short abridgment are sufficiently contained all things that every Christian ought to pray for: yet hath not Christ in this prayer tied us up so short, as that it were not lawful for us to use other words and manner of prayer. But he hath set out in this prayer certain principal[2] points, whereunto all our prayers should be referred. But let each man ask of God as his present need requireth,

[1 quod, in the original.]   [2 Original, *principle.*]

Whatsoever ye ask the Father in my name (saith Christ), he shall give it you.

Master. Forasmuch as there is in all this prayer nothing doubtful or beside the purpose: I would hear thy mind of it.

Scholar. I do well perceive what the words do signify.

Master. Thinkest thou then that there is in it nothing dark, nothing hid, nothing hard to understand?

Scholar. Nothing at all. For neither was it Christ's pleasure, that there should be any thing in it dark or far from our capacity, specially since it belongeth equally to all, and is as necessary for the lewd[3], as the learned. Nothing in the Lord's prayer hard to understand.

Master. Therefore declare unto me, in few words, each part by itself.

Scholar. When I say, Our Father which art in heaven; this do I think with myself: that it can not be but that he must hear me, and be pleased with my prayers. For I am his son (although unprofitable and disobedient), and he on the other side is my most bountiful Father, most ready to take pity and pardon me. What we gather of Our Father.

Master. Why dost thou say, he is in heaven? is he in some one certain and limited place in heaven? What meaneth that which he saith of himself, I fill both heaven and earth; again, the heaven is my seat and the earth my footstool? What is meant by, Which art in heaven.

Scholar. Hereof have I spoken somewhat before: whereunto I will join this that followeth. First of all, as oft as we do say (which art in heaven), it is as much to say as heavenly and divine. For we ought to think much higher of our heavenly Father than of our earthly. He is also said to be in heaven for this cause: that in that high and heavenly place the notable and wonderful works of God do the more clearly and gloriously shew themselves: and he is now declared to be in everlasting and full felicity; whereas we abide yet banished in earth full wretchedly. Moreover as the heaven by unmeasurable wideness of compass containeth all places, the earth, and the sea; and no place is there, that may be hid from the large reach of heaven, sith it is at every instant of time to every thing present: so hereby may we understand, that God is likewise present to each thing in each place. He seeth,

[[3] i.e. simple.]

heareth and governeth all things; he being himself a spirit, and most far from all earthly and mortal state. Witness whereof Hieremy the prophet. Am not I (saith the Lord) a God near unto you? And am not I a God far off? Shall any man be able to shroud himself in such a corner, that I can not espy him? This is a pithy sentence, to drive fear into us, that we offend not that Lord of so large a dominion: whereby also we are persuaded assuredly to believe, that God will hear whensoever we shall stand in need. For he is at all times and in all places present. This foundation then laid; and so sweet and pleasant entrance prepared; there followeth the first part of the Lord's prayer: wherein we require, that not only we, but also all other whosoever, may in holiness honour, reverence, and worship his name.

Master. How is that to be done?

Scholar. I shall shew you: then we do that, when leaving all those that have the name of gods, be they in heaven or in earth, or worshipped in temples, in divers shapes and images, we acknowledge him alone our Father; pray to the true God, and Jesus Christ his only Son, whom he hath sent; and by pure unfeigned prayer call upon him alone, with uprightness of life and innocency.

Master. Thou hast said very well: proceed.

Scholar. In the second part we require that his kingdom come. For we see not yet all things in subjection to Christ: we see not the stone hewed off from the mountain without work of man, which all-to bruised and brought to nought the image which Daniel describeth, that the only rock Christ may obtain and possess the dominion of the whole world, granted him of his Father. Antichrist is not yet slain. For this cause do we long for, and pray that it may at length come to pass and be fulfilled, that Christ may reign with his saints, according to God's promises: that he may live and be Lord in the world, according to the decrees of the holy gospel: not after the traditions and laws of men, nor pleasure of worldly tyrants.

Master. God grant his kingdom may come, and that speedily!

Scholar. Moreover, sith it is the children's duty to frame their life to their father's will, and not the father's to bow to the children's pleasure: forasmuch as our will is commonly by tickling [1] of affections, and stirring of lusts, drawn to do those things, that God is displeased with: it is reason, that we hang wholly upon the beck of our heavenly Father, and wholly submit ourselves to his heavenly government. Wherefore, for this cause, we mortal men do pray, that we may in like case be obedient to his commandment, as are the sun and moon and other stars in heaven, which both by ordinary courses, and by lightening the earth with uncessant beams, execute the Lord's will continually: or that we, as the angels and other spirits divine, in all points obey him; which bestow all their travail diligently to accomplish his godly commandments. Next after that he teacheth us, to ask of our heavenly Father our bread: whereby he meaneth not meat only, but also all things else needful for maintenance, and preserving of life: that we may learn, that God alone is author of all things; which maketh the fruits of the earth both to grow and increase to plenty. Wherefore it is meet that we call upon him alone in prayer, which (as David saith) alone feedeth and maintaineth all things.

Master. Some suppose this place to mean that bread, that Christ maketh mention of in the sixth of John: that is, of the true knowledge and taste of Christ, that was born and died for us; wherewith the faithful soul is fed. The reason whereupon they gather this is the Greek word *epiousion*[2], whereby they understand supernatural, ghostly, heavenly and divine. This meaning I refuse not; for both these expositions may fitly agree with this place: but why calleth he it daily bread, which is also signified by this word *epiousion?*

Scholar. We ask daily bread, that might be always present and accompany us continually, to slake and satisfy our thirsty desire, and unsatiate stomach: lest otherwise we should be, as Christ sayeth, careful for tomorrow; because the morrow shall care for itself. For it shall come not without his own discommodity and care. Wherefore it is not reason, that one day should increase the evil of another. It shall be sufficient for us, daily to ask that our most bountiful Father is ready daily to give. Now followeth the fifth request: wherein we beseech the Father to forgive us our trespasses and defaults, that we have committed. This request doubtless is very necessary: sith there is no man living

[1 exciting.]   [2 'Επιούσιον.]

free from sin. Here therefore must we cast away all trust of ourselves. Here must we pluck down our courage. Here must we pray our most merciful Father, for the love of Jesu Christ his most dear and obedient Son, to pardon, forgive, and utterly blot out of his book, our innumerable offences.

<small>Our covenant with God, as we forgive, &c.</small> Here ought we in the mean season to be mindful of the covenant we make with God: That it may please God so to forgive us our trespasses, as we ourselves forgive them that trespass against us. Therefore it is necessary, that we forgive and pardon all men all their offences, of what sort or condition soever they be. If we forgive men their faults, our heavenly Father shall forgive us ours.

<small>Charitable forgiveness one to another ceaseth brawls.</small> *Master.* Were these things (my son) thus used, there should not, at this day, thus violently reign so many brawls, so many contentions, so many and so heinous disagreements, enmities and hatreds of one man to another. But now, whereas each man so standeth in his own conceit, that he <small>The harms of contention.</small> will not lose an inch of his right, neither in honour or wealth, it chanceth oft that they lose both their wealth, their honour, and their life itself withal. Yea they put from themselves and turn away the favour of God, and everlasting glory. But thou (my son) must not be ignorant of Christ's commandment; nor of that which Paul teacheth, that thou suffer <small>Good, not evil, to be rendered for evil.</small> not thyself to be overcome of evil, that is, suffer not thyself so to be seduced by any other man's offence, as to repay evil for evil, but rather overcome evil with good: I mean, by doing him good, that hath done thee evil; by using him friendly, that hath shewed himself thy most cruel foe. Now go forward to the sixth request.

<small>Our weakness.</small> *Scholar.* I will, with a good will, as you command me. Forasmuch as we be feeble, weak, subject to a thousand perils, a M.[1] temptations, easy to be overcome, ready to yield to every light occasion, either to men fraught with malice, or to our own lust and appetite, or finally to the crafty malicious serpent, the devil: Therefore we beseech our Father, that he bring us into no such hard escape and peril, nor leave us in <small>Temptation.</small> the very plunge of danger; but, if it come to that point, that he rather take us away from the present mischief, and engines of the devil, the author and principal cause of all evil, than suffer us to run headlong into destruction. Now have

[1 thousand.]

you, good master, in few words, all that you have taught me, unless peradventure somewhat be overslipped in the rehearsal.

Master. Because thine is the kingdom, power and glory for ever. Amen. Why was it Christ's pleasure to knit up our prayer with this clause in the end?

Scholar. Partly that we should declare our assured trust, to obtain all things, that we before have required. For there is nothing which, if it be asked with faith, he is not able or not willing to give, who ruleth and governeth all things, who is able to do all things, who is garnished with endless glory. These things when we rehearse, of God our Father, there remaineth no cause to doubt, or suspect, that we shall receive denial. Why this is added: For thine is the kingdom, &c.

Partly by so saying, we teach ourselves, how meet it is to make our suit to God, sith beside him none glistereth with so shining glory, none hath dominion so large, or force so great, to be able to stay him from giving that he hath appointed according to his pleasure, or to take away that he hath already given us. And there is no evil of ours so great, that may not be put away by his exceeding great power, glory and wisdom.

Master. I like well (my son) this thy short declaration: and I see nothing left out, that ought to have been spoken.

Scholar. But yet this one thing will I add thereto. The chief and principal thing, required in prayer, is that without all doubting we stedfastly believe, that God our Father will grant what we do ask; so that it be neither unprofitable for us to receive, nor unfit for him to give. For he that is not assured but doubtful, let him not think (as James saith) to get any thing at the hands of God. Faith in prayer. What to be asked in prayer.

Master. I see now (my dear son), how diligently and heedfully thou hast applied thy mind to those things that I have taught thee; how godly and upright a judgment thou hast of God's true service, and of the duties of neighbours one to another. This remaineth, that from henceforth thou so frame thy life, that this heavenly and godly knowledge decay not in thee, nor lie soulless and dead, as it were, in a tomb of flesh. But rather see that thou wholly give thyself continually and earnestly to these godly studies. So shalt thou live, not only in this present life, but also in the life to come, which is much better and blesseder than this life pre- Honest frame of life.

sent. For godliness (as Paul saith) hath a promise, not in this life only, but in the other. It is convenient therefore, that we earnestly follow godliness, which plainly openeth the way to heaven, if we will seek to attain thereunto. And the principal point of godliness is (as thou hast declared even now very well) to know God only: to covet him only as the chief felicity: to fear him as our Lord: to love and reverence him as our Father: with his Son our Saviour Jesus Christ. This is he that hath begotten and regenerated us. This is he which at the beginning gave us life and soul: which maintaineth: which blesseth us with life of everlasting continuance. To this godliness is directly contrary godlessness. As for superstition and hypocrisy, they counterfeit indeed, and resemble it, whereas nevertheless they are most far different from all true godliness: and therefore we ought to avoid them, as a pestilence, as the venom, and most contagious enemies of our soul and salvation. The next point of godliness is to love each man, as our brother: for if God did at the beginning create us all; if he doth feed and govern us; finally, if he be the cause and author of our dwelling in this wide frame of the world: the name of brother must needs most fitly agree with us; and with so much straiter bond shall we be bound together, as we approach nearer to Christ, which is our brother, the first begotten and eldest: whom he that knoweth not, he that hath no hold of, is unrighteous indeed, and hath no place among the people of God. For Christ is the root and foundation of all right and justice, and he hath poured into our hearts certain natural lessons, as: Do that (saith he) to another, that thou wouldst have done unto thyself. Beware therefore, thou do nothing to any man, that thou thyself wouldst not willingly suffer. Measure always another by thine own mind, and as thou feelest in thyself. If it grieve thee to suffer injury; if thou think it wrong that another man doth to thee; judge likewise the same in the person of thy neighbour that thou feelest in thyself: and thou shalt perceive, that thou dost no less wrongfully in hurting another, than other do in hurting thee. Here if we would stedfastly fasten our foot; hereunto if we would earnestly travail; we should attain to the very highest top of innocency. For the first degree thereof is to offend no man: the next to help, as much as in us lieth, all men:

at least to will and wish well to all: the third (which is accounted the chief and perfectest) is to do good even to our enemies that wrong us. Let us therefore know ourselves: pluck out the faults that are in us, and in their place plant virtues: like unto the husbandmen, that first use to shrubbe and root out the thorns, brambles and weeds, out of their lay-land and unlooked to; and then each where therein scatter and throw in to the womb of the earth good and fruitful seeds, to bring forth good' fruit in their due season. Likewise let us do. For first let us labour to root out froward and corrupt lusts: and afterward plant holy and fit conditions for Christian hearts. Which, if they be watered, and fatted with the dew of God's word, and nourished with warmth of the Holy Ghost, they shall bring forth doubtless the most plentiful fruit of immortality and blessed life: which God hath by Christ prepared for his chosen, before the foundations of the world were laid. To whom be all honour and glory. Amen.

Degrees of charity.

Vices to be rooted out that virtues may be planted in their place.

The bliss of the godly.

The end of the Cathechism.

ARTICLES

AGREED UPON IN THE CONVOCATION,

AND

PUBLISHED BY THE KING'S MAJESTY.

¶ *Of faith in the holy Trinity.*

THERE is but one living, and true God: and he is everlasting: without body, parts, or passions: of infinite power, wisdom, and goodness: the maker, and preserver of all things, both visible, and invisible. And in unity of this Godhead there be three persons, of one substance, power, and eternity: the Father, the Son, and the Holy Ghost.

¶ *That the Word, or Son of God, was made very man.*

THE Son, which is the Word of the Father, took man's nature in the womb of the blessed virgin Mary: of her substance: so that two whole and perfect natures, that is to say, the Godhead[1] and manhood, were joined together into one person, never to be divided: whereof is one Christ very God, and very man: who truly suffered, was crucified, dead, and buried, to reconcile his Father to us, and to be a sacrifice for all sin of man, both original, and actual.

¶ *Of the going down of Christ into Hell.*

As Christ died, and was buried for us: so also it is to be believed, that he went down into Hell. For the body lay in the sepulchre, until the resurrection: but his ghost departing from him, was with the ghosts that were in prison, or in Hell; and did preach to the same: as the place of S. Peter doth testify.

[1 godhode, in the original.]

¶ *The Resurrection of Christ.*

CHRIST did truly rise again from death: and took again his body: with flesh, bones, and all things appertaining to the perfection of man's nature: wherewith he ascended into heaven, and there sitteth, until he return to judge men at the last day.

¶ *The doctrine of holy scripture is sufficient to Salvation.*

HOLY Scripture containeth all things necessary to salvation: so that whatsoever is neither read therein, nor may be proved thereby, although it be sometime received of the faithful, as godly, and profitable for an order, and comeliness; yet no man ought to be constrained to believe it as an article of faith, or repute it requisite to the necessity of Salvation.

¶ *The Old Testament is not to be refused.*

THE Old Testament is not to be put away, as though it were contrary to the new; but to be kept still. For both in the old, and new Testaments, everlasting life is offered to mankind by Christ: who is the only mediator between God and man, being both God and man. Wherefore they are not to be heard, which feign, that the old fathers did look only for transitory promises.

¶ *The three Creeds.*

THE three Creeds, Nicene Creed, Athanasius' Creed, and that which is commonly called the Apostles' Creed, ought throughly to be received: for they may be proved by most certain warrants of holy Scripture.

¶ *Of original, or birth sin.*

ORIGINAL sin standeth not in the following of Adam, as the Pelagians do vainly talk, which also the Anabaptists do now-a-days renew: but it is the fault and corruption of the nature of every man, that naturally is engendered of the offspring of Adam: whereby man is very far gone from his former righteousness, which he had at his creation, and is of his own nature given to evil; so that the flesh desireth always contrary to the spirit: and therefore in every person, born into this world, it deserveth God's wrath and damnation. And this infection of nature doth remain, yea, in them that are baptized: whereby the lust of the flesh, called in Greek φρόνημα σαρκὸς, (which some do expoune, the wisdom, some sensuality, some the affection, some the desire of the flesh,) is not subject to the law of God. And although there is no condemnation for them that believe, and are baptized: yet the Apostle doth confess, that concupiscence and lust hath of itself the nature of sin.

¶ Of Free will.

WE have no power to do good works, pleasant, and acceptable to God, without the grace of God by Christ, preventing us, that we may have a good will, and working in us when we have that will.

Of Grace.

THE grace of Christ, or the Holy Ghost by him given, doth take away the stony heart, and giveth an heart of flesh. And although those that have no will to good things, he maketh them to will; and those that would evil things, he maketh them not to will the same: yet nevertheless he enforceth not the will. And therefore no man, when he sinneth, can excuse himself, as not worthy to be blamed or condemned, by alleging that he sinned unwillingly, or by compulsion.

¶ Of the Justification of Man.

JUSTIFICATION by only faith in Jesus Christ, in that sense as it is declared in the homily of Justification, is a most certain and wholesome doctrine for Christian men.

¶ Works before Justification.

WORKS done before the grace of Christ, and the inspiration of his Spirit, are not pleasant to God; forasmuch as they spring not of Faith in Jesu Christ: neither do they make men meet to receive grace, or (as the School-authors say) deserve grace of congruity: but because they are not done as God hath willed and commanded them to be done, we doubt not but they have the nature of sin.

¶ *Works of Supererogation.*

VOLUNTARY works besides, over, and above God's commandments, which they call works of Supererogation, cannot be taught without arrogancy, and iniquity. For by them men do declare, that they do not only render to God, as much as they are bound to do; but that they do more for his sake, than of bounden duty is required: whereas Christ saith plainly: When you have done all that are commanded, say, We be unprofitable servants.

¶ *No Man is without Sin, but Christ alone.*

CHRIST, in the truth of our nature, was made like unto us in all things, sin only except, from which he was clearly void both in his flesh, and in his spirit. He came to be the Lamb without spot: who by sacrifice of himself, made once for ever, should take away the sins of the world: and sin (as Saint John saith) was not in him. But the rest, yea, although we be baptized, and born again in Christ, yet we offend in many things: and if we say, we have no sin, we deceive ourselves, and the truth is not in us.

¶ *Of Sin against the Holy Ghost.*

EVERY deadly sin, willingly committed after Baptism, is not Sin against the Holy Ghost, and unpardonable. Wherefore the place for penitents is not to be denied, to such as fall into sin after Baptism. After we have received the Holy Ghost, we may depart from grace given, and fall into sin: and by the grace of God we may rise again, and amend our lives. And therefore they are to be condemned, which say, they can no more sin, as long as they live here; or deny the place for penitents, to such as truly repent, and amend their lives.

¶ *Blasphemy against the Holy Ghost.*

BLASPHEMY against the Holy Ghost is, when a man of malice and stubbornness of mind doth rail upon the truth of God's word, manifestly perceived; and being enemy thereunto persecuteth the same. And because such be guilty of God's curse, they entangle themselves with a most grievous and heinous crime; whereupon this kind of sin is called and affirmed of the Lord unpardonable.

¶ *Of Predestination, and Election.*

PREDESTINATION to life is the everlasting purpose of God, whereby (before the foundations of the world were laid) he hath constantly decreed, by his own judgment, secret to us, to deliver from curse and damnation those whom he hath chosen out of mankind; and to bring them to everlasting salvation by Christ, as vessels made to honour. Whereupon such as have so excellent a benefit of God given unto them, be called, according to God's purpose, by his Spirit working in due season: they through grace obey the calling: they be justified freely: they be made sons by adoption: they be made like the image of God's only begotten Son, Jesus Christ: they walk religiously in good works: and at length, by God's mercy, they attain to everlasting felicity.

As the godly consideration of Predestination, and our election in Christ, is full of sweet, pleasant, and unspeakable comfort to godly persons, and such as feel in themselves the working of the Spirit of Christ, mortifying the works of the flesh, and their earthly members, and drawing up their mind to high and heavenly things; as well because it doth greatly establish and confirm their faith of eternal salvation, to be enjoyed through Christ, as because it doth fervently kindle their love towards God: So for curious, and carnal persons, lacking the Spirit of Christ, to have continually before their eyes the sentence of God's predestination, is a most dangerous downfal: whereby the Devil may thrust them either into desperation, or into a rechlessness of most unclean living, no less perilous than desperation.

Furthermore, although the decrees of predestination are unknown unto us; yet we must receive God's promises in such wise as they be generally set forth to us in holy scripture: and in our doings that will of God is to be followed, which we have expressly declared unto us in the word of God.

¶ *We must trust to obtain eternal Salvation, only by the name of Christ.*

THEY also are to be had accursed, and abhorred, that presume to say, that every man shall be saved by the law, or sect which he professeth, so that he be diligent to frame his life according to that law, and the light of nature. For holy scripture doth set out unto us only the name of Jesu Christ, whereby men must be saved.

¶ *All men are bound to keep the Moral commandments of the Law.*

THE Law which was given of God by Moses, although it bind not christian men, as concerning the ceremonies and rites of the same: neither is it required that the civil precepts and orders of it should of necessity be received in any commonweal: yet no man (be he never so perfect a Christian) is exempt and loose from the obedience of those commandments, which are called Moral. Wherefore they are not to be hearkened unto, who affirm that holy scripture is given only to the weak, and do boast themselves continually of the Spirit, of whom (they say) they have learned such things as they teach, although the same be most evidently repugnant to the holy scripture.

¶ *Of the Church.*

THE visible Church of Christ is a congregation of faithful men, in which the pure word of God is preached, and the sacraments be duly ministered, according to Christ's ordinance, in all those things that of necessity are requisite to the same.

As the church of Jerusalem, of Alexandria, and of Antioch hath erred: so also the Church of Rome hath erred, not only in their living, but also in matters of their faith.

¶ *Of the authority of the Church.*

IT is not lawful for the church to ordain any thing, that is contrary to God's word written. Neither may it so expoune one place of scripture, that it be repugnant to another. Wherefore although the church be a witness and a keeper of holy writ, yet as it ought not to decree any thing against the same: so besides the same ought it not to enforce any thing to be believed, for necessity of salvation.

¶ *Of the authority of general Councils.*

GENERAL councils may not be gathered together, without the commandment and will of princes: and when they be gathered (forasmuch as they be an assembly of men, whereof all be not governed with the Spirit and word of God) they may err, and sometime have erred, not only in worldly matters, but also in things pertaining unto God. Wherefore things ordained by them, as necessary to salvation, have neither strength nor authority, unless it may be declared, that they be taken out of holy scripture.

¶ *Of Purgatory.*

THE Doctrine of School authors concerning purgatory, pardons, worshipping and adoration as well of images as of relics, and also invocation of Saints, is a fond thing, vainly feigned, and grounded upon no warrant of scripture, but rather repugnant to the word of God.

¶ *No man may minister in the Congregation, except he be called.*

IT is not lawful for any man to take upon him the office of public preaching, or ministering the sacraments, in the congregation, before he be lawfully called, and sent to execute the same. And those we ought to judge lawfully called, and sent, which be chosen, and called to this work by men, who have public authority given unto them in the congregation, to call, and send ministers into the Lord's vineyard.

¶ *Men must speak in the Congregation in such tongue, as the people understandeth.*

IT is most seemly, and most agreeable to the word of God, that in the congregation nothing be openly read or spoken in a tongue unknown to the people. The which thing Saint Paul did forbid, except some were present that should declare the same.

¶ *Of the Sacraments.*

OUR Lord Jesus Christ hath knit together a company of new people with Sacraments most few in number, most easy to be kept, most excellent in signification: as is Baptism, and the Lord's Supper.

The Sacraments were not ordained of Christ to be gazed upon, or to be carried about: but that we should rightly use them. And in such only, as worthily receive the same, they have a wholesome effect and operation; and yet not that of the work wrought, as some men speak. Which word, as it is strange, and unknown to holy scripture; so it engendereth no godly, but a very superstitious sense. But they that receive the sacraments unworthily, purchase to themselves damnation, as Saint Paul saith.

Sacraments ordained by the word of God be not only badges and tokens of Christian men's profession: but rather they be certain sure witnesses, and effectual signs of grace, and God's good will toward us, by the which he doth work invisibly in us; and doth not only quicken, but also strengthen, and confirm our faith in him.

¶ *The wickedness of the Ministers doth not take away the effectual operation of God's ordinances.*

ALTHOUGH in the visible church the evil be ever mingled with the good, and sometime the evil have chief authority in the ministration of the word and sacraments: yet forasmuch as they do not the same in their own name, but do minister by Christ's commission and authority, we may use their ministry both in hearing the word of God, and in the receiving the sacraments. Neither is the effect of God's ordinances taken away by their wickedness; nor the grace of God's gifts diminished from such, as by faith and rightly receive the sacraments ministered unto them: which be effectual, because of Christ's institution and promise, although they be ministered by evil men. Nevertheless it appertaineth to the discipline of the Church, that inquiry be made of such, and that they be accused by those that have knowledge of their offences; and finally being found guilty by just judgment, be deposed.

¶ *Of Baptism.*

BAPTISM is not only a sign of profession, and mark of difference, whereby christian men are discerned from others that be not christianed: but it is also a sign and seal of our new birth; whereby, as by an instrument, they that receive

Baptism rightly are grafted into the church: the promises of forgiveness of sin, and our adoption to be the sons of God, are visibly signed and sealed: faith is confirmed: and grace increased, by virtue of prayer unto God. The custom of the church to christen young children, is to be commended, and in any wise to be retained in the church.

¶ *Of the Lord's Supper.*

THE supper of the Lord is not only a sign of the love that Christians ought to have among themselves, one to another; but rather it is a sacrament of our redemption by Christ's death: insomuch that, to such as rightly, worthily, and with faith receive the same, the bread which we break is a communion of the body of Christ: likewise the Cup of blessing is a Communion of the blood of Christ.

Transubstantiation, or the change of the substance of bread and wine into the substance of Christ's body and blood, cannot be proved by holy writ: but it is repugnant to the plain words of scripture, and hath given occasion to many superstitions. Forasmuch as the truth of man's nature requireth, that the body of one, and the self same man, cannot be at one time in divers places, but must needs be in some one certain place: therefore the body of Christ cannot be present at one time in many and divers places. And because (as holy scripture doth teach) Christ was taken up into heaven, and there shall continue unto the end of the world; a faithful man ought not, either to believe, or openly to confess the real and bodily presence (as they term it) of Christ's flesh and blood in the sacrament of the Lord's Supper.

The sacrament of the Lord's Supper was not commanded, by Christ's ordinance, to be kept, carried about, lifted up, nor worshipped.

¶ *Of the perfect Oblation of Christ made upon the Cross.*

THE offering of Christ, made once for ever, is the perfect redemption, the pacifying of God's displeasure and satisfaction for all the sins of the whole world, both original and actual: and there is none other satisfaction for sin, but that alone. Wherefore the sacrifices of masses, in the which, it was commonly said, that the priest did offer Christ for the quick and the dead, to have remission of pain or sin, were forged fables, and dangerous deceits.

¶ *The state of single life is commanded to no man by the word of God.*

BISHOPS, Priests, and Deacons are not commanded to vow the state of single life without marriage: neither by God's law are they compelled to abstain from matrimony.

¶ *Excommunicate persons are to be avoided.*

THAT person, which by open denunciation of the church is rightly cut off from the unity of the church, and excommunicate, ought to be taken of the whole multitude of the faithful, as an heathen and publican, until he be openly reconciled by penance and received into the church by a judge that hath authority thereto.

¶ *Traditions of the Church.*

IT is not necessary that traditions and ceremonies be in all places one, or utterly like. For at all times they have been divers; and may be changed, according to the diversity of countries and men's manners, so that nothing be ordained against God's word. Whosoever through his private judgment willingly and purposely doth openly break the traditions and ceremonies of the church, which be not repugnant to the word of God, and be ordained and approved by common authority, ought to be rebuked openly (that other may fear to do the like), as one that offendeth against the common order of the church, and hurteth the authority of the magistrate, and woundeth the consciences of the weak brethren.

¶ *Homilies.*

THE Homilies of late given, and set out by the king's authority, be godly and wholesome, containing doctrine to be received of all men: and therefore are to be read to the people diligently, distinctly, and plainly.

¶ *Of the book of Prayers, and Ceremonies of the Church of England.*

THE book, which of very late time was given to the church of England by the king's authority, and the Parliament, containing the manner and form of praying, and ministering the sacraments in the church of England, likewise also the book of ordering ministers of the church, set forth by the foresaid authority, are godly, and in no point repugnant to the wholesome doctrine of the gospel, but agreeable thereunto, furthering and beautifying the same not a little: and therefore of all faithful members of the church of England, and chiefly of the ministers of the word, they ought to be received, and allowed with all readiness of mind and thanksgiving, and to be commended to the people of God.

¶ *Of civil Magistrates.*

THE king of England is Supreme head in earth, next under Christ, of the church of England and Ireland.

The Bishop of Rome hath no jurisdiction in this realm of England.

The civil magistrate is ordained, and allowed of God: wherefore we must obey him, not only for fear of punishment, but also for conscience sake.

The civil laws may punish Christian men with death, for heinous and grievous offences.

It is lawful for Christians, at the commandment of the magistrate, to wear weapons, and to serve in lawful wars.

¶ *Christian men's goods are not common*[1].

THE riches and goods of Christians are not common, as touching the right, title, and possession of the same, (as certain Anabaptists do falsely boast:) notwithstanding every man ought of such things, as he possesseth, liberally to give alms to the poor, according to his ability.

¶ *Christian men may take an Oath.*

As we confess that vain and rash swearing is forbidden Christian men, by our Lord Jesu Christ, and his Apostle James: so we judge that Christian religion doth not prohibit, but that a man may swear, when the magistrate requireth, in a cause of faith and charity; so it be done (according to the Prophet's teaching) in justice, judgment and truth.

[1 commune, in the original.]

¶ *The resurrection of the dead is not yet brought to pass.*

THE resurrection of the dead is not as yet brought to pass; as though it only belonged to the soul, which by the grace of Christ is raised from the death of sin: but it is to be looked for at the last day. For then (as scripture doth most manifestly testify) to all that be dead their own bodies, flesh, and bone shall be restored; that the whole man may (according to his works) have either reward or punishment, as he hath lived virtuously or wickedly.

¶ *The souls of them that depart this life do neither die with the bodies, nor sleep idly.*

THEY which say, that the souls of such as depart hence, do sleep, being without all sense, feeling, or perceiving, until the day of judgment; or affirm that the souls die with the bodies, and at the last day shall be raised up with the same; do utterly dissent from the right belief, declared to us in holy scripture.

¶ *Heretics called Millenarii.*

THEY that go about to renew the fable of heretics called Millenarii, be repugnant to holy scripture, and cast themselves headlong into a Jewish dotage.

¶ *All men shall not be saved at the length.*

THEY also are worthy of condemnation, who endeavour at this time to restore the dangerous opinion, that all men, be they never so ungodly, shall at length be saved, when they have suffered pains for their sins a certain time appointed by God's justice.

The end of the Articles.

[PRAYERS.]

¶ *A General Confession to be said in the Morning.*

ALMIGHTY and most merciful Father, we have erred and strayed from thy ways, like lost sheep. We have followed too much the devices, and desires, of our own hearts. We have offended against thy holy laws. We have left undone those things which we ought to have done : and we have done those things which we ought not to have done : and there is no health in us. But thou, O Lord, have mercy upon us, miserable offenders. Spare thou them, O God, which confess their faults. Restore thou them that be penitent, according to thy promises, declared unto mankind, in Christ Jesu our Lord. And grant, O most merciful Father, for his sake, that we may hereafter live a godly, righteous, and sober life, to the glory of thy holy name. Amen.

A prayer to be said in the morning.

O MERCIFUL Lord God, heavenly Father, I render most high lauds, praise and thanks unto thee, that thou hast preserved me both this night, and all the time and days of my life hitherto, under thy protection; and hast suffered me to live until this present hour. And I beseech thee heartily, that thou wilt vouchsafe to receive me this day, and the residue of my whole life from henceforth, into thy tuition; ruling and governing me with thy holy Spirit: that all manner of darkness, of misbelief, infidelity, and of carnal lusts and affections, may be utterly chased and driven out of my heart; and that I may be justified and saved both body and soul through a right and a perfect faith; and so walk in the light of thy most godly truth, to thy glory and praise, and to the profit and furtherance of my neighbour, through Jesus Christ our Lord and Saviour. Amen.

¶ *A prayer to be said of Children before they study their lesson at school.*

O BLESSED Lord, which art the well-spring of all wisdom and knowledge, since it hath pleased thee of thy mercy to provide for me such means to be instructed in my tender age, as whereby I may have knowledge to use myself honestly, and to behave myself godly, to lead the whole course of my life in thy holy service: let it be thy pleasure also to illuminate my dark wit and blind understanding, so that it may be able to receive accordingly the learning that shall be uttered: refresh thou my memory, yea, imprint thou it in my remembrance, that I may keep it assuredly: dispose thou my heart also (good God) and frame my will, that I may apply my mind to receive it with such affection and fervent desire, as it behoveth; to this end, that the most happy occasion which thou offerest unto me, do not perish through my unthankfulness: and that these things may come to pass, let it stand with thy gracious pleasure to pour out thy holy Spirit into my heart, thy Spirit, I say, of understanding, of truth, judgment, wisdom and knowledge: whereby I may become apt to learn, and my schoolmaster not lose his pain in teaching me; and what study soever I apply my mind unto, I may reduce and bring it to the right end (that is) to glorify thee in our Saviour Christ, to whom with thee and the Holy Ghost be all honour and glory for ever and ever. Amen.

¶ *A Prayer for the King's Majesty.*

ALMIGHTY God, whose kingdom is everlasting, and power infinite: have mercy upon the whole congregation, and so rule the heart of thy chosen servant Edward the sixth, our king and governor, that he (knowing whose minister he is) may above all things seek thy honour and glory; and that we his subjects (duly considering whose authority he hath) may faithfully serve, honour, and humbly obey him, in thee, and for thee, according to thy blessed word and ordinance: Through Jesus Christ our Lord, who with thee and the Holy Ghost liveth and reigneth ever one God, world without end. Amen.

¶ *A prayer to be said at night going to bed.*

O MERCIFUL Lord God, heavenly Father, whether we sleep or wake, live or die, we are always thine. Wherefore I beseech thee heartily, that thou wilt vouchsafe to take care and charge of me, and not to suffer me to perish in the works of darkness, but to kindle the light of thy countenance in my heart, that the godly knowledge may daily increase in me, through a right and pure faith, and that I may always be found to walk and live after thy will and pleasure, through Jesus Christ our Lord and Saviour. Amen.

Lord into thy hands I commend my spirit: thou hast redeemed me, Lord God of truth.

ℭ IMPRYN-

ted at London by Jhon Day dwelling ouer Aldersgate beneth Saynct Martyns.

☞ These Cathechismes are to bee solde at hys shop, by the litle Counduit in Chepesyde at the sygne of the Resurreccion.

Cum priuilegio ad imprimendum solum.

CATECHISMUS BREVIS,

CHRISTIANÆ DISCIPLINÆ SUMMAM

CONTINENS,

OMNIBUS LUDIMAGISTRIS AUTHORITATE REGIA COMMENDATUS.

HUIC CATECHISMO ADJUNCTI SUNT ARTICULI, DE QUIBUS IN ULTIMA SYNODO LONDINENSI, ANNO DOM. 1552, AD TOLLENDAM OPINIONUM DISSENSIONEM, &c.

1553.

Catechiſmus
BREVIS, CHRISTI-
ANAE DISCIPLINAE
ſummam continens, omnibus
Ludimagistris authoritate
REGIA
commendatus.

HVIC CATECHISMO AD-
iuncti ſunt Articuli, de quibus in vltima Synodo Londinenſi, Anno Dom.
1552. *ad tollendam opinionum diſſenſionem,*
& conſenſum ueræ religionis firmandum,
inter Epiſcopos & alios eruditos at-
que pios uiros conuenerat: Regia
ſimiliter authori-
tate promulgati.

LONDINI.
Cum priuilegio Sereniſſ. Regis.
ANNO DO. M.D.LIII.

[The copy of this edition, which we have followed, is in the possession of G. Stokes, Esq., Cheltenham.]

Catechismus
BREVIS CHRISTI-
ANAE DISCIPLINAE,
summam continens, omnibus
Ludimagistris authoritate
REGIA.
Commendatus.

HVIC CATECHISMO AD-
iuncti funt Articuli, de quibus in
vltima Synodo Londinenfi
Anno Domini. 1552. ad tollendam
opinionum difsensionem, & con-
sensum uere religionis firman-
dum, inter Episcopos &
alios eruditos atque pios
viros conuenerat: Regia
similiter authori-
tate promulgati.

Londini, cum priuilegio Serenifs. Regis
ANNO DO. M.D.LIII.

[The copy of this edition, which we have collated, is in the British Museum, 851. f. 16.]

EDVARDVS VI.

DEI GRATIA ANGLIÆ FRANCIÆ ET HIBERNIÆ REX, FIDEI DEFENSOR, ET IN TERRIS ECCLESIÆ ANGLICANÆ ET HIBERNICÆ SUPREMUM CAPUT, OMNIBUS LUDIMAGISTRIS ET HIS[1] QUI SCHOLAS GRAMMATICAS APERIUNT.

Cum brevis et explicata Catechismi ratio, a pio quodam et erudito viro conscripta, nobis ad cognoscendum offerretur, ejus pertractationem et diligentem inquisitionem quibusdam Episcopis et aliis eruditis commisimus, quorum judicium magnam apud nos auctoritatem habet. Et quia conveniens cum Scripturis et Regni nostri institutis visa est, Placuit, non solum eam propter convenientiam in aspectum lucemque proferre, sed etiam propter perspicuitatem et brevitatem omnibus ludorum magistris ad docendum proponere, ut rudis adhuc et inchoata ætas, religionis simul et literarum jactis fundamentis, cum sapientia pietatem discat, et regulam habeat in reliquo vitæ cursu, quid sentiendum de Deo sit, ad quem omnis vita nostra confertur, et quomodo accepti Deo simus, in quo omnibus actionibus et vitæ officiis elaborandum est.

Præcipimus itaque et mandamus non modo universis, sed etiam singulis, pro cautione qua auctoritatem nostram sanctam habere, et justam violatæ dignitatis animadversionem devitare studetis, ut sedulo ac diligenter hunc Catechismum in scholis vestris doceatis, ut tenera adhuc et fluens ætas, et præceptorum auctoritate et veræ religionis documentis firmata, magnas opportunitates ad veram Dei venerationem habeat, et magna subsidia etiam ad omnia vitæ officia sequenda: quibus instructi, pietatem in Deum auctorem omnium, observantiam erga Regem pastorem populi, studium in rempublicam communem omnium matrem, melius usurpantes, non sibi solum nasci videantur, sed Deo, Regi, patriæ utiles et officiosi sint. Dat. Grenwici, 20: Maij, Anno regni nostri, 7.

[[1] hiis, B. M.]

CATECHISMUS
CHRISTIANÆ DISCIPLINÆ.

Officium singulorum est, quos Christus morte sua redemerat, non modo ut servi sint ad obedientiam, sed etiam filii ad hæreditatem, ita scire quæ sit vera et complacita Deo vitæ via, ut ad singula religionis interrogata respondere possint, et fidei ac professionis suæ rationem reddere.

Atque hæc apertissima docendi ratio est, quam non modo Socrates in philosophia, sed etiam Apollinarius in nostra religione secutus est, ut et ignorantes interrogationibus quasi punctis erudiantur, et scientes ne amittant quæ didicerunt commonefiant. Nos igitur utilitatis ratione habita, quam in adolescentibus instruendis sequi debemus, et brevitatis etiam, ut nihil neque redundans neque defectum esset, universæ scholæ nostræ summam in dialogum conjecimus, ut tota res magis perspicua esset, et minus digressionibus evagaremur. Itaque ad hunc modum Magister Auditorem suum aggreditur.

Magister. Auditor.

Quandoquidem officii mei magnam partem esse video, carissime fili, non tam ut bonis literis institutus sis curare, quam etiam atque etiam de genere religionis, quodcunque in tenera ista ætate colas, sedulo et diligenter perquirere; consentaneum putavi quæstiunculis quibusdam tecum agere, ut certo sciam, num recte an secus in ea re operam posueris. Age igitur, dic mihi, mi fili, quænam ea sit religio quam profiteris?

Aud. Eam, præceptor venerande, religionem profiteor, quæ est Christi Domini, quæque Actorum undecimo Christiana nominata est.

Mag. Agnoscis igitur te Christianæ pietatis et religionis cultorem, ac Christi Domini nostri discipulum?

Aud. Id equidem agnosco, atque ingenue et libere profiteor: quin et universe gloriæ meæ summam in hoc pono, tanquam in re quæ et honoratior sit, quam ut ad eam ingenii mei tenuitas aspirare, et divinior etiam, quam ut orationis ulla facultate a me facile exprimi queat.

Mag. Dic proinde mihi, carissime fili, quam accurate poteris, religionis Christianæ summam quibusnam in rebus positam esse arbitraris?

Aud. In duabus, nempe vera in Deum fide, ac certa persuasione concepta de rebus illis omnibus, quæ sacris literis continentur; et caritate quæ cum in Deum tum in proximum nostrum tendit.

Mag. Fides illa, quæ ex verbi auditu et lectione concepta est, quid docet te de Deo?

Aud. Illud imprimis docet, in mundo esse certam naturam, unam substantiam, unum animum, et mentem divinam, aut potius Spiritum æternum, absque principio[1] et fine, quem vocamus Deum; quem oportet universos mundi populos colere summo honore ac præcipuo genere adorationis. Ex divinis etiam illis oraculis, quæ per prophetas et amicos Dei Opt. Max. in sanctis libris ad sempiternam nominis ejus gloriam divulgantur, legem disco et comminationes; deinde promissiones et evangelium Dei. Hæc per Mosen ac alios viros Dei conscripta, ad nostram usque ætatem integra conservata sunt et illæsa. Deinde præcipua capita nostræ fidei redacta fuerunt in brevissimum compendium, quod vulgo Symbolum Apostolicum appellatur.

Mag. Fidei compendium cur Symbolum nominarunt?

Aud. Symbolum, si interpreteris, est signum, nota, tessera, aut indicium, quo commilitones ab hostibus dignoscuntur[2]: unde compendium fidei, quo Christiani a non Christianis distinguuntur, recte symboli nomen sortitum est.

Mag. De lege primum quid sentias, aliqua dicas: deinde etiam de Symbolo.

Aud. Faciam quod jubes, præceptor venerande, idque libentissime. Dominus Deus per Mosen nobis præcepit, ne ullum prorsus præter illum, hoc est, ut illum solum habeamus Deum, unicum creatorem et liberatorem nostrum: ne veneremur aut colamus simulacrum aliquod, aut imaginem quamcunque, sive depicta ea sit, sive cœlata aut sculpta, sive ratione quavis alia formata: ne sumamus nomen Domini Dei nostri in vanum, in re scilicet aut levi aut falso: postremo, fixum illud et religiosum perpetuo tenere debemus, ut Sabbathi diem, quæ ad quietem et cultum divinum segregatur, sancte et religiose colamus.

[[1] principo, in G. S. for principio as in B. M.]   [[2] dinoscuntur, B. M.]

Mag. Recte. Recitatæ enim jam sunt a te mihi leges primæ tabulæ, qua cognitio Dei et cultus ejus summatim comprehenditur. Jam dic mihi quæ sint caritatis et dilectionis nostræ officia erga homines?

Aud. Interrogas, mi præceptor, quid de altera parte legis Dei sentiam, quæ vulgo secunda Tabula vocatur?

Mag. Hoc ipsum plane est, mi fili, de quo audire cupio.

Aud. Paucis rem omnem, pro ingenii mei tenuitate, expediam. Moses eam brevi epitome conclusit, nimirum ut omni studio patrem et matrem honoremus atque observemus, ne ullum hominem occidamus, ne adulterium committamus, ne furtum ullum faciamus, ne falsi testes simus contra quemvis: postremo, ne rem ullam desideremus proximi.

Mag. Præceptum illud de patris et matris honore quomodo intelligendum est?

Aud. Honor parentum amorem, timorem, et reverentiam complectitur. Nec non versatur in obediendo, subveniendo, defendendo, ac etiam in fovendo, si necessitas incumbat. Nos quoque astringit ut magistratui summopere obtemperemus, et maxima cum pietate tum ministros ecclesiæ, tum præceptores et omnes majores observemus.

Mag. Quid autem continetur in præcepto illo, Ne occidas?

Aud. Ne odio prosequamur, ne injuria afficiamus quemquam, opprobriave jaciamus: ac præterea jubet ut etiam inimicos amemus, atque illis benefaciamus, qui nos odio prosequuntur, utque hostibus nostris prospera quæque atque felicia precemur.

Mag. Præceptum autem de non committendo adulterio, quid tandem continere tibi videtur?

Aud. Hoc quidem præceptum multa continet: prohibet enim non solum ne alloquamur impudice alienam uxorem, aut mulierem quamcunque, neve petulanter contrectemus, verum etiam respiciamus quidem, seu libidinoso aspectu intueamur, nec quocunque modo inhonesto ambiamus eam ipsi nos, nec nomine nostro alii: et denique omne genus obscenæ vagæque libidinis interdicitur.

Mag. Quid autem tibi videtur de præcepto non furandi?

Aud. Pari compendio dicam, si libet audire, quo antea usus sum. Præcipit autem ne cuipiam imponamus, ne commercia exerceamus illicita, ne suas opes cuiquam invideamus, neve rem quamcunque putemus utilem, quæ aut justa non sit, aut ab æquo et bono aliena. Breviter: potius quod tuum est ut perdas, quam ut rapias aliena, et in tuum vertas commodum.

Mag. Quomodo illud observetur de falso testimonio non dicendo?

Aud. Si mendacia aut falsa aut vana nec loquamur ipsi, nec in aliis vel loquendo vel tacendo, vel etiam præsentia nostra approbemus: sed semper veritatem tueri debemus, quotiescunque aut locus aut tempus id postulat.

Mag. Ultimum jam præceptum relinquitur de rem proximi non concupiscendo: quodnam tandem illud est?

Aud. Hæc lex in universum omnis generis malas cupiditates prohibet, ac voluntatis nostræ appetitionem omnem insatiabilem, quæ intra rectæ rationis limites se non continet, refrænare atque moderari nos jubet: vultque ut quisque sit sua sorte contentus. Quisquis autem plus justo appetit cum detrimento proximi et alterius injuria, is caritatis atque humanæ societatis vinculum rumpit, et plane dissolvit: ac nisi resipiscat, acriter de eo sumet supplicium Dominus Deus, legis suæ violatæ vindex severissimus. Qui autem ex harum legum præscripto vixerit, et laudem et felicitatem, ac ipsum etiam Deum propitium et benignum inveniet.

Mag. Jam video te decalogum breviter explicuisse: deinceps vero dicito mihi, quomodo Christus hæc omnia jam per partes a te explicata paucis est complexus, universam vim legis in summa nobis proponens?

Aud. Vis ut omnia simul compendio connectam, quæ tum ad Deum tum ad homines pertinent?

Mag. Maxime.

Aud. CHRISTUS in hunc loquitur modum: Diliges Dominum Deum tuum ex toto corde tuo, ex tota anima tua, et ex tota mente tua, et ex totis viribus tuis: et hoc maximum est præceptum in lege. Alterum autem est huic simile: Diliges proximum tuum sicut teipsum. Ex duobus hisce mandatis pendent tota Lex et Prophetæ.

Mag. Jam porro volo ut mihi dicas, quænam res sit lex illa quam narras: illane quam nos vocamus legem naturæ? an etiam præter eam altera?

Aud. Id olim me abs te didicisse memini, præceptor, nempe naturæ humanæ a Deo insitam eam fuisse, cum integra adhuc esset et incorrupta: post peccatum vero, tametsi sapientes utcunque eam naturæ lucem non ignorarint, attamen hominum partem maximam ita jam latebat, ut vix ejus umbram sentirent.

Mag. Unde fit, ut Deus eam velit in tabulis describi, utque uni peculiariter populo assignaretur?

Aud. Dicam. Imago Dei in homine per peccatum originis et consuetudinem malam adeo in initio obscurata est, et judicium naturale adeo vitiatum, ut homo ipse non satis intelligat, honestum turpi quid intersit, nec justum injusto. Eam itaque imaginem volens benignus Deus in nobis renovare per legem in tabulis descriptam, effecit primum, ut nos ipsos agnosceremus, et in ea, perinde atque in speculo, contueremur sordes et maculas nostri animi, et præfractam cordis vitiati duritiem, ut vel sic tandem peccato agnito, et perspecta nostræ carnis infirmitate, atque ira sævientis in nos Dei ob peccatum, ardentius desideraremus Servatorem nostrum Christum Jesum, qui morte sua et pretiosa sanguinis sui aspersione purgavit et abluit peccata nostra; placavit iram omnipotentis Patris, atque sacrosancto sui Spiritus afflatu animos[1] in nobis creat novos, mentesque renovat ad imaginem et similitudinem sui Creatoris, in justitia et sanctitate veritatis: quam rem nec justitia legis, nec ulla sacrificia Mosaica poterant efficere. Quod autem nullus ex lege justificetur, patet non inde solum, quoniam Justus ex fide vivit, sed hinc etiam, quod nullus vivit mortalium, qui potest ea omnia præstare quæ decalogus jubet. Impedimenta enim, quæ legi adversantur, sunt infirmitas carnis, appetitus pravus, et concupiscentia ingenita. Quod autem ad sacrificia attinet, quod ad purgationes, ad abluitiones, et reliquas cæremonias legis, umbræ erant, typi, imagines et figuræ veri et æterni sacrificii JESU CHRISTI in cruce facti, cujus solius beneficio omnia omnium credentium peccata, ab ipso usque mundi exordio, ex sola mesericordia[2] Dei, non autem ex ullis meritis nostris, condonata sunt.

Mag. Adhuc non audio unde factum sit, ut uni duntaxat populo (nimirum Isralitico[3]) velit Deus optimus maximus arcanam animi sui voluntatem significare.

Aud. Illud propemodum mihi exciderat: puto autem non proinde factum esse, quasi decalogus non ad omnes homines pertinuerit, cum Dominus Deus noster non solum sit Deus Judæorum, sed etiam gentium[4]. At potius dicendum est:

[1 animosi nobis, B. M.]   [2 misericordia, B. M.]
[3 Israelitico, B. M.]   [4 et gentium, B. M.]

ut agnosceretur verus Messias, qui est CHRISTUS noster, cum veniret in mundum, quem ex gente ista, et non ex altera, ob promissionis veritatem oportuit nasci. Ob quam causam voluit Deus populum aliquem certum, sanctum, et separatum, tanquam sibi peculiarem et proprium, describere, ut nimirum sancta, pura, et illæsa sua oracula et verba perpetuo conservarentur.

Mag. Abunde hactenus mihi satisfactum est, care fili: jam ad Christianam confessionem veniamus, quam mihi volo ut clare recenseas.

<small>Symbolum fidei.[1]</small> *Aud.* Faciam. Credo in Deum Patrem omnipotentem, Creatorem cœli[2] et terræ. Et in JESUM Christum Filium ejus unicum, Dominum nostrum. Qui conceptus est de Spiritu sancto, natus ex Maria virgine. Passus sub Pontio Pilato, crucifixus, mortuus, et sepultus. Descendit ad inferna, tertia die resurrexit a mortuis. Ascendit ad cœlos, sedet ad dexteram Dei Patris omnipotentis. Inde venturus est judicare vivos et mortuos.

Credo in Spiritum sanctum. Sanctam Ecclesiam Catholicam. Sanctorum communionem. Remissionem peccatorum. Carnis resurrectionem. Et vitam æternam.

Mag. Ista a te generaliter et strictim proposita sunt, mi fili; quocirca operæ pretium est, ut quæ dicta sunt per partes, amplifices, quo de singulis quid credas, clare intelligam: ac primo loco de cognitione Dei, post autem de ejus cultu audire cupio.

Aud. Sequar libens voluntatem tuam, carissime præceptor, quoad ingenii mei tenuitas patiatur: sic itaque rem omnem accipe. Ante omnia firmiter credendum tenendumque est, Deum Patrem Opt. Max. initio et ex nihilo creasse et fabricasse universam hanc mundi machinam, et res in ea omnes quæcunque continentur: eaque omnia facta esse per potentiam Verbi sui, id est JESU Christi Filii Dei, quod scripturarum testimonio satis est comprobatum: ubi autem creaturas omnes sic fabricasset, eas deinceps rexisse, gubernasse, conservasse, atque ex bonitate et munifica manu sua, quæcunque ad vitam nostram tuendam conservandamque necessaria requiruntur exhibuisse, atque etiamnum exhibere largissime, ut nimirum perinde illis uteremur, ac memores et pios filios decet.

Mag. Cur autem Deum vocas Patrem?

Aud. Ejus rei duæ sunt causæ: una quod nos omnes

[[1] fiddi, G. S.]   [[2] *cœlum*, G. S. almost invariably; *cœlum*, B. M.]

initio creavit, quodque vitam omnibus est largitus; altera vero majoris est momenti, quod videlicet per Spiritum suum sanctum et per fidem spiritualiter secundo genuerit, adoptando nos in filios, donando itidem regno suo, et vitæ æternæ hæreditate cum Jesu Christo, Filio suo et vero et naturali.

Mag. Cum igitur res alias omnes Deus, homini ut inservirent, condiderit, hominem autem ad obsequium, honorem, et gloriam ipsius propriam, quid habes quod dicas de prima ejus origine et creatione?

Aud. Id quod scripsit Moses: Deum scilicet ex argilla primum hominem finxisse, illique animam ac vitam indidisse: atque deinde, sopore in Adam immisso, detractam ex eo mulierem in lucem produxisse, ut eam et vitæ et fortunarum omnium illi sociam adjungeret. Ac propterea homo Adam vocatus est, quia ex terra traxit originem; mulier autem, quia omnium viventium mater erat futura, appellabatur Eva.

Mag. Imago autem illa, ad cujus similitudinem hominem ais formatum, quænam est?

Aud. Ea est absolutissima justitia et perfectissima sanctimonia, quæ ad ipsam Dei naturam quam maxime pertinet, et in Christo, novo nostro Adamo, præclarissime est demonstrata: cujus in nobis quædam quasi scintillæ adhuc vix relucent.

Mag. Itane? Vix relucent?

Aud. Recte quidem: nam non jam sic splendent ut in initio ante hominis lapsum: quandoquidem homo ob peccatorum tenebras et caliginem errorum imaginis hujus splendorem restinxit. Sic iratus peccati reum ultus est Deus.

Mag. At cur id factum sit, dicas volo.

Aud. Dicam. Cum mundi hujus fabricam creasset Dominus Deus, hortum idem ipse plantavit oblectationis et jucunditatis plenissimum, in loco quodam versus orientem sito, eumque nominavit Eden: in quo præter arbores alias longe pulcherrimas, una fuit in primis non ita procul ab horti illius medio, cujus nomen Arbor vitæ; et altera Arbor cognitionis boni et mali. Hic Dominus Deus, singulari amore ductus, posuit hominem, hortumque illi tradidit curandum et colendum, liberum ei faciens, ut de fructu omnium arborum Paradisi manducaret, excepto eo, quem Arbor scientiæ boni et mali produxisset: hujus arboris fructum si quando degustaret, citra omnem controversiam mortis subiret supplicium. Eva autem a diabolo, serpentis imitante formam, elusa, fructum alioqui vetitum, ob aspectus jucunditatem desiderandum, ob manducandi voluptatem appetendum, et ob boni et mali scientiam vehementer jucundum, decerpsit, edit, ac dedit marito, ut ipse eundem ederet : quo factum est, ut statim uterque mortui sint; hoc est, non tantum morte corporis obnoxii fuerunt, verum animi quoque vitam amiserunt, quæ est justitia : et protinus divina in illis imago offuscata est, ac lineamenta illa justitiæ, sanctitatis, veritatis et cognitionis Dei, longe pulcherrima, confusa sunt et pene deleta : reliqua vero fuit imago terrena, cum injustitia conjuncta, fraude, affectione carnali, et de rebus divinis ac cœlestibus ignoratio summa : inde autem nata est carnis nostræ infirmitas : inde ista corruptio et confusio affectionum et cupiditatum omnium : hinc illa pestis, hinc illud seminarium et nutrimentum peccatorum omnium, quo genus humanum inficitur, et Peccatum originis appellatur. Porro sic natura corrupta est et dejecta, ut nisi bonitas et misericordia omnipotentis Dei nobis tulisset opem per medicinam gratiæ, quemadmodum corpore in universas mortis miserias detrudimur, sic necessarium fuisset, ut omnes omnium generum homines in æterna supplicia, et ignem qui extingui non potest, conjicerentur.

Mag. O hominum ingratitudinem![1] At qua tandem spe primi nostri parentes freti, et deinceps reliqui, levati sunt?

Aud. Jam Dominus Deus et Adamum et Evam cum verbis tum factis castigasset, (de horto enim deturbavit utrosque cum opprobrio gravissimo,) maledixit serpenti, minatus illi tempus olim fore, quo mulieris semen caput illi immineret: postea vero Dominus Deus promissionem hanc magnificam et benignissimam confirmavit: primum, fœdere per circumcisionem cum Abrahamo inito, et in Isaac ejus filio; deinde etiam per Mosen; postremo autem per clarissimorum prophetarum oracula.

Mag. Quid autem sibi vult serpentis caput, ac semen illud de quo loquitur Deus?

Aud. In serpentis capite venenum ejus continetur, ac vitæ et virtutis summa : quo fit, ut mihi caput serpentis universam potentiam et regnum, aut (ut verius loquar) tyrannidem Diaboli, serpentis antiqui, referat : semen vero illud est (uti clarissime nos docet Paulus) Jesus CHRISTUS, Filius Dei, verus Deus, et verus homo, conceptus de Spiritu sancto, et generatus ex beatæ, puræ, inviolatæque Mariæ virginis utero

[[1] ingratitudidem, G. S. for ingratitudinem, as B. M.]

et substantia; ac de ea sic natus et enutritus est, ut reliqui infantes, nisi quod ab omnis peccati contagione esset alienissimus.

Mag. Fundamenta, quæ a te jacta sunt, omnino verissima sunt : jam autem ad eas actiones progrediamur, in quibus et salus et victoria nostra contra serpentem illum antiquum sita est.

Aud. Faciam, carissime præceptor. Postquam CHRISTUS Jesus apostolis suis doctrinam hanc lætissimam, et modis omnibus divinam, quæ Græco vocabulo εὐαγγέλιον nominatur, demandasset; ac postquam signis et miraculis innumeris, quibus tota ejus vita fuit refertissima, idem obsignasset; verberibus tandem acriter cæsus, et vultu et verbis et sputo in faciem immisso illusus, tandem manibus ac pedibus clavorum impulsu perforatis, in crucem actus est. Deinde vere mortuus est, et vere sepultus, ut iratum humano generi Patrem suavissimo sacrificio placaret, atque morte sua eum sibi subjiceret, qui mortis tenebat imperium, hoc est diabolum; quandoquidem non vivi solum, sed mortui etiam, sive in inferno fuerint, sive in alio quocunque loco, mortis illius potentiam et vim senserunt. Quibus in carcere existentibus (ut inquit Petrus) CHRISTUS, licet corpore mortificatus, spiritu tamen vivificatus, prædicavit. Tertio die post resurrexit etiam corpore vivus, et multis testimoniis præclarissimis, quadraginta dierum spatio, inter discipulos versatus est, edens ac bibens cum illis : in quorum conspectu nube obductus, in cœlum ferebatur, aut potius supra omnes cœlos, ubi sedet hodie ad Patris dextram, factus Dominus omnium, sive quæ in cœlo sunt, sive quæ in terra; Rex regum omnium, Pontifex noster et æternus et unicus, unicus advocatus, unicus mediator et unicus reconciliator Dei et hominum. Quoniam autem intravit in gloriam Majestatis suæ, demisso ad nos (uti promisit) sancto suo Spiritu, cæcitatis nostræ tenebras illustrat, mentes nostras movet, regit, docet, purgat, solatur ac juvat, sic usque facturus, quoad mundi fabrica dissolvetur.

Mag. Video te præcipua religionis nostræ capita breviter attigisse, ac veluti in compendiolo explicasse Symbolum modo a te recitatum. Jam igitur volo de certis capitibus quædam a te percontari.

Aud. Fac quod libet, mi præceptor, nam in his quæ minus intelligam, tu me poteris accuratius instituere; quæ autem exciderunt, in memoriam revocare, aut etiam quæ parum fideliter inhæserint, altius imprimere.

Mag. Dic porro mihi: si per mortem suam veniam consequimur peccatorum, an non ea satis erat, nisi etiam a mortuis resurgeret?

Aud. Non erat satis, si vel ejus vel nostri rationem habeas. Nisi enim resurrexisset, minime putaretur Filius Dei: quo factum est, ut illud sibi, dum in cruce penderet, ab his qui viderant exprobraretur. Dicebant enim: Alios servavit, seipsum non potest servare: Descendat nunc de cruce, et credemus ei. Jam autem resurgens a mortuis ad vitæ perennitatem, divinitatis suæ potentiam monstravit majorem, quam si descendendo de cruce mortis terrores refugisset. Mori quidem omnibus est commune; at mortis vincula solvere, et virtute propria resurgere, id unigeniti Jesu CHRISTI, Filii Dei, auctoris vitæ unici, proprium est. Deinde etiam necessarium fuit, ut resurgeret cum gloria, ut Davidis et aliorum prophetarum Dei implerentur oracula: qui prædixerunt fore, ut nec corpus ejus videret corruptionem, nec anima apud inferos relinqueretur. Quod autem ad nos attinet, nec fuissemus justificati, nec resurrectionis nobis spes aliqua fuisset reliqua, nisi resurrexisset, ut multis in locis Paulus clarissime demonstrat. Si enim remansisset in claustris mortis, in sepultura, et corruptione, ut reliqui homines, conclusus; quomodo sperassemus salutem per illum, qui seipsum non servaverit? Fuit igitur consentaneum, et ad eam personam quam sustinebat necessarium, et ad summum salutis nostræ adjumentum, ut primum CHRISTUS seipsum a morte liberaret, post autem ut nos nostræ salutis per resurrectionem ejus faceret certiores.

Mag. Attigisti jam, mi fili, principem causam resurrectionis Christi: nunc de ascensione ejus in cœlos quid censeas libet audire. Quomodo illis respondendum putas, qui dicunt satius fuisse hic in terris maneret nobiscum, ut scilicet gubernaret ac regeret nos præsens, siquidem præter alias causas credibile est, amorem populi[1] erga suum principem, bonum præsertim et benignum, per præsentiam suam fieri auctiorem?

Aud. Res quas faceret præsens, id est, si coram nobiscum versaretur, eas omnes absens facit: regit, tuetur, corroborat, defendit, corripit, punit, corrigit, et reliqua omnia facit quæ talem decent principem, aut etiam Deum ipsum: omnia,

[[1] dopuli, in G. S. for populi, as in B. M.]

inquam, sive quæ ad necessitatem, sive quæ ad utilitatem, sive quæ ad honorem et commodum nostrum spectent. Ad hæc autem Christus non sic, ut multi arbitrantur, huic mundo absens est: nam tametsi corporea illius moles hinc a nobis sublata sit, est tamen divinitas ejus nobiscum perpetuo præsens, etiam si oculorum istorum aspectui non sit subjecta. Res quæ incorporeæ sunt corporis organo non possunt apprehendi. Quis unquam suam ipsius[1] animam viderit? Nullus. At quid nobis præsentius? Quid cuique proquinquius anima sua? Quæ spiritualia sunt, non videntur nisi oculo spiritus. CHRISTI igitur divinitatem qui in terris videre vult, aperiat oculos, non corporis, sed animi, sed fidei, et videbit præsentem, quem oculus non vidit. Videbit præsentem, et in medio eorum, ubicunque sint duo vel tres congregati in nomine ejus: videbit præsentem nobiscum usque ad consummationem seculi. Quid dixi? Christum videbit præsentem? Imo et videbit et sentiet in seipso inhabitantem haud aliter, ac animum suum proprium: habitat enim ac residet in animo ac corde ejus, qui suam omnem collocat in eo fiduciam.

Mag. Optime. At nostra confessio est in cœlos eum conscendisse: illud igitur dic quomodo intelligendum sit.

Aud. Vulgo de eo dici solet, qui celsum aliquem gradum aut dignitatem obtinuerit, quod ascendit et promovetur^e in altum locum, altam sedem aut gradum, quia mutavit conditionem, quodque jam reliquis sit honoratior. Sic porro CHRISTUS ascendit, quemadmodum prius descendebat: descendebat autem a summa gloria ad summam ignominiam, nempe ignominiam servi et crucis: atque ita postea ascendebat a summa ignominia ad summam gloriam, ad eam nimirum quam habuit prius: et ascensus ejus in cœlum, imo supra omnes cœlos, ad thronum usque Dei, ratione justissima constare debet, ut scilicet ad humilitatis et ignominiæ proportionem gloria et majestas responderent. Hoc, scribens ad Philippenses, docet nos Paulus: Factus est obediens usque ad mortem, mortem autem crucis; propter quod et Deus illum in summam extulit sublimitatem, et dedit illi nomen quod est supra omne nomen, ut in nomine Jesu omne genu se flectat, cœlestium, terrestrium, et infernorum. Tametsi autem cœlos jam conscenderit, divina tamen sua natura ac Spiritu semper in ecclesia præsens erit, usque ad orbis dissolutionem. Inde tamen non efficitur, ut nobis corpore sit præsens, cum alia

[1 apsius, G. S.]

divinitatis ejus ratio sit, et humanitatis alia. Hæc enim est creata, illa increata: hæc in aliquo cœli loco, illa autem sic ubique est, ut cœlum et terram impleat. Id autem ut similitudine fiat illustrius. Nulla res Christum verius adumbrat sole; est enim imago lucis ac splendoris Christi propria. Sol cœlum semper occupat, eundem tamen dicimus mundo præsentem. Nam absque lumine nihil unquam cuiquam præsens est, id est, non videtur; implet enim sol lumine suo res omnes. Sic Christus supra omnes cœlos elevatur, ut sit præsens omnibus, utque, Paulo teste, impleat omnia. Quod autem ad corpoream Christi hic in terris præsentiam attinet (si magna parvis componere licet), sic Christi corpus præsens est nostræ fidei, ut sol cum cernatur præsens est oculo, cujus corpus tametsi corporaliter oculum non contingat, atque hic in terris præsens præsenti adsit, tamen corpus solis præsens est visui, etiam reluctante intervalli distantia: sic CHRISTI corpus, quod in gloriosa ejus ascensione nobis sublatum est, quodque reliquit mundum et ad Patrem abiit, ore nostro abest, etiam cum sacrosanctum corporis et sanguinis ejus sacramentum ore nostro excipimus; fides tamen nostra versatur in cœlis, ac intuetur solem illum justitiæ, ac præsens præsenti in cœlis haud aliter illi adest, ac visus adest corpori solis in cœlis, aut sol in terris visui. Quemadmodum autem sol lumine suo adest rebus omnibus, sic etiam et CHRISTUS divinitate sua: non tamen potest lumen solis ab ejus corpore separari, neque porro divinitas Christi ab ejus immortali corpore. Sic ergo CHRISTI corpus adserendum est in uno cœli loco, et divinitas ejus ubique, ut nec de ejus divinitate corpus faciamus, nec de illius corpore Deum.

Mag. Video, mi fili, te neutiquam ignarum, quomodo recte dicatur CHRISTUS corpore absens, et spiritu præsens. Porro hoc unum a te scire volo, cur ita Christus Dominus noster oculorum nostrorum aspectu subtrahitur, atque ex ascensione ejus in cœlum quid capimus commodi?

Aud. Illius rei præcipua causa fuit, ut ea a nobis falsa tolleretur opinio, quæ aliquando apostolos ipsos tenuit: quod scilicet Christus in terris nobis conspicuus regnaret, haud aliter ac reliqui reges ac satrapæ mundi. Hunc in nobis errorem voluit extinctum, ac de regno ejus magis sublimia cogitare: quæ res propterea sibi potior visa est, quia magis ad nostrum commodum et utilitatem spectabat, ut regnum aliquod erigeretur, cujus fundamenta in fide nostra jacerentur.

Quapropter necessarium fuit, ut nobis ab omni sensu corporeo subtraheretur, ut ea ratione fides nostra et excitata et exercitata sit ad intuendum moderationem et providentiam ejus, qui corporeis non cernitur oculis. Cum autem sit rex non alicujus regionis unius, verum etiam et cœli et terræ, vivorum pariter et mortuorum, consultissimum fuit, ut clam sensibus nostris regnum suum administraret: si enim oculorum sensibus subjiceretur, oportuit eum nunc in cœlum erigi, nunc in terram deprimi; nunc in hanc regionem, nunc in aliam migrare; atque ita, ut princeps quispiam terrenus, huc atque illuc negotiorum varietate traheretur. Non enim poterat omnibus una adesse præsens, nisi corpus illius sic abiret in divinitatem, ut ubique aut in quamplurimis locis simul esset, quod Eutyches et consimiles ejus hæretici senserunt. Si vero in eodem momento temporis ubique omnibus præsens adesset, jam non esset homo, sed spectrum : neque corpus habuisset verum sed imaginarium: ex qua re mille continuo nascerentur errores, quos omnes, corpore integro in cœlum evecto, sustulit. Regnum interim et rempublicam suam, id est ecclesiam, cum summa sapientia et virtute administrat, ipse inconspicuus. Hominum est humana quadam ratione respublicas suas moderari, CHRISTI autem et Dei, divina. Quicquid autem a me hactenus dictum est, mediocrem duntaxat particulam ejus utilitatis continet, quam a subvecto in cœlum CHRISTI corpore capimus. Sunt enim plura quæ dici possunt, ex quibus fructus colligitur amplissimus. Ante omnia autem non potest taceri hoc, tanta et tam ampla esse beneficia, quæ nobis a morte, resurrectione, et ascensione CHRISTI adferuntur, ut nulla lingua aut hominum aut etiam angelorum queat exprimere. Atque meam ut in hac re scientiam experiaris, de præcipuis dicam, ad quæ, tanquam ad capita, reliqua omnia referas. Dico igitur, cum ab his tum etiam ab aliis CHRISTI actionibus, duas ad nos commoditates provenire : unam, quod quæcunque fecerit, ea omnia in nostram utilitatem et commodum fecerit, adeo ut perinde nostra sint, modo eisdem firma vivaque fide inhæserimus, ac si nos fecissemus ipsi. Ipse quidem cruci suffixus est, et nos cum ipso crucifixi sumus, et nostra in eo peccata sunt punita. Ipse mortuus est et sepultus; nos itidem una cum peccatis nostris mortui sumus et sepulti, idque ita, ut omnis peccatorum nostrorum memoria penitus deleatur. Ipse resurrexit, et nos cum eo resurreximus, nimirum et resurrectionis et vitæ ejus sic facti participes, ut nobis deinceps mors amplius non dominetur : est enim idem in nobis Spiritus, qui suscitavit Jesum a mortuis. Postremo, uti ille conscendit cœlestem gloriam, et nos cum eo sublevati sumus. Ut demus ista non apparere, tamen tum demum hæc omnia proferuntur in lucem, cum CHRISTUS, qui est lux mundi, ostendet se in gloria sua, in quo felicitates nostræ omnes sunt reconditæ. Ad hæc autem, ab ascensione ejus in cœlum concessa nobis sunt sancti Spiritus dona, uti Paulus testatur abunde Eph. iv. Altera commoditas quam ex CHRISTI actionibus percipimus, est, quod CHRISTUS nobis in exemplum proponitur, ad quod vitam nostram omnem formemus. CHRISTUS si mortuus sit, si sepultus, pro peccato, id fecit semel : si resurrexit, si in cœlum ascenderit, semel tantum resurrexit, semel tantum ascendit ; jam non amplius moritur, sed vivit cum Deo, et regnat in summa gloriæ æternitate. Sic si simus nos mortui, si sepulti peccato, quomodo posthac vivemus in eodem ? Si resurrexerimus cum Christo, si per spem firmam in cœlo cum eo versemur ; cœlestes res et divinæ, non terrenæ et caducæ, nobis erunt curæ. Et quemadmodum terreni hominis hactenus gestavimus imaginem, cœlestis deinceps imaginem gestemus : utque nunquam destitit CHRISTUS Dominus nobis benefacere, et Spiritum suum sanctum nobis largiendo, et ecclesiam suam tot præclaris donis ornando, ac Patrem perpetuo precando pro nobis, par nos ratio excitare debet, ut proximum omni studio juvemus, et caritatis vinculum, quantum in nobis est, tueamur : utque Christum Dominum ac Salvatorem honoremus ; non equidem impiis traditionibus et frigidis hominum inventis, sed cultu cœlesti et revera sprituali, quem et nos qui demus, et illum qui accipiat, deceat maxime, haud aliter atque ille et honoravit et honorat Patrem : qui enim honore illum afficit, honorat et Patrem ; cujus rei ille ipse testis est locupletissimus.

Mag. Finem mundi scriptura sacra consummationem et perfectionem regni ac mysterii Christi, et renovationem rerum omnium appellat. Sic loquitur Apostolus Petrus, 2 Pet. iii. Nos cœlos novos et terram novam expectamus juxta promissionem Dei, in quibus justitia inhabitat. Videtur autem rationi consentaneum, ut corruptio, mutabilitas et peccatum (quibus subjicitur totus mundus) aliquando cessarent. Qua vero tandem via, aut quibus circumstantiarum rationibus ista fient, cupio abs te audire.

Aud. Dicam ut possum, eodem Apostolo teste, Cœli pro-

cellæ in morem transibunt, elementa æstuantia solventur,
terraque et quæ in ea sunt opera exurentur: quasi diceret,
Mundus (uti in auro fieri videmus) totus igne repurgabitur,
atque ad ultimam suam perfectionem reducetur; quem minor
ille mundus, nimirum homo, imitatus, a corruptione itidem et
mutatione liberabitur. Itaque hominis causa, in cujus gratiam
major hic mundus creabatur primum, renovatus tandem faciem
induet multo cum jucundiorem, tum pulchriorem.

Mag. Deinde autem quid superest?

Aud. Ultimum et generale judicium. Veniet namque
Christus, ad cujus vocem mortui omnes resurgent, et anima
et corpore integri, atque in throno majestatis suæ residentem[1]
videbit totus mundus; post excussionem autem conscientiæ
cujusque extrema sententia pronunciabitur. Tunc temporis
filii Dei perfecte possidebunt regnum illud immortalitatis et
æternæ vitæ, quod illis præparatum fuit ante jacta fundamenta mundi, et regnabunt cum Christo in æternum. Impii
vero, qui non crediderunt, abjicientur in ignem æternum, de-
stinatum diabolo et angelis ejus.

Mag. Abunde dictum est a te de resurrectione mortuorum. Jam de ecclesia sancta superest ut dicas: de qua
quid sentias nimis vellem audire.

Aud. Dicam ea paucis quæ scripturæ sacræ fuse explicant
et copiose. Antequam cœlum et terram creasset Dominus
Deus, regnum quoddam sibi pulcherrimum et rempublicam
sanctissimam habere decrevit: eam apostoli et majores nostri
qui Græce[2] scripserunt ἐκκλησίαν appellaverunt: in hanc ad-
scripsit infinitam hominum multitudinem, qui omnes regi uni
et supremo et unico suo capiti subderentur: hunc nos vocamus
Christum, quod perinde est ac si unctum dixeris. Solebant
enim pontifices et reges in populo Judaico, ex præcepto divino,
in sua inauguratione oleo quodam materiali perfundi, qui
Christum Dominum Spiritu suo sancto inunctum figurabant.
Ad hanc rempublicam constituendam proprie pertinent, quot-
quot vere timent, honorant et invocant Deum, prorsus appli-
cantes animos ad sancte pieque vivendum, et quicunque, omnem
spem et fiduciam in eo collocantes, vitæ æternæ beatitudinem
certissime expectant. Qui autem sunt in hac fide firmi, erant
ante electi, prædestinati, et ad vitam æternam designati, quam
mundus esset conditus; atque hujus rei testem habent in corde

[1 residente, B. M.]
[2 græcæ, B. M.]

intrinsecus Spiritum CHRISTI, illorum fidei auctorem, arram et minime fallax pignus : quæ fides sola mysteriorum divinorum capax est, sola cordi pacem adfert, sola apprehendit[1] justitiam quæ est in Christo JESU.

Mag. Itane Spiritus solus et fides, etiamsi dormiamus aut aliter supini et otiosi steterimus, omnia in nostram gratiam sic facient, ut sine ulla ope nostra in cœlum etiam otiosos deportabunt?

Aud. Soleo, mi præceptor, (doctus id a te,) inter causas et effectus discrimen ponere. Prima, præcipua, et perfectissima causa nostræ justificationis et salutis est bonitas et amor Dei, quo ille nos in numerum suorum electos ante ascripsit, quam mundum condiderat. Post nobis datur, ut prædicatione evangelii Jesu CHRISTI vocemur, quocum infunditur nobis Spiritus Domini, cujus ductu et auspiciis trahimur, ut firmam in Deo fiduciam collocemus, et promissionum ejus omnium eventum speremus. Ejusdem electionis comes est mortificatio veteris hominis, id est appetitus et concupiscentiæ nostræ. Illius etiam est sanctificatio nostra, amor Dei et proximi, justitia et innocentia vitæ : atque, ut summatim dicam, quicquid purum, sincerum, verum et bonum in nobis existit, aut a nobis fieri potest, id totum a radice ista suavissima, ab isto fonte largissimo, bonitate, amore, electione, et proposito Dei sanctissimo, nascitur. Ille est causa, reliqua sunt effectus. Sunt tamen bonitas Dei, et electio, et Spiritus, et ipse Christus, causæ inter se conjunctæ et colligatæ, quæ inter salutis nostræ principes causas possunt numerari. Quoties igitur dici solet, sola nos fide justificari et servari, ita dictum est, quia fides, aut potius fiducia sola apprehendit[1], intelligit, et cognoscit nostram justificationem nobis a Deo gratis dari, hoc est, nullis nostris meritis, sed ex gratuita gratia omnipotentis Patris. Porro fides amorem gignit proximi, et actiones quæ Deo placent. Nam si viva et vera sit, et Spiritu sancto animata, mater est eorum omnium quæcunque bene aut dicuntur aut fiunt. Ex hoc brevi orationis compendio clarum est, unde justificatio nostra, et quibus modis paretur : non enim meritorum nostrorum dignitate vel hactenus electi, vel olim salvati erimus, sed per solam misericordiam Dei et CHRISTI Domini meram gratiam, per quam ad bona opera quæ præparavit Deus, ut in eis ambularemus, in ipso conditi sumus. Et licet opera bona nostram justificationem apud Deum mereri non pos-

[1 appræhendit, G. S.]

sunt, sic tamen fidei adhærent, ut neque illa sine ipsis inveniri possit, neque bona opera extra fidem usquam reperiantur.

Mag. Brevis hæc tractatio de fide et operibus vehementer mihi placet; eadem enim clarissime docet Paulus. Potesne adhuc mihi describere ecclesiam, quam dicis rempublicam aut communitatem Christianam, et eam sic mihi ob oculos ponere, ut ab alia quavis hominum societate distincte et diserte discernatur?

Aud. Experiar quomodo quam optime id possim præstare. Tu vis, mi præceptor, si recte intelligo, ut certam aliquam tibi, et quæ videri possit, definiam ecclesiam.

Mag. Hoc ipsum volo, atque ut facias, erit valde commodum.

Aud. Ea ecclesia non est aliud, quam certa quædam multitudo hominum, qui, in quocunque loco sint, puram et sinceram profitentur doctrinam CHRISTI, idque ea forma, qua ab evangelistis et apostolis in testamento sancto CHRISTI fideliter prodita est; quique in omnibus gubernantur et reguntur legibus et statutis sui Regis et Pontificis CHRISTI, in vinculo caritatis, et præterea utuntur ejus mysteriis, quæ communi vocabulo Sacramenta appellantur, eadem puritate et simplicitate (quod ad ipsorum naturam atque substantiam attinet) qua usi sunt et nobis in scriptis reliquerunt Apostoli Christi. Sunt igitur hujus ecclesiæ notæ, primum pura prædicatio evangelii: deinde dilectio fraterna, e qua, ut ex ejusdem corporis membris, mutua benevolentia nascitur: tertio, sincera et pura observatio sacramentorum Domini juxta institutum evangelii: postremo, correctio fraterna, et eorum excommunicatio qui vitam nolunt rectius instituere. Hanc notam sancti patres Disciplinam appellaverunt. Hæc illa est ecclesia, quæ est fundata in firma petra Jesu Christo, atque in ejus fiducia: hæc illa est ecclesia, quam Paulus vocat columnam et firmamentum veritatis: ad hanc claves pertinent quibus cœlum et clauditur et recluditur: id enim fit per ministerium verbi, id quod potestas ligandi solvendique, retinendi ac remittendi peccata proprie spectant. Quo fit, ut quisquis evangelio in hac ecclesia prædicato crediderit, salvabitur: qui vero non crediderit, condemnabitur.

Mag. Hic libet audire, quid de Spiritu sancto credas.

Aud. Illum tertiam personam sanctissimæ Trinitatis esse confiteor, et cum Patri atque Filio sit æqualis, ac ejusdem prorsus naturæ, una cum utroque adorandum.

Mag. Cur sanctus appellatur?

Aud. Non tantum ob suam ipsius sanctitatem, sed quod per eum electi Dei et membra CHRISTI sancta efficiantur. Quare divine literæ illum Spiritum sanctificationis vocarunt.

Mag. Quibus in rebus hanc sanctificationem constituis?

Aud. Primum quidem ejus instinctu regeneramur, et idcirco dixit Christus, oportere nos aqua et Spiritu renasci. Ejus deinde afflatu in filios Dei adoptamur, unde non immerito Spiritus adoptionis est dictus. Ejus luce illustramur ad intelligenda Dei mysteria: ejus judicio condonantur ac retinentur peccata: ejus vi reprimitur et domatur caro cum suis cupiditatibus. Ejus arbitrio multiplicia dona sanctis distribuuntur: ejus denique opera corpora nostra mortalia reviviscent. Proinde in tantorum donorum auctorem non immerito credimus, eumque colimus et invocamus.

Mag. Quæ de Spiritu sancto retulisti, satis esse arbitror. Sed id ex te audire velim, cur statim adjungitur nos credere Sanctam Catholicam Ecclesiam, et sanctorum communionem?

Aud. Duo hæc, ut semper credidi, appositissime connectuntur, quoniam societates et corpora ceterorum hominum cum artibus tum rationibus procedunt atque gubernantur. At ecclesia, quæ cœtus est vocatorum ad æternam salutem, a Spiritu sancto, cujus jam mentionem fecimus, et collecta est et regitur; quod cum neque sensu neque luce naturæ intelligatur, jure meritoque inter ea quæ creduntur hoc loco positum est. Et catholica, id est universalis, ideo appellatur fidelium collectio, quia speciali cuipiam loco non est alligata: Deus enim per universos fines orbis habet sui cultores, qui licet diversitate regionum et provinciarum sint disjecti, ejusdem tamen corporis, cujus caput CHRISTUS est, membra sunt invicem quam conjunctissima, communionemque Spiritus, fidei, sacramentorum, precum, remissionis peccatorum, et cœlestis felicitatis habent, atque dilectionis vinculo sic inter ea comparatum est, ut in nullam rem magis incumbant, quam ut sese mutuo juvent, et in Christo vicissim ædificent.

Mag. Cum jam dictum sit de cognitione Dei et de membris ejus, libet etiam aliquid audire quid sit cultus Dei.

Aud. Imprimis considerandum est, rectam et veram cognitionem Dei esse cultus Dei præcipuum et unicum fundamentum: cognitionem timor fovet ac tuetur, quem sacræ literæ initium sapientiæ appellaverunt: fides autem et spes fulcra sunt et stabilimenta, quibus alia omnia prius a nobis commemorata innituntur. Porro caritas, quam dilectionem vocamus, est vinculi instar perpetui, cujus arctitudine virtutes reliquæ omnes unitæ fiunt auctiores. Et hæ sunt partes cultus Dei interiores, id est animi.

Mag. Quid habes quod de sabbatho dicas, aut de die festo, cujus inter leges primæ tabulæ fecisti mentionem?

Aud. Sabbathum, si interpreteris, requiem significat, ad cultum et obsequium Dei solummodo institutum. Est autem ejus quietis et tranquillitatis typus, quam qui in Christum credunt obtinent. Nam fiducia quam habemus in Christo, liberat animos nostros ab omni servili timore legis, peccati, mortis et inferni, certiores interim nos faciens, quod per illum placeamus Deo, quodque nos filios et hæredes regni sui constituerit, unde pax in corde et vera tranquillitas animi nascitur, quæ res gustus quidam est quietis illius felicissimæ, quam in regno Dei sumus habituri. Quæ vero in die Sabbathi geruntur, ut ceremoniæ et exercitia in cultu Dei, hujus fiduciæ et quietis signa sunt et testimonia. Et CHRISTI fideles æquum est diebus, qui ad sacra sunt destinati, profanis operibus longe semotis, religioni et cultui Dei sedulo vacare.

Mag. Quænam sunt cultus illius exterioris (quem in certis quibusdam exercitiis positum aiebas) partes, et illius etiam interioris indicia?

Aud. Primo, docere et audire doctrinam evangelii, deinde ceremoniarum et sacramentorum sincerus et proprius usus; postremo, precationes ad Deum per Christum et nomine CHRISTI factæ, quæ quidem Spiritum sanctum impetrant, omnis veri cultus et religionis sinceræ auctorem certissimum.

Mag. Dic mihi, quid tu vocas sacramenta?

Aud. Sunt certæ solennes actiones et ceremoniæ a Christo institutæ, ut per eas beneficiorum suorum erga nos admoneret, et nos vicissim professionem ederemus, quod ex illorum simus numero, qui talium beneficiorum sunt participes, et qui in illo fiduciam omnem collocant, quodque nos non pudet nominis Christiani, aut appellationis Discipulorum CHRISTI.

Mag. Sacramenta illa duo, Baptismus, et quæ a Paulo vocatur Cœna Domini, dic, fili, quomodo ministrantur?

Aud. Qui in Christum credit et religionis Christiani articulos profitetur, et vult baptizari, (de adultis jam loquor, nam parvulis parentum aut ecclesiæ professio sufficere potest,) hunc minister pura et simplici aqua intingit aut lavat in nomine Patris et Filii et Spiritus sancti, et precationibus commendat eum Deo, cujus ecclesiæ jam palam adjungitur, ut gratiam suam illi largiatur, qua suæ professioni respondeat.

Mag. Cœnæ vero dominicæ quis est usus?

Aud. Is nimirum qui ab ipso Domino nostro Jesu Christo fuit institutus: qui, ut divus inquit Paulus, ea nocte qua tradebatur accepit panem; et postquam gratias egisset, fregit, ac dixit: Hoc meum est corpus, quod pro vobis frangitur: hoc facite in mei commemorationem[1]. Ad eundem modum et poculum, peracta cœna, eis dedit, dicens: Hoc poculum novum testamentum est in meo sanguine: hoc facite quotiescunque biberitis in mei commemorationem. Hæc erat forma et ratio cœnæ Domini, quam tenere et observare debemus, quo memoria tanti beneficii passionis et mortis CHRISTI conservetur, ut ille veniat et faciat nos post hujus seculi finem suæ mensæ assidere.

Mag. Quam rem nobis repræsentat et ob oculos ponit Baptismus?

Aud. Nos esse per Spiritum Christi renatos et mundatos a peccato, quodque simus membra et partes ecclesiæ ascripti in communionem sanctorum: aqua enim significat Spiritum. Baptismus etiam est figura sepulturæ nostræ in Christo, quodque cum illo una resuscitabimur in nova vita, ut superius tractavimus in resurrectione Christi.

Mag. Quam[2] rem significat et demonstrat nobis cœna, quam celebramus in memoriam Domini?

Aud. Cœna (sicuti paulo ante a nobis explicatur) est grata quædam memoria mortis CHRISTI, cum panis repræsentet corpus ejus ad crucifigendum pro nobis traditi, vinum autem ponatur vice et loco sanguinis, abunde pro nobis fusi. Ac quemadmodum pane et vino vita nostra naturalis sustinetur ac nutritur, sic corpore, id est carne et sanguine, Christi anima per fidem nutritur et vegetatur ad vitam cœlestem et spiritualem.

Mag. Quomodo ista fiunt?

Aud. Ista quidem fiunt occulta quadam ratione et energia Spiritus, quando credimus Christum corpus et sanguinem suum pro nobis semel tradidisse in sacrificium et gratissimam

[1 commemoratiovem, in G. S. and B. M.]   [2 Qam, G. S. and B. M.]

victimam Patri coelesti, et dum confitemur atque agnoscimus illum pro unico salvatore[3], pontifice, mediatore et redemptore nostro, cui debetur omnis honor et gloria.

Mag. Recte rem hanc omnem intelligis. Id videris velle dictum, fidem esse os animæ, quo cibum hunc plane divinum et salutis juxta et immortalitatis plenum, et Spiritus sancti opera communicatum, recipimus. Jam cum de sacramentis tractatum sit, ad reliqua cultus Dei membra transeas.

Aud. Faciam quod jubes. Ad divini cultus perfectionem duo adhuc supersunt. Primum, Dominus noster Jesus CHRISTUS voluit doctores et evangelistas, id est, concionatores evangelii, esse, ut scilicet vox ejus perpetuo in ecclesia sua resonaret. Qui Christiani nomine censeri cupit (id quod omnes cupere deberent) dubitationem habere non potest, oportere eum cum summo studio et desiderio longe ardentissimo operam navare, ut verbum Domini et audiat et imbibat, non tanquam verbum hominis cujuspiam, sed veluti (ut revera est) verbum omnipotentis Dei. Deinde vero, quoniam omne quod bonum est, quodque ab homine Christiano appeti debet, nobis adsit a Deo, atque ab eo conceditur, propterea ab eo rem omnem petere debemus, atque per gratiarum actionem omnia illi accepta referre: quæ res adeo illi placet, ut sacrificii præclari loco ducat, quemadmodum prophetarum et apostolorum testimonio est clarissimum.

Mag. Tunc habes formam aliquam precandi certam et propriam?

Aud. Maxime: nempe illam ipsam quam Dominus noster discipulos suos docuit, et simul cum illis reliquos Christianos omnes. Qui aliquando rogatus ut doceret eos formam orandi, hanc eos edocuit. Quando oratis (inquit), dicite:

Pater noster qui es in coelis, sanctificetur nomen tuum.
Adveniat regnum tuum.
Fiat voluntas tua sicut in coelo et in terra.
Panem nostrum quotidianum da nobis hodie.
Et dimitte[4] nobis debita nostra, sicut et nos dimittimus debitoribus nostris.
Et ne nos inducas in temptationem, sed libera nos a malo: quia tuum est regnum, potentia, et gloria in secula, Amen.

Mag. Arbitrarisne licere ut alia precandi forma utamur?

Aud. Tametsi brevi hoc compendio, quæ Christiano

[3 sulvatore, G. S. and B. M.]   [4 dimite, G. S. and B. M.]

cuivis expetenda sunt, abunde contineantur, non tamen in eas Christus nos hac precatione redegit angustias, ut aliis aut verbis aut orandi formis uti non liceat. Proposuit autem in hac oratione certa quædam et præcipua capita, ad quæ precationes nostræ omnes referantur. Petat autem quisque a Deo juxta præsentis necessitatis rationem. Quicquid petieritis Patrem in nomine[1] meo, dicit CHRISTUS, dabit vobis.

Mag. Postquam autem in ea oratione nihil sit aut ambiguum aut extra propositum, libet audire quid de ea sentias.

Aud. Sentio quod verba præ se ferunt.

Mag. Nihil igitur hic tibi retrusum aut reconditum, nihil difficile intellectu videtur?

Aud. Nihil: siquidem ne CHRISTUS quidem ipse voluit, ut in ea quicquam esset aut obscurum aut procul a captu nostro remotum; præsertim cum ad omnes ex æquo pertineat, ac tam doctis quam rudibus inprimis sit necessaria.

Mag. Proinde expone mihi paucis partes seorsim singulas.

Aud. Cum dicam, Pater noster qui es in cœlis; id mecum cogito, fieri non posse quin me audiat, quin precationes meæ illi placeant: sum enim illi filius (licet inutilis et minime obsequens), et ille contra mihi est benignus Pater, ad ignoscendum et condonandum paratissimus.

Mag. Cur autem in cœlo eum dicis? estne in aliquo cœli certo et definito loco? Quid est quod de se ipso dicit, Ego cœlum et terram impleo? et, Cœlum mihi sedes est, terra autem subsellium pedum meorum?

Aud. De hac re superius quædam, quibus ista adjungere libet: Principio, quoties a nobis dicitur (qui es in cœlis), perinde est ac si dicas cœlestis et divinus. Nam de cœlesti nostro Patre cogitatio nostra sublimior esse debet, quam quæ est de terreno. Et in cœlis etiam ob id esse dicitur, quod in sublimi atque cœlesti regione Dei præclara et admiranda opera se illustrius et magnificentius declarant, atque is jam in æterna et plena felicitate esse demonstratur, cum nos adhuc in terris misere atque calamitose a patria exulemus. Deinde, quemadmodum cœlum immensa capacitatis suæ amplitudine omnem locum amplectitur, circundat terram, circundat maria, nec locus aliquis est qui a cœli capacitate queat abscondi, quoniam omni temporis momento rebus omnibus præsens est: sic ex eo licet intelligere, Deum omni in loco rebus omnibus

[1 nmine, B. M.]

adesse: videt, audit, moderatur res omnes, ipse existens Spiritus ab omni mortali et terrena conditione remotissimus. Cujus rei testis est Hieremias Propheta: Non Deus de propinquo ego? (dicit Dominus) et non Deus de longinquo? Num abscondet se quisquam in latebras, ut eum videre nequeam? Hæc oratio est valde efficax, qua timor nobis incutiatur, ne tam late regnantem Dominum offendamus; quaque adducimur, ut certo credamus eum auditurum nos, si quando necessitas incumbat: est enim et semper et in omni loco præsens. Hoc igitur jacto fundamento, et tam suavi et jucundo ingressu præfixo, sequitur precationis dominicæ prima pars, in qua petimus, ut non solum nos, sed quicunque etiam sunt alii, nomen ejus sancte honoremus, revereamur, adoremus.

Mag. Quomodo hoc fit?

Aud. Dicam. Tum demum hoc fit, cum omissis illis omnibus, qui nomen deorum sortiuntur, sive in cœlo, sive in terra, sive in templis variis figuris et imaginibus adorentur, solum hunc nostrum Patrem agnoscamus, et precemur[2] verum Deum et Filium ejus Jesum Christum quem ipse misit, et eum solum cum vitæ integritate, et innocentia, puris et infucatis precibus solicitemus?

Mag. Recte quidem dixisti. Perge, quæso.

Aud. Secundo loco petimus, ut adveniat regnum ejus. Adhuc enim non videmus res omnes Christo esse subjectas: non videmus ut lapis de monte abscissus sit sine opere humano, qui contrivit et in nihilum redegit statuam descriptam a Daniele; ut petra sola, qui est Christus, occupet et obtineat totius mundi imperium a Patre concessum. Adhuc non est occisus antichristus: quo fit, ut nos desideremus et precemur, ut id tandem aliquando contingat et impleatur; utque solus Christus regnet cum suis sanctis, secundum divinas promissiones; utque vivat et dominetur in mundo, juxta sancti evangelii decreta, non autem juxta traditiones et leges hominum, et voluntatem tyrannorum mundi.

Mag. Faxit Deus, ut regnum ejus adveniat quam citissime.

Aud. Porro cum filiorum sit, ut ad patrum voluntatem vitam instituant; non autem e contra, ut patres ad filiorum voluntates se deflectant (quandoquidem voluntas nostra plerumque[3] affectionum titillatione et cupiditatum motu trahitur ad eas res peragendas, quæ omnino Deo displicent), rationi consentaneum

[[2] precemus, B. M.]　　[[3] plærumque, G. S.; et plerunque, B. M.]

est, ut e cœlestis Patris nutu toti pendeamus, utque divino illius imperio nos penitus subjiciamus. Quare hanc ob causam precamur, ut nos omnes mortales non aliter illius mandatis simus audientes, quam sol et luna et reliquæ stellæ cœlestes, quæ cum statis motibus et perenni agitatione, tum indefessis terram radiis illustrando perpetuo divinam voluntatem exequuntur : aut veluti cœlestes angeli et ceteri divini spiritus, illi per omnia obtemperemus, qui omnem dant operam ad divina jussa sedulo adimplenda. Deinde petere nos docet a cœlesti Patre panem nostrum : quo significat non cibum modo, verum etiam res alias omnes ad vitam tuendam conservandamque necessarias : ut Deum solum intelligamus esse auctorem rerum omnium, qui efficit et ut crescant et ut abundent terræ proventus. Quamobrem par est, ut eum solum precibus compellemus, qui (juxta Davidis oraculum) omnia et pascit et tuetur.

Mag. Sunt qui hunc locum intelligant de pane cujus meminit Christus Joannis sexto, id est, de vera cognitione et gustu CHRISTI, pro nobis nati et mortui, quo fidelis anima pascitur. In causa autem cur sic colligant, est Græcum quod hic legitur vocabulum ἐπιούσιον, qua voce volunt exprimere supernaturalem, spiritualem, cœlestem et divinum. Hunc sensum non rejicio : potest enim utraque interpretatio huic loco apte accommodari. Sed panem cur vocat quotidianum ? quod etiam per vocem ἐπιούσιον significatur.

Aud. Panem sane quotidianum petimus, qui nobis perpetuo adsit et comitetur assidue, ut finem et modum sitienti desiderio et gulæ insatiabili imponeret, ne alioqui essemus (ut Christus loquitur) in crastinum solliciti, quoniam crastinus dies curam habebit sui ipsius: adveniet enim non sine suo incommodo et sollicitudine : quare rationi consentaneum non est, ut dies unus malum alterius aggravet ; satis namque erit id quotidie petere, quod Pater noster benignissimus paratus est quotidie impartire. Sequitur quinta petitio, qua Patrem precamur, ut nobis dimittat debita et delicta quæ commisimus. Hæc certe petitio est vehementer necessaria, cum nemo vivat mortalium immunis a peccato. Hic igitur fiducia omnis nostri abjicienda est, hic cristæ demittendæ : hic precandus est Pater noster clementissimus, ut in gratiam et amorem Jesu Christi, Filii sui et carissimi et obsequentissimi, innumeras nobis offensas condonet, remittat, ac de libro penitus deleat. Memores autem nos hic interim esse decet pacti nobis cum Deo initi, siquidem petimus, ut Deus ita nobis remittat peccata nostra, ut hiis qui nos offenderint ipsi remittimus : proinde necessarium est ut ignoscamus, ut remittamus omnibus offensas omnes, cujuscunque aut generis sint aut conditionis. Si remiserimus hominibus errata sua, remittet nobis Pater noster coelestis errata nostra.

Mag. Si hæc ita fierent, mi fili, non tot lites, non tot contentiones, non aut tot aut tam graves discordiæ, inimicitiæ, atque odia inter homines hodie grassarentur : nunc autem, dum quisque sic sibi placet, ut ne tantillum de suo jure velit discedere, sive de honore loquaris, sive de opibus, sive de re alia quavis, non raro solet usu venire, ut et opes et honores et vitam ipsam una amittant, nec non favorem divinum et æternam gloriam a se prorsus repellant atque avertant. Te autem, mi fili, nec fugere debet præceptum CHRISTI, neque quod docet Paulus, ne sinas te vinci a malo, id est, ne sinas te aliorum offensa eo adduci, ut malum malo rependas; imo vince bono malum, nempe benefaciendo illi, qui tibi male fecit, atque eum benigne tractando, qui hostem se tibi præbuerit etiam acerbissimum. Perge porro ad sextam petitionem.

Aud. Pergam, ut jubes, libenter. Quandoquidem igitur debiles et infirmi, et mille periculis, mille tentationibus expositi, ad succumbendum faciles, ad cedendum parati, occasionibus quibusvis etiam levissimis, vel hominibus malitia instructis, vel concupiscentiæ et appetitioni propriæ, vel tandem serpenti astuto et malitioso, id est diabolo ; oramus Patrem, ne nos in tales difficultates aut periculum adducat, neve in ipso discrimine deserat; quin si eo ventum sit, ut prius nos de imminenti malo et diaboli machinis (auctoris et principis omnis mali) eripiat, quam prorsus in exitium præcipitemur. Habes jam paucis, venerande præceptor, nisi quid inter narrandum exciderit, quæ a te mihi sunt tradita.

Mag. Quia tuum est regnum, potentia et gloria in secula. Amen. Cur ista periodo voluit Christus nostras preces absolvi?

Aud. Partim ut certam nostram fiduciam testaremur obtinendi omnia ea quæ antea postulavimus. Nihil enim est quod is dare vel non possit vel nolit, si ex fide rogetur, qui cuncta regit et gubernat, qui omnia potest, quique infinita gloria est ornatus. Hæc ubi de Deo Patre nostro commemoramus, nullus in animo dubitationi relinquitur amplius locus, qua suspicemur nos repulsam esse passuros. Partim nobis ipsis ostendimus ita dicendo, quam sit consentaneum ab uno Deo petere, cum nullus citra eum tam illustri gloria fulgeat, adeo late regnet, atque tantarum sit virium, ut vel ei obstare possit, quin pro sua voluntate largiatur quæcunque decreverit, vel jam nobis ab ipso donata valeat auferre : nullumque malum nostrum usque adeo magnum est, quod ejus incredibili vi, gloria et sapientia, non sit a nobis propulsandum.

Mag. Probo brevem hanc tuam qualemcunque declarationem, mi fili, nec videtur omissum quicquam quod dictum oportuit. Interim tamen hoc unum addere libet : Summa et præcipua res, quæ in precatione requiritur, est, ut extra omnem dubitationem firmiter credamus, Deum Patrem nostrum id quod petimus daturum, modo nec sit inutile nobis qui accipiamus, nec indignum illo qui det : nam qui non est certus sed dubius, non putet se quicquam a Deo impetraturum, juxta Jacobi sententiam.

Jam video, care fili, quam diligenter et studiose applicasti animum ad ea, quæ a me tibi proposita sunt, quamque pie et sancte de vero Dei cultu, deque mutuis in proximum officiis cogites. Superest, ut deinceps vitam sic instituas tuam, ne cognitio hæc plane cœlestis et divina in te torpeat, ac perinde jaceat atque in carnis tumulo, inanimis et mortua. Imo fac, ut totus piis hiisce studiis continenter ac sedulo incumbas, et vives non in hac solum præsenti vita, verum etiam in futura, quæ multo quam hæc præsens et melior est et beatior : habet enim pietas promissionem, non in hac vita solum, sed etiam in futura, juxta sententiam Pauli. Operæ pretium igitur est, ut pietatem sedulo sectemur, quæ viam plane nobis ad cœlum aperit, si modo eo aspirare velimus. Pietatis autem primum officium est (quod a te quam optime jam est explicatum) cognoscere Deum solum, et solum eum appetere ut summum bonum, timere ut Dominum, amare et venerari ut Patrem, una cum Filio ejus Servatore nostro Jesu Christo. Hic ille est qui nos et genuit et regeneravit : hic demum ille est, qui principio dedit et vitam et animam, qui tuetur, qui salvat, qui vitæ nos beat æternitate. Huic pietati prorsus contraria est impietas : superstitio vero et hypocrisis imitantur quidem eam et præ se ferunt, quum longissime tamen ab omni pietate discrepent; atque ideo ut pestes[1] et venena animæ et salutis nostræ hostes immanissimos evitare debemus. Proxi-

[[1] pestis, B. M.]

mum vero pietatis officium, hominem quemvis veluti fratrem diligere. Nam si Deus nos omnes in initio creaverit, si nos pascat et regat, si denique habitationis nostræ in immensa hac mundi fabrica causa sit et parens, non potest fratris nomen non aptissime nobis convenire; adeoque tanto arctiori invicem vinculo erimus colligati, quanto propius ad Christum accedamus, qui est Frater noster primogenitus et natu maximus : quem qui non novit, qui non tenet, revera injustus est, et in populo Dei locum non habet. Ille enim radix et fundamentum est omnis æquitatis et justitiæ, et mentibus nostris naturales quasdam præceptiones instillavit. Fac idem (inquit) alteri, quod tibi vis fieri : cave igitur ne quicquam illi facias, quod non libenter ipse patiaris. Semper ex proprio ingenio atque sensu metire alienum. Si pati injuriam durum et grave sit, si quod tibi facit alius iniquum videatur, transfer idem judicium in personam proximi quod in te sentis, et videbis te non minus inique facere si noceas alteri, quam alii faciunt qui tibi nocuerint. Si hic pedem fortiter figeremus, si huc omni studio niteremur, ipsum teneremus innocentiæ fastigium : siquidem gradus primus est, nulli offensionem præbere ; proximus, cunctos quantum in nobis est juvare : id si minus poterimus, saltem omnibus bene velle et precari : tertius, qui horum omnium summus et perfectissimus habetur, est etiam inimicis benefacere, qui nos injuriis afficiunt. Cognoscamus igitur nosmetipsos, tollamus quæ in nobis sunt vitia, atque in eorum loco virtutes plantemus : non aliter quam agricolæ, qui primum spinas, tribulos, ac vitiosas herbas ex agris suis incultis et neglectis auferre et penitus eradicare solent; deinde vero, bona et frugifera semina undique dispergunt, et terræ visceribus injiciunt, quæ tempore bonas fruges producant : eundem in modum et nos agamus. Imprimis enim operam demus, ut pravas et vitiosas cupiditates tollamus penitus e mentibus nostris ; postea autem mores sanctos, et Christianis pectoribus dignos, inseramus. Qui si rore verbi divini spargantur et fœcundentur, sique calore foveantur Spiritus cœlestis, fructum haud dubie proferent uberrimum immortalitatis et beatæ vitæ, quam Deus per CHRISTUM electis suis, ante jacta fundamenta mundi, præparavit. Cui sit omnis honor et gloria. Amen.

Catechismi Finis.

ARTICULI,

DE QUIBUS IN SYNODO LONDINENSI, ANNO DOM. M.D.LII.
AD TOLLENDAM OPINIONUM DISSENSIONEM,
ET CONSENSUM VERÆ RELIGIONIS
FIRMANDUM, INTER EPISCOPOS
ET ALIOS ERUDITOS VIROS
CONVENERAT: REGIA
AUTHORITATE IN
LUCEM EDITI.

De fide in Sacrosanctam Trinitatem[1].

1. UNUS est vivus et verus Deus, æternus, incorporeus, impartibilis, impassibilis, immensæ potentiæ, sapientiæ, ac bonitatis: creator et conservator omnium, tum visibilium tum invisibilium. Et in unitate hujus divinæ naturæ tres sunt personæ, ejusdem essentiæ, potentiæ, ac æternitatis, Pater, Filius, et Spiritus sanctus.

Verbum Dei verum hominem esse factum.

2. FILIUS, qui est Verbum Patris, in utero beatæ Virginis ex illius substantia naturam humanam assumpsit, ita ut duæ naturæ, divina et humana, integre atque perfecte, in unitate personæ fuerint inseparabiliter conjunctæ, ex quibus est unus CHRISTUS, verus Deus et verus homo, qui vere passus est, crucifixus, mortuus et sepultus, ut Patrem nobis reconciliaret, essetque hostia non tantum pro culpa originis, verum etiam pro omnibus actualibus hominum peccatis.

De descensu Christi ad Inferos.

3. QUEMADMODUM CHRISTUS pro nobis mortuus est et sepultus, ita est etiam credendus ad inferos descendisse. Nam corpus usque ad resurrectionem in sepulchro jacuit, Spiritus ab illo emissus cum spiritibus qui in carcere sive in inferno detinebantur, fuit, illisque prædicavit: quemadmodum testatur Petri locus.

[1 The Articles are not numbered originally in the B. M. copy: some one has numbered them in ink, but omitted the 25th, and thus made only 41.]

Resurrectio Christi.

CHRISTUS vere a mortuis resurrexit, suumque corpus cum carne, ossibus, omnibusque ad integritatem humanæ naturæ pertinentibus, recepit, cum quibus in cœlum ascendit, ibique residet quoad extremo die ad judicandos homines revertatur. 4.

Divinæ Scripturæ doctrina sufficit ad salutem.

SCRIPTURA sacra continet omnia quæ sunt ad salutem necessaria, ita ut quicquid in ea nec legitur neque inde probari potest, licet interdum a fidelibus ut pium et conducibile ad ordinem et decorum admittatur, attamen a quoquam non exigendum est, ut tanquam articulus fidei credatur, et ad salutis necessitatem requiri putetur. 5.

Vetus Testamentum non est rejiciendum.

TESTAMENTUM Vetus, quasi Novo contrarium sit, non est repudiandum, sed retinendum: quandoquidem tam in veteri quam in novo per CHRISTUM, qui unicus est mediator Dei et hominum, Deus et homo, æterna vita humano generi est proposita. Quare non sunt audiendi, qui veteres tantum in promissiones temporarias sperasse confingunt. 6.

Symbola tria.

SYMBOLA tria, Niceni, Athanasii, et quod vulgo Apostolicum appellatur, omnino recipienda sunt. Nam firmissimis divinarum scripturarum testimoniis probari possunt. 7.

Peccatum Originale.

PECCATUM originis non est (ut fabulantur Pelagiani et hodie Anabaptistæ repetunt) in imitatione Adami situm, sed est vitium et depravatio naturæ cujuslibet hominis ex Adamo naturaliter propagati: qua fit, ut ab originali justitia quam longissime distet; ad malum sua natura propendeat, et caro semper adversus spiritum concupiscat: unde in unoquoque nascentium iram Dei atque damnationem meretur. Manet etiam in renatis hæc naturæ depravatio, qua fit, ut affectus carnis, Græce φρόνημα σαρκὸς, quod alii sapientiam, alii sensum, alii affectum, alii studium vocant, legi Dei non subjiciatur. Et quanquam renatis et credentibus nulla propter CHRISTUM est condemnatio, peccati tamen in sese rationem habere concupiscentiam fatetur Apostolus. 8.

De libero arbitrio.

9. ABSQUE gratia Dei, quæ per Christum est, nos præveniente ut velimus, et cooperante dum volumus, ad pietatis opera facienda, quæ Deo grata sint et accepta, nihil valemus.

De Gratia.

10. GRATIA Christi, seu Spiritus sanctus, qui per eundem datur, cor lapideum aufert, et dat cor carneum. Atque licet ex nolentibus quæ recta sunt volentes faciat, et ex volentibus prava nolentes reddat; voluntati nihilominus violentiam nullam infert. Et nemo hac de causa, cum peccaverit, seipsum excusare potest, quasi nolens aut coactus peccaverit, ut eam ob causam accusari non mereatur aut damnari.

De hominis justificatione.

11. JUSTIFICATIO ex sola fide JESU CHRSTI, eo sensu quo in Homilia de justificatione explicatur, est certissima et saluberrima Christianorum doctrina.

Opera ante justificationem.

12. OPERA quæ fiunt ante gratiam CHRISTI, et Spiritus ejus afflatum, cum ex fide Jesu CHRISTI non prodeant, minime Deo grata sunt. Neque gratiam (ut multi vocant) de congruo merentur: imo cum non sint facta ut Deus illa fieri voluit et præcepit, peccati rationem habere non dubitamus.

Opera Supererogationis.

13. OPERA quæ Supererogationis appellant, non possunt sine arrogantia et impietate prædicari: nam illis declarant homines non tantum se Deo reddere quæ tenentur, sed plus in ejus gratiam facere quam deberent: cum aperte Christus dicat, Cum feceritis omnia quæcunque præcepta sunt vobis, dicite, Servi inutiles sumus.

Nemo præter Christum est sine peccato.

14. CHRISTUS in nostræ naturæ veritate, per omnia similis factus est nobis, excepto peccato, a quo prorsus erat immunis tum in carne tum in spiritu. Venit, ut agnus absque macula esset, qui mundi peccata, per immolationem sui semel factam, tolleret: et peccatum (ut inquit Joannes) in eo non erat: sed

nos reliqui etiam baptizati, et in Christo regenerati, in multis tamen offendimus omnes : et si dixerimus quia peccatum non habemus, nos ipsos seducimus, et veritas in nobis non est.

De peccato in Spiritum sanctum.

15. Non omne peccatum mortale post baptismum voluntarie perpetratum, est peccatum in Spiritum sanctum et irremissibile: proinde lapsis a baptismo in peccata locus pœnitentiæ non est negandus. Post acceptum Spiritum sanctum possumus a gratia data recedere atque peccare, denuoque per gratiam Dei resurgere ac resipiscere. Ideoque illi damnandi sunt, qui se, quamdiu hic vivant, amplius non posse peccare affirmant, aut vere resipiscentibus pœnitentiæ locum denegant.

Blasphemia in Spiritum sanctum.

16. Blasphemia in Spiritum sanctum est, cum quis verborum Dei manifeste perceptam veritatem, ex malitia et obfirmatione animi, convitiis insectatur, et hostiliter insequitur. Atque hujusmodi, quia maledicto sunt obnoxii, gravissimo sese adstringunt sceleri. Unde peccati hoc genus irremissibile a Domino appellatur et affirmatur.

De prædestinatione et electione.

17. Prædestinatio ad vitam est æternum Dei propositum, quo ante jacta mundi fundamenta, suo consilio, nobis quidem occulto, constanter decrevit eos, quos elegit ex hominum genere, a maledicto et exitio liberare, atque ut vasa in honorem efficta per Christum ad æternam salutem adducere : unde qui tam præclaro Dei beneficio sunt donati, illi Spiritu ejus, opportuno tempore operante, secundum propositum ejus vocantur : vocationi per gratiam parent : justificantur gratis : adoptantur in filios : unigeniti JESU CHRISTI imagini efficiuntur conformes : in bonis operibus sancte ambulant : et demum ex Dei misericordia pertingunt ad sempiternam felicitatem.

Quemadmodum prædestinationis et electionis nostræ in Christo pia consideratio dulcis, suavis, et ineffabilis consolationis plena est vere piis, et his qui sentiunt in se vim Spiritus CHRISTI, facta carnis et membra quæ adhuc sunt super terram mortificantem, animumque ad cœlestia et superna sapientem, tum quia fidem nostram de æterna salute consequenda per Christum plurimum stabilit atque confirmat, tum quia amorem nostrum in Deum vehementer accendit : Ita hominibus curiosis, carnalibus, et Spiritu CHRISTI destitutis, ob oculos perpetuo versari prædestinationis Dei sententiam, perniciosissimum est præcipitium, unde illos diabolus pertrudit vel in desperationem, vel in æque perniciosam impurissimæ vitæ securitatem. Deinde licet prædestinationis decreta sunt nobis ignota, promissiones tamen divinas sic amplecti oportet, ut nobis in sacris literis generaliter propositæ sunt : et Dei voluntas in nostris actionibus ea sequenda est, quam in verbo Dei habemus diserte revelatam.

Tantum in nomine Christi speranda est æterna salus.

18. Sunt et illi anathematizandi qui dicere audent, unumquemque in lege aut secta quam profitetur esse servandum, modo juxta illam et lumen naturæ accurate vixerit: cum sacræ literæ tantum JESU CHRISTI nomen prædicent, in quo salvos fieri homines oporteat.

Omnes obligantur ad moralia legis præcepta servanda.

19. Lex a Deo data per Mosen, licet quoad ceremonias et ritus Christianos non astringat, neque civilia ejus præcepta in aliqua republica necessario recipi debeant, nihilominus ab obedientia mandatorum, quæ moralia vocantur, nullus quantumvis Christianus est solutus : quare illi non sunt audiendi, qui sacras literas tantum infirmis datas esse perhibent, et Spiritum perpetuo jactant, a quo sibi quæ prædicant suggeri asserunt, quanquam cum sacris literis apertissime pugnent.

De Ecclesia.

20. Ecclesia CHRISTI visibilis est cœtus fidelium, in quo verbum Dei purum prædicatur, et sacramenta quoad ea quæ necessario exiguntur, juxta Christi institutum, recte administrantur.

Sicut erravit ecclesia Hierosolymitana, Alexandrina, et Antiochena, ita et erravit ecclesia Romana, non solum quoad agenda et ceremoniarum ritus, verum in his etiam quæ credenda sunt.

De Ecclesiæ auctoritate.

21. Ecclesiæ non licet quicquam instituere, quod verbo Dei scripto adversetur : neque unum scripturæ locum sic exponere

potest, ut alteri contradicat: quare licet ecclesia sit divinorum librorum testis et conservatrix, attamen ut adversus eos nihil decernere, ita præter illos nihil credendum de necessitate salutis debet obtrudere.

De auctoritate Conciliorum generalium.

GENERALIA concilia sine jussu et voluntate principum congregari non possunt: et ubi convenerint, quia ex hominibus constant, qui non omnes Spiritu et verbis Dei reguntur, et errare possunt, et interdum errarunt, etiam in his quæ ad normam pietatis pertinent: ideo quæ ab illis constituuntur, ut ad salutem necessaria, neque robur habent neque auctoritatem, nisi ostendi possunt e sacris literis esse desumpta. 22.

De Purgatorio.

SCHOLASTICORUM doctrina de Purgatorio, de Indulgentiis, de veneratione et adoratione tum imaginum tum reliquiarum, necnon de invocatione sanctorum, res est futilis, inaniter conficta, et nullis scripturarum testimoniis innititur, imo verbo Dei perniciose contradicit. 23.

Nemo in ecclesia ministret nisi vocatus.

NON licet cuiquam sumere sibi munus publice prædicandi, aut administrandi sacramenta in ecclesia, nisi prius fuerit ad hæc obeunda legitime vocatus et missus. Atque illos legitime vocatos et missos existimare debemus, qui per homines, quibus potestas vocandi ministros atque mittendi in vineam Domini publice concessa est in ecclesia, cooptati fuerint et asciti in hoc opus. 24.

Agendum est in ecclesia lingua quæ sit populo nota.

DECENTISSIMUM est, et verbo Dei maxime congruit, ut nihil in ecclesia publice legatur aut recitetur lingua populo ignota. Idque Paulus fieri vetuit, nisi adesset qui interpretaretur. 25.

De Sacramentis.

DOMINUS noster Jesus CHRISTUS sacramentis numero paucissimis, observatu facillimis, significatione præstantissimis, societatem novi populi colligavit, sicuti est Baptismus et Cœna Domini. 26.

Sacramenta non instituta sunt a Christo ut spectarentur aut circumferrentur, sed ut rite illis uteremur : et in his duntaxat qui digne percipiunt, salutarem habent effectum, idque non ex opere (ut quidam loquuntur) operato, quæ vox ut peregrina est et sacris literis ignota, sic parit sensum minime pium, sed admodum superstitiosum : qui vero indigne percipiunt, damnationem (ut inquit Paulus) sibi ipsis acquirunt.

Sacramenta per verbum Dei instituta non tantum sunt notæ professionis Christianorum, sed certa quædam potius testimonia, et efficacia signa gratiæ, atque bonæ in nos voluntatis Dei, per quæ invisibiliter ipse in nobis operatur, nostramque fidem in se non solum excitat, verum etiam confirmat.

Ministrorum malitia non tollit efficaciam institutionum divinarum.

27. QUAMVIS in ecclesia visibili bonis mali sint semper admixti, atque interdum ministerio verbi et sacramentorum administrationi præsint, tamen cum non suo sed Christi nomine agant, ejusque mandato et auctoritate ministrent, illorum ministerio uti licet, cum in verbo Dei audiendo, tum in sacramentis percipiendis: neque per illorum malitiam effectus institutorum Christi tollitur, aut gratia donorum Dei minuitur quoad eos, qui fide et rite sibi oblata percipiunt, quæ propter institutionem CHRISTI et promissionem efficacia sunt, licet per malos administrentur.

Ad ecclesiæ tamen disciplinam pertinet, ut in eos inquiratur, accusenturque ab hiis, qui eorum flagitia noverint, atque tandem justo convicti judicio deponantur.

De Baptismo.

28. BAPTISMUS non est tantum signum professionis ac discriminis nota, qua Christiani a non Christianis discernuntur; sed etiam est signum regenerationis, per quod, tanquam per instrumentum, recte Baptismum suscipientes ecclesiæ inseruntur, promissiones de remissione peccatorum atque adoptione nostra in filios Dei per Spiritum Sanctum visibiliter obsignantur, fides confirmatur, et vi divinæ invocationis gratia augetur. Mos ecclesiæ baptizandi parvulos et laudandus est, et omnino in ecclesia retinendus.

De Cœna Domini.

29. Cœna Domini non est tantum signum mutuæ benevolentiæ Christianorum inter sese, verum potius est sacramentum nostræ per mortem Christi redemptionis. Atque adeo rite, digne et cum fide sumentibus, panis quem frangimus est communicatio corporis Christi: similiter poculum benedictionis est communicatio sanguinis CHRISTI.

Panis et vini transubstantiatio in Eucharistia ex sacris literis probari non potest, sed apertis scripturæ verbis adversatur, et multarum superstitionum dedit occasionem.

Quum naturæ humanæ veritas requirat, ut unius ejusdemque hominis corpus in multis locis simul esse non possit, sed in uno aliquo et definito loco esse oporteat, idcirco CHRISTI corpus in multis et diversis locis, eodem tempore, præsens esse non potest. Et quoniam, ut tradunt sacræ literæ, CHRISTUS in cœlum fuit sublatus, et ibi usque ad finem seculi est permansurus, non debet quisquam fidelium carnis ejus et sanguinis Realem et Corporalem (ut loquuntur) præsentiam in Eucharistia vel credere vel profiteri.

Sacramentum Eucharistiæ ex institutione CHRISTI non servabatur, circumferebatur, elevabatur, nec adorabatur.

De unica Christi oblatione in cruce perfecta.

30. Oblatio Christi semel facta perfecta est redemptio, propitiatio, et satisfactio pro omnibus peccatis totius mundi, tam originalibus quam actualibus: neque præter illam unicam est ulla alia pro peccatis expiatio. Unde Missarum sacrificia, quibus vulgo dicebatur, sacerdotem offerre Christum in remissionem pœnæ aut culpæ pro vivis et defunctis, figmenta sunt et perniciosæ imposturæ.

Cœlibatus ex verbo Dei præcipitur nemini.

31. Episcopis, presbyteris, et diaconis non est mandatum ut cœlibatum voveant: neque jure divino coguntur matrimonio abstinere.

Excommunicati vitandi sunt.

32. Qui per publicam ecclesiæ denuntiationem rite ab unitate ecclesiæ præcisus est et excommunicatus, is ab universa fidelium multitudine, donec per pœnitentiam publice reconciliatus

fuerit, arbitrio judicis competentis, habendus est tanquam ethnicus et Publicanus.

Traditiones Ecclesiasticæ.

33. TRADITIONES atque ceremonias easdem non omnino necessarium est esse ubique aut prorsus[1] consimiles: nam et variæ semper fuerunt, et mutari possunt pro regionum et morum diversitate, modo nihil contra Dei verbum instituatur.

Traditiones et ceremonias ecclesiasticas, quæ cum verbo Dei non pugnant, et sunt auctoritate publica institutæ atque probatæ, quisquis privato consilio volens et data opera publice violaverit, is ut qui peccat in publicum ordinem ecclesiæ, quique lædit auctoritatem magistratus, et qui infirmorum fratrum conscientias vulnerat, publice, ut ceteri timeant, arguendus est.

Homiliæ.

34. HOMILIÆ nuper ecclesiæ Anglicanæ per Injunctiones Regias traditæ atque commendatæ, piæ sunt atque salutares, doctrinamque ab omnibus amplectendam continent: quare populo diligenter, expedite, clareque recitandæ sunt.

De libro Precationum et cæremoniarum Ecclesiæ Anglicanæ.

35. LIBER qui nuperrime auctoritate Regis et Parliamenti ecclesiæ Anglicanæ traditus est, continens modum et formam orandi, et sacramenta administrandi in ecclesia Anglicana; similiter et libellus eadem auctoritate editus De ordinatione ministrorum ecclesiæ, quoad doctrinæ veritatem, pii sunt, et salutari doctrinæ evangelii in nullo repugnant, sed congruunt, et eandem non parum promovent et illustrant: atque ideo ab omnibus ecclesiæ Anglicanæ fidelibus membris, et maxime a ministris verbi, cum omni promptitudine animorum et gratiarum actione recipiendi, approbandi, et populo Dei commendandi sunt.

De civilibus Magistratibus.

36. REX Angliæ est supremum caput in terris, post CHRISTUM, ecclesiæ Anglicanæ et Hibernicæ.

Romanus Pontifex nullam habet jurisdictionem in hoc regno Angliæ. Magistratus civilis est a Deo ordinatus atque

[[1] prosus, in G. S. and B. M.]

probatus: quamobrem illi non solum propter iram, sed etiam propter conscientiam obediendum est.

Leges civiles possunt Christianos propter capitalia et gravia crimina morte punire.

Christianis licet ex mandato magistratus arma portare, et justa bella administrare.

Christianorum bona non sunt communia.

FACULTATES et bona Christianorum non sunt communia, quoad jus et possessionem, ut quidam anabaptistæ falso jactant: debet tamen quisque de his quæ possidet, pro facultatum ratione, pauperibus eleemosynas benigne distribuere. 37.

Licet Christianis jurare.

QUEMADMODUM juramentum vanum et temerarium a Domino nostro Jesu Christo et ab apostolo ejus Jacobo Christianis hominibus interdictum esse fatemur; ita Christianam religionem minime prohibere censemus, quin jubente magistratu, in causa fidei et caritatis, jurare liceat, modo id fiat juxta prophetæ doctrinam, in justitia, in judicio et veritate. 38.

Resurrectio mortuorum nondum est facta.

RESURRECTIO mortuorum non adhuc facta est, quasi tantum ad animum pertineat, qui per CHRISTI gratiam a morte peccatorum excitetur, sed extremo die, quoad omnes qui obierunt, expectanda est: tunc enim vita defunctis (ut scripturæ manifestissime testantur) propria corpora, carnes et ossa restituentur, ut homo integer, prout vel recte vel perdite vixerit, juxta sua opera sive præmia sive pœnas reportet[2]. 39.

Defunctorum animæ neque cum corporibus intereunt, neque otiose dormiunt.

QUI animas defunctorum prædicant usque ad diem judicii absque omni sensu dormire, aut illas asserunt una cum corporibus mori, et extrema die cum illis excitandas, ab orthodoxa fide, quæ nobis in sacris literis traditur, prorsus dissentiunt. 40.

[2 repotet, B. M.]

Millenarii.

41. Qui millenariorum fabulam revocare conantur, sacris literis adversantur, et in Judaica deliramenta sese præcipitant.

Non omnes tandem servandi[1].

42. Hii quoque damnatione digni sunt, qui conantur hodie perniciosam opinionem instaurare, quod omnes, quantumvis impii, servandi sunt tandem, cum definito tempore a justitia divina pœnas de admissis flagitiis luerunt.

Κύριε σῶσον τὸν Βασιλέα[2].

---

*Excusum Londini apud Reginaldum
Wolfium, Regiæ Maiestatis
in Latinis Typo-
graphum.*

ANNO DOMINI. M.D.L.III.

[1 servandi sunt, B. M.]
[2 Κύριε, &c. omitted B. M. and colophon.]

CORRIGENDA.

Page 18. Note 1, for been, Grafton, 2, "been altered, Grafton, 2, and C."
    20. Note 1, insert "and C," after Grafton, 2.
    21. In the table, ivth day, the C copy has 20, by mistake for 21.
    24. 7th day, Evensong, for Ruth 3, C copy has Ruth 2; and 8th day, Matins, for Ruth 4, C copy has Ruth 3.
    28. Note 1, for Is. it should be Esay.
    30. In the C copy, *Te Deum Laudamus* is not given in versicles; also the eighth versicle, "the goodly fellowship of the Prophets, praise thee," is wanting.
        Note 1, insert "and C," after Grafton, 1.
   502. Margin, for the name, "the names of."
   509. Margin, for Christ's example, "Christ an example."
   520. For God always, "God alway."

N.B. The Cashel copy was not collated until after the second sheet had been printed.

www.ingramcontent.com/pod-product-compliance
Lightning Source LLC
Chambersburg PA
CBHW071216290426
44108CB00013B/1199